FORECAST 2021

FORECAST

2021

Merriman Market Analyst, Inc. / PO Box 14934/ Scottsdale, AZ 85267
Phone 1-800-MMA-3349 / Fax: 1-248-538-5296

E-Mail: customerservice@mmacycles.com
Website: http://www.mmacycles.com

DEDICATION

This year's book is dedicated to our newest Merriman Market Timing Academy (MMTA) Graduate, Gianni di Poce of Grosse Isle, Michigan. Gianni completed all eight courses this year, passed all the exams and the final exam. He started work as an MMA Analyst in 2019, covering T-Notes and the Crude Oil markets in the monthly MMA Cycles Report. Gianni also covers the analysis on the Euro/Yen and T-Notes for MMA's Weekly subscription reports. Additionally, he also writes the monthly analysis of the Australian Dollar and Australian stock market for the ICR Financial Report and Live Cattle and a Cannabis ETF in the ICR Commodities Report.

Gianni is a young man, born on June 10, 1993. However, prior to joining MMA in 2019, he attained a bachelor's degree in Economics from the University of Michigan and worked five years as a financial advisor for a wealth management firm. He started his studies of MMA's market timing methods in 2016, and it changed his life. He was inspired to learn more and eventually started his training to become an apprentice of the MMTA. With his studies now completed, Gianni will serve as MMTA's Educational Director. Along with founder, Raymond Merriman, they will offer the next 2-year study program of MMTA courses to the public starting January 16, 2021. It will be the first time these courses will be offered online, and the first time a new class will be assembled in seven years.

Gianni may be reached at gianni@mmacycles.com.

Special thanks this year goes to Teresa Detrich, Dan McCamman, and Beth Woody for editing this year's book. Special thanks to Daniel Gordon (dmhgordon@hotmail.com) for his research on historical dates of long-term planetary aspects used in this work. The weekly planetary calendar guide in the back of the book is from the Pathfinder Astrology System, created by John Woodsmall of Astro Cybernetics. He can be contacted at john@astrocye.com and via his website, http://www.astrocye.com. The ephemeris tables are reproduced from The New American Ephemeris, 2020–2030: Compiled and Programmed by Rique Pottenger, based on the earlier work of Neil F. Michelsen of Astro Computing Services (ACS) and copyright by the Michelsen-Simms Family Trust. ACS may be reached at 866-953-8458, or www.astrocom.com.

Cover Design: Lara Baum, Digital Media Designer, Dusseldorf, Germany, www.lara-baum.de. Book Formatting and Technical Execution: Stefanie Deutsch, Ulm, Germany.

ISBN 978-1-7353437-0-9
Phone: 1-248-626-3034 or 1-800-MMA-3349 / Fax 1-248-538-5296
Merriman Market Analyst, Inc. – PO Box 14934 – Scottsdale, AZ 85267
Website: https://www.mmacycles.com
Email: customerservice@mmacycles.com

TABLE OF CONTENTS

TERMINOLOGY OF MARKET TERMS USED IN THIS BOOK

The following are terms that the reader will find throughout this book, especially in the Financial Markets sections.

1. Cycle: A measurable phenomenon that recurs consistently at regular intervals of time. In markets, cycles are measured from trough (low) to trough, unless specified otherwise.

2. Trough: a low in price; the bottom of a cycle, from whence the cycle ends and begins.

3. Crest: the peak of a cycle; the highest price between the troughs that define the cycle.

4. Phase: These are sub-cycles within each cycle. Each cycle is comprised of two or three sub-cycles or phases that are approximately 1/2 or 1/3 of the greater cycle's length.

5. Cycle Pattern: There are three common cycle patterns: 1) the classical "three-phase" pattern, in which there are three sub-cycles (or phases) of approximately 1/3 the greater cycle length; 2) the classical "two-phase" pattern consisting of two sub-cycles (or phases) of approximately 1/2 the greater cycle length; and 3) a "combination" pattern, which has sub-cycles at the 1/2 and 1/3 intervals of the greater cycle.

6. Bull Market: Consecutively higher crests and higher troughs of the same cycle type; "right translation" patterns of primary cycles. "**Right Translation"** means the crest occurs in the second half of the cycle, past the midway point of the cycle.

7. Bear Market: Consecutively lower troughs and lower crests of the same cycle type; "left translation" patterns of primary cycles. "**Left Translation"** means the crest occurs in the first half of the cycle.

8. Trend: Bull or bear (as above). Trends depend upon the cycle you are studying. The first phase of a cycle is always bullish, and the last is usually bearish.

9. Support: An area below the current market price where we expect prices to hold on declines, a "floor" for prices.

10. Resistance: An area above the current market price where we expect prices to hold on rallies, a "ceiling" for prices.

11. Treasury Values: In the chapter under T-Notes and Interest Rates, prices for T-Notes are given in values of 1/32 of a point. For instance, a value of 130/25 really means 130 and 25/32 of a point. This is how prices are quoted in Treasuries.

For further information on understanding market and cycles' terminology, the reader is advised to read the author's work, titled Merriman on Market Cycles: The Basics.

TERMINOLOGY OF GEOCOSMIC TERMS USED IN THIS BOOK

1. **Conjunction:** An aspect or phenomenon that occurs when two planets are in the same sign and degree of the zodiac. They "appear" to be together. A conjunction is the starting point for a cycle involving those two planets.

2. **Opposition:** An aspect or phenomenon that occurs when two planets are in opposite signs and degrees of the zodiac. They "appear" to be in the opposite part of the sky. When one sets in the west, the other rises in the east. An opposition is the halfway point for a cycle involving those two planets. It represents the "culmination" of the themes, or peak of the cycle, that began at the time of their conjunction.

3. **Square:** An aspect or phenomenon that occurs when two planets are 90 degrees apart in the zodiac. They "appear" to be at a right angle, perpendicular to one another. A square represents the first (opening) and last (closing) quarter phase of a cycle involving those two planets.

4. **Trine:** An aspect or phenomenon that occurs when two planets are 120 degrees apart in the zodiac. A trine represents the first third and last third phase for a cycle involving those two planets. Trines are considered "soft" or "harmonious" aspects, along with the sextile (1/6 of the zodiac circle).

5. **Hard aspects:** The conjunction, squares, and opposition are considered the "hard aspects" in astrology. They are challenging and difficult and represent the urge to force conflicting dynamics to work together.

6. **T-square:** This is a pattern in which two planets are in opposition, and both are in square aspect to a third planet.

7. **Grand square:** This is a pattern in which four planets are in consecutive squares to one another. It is two pairs of oppositions, with each pair also square to the other pair.

8. **Grand trine:** This is a pattern in which three planets are in consecutive trines to one another. It appears as an equilateral triangle in the heavens and is considered the most fortunate of all planetary configurations.

9. **Cardinal signs:** Every third sign, starting with Aries, and then Cancer, Libra, and Capricorn. Cardinal signs start each season. Cardinal signs are the signs of action.

10. **Fixed signs:** Every third sign, starting with Taurus, and then Leo, Scorpio, and Aquarius. Fixed signs are the middle of each season. Fixed signs maintain the energy initiated by cardinal signs. They are said to be fixed, stable, and/or stubborn.

11. **Mutable signs:** Every third sign, starting with Gemini, and then Virgo, Sagittarius, and Pisces. Mutable signs are the last signs of each season and represent changes and flexibility.

ABOUT THIS YEAR'S BOOK COVER

The idea behind this year's book cover is to convey awareness that the decade of the 2020s is the birth of a new era in human activity.

It started with the Grand Conjunctions of 2020, as Jupiter, Saturn, and Pluto all conjoined one another. The first was the 32–37 year conjunction cycle of Saturn and Pluto at 22° Capricorn on January 12, 2020. This was followed by the three-passage series of the 14-year Jupiter/Pluto cycle on April 4, June 20, and November 12, 2020. The culmination occurred with the 20-year Jupiter/Saturn conjunction on the winter solstice of December 21, 2020. This last of the outer planet synodic cycles is also important because it begins a series of Jupiter/Saturn conjunctions in air signs over the next 140 years. This phenomenon only occurs approximately every 800 years. The December 21, 2020 case additionally unfolds at 0° Aquarius, as if to announce the cosmic start of "The Age of Aquarius."

Thus, from the cosmic perspective, this celestial arrangement symbolizes the birth of a New Era for humanity.

As I look at this image, I see what appears to be a volcanic eruption—an explosion of fire out of water from somewhere deep in the earth. In the sky, there is a solar eclipse—with a corona around it no less— rising at daybreak. A volcanic eruption from the bowels of the earth is an expression of the power of Pluto. Pluto has been in Capricorn from 2008, which actually began the Cardinal Climax of 2008–2015 that is undergoing its second coming as of 2020–2021. Capricorn rules earth (terra firma), and in particular, mountains. When volcanoes erupt, new lands—even mountains—can be birthed or taken down. Pluto is considered the planet of destruction and rebirth. One can look back on the year 2020, and even back to 2008 when Pluto first entered Capricorn and began its 16–year trek through the sign of the sea-goat and easily sense that humanity has entered a new era.

The total solar eclipse likewise symbolizes the end of a period and the start of a new one. This is when the Moon (the past) blackens out the Sun (the future), meaning that a new path for the future is emerging. Light turns to darkness and then returns once more to light after an interval of time has passed. The depiction of the eclipse occurring at daybreak also adds to the image of a "new day" beginning. The idea of a corona around the Moon is obvious: we have just experienced the worst pandemic of our lifetime, the COVID-19 corona-virus. It has completely transformed the way we conduct ourselves and business with one another. Indeed, it is a new world we are learning to adjust to as we start this new decade.

Although the picture impressed me as a volcanic eruption, it is actually the famous Seljalandsfoss Waterfall in Iceland. The solar eclipse was photoshopped into it to create this stunning book cover, created by gifted graphic designer, Lara Baum, of Dusseldorf, Germany.

HIGHLIGHTS OF THE FORECAST 2021 BOOK

- **"The Capricorn Stellium" – Jupiter, Saturn, and Pluto conjoining one another in 2020 – comes to an end; the start of a new era**
- **The emergence of new world leadership, new international treaties, trade deals, and laws, as well as a monumental shift in world education related to the 20-, 200-, and 800-year cycle of Jupiter conjunct Saturn**
- **Saturn square Uranus: Worldwide political insurrections; protests regarding systemic racism and denial of human rights; conflict between government and technology companies over new regulations and attempts at censorship**
- **Uranus in Taurus: Changes in banking; efforts to revaluation and status of world currencies, including the U.S. Dollar**
- **Pluto return in the chart of the U.S.; America at another crossroads regarding its survival and future direction**
- **The bull market in world stocks and economies, with possibilities of large price swings or long-term trend reversals in many financial markets like stocks and precious metals**

These are the key bullet points for Forecast 2021. They are based on the history of the most important long-term geocosmic signatures in effect in 2020–2021 and what happened previously during the times these planets were in the same or similar aspects or positions in the cosmos. They also consider the astrological meanings—the dynamics and themes—related to the planets, the type of aspect in effect, and the signs involved.

Keep in mind these are "forecasts," not "predictions." The forecasts presented in this book are the result of research correlating planetary cycles with the history of cycles in human activity, most of which have correlations of 80% or greater. Therefore, the art of forecasting is a projection of these cycles in terms of historical probabilities—not inevitabilities. In other words, planetary cycles represent *correlations, not causations*, to cycles in human activity. One should understand that astrology, cycle studies, and/or technical analysis studies do not make forecasts. Humans do, based upon historical rates of frequency denoted by these studies. And because we are human, our judgment of how these factors will manifest is fallible. Our forecasts are educated, well-researched, and mostly accurate. But no human is always correct in the interpretation of how indicators will actually interact with one another and manifest as an outcome. Additionally, there are choices that humans make when conditions arise related to these themes. The element of "choice" or "free will" can also affect the forecasts given in this book.

With these disclaimers in place, may this annual book continue to serve you as a most valuable reference and planning guide for the year ahead.

REVIEW OF 2020: WHAT JUST HAPPENED?

The pandemic is a story not only about our health but our humanity. — Peggy Noonan, "Scenes from the Class Struggle in Lockdown," Wall Street Journal, May 16, 2020.

"It's either Evolution or Revolution. In fact, it is probably both, for with Saturn and Pluto, structural changes are very likely, even if forced. And such changes will require a period of rebuilding, and that is where the forces of evolution will take hold. Something new is about to be born." — Raymond Merriman, Excerpt from the Forecast 2020 Book.

It was a year unlike any we have lived before. And it will alter the way we will live from now on.

Between February 12 and February 20, 2020, many of the world's stock indices were making new multi-year highs. In the United States, the Dow Jones Industrial Average had reached a new all-time high of 29,568. One week later, the S&P and NASDAQ did the same. Both the world and national economies were humming along, with unemployment in the United States at its lowest level in 50 years. The U.S. added a record 103 straight months of job gains, and the economic expansion showed little sign of slowing down.

All that would change dramatically during the next month.

Astrologers across the world knew something big was about to happen, which would transform systems and structures on a huge scale. There would likely be an enormous economic impact, along with powerful social and political transformations. Astrologers aren't psychics, so they don't necessarily see the specifics of the details that would cause such a huge transition, but they knew 2020 would be the year of "The Grand Conjunctions," "The Synodic Convergence," "The Capricorn Stellium," or a host of other cosmological titles used to describe this rare combination of outer planets conjoining in the sign of Capricorn.

We hadn't experienced a period of "Grand Conjunctions" or a "Synodic Convergence" of the outer planets like this since 1988–1993, when Saturn, Uranus, Neptune, and the Moon's North Node all conjoined in Capricorn. This was a 5-year period I coined as "The Capricorn Climax" at the time. There had been no conjunctions—the beginning of synodic cycles—involving Saturn, Uranus, Neptune, and/or Pluto to one another since 1993. It was a very long stretch of time. Hence, this would be a momentous development in the arrangement of the cosmos to astrologers.

Finally, in 2020, the first of the Grand Conjunctions occurred. Saturn made its 32–37-year conjunction to Pluto on January 12, 2020, in 22°47' Capricorn. Just one week before this cosmic event, the United States military assassinated Iranian major general, Qasem Soleimani, who was planning on meeting the Iraqi prime minister that day. At the time, many people thought this assassination was the event that would start the process of tearing down and rebuilding the political structures of the world, symbolized by the Saturn/Pluto conjunction in Capricorn. After all, Saturn and Capricorn rule governments and political leaders, and Pluto is often referred to as the planet of the underworld, where such acts as assassinations occur. Events often follow, threatening the lives of many people. Surely, this assassination could start a major international conflict, perhaps even commence a major war. A conflict began to arise. But something even overwhelming was about to begin, and it would diminish the importance and attention of that first Saturn/Pluto act.

On February 16, 2020. Mars—quietly, at first—entered Capricorn. It was right in the middle of the global economic peak of growth and prosperity and right in the middle of record highs in many world stock indices. Little did the world know at the time that all of that optimism would suddenly evaporate. Few noticed the dark, foreboding cloud looming on the horizon, signaling a tempest was coming to transform the light of sunshine and confidence into anxiety and fear. A pandemic panic was about to unfold over the next several weeks that was unlike anything anyone alive had ever experienced.

THE CAPRICORN STELLIUM #1

From 1988–1993, three of the five outermost planets (Saturn, Uranus, and Neptune) transited through the sign of Capricorn, along with the Moon's North Node. The lunar nodes do this approximately every 18.6 years. Saturn will enter Capricorn approximately every 29 years. The orbital cycles of Uranus and Neptune are 84 and 164 years, respectively. As one can see, having all four of these orbital cycles going through Capricorn in a 5-year interval is quite uncommon. As postulated in these Forecasts Books at the time, this "Capricorn Climax" would likely coincide with a massive shift in human activity. Indeed, it did. The way we communicated and did business began to change dramatically with the application of the fax machine, cell phones, and the internet. It was the liftoff to the "Information Superhighway" that revolutionized our personal and professional lives. Nothing would ever be quite the same again.

The revolution was not only in the field of business and communications. It was also in the world political arena. Russian Communism came crashing down, and with it, the Berlin Wall. Over 300 million new consumers entered the world's free-market economy, and stock markets everywhere surged. The demand for products and services just exploded as the cold war between the U.S.S.R. and the U.S.A. ended. World peace was suddenly no longer just an abstract ideal. It was becoming a reality, and people worldwide celebrated this historic transition emphasizing individual freedom.

This first "Capricorn Climax of 1988–1993" was a jubilant time for many, an economic boom leading to technology euphoria, which in turn eventually led to the dot-com bubble of 1999–2000. That was when Jupiter and Saturn conjoined (came together) in Taurus, the sign of money. And this duo formed a square aspect to Uranus in Aquarius—the planet and its ruling sign have dominion over chaos and technology. The bubble burst, and a severe bear market began that lasted over two years and witnessed a 39% decline in the DJIA and an 80% decline in the NASDAQ. Why is that important to us today? Because the position of those three planets is exactly reversed in 2021. That is, Jupiter and Saturn will be in Aquarius, the sign of technology and chaos, and both will form a square to Uranus in Taurus. With Uranus ruling disruptions, social unrest, and revolutions, as well as technology and innovation, and Taurus ruling money and currency values, many of the themes of the bursting of the dot-com bubble of 1999–2000 may be upon us again.

THE CAPRICORN STELLIUM #2

There is more to this story and how it relates to the "Capricorn Stellium" and "Synodic Convergence" of 2020. It was pointed out earlier there had been no conjunctions since 1993 involving the outer planets of Saturn, Uranus, Neptune, or Pluto. However, if we add Jupiter, which can also be considered an outer planet, but whose orbit around the Sun is only about 12 years, we will see there was an outer planet conjunction in 2000. That was when Jupiter and Saturn conjoined in Taurus, the last time that planetary conjunction (also known as "The Great Chronocrator") will happen in earth signs for over 570 years.

With the addition of Jupiter to our list of outer planets, we have the cosmic framework for the 2020 Capricorn Stellium. That is, Jupiter, Saturn, and Pluto were all in Capricorn. Not only that, but they each formed a conjunction with one another during the year. Firstly, Saturn conjoined Pluto on January 12, 2020. Next, Jupiter made a three-passage conjunction to Pluto on April 4, June 30, and November 12, 2020. Finally, Jupiter ended the year with its conjunction to Saturn, the "Great Chronocrator," on December 21, 2020.

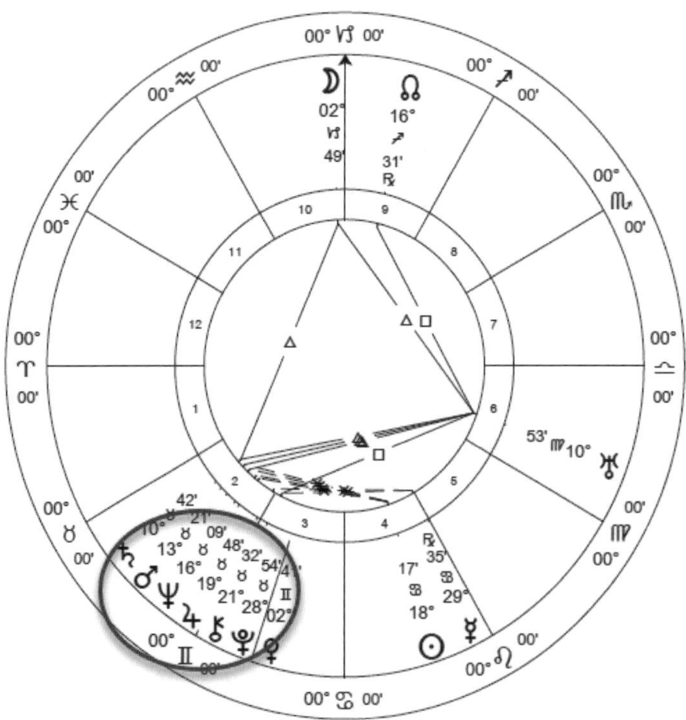

The "Grand Conjunctions" of 1881–1882

There are only ten possible conjunctions—or synodic cycles—involving these outer five planets, and three occurred in 2020. Three synodic cycles involving these five outer planets occurring in one year haven't happened since 1881–1882. And even that involved a 2-year span (that stellium was in Taurus and involved Jupiter, Saturn, and Neptune conjoining one another). As a side note, in 1881, Alexander II, Emperor of Russia and King of Poland, was assassinated. In the U.S., President James Garfield was also assassinated. The fifth cholera pandemic of 1881–1896 broke out then as well. It was the last serious European cholera outbreak of the century. Does this sound eerily similar to what happened in 2020?

MARS THE ACTIVATOR

Now let's add Mars to the list of outer planets. Technically, Mars is an outer planet because it is outside the orbit of the Earth. But its orbital cycle is only 26 months, and thus it is seldom referred to as an outer planet. However, when it enters the same sign as an outer planet stellium, it can serve as an activator mechanism, setting off the themes of the planets making up the stellium and the sign they are in. That is precisely what happened in February and March 2020.

As stated earlier, Mars entered Capricorn on February 16, 2020, right at the peak of the U.S. stock market's all-time high at the time and just before the historically swift plunge that immediately followed. All-time highs were also recorded during the same period in the Australian ASX, German DAX, and Zurich SMI stock indices. Brazil's Bovespa and India's NIFTY indices made their all-time highs about three weeks earlier. But all came crashing down as Mars entered Capricorn and approached the Jupiter/Pluto/Saturn conjunctions. By March 20–31, when Mars actually conjoined all three planets, the COVID-19 virus had turned global euphoria into global hysteria. Stock markets entered a panic. In just one month, these same indices had lost approximately 40% of their value. There had never been a case in the U.S. where stock markets lost so much value in such a short amount of time. For that matter, there had never been a case where the unemployment rate had skyrocketed, and the GDP had fallen so sharply and so quickly, all as a result of the pandemic and the business lockdowns imposed by the governments of nations around the world. Business stopped, and many companies went bankrupt and closed for good, typical of the 4 D's ascribed to Pluto: debt, deficits, downgrades, and defaults (bankruptcies).

The outbreak of the novel coronavirus expanded to include restrictions in travel and education too. Schools and universities were closed. Children were forced to stay home, and with them, their parents and others had to learn to work from home as offices were closed, and someone needed to home-school the children. The travel and tourism industries of many countries suffered significantly as people were not allowed to travel from one country to another or even from one state to another. Jupiter rules travel and education. Saturn and Capricorn pertain to restrictions and bans. You couldn't go to work, you couldn't go to school, you couldn't travel by air, bus, train, and you couldn't go to conferences in person. You had to abide by new social distancing mandates and wear masks in public where no more than ten people at a time were allowed to gather. What was happening? No one really knew, except many people were getting sick, dying, while the economic and social life we had all enjoyed and perhaps taken for granted was suddenly gone. It was no more. In its place, fear took dominance over confidence.

The worldwide economic and pandemic health crises were challenging enough. But they were not the only two crises experienced in the U.S. On May 25, 2020, a white police officer in Minneapolis, MN, named Derek Chauvin, arrested an African-American named George Floyd for forgery. Chauvin kneeled on Floyd's neck as he was being detained on the ground crying, "I can't breathe!" for over 8 minutes. Shockingly, as a result of being unable to breathe, George Floyd died. This tragedy between a white police officer and an African-American citizen set up a wave of national protests—the largest protests in U.S. history—against police brutality, especially targeting African Americans and systemic racism. The protests soon turned violent with looting and destruction of property in scores of U.S. cities, turning many into centers of dangerous social unrest persisting as this is being written several months later.

These dramatic events of 2020 were not an economic or political cycle correlation. This was purely a geocosmic cyclical correlation. It was a rare "Synodic Cycle Convergence" and "Grand Conjunction," a new "Capricorn Climax," involving three outer planets conjoined by a fourth: Mars, the activator. And it was all taking place in a single year: 2020.

THE PANDEMIC

There have been several astrological theories proposed as to its correlation with the COVID-19 Pandemic of 2020. The most frequent espoused is that the pandemic relates to the Saturn/Pluto conjunction, a synodic cycle happening every 32–37 years. Proponents of this theory point out the last four times Saturn and Pluto conjoined also coincided with major pandemics or epidemics in which large numbers of people died. But is that true?

The previous occurrence of this conjunction took place in November 1982, which proponents point out coincides with the onset of the HIV-AIDS pandemic. Before that, Saturn and Pluto conjoined in August 1947, which they assert correlated with the polio outbreak in the U.S. They also state the time before that coincided with the Spanish Flu Pandemic of 1918.

Let's look back in time and see what the geocosmic set up was during those times and determine if Saturn/Pluto in conjunction was the primary correlate.

HIV/AIDS

The first reported case of HIV/AIDS occurred on April 24, 1980, in San Francisco, when Ken Horne, a San Francisco resident, was reported to the Centers for Disease Control and Prevention (CDC). *Horne was the first US resident officially diagnosed with a disease that would soon span the city of San Francisco, and indeed the wider world.*[1]

Notice Saturn and Pluto were one full sign apart. They would not conjoin one another for another 2 - 1/2 years.

Notice Saturn was at 20° Virgo, the sign of health, square to Neptune at 22° Sagittarius. Also, notice the outer planets of Jupiter and beyond were in a tight orb of 112° of one another (Jupiter at 0° Virgo through Neptune at 22° Sagittarius). The importance of these positions will be discussed shortly.

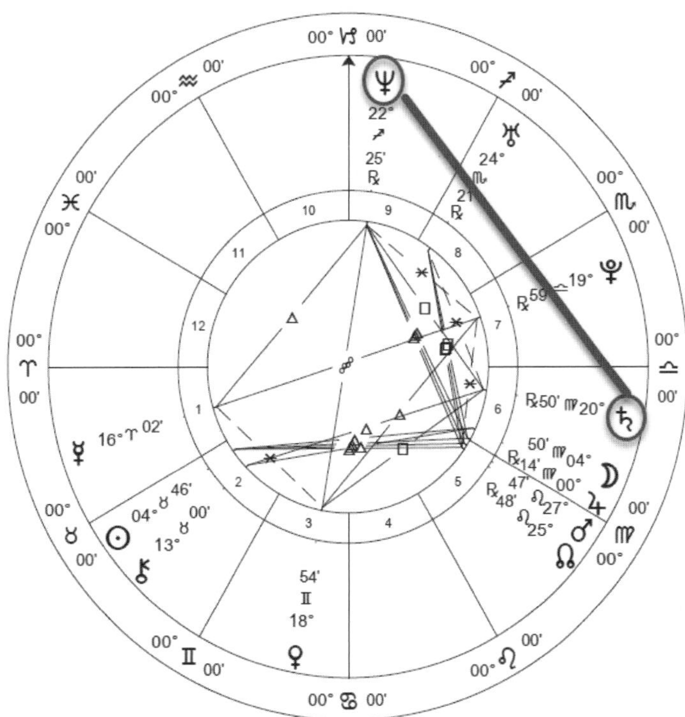

First reported case of AIDS, April 24, 1980, San Francisco, CA, time unknown

To date, 32 million people have died of AIDS. It is the fourth deadliest pandemic in world history, according to PublicHealthOnline.org, which also states, *"Despite extensive research, medical experts have yet to come up with a vaccine."*

POLIO OUTBREAK

According to the CDC (Center for Disease Control and Prevention), *"Polio was once one of the most feared diseases in the U.S. In the early 1950s, before polio vaccines were available, polio outbreaks caused more than 15,000 cases of paralysis each year. Thanks to the polio vaccine, dedicated health care professionals, and parents who vaccinate their children on schedule, polio has been eliminated in this country for more than 30 years. Since 1979, no cases of polio have originated in the U.S."* (www.cdc.gov/vaccines.com)

According to www.npr.org and google.com, *"In 1952, the polio epidemic reached a peak in the U.S.: almost 58,000 reported cases and more than 3,000 deaths."*

Polio had been present long before reaching its peak in 1952. The first reported case was in England in 1789. The first outbreak of polio in the U.S. was in Vermont in 1894 when 132 cases were reported. In 1916, according to the National Museum of American

History (NMAH) Polio timeline (https://amhistory.si.edu/), there was a massive epidemic in the U.S. in 1916. It was not eradicated until 1979 after Dr. Jonas Salk developed a vaccine in 1953 and began administering it in mass in 1955. However, prior to that, in the early 1950s, polio exploded in the U.S., reaching a peak of 57,859 cases in 1952. For this reason, we will use November 1, 1952, as the period of the epidemic's peak.

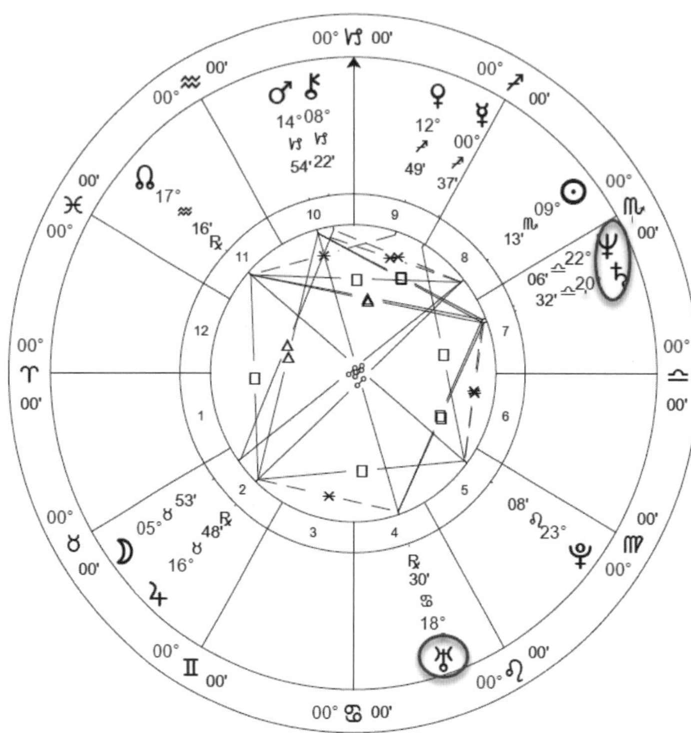

Polio Epidemic, date unknown, but here we use November 1, 1952

In this chart, Saturn and Pluto are now two signs away from their conjunction. In fact, they are in a 60° sextile aspect. Their last conjunction was five years earlier in August 1947, too far away to be considered in conjunction.

However, note that Saturn and Neptune are conjunct in 20–22° Libra, in a square aspect to Uranus at 18° Cancer. If we eliminate Jupiter, we will see four outermost planets (Saturn, Uranus, Neptune, and Pluto) are within only 94° of one another. The importance of these positions will be discussed shortly.

Polio was the most feared disease of the 20th century. There are no references as to how many people died from polio over the years, but it is not considered one of the seven deadliest pandemics in world history.

THE SPANISH FLU

It was also known as the 1918 flu pandemic, and it did not originate in Spain, as the name implies. The first occurrence of the Spanish flu is disputed, but www.history.com states the first case in the U.S. was reported on March 11, 1918, at Ft. Riley, KS. The CDC website (www.cdc.com) states, *"The 1918 influenza pandemic was the most severe pandemic in recent history. It was caused by an H1N1 virus with genes of avian origin. It is estimated that about 500 million people or one-third of the world's population became infected with this virus. The number of deaths was estimated to be at least 50 million worldwide with about 675,000 occurring in the United States."* The Spanish flu is rated the third most deadly pandemic in world history by www.publichealthonline.org.

Once again, there was not a case of Saturn conjunct Pluto. These two powerhouses were 35° apart. They were last conjunct October 4, 1914–May 13, 1915, three years earlier. However, note once again, Saturn conjoins Neptune. Also, note the outer planets are more spread out in this instance. They are not located in a tight orb to one another. If we include Jupiter, however, we can observe four of the five outer planets are only 64° apart. Plus, Uranus at 25° Aquarius is far away from the other four planets.

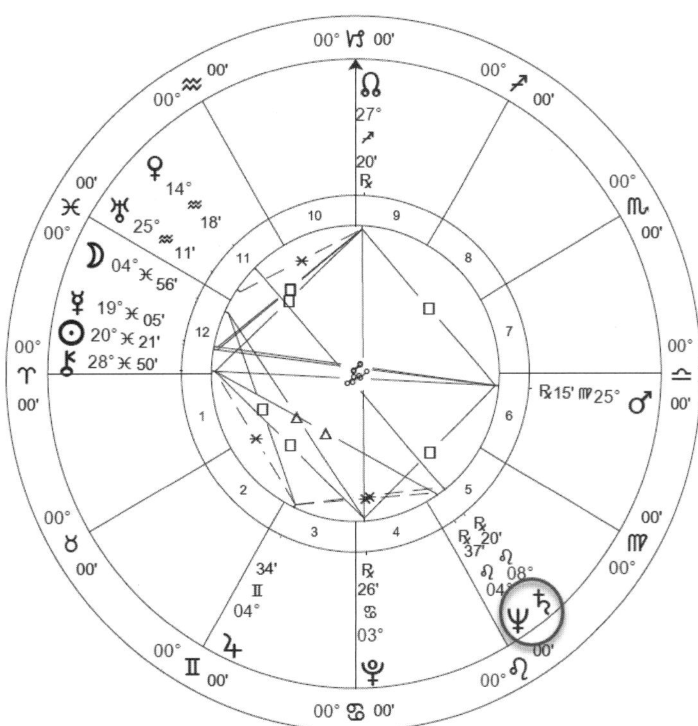

First reported case of Spanish Flu in the U.S. on March 11, 1918, in Ft. Riley, Kansas

Thus, the recent occurrences of Saturn/Pluto conjunctions have not correlated well with the onset or peak of global pandemics. But what about the other seven most deadly pandemics in history? Let's briefly discuss them and see if there are further correlations between geocosmic factors and the onset or peak of pandemics throughout history.

PANDEMIC HISTORY AND THE SEVEN DEADLIEST CASES

Here we will simply show charts for the other deadliest pandemic outbreaks in history. The exact dates of the outbreak are unknown, so I simply approximated a time in the year or years when it reflected the points I think are relevant to this discussion (I know, this is selective bias, but I think the study still has merit). I will summarize the importance of these charts at the end of this section.

The worst and most deadly pandemic in world history was smallpox. No one knows exactly when smallpox began, but according to www.google.com, it probably emerged in humans about 10,000 BC. It came to North America from European settlers in 1633–1634. Cases began arising in worrisome numbers in 1870–1874 but became a full pandemic in 1877, even after a vaccine was discovered in 1796, by English physician Edward Jenner, over 70 years earlier. According to Aaron O'Neil of www.statista.com, *"The Great Smallpox Pandemic of 1870 to 1875 was the last major smallpox epidemic to reach pandemic level across Europe."* The disease was not declared eradicated until 1980 by the World Health Organization (WHO). The last naturally occurring case was reported in 1977. An estimated 300–500 million people were killed before 1977.

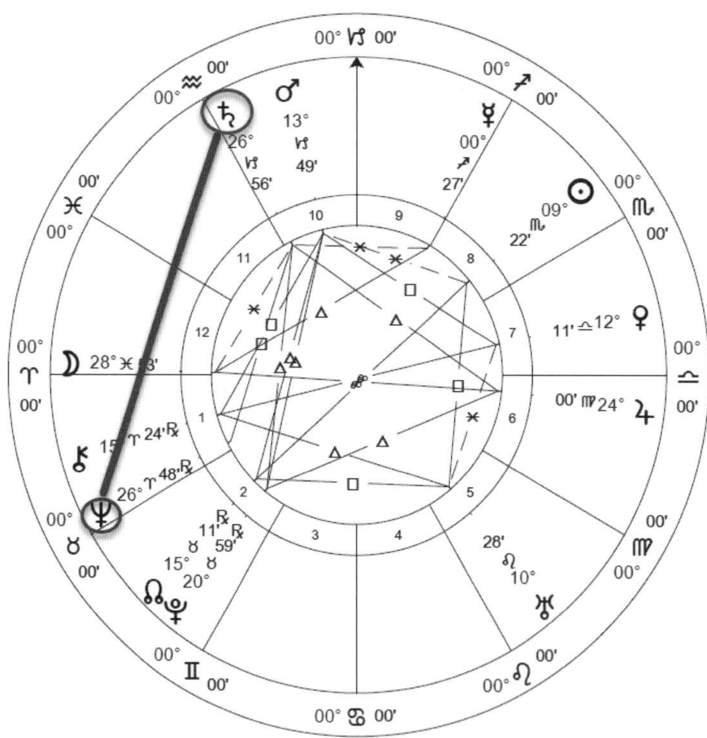

Smallpox outbreak, November 1, 1873

The second worst pandemic in world history was the Black Plague of 1347–1351. It actually started in 1346. Also known as the Bubonic Plague, it killed an estimated 75–200 million people in Eurasia and North Africa, according to www.wikipedia.com.

Some sources say this was the deadliest pandemic recorded in human history. The fatalities over these four years averaged more per year than the total of smallpox over a 100-year period.

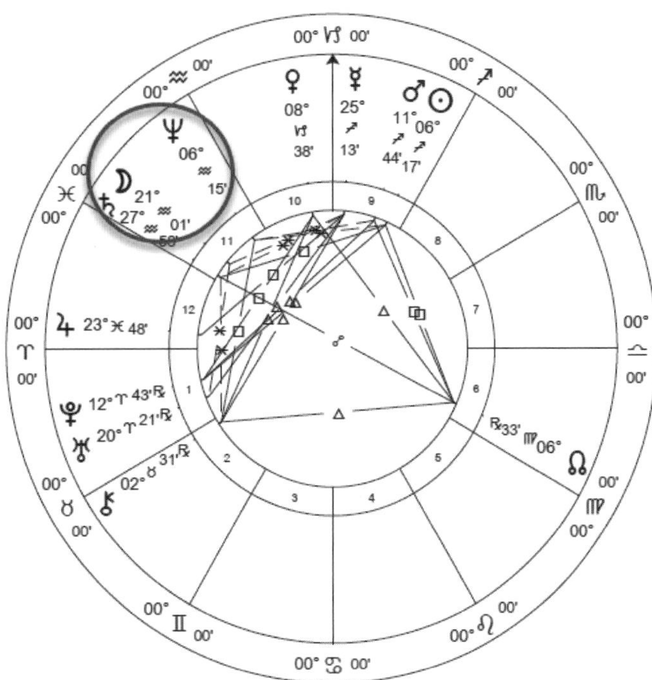

Black Death Plague, November 20, 1346

The Spanish Flu Pandemic of 1918 is ranked the third deadliest pandemic in history.

The HIV/AIDS pandemic is ranked number 4 in terms of the deadliest pandemics.

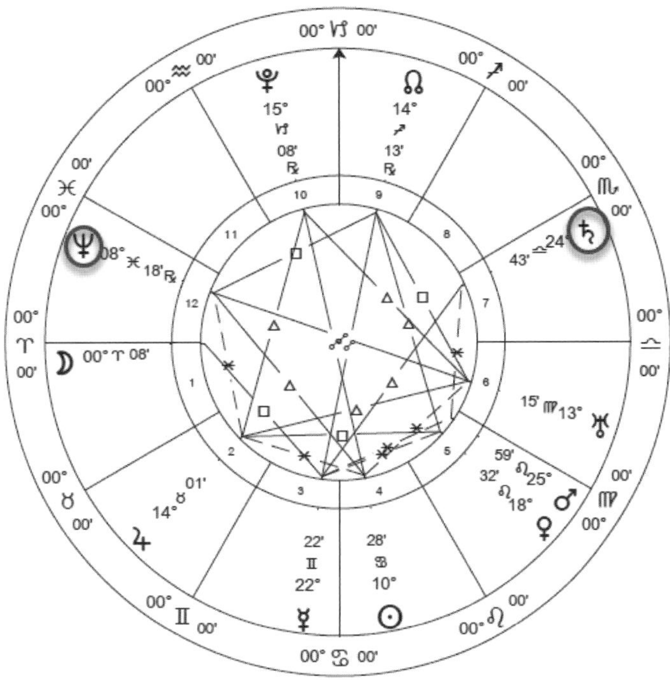

Plague of Justinian, July 1, 541. Saturn/Neptune solstice point conjunction, or antiscia

Number 5 on the list of deadliest pandemics in world history is known as The Plague of Justinian, 541–542, in which 25–100 million people died. This bubonic plague victimized 13–51% of the world's population.

According to www.google.com, the Plague of Justinian arrived in Constantinople, the capital of the Byzantine Empire, in 541 CE. It was carried over the Mediterranean Sea from Egypt, a recently conquered land paying the tribute of grain to Emperor Justinian. Plague-ridden fleas hitched a ride on the black rats snacking on the grain. Recurrences over the next two centuries eventually killed several million more people. It is believed to be the first significant appearance of the bubonic plague.

The 6th most deadly pandemic in world history is known as The Third Plague Pandemic of 1855–1945. It started in Yunnan Fu, China, in 1855 and lasted mostly through 1945, and to some extent into 1960, during which more than 15 million people died.

Notice the square between Saturn and Neptune in this chart, calculated for June 7, 1855. Also, notice how all the outer planets are in a tight orb of space with one another. The importance of these two factors will be shown shortly.

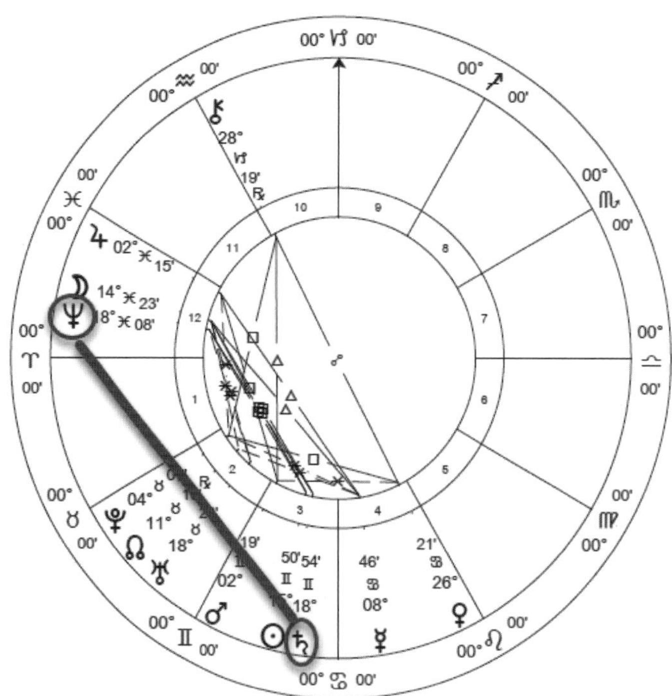

Third Plague Pandemic, July 7, 1855, Yunnan Fu, China

This was followed by the Hong Kong Flu of 1968–1969, killing an estimated one to four million people, according to www. wikipedia.com. Here, we have an exact date of the first reported case on July 13, 1968, in Hong Kong.

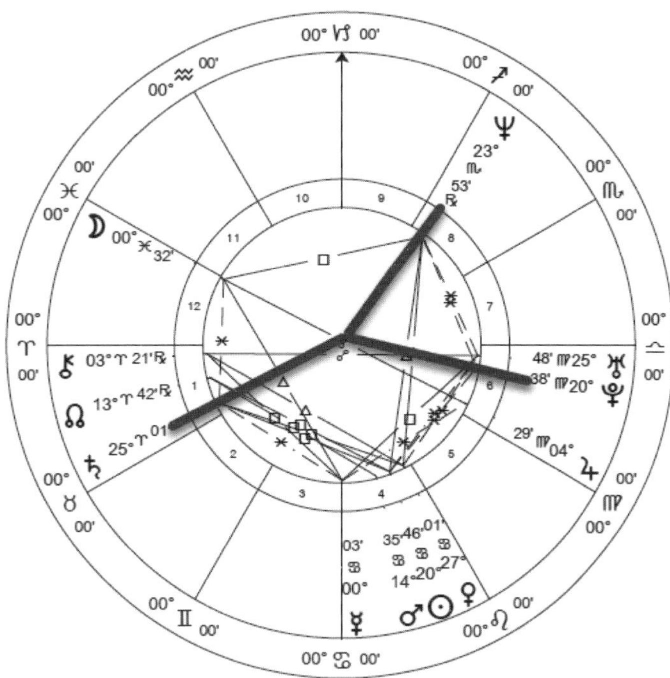

The Hong Kong Flu, July 13, 1968, Hong Kong, China

Once again, we see Saturn and Neptune involved. In this case, they are part of a powerful aspect pattern known as Yod formation. There will be more on this below.

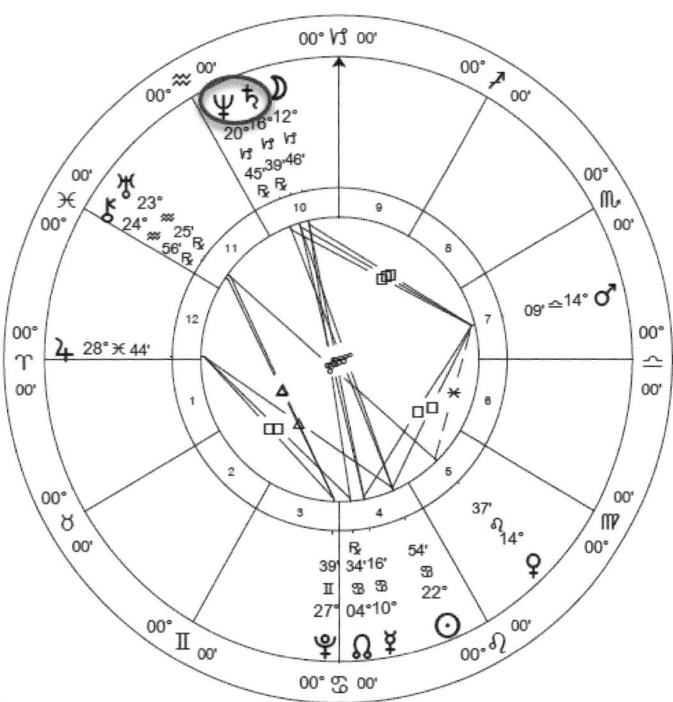

The Great Plague of London, July 15, 1666, London, England

To these eight health crisis cases, I would like to add two more charts. The first is the Fifth Cholera Pandemic of 1881–1896, which was shown earlier in this section as the last time in which a Grand Conjunction occurred involving at least three outermost planets in a single year (actually spanning two years in this case). This pandemic claimed 200,000 lives in Russia between 1893 and 1894, and 90,000 in Japan between 1887 and 1889, as well as several thousand in Germany.

The second chart added is for the Great Plague of London in 1665–1666 (shown on the prior page). It was one of the most well-known plagues in history, with deaths exceeding 100,000 in a city whose population was about 460,000. It was the last major epidemic of the bubonic plague to occur in England. Once again, note the importance of Saturn and Neptune.

RESULTS

We have ten cases here of historically important pandemics/epidemics in which large numbers of people died. Was Saturn conjunct Pluto? Were these two planets even in the same sign? Yes, but only once in the case of the cholera outbreak in 1881, which was not really a pandemic, but we used it because there was an epidemic, and it was the last time a "Great Conjunction" involving three or more outer planets occurred within 1–2 years.

With these results, the idea can be dismissed that the Saturn/Pluto conjunction has any historical correspondence with deadly pandemics and even the COVID-19 pandemic. The correlation with the events of 2020 and Saturn conjunct Pluto has more to do with the threat to the worldwide economy and financial system, the overhaul of socio-political and governmental systems and structures, and perhaps the disruption to the daily lives of humans. It may have some correspondence to a rise in high-profile political assassinations or natural catastrophes, like wildfires, volcanoes, earthquakes, etc., that may threaten the lives and homes of many people. Saturn and Pluto in hard aspect have often been considered a "threat" signature to human lives, but not necessarily due to pandemics. In fact, there is no compelling historical evidence that, by itself, the conjunction of Saturn and Pluto can be associated with pandemics.

So, what does stand out in the history of pandemics related to geocosmic factors? The most outstanding feature is Saturn/Neptune in hard aspect—especially the conjunction—followed by the outer planets compressed into a tight section of the zodiac.

In eight of these 10 cases, Saturn was either in a conjunction (same sign, five times) or a square aspect (three times) to Neptune. In the other two cases, these planets were still in a strong relationship with one another. In the case of the Plague of Justinian in 541, Saturn was in 24° Libra, and Neptune was in its ruling sign of Pisces at 8°, which means they were conjunct by solstice point (equidistant from the winter solstice, also known as "antiscia" points). In the case of the Hong Kong Flu of 1968–1969, Saturn was the focal point of a Yod configuration with the sextile between Neptune and the Uranus/Pluto conjunction. It formed a quincunx (150° aspect) to the other outer planets that were sextile to one another. Thus, Saturn and Neptune were highlighted in all ten charts.

It is also important to note that in five of these cases, the five outermost planets were in close proximity to one another, with more than 120° apart between the first and last of the five planets. In four of these cases, the distance separating the grouping was less than 94° apart. If we only included four of the five outmost planets in this field, we found 8 of the ten cases fell into a zodiacal region where less than 120° separated the first and the last planet of this group. In fact, in 6 of the ten charts, the distance separating the first and last outer planet of the group was 90° or less.

BARBAULT'S CYCLICAL INDEX

This latter factor supports the work of legendary Mundane Astrologer, Andre Barbault.

In an article published in 2012 titled "Survey of Pandemics" (Aperçu sur les Pandémies), Barbault graphically demonstrated outer planet positions close to one another (essentially in a 100º orb) coincided with major social, cultural, and economic events. He also included pandemics as a possibility in this grouping. Applying his index, aptly called the "Barbault Cyclic Index," over the past century, Barbault forecasted in this article the next such alignment would occur around 2020–2021, and it could coincide with a major pandemic. Specifically, he stated:

"Going back to the pandemics and going back to the past century, the four crises of 1918, 1954, 1968 and 1982 are obvious, the two considerable being the first, the famous "Spanish flu" which is said to have claimed 25 million lives, and the last one in which AIDS, which is even more devastating and continues to be deadly. Since then, there has also been a small influenza surge in 2009, against the last lowest cyclical index (2010). We may well be in serious danger of a new pandemic at the 2020–2021 mark, at the lowest peak of the cyclical index of the 21st century, with the quintet of outer planets gathered over a hundred degrees, a conjunction Jupiter-Saturn-Pluto can more specifically, and even specifically, lend itself to the "tissue" of this imbalance. Nevertheless, this configuration can also transfer its core of dissonances to the terrain of geophysical disasters, without ultimately sparing the international affairs scene, Nature and Society being indiscriminately affected."[2]

Just to make sure there is no confusion here, Andre Barbault, a well-known Mundane Astrologer from Paris, France, forecasted a pandemic would occur in 2020–2021 based on his "Cyclical Index" studies, stating such occurrences can happen when outer planets are within 100° of one another. So, let us dismiss at once any arguments stating *no* astrologer forecasted a pandemic in 2020. In truth, Barbault exactly predicted the coming catastrophe eight years before it occurred.

If we apply his cyclical index criterion to the 10 cases of pandemics and epidemics cited here and use the idea that at least 4 of the five outermost planets must be within 100° for this to apply, we find this criterion was present in 6 of those 10 cases. If we expand his limits and allow up to 120°, his conditions were met in 8 of the 10 cases.

Barbault's study is impressive. But so is the correlation of Saturn and Neptune to global pandemics in history.

COVID-19

The novel coronavirus disease of 2019 is abbreviated as COVID-19, where "CO" stands for "corona," VI stands for "virus," D stands for "disease," and "19" stands for the year it was first reported (2019). It will likely rank in the top eight of the world's deadliest pandemics before it ends. It has already claimed over 1 million lives, equal to the lowest estimated number of deaths recorded with the Hong Kong Flu of 1968–1969, the seventh deadliest pandemic. As of this writing (October 1, 2020), there is still no cure or vaccine, although progress on each is underway and reportedly close at hand. Still, judging by the history of global pandemics, COVID-19 may be with us for a while. More deaths are likely.

According to the South China Post, the first case of someone suffering from COVID-19 can be traced back to a 55-year old person from the Hubei province of China on November 17, 2019.[3]

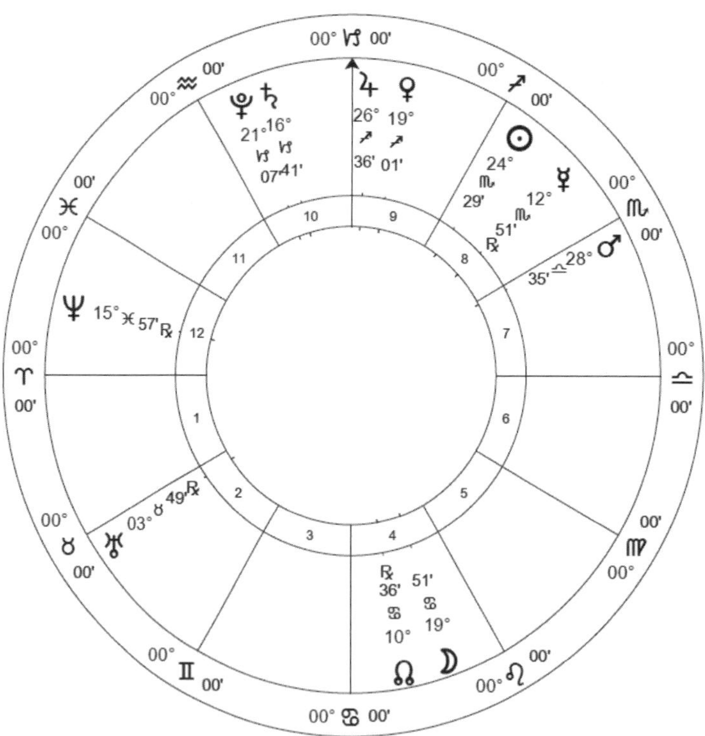

First Reported Case of COVID-19, November 17, 2019, Wu-Han, China

I remember when I first looked at this chart and thought: "Where is Neptune? It is not in a hard aspect to Saturn." In fact, it was in a benign sextile to the Saturn/Pluto conjunction. This just wasn't fitting the theory that Neptune—the planet of disease and weakness of the immune system—would be prominent. But it wasn't. Yes, it was in a square aspect to Jupiter throughout most of 2019, but that was not a signature showing in most cases of worldwide pandemics throughout history. By solstice point, Saturn was in a square aspect to Neptune (Saturn's solstice point was 13° Sagittarius, and Neptune was located at 15° Pisces). I didn't think that was compelling enough. With solstice points, I like to see conjunctions and oppositions, as in the case of the Plague of Justinian in 541 CE. "There must be something else missing," I thought. *But what?*

Perhaps it was Uranus making a semi-square to Neptune, as postulated by MMTA (Merriman Market Timing Academy) graduate Nitin Bhandari of Mumbai, India, in an article he posted on the ISAR financial E-zine. Uranus had already made this aspect five times from August 11, 2017, through its final exact passage on May 2, 2019. It was still within a 3-degree orb on November 17, 2019, so it was possible. But again, Uranus/Neptune aspects did not show up in the previous cases of worldwide pandemics, and this was a relatively minor aspect compared to say a conjunction, square, or opposition.

Looking at the Barbault Cyclical Index, we can see the five outermost planets were in a tight orb of 101° in March 2020. This is slightly outside of Barbault's studies allowing up to 100°, but well within our studies of ten epidemics and/or pandemics in which the planets fall within a range of 120°. Thus, Barbault's Cosmic Index indeed was in effect for this COVID-19 Pandemic of 2020.

But the Saturn/Neptune historical correlation, which was even more impressive in these 10 cases, was not present. This suggests one of three things, or maybe a combination: 1) Nothing is 100%, and this was one of those cases where it simply did not apply. It doesn't alter the fact that the Saturn/Neptune factors are still a very impressive correlation historically, and maybe still the most consistent. 2) There may be some other Neptune relationship no one is seeing. Or 3) it may mean the COVID-19 Virus was not a natural, organic virus, but rather something created in a chemical laboratory, perhaps as a biological chemical weapon for the purpose of threatening the lives of a nation's enemies. This latter possibility sounds like a conspiracy theory. However, the idea of a biological weapon to harm and kill humans fits more with darker principles of Saturn conjunct Pluto in Capricorn.

It was the second possibility, however, motivating me to seek further. What was it about Neptune turning retrograde at 15° 57' Pisces? In fact, it was stationary retrograde, about to go direct 9–10 days later at 15° 55' Pisces. What was so important about that degree and sign?

Then….Bingo! It came to me!

PLANETARY PAIR CYCLES

This degree of Pisces ignited the memory of a concept I introduced in 1977 in the first astrology book I ever wrote, titled Evolutionary Astrology: The Journey of the Soul Through the Horoscope.[4] This book is out of print, but a second volume was written and published in 1991, containing some of the chapters from the first book. The second volume in this series was titled Evolutionary Astrology: The Journey of the Soul Through States of Consciousness.[5] It was these books I now retrieved from my library to review. And there it was, in Chapter 20 of the latter publication (Chapters 13 and 14 of the first out-of-print series) titled "Planetary Pair Cycles: Breaking Through the Collective Pattern." The concept—the technique—was introduced in two points as follows:

- *The point of conjunction between two planets involved in a planetary pair cycle becomes a "charged" point in the zodiac (signs). That degree of the conjunction takes on a synthesis of the two planetary principles involved and will remain in effect until the next cycle of the two planets commences. At that time, the degree of the new conjunction becomes the "charged" point of the signs for that planetary pair cycle.*

- *Every time a major planet transits in an aspect to this "charged degrees" point, it potentially coincides with an event related to the nature of the planetary pair cycle.*

Today, the phrase "planetary pair cycles" is more commonly referred to as "synodic cycles." When "synodic cycles" or "planetary pair cycles" involve three or more outer planets, they are also referred to as "Grand Conjunctions."

There was a corollary to this theory. As stated in the Evolutionary Astrology books:

- *Not all planetary pair cycles are equal in their potential impact. Some are potentially more powerful than others. This leads to a basic assumption regarding planetary pair cycles: The longer the periodicity of a planetary pair cycle, the more profound and long-lasting its potential impact is likely to be upon the affairs of humankind.*

In other words, the further out the planets involved in the conjunction were, the more "profound" their correlation would be to major cycle turning points in human activity. Let's see how this worked in 2020, the year of COVID-19, and the year that changed the arc of human activity in ways never imagined before.

SUPER CHARGED DEGREES

We humans are pattern-matching animals, and astrology is the universe's grand pattern-matching game. Acknowledging this and recognizing some of the patterns that characterize our own pattern-matching tendencies, is hardly without relevance in a world that puts every more stock in the ability to pick out just the right patterns from all the information around us. — Alexander Boxer, "A Scheme of Heaven," W.W Norton and Company, New York, NY, 2020.

The most important of the planetary pair cycles, or synodic cycles, would be the three possible conjunctions between Uranus, Neptune, and Pluto. They will be considered "Tier One" synodic cycles. They last anywhere from 111 to 492 years in duration. The Tier One synodic cycles are listed here:

1. Neptune / Pluto 492 years
2. Uranus / Neptune 171 years
3. Uranus / Pluto 110–143 years

Next in importance would be conjunctions involving Saturn to either Uranus, Neptune, or Pluto. There would be three of these possibilities too, and they are considered "Tier Two" synodic cycles. Their cycles last anywhere from 32–45 years. The Tier Two synodic cycles are listed here:

4. Saturn / Uranus 45 years
5. Saturn / Neptune 36 years
6. Saturn / Pluto 32–37 years

Conjunctions of Jupiter to Saturn, Uranus, Neptune, or Pluto are considered "Tier Three" types. These four possibilities last 13–20 years. The Tier Three synodic cycles are listed here:

7. Jupiter / Saturn 20 years
8. Jupiter / Uranus 14 years
9. Jupiter / Neptune 13 years
10. Jupiter / Pluto 13 years

In all, there are ten possible planetary pair cycles (or Synodic Cycles) involving the outer planets of Jupiter, Saturn, Uranus, Neptune, and Pluto. And three of them just occurred in 2020. This is the first time that three or more outer planet conjunctions have occurred in even a 2-year period since 1881–82, as discussed before. But I was mostly interested in the Tier One signatures, and these were Tier Two and Tier Three types.

The theory postulates that any Tier One, Two, or Three synodic cycle will "super-charge" the degree of the sign in which the conjunction occurs. It imbues that segment (degrees) of the sign with the qualities—the dynamics—associated with those two planets and the sign in which the conjunction takes place. The influence of that degree area remains in effect until the next synodic cycle of those two planets unfolds. Thus, the super-charged degrees of the Tier One conjunctions will not only be powerful, but they will last for a considerable period (over 100 years). In the case of Uranus/Pluto, the super-charged degrees will carry those dynamics for 110–143 years. In the case of Uranus/Neptune, the period will last 171 years. The super-charged degrees of the Neptune and Pluto conjunction influence will last 492 years.

The Uranus/Pluto conjunction of 1965–1966 was pertinent to the placement of Neptune on November 17, 2019, at 15° 57' Pisces. The conjunction occurred three times as follows:

— October 9, 1965, at 17°10' Virgo
— April 4, 1966, at 16°28' Virgo
— June 20, 1966, at 16°08' Virgo

The orb can be expanded slightly to consider the range of each planet's motion from the first to the last passage, based on the degrees of their retrograde and direct stations occurring between the first and last passage of the conjunction. Thus, the Uranus/Pluto super-charged degrees from their 1965–1966 conjunction would be 15°29'–19°38' Virgo. On November 17, 2019, Neptune was stationing right there, in direct opposition to this super-charged degree zone. Virgo is important in this case because it is the sign of health, and Neptune was the planet of disease, especially involving the weakness of the immune system. It fits!

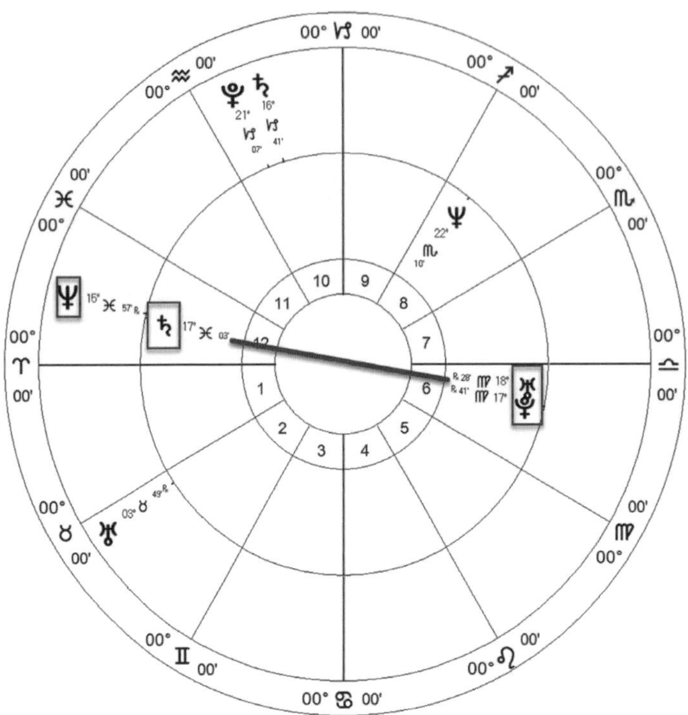

Inner wheel is transits February 15, 1966, Saturn opposition to Uranus/Pluto. Outer wheel shows transit Neptune on day of first COVID-19 case, November 17, 2019, in Wu-Han, China

However, what about Saturn? Our studies indicated Neptune needed to be associated with Saturn. In medical astrology, hard aspects between the two referred to physical vulnerability. In cosmobiology, the midpoint of Saturn/Neptune in a natal chart is considered the weakest part of one's physiology. A look at the period of the Uranus/Pluto conjunction in 1965–1966 will reveal from February 6–27, 1966, Saturn was in 16–18° Pisces, in exact opposition to the Uranus/Pluto conjunction, and close enough to a conjunction with the transit of Neptune on November 17, 2019. That is, transiting Neptune was turning stationary direct on the degree Saturn held in February 1966, when it was also in exact opposition to the Uranus/Pluto conjunction in Virgo.

Now, I had my Saturn/Neptune correlation!

However, there is more to this story. The 171-year Uranus/Neptune conjunctions occurred three times in 1993, in 18–22° Capricorn. Where was Saturn in late 2019, early 2020? Right there in the super-charged 18–22° Capricorn! In fact, the Saturn/Pluto conjunction that preceded the hysteria of the COVID-19 pandemic occurred on January 12, 2020, at 22° Capricorn.

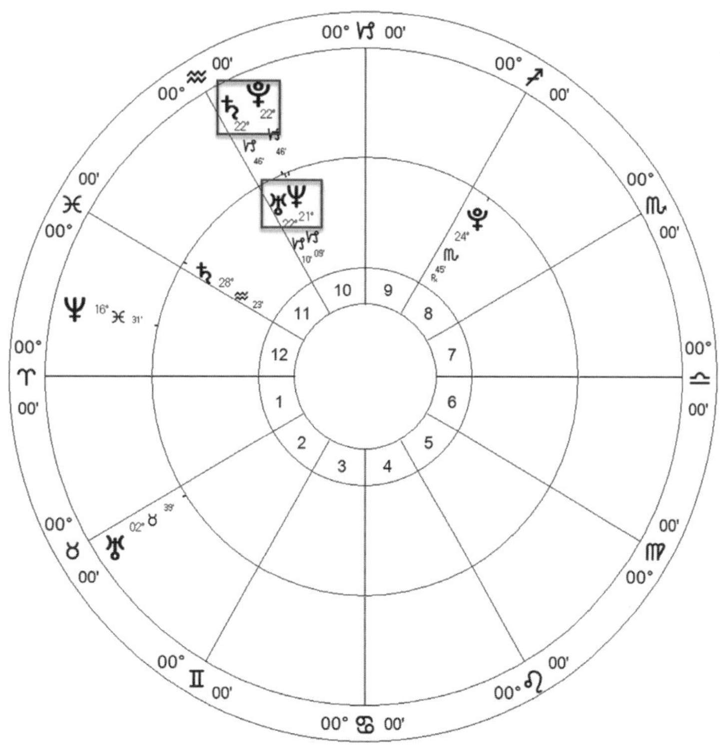

Inner wheel is Uranus/Neptune conjunction, April 21, 1993.
Outer wheel is Saturn/Pluto conjunction, same degrees of Capricorn, January 12, 2020.

Thus, we had two of the three Tier One synodic cycles' super-charged" degrees being conjoined by both the transit of Saturn and Neptune. The correlation to major shifts in the cycles of human activities, shown by the presence of Tier One super-charged degrees being activated, was in effect. Additionally, the presence of transiting Saturn and Neptune to these super-charged degrees fit the correlation of these two planets being highlighted in past historical cases of deadly world pandemics.

FUTURE THOUGHTS ABOUT COVID-19 AND PANDEMICS

History shows pandemics don't just end suddenly or miraculously. As of this writing, there is no vaccine or treatment available to the public, although reports indicate either one or both could be available soon, maybe even by the time you receive this year's Forecast Book. However, keep in mind that in many of these studies, the pandemics have not been totally eradicated until several years after a treatment or vaccine has been found.

Still, as the Grand Conjunctions of 2020 come to an end with the Jupiter/Saturn conjunction in 0° Aquarius on the winter solstice of December 21, 2020, there is hope that life will begin to return to somewhat more normal conditions, realizing, of course, it may never fully return to the normalcy enjoyed before February 2020. But Jupiter—the planet of freedom, social activities, travel, and education—will start to separate from Saturn and leave Capricorn—the planet and sign of restrictions and lockdowns. Both Jupiter and Saturn will enter the freedom-loving sign of Aquarius. This suggests the restrictions caused by the pandemic may end within three months after December 2020.

We also note Neptune will leave its opposition to the Uranus/Pluto super-charged degrees of 15–19° Pisces in February 2021. Again, this suggests a return to more "normalcy" within three months. Saturn has already passed its conjunction with the Uranus/Neptune super-charged zone at 18–22° Capricorn.

As you will see in the "Seasons" section of this year's book, the spring and summer ingresses will find Jupiter conjunct the ascendant in the chart for Washington D/C., indicating a greater sense of openness and social activity during those two seasons. All of these studies indicate that by spring and summer of 2021, business and social activities are opening up, and there is likely a sigh of relief from the world's collective by then.

However, it doesn't mean the virus has been eradicated. First, there is the strong possibility of a "second wave" occurring within three months of Neptune turning stationary direct on November 29, 2020. More importantly, we note Saturn and Neptune will form their next conjunction at 0° Aries on February 20, 2026. In the year prior to that, they will be in orb of conjunction in Pisces, the sign of infections. We cannot rule out a future wave then, or even the advent of another pandemic threat. However, there are other possible manifestations to these planetary dynamics (oil spills affecting the ecological balance of the earth, major floods, and heavy rains, etc.).

Second, the Barbault Cyclical Index, in which four or more outer planets remain within an orb of 120° (by our research, whereas 100 ° in his own publications), remains in effect through June 2027 when Uranus in Gemini trines Pluto in Aquarius. Not only is this trine important from the Barbault Cyclical Index study, but it is important because Uranus will conjunct the Neptune/Pluto super-charged degrees of 6–9° Gemini. The last time this occurred was in 1944 when the Bretton Woods agreement determined the U.S. Dollar would become the world's standard currency for trading. Also, the most extensive vaccination program up to that time was administered in Bengal, India, in 1944 too. It ushered in the final months of World War II. These are topics for another book, but it may also support the symbology for the eradication of COVID-19 through discoveries and new treatment programs. Thus, there is hope for the future of humanity.

References:

1. Nattress, Katrina, "A Closer Look at San Francisco's Powerful AIDS Memorial," www.theculturetrip.com, February 7, 2019.
2. Barbault, Andre, "Survey of Pandemics" (Aperçu sur les Pandémies), 2012
3. Davidson, Helen, "First COVID-19 Case Happened in November, China Government Records Show, www.theguardian.com, March 13, 2020.
4. Merriman, Raymond, Evolutionary Astrology: The Journey of the Soul Through the Horoscope, Seek-It Publications, Rochester, MI, 1977 (out of print).
5. Merriman, Raymond, Evolutionary Astrology: The Journey of the Soul Through States of Consciousness, Seek-It Publications and MMA, Inc, Scottsdale, AZ, 1991.

JUPITER/SATURN AND
"A NEW AIRA"

Planetary cycles preside over the destiny of the world with each conjunction being a honing point at the heart of the planetary whole. — Andre Barbault, "Planetary Cycles: Mundane Astrology," The Astrological Association, London, UK, 2016.

Modern science began from studying the heavens, and in this sense we can say that, yes, the stars really have communicated to us many profound truths about the nature of things. The bigger question isn't whether the universe is speaking but, instead, how far can we ever hope to comprehend what it might be saying. Alexander Boxer, "A Scheme of Heaven: The History of Astrology and the Search for Our Destiny in Data," W.W. Norton & Co., New York, NY, 2020.

I missed my friends.

We used to go out every Saturday night. We'd meet for a sundowner at my house, sit out on my pool deck watching the majestic sunsets of Arizona. We would either go out to a restaurant, or I would cook for everyone, and we would catch up on what we did over the past week or month, discuss markets, astrology, family, politics, etc. But when social distancing, meeting-size restrictions, quarantines, and lockdowns began in March 2020, we stopped doing that. It was Jupiter (social) and Saturn in Capricorn (distancing, face masks, lockdowns, and other restrictions). The fun with friends stopped, and in its place, fear to congregate began.

I missed my wife.

Antonia, my beautiful companion and fellow astrologer, lives in Cologne, Germany. Due to travel bans between the U.S. and Europe, she couldn't come to the U.S. and I couldn't go to Germany for five months. We had never been apart for five months in the 18 years we have known one another. But with Jupiter (travel) and Saturn in Capricorn (restrictions and bans), it wasn't allowed. I started to become a little grouchy (Saturn and Capricorn, both highlighted) and restless. But I also had more time to accomplish projects (also Saturn in Capricorn).

I missed my children.

My eldest daughter Aimee and her family live in Evanston, Illinois, outside of Chicago. My son Sean and his wife live in Los Angeles. We would get together for vacations somewhere nice every winter and summer. But with COVID-19 running rampant last spring and summer, it wasn't wise for us to travel (Jupiter and Saturn in Capricorn again, along with Pluto—danger). On the other hand, my youngest daughter Alie and her husband, Richard, had to rebuild their house here in Scottsdale. It was damaged during one of those summer storm outbursts that cause major flooding in the desert. They moved in with me for almost a year while their house was being rebuilt. It was wonderful to re-connect in a family setting with my daughter and her husband. But the most wonderful event during this period was when Alie became pregnant and gave birth to Gabriella. I had the awesome experience of living with Gabriella for the first 100 days of her life. How many people my age ever get that kind of experience? It was indescribable. It was transformative (Pluto). It was a lot (Jupiter) of new responsibilities (Saturn in Capricorn), for me, the elder (Saturn) of the family. But it created a new level of joy and reverence for life to witness the first 100 days of a newborn child. It produced a memory (Saturn in Capricorn) for which I will forever be grateful.

The point of sharing my personal story of 2020 is two-fold. First, to illustrate that Jupiter, which rules "fun" and "enjoyment," was approaching Saturn in Capricorn, which rules restrictions, duty, even being alone and isolated. Together, this combination is not much fun, unless you can adjust your mindset and make your responsibilities become a source of enjoyment. Otherwise, fun is limited with Jupiter conjunct Saturn in Capricorn. Jupiter rules expansion and increase, but the things that expanded and increased were of a Saturn in Capricorn variety: responsibilities, restrictions, travel bans, lockdowns, social distancing, feelings of isolation, loneliness, and depression for many people. I was fortunate as I had the blessing of a newborn in my house for the first 100 days of her life, plus my youngest daughter and her husband for several months during the pandemic. Many others were not so fortunate. Many people were unable to share enjoyable activities with friends or other family members because of the pandemic and the restrictions it created.

The second point of sharing this personal experience is to acknowledge that Jupiter and Saturn in Capricorn were both in the balsamic (ending) phase of their synodic cycle. They were moving closer and closer to their conjunction that would take place on December 21, 2020. The most challenging, difficult part of a cycle is just before it ends. Basic cycles' theory postulates that the first stage of a new cycle is usually bullish. It can be exciting, as one sees new inventions and discoveries, or applications to existing inventions and discoveries begin to blossom. But the last stage—in fact, the very last stage—of a cycle is bearish. The same principle applies to planetary cycles, and the longer the planetary pair cycle (synodic cycle), the more difficult matters become as the two planets approach their conjunction. The year 2020 hosted three Grand Conjunctions of synodic cycles, each lasting between 14 and 37 years. Until the very end of 2020, two of these three synodic cycles were in their balsamic, or final stages. That ends in 2021.

As noted in the introduction, there were three "Grand Conjunctions" in 2020 involving the outer planets of Jupiter, Saturn, and Pluto. If we include Mars, then we experienced four synodic cycles. Mars conjoined the other three outer planets between March 20 and March 31, right at the peak of the hysteria surrounding both the COVID-19 pandemic, the lockdown of the economy, and the selloff in the world stock markets. It was the most powerful cosmic gathering of 2020. In fact, it was the most powerful cosmic combination since the Cardinal Climax of 2008-2010 that coincided with the Great Recession of 2007-2009.

The Long and Even Longer Cycles of "The Great Chronocrator"

Of these four synodic cycles, the last one may be the most important. It is the 20-year Jupiter/Saturn conjunction of December 21, 2020. As a 20-year cycle, it is the 7th longest of the planetary pair cycles. But this particular instance will also represent the start of a new 140-year period consisting of seven successive cycles in air signs as it takes place at 0° Aquarius. It breaks the earth sign dominance of the Jupiter/Saturn synodic cycle that began in July 1802, which was interrupted in its next conjunction in 1821, but then resumed its passage through earth signs approximately every 20 years between 1842 and 1961. Once again, it was interrupted when it occurred in an air sign in 1980–1981 before returning for its last passage in an earth sign (Taurus) for this series on May 28, 2000. Thus, we could say that the 200-year Jupiter/Saturn earth sign era finally ended on December 21, 2020, when the air sign era fully commences without interruptions for the next 139 years.

However, the December 21, 2020 conjunction of "The Great Chronocrator," as the Jupiter/Saturn 20-year cycle is often called, is actually a longer elemental cycle than that. Approximately every 200 years, the Jupiter/Saturn synodic cycle changes elements, as just noted. But the last time it started, a series of consecutive occurrences in air signs was in 1226, also in early Aquarius. Just as in 1980–81 when it had its first conjunction in the air sign of Libra, it also had its first entrance into the air element (Libra again) in 1186, after which it then returned to Taurus, an earth sign in 1206, just like it did in 2000. But the following six conjunctions between Jupiter and Saturn were in air signs from 1226 through 1345. There was an interruption into a water sign in 1365, after which the next two conjunctions were back in air signs once more (1385 and 1405). Thus, the entrance of Jupiter and Saturn, both into Aquarius, December 17–19, 2020, and especially their conjunction on December 21, 2020, represents the return of the approximately 800-year air sign elemental cycle of the "Great Chronocrator."

In short, this means the Jupiter/Saturn conjunction on December 21, 2020, is a combination of the end and beginning of 20-, 200-, and 800-year cycles. The most challenging part of any cycle is its end, and here we have the end and beginning of three longer-term cycles involving Jupiter and Saturn. The most bullish or growth-oriented phase of a cycle is its beginning stages. Symbolically, this suggests that the severe restrictions, bans, lockdowns, etc., represented by Jupiter in Capricorn approaching Saturn in Capricorn will give way to a "New Aira[1]" after the winter solstice of 2020.

"A New Aira"

The implications of a new air sign era ("New Aira") are huge.

The meaning of earth signs in astrology pertains to logic, common sense, business, agriculture, mining, materialism, and governance. The 200+ -year period of 1800–2020 was typified by society's value placed on wealth, accumulation of material possessions, and power, especially attained through business and/or government. It started as a mostly agrarian society and economy in many of the developing nations of the world, where industries and businesses were created as populations moved from rural settings to urban cities. That's where the power shifted from and to. If you wanted to change the world, and achieve great status in the world, you mostly had to do it through the power afforded in politics and government, or the accumulation of wealth through business enterprise. And you had to do it from the rapidly growing urban locations (cities). Those who acquired the most power or possessions had access to avenues to change the world where major populations were gathered. These factors were held in high esteem by societies everywhere. It was the era of capitalism and the striving towards control in governance either by democracy or dictatorship.

That model of societies, economies, and governance defined by the 200-year earth sign presence of Jupiter and Saturn began to change dramatically with the first occurrence of the "Great Chronocrator" in air signs in 1980–81, primarily when the "Capricorn Climax" unfolded in 1988–1993 during, the middle of this first 20-year air sign experiment. As described earlier, models for both governance and business began to change. The Berlin Wall came tumbling down as Russian Communism went broke, and 300 million new consumers entered the capitalistic, free-market economies of the world. This was also the period when the way the world conducted business began to shift from brick and mortar buildings to cyberspace and the internet. It was a "Communications Revolution," which describes the way the approximate 54-year Kondratieff Cycle (named after famed Russian economist and cycles' analyst Nicholai Kondratieff) ends and begins. Now the idea of wealth and power began to shift from governance, politics, manufacturing, and control of natural resources to knowledge and technology.

♃	☌	♄	(X)	Nov 5 1782	N:28°♐06' D	28°♐06' D
♃	☌	♄	(X)	Jul 17 1802	N:05°♍07' D	05°♍07' D
♃	☌	♄	(X)	Jun 19 1821	N24°♈38' D	24°♈38' D
♃	☌	♄	(X)	Jan 26 1842	N08°♑54' D	08°♑54' D
♃	☌	♄	(X)	Oct 21 1861	N18°♍22' D	18°♍22' D
♃	☌	♄	(X)	Apr 18 1881	N01°♉35' D	01°♉35' D
♃	☌	♄	(X)	Nov 28 1901	13°♑59' D	13°♑59' D
♃	☌	♄	(X)	Sep 10 1921	26°♍35' D	26°♍35' D
♃	☌	♄	(X)	Aug 7 1940	14°♉27' D	14°♉27' D
♃	☌	♄	(X)	Oct 19 1940	12°♉27' ℞	12°♉27' ℞
♃	☌	♄	(X)	Feb 15 1941	09°♉07' D	09°♉07' D
♃	☌	♄	(X)	Feb 18 1961	25°♑12' D	25°♑12' D
♃	☌	♄	(X)	Dec 31 1980	09°♎29' D	09°♎29' D
♃	☌	♄	(X)	Mar 4 1981	08°♎06' ℞	08°♎06' ℞
♃	☌	♄	(X)	Jul 24 1981	04°♎56' D	04°♎56' D
♃	☌	♄	(X)	May 28 2000	22°♉43' D	22°♉43' D
♃	☌	♄	(X)	Dec 21 2020	00°♒29' D	00°♒29' D

Table of Jupiter and Saturn in earth signs in the red frame. The first instance was actually July 17, 1802 (outside the red frame). But it wasn't until January 26, 1842, that series of conjunctions in earth signs began that lasted until December 31, 1980. It returned for its last passage in an earth sign on May 28, 2000, the last entry shown in the red frame above.

In 2000, Jupiter and Saturn returned to Taurus for their last jaunt through an earth synodic cycle that would last for the next 20 years, after which it would advance through the other elements of the signs for the several centuries starting December 21, 2020. But in its return to its final foray into the earth element (2000–2020) following its first foray into the air element cycle of 1981–2000, the new "information superhighway" crashed. It coincided with the dot-com bubble burst of 2000–2002. It also coincided with the return of the old earth sign themes prior to 1981. Russian Communism and dictatorial governance in many parts of the world regained their control. You couldn't trust technology any longer as an abundance of computer viruses, hacks, worms, ransomware, and the likes became all too common. All governments realized the power of technology and began developing very sophisticated tools to harness that power for their nation's interests, often at the expense of other nations whose computer programs were frequently hacked. Money was needed for these imperialistic endeavors, and so the accumulation of wealth and political power once again became paramount in determining one's status in the world. Populations, which had moved out to the suburbs in the three decades before the new century, once again returned to urban areas. The cities became the meccas for another migration of people who sought careers that would lead to greater power, wealth, and influence in society.

That is all about to shift again as the "New Aira" commences on December 21, 2020. The changes won't happen overnight. When Jupiter and Saturn made a conjunction in Libra, an air sign for the first time on December 31, 1980, the monumental changes of the next 20 years did not erupt immediately. It took 8–13 years before these new discoveries began to be applied on a large scale, and new shifts in status began to take hold in both business and government arenas. It may take another 8–13 years before the application of new inventions and forms of governance take shape on a meaningful level this time as well.

♃	☌	♄	(X)	Dec 11 1166	21°♑42' D	21°♑42' D
♃	☌	♄	(X)	Nov 8 1186	12°♎03' D	12°♎03' D
♃	☌	♄	(X)	Apr 16 1206	25°♉46' D	25°♉46' D
♃	☌	♄	(X)	Mar 4 1226	02°♒58' D	02°♒58' D
♃	☌	♄	(X)	Sep 21 1246	19°♎07' D	19°♎07' D
♃	☌	♄	(X)	Jul 25 1265	09°♊41' D	09°♊41' D
♃	☌	♄	(X)	Dec 31 1285	08°♒01' D	08°♒01' D
♃	☌	♄	(X)	Dec 25 1305	00°♏49' D	00°♏49' D
♃	☌	♄	(X)	Apr 20 1306	28°♎05' ℞	28°♎05' ℞
♃	☌	♄	(X)	Jul 19 1306	26°♎00' D	26°♎00' D
♃	☌	♄	(X)	Jun 1 1325	17°♊52' D	17°♊52' D
♃	☌	♄	(X)	Mar 24 1345	19°♒01' D	19°♒01' D
♃	☌	♄	(X)	Oct 25 1365	07°♏00' D	07°♏00' D
♃	☌	♄	(X)	Apr 8 1385	25°♊53' D	25°♊53' D
♃	☌	♄	(X)	Jan 16 1405	23°♒46' D	23°♒46' D
♃	☌	♄	(X)	Feb 14 1425	17°♏18' D	17°♏18' D

Table of Jupiter and Saturn in air signs in the red frame. The first instance was actually November 8, 1186 (outside the red frame). It returned to an earth sign (Taurus) on April 16, 1206. But it wasn't until May 4, 1226, that a series of conjunctions in air signs began that will last until March 24, 1345. It advanced to a water sign on October 25, 1365, before returning for two more cycles in air signs on April 8, 1385, and January 16, 1405. It finally ended its air cycle on February 14, 1425, when the "Great Chronocrator" entered Scorpio for the next several 20-year conjunction periods.

The "Great Chronocrator" and the "Great Mutation"

Jupiter and Saturn are known as the "Great Chronocrator" because they conjoin one another regularly at approximately 20-year intervals (they actually conjoin on average every 19.6 years). The term means "Marker of Time." Until the discovery of Uranus on March 13, 1781, by German-born British astronomer, Frederick William Herschel, Jupiter and Saturn were the furthest-out planets in the solar system visible to the naked eye. They appeared as very bright stars, especially when in opposite signs as the Sun. But most remarkable was the fact that they moved closer and closer to one another until they appeared together in the same sector of the heavens approximately every 20 years. Astrologers gave this 20-year interval great significance throughout history as portending significant changes for the world. For instance, many astrologers believe it was the conjunction of Jupiter and Saturn in the sign of the Fish (Pisces) in 7 BC that created the bright star which led the "wise men" (astrologers) to Bethlehem when Jesus of Nazareth was born, and thus the origin of Christianity.

This 20-year synodic cycle finds the "Great Chronocrator" advancing about 248–249° forward from one cycle to the next. If it were exactly 240°, these planets' conjunction would always occur in the same element (fire, earth, air, or water). Hence, approximately every 200 years, this synodic cycle will switch to a series involving another element sign. There are interruptions at the beginning and end of each element change where the conjunction will occur in the next element sign. Then in the next 20-year instance, it will revert to the former element sign, only to next be followed by a series of 6–8 successive 20-year occurrences in the following element sign.

We witnessed this cosmic ballet from February 1961 through December 2020. That is, the "Great Chronocrator's" synodic cycle in February 1961 was in the earth sign of Capricorn. The next cycle in December 1980 occurred in Libra, an air sign. It then returned for its final passage in an earth sign on May 28, 2000, when the two planets conjoined in Taurus. But then they returned to the air signs on December 21, 2020, as both entered Aquarius. They will continue to conjoin in air signs through 2140. In 2159, Jupiter and Saturn will advance into Scorpio, a water sign. But the next two cycles in 2179 and 2199 will return to air signs before that cycle finally ends in 2219. The "Great Chronocrator" then moves fully into water signs for the next several cycles.

When the Jupiter/Saturn synodic cycle changes elements, it is referred to as a "Great Mutation." This means an old 200-year era has ended, and a new one begins. But the most important of the "Great Mutations" is when the "Great Chronocrator" moves into the same elemental cycle where it last commenced approximately 800 years ago. That is what happened on December 31, 1980, when Jupiter and Saturn conjoined in Libra, an air sign that last began an air elemental cycle on November 8, 1186, nearly 800 years before. Now that is what is happening on December 21, 2020, when this great cycle returns to air signs—to 0° Aquarius, where it will begin a series of seven synodic cycles in air signs, much like it did on March 4, 1226, and lasted until the final one of that elemental series commenced January 16, 1405; except for the one interruption in 1365 when it advanced to a water sign before returning back to the air element in the following two cycles.

The purpose of this astronomy/history lesson is to identify a time band that has a pattern similar to what we are experiencing today and relative to the cycles of the "Great Mutation." That is, the period of 1961–2020 exhibits a Jupiter/Saturn pattern similar to 1166–1226. And the period of 2021–2219 will show a Jupiter/Saturn pattern similar to 1126–1425. In the study of Mundane Astrology, these periods are likely to exhibit themes that are similar to one another. *As above, so below.*

So, what are those themes?

The Themes of Jupiter/Saturn in Aquarius

The only real prison is fear, and the only real freedom is freedom from fear.
— Aung San Suu Kyi

There are two ways to forecast potential themes of the future using astrology. The first is to perform pattern-matching studies. That is, identify the geocosmic cycles in effect and then go back in time and examine the conditions and events that took place during the previous instances of those same geocosmic cycles. In this exercise, we are looking for the re-occurrence of specific planetary cycles to cycles in human activity, which is the very definition of how astrology works to those who research the data available. The second is to simply apply astrological dynamics of planets, signs, and aspects and then project how they might manifest at a time when certain combinations are present. We will use both to construct a glimpse of what the future might hold in 2021 and beyond.

The Dynamic Themes of Aquarius

Harmony and understanding
Sympathy and trust abounding
No more falsehoods or derisions
Golden living dreams of visions
Mystic crystal revelation
And the mind's true liberation
— The 5th Dimension, "Aquarius/Let the Sunshine In," James Rado, Gerome Ragini, Gait MacDermot, Soul City, Los Angeles, 1968

What is the difference of Jupiter and Saturn in Capricorn in 2020 versus Jupiter and Saturn in Aquarius in 2021? Also, what is the difference between the ending phase of the Jupiter/Saturn synodic cycle versus its beginning phase? Let's make a list.

Education

"*More than young people in the past, millennials have friends they can count on in tough times. More millennials have college degrees than do prior generations, and there is no better predictor of functioning well at advanced ages than education.*" Sightline Project at Stanford University's Center on Longevity, as quoted from "2030: How Today's Biggest Trends Will Collide and Reshape the Future of Everything," by Mauro Guillen. St Martin's Press, New York, NY 2020.

Jupiter rules education. Saturn and Capricorn rule structure, boundaries, limits, closures, and restrictions. Aquarius rules technology and cyberspace. As Jupiter and Saturn move out of Capricorn and into Aquarius December 17–21, 2020, the focus on education—especially higher education—moves from traditional structures, rules, and guidelines of the past 200 years to new formats that will increasingly involve technology, computers, and online learning applications.

In 2020, with Jupiter and Saturn in Capricorn, schools at all education levels were closed for long periods. Children and university students were restricted from entering the classrooms of school buildings. Classes at both the grade school and college level began to take place online. The transition was resisted at first. It was not easy to adjust the routines of children, let alone the working schedules of the parents. It was equally difficult to adjust if you were an independent adult taking courses at the college and university level or a teacher/professor at those institutions. You had to learn to teach online, or you had to learn to use the avenues of online learning to continue your education. This required significant adjustment in schedules, routines, and computer skills for many.

Under the Capricorn stellium, adjustments do not take place willingly. It calls for sacrifices, to which the first response is to resist. But Capricorn instructs that reality prevails, and grudgingly we start to adapt to the new reality. Now online learning is becoming accepted as a vital component of the new world of education as these planets move into Aquarius.

This trend will continue evolving now that Jupiter and Saturn are fully into their air sign element series. In fact, online education and vocational training beyond the secondary school level will likely provide one of the most excellent opportunities for economic growth and individual wealth. Expenses in providing and receiving higher education online will be much less than conducting in-person classes that require traveling and housing expenses for both students and instructors. Colleges and universities may see an increase in profits due to online education, thereby reducing the dependence on government subsidies to stay open. This may indirectly affect the budgets of communities, states, and countries, especially pertaining to the financial support required of governments to operate.

Of course, politicians will continue campaigning for more taxes to support higher education for a while. But soon, this may pass away as more and more colleges and universities of higher education become progressively more self-sufficient. Aquarius is one of the more independent signs in astrology. An additional benefit is that as the costs of online higher education come down, future college students will be required to take on less student debt. There are several details to work out between governments, schools, and students in this vision of the future of education in order to get this right. But with the synodic cycles of Jupiter and Saturn occurring in air signs for the next 140 years, I believe it will work out. And I think the day is fast approaching when students will be able to attain an online higher education degree for free. Aquarius rules freedom. Jupiter rules education, and Saturn rules government. Put it all together, and the next 20 years indicate a movement towards greater freedom in education, even to the point of cost-free education in many cases.

This projection may not be the same for secondary schools and younger students because of the need to 1) focus on the social development of children, much of which takes place in the school setting, and 2) the need for parents to work while their children are at school. But changes in this arrangement are likely to start over the next 20 years, too. Secondary school teachers who are proficient in computer skills may also be more in demand as private tutors for parents who wish their children to become more home-schooled and avoid the health risks associated with the socializing that takes place in the school buildings of early education. With Aquarius, we may see a new form of "school groups" forming, something like "commune schools," maybe out of one parent's home or a rotating home setting environment with small groups of students who study together under the direction of one well-qualified and well-paid instructor for several years.

Consistent with the principles of Jupiter and Saturn in air signs, more people will be able to afford a higher education, and intellectual competency will become the basis for a higher standing in one's community. Teachers, professors, and "career trainers" who master the new form of online teaching—the "cyber classroom"—will be valued. They will demand and receive greater compensation for their training and ability to educate online. Teaching will once again be a profession that is equated with a higher status in societies everywhere over the next 140 years, and it is starting now. If you are young and looking for a career that has a bright future, consider mastering computers, technology, and especially hosting online webinars, and becoming a teacher.

Historically, major advances in education have taken place under the conjunctions of Jupiter and Saturn. Astrologer Omari Martin of Chicago gave a very insightful talk on this subject at the ISAR 2020 "Virtual Conjunction" online conference in September 2020 (www.isarastrology.org).

As an example, the English High School of Boston became the first public school in the U.S. It was established in 1821, the year of a Jupiter/Saturn conjunction.

In 1861, under another 20-year Jupiter/Saturn conjunction, Vassar College was founded. "*For the first time, women were offered courses in art history, physical education, geology, astronomy, music, mathematics, and chemistry, taught by the leading scholars of the day.*"[2]

The Elementary Education Act of 1880 ("The Mundella Act") required school attendance of everyone ten years old or more in England and Wales. This was the year just before the Jupiter/Saturn conjunction of 1881.

In 1901, during the next Jupiter/Saturn cycle, the first public community college in the U.S. opened in Joliet, IL (Joliet Junior College).

On November 14, 1960, just four months before the Jupiter/Saturn conjunction of February 18, 1961, "*Ruby Bridges became the first African American child to integrate an all-white public elementary school in the South. She later became a civil rights activist.*"[3]

In 1979, Congress established the Department of Education as a cabinet-level agency. It began operations in 1980.

These are just a few of the crucial developments in the history of education related to the presence of the "Great Chronocrator."

The message is that education, as we know it, is undergoing massive changes. The form in which education is delivered, and the impact it will have on society will likely be substantial not only for this decade but, in fact, for the next 140 years. Opportunities (Jupiter) abound for those who get engaged in this new direction of education, learning, and career training. Companies that host online meetings, conferences, and classes are poised to do exceptionally well over the next decade. And so will those instructors who master these online platforms and efficiently deliver knowledge and education to a new generation of students who will be transitioning from learning in traditional schools and colleges to that of the cyber world.

Conferences and Seminars

Related to education are conferences and seminars, where learning also occurs and is therefore associated with Jupiter. With Jupiter and Saturn ingressing into Aquarius, these will also be conducted more often via an online venue. Once again, this will result in enormous profits (revenues and savings) for the organizers, speakers, and attendees because it means a considerable reduction in costs to conduct. This will provide an economic boom for those who efficiently manage to navigate this new forum for educating and teaching skills to others. It is already happening.

Travel

This is a two-pronged issue. Travel for leisure and social or family activity will increase now that Jupiter is leaving Capricorn and separating from Saturn. Airlines will begin to come back after the Capricorn stellium and Grand Conjunctions of 2020.

However, the use of hotels and convention centers will likely struggle as organizers of those events realize the enormous profit differences of hosting such events online versus in person.

Sports

Jupiter and Mars rule sports. Aquarius rules large gatherings of people. After both Saturn (restrictions related to the size of group gatherings) and Jupiter (fun, sports, social activities) leave Capricorn (restrictions and bans), stadiums are likely to fill up again for sporting events. Sports, as entertainment and recreation, will return.

Communes and Fractional Home Ownership

Aquarius and air signs, in general, are communal-oriented. Aquarius gravitates toward sharing life's activities in groups, with friends, with those who share common interests.

Aquarius is also very independent-minded, preferring camaraderie above formal commitment. For this reason, an increase of property and land purchased by groups of people who are part of a nuclear family, rather than individuals or families, is likely to appear. Fractional ownership is where multiple people split the cost of the purchase and share proportionately in the ownership. Taking this one step further, many of these purchases will create communities to live together, or housing to share, as in a commune model. With Saturn involved, responsibilities and duties will be clearly defined so that the effort to maintain the commune is divided equally, which is another concept (equality) related to Aquarius. The Aquarian disposition is to "think out of the box," but their living structures, however, are likely to appear as anything but a box. Aquarius is very inventive and likes space, air, and light. Hence the architecture of new homes supporting this concept of communal living is likely to be very interesting if not also very original.

Planes, Drones, and Fractional Ownership

Fractional ownership arrangements may also apply to purchases of other needed aspects of daily living, such as automobiles and airplanes, and even drones for the transportation and delivery of goods. With Aquarius, societies may be moving from a concept of individual ownership to one that is more group-oriented. People will band together in tight-knit groups that place a high value on the enjoyment of one another's friendship. They will be willing to invest in a variety of assets together, as a group body, to enhance the quality of life for all involved. Finances will not be the motivating factor. Friendship, communication, and quality of life shared with like-minded contacts will be the driving force. With Saturn involved, this may appeal more to the young elders of society, especially those who do not want to burden their children (Aquarius is independence-minded), nor do they wish to live in assisted living or nursing facilities where they do not know anyone. They will be more likely to create their own communities with those they have grown to share many of their life experiences with—their personal "network" developed over many years of life.

Protests for Freedom, Social Justice, and Equality

Other keywords related to Aquarius and Jupiter are freedom, social justice, and equality. Aquarius also rules mass gatherings for a purpose, usually attached to one of the concepts just mentioned. If peaceful, these gatherings of protest demanding freedom, social justice, and equality will accomplish their goals (see the section below on Court decisions and actions). If not peaceful, they will likely result in great divisions (already apparent) and, at worse, civil wars, at least at first. That means the first half of the Jupiter/Saturn synodic cycle (2020–2030) in Aquarius may be chaotic and dangerous as different ideologies clash. Eventually, the proponents of "thinking for the good of the greater whole" will prevail. Aquarius can bring forth revolutionary thoughts and even revolutions. Still, in the end, the victors are usually those who hold the well-being of the greatest number of people foremost in their actions. Aquarius wants change, but not necessarily war. We will discuss that further in the next chapter on Saturn/Uranus and social unrest.

Major Court Decisions and Changes of Laws

Jupiter and Saturn represent the laws of the land and the highest courts where decisions are made to uphold or enforce those laws. In Aquarius, laws that support individual human rights, such as freedom and equality, are likely to prevail.

If we go back to 1226, the last time the Jupiter/Saturn cycle started their air sign series in Aquarius, we will find that the Magna Carta was adopted and then applied in 1225. This served as the foundation of the English system of common law. It abolished older oppressive laws and outlined policies that would respect liberties and equality for everyone.

In another powerful case that changed the arc of equal rights, President Abraham Lincoln signed the Emancipation Proclamation on September 22, 1862, within a year of the Jupiter/Saturn conjunction in late 1861. He declared, *"...that all persons held as slave are, and henceforth shall be free."*

In 1801, John Marshall was appointed the fourth chief justice of the Supreme Court, and the "Judiciary Act of 1801" was established, which allowed the outgoing president to nominate 50 new judges. *"The incoming Democratic-Republicans, who controlled Congress, promptly repealed the measure"* (https://oxfordre.com/americanhistory/

In 1880, the Supreme Court unanimously voted to protect black voting rights.

In 1961, the Court voted on safeguards against unreasonable search and seizures.

These illustrate just a few samples of cases where the government passed laws, or the Court (Jupiter and Saturn) made important decisions to protect individual rights. Equally important decisions along these lines are likely to occur within two years of this current Jupiter/Saturn conjunction, especially as it takes place at 0° Aquarius. In fact, there is a possibility that major changes in the composition of this Supreme Court of the U.S. or the highest courts in other countries may take place. We may even see the creation of new world judicial systems or bodies. For example, on June 12, 1941, just months after the conjunction of Jupiter and Saturn, the "Declaration of St James Palace" was made that became the precursor to the creation of the United Nations. It stated, *"The only true basis of enduring peace is the willing cooperation of free peoples in a world in which, relieved of the menace of aggression, all may enjoy economic and social security; It is our intention to work together, and with other free peoples, both in war and peace, to this end."*[4]

The Peculiar Relationship Between the 2000 and 2020 Instances

The 20-year cycle of the Jupiter/Saturn conjunction may be particularly important this year due to the similarity of planetary sign positions that were present in 2000. In fact, it is not just Jupiter and Saturn, but also their square to Uranus.

On May 28, 2000, Jupiter and Saturn conjoined at 22° Taurus. Uranus was at 20° Aquarius.

On December 21, 2020, Jupiter and Saturn conjoin at 0° Aquarius, approaching a square with Uranus in Taurus. In January and February 2021, Jupiter and Saturn both form exact squares to Uranus.

One can easily observe that the same signs were involved in both instances, and only the planets were reversed. In 2000, Jupiter and Saturn were in Taurus, and Uranus was in its ruling sign of Aquarius. In 2020–2021, Jupiter and Saturn are in Aquarius. Saturn co-rules Aquarius. Uranus is in Taurus. The planets now reverse the signs they occupied. The 2000 instance was a waxing or opening square of the Jupiter/Saturn conjunction to Uranus. In 2020–21, Jupiter and Saturn are in a waning or closing square relationship to Uranus.

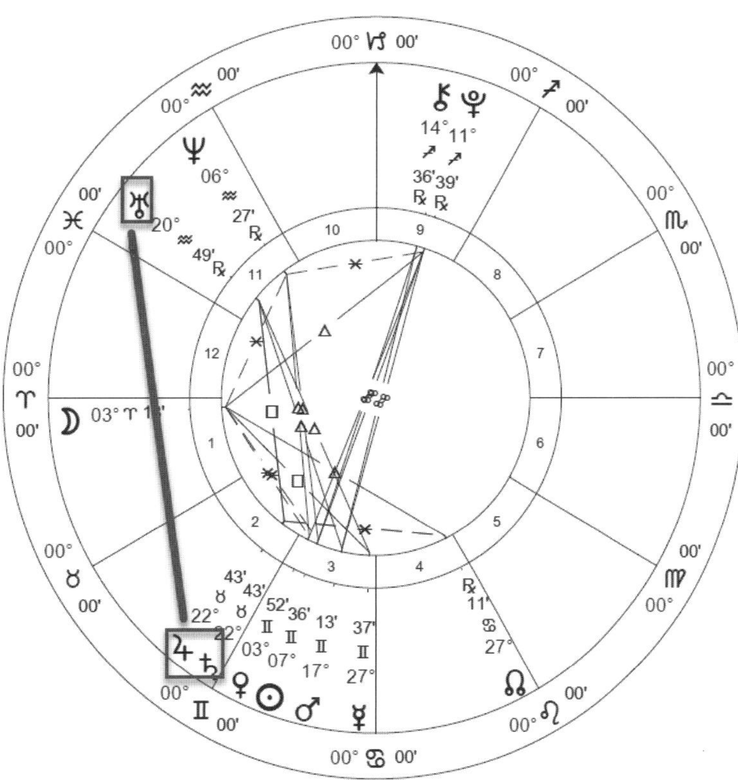

Jupiter/Saturn conjunction, May 28, 2000, in square aspect to Uranus in Aquarius

Both types of squares are challenging. The waxing square indicates a crisis in action related to the nature of the planets involved. In 2000, the crisis related to the dot-com bubble burst, which disrupted the progress of the new technology economy that was underway. After a 2-year recession, the new technology economy resumed. The waning square represents a crisis in consciousness. It is an awareness that matters related to the planets are getting mature, and new forms of expression are needed as the old forms become outdated and will soon become obsolete. But no one knows yet what the new form will be. The inventions start to percolate in the minds of the future innovators.

In 2000, this square coincided with a deep economic recession and a stock market decline that lasted over 2.5 years. The NASDAQ lost 80% of its value from its all-time high in March 2000 to its bear market low in October 2002.

As we leave 2020 and enter the waning square aspect of these same three planets 20 years later, many of the world's stock indices are again making new all-time highs, such as in the NASDAQ and S&P. Is the world in danger of another economic and stock market collapse as in 2000–2002? Given that astrology is humankind's most extraordinary pattern-matching study of correlations to history, we cannot dismiss the possibility.

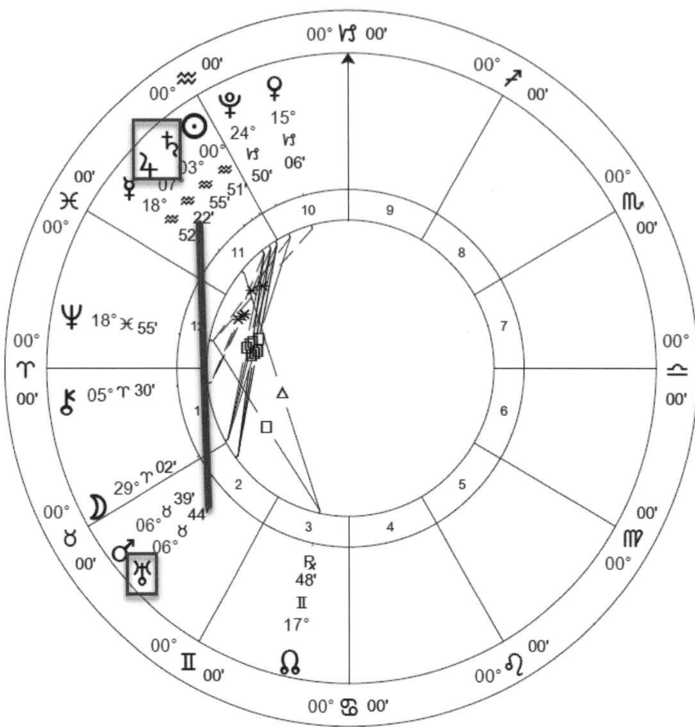

January 20, 2021. Note the square between Jupiter/Saturn in Aquarius to Uranus in Taurus

References:

1. "A New Aira" is a term coined by Kat Powell of Scottsdale, AZ as the theme of the ISAR 2021 conference, https://isarastrology.org/
2. "A History of Vassar College," Info.vassar.edu
3. "Ruby Bridges," www.biography.com
4. "History of the United Nations," www.un.org

SATURN/URANUS WANING SQUARE: CROSSING THE LINES OF TIME, SPACE, AND PLACE

"Those who make peaceful revolution impossible will make violent revolution inevitable." – John F. Kennedy, 1962 speech.

"It has become appallingly obvious that our technology has exceeded our humanity. It is harder to crack a prejudice than an atom." – Albert Einstein

One of the most challenging of all planetary cycles involves hard aspects between Saturn and Uranus. And the most demanding of all aspects to experience is the waning square. In 2021, Saturn and Uranus will go through a three-passage series of its waning square, a cosmic phenomenon happening approximately every 45 years.

The importance of the 20-, 200-, and 800-year Jupiter/Saturn cycles (conjunctions) starting December 21, 2020, was examined in the previous section. We described it as the start of a "New Aira" because it took place at 0° Aquarius, an air sign symbolizing a new era, for the first time in several centuries. The next six 20-year Jupiter/Saturn synodic cycles would also unfold in air signs until 2159.

As discussed previously, the end of synodic cycles is difficult and challenging. The early stages of synodic cycles contain elements of hope and optimism about the future. However, the switch from "difficult" to "hope" doesn't take place overnight. It may take some time before the positive qualities of the new cycle become realized. The first phase of a new cycle can therefore be rocky or erratic, with many ups and downs as there are glimpses of the new possibilities intermingled with resistance and the realities of struggles that prevailed at the end of the older cycle. It is likely to be that way in this first decade, especially the first year of this new Jupiter/Saturn "Aira," for during this same period, Saturn and Uranus will be in the last quarter phase of their 45-year cycle.

The Challenge of Waning Squares

In the study of astrology, all planetary pair cycles begin with their conjunction and peak with their opposition. As planetary pairs move from conjunction to opposition, they are in their "waxing phase" to one another, which means they are in a "growth cycle." It is similar in essence to how the Moon grows in light from its new Moon (conjunction) to the full Moon (opposition) phase. "Growing in light," or "waxing," also means increasing in influence. It is the "growth" half of the planetary pair cycle.

The period from opposition to conjunction is the "waning" phase of those two planets in relation to one another. The ascent of growth is diminishing, just as the Moon's light decreases from its full Moon status to its new Moon phase (opposition to conjunction). Symbolically, the planetary pair cycle is losing its power or its effectiveness in world affairs. It still has an influence or correlation, of course, but it is less and less a force in the cycle of growth.

The two points midway between the conjunction and opposition are known as the waxing and waning square. The waxing square is the first quarter cycle, midway between the conjunction and opposition. It is also called an "opening square." The waning square is the midway point between the opposition and conjunction, sometimes referred to as the "closing square" between those two planets. Both squares symbolize a time of crisis related to the dynamics and areas of human activity associated with the two planets and the signs they occupy.

The opening square can be harsh. It is referred to as "crisis in action" but is usually managed and resolved, after which the cycle continues to grow.

The closing or waning square can also be harsh. It is referred to as a "crisis in consciousness" or "awareness." This time of crisis is more difficult because it comes with the realization there may be issues not easily resolved. There is an awareness something fundamental must change related to the dynamics and areas of human activity associated with the two planets. It is as if these dynamics are becoming obsolete, and until a replacement is discovered or invented, these matters become a source of greater frustration and stress. Conflicts are apparent and tend to increase into the conjunction period when the new cycle is ready to commence. But even then, it takes time to adjust to the new realities.

Specifications of the Saturn/Uranus Waning Square of 2021

The Saturn/Uranus cycle enters its waning square phase in 2021. The aspect will be exact three times: February 17, June 14, and December 24. Hence, it is a 3-passage series.

Saturn will be in 7–13° Aquarius during these three passages. Uranus will be in 7–13° Taurus. Saturn and Uranus are the co-rulers of Aquarius. Thus, this is expected to be a significant, highly-charged Saturn/Uranus waning square cycle, as we will explain.

Recent History of the Saturn/Uranus Waning Square

The last occurrence of the Saturn/Uranus waning square was a five passage series that began October 4, 1975 and lasted through April 22, 1977.

In the United States, this followed the resignation of President Richard Nixon due to the Watergate scandal when he—and the U.S. government—lost its trust and bond with the American population. Richard Nixon was a law and order president. He also opened up trade relations with China for the first time in many years. However, for the first time in many years, Americans realized the head of its government was guilty of a cover-up, breaking the law and flouting the very principles of law and order he championed. The trust of the people in its government has never fully recovered from that experience.

Nixon's resignation and violation of trust with the American public led to a severe recession and the steepest decline in the U.S. stock market since the Great Depression.

After the aspect began in earnest, Jimmy Carter was elected president, and the Democrats took control of the White House from the Republicans. A period of stagflation began, eventually erupting into historical inflation. Commodities, like Gold and Silver, soared over the next three years, along with record-high interest rates. But the seeds for this implosion in the economy began during the Saturn and Uranus waning square passage. Jimmy Carter ended up being a one-term president.

The Saturn/Uranus waning square before that was even more cataclysmic. They entered a five-passage series of waning square aspects on February 22, 1930, which lasted through October 16, 1931. The peak of the stock market occurred just five months before, in September 1929. But by July 1932, the Dow Jones Industrial Average (DJIA) had lost approximately 90% of its value as the Great Depression ravaged the American lifestyle, and millions of people lost jobs.

The president at the time was Herbert Hoover, who had little previous political experience. He was a successful businessman, and he was not liked by Congress or even by members of his own party. Under his watch, Congress passed the Smoot-Hawley Tariff Act (June 17, 1930) with the idea of protecting American businesses and farmers. However, it only exasperated the strain on the international economy and made things worse. Herbert Hoover ended up being a one-term president and was voted out of office in the 1932 election. The victor was Franklin D. Roosevelt, a Democrat, who began a series of major legislative acts radically transforming the American society and workplace.

The time before that was a three-passage series lasting from June 28, 1885, through April 29, 1886. Grover Cleveland had just begun his first 4-year term as president on March 4, 1885; the first Democrat elected to the nation's highest office since the Civil War. He was defeated in the next election in 1888, even though he won the popular vote. He then became the first president in history to win the election in non-consecutive terms, as he won again in 1892.

The previous instance of the Saturn/Uranus waning square coincided with another terrible economic crisis in America. It was also a three-passage series, starting on December 3, 1839, and lasting through October 10, 1840. And it occurred in the middle of one of the most prolonged and most paralyzing economic depressions in the United States, starting with the Panic of 1837. There was a brief recovery in 1838, but then the depression returned with a vengeance in 1839 through 1844. Banks collapsed, businesses failed, deflation set in, and thousands of workers lost their jobs as unemployment soared to about 25%. Many believe this depression was actually caused by President Andrew Jackson's decision in 1832 to terminate the nation's central bank, the Second Bank of the United States. As the bank completed its term in the next four years, major banks and financial institutions then had to scale back their loans, which led to the financial panic in 1837 and a real estate crash soon afterwards. The Great Depression of 1837–1844 was on.

Although there are only a few cases so far in the United States' brief history, it is interesting to observe that the two most devastating instances were in the 90-year alternating (non-consecutive) cases of 1839–1840 and 1930–1931. The theme in all episodes was "change." The Saturn/Uranus square disrupted the patterns and traditions of the American lifestyle. New political ideologies were enacted, and financial markets, as well as the economy struggled, especially in the alternating cases that were approximately 90 years apart. The 2021 instance is next in line with this potential 90-year cyclical geocosmic pattern.

The Astrological Dynamics of the 2021 Saturn/Uranus Waning Square

There is only one sin, only one. And that is theft. Every other sin is a variation of theft. When you kill a man, you steal a life... you steal his wife's right to a husband, rob his children of a father. When you tell a lie, you steal someone's right to the truth. When you cheat, you steal the right to fairness... there is no act more wretched than stealing. — Khaled Hosseini, "The Kite Runner," Riverhead Books, New York, NY, 2003.

The 2021 Saturn/Uranus waning square is the first in the U.S. history involving Saturn in Aquarius. As stated above, Saturn and Uranus co-rule Aquarius, so the 2021 episode is apt to be very special, perhaps even dramatic, as the two rulers are in a difficult square aspect to one another. In addition to the fact this will be the 90-year alternate interval of their 45-year waning square aspect, when economic crises have happened before, this instance also finds Uranus, the disruptor, in the financial sign of Taurus. Therefore, it doubly highlights the U.S. economy's vulnerability to a financial crisis in the next 1–4 years via historical correlations to geocosmic studies.

Yet, there are several other themes in human activity relating to this unique and powerful astrological cycle.

Let's start with Saturn in Aquarius. Saturn is the "line" referred to in the title of this section. Saturn rules boundaries, limits and limitations, structures such as buildings, and the "form" of almost everything, including the physical body and its skin and bones. But "boundaries" pertain to the psychological and geopolitical sphere as well.

When we talk about a "physical" or "geopolitical line," like a "red line in the sand," we are referring to a boundary, a limit that must be respected. If not, then Saturn's next level usually takes over, and that is "consequence." When a line is crossed, and a limit or law or principle has been violated, a consequence is meted out, often in severe punishment, restriction, and even incarceration or imprisonment. You may be detained, even locked up. You are guilty of a violation, of breaking the law or a rule. Saturn is the law, the rule, and the consequences (results) that will follow. Saturn is karma.

The opposite dynamic of Saturn and karma is Uranus and freedom. Uranus' primary dynamic and the sign it co-rules, Aquarius, is to "cross over the line," to move the idea or activity to another level outside the boundary. In some cases, this may mean violating the law or the rule, rebelling against it as too confining and restrictive to the human quest to be free and liberated.

Uranus and Aquarius also rule the masses, the collective, and the urge to either disrupt or do what is best for the greatest number of people—usually in the name of freedom and equality. Hence, the merging of these two principles, Saturn and Uranus (in Aquarius, no less), is the basic underlying dynamic leading to protest movements. When carried out to extremes, they can lead to violence and the threat of rebellion or revolution, civil unrest, and disobedience. Chaos and anarchy can erupt. People go to jail, get hurt, pay fines when caught acting out in violence, and breaking the laws represented by Saturn. There are consequences when breaking the law if caught, and with a strong Uranus and Aquarius present, people are often willing to risk their freedom and even their lives in the pursuit of a belief in a cause. In some cases, they are willing to inflict violence on others to get their cause known. They are like "riders in a storm," wreaking havoc and danger to those obstructing their path. With Uranus and Aquarius highlighted, especially in a square aspect to Saturn (or Pluto or Mars), some people may behave as if crazed, out of control. Uranus and Aquarius can completely detach from normal behavior, which means they can act out in psychologically inappropriate and even socially abnormal, and perhaps criminal ways.

Protests: Peaceful versus Dangerous and Life-Threatening

Into this house we're born
Into this world we're thrown
Like a dog without a bone
An actor out alone
Riders on the storm

There's a killer on the road
His brain is squirmin' like a toad
Take a long holiday
Let your children play
If ya give this man a ride
Sweet memory will die
— The Doors, "Riders on the Storm," Elektra Records, 1971.

But take note, for here is also where it gets fascinating. This "abnormal" behavior may be perceived as an act of independence and individuality, even brilliance (like an unstable, unpredictable genius), which creates a sense of charisma and magnetism about a person. They can attract a following of ardent "believers." They have a strange, non-conforming vision about "truth" and higher principles for humanity couched in the concept of independence, freedom, and social equality, where the means to the end is to proclaim social injustice and repression by authoritarian leaders. They abhor authoritarianism, and Saturn is the classic symbol of authority and hence the object of their disdain.

If the Uranian leader says, "Fight these authoritarians who repress you and deny your freedom!" then their believers may want to band together and do just that. At first, they may just protest but then take more forceful action against their oppressors (in their view). If they have organized a strong enough community, the group can lead a successful revolt. If not, the members are often squashed and thrown into prison, jails, or worse. Plus, if these people cannot conduct peaceful protests to enact change, they end up losing their freedom in most cases. In 2021, with Saturn square Uranus, there will be many cases like this. But there may be some cases where they successfully overthrow their nemesis, succeeding at the overthrow of a government or enterprise. There may even be a case or two of civil war ignited by these dynamics of Saturn in Aquarius square Uranus. It is conducive to a revolutionary fervor, especially in those countries whose founding charts have planets or angles in 7–13° of fixed signs. The U.S. does not. But it has its own issues with its Pluto return in 2021–2024 to be discussed in the U.S. chart section.

Nevertheless, the Saturn in Aquarius, square Uranus in Taurus signature, manifested as the third leg of what went wrong (especially in the U.S.) during its brief run there in 2020. The first leg was the pandemic and the resulting deaths and lockdowns. The consequence was the second leg: an economic crisis where people lost their livelihood, and the pandemic took more lives. The third leg was—and still is—the social unrest and civil disobedience following the killing of George Floyd, an African American, by police in Minneapolis in late May 2020. Other cases of killing African-Americans by police occurred shortly after. Protests against police brutality and systemic racism quickly turned into looting and violence. New protests began to "defund the police." The government of several major cities in the U.S. lost control of the situation, which became chaotic and dangerous, with many killings taking place. There began a migration of citizens from urban centers back to the suburbs. These events of this third leg happened mostly when Saturn briefly entered Aquarius, March 21–June 30, within orb of its square to Uranus.

The aspect is not over. In fact, it does not even become exact until February 2021. Saturn returns to Aquarius on December 17, 2020 and will make three exact squares to Uranus through December 24, 2021. The climate for civil disobedience, destruction of property, potential violence to innocent people, and the violation of laws is heightened while these geocosmic dynamics are in force. It is not a safe environment, as the battle between advocates of law and order clash with protestors demanding freedom, equality, and social justice, of which some may be willing to destroy property, steal, and inflict harm on innocent bystanders in order to carry out their agenda.

The Psychological "Line in the Sand"

President Barack Obama infamously drew a "red line" with the regime of President Bashar al-Assad in Syria only to back away from it. — Pamela Engel, "Obama Reportedly Declined to Enforce Red Line in Syria After Iran Threatened to Back Out of Nuclear Deal," Business Insider, August 25, 2016.

New books about therapy unpack the private lives of patients—do they cross a line?" — Ellen Gamerman, "What If Your Therapist's Tell-All Is About You?" Wall Street Journal, October 20, 2020.

The Saturn/Uranus's hard aspects often require us to define exactly the ideals for which we stand: the ones for which we are willing to fight and perhaps sacrifice our lives. What are the principles we cherish and will defend, even if it means a loss of opportunity elsewhere in our life?

Saturn is that "line" defining the principles, beliefs, and values we hold sacred. Uranus is the force (usually external) pushing us to compromise those principles, to cross that "red line" or "line in the sand," to go against that which we hold sacred and believe to be the "right action" to enact. These represent times when we are apt to be caught in a conflict of interests or values, where someone or some situation demands us to violate that psychological line we have developed called *our conscience.*

For instance, Americans as a whole, experienced this conflict in the recent election. Many felt forced to choose between the character of one candidate versus the policies of the other. Many deplored the behavior, actions, and temperament of one candidate, and others deplored what they perceived as the extreme ideologies, economic policies, and potential financial dangers to the nation from the other candidate. This type of conflict is typical of Saturn square Uranus during an election, or even when Saturn is in Aquarius, the sign both Saturn and Uranus co-rule.

Another example would be when an employer asks you to do something you believe is wrong, maybe even immoral, but you don't want to lose your job. It comes down to *principle,* which is Saturn. If you cross that line, violate a principle you have held as central to your character, then you lose an essential core of your identity. You are no longer "you." Furthermore, others will change their opinion of who you are, for you are no longer the person they knew. If they were your friend, the friendship is likely terminated. If they were someone you trusted, that is no longer the case. They are now foreign to you or whoever you have now become. You are foreign to them. You are divorced from the relationship due to this "crossing of the line."

In the election of 2020, many Americans expressed dismay that "America is no longer America," or the Republican (or Democratic) party is no longer the party they once belonged to—because of the "crossing of a line." The extremist policies espoused by one (or the other) and the personal conduct accepted and even enabled of the other, "crossed the line" in their mind. They felt compelled to take a stand on one principle or the other, and it was difficult to accept both sides of "the line."

Let's put it in simple terms. Saturn represents "promises." It is one's word of honor. Uranus can represent the "break" or "violation" of a principle. Together, when in conflict, the combination can define a time or situation in which there is a "broken promise," a time when someone "crosses the line" and violates the honor of their word. Saturn also represents "respect' for others. Uranus has very little respect for anything other than originality and invention, which inherently means it respects matters and ideas that are new but not old or traditional. Thus, when one breaks their promise or their word, it is a sign of disrespect to others who expect the person to honor their word, that promise.

In 2021, we could see a lot of "broken promises." This is Saturn square Uranus. And that behavior could be met with great angst by those expecting promises to be kept. The reaction can become the basis for scorn, disdain, disrespect, outrage, and rebellion. It can lead to protest movements, which can then escalate to social unrest and civil disobedience if the perpetrator of the broken promise is a government or community leader.

The "Line in Time:" The Clash Between the Past and the Future

Under Saturn square Uranus, the masses (Uranus) want change (Uranus) and a break from the past (Saturn), especially if certain parts of the past are seen as oppressive (Saturn). But Saturn rules traditions and control, so those in positions of power don't want to change those traditions or lose their control. The challenge becomes how to define the aspects of those traditions still having value. And the next question: What should be preserved, versus what aspects of tradition no longer serve a useful purpose to society's future?

This is similar to the waning square dynamics or the phase of a planetary pair cycle as it moves from its waning square to its conjunction. It is the evolving awareness something related to these planetary dynamics is becoming obsolete, and a new dynamic related to those planetary qualities needs to be birthed. In Saturn/Uranus's case, the waning square and conjunction period will last nearly 12 years, from February 2021 through January 2032. However, with Saturn already having visited Aquarius March–June 2020, these dynamics have already begun to manifest.

The danger is those who push for change too radically or too quickly (Uranus and Aquarius) will be resisted by those not wanting change, losing control, or who wish to move at a more measured pace (Saturn). There is a need to draw a line—a timeline—to which all parties must agree.

One area where this is apt to manifest is over the line of control between the agents of government and entrepreneurs, over the application of certain business applications of technology.

The fear is that control of the world of technology is falling into the hands of a select few companies who thwart competition from others. These corporate behemoths like Google, Facebook, Twitter, Apple, Microsoft, and perhaps a few others are building monopolies that restrict access to entrepreneurial growth of other companies trying to launch themselves in the same field. This will likely result in a clash between government agencies and their newly appointed regulators who want to control these established technology companies and restrict the potential monopolies. As this battle gets underway, these companies' services may be disrupted, causing frustration from the population of users who depend upon those services. This is compounded by the frustration and complaints of those other businesses trying to break through these "lines" and barriers to makes their services more available to consumers.

New entrepreneurs cannot break through to these markets. They cannot overcome the consumer's dependence upon the established leaders in these fields who have built a monopoly designed to prevent competition. On the other hand, the government (Saturn) may create restrictions on those established companies, perhaps forcing them to break up into smaller companies. Therefore, this levels the playing field, and it makes room for other entrepreneurs who want to compete. It's a classic clash between control (Saturn) and freedom (Uranus), between government (Saturn) and technology (Uranus and Aquarius).

The "Line in Place"

Saturn rules the boundaries between nations, or municipalities, or any land mass and/or piece of property. Uranus wants to "change" those boundaries. It may even "trespass" those boundaries. The waning square indicates those involved in this negotiation may disagree on how it should be done. In fact, there may not even be a negotiation, for

Uranus and Aquarius do not care for such formalities. They may simply "cross the line" and claim the other side as their own.

Any nation whose boundaries are in dispute is likely to experience outrage over one another's actions in 2021.

This also pertains to governments whose legitimacy is in dispute, perhaps due to perceived (or real) violations in voting or vote counting. Once again, it is a battle between the forces of change who dispute the control of the leaders versus those who resist giving up their controls to what they perceive as "mob rule."

In such situations, one form of conflict resolution would be to have an outside, independent agency oversee the election (i.e., the voting process legitimacy). Or, if too late, then to serve as independent arbitrators in trying to find ways to bridge the gap between the two forces. There is a need to build "a line" or a "bridge" between opposing sides. Otherwise, "the line" or "the bridge" will be violated and destroyed, and in its place will be born rebellion and civil discord. Saturn and Uranus are either a new order finding a way to build a bridge between opposing views or revolution where either the forces of control (Saturn) shut down the voices of opposition (Uranus), or the voices of opposition successfully overthrow the forces of control. This could end up being a 12-year process.

The "Line" in Space

Starlink's key difference is that it will be utilizing thousands of low-orbit small table-size satellites, which will provide faster transmission rates over the older high-orbit satellite networks. Instead of orbiting at over 22,000 miles above the earth, Starlink will be orbiting at 340 miles. — Ken Colburn, "Coming Soon: Fast Satellite Internet from Musk's SpaceX," Arizona Republic, November 2, 2020.

Images of broken light
Which dance before me like a million eyes
They call me on and on across the universe
Thoughts meander like a restless wind inside a letter box
They tumble blindly as they make their way across the universe
Jai Guru Deva, Om
Nothing's gonna change my world
Nothing's gonna change my world
Nothing's gonna change my world
Nothing's gonna change my world
— The Beatles, "Across the Universe," EMI, London, 1969

Uranus rules space, as in outer space. It also rules technology and telecommunications. Saturn rules control, property, governments, and their laws. Who owns outer space? Who owns the satellites and the stations they occupy in space as they orbit around the globe? Who determines which companies or persons are allowed to claim a part of space for their ventures and satellites? This is apt to become a source of great conflict between nations and private enterprises in this decade and perhaps even in 2021.

For example, what if a company launches a satellite or "space station" occupying an orbit in space around the earth upon which other companies—or even nations—soon depend upon for its proper functioning (think Space X)? And what if that space station has a mishap? Perhaps it has an electrical or technological failure, or is (God forbid) attacked and disabled? And what if there is no secondary backup to that space station so many depend upon for their existence? What happens to those companies and nations depending upon that satellite for its proper functioning? This is not just a security threat for a company or even nations. It could conceivably become a security threat to the entire world.

New laws and policies involving the entire world will have to be developed and enforced to ensure: 1) such locations in space are delegated fairly and safely, 2) there is a backup plan in the event of a satellite or space station failure that would disrupt life on earth as we know it, or will soon realize it due to our increasing dependency upon such technological advances into space.

Space is the future. It is ruled by Uranus and Aquarius. It is also the frontier ruled by the Great Mutation (Jupiter and Saturn) into air signs for the next 140 years. There is a race for time and space, and it also involves the quest for freedom, independence, equality, and truth (Uranus and Aquarius). With Saturn in Aquarius, square Uranus in 2021, we will have to understand these liberties and quests for truth and freedom come with responsibilities (Saturn). There are limits (Saturn) to freedom (Uranus). And there is no freedom, even in space, without responsibility. There will be conflicts between the old ways and the new visions. We cannot have a future without connecting the dots, respecting the lines, or building a solid bridge with the past. You cannot have Uranus (future) without Saturn (past). When their dynamics integrate, there is no end to what humankind can accomplish. The Saturn/Uranus aspect is the most remarkable and stunning of all geocosmic signatures of accomplishment. It is potential, which is why it is also our future when built upon the solid foundations of our past.

It is part of the cosmic plan as we evolve.

URANUS IN TAURUS
THE COLOR OF MONEY

"The time will come that Gold will hold no comparison in value to a bushel of wheat."
— Brigham Young

"Money is a terrible master but an excellent servant." — P.T. Barnum

Uranus, the Disruptor

Uranus, the disruptor as well as the revolutionary inventor, is still in the early degrees of Taurus, the sign of money, currencies, and agriculture.

In prior books, we have illustrated how Uranus correlates with periods of boom and bust in the sectors of the economy related to the sign it is in. Its seven-year trek through Aquarius, 1995–2003, coincided with the dot-com bubble in which tech stocks exploded into early 2000. Then, just as quickly, the boom went bust, and the tech-heavy NASDAQ lost 80% of its value by October 2002, right before Uranus departed Aquarius. It then entered Pisces, 2003–2010, the sign co-ruling Crude Oil, which soared to a record high of 147.17 in July 2008. By the end of that year, the boom once again went bust as Crude Oil lost nearly 80% of its value. Uranus then ingressed into Aries, 2010–2018, which rules guns and bullets. Sales of firearms soared, and so did the companies involved in producing and bringing them to the market. However, before Uranus ended its journey through Aries, sales of guns plunged, and gun manufacturers struggled, with many going bankrupt.

In 2018, Uranus began its current seven-year occupation of Taurus. At the time, we speculated this combination would affect currencies, banks, and foods (like meats and vegetables) substantially. They would be the candidates to exhibit a boom-bust cycle over the next seven years. Of particular interest would be digital or cryptocurrencies, like Bitcoin, which combined the principles of Uranus (digital, technology-based) with a new and revolutionary (also Uranus) form of currency, or a new form of exchange for goods and services (Taurus). We also speculated this would begin a concerted reexamination of the U.S. Dollar's role as the international standard currency used in world trade.

This section reviews and projects for each of these areas of human activity and financial markets related to Uranus in Taurus, 2018–2019 through 2025–2026. The reason there are two years given at the beginning and end is because Uranus went retrograde for a short time back into Aries (November 6, 2018–March 8, 2019). It will also exhibit the same pattern at the end when it advances into Gemini but then retrogrades back into Taurus for a short time (November 6, 2025–April 26, 2026). Most of the "boom" part of this cycle will take place after Uranus has entered the new sign for the second time. Most of the "bust" part of the cycle will occur before Uranus enters the next sign for the first time. In this case, we anticipate the "boom" will not top out until after March 8, 2019, and the "bust" will mostly bottom in price before November 6, 2025. But which sectors will be affected this time, and how will this combination manifest in other areas of human activity?

Taurus, the Resister

Let us first of all review our understanding of the principles associated with Uranus and Taurus.

We begin with the idea that Uranus and Taurus are a clash of opposites. This should be interesting in 2021 as Uranus is squared by Saturn in Aquarius, for these (Uranus and Saturn in a hard aspect) also indicate a clash of opposites.

We already discussed the dangers of Saturn in Aquarius (the sign is ruled by both Saturn and Uranus) in terms of civil unrest, disobedience, protests turning deadly and into destruction of property, and even revolutionary movements against authoritarian leadership. Uranus, the other ruler of Aquarius, is in the sign of Taurus, thus combining similar principles. Uranus wants change, but Taurus likes stability and will tend to resist change unless it offers something of greater value to its predicament. Taurus isn't going to get off the couch and change the station on the TV unless it is convinced there is a more interesting program on another channel. Fortunately, with the invention of remote control, this act of initiative is a lot easier these days. Although this is an exaggeration of the Taurus tendency to stand firm at all times, the fact is the nature of Taurus sees value in tradition and things that have been built, which continue to serve a useful purpose. Taurus is sturdy and firm. But with Uranus in Taurus, those traditions and that sturdiness and firmness will likely be challenged. And Taurus is likely to resist those challenges unless it sees a greater value in making the change.

Thus, we see the sociological conflict of Uranus in Taurus, being squared by Saturn in Aquarius, setting up in 2021. In fact, it started in 2020 with the emergence of the COVID-19 pandemic, and the explosion of protest movements against social inequities and authoritarian leadership (i.e., police brutality against African-Americans) that surged dramatically when Saturn briefly entered Aquarius for the first time in March–June 2020. Saturn will return to Aquarius on December 17, 2020, where it will remain uninterrupted through March 7, 2023. This promises to be the most challenging period of the 7-year trek of Uranus through Taurus.

It is also a time when the conflict between science and science fiction (e.g., conspiracy theories), or between government policies and the guidelines for societal and individual protection recommended by science reaches a crescendo. The presence of Taurus may only increase this conflict because the Taurean nature may resist the guidelines proposed by science if it means altering their traditions, routines, and zones of comfort. They (societies) will, however, make the adjustment if the alternative threatens health and life. Taurus is, after all, practical-minded. It knows you cannot have comforts or maintain traditions in life if one's life and well-being itself are threatened. But until that realization is evident, resistance is the normal first response to change when Taurus is highlighted. Thus, Uranus in Taurus may be a case of "push comes to shove" for the masses in adjusting to the terms of the "New Aira" the world is now entering.

If the revolutionaries and scientists represented by Saturn in Aquarius want to be heard and succeed with engineering social change they believe will benefit the world, they must proceed at a measured pace. They will need to refrain from forced or mandatory acts that are rushed without consensus or adequate time to understand mentally and then adjust. Making demands on populations without properly making a convincing case will only exasperate and delay the inevitable. Whether one is talking about policy changes involving climate change, COVID-19 prevention, currency and banking changes, or the production and distribution of foods, major changes cannot be easily forced upon societies without risk of revolt between now and 2025 with Uranus in Taurus.

However, the risk of revolt is great too. After all, Saturn is in Aquarius, and it makes a powerful waning square to Uranus, beginning the last quarter cycle between these two planets into 2032. It's just a matter of whether world and local leaders can work with their populations to find common ground in the process—to make this a smooth and non-violent social and economic revolution—or they give into frustration and start making demands resisted by their citizens. If the latter, we may embark upon a period of prolonged chaos. The hope is the Taurus energy will not be inflexible or resistant to changes necessary and beneficial to one's society. While at the same time there is hope, the Saturn in Aquarius energy is not so demanding of others to comply before they feel "comfortable" with the changes they view as necessary.

"Show Me the Money"

Taurus rules money and assets of value, like stocks and currencies. The value of these assets is vulnerable to extreme changes in price. For instance, stock markets can go through peaks and valleys of great amplitude, as witnessed in 2020, when Saturn moved briefly into Aquarius in March–June. In 2021, Saturn will be in Aquarius; only this time, the square to Uranus will be even more exact. The implication is another severe decline will unfold, either during 2021 or from a high completed in 2021 and a plunge that could extend through the following 1–2 years.

Currency values could also be in line for a huge reversal. Their price is relative to other currencies, the standard of which remains the U.S. Dollar for global trading purposes. But that standard is being questioned now in lieu of tariffs imposed by the U.S. government onto other nations wishing to trade with the U.S. over the past two years. Tariffs have created a deterrent for other nations feeling forced to trade in U.S. Dollars because of its unique role as the standard world currency since the Bretton Woods agreement in 1944. That agreement is vulnerable to being upended this decade to allow for a new (Uranus) form of exchange or a new currency for international trading purposes that removes the U.S. from its position of control and/or coercion over other nations who wish to trade with one another but not be subject to transactions based solely in terms of U.S. Dollars.

The set up between Jupiter, Saturn, and Uranus, and their sign positions, is the inverse of the case in 2000. Uranus is in Taurus in 2021, squared by Jupiter and Saturn in Aquarius. In 2000, Uranus was in Aquarius, squared by Jupiter and Saturn in Taurus. In 2000, a steep recession and a 2.75-year bear market in stocks began in the U.S. The Dow Jones Industrial Average (DJIA) plummeted to its steepest decline since 1987 and 1974. In the case of the tech-heavy NASDAQ, the decline was a stunning 80% loss of value, with many dot-com companies going bankrupt.

A major trend reversal materialized in world currencies as well. The Euro currency bottomed in 2000 and commenced an 8-year rally to its all-time high in July 2008. During much of this same period, the U.S. Dollar topped out (in mid-July 2001) and began a prolonged bear market into early 2008. In other words, the Taurus areas of the stock and currency markets underwent major disruptions in 2000–2001. They could do so again in 2021 +/- 1 year, as these same three planets are in a similar aspect configuration involving the same signs of Aquarius and Taurus. Taurus rules money, and both Uranus and Aquarius are significators of sudden changes and disruptions.

We should point out one important difference this time, however. That is, Saturn is in Aquarius, the sign it co-rules (with Uranus). Therefore, there is an alternate scenario possible that takes into account Saturn holding dominance over Uranus, as opposed to 2000 when Uranus was in Aquarius (a sign it co-rules), and therefore Uranus was more dominant then. This is a significant difference because if Saturn holds power over Uranus, the sharp price swings of 2000 may not manifest in 2021. Instead, we may find the strength of resistance more powerful than the force of radical change. There may be much talk about major changes that are imminent, but in fact, action on those ideas may be stalled. Resistance might be massive, and the result may be a standoff. Therefore, much of the next year's market activity may experience lower volatility than this year's unprecedented high volatility. Instead of momentous disruptions, the world and its leaders may experience overwhelming frustration because everything seems stuck in gridlock. My bias is that we will see long stretches of gridlock with frustration, but then sudden and dramatic breaks in financial markets along the lines of the alternating 90-year Saturn/Uranus waning square cycle described in the previous section. Saturn will demand patience as it is strong in Aquarius. Uranus will demand changes, but they will be resisted in Taurus. The forces of resistance will be frustrated at first, but it won't stop the demands for change. In fact, as the frustration grows, the intensity of demands will also increase, creating an even more highly charged atmosphere during 2021.

Digital Currencies/Bitcoin

The Federal Reserve Bank (FRB) wants to communicate that it takes CBDCs (central bank digital currency units) seriously and is engaged in efforts to research a path toward implementation... The Fed's primary purpose is to ensure the financial stability of the US in the service of its citizens. Federal Reserve chairman Jerome Powell made it clear that as CBDC is an extremely important part of the national infrastructure and under the purview of the Fed, the Fed would be in charge of the core infrastructure of CBDC.... Central Bank Digital Currency will complement cash, not replace it entirely. An impetus for the Fed's efforts is the possibility of widespread global adoption of Libra, which can threaten the Fed's control of monetary policy. Digital Currency Electronic Payments (DCEP) from China is much further ahead in terms of implementation. DCEP and Chinese international strategy threatens the primacy of the dollar as the international unit of account and means of payment. — Vipin Bharathan, "Fed Partners with MIT Based Digital Currency Initiative to Explore Central Bank Digital Currency," Forbes, August 30, 2020.

This now leads us into the discussion on alternative and new forms of currencies, like Bitcoin and other cryptocurrencies. They have survived longer than many thought possible. Even the central banks of the world are now considering their use in the not-so-distant future. But before cryptos can be genuinely considered viable currencies, their huge spikes in price will have to be contained. Nobody wants an unstable currency, and so far, Bitcoin and other cryptocurrencies have been anything but stable compared to other world currencies. Consider in 2020 alone; Bitcoin vacillated between a low of $3850 on March 13, 2020, to a new all-time high of 19,510 as this is being written at the end of November 2020, a gain of over 300%. In comparison, the Euro currency traded between 1.0600 and 1.2000, a range of only 13%.

The possibility of a boom/bust pattern in Bitcoin related to Uranus in Taurus is present. Notice on the weekly chart after its all-time high of 19,458 on December 18, 2017, Bitcoin plunged to a low of 3122 one year later, on December 15, 2018. This was a loss of approximately 84%, which is in the 77–93% range we have observed often happens at the end of a boom/bust cycle. The only problem was Uranus was in Aries then, and not the money sign of Taurus. But shortly after that dramatic decline to 3122, Uranus did begin its uninterrupted journey into Taurus on March 6, 2019. It was still trading as low as 3666 then. Our observation is a market will appreciate 5–8 times (or more) above its low preceding the "boom" part of a boom/bust cycle, and sometimes much more. In this case, we can project Bitcoin to rise from 3122 to $15,600–25,000 or higher before falling below $4000, while Uranus is in Taurus. Once the high is in, we can project that Bitcoin will decline 77–93%, a gain before leaving Taurus in 2025–2026. ***(*Note, as we go to press, Bitcoin has just made a new all-time high of 19,510 on November 25, 2020. At the time this section was written in October 2020, the high was slightly above 13,000).***

Identifying the exact time of the high is never an easy task. Usually, the boom part of a cycle will occur in years 2–5 after Uranus enters the sign. Starting from March 6, 2019, this suggests the high will be somewhere between 2021–2024.

Looking at the founding chart of Bitcoin may help. The most accepted "birth" of Bitcoin was on January 3, 2009, also referred to as its "Ledger start." This followed the invention of the concept of Bitcoin as a cryptocurrency in 2008 by a person or group of people using the name Satoshi Nakamoto. The chart used here is that of January 3, 2009, at midnight, in London. Since we do not know the exact time Bitcoin was actually launched, we will use an Aries chart (with 0° Aries on the Ascendant). Of more practical use to us will be the planets' sign and degree positions, to which we will apply our knowledge of the transits of the outer planets to this chart.

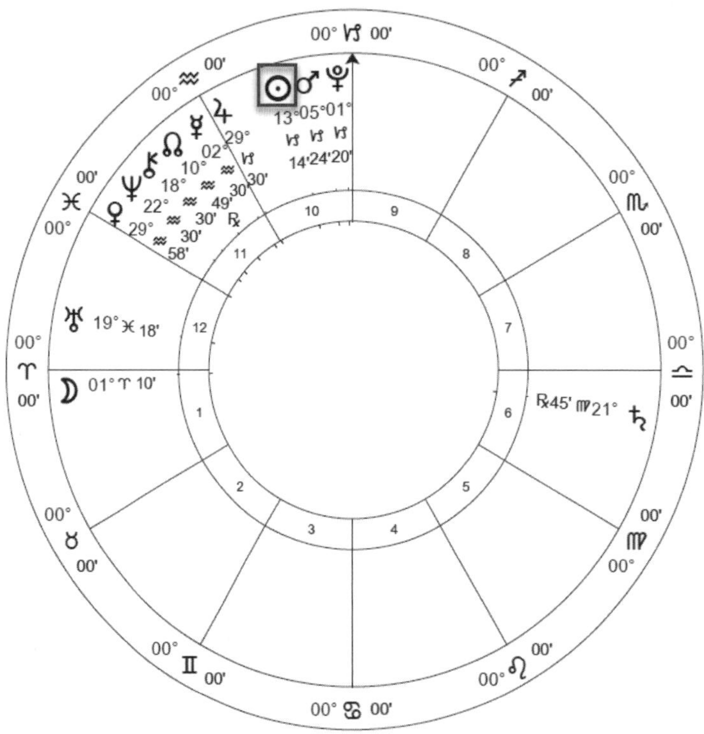

Bitcoin's founding chart, January 3, 2009, Aries chart for midnight, London

In financial astrology, Jupiter's transit is considered to represent a favorable time of gain (price) and demand (or supply) when posited in a conjunction, sextile, or trine aspect to the faster moving planets in the natal chart. The Bitcoin chart contains 7 of the ten planets (we include the Sun and Moon along with the eight other planets in this concept) in the signs Capricorn and Aquarius. Between December 2, 2019, through December 29, 2021, Jupiter will transit through Capricorn and Aquarius, except for a brief stint in Pisces, May 13–July 28, 2021. By itself, this would suggest a period of mostly rising prices. Indeed, except for the one-month selloff of mid-February through mid-March 2020 during the panic of COVID-19 in which prices dropped to 3850, Bitcoin has been in an uptrend. As this is being written in late October 2020, Bitcoin is testing 14,000. It is nearing our upside projection range of 15,600–25,000.

The opposite of the growth and expansion inherent in a Jupiter transit is the contraction and potential loss of value represented by Saturn's transit in hard aspect to a founding chart. When Bitcoin dropped to 3850 on March 13, 2020, transiting Saturn was at 29° Capricorn, right on the natal position of Jupiter. Both Saturn and Jupiter return there again December 6–19, 2020, just before they both exit Capricorn and enter Aquarius together.

While Jupiter contacts all the planets in Aquarius for most of 2021, Saturn will only conjoin Mercury in the first two weeks of January. It would appear Bitcoin will be mostly bullish in 2021 as well.

The transit of Uranus in Taurus further supports the idea of a rising Bitcoin. Not only is that combination suggestive of a boom/bust cycle for cryptos like Bitcoin, but because it will trine the natal Sun of the Bitcoin chart, it identifies a period when it may be most prone to explosive rallies. Uranus will transit 13° Capricorn (trine Bitcoin's natal Sun at 13° Capricorn) off and on between June 2021–April 2022. The overlap with the favorable Jupiter transit is June–December 2021, pointing to a high probability period when Bitcoin may climax in its "boom" stage.

Once transiting Saturn enters the last decanate of Aquarius, where it will conjoin its natal Neptune and Venus, Bitcoin may experience pressure. This will be the geocosmic situation April 2022–March 2023.

Even though central banks are seriously considering the use of cryptocurrencies in their future thoughts about its potential as a means of exchange for goods and services, dangers still remain to Bitcoin's safety and credibility as a stable investment. Note that Neptune will transit 19–21° Pisces, January 2021, through February 2022. In these degrees, Neptune will conjunct Uranus and oppose Saturn in the founding chart. This conveys the possibility of fraud and deception, with the possibility of money (value) suddenly disappearing or being lost, even stolen through cybercrime. These studies show the potentiality of Bitcoin soaring in price next year. Yet, they also indicate the vulnerability of loss through activities of intruders who are not abiding by the rules. They are breaking the law (Neptune and Saturn), causing a loss of faith in cryptocurrencies' safety and stability as a legitimate currency. For this reason, we view cryptos as an interesting arena for speculation in 2021, with considerable prospects of gain, but not an area where one should place a substantial portion of their net worth until these issues of deception, cybertheft, and vulnerability are resolved.

Live Cattle Update

Three years ago, when Uranus first entered Taurus, we speculated that a potential candidate for a boom/bust cycle might be Live Cattle. After all, the Taurus symbol is the bull, and the bull, cow, steer, and heifer all fall under the title of cattle. Although there may be a connection to the sign of Taurus and bulls (cattle), it doesn't seem to translate to the price of cattle. At this point, there is no sign of a "boom" in Live Cattle prices since Uranus entered Taurus. In fact, as of this writing in late October, the price of Live Cattle futures has been falling under Uranus in Taurus.

It looked like Live Cattle might have been a prime candidate for a bull run when Uranus first entered Taurus, May 15, 2018, through November 6, 2018. Live Cattle prices had dropped to a 6-year low of 94.30 in October 2016 (see [1] on monthly chart) and then rose sharply to 138.90 six months later in April 2017 (see [A] on monthly chart). Prices then dropped again to a secondary low of 101.375 as Uranus made its first entrance into Taurus in May 2018 (see [1-A]). Another rally began then peaked in March 2019 at 130.45 as Uranus re-entered Taurus (see [B]), where it will remain through July 7, 2025. Since it's re-entrance into Taurus, the price of Live Cattle has plummeted, with a low so far down to 81.45 in April 2020 (see [2]), its lowest mark since December 2009.

This has not been a pattern of a bull market. To the contrary, the trend has been bearish since Uranus entered its uninterrupted period in Taurus that will last six years. In fact, Live Cattle is trading in a downward channel of successively lower cycle highs and lower cycle lows since the high of April 2017.

It is not impossible for Live Cattle to begin a boom as Uranus will still be in the first 1/3 of Taurus until February 2022, but it would be unusual. In most cases, the low that forms shortly before Uranus moves into its boom/bust sign will not be taken out. That would be the low of October 2016 at 94.30 (see [1]). As one can see, that low has been taken out in April 2020 (see [2]). Additionally, the high preceding the entrance of Uranus in a boom/bust sign is usually taken out within the first three years. That has not happened yet. The high of April 2017 (see [A] on the chart) has not been taken out. If it is taken out soon, then Live Cattle will return to the discussion as a possible boom/bust market.

In the meantime, traders and investors may note Live Cattle tends to trade in 6-year cycles with a 1-year orb. You can see these cycle lows in 1985, 1991, 1996, 2002, 2009, and 2016. The 6-year cycle breaks down into two 3-year phases usually, with an orb of 6 months. The low of April 2020 was probably the 3-year cycle, the half-cycle to the greater 6-year cycle. It was 42 months into the 6-year cycle, which is within the allowable range. Thus, a sharp 5–12-month rally may be underway to the crest of the second half of the 6-year cycle, with an upside price target of 107–131. As of this writing, it is already in the lower part of this range (above 110 in October 2020, the 6th month). Once the crest is completed, we will look for a new low, below 81.45, into its 6-year cycle low, due 2021–2023. It would likely overlap with the 3-year cycle low due April 2023 +/- 6 months. Perhaps it will happen nearby to the Jupiter/Pluto square of May 18, 2023, given the low in April 2020 occurred in the same month as the first passage of the Jupiter/Pluto conjunction.

In any event, our advice would be to sell this rally in Live Cattle in the price range given above, sometime before April 2021. In the event Live Cattle exceeds 131, and especially if it takes out 138.90, reverse to bullish strategies because then Live Cattle is on track to increase 5–8 fold from the low of 81.45.

Agricultural – Grains

Taurus is one of the signs ruling foods (Cancer is the other). In particular, Taurus rules foods grown on farms, like grains, such as Corn, Wheat, and Soybeans. Here, we see the pattern associated with a boom/bust cycle, as will be explained in greater detail in the Grains section of this year's Forecast Book.

To illustrate, note that Wheat made its most recent long-term cycle low in August 2016 at 360, its lowest mark in 10 years. It remained relatively depressed as Uranus began the uninterrupted portion of its journey through Taurus in March 2019. Between March and May 2019, Wheat was making a secondary low at 416–422. This is the usual pattern for a boom/bust market. It makes a long-term cycle low shortly before Uranus enters the sign associated with its sector. Then it makes a secondary low nearby to the time it actually enters that sign, especially the uninterrupted portion of that sign, as was the case in March–May 2019. As of this writing in October 2020, Wheat has soared to 638, its highest price since December 2014, nearly six years ago. Can Wheat continue to explode 5 or 8 fold in the next three years? That would put it up to 1800–3000 (that $18.00=30.00/bu.), exceeding its all-time high of 1335 in February 2008.

The pattern is similar, but not quite the same, in Soybeans and Corn, which will be discussed later in this year's book. For now, however, it appears that Wheat is form-fitting the boom/bust pattern more than any other of the markets we follow. This also fits our understanding of planetary rulerships, for we have assigned Uranus to Wheat for many years. Thus, Wheat is now our favored market for the boom/bust scenario associated with Uranus in Taurus.

This would furthermore indicate inflation may soon be on the way. It usually starts with commodities, and Wheat is one of the founding fathers of commodity markets.

THE ECONOMY AND THE LUNAR NODAL CYCLE

We have now passed the midpoint of the economic growth cycle denoted by the 18.6-year Lunar Nodal cycle. The idea for the Nodal cycle's correlation to the U.S. economy comes from the work of Louise McWhirter in her book titled McWhirter's Theory of Stock Market Forecasting (American Federation of Astrologers, 1938, Tempe, AZ). She observed the American economy and stock market often bottomed when the Moon's North Node was in Aquarius and peaked when it was in or near mid-Leo.

This correlation was accurate at the time of her research in the late 1930s. The nadir of the business cycle had occurred nearby to the times when the Moon's North Node was in Aquarius.

As discussed in our previous Forecast books, the correlation was also present when the stock market and economy last bottomed in March 2009. The Moon's North Node was then at 8° Aquarius. Prior to that, the Moon's North Node was in Aquarius in 1989–1990. There was a recession in 1990, too. However, the previous time containing the North Node in Aquarius was October 1970–May 1972. A major recession did not occur then, but one did unfold a year later, lasting November 1973 through March 1975 when the Moon's North Node was transiting through the signs of Capricorn and Sagittarius. In fact, a review of the four recessions in the USA since McWhirter published her research shows three bottomed with the Moon's North Node in Aquarius, and the other occurred when the Node transited into the next sign of Capricorn.

We pursued this study further and examined all 13 recessions since the Great Depression of 1929–1933. We found a recession occurred in all five instances of the Moon's North Node's transit between 15° Aquarius and 15° Scorpio. This 90° transiting period lasts about 4.6 years out of the 18.6-year nodal cycle. In fact, in two cases, there were two recessions during this 4.6-year time span, which means over half of the recessions in the USA since 1933 had occurred when the Moon's North Node transited between the middle of Aquarius and the middle of Scorpio. This led us to modify the McWhirter wheel, where the adjusted correlation is displayed on the next page.

Instead of an economic low occurring near the middle of Aquarius, these more recent studies indicate a recession is more likely to occur within 45° of 0° Capricorn, or 15° Aquarius to 15° Scorpio. Furthermore, these studies reveal an economic peak tends to happen when the Moon's North Node is transiting within 45° of 0° Cancer, or 15° Leo through 15° Taurus, instead of near 15° Leo postulated by McWhirter's studies.

The Lunar North Node is in that sector of the signs, now correlating with a peak in the economy. Indeed, the economy may have peaked out just before the COVID-19 pandemic struck in January–February 2020 when the Moon's North Node was posited in approximately 6° Cancer. The pandemic caused the economy to contract at its steepest quarterly rate ever in the second quarter of 2020 as the Node ingressed over 0° Cancer and into Gemini in late May, early June 2020. The actual quarterly high of the GDP took place in the last quarter of 2017 and the first quarter of 2018 when the lunar North Node was in mid-Leo, where McWhirter's studies projected the peak, but still within the zodiac sector shown by the revised chart here.

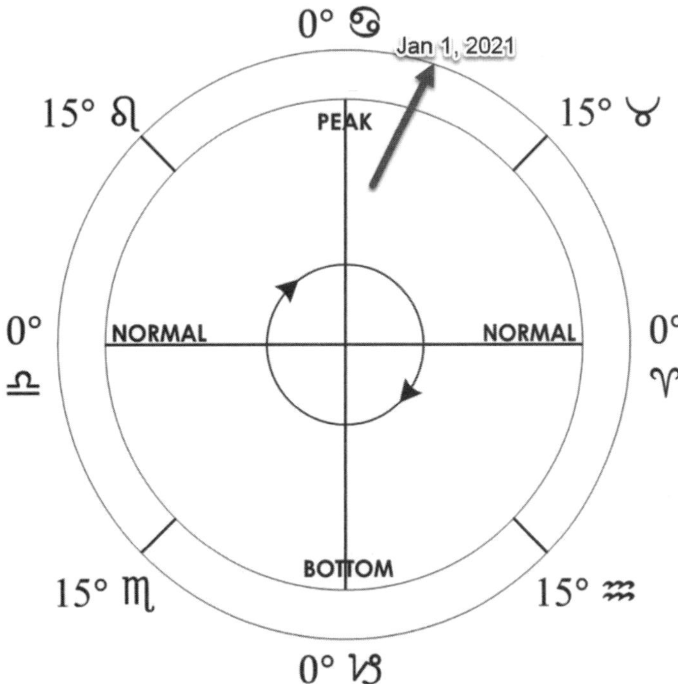

As we enter 2021, the Moon's North Node is located at 19° Gemini, shown on the figure with the arrow's point. It is on its way down from the peak of the cycle, although it is still within the time band when the peak occurs through 15° Taurus, which ends August–September 2022. That doesn't mean the economy remains strong throughout that time. In fact, with Saturn in Aquarius square Uranus in Taurus, there is certainly the possibility of an economic decline in 2021. It simply means the peak of the economy will likely occur between late 2017 and September 2022, and so far, that is the case.

Interestingly, the last time the Moon's North Node was in this "peak" sector of the zodiac (15° Leo through 15° Taurus) was June 1999–February 2004. The economy topped out in the early part of that period, too, along with the dot-com bubble in U.S. stocks in January–March 2000. This was followed by a sharp economic downturn leading to a recession through most of 2001 and into 2002. The stock market didn't bottom until October 2002, with the Lunar North Node at 10° Gemini. After a secondary rebound into late 2007, it fell even further when a deeper recession struck that bottomed in early 2009, but it didn't really end until the fourth quarter of 2009. This was during the time the Lunar North Node was in early Aquarius through late Capricorn (the Moon's Nodes move backwards through the zodiac, like a retrograde planet).

The next time the Lunar North Node cycle is scheduled to enter the zodiac band coinciding with a recession is May 2027 through January 2032. It will be at 0° Capricorn in September 2029, which is the center correlating with a low point in the economy +/- 2.3 years. Our "ideal" time for this low would be January 2027 through September 2029.

Although the Moon's North Node by sign position is one of the most reliable geocosmic indicators of an economic peak and trough, it is by no means the only one. Hard aspects involving Saturn/Uranus and Saturn/Pluto are also signatures of economic duress, especially when they unfold within a calendar year of one another. That is the case in 2020–2021, and there was a sharp economic contraction in the first two quarters of 2020. In my view, there could be a second recession in 2022 +/- 1 year. If so, the decade of the 2020s may witness three economic recessions in the U.S., which would be very rare, but certainly consistent with Uranus (planet of volatility and instability) transiting through Taurus (the sign of economic and financial stability), especially in a square aspect with Saturn in Aquarius. This combination symbolizes peaks and valleys, periods of tremendous growth, and sudden declines, much like the world experienced in 2020.

One reason why I think there could be another recession in the next two years is because the 2020–2021 geocosmic case is very similar to that of 1999–2000. That is, in 1999–2000, we had Jupiter conjunct Saturn in Taurus, square Uranus, in Aquarius. The economy topped out and then began a 2.5-year swoon. The inverse of that planetary/sign relationship is in effect in 2021, when Jupiter and Saturn conjoin in Aquarius and form a square aspect to Uranus in Taurus. It's possible that coincided with the steep economic decline in 2020. But I think there may be another episode to go through before 2023. A case can be made for a secondary economic and stock market crest between late 2020 and mid-2021 (much like late 1999–early 2000). That often happens when Saturn and Uranus form a hard aspect. That is, the economy and stock market make a high or secondary high during that hard aspect (January–December 2021), but then both reverse. Thus, from a secondary peak in late 2020 through 2021 (and ideally by the middle of 2021), another decline is scheduled to commence in the U.S. and possibly the entire global economy and equity markets. We will discuss this further in the Stock Market section of this year's book.

AMERICA AT THE CROSSROADS PART 2
THE UNITED STATES CHART IN 2021

"At what point shall we (the USA) expect the approach of danger? By what means shall we fortify against it? Shall we expect some transatlantic military giant, to step the Ocean, and crush us at a blow? Never!—All the armies of Europe, Asia and Africa combined, with all the treasure of the earth (our own excepted) in their military chest, with a Bonaparte for a commander, could not by force, take a drink from the Ohio, or make a track on the Blue Ridge, in a trial of a thousand years.

"At what point then is the approach of danger to be expected? I answer, if it ever reaches us, it must spring up amongst us. It cannot come from abroad. If destruction be our lot, we must ourselves be its author and finisher. As a nation of free men, we must live through all time, or die by suicide." —Abraham Lincoln, his Lyceum Address, January 27, 1838, Springfield, IL. He was only 28 years old at the time.

In the Forecast 2015 Book, I wrote a section titled: "America at the Crossroads: Will America Survive, Perish, or Transform?" The modified version of that section of the book can be found on the MMA website at www.mmacycles.com under Events and Articles. The article, written in September 2014, concluded the following:

Right now, you can see that the danger to the USA (and even the world) is both external and internal. But coming up in a few short years is a classic aspect of survival that originates from within, just as Abraham Lincoln predicted nearly 200 years ago.

The aspect I am referring to is the conjunction of Saturn and Pluto in late Capricorn in 2020, conjunct the July 2, 1776 conjunction of the Moon and Pluto.

Here is when the dark side of America's psyche rises to the surface. Here is when the enemy from within is most likely to strike. Here is when America will likely decide if it is to survive, perish, or transform.

America has been seriously challenged from within and without since the start of the 21st century. An external threat alarmingly struck on September 11, 2001, when the nation was jolted by an aerial attack of foreign terrorists on the World Trade Center, killing 2977 people and injuring more than 6000 others. The U.S. suddenly came together in an incredible display of patriotism and unity behind its leadership at that time.

However, that support and unity were short-lived. Soon afterwards, in March 2003, the U.S. invaded Iraq and overthrew its leadership (Saddam Hussein) based on false intelligence claiming Iraq had weapons of mass destruction. A Joint Chief of Staff report concluded, on September 9, 2002, *"Our knowledge of the Iraqi (nuclear) weapons program is based largely—perhaps 90%—on analysis of imprecise intelligence."*[1] The 8-

page report was buried and never shared with key members of the George W. Bush Administration, such as then Secretary of State Colin Powell, until it was declassified years later. The decision to go to war with Iraq under false or incomplete intelligence started a course of sharp divisiveness in the American political arena that has grown increasingly more bitter in the years following and continues to this day. The threat to the integrity, safety, and even the very survival of America is no longer external, as feared in 2001–2003. The much more significant threat today is internal, just as Abraham Lincoln warned in 1838.

THE CHART OF THE UNITED STATES

There is no consensus on the time, or even the date, of the actual beginning of the United States of America. As long-time readers of the Forecast books know, I have chosen to use the date of July 2, 1776, at 11:50 AM in Philadelphia for many years. The events of 2020 have only strengthened the defense supporting this choice of dates and time.

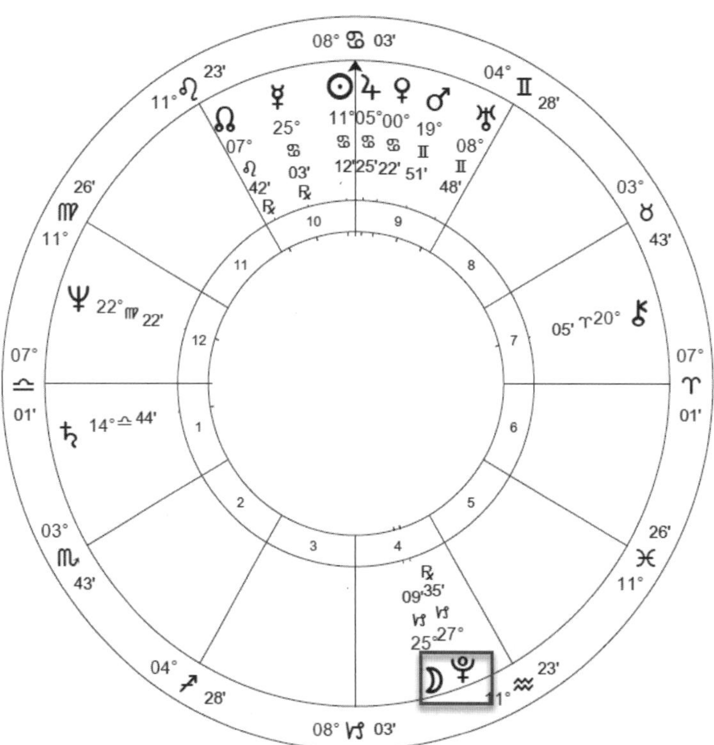

Vote for U.S. Independence, July 2, 1776, 11:50 AM, Philadelphia, PA

The United States celebrates its independence on July 4, 1776. That is the date General George Washington was notified of Congress' vote for independence. It was the date that the American Revolutionary War began. The vote for the Declaration of Independence, however, is arguably more of "birth" than the delivery of the vote to General Washington. The vote—the decision of the new nation to declare itself independent—was completed on July 2, 1776, according to David McCullough, historian and author of the book "1776."[2] The exact time of the vote's completion is not known. It is likely that the vote took place before noon because the vote was announced in the evening newspaper according to astrologer Gary Noel. In order to make the evening edition, articles needed to be in before noon. A vote before noon on July 2 would give a chart with Virgo or Libra rising.

I have chosen to use Libra rising because I believe Libra, and not Virgo, represents the core principles of the United States as written in its Declaration of Independence, which states, *"We hold these truths to be self-evident, that all men are created equal."* Throughout the document, the importance of equality and the right of all people to *pursue liberty, justice, and happiness* are highlighted. Therefore, I believe Libra is rising, for Libra pertains to the concepts of "liberty," "equality," and "justice for all."

The major difference between the July 2 and July 4, 1776, charts is the Moon's position. On July 4, the Moon is located in the middle of Aquarius. In the July 2 chart, 11:50 AM, the Moon is located 25° 09' Capricorn, conjunct Pluto at 27° 35' Capricorn. The difference between a natal Moon in Aquarius and one in Capricorn in conjunction with Pluto is monumental. The Moon in Capricorn (its detriment) conjunct Pluto speaks to the deep stain on the soul of the nation related to slavery (bondage, Capricorn) and racism (Pluto), as issues that are very much in the foreground today as transiting Saturn and Pluto conjoin this natal Moon and Pluto in Capricorn.

Additionally, the U.S. has just elected a president and vice president, where the latter is both an African-American and Asian-American female. The Moon is the feminine principle. It is the first time the U.S. has elected a female and African-American or an Asian-American to an office this high in American government. It fits exceptionally well with the chart of July 2, much closer than a Moon in Aquarius that is unaspected in 2020.

There is more—Kamala Harris, the new Vice-President, is not only a female (Moon) and born of two minority groups (Pluto), but her natal Sun-Moon opposition (27° Libra-Aries) is being T-squared by transiting Saturn and Pluto in 2020. Pluto will remain in this aspect through 2023. In other words, she has a Moon/Pluto narrative unfolding in her own chart in the next three years that is similar to the cosmic narrative of the U.S., as it undergoes transiting Saturn (2020) and Pluto (through 2023) to its natal Moon/Pluto. Her personal drama aligns with the nation's collective drama in 2020–2023, especially as it pertains to America's history of racism and the current issue of systemic racism (i.e., "Black Lives Matter," and the protests of police killings of several African-Americans in 2020). Pluto on the U.S. Moon/Pluto is also indicative of rioting, looting, destruction of property, and the ruination of businesses, which have evolved out of protests that quickly escalated out of control and threatened the lives of innocent people. It has become a dangerous setting domestically (Moon), indicative of Pluto returning to its natal position, and also conjunct the nation's own natal Moon.

America is indeed at a crossroads regarding this deep emotional wound in its collective psyche. And it has begun to erupt, demanding uncomfortable attention and healing. The progressions and transits to the U.S. chart of July 2, 1776, tell a story that will either lead the nation into a more profound crisis or a collective transformation and healing. The existence of this experiment, known as the United States of America, can either end in the next 15 years or be empowered to continue along this path of destiny it began 245 years ago. I am optimistic. I think America will survive.

THE U.S. PROGRESSED CHART

The progressed Sun has now advanced to 14° Pisces. It is, therefore, in the middle of its 30-year trek through this sign that desires peace. Mars, the god of war, is in Libra, another sign that desires peace. It will be in Libra for a very long time, until 2171. But Mars turned retrograde in 2008, nearby to the time when the U.S. started to dismantle its military might and other nations began to build up their defenses. As it retrogrades, it will conjoin with Saturn in 2024–2035. This could be a period of increased military threats against the country, at a time when the leadership continues to desire peace and non-military confrontation. It will be interesting to see how that plays out.

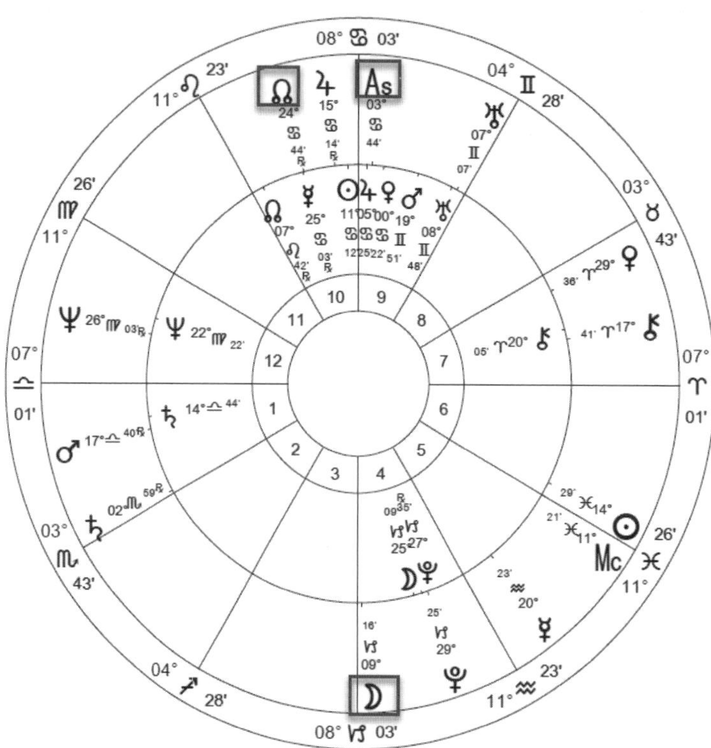

The U.S. Progressed chart, outer wheel, as of July 2, 2021

For the year 2021, there are a few progressions that stand out. Let's start with the positives. The progressed ascendant, which is questionable because the time of birth is uncertain, is around 3° Cancer, between the Venus/Jupiter conjunction of the founding chart. This is favorable and speaks to the booming economy the U.S. enjoyed over the last three years when it entered Cancer, conjunct the U.S. Venus. It will conjoin natal Jupiter in 2022–2023, which could continue the economic growth, supported by renewed trade agreements that enhance both the nation and its allies. We have to observe this because it appears to conflict with the Saturn/Uranus waning square cycle that poses the danger of a sharp economic decline sometime between 2020–2024. Every four minutes, this chart is off, the progressed ascendant will be off, on average, by one year. Thus, the exact position of the progressed ascendant (AS) and midheaven (MC) are uncertain because the time used here may be more than four minutes off.

However, the exact time will not matter as much with progressed planets, but only the progressed angles like the AS and MC, providing we are not off by more than, say, two hours.

Progressed Venus is in 29° Cancer, square to progressed Pluto at 29° Capricorn in 2021. This reinforces the ascendancy of a minority female to a position of power (Kamala Harris) in the nation, with deep-seated issues to confront in the national psyche regarding females and minorities—especially minorities that have been historically discriminated against in the minds of many Americans. There are other possible manifestations of this combination too. Pluto rules debt, and Venus rules credit and money (the nation's treasury), and they are in a hard aspect to one another. This combination could correlate with an economic downturn while in orb of the square aspect, or at some point in 2020–2022. It is possible it already happened with the pandemic crisis of 2020, but it is by no means out of danger of happening again while in orb. On the plus side, the progressed Venus ingresses into its ruling sign of Taurus in December 2021, where it will remain for the following 30 years (late 2051). Venus in Taurus is favorable for financial matters, and also for women in general, as Venus is the "other" feminine cosmic entity.

The progressed Moon entered Capricorn in late 2020 and will remain there until January 2023. The last four months of this progression could be very challenging. It will conjoin the U.S. natal Moon/Pluto in Capricorn and progressed Pluto, September 2022–January 2023. All of the systemic racism issues, and matters around police brutality against Blacks, may peak during that time if healing doesn't occur before. But a healing could take place, for as dangerous, threatening, and uncomfortable as Pluto is; it also contains forces that can lead to a transformation and recovery. It is worth noting that no one and no nation is likely to escape a hard Pluto transit unscathed. You can't hide from Pluto. You end up surrendering to its demand for a change, or it will bring about conditions that will force the change. This applies both to society and the economy, particularly in matters of debt. Pluto, as a transit, is a symbol of death and rebirth, at least metaphorically-speaking. There is an ending, and if accepted and dealt with, there is a rebirth.

TRANSITS TO THE U.S. CHART IN 2021 (AND ITS SOLAR RETURN)

Transits are more revealing than progressions. They often represent events or changes in one's situation. Progressions are more indicative of psychological, internal changes taking place where decisions are made that alter the course of one's direction. With transits, how one reacts to circumstances in life leads to an alteration of life's path. It is more of a choice with progressions, although events can heighten the need to make those choices.

We will use the transits in effect on July 2, 2021, to get an idea of what is in store for the U.S. When a chart is cast for the date of one's birth each year, it is also known as a "solar return." It is the time of each year when the Sun returns to the same position it occupied to the earth at the time of one's birth. Thus, the transits of July 2, 2021, are pertinent to understanding what conditions the U.S. is undergoing in 2021 and even the first half of 2022.

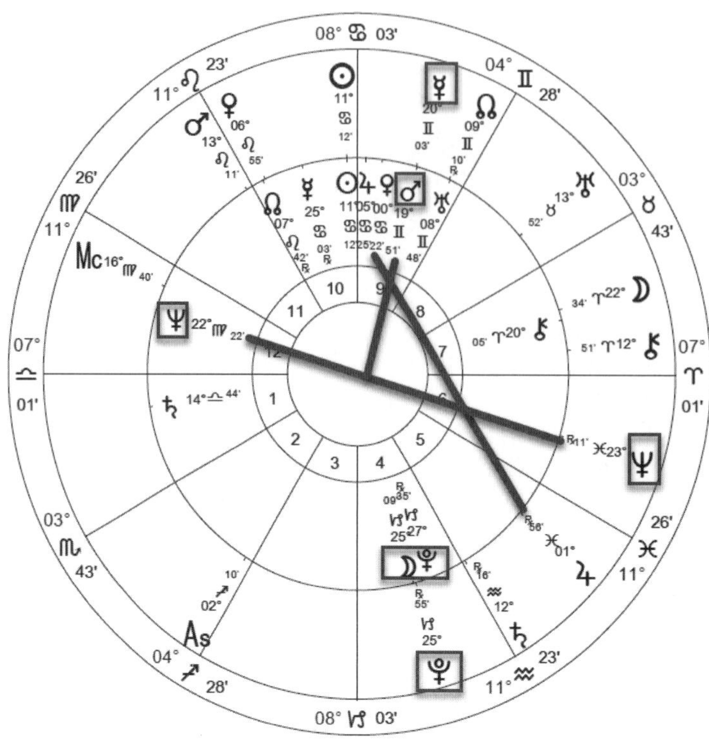

Transits on July 2, 2021, to the U.S. founding of July 2, 1776.
Also known as the U.S. solar return for July 2021-through July 2022

Of most importance in delineating transits to the U.S. chart of 2021 are the outer planets (Jupiter, Saturn, Uranus, Neptune, Pluto, and perhaps Chiron) to planets and angles in the natal or founding chart. The further out the transiting planet, the more profound its impact is on the nation's conditions and issues.

Thus, we start our analysis with transiting Neptune and Pluto, and both are in critical positions relative to the founding chart of the U.S. in 2020–2022. And I begin with a warning: the next few pages may be hard to read and digest. They may appear alarming, but these pages are written with the intent to inform readers of the potentially dire situation in the U.S. over the next 1–2 years if remedies to current conditions are not addressed. Hard aspects from transiting Pluto are not to be taken lightly.

In 2021, Pluto mostly transits between 24–27° Capricorn. This conjoins the U.S. natal Moon/Pluto conjunction at 25–27° Capricorn and is in opposition to the U.S. natal Mercury, retrograde at 25° Cancer. Pluto moves slowly. In fact, it will not wholly pass 27° Capricorn until November 2023. The U.S. is undergoing its first Pluto return for three years, 2021 through 2023. This is a serious time for the U.S.—Pluto, as mentioned before, is symbolic of a death and a rebirth, and no individual or national chart undergoing such a transit is likely to escape unscathed.

Think of Pluto like a volcano readying to erupt. Think of the natal Moon as the nation's soul—its pulsating core giving rise to its collective emotional state of being. Think of

Mercury as its mind, how it communicates with others, seeks information, knowledge, and conducts commerce or business with others. It also represents the media, the source of news, and information in the nation. Right away, we see a wide division between the intellect (mind, mental functioning, business, and news media centers) and the emotions, the culture, and traditions that bind the nation's people together.

With Pluto, all these areas are being threatened—threatened to be extinguished, to be removed, to be canceled—amidst demands that those traditions and cultural norms are somehow wrong, evil, and must be cast aside in order to build a new and "better" model of who we are and/or want to be. The past, we are told, has been fabricated too much on hatred, bondage, and repression of others (Moon and Pluto in Capricorn), and that stain—and anything that represents or reminds us of it—must be removed from our awareness.

The only problem is those who represent the heart and soul of the nation disagree. The heart of a country is its Sun. The soul is its Moon. The U.S.'s Sun (heart) is posited in Cancer, which is ruled by the Moon (soul, emotional self). As one who has studied the interplay of geocosmic energies for almost a lifetime, I present a forewarning. At this moment—the heart and soul of the U.S. are under attack, and its survival is at risk. Take heed—for America as we have known it for 245 years is endangered—and it is from within (Moon).

Pluto in Capricorn is not only a threat, but in action, it can be very demanding, forceful, coercive, and even violent. At its worst, it is an organized, conspiratorial, underground movement whose purpose is no less than to overtake the nation. As suggested before, and by Abraham Lincoln, this is not a force from the outside, but within the country itself. It is deeply divided as indicated by the opposition of the Moon and Mercury natally, in other words, between the nation's head (cerebral nature) and its heart and soul. To say this may be a perilous time ahead for America probably is an understatement. The nation's very existence could be at stake, for there is a continuing and escalating demand to tear down its institutions, culture, security systems of protection (i.e., police and military), and any reminders of its proud or tarnished history.

The source of these demands to extinguish the U.S. lies in the negatives of its past, symbolized by grievances reflective of the Moon/Pluto in Capricorn. These include slavery, discrimination and violence of minority groups, displacement of Native Americans, and probably a host of other violations attributed to the nation's past behavior by those who believe America is cruel, hateful, and arrogant. There is also the issue of envy and jealousy that fall under the heading of Pluto. But are America and its history and culture only negative? Is there any nation whose history and culture are so detrimental that it deserves to be completely torn down? No. Every country, every person, has "positive and negative" qualities and aspects in its make-up and its history. The positives are worth preserving. The negatives will require acknowledgment and willingness to change and reform. Pluto has the power to transform for the better or the worst.

If the U.S. survives these next two years under Pluto's transit, it will require acknowledging its historical "dark side" (Pluto) and willingness to create a pathway forward. It will also require revealing those who would only want to destroy the nation, who are filled with hate towards it, and wish no protection or perseverance despite the positive features of its history and culture. It will also require they be removed from positions of power and influence over those who wish to heal, reform, and rebuild with honest intent, without violence and property destruction and lives. It can be done. It is the only way society stays intact under such a potent Pluto combination and avoids revolution and annihilation of everything it has built and stands for as a force of goodness to the world at large.

There is more. There is Neptune's transit, which is just as dangerous as Pluto in its aspects to critical planets in the U.S. founding chart, but differently. In fact, the transits of both Pluto and Neptune have already begun in 2020. Neptune transits between 19° and 22° Pisces, April 2020 through February 2022. During that time, it will be in opposition to the U.S. natal Neptune and square its natal Mars at 22° Virgo and 19° Gemini, respectively. Whereas Pluto as a transit is often coercive, forceful, and nearly impossible to placate until it makes its power known, Neptune is complacent and laid back, even to the point of being delusional and convincing itself that all is well, and nothing is amiss.

The height of complacency, fantasy, and unrealistic thinking can arguably be ascribed to Neptune's transits in hard aspect to its natal position. Neptune also symbolizes the desire not to be seen, to work in the shadows, undermining or betraying those situations and people it is involved with, often appearing to be harmless and innocent. Mars, in a nation's chart, represents its military and the urge to take aggressive action, to take the offensive. Neptune is the opposite. It is the wish to avoid conflict and aggression. The result is confusion over the role or activity of the military, while at the same time, the military may be subject to unseen forces to undermine it. There may be an effort to initiate a military offensive. However, there may be considerable disagreement over how to do it or even whether to do it and puzzlement on who calls the orders. One leader may issue the command to "attack," while another directs to "stand down." Or, at worst, there is a behind-the-scenes movement to engage the military for dubious purposes. Does someone (Commander in Chief?) think the nation's military force is their own personal army, ready to act on their beck and call without any consultation with other members of the defense department? Is the military baited to enter into a conflict based on false intelligence (again) or in which it may be ambushed or sabotaged? These are just a few examples of the danger that might be posed by this transiting aspect.

The solar eclipses of December 14, 2020, and June 10, 2021, take place at 23° Sagittarius and 19° Gemini, making a T-square with transiting Neptune, and further illuminating the U.S. natal Mars/Neptune square described above. Solar eclipses are powerful symbols of changes too. They give an even greater thrust to the dynamics of the Neptune transits just described. Thus, we can anticipate that 2020–2021 and even beyond will be filled with conspiracy theories and efforts to undermine the U.S., during which the population will be pulled between taking drastic action to deal with explosive conditions in society versus standing down and being completely complacent. It is like the picture of Nero playing the fiddle while Rome burned.

However, just as is the case with Pluto, nothing in the study of astrology is totally negative. All planetary aspects have the challenge to successfully integrate the dynamics of expression that each planet and its sign require. Mars is aggressive, and Neptune is passive. Mars wants action, while Neptune wants peace, quiet, and harmony. They work well together in circumstances requiring empathy and understanding that call for rescue from duress. That is why those with natal Mars/Neptune aspects often make effective counselors, psychologists, and healers. There may be a nation or a state of affairs involving many people needing aid in terms of military actions. The nation's armed forces can come to the rescue. They just need to make sure that their response to a call for help is not a set up for sabotage. They also need to make sure that the Commander in Chief is indeed making decisions based on incontrovertible evidence and facts and not rumor or personal scores to settle. Any hard aspect involving Neptune carries with it the possibility for deception.

Transits of the other outer planets carry less weight to the U.S. chart in 2021–2022 than Neptune and Pluto. Uranus makes a sextile to the U.S.'s Sun in 2021, indicating tremendous discoveries in science, finances, technology, and perhaps new developments in electric vehicles and aviation. Transiting Saturn will make a grand trine to the U.S. natal Saturn and Uranus, which also indicates accomplishment in science and technology, perhaps applied to the banking industry. These two transits are welcomed because, during the year, they will be in square to one another. But, to the U.S. chart, they are favorable, which means any economic havoc in 2021 may pertain more to other nations than to the U.S.—at least for much of 2021. Keep in mind, though, that these transits are not as potent as those of transiting Pluto and Neptune. There may be advances in science and technology and new applications in banking that are received well. Yet, the threats posed by increases in the national debt (Pluto) or conspiracies to undermine the country (Pluto and Neptune) can diminish the impact of these more supportive transits if not handled well.

Finally, Jupiter will briefly enter the first two degrees of Pisces, May 13–July 28, making a favorable trine aspect to the U.S. natal Venus/Jupiter 2021. This is a benevolent combination, favoring gains and enriching experiences socially, romantically, and financially. It would seem that the nation is in a festive mood, feeling free and liberated, perhaps from the restrictions experienced under the COVID-19 pandemic. There may be a cure or treatment with good results, and people are much happier about that.

Now, if we can just make sure that the foundation of the United States remains intact, and its citizens can be safe throughout 2021 by exposing corruption and conspiracy of those who hate the nation and would wish it to fail, and by addressing the sins of our past with actions designed to reform and rebuild in a manner that allows everyone the equal right to *pursue liberty, justice, and happiness,* as advocated in the nation's Declaration of Independence, the future will look bright.

CONCLUSION

Let's conclude this section with the same paragraphs that concluded "America at the Crossroads" written in 2014 as follows:

Yes, America's survival is threatened right now. America's survival could remain threatened in 2015, and perhaps even into the next decade. This is indicated by the potent and extremely challenging and dangerous set up of Uranus in a waxing square to Pluto, which creates a grand square to the USA natal Sun-Saturn square, especially 2013–2015. It is no doubt a difficult time, when the experiment of America is at risk.

But this is a transit, not a natal placement.

And even as a transit, it is a waxing square, not a waning square. As I have stated in many writings, a waxing square is a birthing principle, unlike the waning square, which is more of an ending principle. What the USA is going through is like the pains of birth or rebirth, and not the pain or loss from death. This is not the end. This is a threat, a crisis, but I believe the USA, as born on July 2, 1776, at 11:50 AM, is built to last and will survive this threat.

As mentioned before, I also believe the aspects of 2020 portend a new leader who will be a unifier. The divisions within the USA will give way to the more common sense of a shared struggle, and a crisis that will require the USA to become more united and less divided. The nation will heal. It will recover from the pains of the Cardinal Climax, and even from those that began at the start of the 21st century.

How will that happen? I don't know. Maybe it will be a world war that brings Americans and its allies together once again. Maybe it will be natural calamity. With Pluto, there is almost always a threat to human life, either by nature or by human-initiated violence.

Maybe it will be new treaties between the USA and other world leaders that provide more security worldwide for everyone. Maybe there really is a reset between the USA and other leading military powers, like Russia, and perhaps China too.

Maybe multiple countries have a surge of realism and common sense and figure out that it is in everyone's best interest to have world peace, and not ongoing senseless conflict with one another.

Maybe, in the end, we just figure out what Nelson Mandala meant, when he spoke: "Our human compassion binds us the one to the other— not in pity or patronizingly, but as human beings who have learnt how to turn our common suffering into hope for the future... If you want to make peace with your enemy, you have to work with your enemy. Then he becomes your partner."

References

1. Wolcott, John, "What Donald Rumsfeld Knew We Didn't Know About Iraq," Political Magazine, January 24, 2016.
2. McCullough, David, *1776,* Simon and Shuster, New York, NY 2005 (page 135).

THE U.S. PRESIDENT AND VICE-PRESIDENT IN 2021

"Never let yourself be persuaded that any one Great Man, any one leader, is necessary to the salvation of America. When America consists of one leader and 158 million followers, it will no longer be America." — Dwight D. Eisenhower

REVIEW

Joe Biden won the 2020 Presidential election with the largest number of votes in the history of the U.S. The Forecast 2020 Book written in October–November 2019, well before it was known Joe Biden would even be the nominee, stated the following:

Biden's natal Jupiter makes a trine to his natal Sun/Venus, while at the same time it conjoins the U.S. Mercury. He is likely to receive much more support from the press than President Trump. But it won't be all positive because of the U.S. Moon/Pluto conjunctions opposite Biden's natal Jupiter. Biden is vulnerable to embarrassing revelations about his financial dealings in the past, or debts currently, or "cover-ups," both present and past and related to Pluto. He may have made "deals" that are questionable and could cause him problems in the 2020 election.

Indeed, he received much more support from the press and media than President Trump. He also had to endure damaging allegations about special financial favors he arranged for his son, Hunter Biden. It was also alleged Joe Biden received questionable "kickbacks" financially from these arrangements. These allegations were never proven (nor disproven), but they nearly cost him the election. The book went on to state:

He is also on the wheel with his natal Saturn conjunct the U.S. Uranus. However, this is not a "personal" contact. It implies that anything he tries to establish is likely disrupted by more radical forces than his more traditional or moderate approach to matters. He is not comfortable with radical forces who are likely to try to get him to do things he doesn't want to do. His resistance, and their push, do not make for an easy governance. In the end, Mr. Biden is "on the wheel," but not in the strongest of ways. He is popular with the American people, and if nominated, could win the popular vote.

He won both the popular and the Electoral College vote. Already, before he takes office, different groups are claiming to be responsible for his victory and "expecting" something in return for their support. Demands will likely be made for him to do things he doesn't want to do. Given that he was born in the last degrees of Scorpio, where the "stinger" of the Scorpion is located, he may not honor those promises made to others for their support. They may feel "stung." This could create resentments within his own party by the end of the year if he cannot effectively navigate this division.

BIDEN'S PROGRESSED CHART FOR 2021

According to a conversation with legendary astrologer, Marion March, Joe Biden was born November 20, 1942, 8:30 AM, Scranton, PA. We will use this time and progress President Biden's chart to July 2, 2021, to the middle of the year, when it coincides with the founding birthdate of the U.S. in 1776.

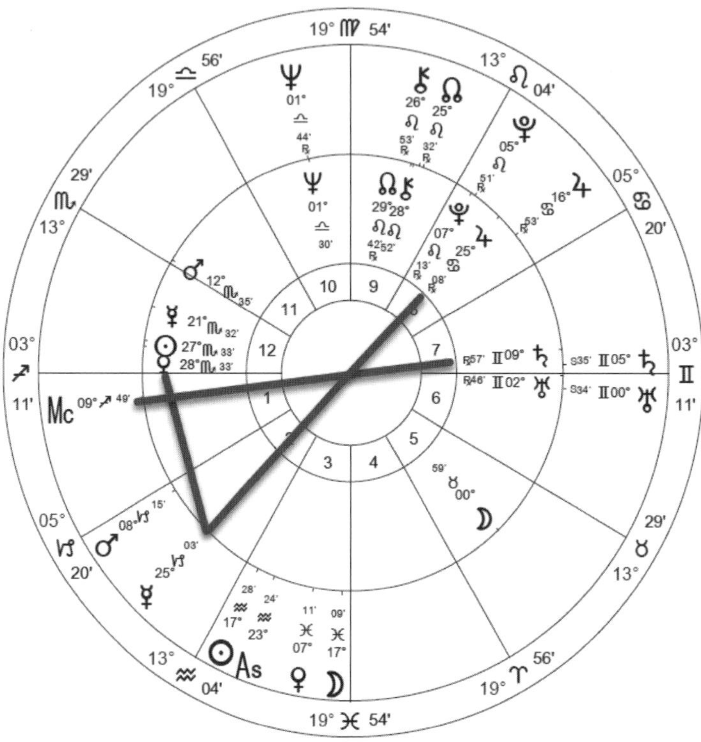

Joe Biden's Progressed Chart (outer wheel) for July 2, 2021. The inner wheel is his Natal Chart, born November 20, 1942, 8:30 AM, Scranton, PA.

The most notable progression is the Midheaven, which is in opposition to his natal Saturn. This highlights the demands (Saturn) of others who expect him to honor their support and perhaps the agreements he made with them. But the opposition also refers to his resistance to keeping these demands and their possible disappointment in him. The aspect further denotes a fight for control between progressives (Uranus) and traditionalists (Saturn) in the Democratic Party. This conflict can be resolved with an honest discussion in which both parties find common ground on what is realistically advantageous for all concerned. But that will not be easy, for others will want to hold him to his word or force him to make new promises or concessions. Neither side wants to relinquish control. President Biden will need to make the boundaries very clear and get other parties to agree with these "lines" (boundaries, limitations), or the fight for control will escalate as his term unfolds. If he is seen as being too crystallized and unwilling to budge, or if that is the case with those who make demands on him, it could become a source of considerable frustration, stress, and exhaustion, possibly even affecting his health and level of vitality. That's how Saturn operates when blocked from doing what it wants.

Progressed Mercury is important too. Along with transiting Pluto in the same position, it opposes his natal Jupiter in Cancer and moves towards a sextile with his natal Sun/Venus in 2–3 years. The opposition to Jupiter is very important because Jupiter is his ruling planet. Any time the ruling planet is in a hard aspect, it can pertain to matters of health. In the 2nd and 8th houses of money and debt it can also indicate that he may still be the target of accusations or even formal investigations related to his handling of money involving family members (Cancer). Biden may not be a good manager of finances. With Jupiter, he may be overly optimistic with a tendency to over-estimate or inflate numbers and projections. When the actual results come in at much less than what he stated, it creates conflicts in 2021. He ran on a platform of honesty and accuracy of facts, but this aspect implies he may have difficulty following through on those promises and projections. It would be essential for him not to over-estimate but rather underestimate, so he has room to maneuver later on in his negotiations with others. If he inflates figures, he will lose the trust of those with whom he is dealing. On the positive side, this is an aspect of optimism and goodwill, which may open doors in discussions with foreign leaders (Jupiter). This can be a friendly signature, which makes it easier for others to deal with him. But he needs to see things accurately, get his facts straight, or else this aspect can cause him extreme embarrassment with those who want to hold him accountable for his words and promises.

The progressed Moon is in Pisces through the middle of 2022. This is not an easy signature either for accuracy or full, honest disclosure. On the one hand, it may be friendly, kind, and compassionate. On the other hand, it is not inclined to be very specific or even realistic. It can be withdrawn at times (perhaps too often) and seemingly out of step with what is going on, as if confused and disoriented. Biden may need help from others who can keep him focused. Otherwise, he may tend to "drift" off point, and crucial matters get "lost in translation." If he can get past 2022, this may start to correct itself.

Progressed Mars is making a Yod formation (quincunx) to his natal Saturn and Pluto (sextile). This points to many adjustments. Nothing is perfect. Matters do not proceed exactly as planned, or as they should, and he is forced to adjust. At first, this can be annoying, even frustrating. But once he makes the changes, those situations become better than they were before. This probably involves personnel he has appointed to important positions but then discovers they do not work out. Or perhaps several of his appointments are not even confirmed. But he is determined to work through these issues and get organized with progressed Mars in Capricorn.

TRANSITS TO BIDEN'S CHART IN 2021

Transiting Pluto will be conjunct President Biden's progressed Mercury in the 2nd house of money. Both will oppose his natal Jupiter (ruling planet) in the 8th house of debt. As discussed last year, this is a classical bankruptcy aspect if one is not careful. Since natal Jupiter is in the 8th house of other people's money (such as the nation's), an unsustainable spending program could have dire consequences for the nation's debt during his first 1-3 years in office. There may be a massive difference between revenues coming in and expenses going out.

This aspect may also represent challenges in trade deals. Is he giving away too much in concessions? Or is he raising new tariffs, which in turn hamper trade deals with other nations? Jupiter is trade, and Pluto is the need to restructure trade agreements with foreign powers using tactics that don't put America at a financial disadvantage. Mr. Biden himself may not be the best person to oversee these matters, so the hope is he appoints someone who is. This is one of those positions (appointments) that may have to be reconsidered afterwards, hopefully before any damage has been incurred. When you see Pluto in a hard aspect like this, there is often a situation (or two) requiring a major change, such as terminating someone's position because of costly errors committed. Again, it could also be a situation where the history of financial arrangements involving his family is revealed and have to be explained. If not handled well, it could be more than just embarrassing. It could lead to further investigations that might become very problematic.

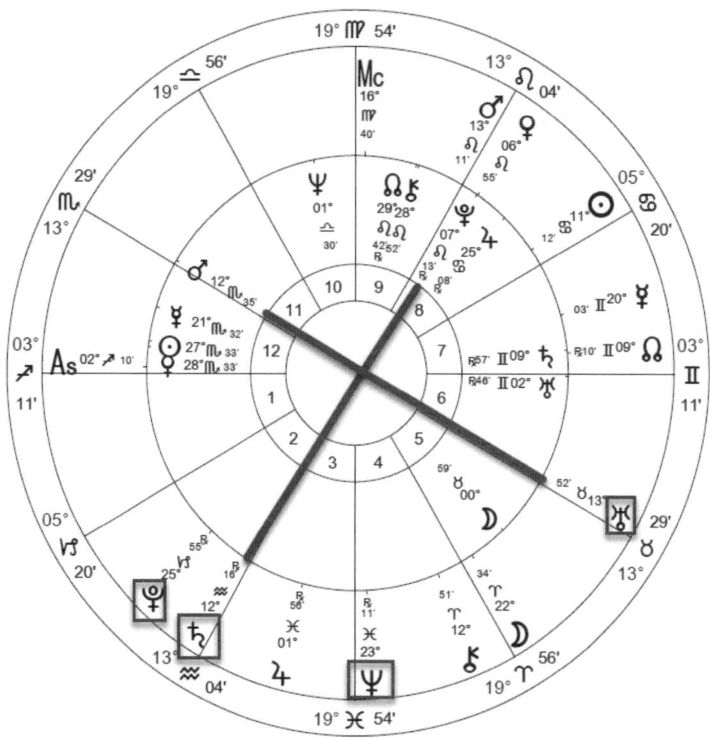

Joe Biden's transits for July 2, 2021
The U.S. Solar Return Chart for 2021 is in the outer wheel, Biden's Natal Chart is the inner wheel

Transiting Neptune is also critical in 2021 and beyond. It is moving into the natal fourth house of his family, home, and living conditions. There could be something unrealistic and strange about these areas of his life. It is hard to say exactly what the issue is. It could relate to several areas, such as someone eavesdropping or spying on him (is the White House bugged?). It could indicate he needs assistance in his residence to get by (Is he hospitalized? Does he need a caregiver?). It may indicate he conducts much of his business in a location other than the White House, or in secret meetings with others. Neptune can be very secretive. It can also indicate efforts to distract and mislead from the reality of what is really going on. Neptune can create an image that is not real or accurate.

It is not usually very transparent, but that is exactly what it needs to be lest one risk losing the trust of others. Thus, the public may want to know what is truly going on because something may seem very peculiar and unreal. President Biden will need to be transparent with the nation, or he courts issues of trust versus mistrust from the populace and even members of his party.

The Saturn/Uranus square of 2021 falls in a critical sector of President Biden's natal chart. It will form a Grand Square to his natal Mars/Pluto square in fixed signs during the year. This cosmic indicator for 2021 perhaps could be one of great magnitude. It underscores the battle between power and control and the potential for disruption and interference. Biden's natal Mars in Scorpio, square his natal Pluto in Leo (with both Mars and Pluto ruling Scorpio), reveals his ability to be either a ruthless, coercive force or someone who works extremely hard to correct and heal sensitive situations that could explode if not handled properly. He can be a healer or destroyer. This is not a sign of weakness. But it may also involve attraction to people who have ulterior motives, hidden agendas, even violent or mob-like tendencies. He will need to recognize who those people are and work hard to keep them out of influence in his administration. Once again, there may be occasions where he does recognize this and terminates their involvement. There may be power plays and threats (Mars/Pluto has a propensity for issuing or receiving threats). This can be a dangerous situation to one's well-being.

Transiting Saturn square Uranus making the T-square to his natal Mars can also be a sign of danger, accidents and/or anger. His natal Mars wants to do something, wants to make major reforms. But the square from Saturn indicates he may feel blocked, and this causes both frustration and potential anger. He doesn't want to waste his effort and time on something that isn't going to happen, but that is precisely what this aspect suggests. He will need patience or recognize it is not going to happen and be prepared to cut his losses before he gets too invested in a losing effort. Because it is Mars in Scorpio, the public may see an angrier side to President Biden that it never knew existed. As a late Scorpio Sun sign, He is not someone you want to upset. But in 2021, he is apt to be upset and feel compelled to exercise his own power, which will likely have mixed results of significant support on the one hand and opposition on the other. The "Mr. Nice Guy" image of Sagittarius rising may be severely tested with Uranus T-squaring his natal Mars/Pluto in fixed signs.

As one looks at these challenging aspects from each of the four outermost transiting planets, one can only wonder what surprising events and situations will arise in 2021 that might roil his presidency. These are not smooth or easy dynamics to integrate constructively. It can be done, especially if he can identify those who have hidden agendas and wish to wrestle power away from him and then remove them before they cause harm. Or if he can lead the charge for changes in such a transparent way that most people understand what he is doing, rather than trying to force changes most people do not understand or accept, he can also succeed in his tasks. These are very coercive and forceful dynamics, but people do not want to be forced to accept changes they do not agree with or understand. Recognizing this and developing a plan that "rolls out" changes in a deliberate and gradual way that doesn't overwhelm people will help his efforts to succeed. Otherwise, Uranus and Pluto will have their way, and he could fall hard to those who wish to usurp his power.

KAMALA HARRIS

The most intriguing chart in the U.S. drama these next three years could be that of Vice-President Kamala Devi Harris. According to her birth certificate, she was born on October 20, 1964, at 9:28 PM in Oakland, CA. She was born to a Tamil Indian (southern India) mother and a Jamaican father. She is the first female, African American, and Asian American person to be chosen as the Vice-President of the United States. Thus, she is already historical, which may be illustrated in her very unusual birth chart based on this exact birth time.

As a matter of disclosure, let me state I am neither a supporter nor an adversary of her political positions (yet). I am, however, very intrigued by the arrangement of planets and angles in her birth chart. It is extremely rare in my experience to see such an arrangement and suggests to me someone who has a sense of destiny and high purpose in life. She is not someone to be taken lightly, and she may be capable of achieving greatness or notoriety.

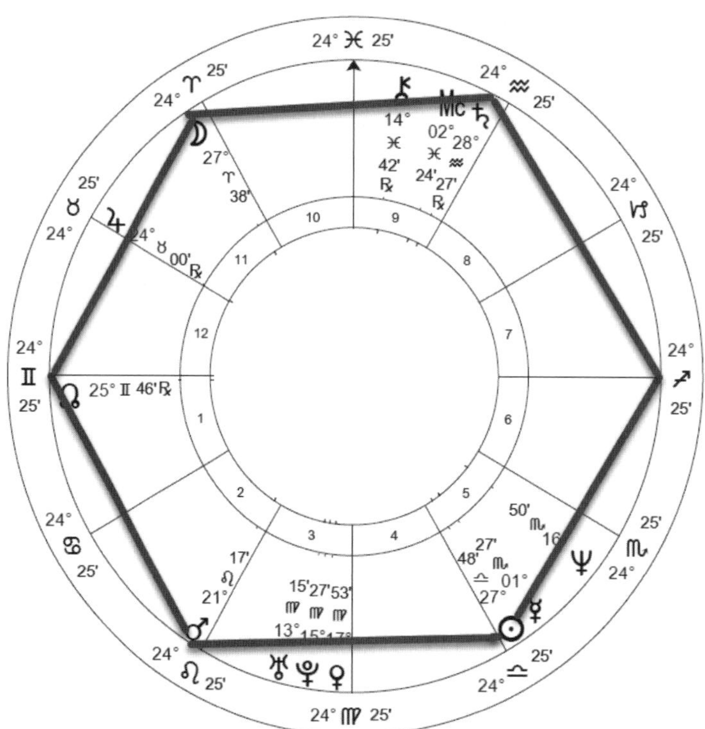

Kamala Devi Harris, October 20, 1964, 9:28 PM, Oakland, CA, from birth certificate

The uniqueness of her chart can be illustrated most clearly by using the "equal house" method. In this chart is a very rare natal configuration known as a "Star of David," or "Grand Hexagon." Using the Ascendant/Descendant axis (which changes degrees on average every 4 minutes), one can observe this arrangement starting with her Ascendant at 24° Gemini conjunct her natal Lunar North Node. From there follows a series of consecutive sextile aspects: Mars in Leo/ Sun in Libra/ Descendant in Sagittarius/ Saturn in Aquarius/Moon in Aries (see chart above). This is an extraordinary pattern highlighting the potential for intelligence and remarkable organizational skills, especially if one of these planets is further in hard aspect to another not listed. And this is the case with Mars, which is not only in opposition to Saturn but also in a fixed T-square aspect to Jupiter in Taurus. Thus, Mars in Leo becomes very important and further supported because it disposes her natal Moon in Aries, and it is also part of the Grand Hexagon. Furthermore, the Grand Hexagon is actually comprised of two Grand Trines: one in air (Sun-Saturn-Ascendant) and one in fire (Moon-Mars-Descendant).

The Grand Trine in air signs, especially involving her Sun in Libra, suggests she can be persuaded to take a position: 1) with sound arguments she sees as benefitting a larger amount of people, and 2) will garner greater support for her own personal ambitions. These two factors are tied together. She is ambitious and wants to get ahead. To accomplish this, she recognizes she must get behind policies and positions supported by the majority of people, especially those that can affect her own standing. This is both good and challenging. It is favorable because she may not be so entrenched in any particular idea that she is unbending despite her fixed T-square. She will recognize the importance of compromise and modification to any stance if it means getting the idea, and her position moved forward. As a Libra, she can support any side of an issue once she sees its potential and decides to get behind it.

The Grand Trine in the Fire element means she can muster passion behind whatever position she takes. She can be a formidable fighter once she makes up her mind about what is worth fighting for. This is doubly highlighted with Mars in Leo as part of a fixed T-square with Jupiter and Saturn. Sometimes, however, she might fight too hard (Jupiter), resulting in others holding back their support (Saturn), thus causing delays and frustrations.

KAMALA HARRIS PROGRESSED CHART FOR 2021

Her progressed chart in late 2020 through 2021 is very active. The most outstanding feature is the progressed Sun at 24° Sagittarius, conjunct her Descendant, and Lunar South Node, which is part of her natal Grand Hexagon formation.

The reason why this progression is highlighted is because the solar eclipse of December 14, 2020, also unfolds there. The progressed Sun is now moving above the horizon in her natal chart for the rest of her life. She will now be more in the public eye than ever before again, for the rest of her life. Life, as she knew it, will never be the same. However, that is usually a positive cosmic event. She now has a partner, besides her husband, and it is the President of the U.S. She sees herself as a partner, and he is likely to treat her as a partner. For the next four years, the progressed Sun makes favorable aspects to all the planets in her natal Grand Hexagon.

The December 14, 2020, solar eclipse on her progressed Sun and natal Descendant is also a matter of concern. Solar eclipses denote a time of three months before through at least a year afterwards where one's life undergoes a radical change. In this case, it involves the Sun, which is her career and standing in the world. No doubt that has now changed dramatically. But it also pertains to changes in her partnerships, which means her husband (who has terminated his job to be with his wife as she serves the nation as its VP) and Joe

Biden, her partner, in leading the U.S. over the next four years. This can either be a time of impressive success and recognition. Or it can be a time of great changes and personal transformation, which can be challenging to navigate. Think of an eclipse where the Moon (the past) blocks out the Sun (the path, the future). There is a new future path as one seems forced to recognize and move beyond their current conditions and plans. Her relationships of the past give way to new relationships of the future. Her daily routines change. Becoming the Vice-President may suggest this, of course. But the aspect will be in effect for at least another year, and other circumstances may arise which pertains to this dynamic.

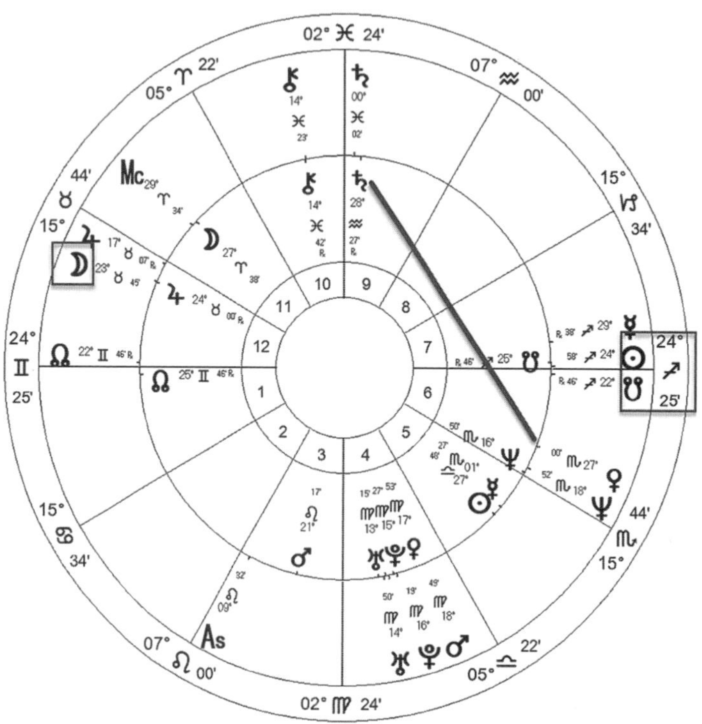

Kamala Harris' Progressed Chart (outer wheel) as of July 2, 2021

The progressed Moon is in Taurus and will conjoin her natal Jupiter in July 2021. This is a favorable indicator for three months on either side. It may get more challenging when it reaches the square to her natal Saturn and opposition to her progressed Venus in Scorpio in November-December. Things start to change then. Her positions on matters become more complicated and conflicting. This may continue over the next 1–2 years as Venus (ruler of her Sun) squares natal Saturn, and the progressed Moon travels through the 12th house of behind-the-scenes activities. She has to decide between two contradictory forces. Maybe the choice is between supporting the President versus the demands made by the more extreme elements of her party who are demanding her support in the name of "leadership." With Venus in Scorpio (and conjoint Pluto in her natal chart, which is the ruler of Scorpio), there may be a situation of loss in a relationship. This is further highlighted by the progressed Venus forming a square aspect to her natal Saturn (loss of a meaningful relationship, loss of support she values).

KAMALA HARRIS TRANSITS FOR 2021

As mentioned earlier, Vice-President Harris' chart shows a similar narrative these next three years as that of the United States. It is a drama involving the transit of Pluto. President Biden has it to Jupiter, his ruling planet, and so does former President Donald Trump to his natal Venus/Saturn conjunction. No one escapes unscathed from a challenging Pluto transit. All three of these leaders are undergoing this Plutonian transit in 2020–2022. Ex-President Trump already received his Pluto judgment in 2020. He lost the election, and he has not lost anything before. Trump doesn't like to lose. Also, Pluto doesn't like to lose either, and under Pluto, one usually suffers a severe loss somewhere in their life, whether in terms of health, well-being, career, or relationships. The loss forces a transformation, a major rebirth in life. With a major transformation, or reformation of one's life and character, it is possible to rebound more strongly than before. Without this transformation, Pluto is relentless. It is like a slow death march that never seems to end, like being caught in a vise that just keeps getting tighter and tighter.

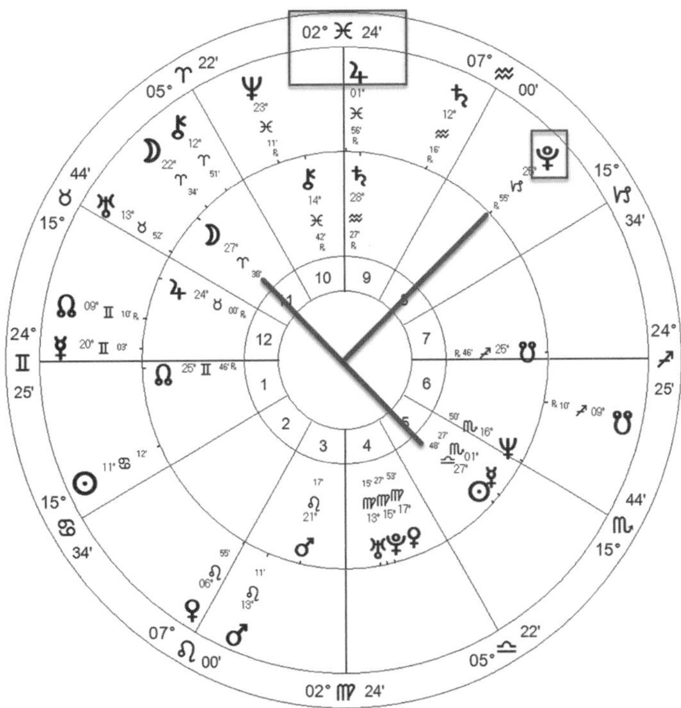

Kamala Harris transits for July 2, 2021

Pluto is transiting through Kamala Harris' natal 8th house. The planet of change and transformation is in the house of change and transformation. Both also represent endings in life, the end or finalization of matters and/or relationships. No doubt, the life she has known has ended.

But there may be more to this story because transiting Pluto also makes a cardinal T-square to her natal Sun/Moon opposition. She was born under a Full Moon, just like Donald Trump, but his Full Moon was also a lunar eclipse. Her Full Moon is not. His Full Moon is under a T-square with transiting Neptune in 2020-2023, which can correspond to a period of disconnection from reality. He can't believe what is happening as his world becomes surreal and seems to disintegrate right before his eyes, and he can't seem to stop it or himself. The Full Moon in Harris' chart is under a T-square from Pluto. This also corresponds to a period where one cannot seem to stop the momentum that is upending their life, where reality is ripped out from underneath, and now a major transformation must occur. It is like an end, a death of one's past, and a rebirth into a new future.

The importance of this Plutonian transit to the VP's natal chart is similar to what is happening simultaneously in the U.S. chart. Pluto is conjunct the natal U.S. Moon and Pluto. The nation is having its Pluto return over the next 1–3 years. The U.S. is in the throes of a momentous rebuilding and transformation, just like the VP is in her personal life. But with Pluto in a hard aspect to one's Sun and Moon, this will not be an easy path to navigate. There is danger on many fronts, whether professional, relationship-wise or even to one's own physical well-being and safety. She is apt to feel pressured, forced to make concessions to her very sense of self-identification. The U.S. set up speaks to issues involving systemic racism and inequalities in the population. She may be called upon to make a difficult choice here, between support for the president, the nation, and her own racial and gender heritage, which may not all be on the same page.

She may be coerced to choose between the forces within her own political party who desire to overthrow or radically change the nation's history, culture, and past governance or consider what is valuable and worth preserving. With Pluto in Capricorn, she may be asked to take a strong stand regarding defunding the police, see protests turning violent or withdraw the U.S. military presence around the world, and other matters of national security. Her reactions may lead to a much stronger backlash than she anticipated. Her opinion and positions matter, and she wants to do what is right for the greatest number of people (Libra with Saturn in Aquarius at the top of her chart). Still, she also has her own set of personal values and ambitions to consider. It is a tricky balancing act for a Libra born under Full Moon being T-squared by transiting Pluto. She will not likely get through this period unscathed. No one does. But she can become stronger due to these critical situations if she is willing to undergo the transformation Pluto requires to be truly empowered and not disempowered. With Pluto, it is all about power. It either gives you power, or it takes it away. Actually, the choice is yours.

On a lighter note, Jupiter will be stationary on her natal Midheaven (MC) May 13–July 28, 2021. This is a period in which she is likely to have huge support and a sense of happiness related to what she is doing. It is a time of opportunity and success. It may be a break from the otherwise harsh Pluto transits in effect for the next 1–2 years. Kamala Harris likes to dance, and with Jupiter in Pisces, she may get an opportunity to dance.

In summary, the year 2021 (and even 2022–2023) promises to be extraordinary for the U.S. President, Vice-President, and the entire nation. It is a make-it or break-it time. It is either reform and transform by choice, with agreement from the majority of people or try to force changes on others who then resist, resulting in losses and the need to accept the changes that were resisted. In short, America is at the next stage of its crossroad, as the consequences of the Cardinal Climax of 2008–2020 finally come home to roost.

THE UNITED STATES STOCK MARKET IN 2021

In the course of their lifetime, Millennials have already seen 9/11 and the dot-com bubble burst, the Great Recession of 2007–2009, and now Pandemic crash of the economy and stock market, and no sense of safety as they watch an urban flight to the suburbs to find refuge from civil unrest. It does not lend itself to a very secure feeling about the future.
– Raymond Merriman, author, in his weekly column at www.mmacycles.com.

REVIEW

The Great Conjunctions of 2020 corresponded with arguably the most turbulent year in the U.S. stock market history.

On February 12, 2020, as Mars was about to enter Capricorn and join Jupiter, Pluto, and Saturn as the fourth member of the Capricorn Stellium over the next month, the Dow Jones Industrial Average made a new all-time high of 29,568. One week later, on February 20, shortly after Mars entered Capricorn, the S&P and NASDAQ made new all-time highs of 3393.52 and 9838.37, respectively. Each suffered their steepest decline in the following month since the Great Recession low of March 9, 2009. By March 23, the DJIA had declined 38% from its all-time of February 12, while the S&P and NASDAQ plummeted 35% and 32%, respectively. The low on March 23 was significant because it was right in the middle of the period when Mars conjoined Jupiter, Pluto, and Saturn in Capricorn, March 20–31, a very rare cosmic phenomenon. During the week that ended March 20, 2020, the DJIA fell over 4000 points, its largest weekly loss on record.

Then, to everyone's surprise, a massive reversal took place. All three indices rallied to new all-times. The NASDAQ's new high came first, in early June, less than three months after its low. The S&P followed in late August. Finally, the DJIA took out its February high on November 9, 2020. All the losses – and more – had been recovered. As this is being written in mid-November 2020, the DJIA is testing 30,000, a gain of nearly 65% in less than eight months. It has been a stunning turnaround, unlike anything ever seen in a single year. Then again, nothing quite like the Great Conjunctions of 2020 had been experienced since the early 1880s. It was a rare cosmic configuration. In turn, it was also a rare and unprecedented year of stock market turbulence, once again demonstrating the correlation between cycles in the cosmos and cycles in human activity.

No one called for such a year going into 2020. Not even myself. However, the *timing* of the reversal from March 23 was quite in line with last year's Forecast 2020 Book, as illustrated by the following excerpts:

"*Thus, the (50-week cycle) is due to bottom again within 12 weeks of December 13, 2019 (September 16, 2019–March 7, 2020), although this could distort and occur as late as April 10, 2020. This low will probably coincide with the 15.5-month stock market cycle. It will also likely coincide with the "Pre-Presidential Election Year Cycle Trough," which tends to happen between October and March preceding a U.S. Presidential Election."* The low of March 23 was in the 15th month of the 15.5-month intermediate-term cycle in the DJIA. The low was right on time. However, the amplitude of the decline was much greater than anticipated.

"This conjunction (Saturn/Pluto on January 12) takes place in a cardinal sign (Capricorn), and hence another geocosmic indicator supporting that a long-term cycle crest is likely to form in 2020 (if not in late 2019, but the four-year cycle also suggests the high is most likely due after April 2020)." We can now confirm that February 12–20, 2020 was the crest of the 4-year cycle, and the plunge on March 23, 2020, was its 4-year cycle trough. And now, after April 2020, the U.S. stock market is making new all-time highs.

"This too (Jupiter conjunct Pluto) is an important geocosmic signature related to the stock market, especially when it occurs in a 3-passage series... if the conjunction unfolds in a series of three passes due to retrogradation, then it tends to correspond with a longer-term cycle — like a 4-year cycle type. Thus, we should not be surprised if a long-term stock market cycle crest happens again in 2020 during this 3-passage series." The first passage was on April 4, 2020. The 4-year cycle low is confirmed as of March 23, just a week earlier. The third passage of the Jupiter/Pluto conjunction occurred on November 12, as this is being written, and the DJIA is making a new all-time high.

"Jupiter will conjunct Saturn in a single passage in 0° Aquarius on December 21, 2020. When the aspect forms only once, the cycle culmination will tend to be 1-9 months away from the exact date, and usually five months or less. Thus, investors may use this aspect to time a 4-year or greater cycle in U.S. stocks, using an orb of 5 months either side of the contact. Whatever 4-year cycle trend is in effect going into this time band, investors may look to take contrary action (plan to purchase if going down, or plan to sell if trend is going up into this time band)." This 5-month orb is now in effect as this is being written. Last year's book went on to state, *"... this does imply that a 4-year cycle trough or crest is likely within 5 months of December 2020. That is too soon for a 4-year cycle low, so if it indeed is to correlate with a 4-year cycle within 5 months of December 2020, it would be from a crest."* We shall see. And this is an excellent point to start our forecasts of the U.S. stock market in 2021.

LONG-TERM PLANETARY CYCLES

Let's begin this year's stock market analysis with an overview of the long-term planetary cycles that will be operative in 2021. The two most important are the 20-year Jupiter/Saturn conjunction of December 21, 2020, and the three-passage series of the Saturn/Uranus waning square of February–December 2021.

The Jupiter/Saturn conjunction is a single passage event this time. As noted above and in last year's book, this aspect has a very high correlation to 22.5-month or greater cycles within five months (91%). Most of those will be even greater than a 4-year (72.7%). When it is a single passage, as this one will be, the long-term stock market cycle culminates within 1–9 months of the conjunction, and usually five months or less. In 7 of the 11 historical instances so far, it has been a long-term cycle crest. Since the stock market is making new all-time highs as this is being written in November 2020, the Jupiter/Saturn synodic cycle projects a crest no later than September 2021, and most likely by May 2021.

There is a less likely, alternate possibility. The low of March 23, 2020, was nine months *before* the aspect unfolds in December 2020. That low was at least a 4-year cycle, and possibly a 6.5- or even 9-year cycle (half-cycle to the 18-year cycle). There is one case where the longer-term cycle topped nine months *after* the aspect (February 1961 to November 1961). Thus, there is an outside possibility one could occur nine months before the aspect too. However, that would be a low, and the majority of longer-term stock market cycles related to Jupiter/Saturn are crests. Thus, this is a possibility, but not the preferred outlook suggested by the Jupiter/Saturn conjunction. If the stock market continues making new highs after September 2021, then the low of March 2020 will be labeled as the correct correlation. Until then, we will look for the correlation to be a long-term cycle crest.

We would also like to point out that there was also a Jupiter/Saturn conjunction within a year of "Great Conjunctions" on April 4, 1881. The 2020 case is also a "Great Conjunctions" year. In 1881, a half-cycle crest to the 18-year cycle (i.e., a 9-year cycle crest) occurred in June 1881, two months after the aspect.

Another similarity occurred with the last Jupiter/Saturn conjunction on May 28, 2000. That was also a single passage event. It too correlated with a long-term cycle crest in the DJIA four months earlier, and in the NASDAQ, two months earlier. More importantly, it occurred near another quarter cycle of the Saturn/Uranus cycle, the three-passage series of the waxing square of July 1999–May 13, 2000. That too correlated with a crest – the all-time high of January 14, 2000 – that was followed by the dot-com bubble burst in which the DJIA lost 39.7% of its value by the time it bottomed in October 2002, and the NASDAQ dropped 80%. The 2020–2021 instance will be the inverse of the 1999–2000 setup. Then, the Jupiter/Saturn conjunction was in Taurus, and the market peaked four months earlier (the NASDAQ topped out two months before the conjunction). This time the Jupiter/Saturn conjunction is in Aquarius. Then, Uranus was in Aquarius. This time it will be in Taurus. The planets' signs are reversed, and the aspect to Uranus switches from a waxing square to a waning square. As we enter this time band of +/- 5 months from the Jupiter/Saturn conjunction (July 2020–May 2021), the stock market is again making a new all-time high.

Now let's consider the Saturn/Uranus waning square of February 17–December 24, 2021. This is the next quarter phase of the 45-year Saturn/Uranus cycle. This will only be the 6th time it has occurred in the history of the U.S. stock market. Within the central time band (February–December 2021), it has a slight preponderance to long-term crests over troughs (3 versus 2). However, as discussed in an earlier section, what is most interesting is what happens in every other instance. That is, the two largest declines in the history of the U.S. stock market happened during the alternating Saturn/Uranus waning square periods: 1839-1840 (the middle of the 80% decline from the crest to the trough of 1835-1842) and 1930-1931 (90% decline from crest to trough, September 1929–July 1932). In both cases, the crest happened *before* the aspect began. In both cases, the bottom wasn't until at least 1–2 years after the aspect ended. This gives rise to the possibility there may be a 90-year cycle in U.S. stocks. If so, the Saturn/Uranus waning square is the only long-term geocosmic signature present in each instance. And it is due again in 2021.

Putting these two long-term planetary cycles together (and they are the only two longer-term planetary aspects in effect in 2021) serves as an alert. The all-time high in the U.S. stock market could be completed by September 2021, and if so, most likely by May 2021. A 1–3 year plunge would then follow according to the limited history of these two planetary cycles.

THE JUPITER EFFECT

Another geocosmic cycle to consider is the 12-year transit of Jupiter through the signs. It spends approximately one year in each sign in its 12-year orbit around the Sun.

In last year's book, studies were provided showing intermediate or long-term cycle crests occurred when Jupiter transited between 15° Sagittarius and 20° Capricorn. Based on this, an important cycle crest was due January 14, 2019–October 31, 2020. As we look back, we see this corresponded to the 4-year cycle crest in February 2020. Jupiter was posited at 15–17° on February 12–20, 2020, when the highs occurred.

These studies also revealed that lows related to Jupiter's sign position were more significant than highs. In 9 of the ten previous instances, long-term cycle lows occurred when Jupiter transited between 0° Aquarius through 24° Pisces, and 8 occurred when Jupiter transited 14° Aquarius through 24° Pisces. Jupiter will be in this sector of the signs again in February 2021–April 2022.

Thus, although long-term geocosmic cycles can support a new high in stock indices as we enter 2021, they also indicate a sharp sell-off at some point to begin by October 2021, and more likely by May 2021, lasting into late 2021 through early 2022, and possibly continuing as late as August 2023.

LONG-TERM CYCLES IN U.S. STOCKS

Our market timing methodology attempts to integrate geocosmic indicators of a long-term cycle high or low with our knowledge of historical market cycles. In many cases, the correlation is very clear. In some cases, they conflict. We may be in such a conflict as we enter 2021. The geocosmic cycles clearly point to another long-term cycle crest by October 2021, and most likely by May 2021. But some of the longer-term stock market cycles start the new year with a greater bullish potential.

Before we discuss longer-term stock market cycles, let's pause to reflect on how these cycles may be applied to enhance maximum long-term performance results.

If you are an investor, your focus is on the long-term cycles in the stock market. You are what is known as a "buy and hold" owner of equities. However, you still have the challenge of figuring out *when* to buy. Knowing when long-term cycle troughs in the stock market are due can aid greatly to one's long-term profits.

Generally speaking, the idea is to buy an 18-year cycle low and its 4- and 6.5-year cycle phases and just hold these positions. That is known as the "core" position. You don't want to exit your "core" positions unless something fundamental has changed drastically.

Until then, you only look to buy on corrective declines into other important cycle troughs. And you adopt this strategy because it is a fact that the U.S. stock market has appreciated over every ten-year period since the Great Depression low of 1932. That is, if you had bought a basket of stocks that tracked the performance of the DJIA or S&P at any time since mid-1932, the value of the index was always higher 10 years later. Thus, there is value in being a "buy and hold" investor. But even that performance can be improved if one times their purchases during the lows of the 18-year cycle and its phases.

We refer to the 18-year cycle in stock prices because that is the common denominator for the very long-term 90-, 72- and 36-year cycles. We do not really know if there is a 90-year cycle yet, because there have only been two instances in the history of the New York Stock Exchange dating back to its founding in 1792. In both cases, the stock market declined by over 80%. Looking at other financial markets over the last 200 years, we note that very long-term cycles usually witness a 77-93% decline in value from their crests to these lows. If there is a 90-year cycle in U.S. stocks, it is due again within the next 15 years (all cycles have an orb equal to 1/6 of its mean length). The Saturn/Uranus cycle indicates it could even happen in the next three years.

Let's briefly list the very long-term cycles multiplying 18-year cycle, their next due dates, and the current trend of each:

The 90-year cycle: It last unfolded in July 1932. It is next due in 2022, or any time between 2021–2037 and, more specifically, before 2032. It is late in the cycle, and thus a top is due. Investors are advised to prepare for a buying opportunity on a 77–93% decline.

The 72-year cycle: It has occurred four times, with a range so far of 73–77 years. So far, it has been closer to a 75-year cycle with a 2-year orb. It last occurred in March 2009 when the DJIA bottomed at 6470. It is early in its cycle and therefore bullish for the next several years, especially if there is no 90-year cycle. Investors are advised to buy all declines of 20-50% to an 18-year cycle trough or phases of the 18-year cycle, including 4-, 6.5-, or 9-year cycles.

The 36-year cycle: With a range of 30–42 years, it last bottomed in 1932, 1974, and 2009. It is not due again until 2045 +/- 6 years. It is in its bullish stage, too, as 2021 begins only the 12th year.

The 18-year cycle: This is the most important of the very long-term cycles in U.S. stocks. It has occurred 12 times since the U.S. stock market was founded in 1792.

The last 18-year cycle also bottomed with the "Great Recession" low of March 9, 2009. This coincided with the Saturn/Uranus opposition (November 2008–July 26, 2010). This is important because, as explained earlier, every quarter cycle of the 45-year Saturn/Uranus cycle has a very high correlation to a 4-year or greater cycles. One will take place in a 3-passage series from February–December 2021. It will be the first Saturn/Uranus quarter cycle since the opposition of 2008-2010, and the second since the dot-com bubble burst of 2000, leading to the recession low of October 2002.

The 18-year cycle trough has a normal range of 15–21 years. Measured from the low of March 2009, it is next due in 2027 +/- 3 years. This coincides when the Lunar North Node occurs in Aquarius–Capricorn, the "trough" part of its correlation to the economic and stock market cycle, January 2027 through September 2029.

There are two historical instances when the 18-year contracted to only 13 years, which would equate to 2022. We need to be aware of this possibility again since the low of March 2009 was the longest 18-year cycle on record, lasting 21 years, 5 months. When a cycle occurs very early or late in its normal periodicity, the next cycle will often do the opposite. The low of 2009 was long, and therefore the next instance may be on the shorter side. Additionally, 2022 corresponds with the time band related to the downside of the Saturn/Uranus waning square cycle. It is also the major geocosmic aspect present in a potential 90-year cycle as described earlier (1842, 1932, and maybe 2022 +/- 1 year). Unfortunately, there are only two historical points from which we can draw. But every eventual cycle has to start somewhere.

THE "PHASES" OF THE 18-YEAR CYCLE

All cycles sub-divide into two or three phases of approximately equal length to the greater cycle. An 18-year cycle is either comprised of two **9-year cycles** with a range of 7-11 years, or three **6-year cycles** with a range of 5–8 years (more like a 6.5-year cycle), or both. Sometimes there is a variation, such as a 9-year half cycle followed by a–6-year cycle phase. The point is that we have to watch the 1/3 and 1/2 subdivisions of every cycle.

Here is where it gets interesting and challenging because the U.S. stock market is currently in the middle of its 18-year cycle where the 6- and 9-year cycles are not always clear. This is the case right now, given the historic plunge into the low of March 23, 2020. That low was in the 11th year, within the time band of a half-cycle to a normal 18-year cycle (7–11 years). It was also in the fifth year of the second 6-year cycle phase as measured from its previous low in August 2015 (shown as "7" on the monthly chart).

If you look closely at the monthly chart, you will see the low for March 23, 2020, (shown as "8) broke below the upward trendline connecting the lows of March 2009 ("6) and the double bottom lows of August 2015 and February–January 2016 ("7" and "7-a"). When a market breaks below a trendline, it usually means a cycle greater than the lesser of the cycle lows on the trend line is unfolding. The low of "6" is a 72-year cycle. The lows of "7 and 7-a" are the six-year cycle and its double bottom. Therefore, according to trendline analysis, the low of "8" is a greater cycle than the 6-year cycle. The cycle above the 6-year cycle is the 9-year cycle, which is the half-cycle to the 18-year cycle. Thus, the idea that the low of "8" could have been a 9-year cycle. It's too early to be the next greatest cycle, which would be the 18-year cycle.

What do we know about half-cycles in bullish markets? They are usually very sharp and very brief. The decline from the then-all-time high of February 12, 2020, to the low of March 23, 2020, was both. The decline lasted only 6 weeks, and the DJIA lost 38% of its value, the greatest loss since the 72-year cycle low of March 2009. In other words, it fits the characteristics of a half-cycle trough to the 18-year cycle. It strongly suggests that it was both a 9- and 6-year cycle low. They converged, which is not unusual. It means this 18-year cycle will likely be a "combination" pattern, consisting of three 6-year cycles and two-year 9-year cycles.

It also means that 2021 is the first year of both the 6- and 9-year cycles. The first stage of all cycles is bullish. This represents a conflict with the preferred outlook suggested by the long-term planetary cycles, which calls for a long-term cycle crest by September and probably by May 2021.

From our studies published in The Ultimate Book on Stock Market Timing, Volume 1: Cycles and Patterns in the Indexes,[1]" we know the following:

1. In all 12 cases of 18-year cycles, there has been an important low at the first 5–7 year interval. That was also the case in the current 18-year cycle, which bottomed in March 2009 and had its first 5–7 year cycle trough in August 2016.
2. In 10 of the 12 cases, there was a half-cycle low at the 7–11 year interval. Since 1857, all 18-year cycles have exhibited a 7–11 year cycle trough. This could be the 11th case with the low of March 23, 2020.
3. In 80% of those ten previous cases, the stock market exploded to much higher prices following the half-cycle low. In 20% of cases, the market only re-tested the highs of the first half of the cycle (double top).

Allowing a 2% range for a double top would put the DJIA at 30,160. Above there, the DJIA has an upside price target of 32,487 +/- 3070 and 32,411 +/- 2010 for its second half-year cycle crest. But once that crest is in, an even sharper decline is due into the 18-year cycle trough, scheduled for 2027-2031, unless it is due to bottom in the third and final 6-

year cycle. Measured from March 2020, that final 6-year cycle trough is due 2025-2028. It is interesting to note they overlap 2027-2028, which is also when the Lunar Nodal cycle low is due for the economy and stock market is due (2026-2029).

So, how do we rectify the difference between the preferred bearish scenario suggested by long-term planetary cycles for a long-term stock market cycle low in 2021-2023 and the bullish labeling of the 6-, 9- and 18-year longer-term stock market cycles? We can't at this time. One will predominate over the other. Perhaps the planetary cycles of Jupiter/Saturn and Saturn/Uranus will correlate with a lesser cycle low in 2021-2023. Or, perhaps, there will be another huge decline equal to or greater than the decline of February–March 2020, and will be the 6-year cycle low, and it will not be labeled as of March 2020. With Saturn square Uranus, we cannot rule out these possibilities. But for now, our cycle studies suggest the U.S. stock market made a 9-year cycle low in March 2020, and it is bullish, at least until it breaks below the 23- and 36-month moving averages. That would be the first sign of trouble in the bullish trend of the long-term stock market cycles.

We can get further insights by analyzing the 4-year cycle.

THE 4-YEAR STOCK MARKET CYCLE

We can also confirm the low of March 23, 2020, was a 4-year stock market cycle. In many cases, the 4-year cycle will coincide with a 6- and/or 9-year cycle. It appears to have done so in March 2020, which was almost exactly 4 years after the double bottom low of February 2016 in the S&P and 55 months after the prior DJIA low of August 2015.

Historically, all 4-year cycles have bottomed in a range of 31–68 months, with 81.8% occurring in the range of 36–56 months, thus making it actually a 46-month cycle with a 10-month orb. It is therefore due next in January 2024 +/- 10 months (March 2023–November 2024). In over 90% of cases, the rally from the start of the cycle to its crest lasted at least 12 months, and usually 12–49 months. Thus, there is a less than a 10% historical rate of frequency indicating this current market will peak before March 2021. This also challenges the Jupiter/Saturn synodic cycle that calls for a crest before the end of May 2021. An ideal time for a crest combining these two studies would be March–May 2021. It's a very narrow time window for a 4-year cycle crest, but it is possible.

There is an 80+% probability the DJIA will appreciate at least 50% off the low that started the cycle. That has already been achieved in the current case since a 50% appreciation above the 18,213 low of March 23, 2020, would be 27,320. The majority of these rallies will show an increase of 70-189%. This range would yield a DJIA 4-year cycle crest of 30,962–52,635. The average appreciation is 103.9%, or in this case, 37,136.

THE 2- AND 3-PHASE COMPONENTS OF THE 4-YEAR CYCLE

We were able to forecast the low of March 2020 based largely on the three-phase pattern within the 4-year cycle, comprised of 15.5-month sub-cycles. Measured from the previous low of December 26, 2018, this cycle was ideally due in March–April 2020 +/- 3 months. It was right on time.

The first phase of a 4-year cycle has a slightly longer interval of 16.5 months, with a range of 13–20 months. Therefore, the first phase of this new 4-year cycle is due April–November 2021. It has an 80% rate of frequency.

The first 15.5-month phase of the 4-year cycle exhibits "right translation" (high is in the second half of the cycle, or past the 8th month) with a 96+% rate of frequency. Most rallies have lasted 9–18 months. Therefore, we look for the crest of the first phase of the 4-year cycle to culminate December 2020–September 2021. The decline from that crest usually lasts 1–6 months, with an average decline of 3.3 months.

The two-phase pattern is not as common in the 4-year cycle as the three-phase pattern. Of the 32 cases of 4-year cycles since 1893, a two-phase pattern has only happened 15 times. Still, one must be aware of its possibility. The mean length of this cycle is 22.5 months, with a normal range of 18–27 months. If it occurs in the current case, it would be due September 2021–September 2022. The rally from the start of the 4-year cycle to its first half-cycle crest usually lasts 12–21 months, which means the first 22.5-month cycle crest (if it occurs) would be due March–December 2021.

Combined with other studies referenced in this section, we like the idea of a stock market crest March–May 2021. If the 4-year cycle is bullish, as it suggests, then a crest during that time would be for a 16.5- or 22.5-month cycle. It may be the crest of a greater cycle if prices drop below the 23-month moving average.

THE 50-WEEK CYCLE

The last intermediate-term cycle to examine is the 50-week cycle in the DJIA. The range of a 50-week cycle is 34–67 weeks (91.1% historical rate of frequency), with the majority of cycles (74.4% frequency) unfolding in a 38–62 week interval.

The start of the current 50-week cycle also began with the longer-term cycle lows of March 23, 2020. Thus, it is due to bottom next within 12 weeks of March 8, 2021 (December 14, 2020–June 4, 2021), although this could distort and occur as late as July 9, 2021.

Rallies to the crest of bullish 50-week cycles usually last 30–52 weeks, which means in the current case, the crest is due any time before March 26, 2021. Our attention will be focused on March 2021, for that is a month that stands out with many of these studies as a possible crest.

GEOCOSMICS PART TWO

We need to keep in mind one more study from The Ultimate Book on Stock Market Timing Volume 2: Geocosmic Correlations to Investment Cycles[2] as referenced in last year's Forecast 2020 Book: "*Long-term cycle crests in U.S. stock indices tend to top out when the* ***Moon's North Node*** *transits from 21° Leo through 2° Aries. This occurs October 2017–December 2024. It happens most often when the Node transits 28° Gemini through 14° Taurus, which takes place May 2020–September 2022.*" Once again, geocosmic studies point to the possibility of an important crest even by May 2021.

STOCK SECTORS

Jupiter enters Aquarius on December 19, 2020, through December 29, 2021, except for a brief two-month period when it enters Pisces May 13–July 28, 2021. The sign Jupiter occupies identifies stock sectors that tend to outperform the overall market. However, Saturn will also enter Aquarius December 17, 2020, through March 7, 2023, and tends to depress stocks in those same sectors, so it is probably a wash for much of 2021. Stock sectors ruled by Aquarius will be highlighted and includes computers, technology, software companies, media, science, and anything pertaining to outer space and satellites. Those companies not being investigated and suppressed by governments (Saturn) will likely do well. Those that are targeted by governments may perform poorly and possibly even broken up. They may be the subject of severe financial penalties and forced into an expensive legal defense of their business. These companies may be subject to a "shakedown" by government regulators in many regions of the world, perhaps due to alleged monopolistic practices.

CONCLUSIONS

With Saturn square Uranus in 2021, the U.S. stock market could be in store for wild price swings. Along with the Jupiter/Saturn conjunction on December 21, 2020, these two signatures point to a cycle crest of importance sometime by September, and ideally by May 2021. But what type of cycle crest?

The majority of the longer-term cycles are in their bullish phase. The low of March 23, 2020, was a 4-year cycle trough, and very possibly a 6-year and 9-year cycle low too. Those cycles' lows are not due in 2021, and not even until at least the latter half of 2022. They are not expected to top out this early in their new cycles.

There are reasons to support a continuation of the bull market off the lows of March 2020. For one, our studies on pandemics indicate the nation may get COVID-19 under control with the development and distribution of new vaccines and treatments by spring–summer 2021. The threat of lockdowns and social distancing may very well end by then, and that will support economic growth and employment. Second, the Federal Reserve has stated they will continue monetary stimulus efforts to support the economy by making purchases in both the bond and security markets. This will help buttress any serious threat to the stock market. There is also talk of further fiscal stimulus relief aid for those businesses and individuals who have suffered financial losses due to the pandemic. More liquidity will also fuel rallies in equity prices.

However, with Saturn square Uranus, there is a possibility of a "Black Swan," a sudden and unexpected event that turns the world and its economies on its heels. With Uranus and "Black Swans," you never know ahead of time what the event is. We can speculate that it could be something dramatic and/or traumatic affecting the leadership of the U.S., given the hard Pluto aspects to the Moon/Pluto conjunction in the U.S. founding chart. It could pertain to civil unrest growing into an extreme existential crisis that undermines the nation's security. With Pluto involved, it could relate to policy measures, such as an abundance of new taxes (business and individual) and onerous regulations that force businesses to cut back their expenses or depress the urge to hire new people and invest in research and other growth activities. If the new administration treats the business community as immoral, corrupt, and destructive to the well-being of the nation whose evil activities must be reined in, as they have charged during the 2020 election campaigns, then Pluto's nature may slowly suck the vitality out of those in business. It would be just a matter of time before the business community — and treasury revenues it provides — shrink. Combined with massive new spending programs, this could also result in another issue related to Pluto: a massive increase in the national debt. The Dollar could plunge as other nations lose trust in the nation's ability to pay its debts much longer. Also, these are possibilities that could result in a sudden downturn in the stock market that begins near the Saturn/Uranus square, as it has coincided with the two previous instances of a 90-year stock market cycle (1842, 1932). If that is the track the economy, government, and the stock market take, then it is possible the high that forms before October 2021 might be a super-long all-time cycle crest. The market could enter a sharp bear market that won't end before 2022–2023. That is not my bias, but it is a possibility.

The next sign of potential trouble for the bull market in the U.S. stock market will happen if and when the DJIA takes out support at 25,000–26,000. The 23- and 36-month moving average also offer support to the bullish trend. Until then, our advice for investors is to stay with bullish strategies. That is, buy corrective declines (even if sharp) into the 50-week and 16.5-month cycle lows due in 2021. Each is expected to be at least a 10% decline. The 50-week cycle low is due within 12 weeks of March 8, 2021. The 16.5-month cycle low is due within three months of March–April 2021. These will be the first instance of both cycles within the greater 4-year cycle, so these declines may happen fast from a crest that precedes them by only 1–3 months. For example, we expect a crest before the end of May 2021 based on the Jupiter/Saturn cycle. A 10+% decline from that crest can happen quickly, creating a mini-panic in the trading community. But as long as the DJIA does not fall below 25,000–26,000, it is probably a buying opportunity. If it does break below 25,000, then the selloff could gain momentum and turn ugly during Saturn square Uranus.

THREE-STAR CRITICAL REVERSAL DATES FOR 2021 – STOCK MARKET

The following a list of three-star geocosmic critical reversal dates (CRDs) used in MMA's market timing calculations. They are mostly valid when a market is also in the time band for a primary or half-primary cycle crest or trough. They are also primarily accurate if a technical momentum indicator (oscillators) is in overbought or oversold conditions or if there are any cases of intermarket or oscillator divergence readings at the time, as reported in MMA's daily, weekly, and monthly reports. The best trading set ups occur when these market timing, technical, and chartings studies overlap one another. Allow a range of 3 trading days (sometimes as much as 6) to these dates for a reversal.

In addition to the three-star CRDs, there are also 2- and 1-star geocosmic CRD dates that do not show up here but are reported in the MMA daily, weekly, and monthly reports. These will more often correspond with major or trading cycle lows and highs, which more aggressive traders can use to time short-term trades.

Dec 28, 2020
Jan 15–18, 2021

Jan 29–Feb 1 (this may be just volatile and not a market cycle reversal)
Feb 12–15
Apr 23
May 26
July 2 (may need 1-week orb; June 23 & July 9 also highlighted)
Aug 4–5
Aug 20–23
Sep 3–6
Oct 15–18 (may need 1-week orb; also watch Sep 26–27 and Oct 27–28)
Dec 3–6
Dec 22

References:

1. Merriman, Raymond, The Ultimate Book on Stock Market Timing, Volume 1: Cycles and Patterns in the Indexes, 3rd edition, Seek-It Publications, Scottsdale, AZ, USA, September 2017.
2. Merriman, Raymond, *The Ultimate Book on Stock Market Timing, Volume 2: Geocosmic Correlations to Investment Cycles*, 2nd edition, Seek-It Publications, Scottsdale, AZ, USA, 2012.

GOLD AND SILVER IN 2021

GOLD REVIEW

The Great Conjunctions (Capricorn Stellium) of 2020 correlated with a huge rally to new all-time highs in Gold. On August 7, 2020, Gold peaked at 2089.20, exceeding its previous all-time high of 1923.70 that was achieved on September 6, 2011, which was made during the Uranus/Pluto square aspect, another very rare geocosmic signature that had not occurred since 1876–1877. The last time Great Conjunctions (involving at least 3 of the outer planets Jupiter, Saturn, Uranus, Neptune, and Pluto) occurred was in 1881–1882.

The low of 2020 unfolded during the first wave of the COVID-19 panic when Gold fell to a double bottom low of 1450.90 and 1457.50 on March 16 and 20, just as Mars was entering into its conjunction with Jupiter, Pluto, and Saturn, on March 20–31.

Last year's book pointed out, *"Whichever of those two areas break first (1350 or 1575) will determine the longer-term trend status of Gold. If it breaks above 1575, it means the 23.5- and 7.83-year cycles are still bullish, and the all-time high of September 2011 can be revisited, or higher."* It broke above 1575 in early January, near the 32-37 year Saturn/Pluto conjunction (January 12, 2020), making its first peak at 1709 on March 9 before collapsing to the 1450 area during the pandemic crisis. A steady march followed this to the new all-time high in early August. As of this writing, Gold has been trading between 1850 and 2000, but is threatening to break below 1850 as we head into 2021 and the Saturn/Uranus square. ***(Note: as we go to press in late November, Gold has dropped below 1800).***

GEOCOSMICS

Let's begin with analyzing the longer-term planetary cycles in effect in 2021 and their historical relationship to Gold prices. The most important is the 45-year waning square between **Saturn and Uranus**, a three-passage series from February 17 through December 24, 2021. The waning square of these two planets has only happened once since Gold began trading freely on the futures exchanges in 1971. That instance was also a five-phase passage starting in October 1975 and lasted through April 1977. In August 1976, Gold dipped to $99, a level not seen since, and the start of the first of two 23.5-year long-term cycles in Gold. It was obviously historic.

Although that is the only instance of this aspect in the modern history of Gold prices to draw from, we can find similar strong correlations to the other "hard" aspects between Saturn and Uranus since then. For instance, the next "hard" aspect was the Saturn/Uranus conjunction of February–October 1988. Just four months earlier, in October 1987, Gold completed its 7.83-year cycle crest. The next case was the waxing square of July 1999–

May 2000, which correlated with the next 23.5-year cycle low of July 1999. The fourth and last instance of the hard aspect between these two powerhouses was the five-passage series of the opposition, November 2008 through July 2010. One month prior, in October 2008, Gold formed its first 7.83-year cycle within the greater 23.5-year cycle. Thus, in all four previous cases of hard Saturn/Uranus aspects (about every 11 years), Gold has formed a 7.83- or 23.5-year cycle. In two cases, the cycle culminated within the central time band, between the first and last passage. In the other two cases, the cycle unfolded 1 and 4 months before the first passage.

Although there are only four cases to date, the Saturn/Uranus quarter cycle suggests a long-term cycle trough or crest could occur either during February–December 2021 or within four months of the first or last passage. As shown under the Cycles section, that could be either a 31.33-cycle trough or the crest (or double top) of the even greater 23.5-year cycle. We cannot rule out the long-term cycle crest that may have occurred in August 2020, six months before the waning square begins.

The next most important long-term planetary cycle in effect will be the **Jupiter/Saturn conjunction** of December 21, 2020. There has not been a consistent correlation to long-term Gold price cycles nearby in the two prior instances of this synodic cycle. The closest was the secondary high to Gold's then all-time high of January 1980, which happened in September 1980. That three-passage series began on December 31, 1980, three months later, and lasted through July 23, 1981. That could be a correlation. But the next conjunction was on May 28, 2000, which was ten months after the 23.5-year cycle low of July 1999 and 9–11 months before its double bottoms in February and April 2001. If anything, it might correspond to a long-term cycle high or low if given an orb of 11 months. The all-time high of August 7, 2020, could be a 23.5-month cycle crest falling within this time band. It was four months prior to the December 21, 2020 conjunction.

The **Jupiter/Uranus conjunction** of January 17, 2021 deserves some consideration as a possible planetary cycle correlating with a long-term Gold market cycle. This 14-year geocosmic cycle has occurred three times as follows, with the results listed below:

1. July 29, 1979 (single passage): 23.5-year cycle crest was six months later in January 1980.
2. September 16, 1993 (single passage): 7.83-year cycle low was six months earlier in March 1993.
3. January 22–October 9, 2007 (three passes): 7.83-year cycle crest five months later in March 2008.

Although this aspect has only occurred three times, it shows promise as a correlate to long-term cycles in Gold prices within an orb of 6 months. The all-time high of August 2020 could fit as a long-term cycle crest, as it was five months before this aspect unfolds. Or it could coincide with the 31.33-month cycle trough that is due. Or both.

A shorter-term astrological correlation to note is Mars in Scorpio, which will take place from October 30 through December 13, 2021. This planet-sign combination has a strong correlation to robust rallies in Gold peaking before the transit ends.

LONG-TERM CYCLES IN GOLD

We have only two very long-term lows to consider: the low of August 1976 and the double bottom episode in July–August 1999 and April 2001. Those cycles were 23 and 24.7 years apart, depending on which of the two double bottom lows one chooses as the start. We will consider this an early sign of a possible 23.5-year cycle, based on an analysis of these cycles' phases.

Within all cycles are sub-cycles of the greater cycle, known as phases. These sub-cycles usually occur at the ½ or ⅓ interval of the greater cycle. So far, the longest-term cycle in Gold has been sub-dividing into a three-phase pattern, with each low consisting of a 7.83-year periodicity, or 94 months, with a historical orb of 8 months. Starting from the low of August 1976, there have been six instances of this cycle in Gold occurring at intervals of 86–102 months. The midpoint is thus 94 months, or **7.833 years**, +/- 8 months. If we multiply that cycle by 3, we get the longer-term **23.5-year cycle**, with an estimated orb of 4 years. This, then, is the longest-term cycle we currently use in Gold.

If the 23.5-year cycle began with the low of August 1999, it is due to unfold again in February 2023 +/- 4 years. If it started with the double bottom in April 2001, it is next due in October 2024, +/- 4 years. The overlap is **October 2020–February 2027.**

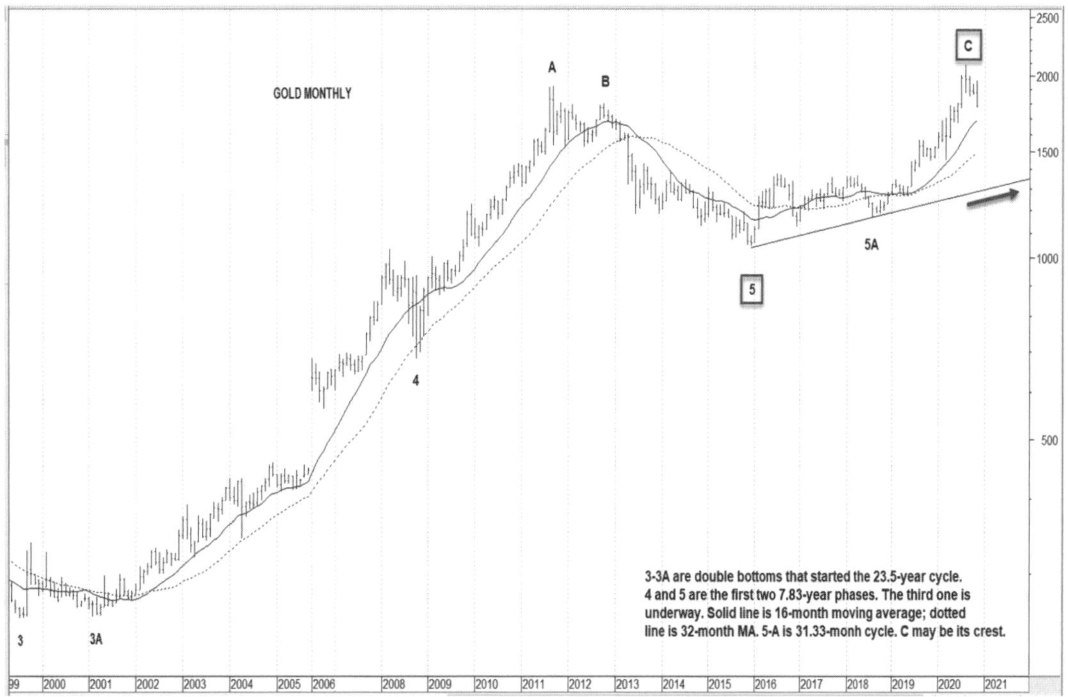
GOLD MONTHLY
A
B
C
4
5
5A
3
3A
2500
2000
1500
1000
500
99 2000 2001 2002 2003 2004 2005 2006 2008 2009 2010 2011 2012 2013 2014 2015 2016 2017 2018 2019 2020 2021
3-3A are double bottoms that started the 23.5-year cycle. 4 and 5 are the first two 7.83-year phases. The third one is underway. Solid line is 16-month moving average; dotted line is 32-month MA. 5-A is 31.33-monh cycle. C may be its crest.

Starting from the double bottom lows of 1999–2001, we can see the first 7.83-year cycle trough occurred in October 2008, shown as "4" on the monthly chart. The second 7.83-year cycle low then unfolded in December 2015 ("5" on the chart). The third and final 7.83-year cycle low is thus due October 2023 +/- 8 months or **February 2023–June 2024.**

What do we know about the third phase of bullish cycles? That they can exhibit "boom/bust" characteristics. That is, they can have explosive rallies to new all-time highs, followed by the steepest decline of the entire greater cycle. As stated in last year's Forecast 2020 Book, *"Third phases of cycles are the most difficult to forecast. If the first two phases have been bullish, as was the case in Gold (2001–2008 and then 2008–2015), the third phase can be either extremely bullish, moderately bullish, or bearish. Extremely bullish would mean a new all-time high, with an upside potential of 2077.50 +/- 215.50, or 2285.40 +/- 189.40, or much higher. Moderately higher means Gold would test the high of its previous cycle phase, which was the all-time high of 1920.80 in September 2011, +/- 2%. Bearish means only a corrective rally off the low of December 2015 at 1045.70, which would be 1483 +/- 103.50."* Last year's high was 2089.20, which qualifies as "extremely bullish." This could pose a problem for Gold shortly.

The explosive rally to new all-time highs in Gold may have already happened or could still be underway. If the high of the 7.83-year cycle is in as of August 7, 2020, then it is also the high of the greater 23.5-year cycle, and the largest decline since 2001 has begun. So far, the most considerable decline within the 23.5-year cycle has been 45.65%. Once the crest is confirmed, a decline exceeding 45% from that high is to be anticipated. In many cases, the third phase low will fall near the second phase low of 1045 (in this case).

We also know in bullish 18-year or greater cycles the low will tend to be 2–5 years after the high. If the high occurred in August 2020, then the low would most likely be due 2022–2025. This fits with the time band for both the 23.5-year cycle low and 7.83-year cycle low given above. The only issue is whether the all-time high of August 2020 is the end of the rally, completing the crest to the 23.5- and 7.83-year cycles. There is no confirmation these cycles have topped out yet. They are due, but there is still time for them to go higher until they are confirmed. To gain further insight, we look to the intermediate-term phases within the 7.83-year cycle.

THE INTERMEDIATE-TERM CYCLES IN GOLD

The 7.83-year cycle also tends to sub-divide into three phases of approximately **31.33-month sub-cycles** with a range of 26–37 months. The first of these three phases was completed with the low of August 16, 2018, at 1167, which was 32 months following the start of the 7.83-year cycle on December 2015, and right on time.

Gold is now in its second 31.33-month cycle phase. Its next trough is due April 2021 +/- 5 months. The crest happened with the all-time high of 2089.20 on August 7, 2020. If Gold makes a "normal" corrective decline of the 31.33-month cycle, the price target is 1628 +/- 109. If the market is still bullish and another new all-time high is still ahead in the next 31.33-month cycle, then Gold may not fall much yet. It may find support at the higher end of this range or into another downside price objective of a shorter cycle.

The 31.33-month cycle, like all cycles, can also sub-divide further into a two– or three–phase pattern, consisting of two **16-month**, or three 10.5-month cycle lows, or a combination of both. It appears this current 31.33-month cycle will be a two-phase pattern, with its half-cycle low occurring on November 12, 2019, at 1446.20, the 15th month (it can have an orb of 2.5 months). It re-tested that with a double bottom at 1450.90 on March 16,

2020, as the first wave of the COVID-19 pandemic was peaking. If measured from the first low of November 12, 2019, it is next due to bottom in March 2021 +/- 2.5 months. The price objective for a corrective decline is this case would pull Gold back down to 1768 +/- 76. Notice how this price overlaps with the 31.33-month cycle low price target, which is also due in this same time frame, at 1692–1737.

CHART PATTERNS AND TECHNICAL CONSIDERATIONS

The weekly chart shows an upward trendline connecting the 7.83-year cycle low of December 3, 2015, to the low of the first 31.33-month phase on August 16, 2018. A close below that line means the next longest-term cycle has topped out. That would be the 23.5-month cycle. That trendline begins the year around 1275 and rises about $5/month. It is unlikely to drop that far in the forthcoming 31.33-month cycle. And, as long as it doesn't fall below the price target ranges given above (1692–1737), these cycles are still bullish. Below that range, Gold is downgraded to neutral. Below the trendline(1–2), it is bearish.

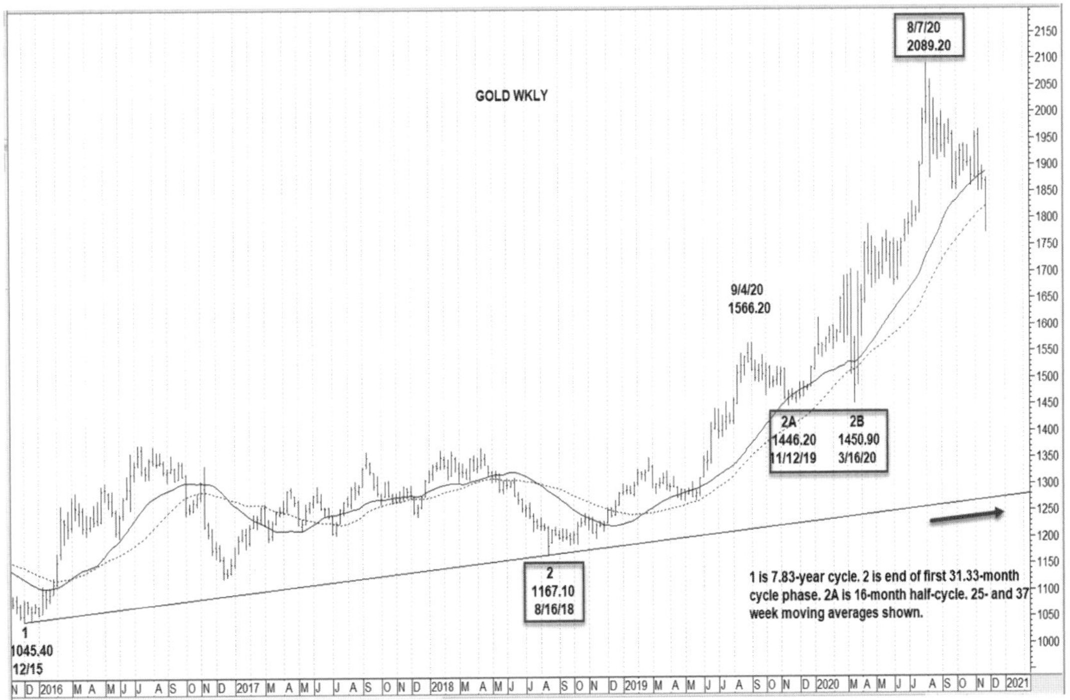

Once the 31.33-month cycle low is completed, Gold will start its third 31.33-month phase within the greater 7.83-year cycle, which is already in its third phase of the greater 23.5-year cycle. Remember what we said about third phases: they can be very explosive, which means another new all-time high, or they can re-test the high of the prior phase (2089 +/- say 60), or they can be bearish, which means the rally is only a correction of the move down from 2089 to whatever the low of the 31.33-month cycle turns out to be. But once the crest of the third phase is in, the steepest decline since 2001 is likely to begin.

Another technical study to watch are the moving averages. Both the weekly and monthly charts show two moving averages. As long as the faster moving average is above the slower one and prices above each, the market is bullish. Even if the price falls below each, the trend is still neutral as long as the faster MA is above the slower one. The trend is not bearish until: 1) prices are below both moving averages, and 2) the faster-moving average is below the slower one. The monthly chart is still bullish via this study as this is being written in mid-November. The weekly chart is bullish but starting to turn neutral. A close below 1815 will turn it neutral, which would not be unusual as the 31.33-month cycle bottoms April 2021 +/- 5 months, and ideally March 2021 +/- 2.5 months. We want to buy that low, especially if Gold holds in the corrective price targets zones given before.

CONCLUSIONS

Gold's 31.33-month cycle trough is due anytime by September 2021, and ideally December 2020–June 2021. The price target is 1628 +/- 109 or 1768 +/- 76. The overlap (ideal) is 1692–1737. If the price falls below these ranges, it is a concern to the bullish case. Below 1275 is bearish. Anything above 2089 (and probably above 2030) means the low is in, and the next cycle is underway.

Once the low is in, we look for Gold to re-test its all-time high again (2089), or much higher. But the next rally may not last more than 8–16 months and be followed by the steepest decline since 2001, over 45%, to the 23.5-year cycle low due by 2024.

With these thoughts in mind, traders are advised to buy declines into primary or half-primary cycle lows in the first nine months of 2021, especially into any three-star critical reversal dates (CRDs) given below. Specific strategies are shown in the monthly, weekly, and daily MMA Cycles Reports.

SILVER REVIEW

Silver had a remarkable year in 2020, perhaps not surprising given it was also the year of the very rare Grand Conjunctions or Capricorn Stellium. The first "shock" came with the collapse of Silver during the COVID-19 crisis of March 2020. After posting a three-year high of 19.75 on September 4, 2019, and re-testing it (18.92) on February 24, Silver plunged to a low of 11.64 on March 18, 2020. That was its lowest price since January 2009, and near its 7-year cycle low in October 2008. A massive rally then followed that low to 29.91 less than five months later, on August 7, 2020, its highest price since February 2013. What was that all about? It was about the panic related to the pandemic and Mars' approach to the Grand Conjunction planets of Jupiter, Pluto, and Saturn in Capricorn—bizarre market behavior related to extremely rare and powerful long-term synodic cycles converging in the cardinal sign of Capricorn.

More importantly, to our work, what kind of cycle was that low on March 18, 2020? A break down that steep (lowest level in over 11 years), followed by a rally that strong usually means it was a long-term cycle trough, and Silver is now bullish. But what cycle was it, since it was not in a "normal" time band for any of conventional cycle studies? Was it a distortion (yes)? And if so, was it a contraction or an expansion to a longer-term cycle in Silver? Let's look at the longer-term cycles in Silver and see if we can piece this together in a way that will give us view as to how Silver might trade this year.

THE 18.5-YEAR CYCLE IN SILVER AND ITS PHASES

The longest cycle throughout the history of Silver has been the **18.5-year cycle**, with a range of 15–22 years. As with all market cycles, this cycle can expand or contract up (my observation is about 20% of the time) The double bottom lows of 1991–1993, shown as 1–1A on the monthly chart, is an example of the 18.5-year cycle, when Silver fell to $3.50/ounce (February 1991) after peaking close to $50.00/ounce in 1980. That was 19 years and four months after its previous 18-year cycle trough of November 1971.

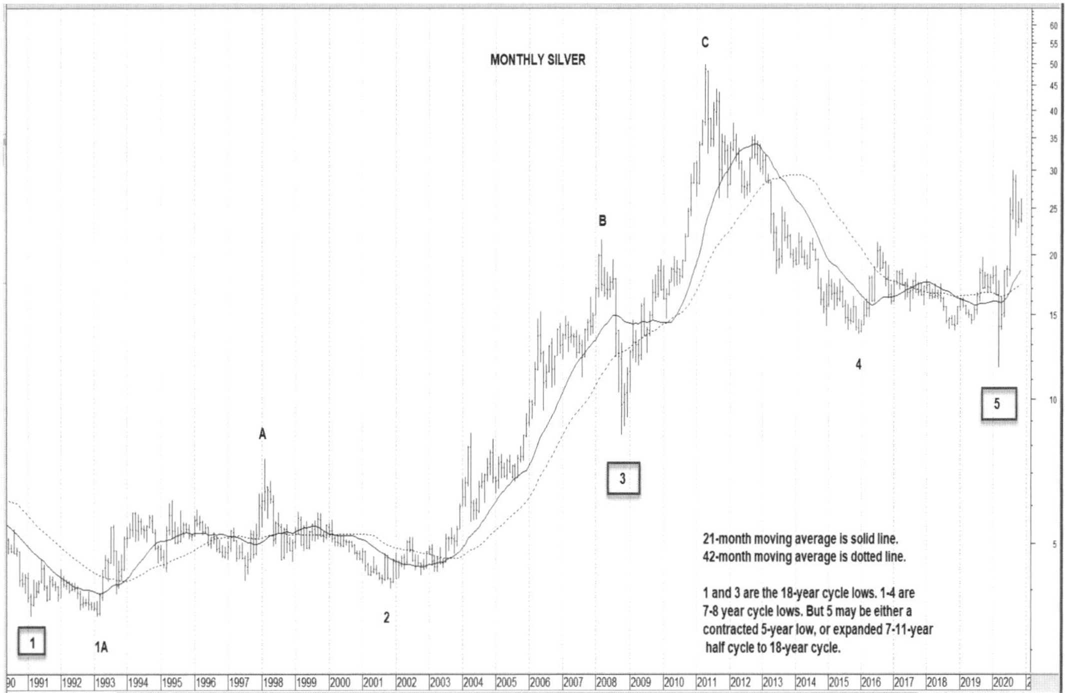

The next occurrence of this long-term cycle was in October 2008, which was 17 years and eight months later, shown as "3" on the monthly chart, when Silver fell from 21.44 in March 2008 to 8.40 in October of the same year as the Great Recession got underway—and Saturn began its opposition to Uranus.

The low of last March was 11 years and four months into the 18.5-year cycle measured from October 2008. Previously this cycle was unfolding in the classical 6-year cycle phases with a range of 5–8 years, and it appeared that was the case with the low in December 2015 ("4" on the monthly chart). But the low of March 2020 took out that low and then exceeded the high following that low in July 2016 at 21.22. Because the decline was so steep and so quick, we will label it as a 7–11 year half-cycle trough to the 18.5-year cycle. Half-primary cycles have those characteristics of a sharp but short-lived decline.

When there is a pronounced cycle low at the 1/3 interval, followed by an even steeper decline at the 1/2-cycle interval, it is known as a "combination" cycle pattern. That means there will probably be another important cycle low at the 5–7-year period following the low of December 2015, or due December 2020 and December 2022. It also means we will see the final 18.5-year cycle 5–7 years after that and 7–11 years after the low of March 2020. That will bring us to the time when the Moon's North Node is in Aquarius, August 18, 2026, through March 7, 2028. We will explain shortly why that is important.

For now, 2021 begins the 5th year of the second 5–7 year cycle phase in Silver and the 1st year of its second 7–11 year half-cycle. It's bullish, as long as it doesn't fall below 11.64. But it is also due for a corrective decline to the next 5–7 year cycle within the next two years (but not below 11.64).

THE 7-YEAR CYCLE IN SILVER

The 7-year cycle in Silver had been evident since the long-term double bottom lows of 1991–1993. These cycle lows are shown as 2, 3, and 4 on the enclosed chart as having bottomed in 2001, 2008, and 2015. That cycle got crushed in 2020 when the pandemic struck, and panic set in, driving Silver sharply lower in March 2020. Whether it starts up anew from the low of March 2020 or continues from its last occurrence in December 2015 is unknown. I suspect, as stated before, we will see it again in 2021–2023. As a result, the smaller cycle phases of the 7-year cycle may have been compromised as well.

THE 40-MONTH CYCLE IN SILVER

Silver's 7-year cycle has been sub-dividing into a two-phase pattern of 40-month sub-cycles with a range of 7 months. A 40-month half-cycle off the low for December 2015 occurred November 14, 2018, at 13.86. If the collapse into March 2020 was an aberration, it is due again March 2022 +/- 7 months.

But I think we need to consider a long-term cycle that used to be present before 2001. This would be the 4.25-year cycle (51 months), which was also a half-cycle to the 9-year cycle, which itself used to be a half-cycle to the greater 18.5-year cycle. The low of March 2020 was exactly 51 months (4.25 years) from the low of December 2015. It is too complicated to get into much detail here about this possibility, and it is still speculative, but I offer it for those readers who want to consider all the cyclical options.

Until this pattern clears up, we will consider the low of March 18, 2020, as a half-cycle low to the greater 18.5-year cycle, and we will consider that this current 18.5-year cycle will break down into a "combination" pattern consisting of three 6–7 year sub-cycles and two 7-11 year half cycles. Beyond that, we are going to focus on the relationship of Silver prices to long-term geocosmic cycles.

GEOCOSMICS

Unlike Gold, there appears to be an inconsistent correlation of long-term Silver cycles (highs or lows) to long-term planetary cycles. The quarter cycles of Saturn and Uranus, which were strong with Gold, are only half consistent with Silver. There is a stronger correlation with the Jupiter/Uranus conjunction, but it requires an orb up to 7 months, whereas with Gold, it required 6 months. The bottom line is Silver could form its 5–7 year cycle low, or some phase of it, by August 2021, but it is not a high probability.

However, there is a strong Nodal and planet/sign correlation with Silver prices. Long-term cycle lows are more common with the Moon's North Node transiting through an air sign than any other element. The Lunar North Node is in Gemini, an air sign, May 2020, through December 2021. The correlation to a long-term cycle low is especially strong when it is in Aquarius (August 2026–May 2028), when the 18.5-year cycle trough is due.

Jupiter also has a strong correlation to longer-term Silver cycles. Lows tend to occur when Jupiter is in a fixed sign. Jupiter will be in Aquarius, a fixed sign, from December 19, 2020, through May 13, 2021. It then moves into Pisces until July 28, 2021, before retrograding back into Aquarius, where it remains until December 28, 2021. After that, it returns to Pisces until December 20, 2022, with a brief interruption into Aries May 10–October 28, 2022. In Pisces, Silver often makes a long-term cycle high and low, and more frequently a high. Thus, we look for a low of importance in 2021, followed by another rally to a crest in 2022.

A shorter-term astrological correlation to note is Venus in Libra, which will take place from August 15 through September 10, 2021. This planet-sign combination has a strong correlation to primary or half-primary cycle troughs in Silver.

CONCLUSIONS

Silver's monthly chart pattern is bullish as of March 2020, as long as prices remain above 11.64 and probably above 18.50. However, the Jupiter and Nodal cycles suggest a low of importance is due in Silver in 2021, most likely before May 13 or after July 28. It may be a 5–7 year cycle trough, but likely to remain above 18.50. A close below 17.00 would be a concern. Until then, traders are advised to buy all declines into critical reversal date-time bands (CRDs), with the idea by 2022, Silver prices could very well be considerably above 30.00.

THREE-STAR CRITICAL REVERSAL DATES FOR 2021 — GOLD AND SILVER

The following is a list of three-star geocosmic critical reversal dates (CRDs) used in MMA's market timing calculations for Gold and Silver. You may also use the CRDs given for the stock market, as others may appear there.

Jan 22–25
Feb 2
Feb 19–22
Mar 23
Apr 27
May 20
July 2 (watch June 22–23 and July 11–12 too – all part of the same grouping)
Aug 4–7
Aug 20–23
Sep 3–7
Oct 1–4 (watch Oct 14 as well; part of the same grouping)
Nov 9–10
Dec 17

CURRENCY MARKETS IN 2021

The riddle once posed in the 1960s by former French finance minister (eventually president) Valéry Giscard d'Estaing is about to be solved. Giscard bemoaned a U.S. that took advantage of its privileged position as the world's dominant reserve currency and drew freely on the rest of the world to support its over-extended standard of living. That privilege is about to be withdrawn. A crash in the dollar is likely and it could fall by as much as 35 per cent by the end of 2021. The reason: a lethal interplay between a collapse in domestic saving and a gaping current account deficit. In the second quarter of 2020, net domestic saving—depreciation-adjusted saving of households, businesses, and the government sector—plunged back into negative territory for the first time since the global financial crisis. – Steven Roach, faculty member at Yale University and former Morgan Stanley Asia chair, "The End of the Dollar's Exorbitant Privilege," Financial Times, www.ft.com, October 4, 2020.

REVIEW – THE U.S. DOLLAR

The U.S. Dollar ended its rally on March 20–23, 2020, at 102.99 that began with the 5.5- and 3.25-year cycle low of 88.25 on February 16, 2018. That was the high of the year and a double top to the 16-year cycle crest of 103.82 on January 3, 2017. The low of 2020, as of this writing, has been 91.74 on September 1, but that is being tested again in late November. The high of the year was right in the midst of Mars conjoining the Great Conjunction planets of Jupiter, Pluto, and Saturn, March 20–31, 2020. The low of the year, as of September 1, unfolded as Venus (one of the currency-ruled planets along with Pluto) was in opposition to the Capricorn Stellium planets, and one week before Mars turned retrograde.

LONG-TERM CYCLES IN THE U.S. DOLLAR

The longest cycle we use for the U.S. Dollar is a 16.5-year crest and trough cycle, which has also corresponded with the U.S. presidential election and the party that has been voted into office since 1984. Basically, the cycles go as follows: Since the U.S. election in 1984, every 16 years has corresponded to an important long-term crest. It has also corresponded to the election of a Republican to lead the nation. The crest occurs within six months of the president's inauguration on January 20 following the election. The all-time high in February 1982 was one month after Ronald Reagan was elected in November 1984. The next 16-year crest was in July 2001, six months after Republican George W. Bush was inaugurated. Donald Trump (Republican) was inaugurated in January 2017, the same month as the next long-term cycle crest in the Dollar.

After the crest, the U.S. Dollar then falls about eight years into a 16-year cycle trough. This bottom also occurs within six months of a presidential election in which the Democrat candidate prevails. The monthly chart will show long-term cycle troughs occurred in September 1992, two months before the election of Bill Clinton, and then in March 2008. This latter case was eight months before Barack Obama won the 2008 election, so it is a little outside the time band. However, there was a double bottom in July 2008, and that does fit the normal time band for a 16-year cycle low, corresponding to the election of a Democrat to the White House.

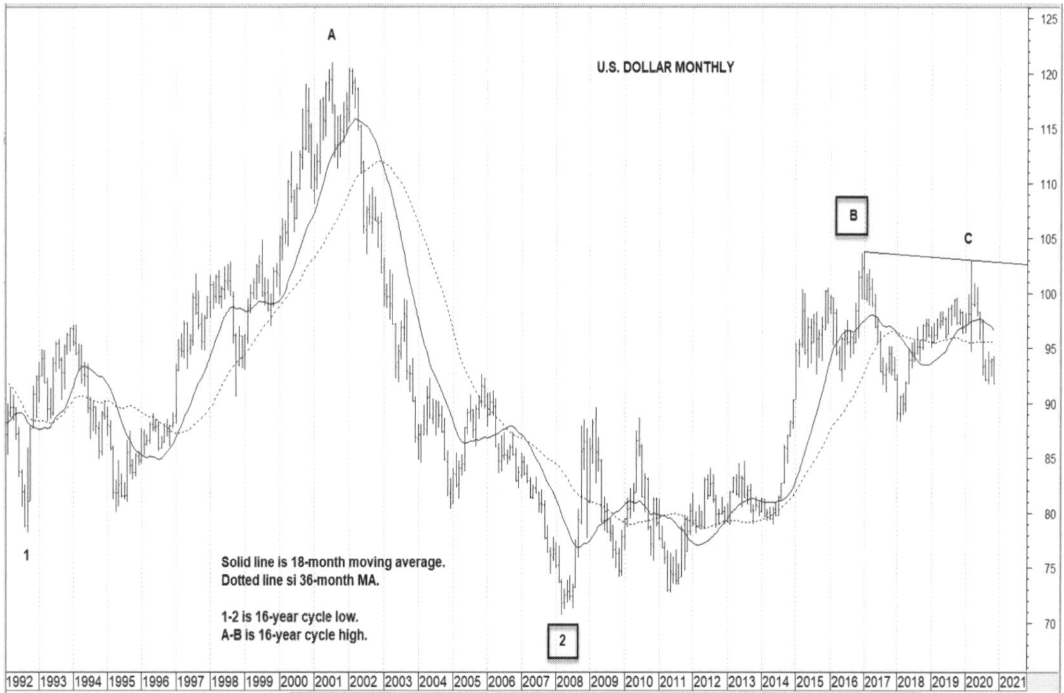

The next 16-year cycle low is due within six months of January 2025, following the November 2024 election. The cycle's correlation to the party winning the White House may be tested this time, for a Democrat (Joe Biden) won the 2020 election. Under a Democrat administration, the Dollar tends to rally into the 16-year cycle crest. Under a Republican, it tends to fall into the 16-year cycle low. The correspondences are in conflict for 2024. The 16-year cycle is due for a low then, but under a Democrat presidency, the U.S. Dollar tends to rise. Thus, either the cycle wins out, and the Dollar continues to fall, as Dr. Steven Roach suggests in the quote that started this section, or in this case, under a Democrat, the Dollar will rise and break the 16-year cycle pattern. Maybe it will depend upon the party whose majority rules the Senate. Since we are cycles' analysts, we will go with the 16-year cycle, pointing to low due in 2025, +/- 1 year.

The downside price targets for the 16-year cycle low are 87.25 +/- 3.91, 87.42 +/- 1.94 or 77.80 +/- 3.07. In the event it is very bearish, we could see 53.49 +/- 7.97. Any move above the double top of 102.99–103.82 will negate this bearish outlook for the Dollar. Instead, it would suggest the historical correspondence of a rising Dollar to a Democrat presidency will be dominant, in which case the upside potential going into 2025 +/- 1 year would be 108.72 +/- 4.48. However, it could go even higher as the monthly chart shows the development of an inverse (bullish) head and shoulders pattern. A break to new multi-year highs (above 103.82) gives an upside measuring target of 116.83 +/- 3.37.

THE INTERMEDIATE-TERM CYCLES IN THE U.S. DOLLAR

The U.S. Dollar also exhibits a 4–6 year cycle. It is probably more like a 5.5-year cycle that is found in other currency markets (range 55–77 months), but we note the double bottom lows of March and July 2008, which marked the 16-year cycle trough, were on the short side from the previous low in November 2004. That may be a case of contraction because it coincided with the longer-term 16-year cycle. When a cycle low occurs, it is not unusual for its last phase to distort.

This cycle might be bottoming soon if it didn't also happen in February 2018. That is, the last confirmed instance of a 5.5-year cycle low was in March 2014. With a range of 4–6 years, it was due again 2018–2020. February 2018 was in this range as the Dollar fell to 88.25. But as we end 2020, the Dollar is falling again to the low 90's. It may be trying to form a 5.5-year cycle low due by early 2021. If so, the downside price targets are the same as given above: 87.25 +/- 3.91, 87.42 +/- 1.94 or 77.80 +/- 3.07.

The U.S. Dollar also appears to exhibit a 3.25-year cycle too, with the lows of 2008, 2011, 2014, and February 2018. Possibly these lows made up a greater 9-year cycle trough with the 88.25 low in February 2018. That low of February 2018 may have also been a 5.5-year cycle trough. In any event, as discussed in last year's book, we note since 1992, the U.S. Dollar has exhibited nine intermediate-term cycle lows at intervals of 27–47 months. Eight of these occurred at the 31–47 month interval, which we will consider the "normal" range of a 39-month cycle, with an orb of 8 months. Measured from the low of February 2018, it is next due to bottom in May 2021 +/- 8 months. We are in this range as we approach 2021, and the Dollar is falling.

The question is, will it break below the 88.25 low that started the 3.25-year (and possible 4–6 year) cycle, which would confirm a bearish trend? Given that both the incoming president (Joe Biden) and the Federal Reserve Board seem to be committed to additional financial stimulus programs, there is reason to think the Dollar will continue lower, to one of the downside price targets given above, due sometime before February 2022.

However, there is no guarantee the Dollar will go lower than the low of September 1, 2020, at 91.74. As stated in the last two Forecast books (2019 & 2020), *"Since the last occurrence was on the long side, this one may be on the short side. We note that it will overlap the 5.5-year cycle time band **August–October 2020.** This would be an excellent time for a low in the U.S. Dollar... A move above there gives another upside price range of 99.20 +/- 1.29 or 102.54 +/- 1.68. A close below 94.75 is a strong indication the top is in, and the decline to the 5.5-year cycle low may be underway."* The Dollar did move up to a high of 102.99 on March 20, 2020. And then it fell to the yearly low of 91.74 on September 1, right into this time band for a low. *Therefore, 91.74 is the key area of support for the Dollar*. With a new Democrat president, it is possible that this low could hold, and the Dollar will rally, maybe even to a new multi-year high.

Our bias for the U.S. Dollar is bearish. But it needs to close below 91.74 to support this bias.

REVIEW: U.S. DOLLAR/YEN

The Dollar/Yen was bearish for most of 2020, but the year's high and low occurred during the pandemic crisis of February 2020. First, it rallied to its yearly high of 112.21 on February 20. It then fell to its yearly low of 101.17 just two weeks later, on March 9. A very quick and sharp rebound followed this to a double top for the year at 111.71 on March 24. The rest of the year trended down, with every primary and major cycle low and every primary and major cycle crest falling lower than the same type that preceded it. By November 9, it was down to 103.16, its lowest price since March.

The price and time for the lows of the year in March fit with our forecast of last year, stating, *"The downside price target for the second 22.5-month cycle low would be 100.43 +/- 2.15 or 95.11 +/- 2.30. It would be due to bottom August 2019–June 2020."*

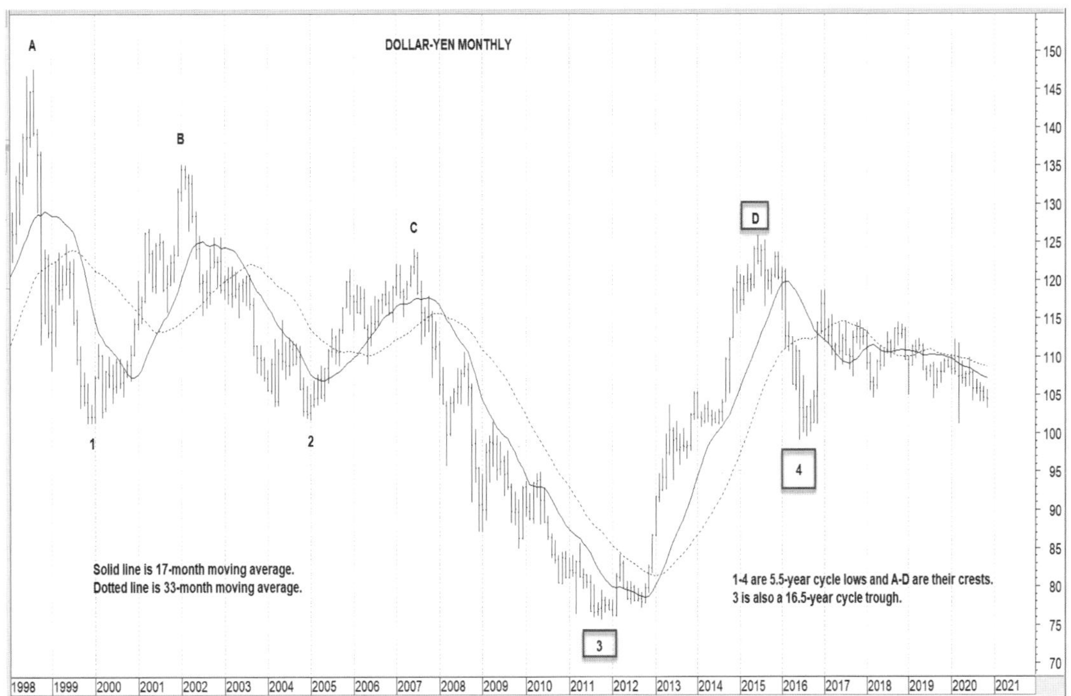

THE LONG-TERM CYCLES IN THE DOLLAR/YEN

The Dollar/Yen, like the U.S. Dollar, has a long-term 16.5-year cycle. The current 16.5-year cycle in the Dollar/Yen started with the low on October 31, 2011, at 75.55. It is not due to bottom again until April 2028 +/- 3.5 years. Its crest will occur before then.

The 16.5-year Dollar/Yen cycle has a consistent history of unfolding in a classic 3-phase pattern of 5.5-year cycles. The first 5.5-year cycle phase of the current 16.5-year cycle was completed at 99.08 on June 24, 2016, with the Brexit vote in the U.K. With a range of 55–77 months, it is next due December 2021 +/- 11 months. The year 2021 will begin its 5th year of this cycle, so its low is approaching this year or next.

It appears the crest of the current 5.5-year cycle occurred at 118.66 and 118.60 in December 2016 and January 2017, respectively. However, prices have yet to take out the low that started the cycle at 99.08 in June 2016. My bias is that they will, and if so, the downside price target for the 5.5-year cycle trough is 91.89 +/- 4.01. However, as stated last year, *"That high (December 2016 and January 2017) occurred only 6-7 months into the 5.5-year cycle, which is unusually short."* If last year's low of 101.17 holds, and the Dollar/Yen can break above 112.21 (last year's high), then this market may not fall to our downside price target range for a bearish 5.5-year cycle. We must keep in mind a Democrat, and not a Republican, is in the White House now. Over the past 36 years, that situation has corresponded with a rising Dollar, making U. S. goods more expensive in world trading markets. Hence, it is more difficult for U.S. corporations to maintain their share of world markets.

THE 22.5-MONTH INTERMEDIATE-TERM CYCLE IN THE DOLLAR/YEN

Within the 5.5-year cycle, are either two 33-month half-cycles or three 22.5-month cycle phases. This current 5.5-year cycle appears to be unfolding in a classic 3-phase pattern.

The first of three 22.5-month cycles bottomed at 104.55 on March 26, 2018, which was 21 months after the 5.5-year cycle started in June 2016. This was normal. Then, as stated in the Forecast 2020 Book, *"The downside price target for the second 22.5-month cycle low would be 100.43 +/- 2.15 or 95.11 +/- 2.30. It would be due to bottom August 2019–June 2020."* The low was right there at 101.17 on March 20.

Thus, the third and final 22.5-month cycle phase to the greater 5.5-year cycle is due September 2021–June 2022. In the meantime, the question is whether the crest to this third phase already happened on March 24, 2020, at 111.71. That was only two weeks after the low, which is extremely short. But, in last phases of longer cycles, markets can exhibit very bearish characteristics. If that were the crest, then the price target for the final low would be 100.90 +/- 1.61, 98.34 +/- 1.91, or 91.89 +/- 4.01. However, as shown on the weekly chart, there is a downward channel in effect with resistance along the top line around 110–111 as we enter 2021. A break above there may mean the crest was not that high of 111.71 on March 24, 2020. In fact, price could go much higher. The upside measuring breakout would give a target of 123.00 +/- 2.60.

My bias is that any rallies this late in the 5.5-year cycle may be modest. A rally in a still-bearish 5.5-year cycle could see the Dollar/Yen back to 109.91 +/- 2.06. This, then, would be a more likely target for a rally, which is basically a test of the upper channel line.

REVIEW - SWISS FRANC

The Swiss Franc was bullish in 2020. As of this writing in late November, the high of the year has been 1.1144 on November 6, 2020, within a week of the third Jupiter/Pluto conjunction (November 12) and Mars turning direct (November 13–14, 2020). That was its highest price since January 2015. The yearly low was 1.0138 on March 23, right in the middle of Mars conjunct the Capricorn Stellium planets and the pandemic panic. Last year's book stated, *"(The low of 2019) was the double bottom troughs of April 26 and May 7 at .9814 and .9816, respectively. It is possible that was the first 26-month cycle trough of a new 16.5-year cycle that started in December 2016. If so, those lows will hold, and the Swiss Franc will shortly start an impressive rally that will exceed last year's high of 1.0392."* It held, and the Swiss Franc blasted well above the high of 2019.

THE LONG-TERM CYCLES IN THE SWISS FRANC

Like all currencies, the Swiss Franc has a **longer-term 16.5-year cycle**. The last confirmed instances of this cycle were the double bottom lows October 2000 and July 2001 at .5488 and .5492, respectively (shown as 1 and 1-A), and the double bottom lows of .9686 and .9669 on November 27, 2015, and December 15, 2016, respectively, shown as '5' and 5-A in the monthly chart enclosed. The Swiss Franc seems to like to make double bottoms before it starts a new bull run.

Last year's book stated, *"The monthly chart shows a descending wedge formation. The upper line is steep, and prices did trade slightly above it last year, but could not develop a pattern of higher highs on the primary cycles before falling back into it. It needs to not only start closing above this line in consecutive months, but it also needs to start exceeding the prior highs of primary cycles. For now, that type of bullish pattern would begin with a close above 1.0392.... investors and traders need to keep in mind that the long-term 16.5-year cycle low is due, and once completed, a powerful multi-year rally is due to follow."* It broke well above the downward trendline of the triangle, thus confirming the lows of 2015 and 2016 as the 16.5-year cycle troughs. Therefore, this long-term cycle is bullish. Even a corrective rally in this cycle is due to reach 1.1832 +/- .0510 before falling below .9669.

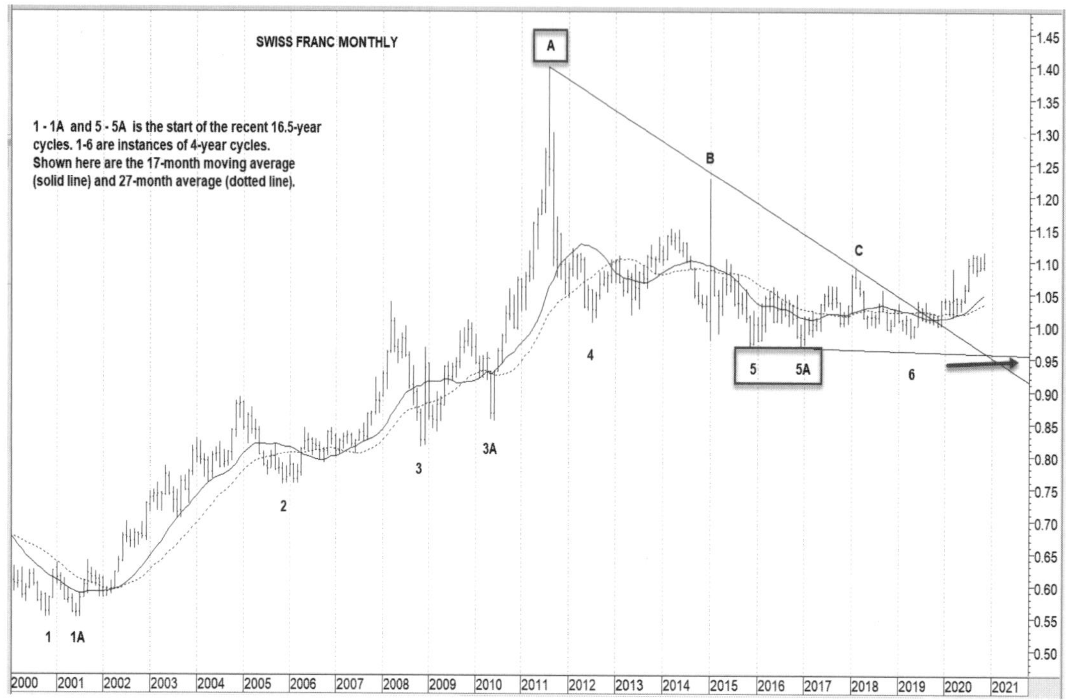

The 16.5-year cycle is comprised of two **8.25-year half-cycles**. It is also labeled as last having unfolded with the double bottom lows of November 2015 and December 2016. It is not due again until 2024 +/- 2 years. In the meantime, a rally to 1.1832 +/- .0510 before falling below .9669 is anticipated here too.

Just as important is the 5.5-year cycle, which is a classic three-phase pattern within the 16.5-year cycle. The current 5.5-year cycle also began with the double bottom lows of November 2015 and December 2016. The low of November 2015 fits best, as it was a 64-month interval. The December 2016 instance lasted 77 months. With a range of 55–77 months, either could be the correct starting point. In the first case, the next 5.5-year cycle is due May 2021 +/- 11 months. In the second case, it is due June 2022 +/- 11 months. The overlap would be July 2021–April 2022. If this cycle occurs on time, then it is possible it could top out in 2021. The price targets for the crest are 1.1053 +/- .0163, 1.1819 +/- .0253, or 1.1832 +/- .0510. The first level has already been achieved with the high so far of 1.1144. If it can exceed 1.1250, then we will look for the next price targets to be attained.

One of the issues confronting the bullish or bearish outlook in 2021 is the cycles' labeling and the policies of a new White House administration and its relationship with the Federal Reserve Board. Under a Democrat administration, the Dollar will usually rise, which would mean the top of the 5.5-year cycle is forming now as we end 2020 and start 2021. But the Fed and President-elect Biden seem in agreement on further spending programs and continued monetary easing policies, which would tend to depreciate the

Dollar, which is also in accordance with the Dollar's 16-year cycle (bearish). We will take the bullish outlook for the Swiss Franc (bearish for the Dollar) until proven otherwise. Therefore, our bias is that the Swiss Franc will reach the higher price targets given above in 2021 unless: 1) it fails to exceed 1.1250, or 2) it breaks below .9814. But we also think the 5.5-year cycle could top out in 2021 and be followed by a decline by the end of 2022.

THE INTERMEDIATE-TERM CYCLES IN THE SWISS FRANC

The 8.25-year cycle has two **4.125-year half-cycle phases**, with a range of 44–55 months. The current 4.125-year cycle low occurred in December 2016 at .9669, shown as (5A) on the monthly chart. It is not due to bottom again until August 2020–July 2021. As this cycle bottoms, it will likely test or fall below the 27-month moving average shown on the monthly chart with the dotted line. That average is around 1.0340 in late 2020.

The 4.125-year cycle unfolds further in a 2-phase pattern of two **26-month phases**. The double bottom troughs of April 26 and May 7, 2019, at .9814 and .9816, respectively, fit this cycle. As stated last year, *"It is possible that was the first 26-month cycle trough of a new 16.5-year cycle that started in December 2016. If so, those lows will hold, and the Swiss Franc will shortly start an impressive rally that will exceed last year's high of 1.0392."* It did that and soared to 1.1144 by November 2020.

The next 26-month cycle trough is due June–July 2021 +/- 5 months. If the high is already in at 1.1144, then the price target for the 26-month cycle low is 1.0480 +/- .-157. Traders and investors would be advised to look for buying opportunities in this range if offered in 2021, with a stop-loss on a close below .9814.

REVIEW – EURO CURRENCY

The Euro took out both the low and high of 2019 last year. The low was 1.0635 on March 23, right in the middle of Mars conjoining the Capricorn Stellium and the COVID-19 pandemic panic. That was its lowest price since the 16.5-year cycle trough of 1.0339 on January 3, 2017. However, it then rallied to its yearly high, as of this writing, on September 1, 2020, at 1.2011. In fact, that was its highest price since May 2018.

Last year's book stated, *"Bottom line: The Euro is in the time band and price range for a 33-month cycle low, due no later than May 2020. Once that low is in, a multi-month rally is due to the crest of the next 33-month cycle. If the 16.5-year cycle low did bottom January 3, 2017, then the rally to that next 33-month cycle is likely to exceed the 1.2550 high of February 2018."* It made its 33-month cycle low on time in March 2020, and then the rally began. It remains to be seen if prices can exceed 1.2550.

THE LONG-TERM CYCLES IN THE EURO CURRENCY

The Euro has a 16.5-year long-term cycle similar to the Swiss Franc, U.S. Dollar, and Dollar/Yen. Like those other currencies, the Euro completed its long-term cycle low on January 3, 2017, with the Euro (bottom), whereas the U.S. Dollar made its crest. Unlike the Swiss Franc, the Euro did not post a new high last year for this new 16.5-year cycle. Its high remains 1.2550 in February 2018. But it is still early (bullish) in this long-term cycle.

It is too early to say if this 16.5-year cycle will be bullish or bearish. If bullish, it is not likely to top out before the 8th year (2025). If bearish, it will likely top out in years 2–5 (2019–2022). As stated last year, *"The high since January 3, 2017, has been 1.2550 one year later, on February 16, 2018." These guidelines suggest that the top is not in yet if January 3, 2017, was indeed the 16.5-year cycle trough. It is most likely to exceed 1.2550 before falling below 1.0339."*

Like most cycles, the 16.5-year cycle divides into either two 8.25-year or three 5.5-year sub-cycles or phases. For reasons to be given shortly, it already appears this will be a three-phase pattern, which means the first 5.5-year cycle trough is likely due July 2022 +/- 11 months. The crest will come first, and it is likely to be higher than 1.2550. The upside price targets are 1.2846 +/- .0295, 1.3188 +/- .0336, or 1.4212 +/- .0457. Any break below the three-point trendline of 1-2-3 will jeopardize this outlook. The new Democrat leadership in the U.S. is not historically conducive to a rising Euro currency. But Janet Yellen, as the new Treasury Secretary and the stated accommodative monetary policies of the Federal Reserve Board, supports the idea of a rising Euro. Therefore, we stay with the idea the 5.5-year cycle and the longer-term 16.5-year cycles will be bullish for the Euro.

THE INTERMEDIATE-TERM CYCLES IN THE EURO

The reason why the 16.5-year cycle is likely to consist of three 5.5-year cycle phases is because last year's steep decline to 1.0635 on March 23, 2020, was in the range of a 33-month half-cycle to the 5.5-year cycle. That low doesn't fit well with a breakdown into a 2-phase pattern of 8.25-year cycle lows, which breaks down into two 4.125-year sub-cycles. Furthermore, the 8.25-year cycle can subdivide into three 33-month phases too.

Thus, for students of cycle studies, the 16.5-year Euro cycle could very well be a "combination" pattern, consisting of two 8.25-year phases and three 5.5-year phases. The 8.25-year cycle can then break down into three 33-month phases, and the 5.5-year cycle can break down into two 33-month cycle phases. The low of March 2020 was the first 33-month cycle phase of either (or both) the 8.25-year cycle as well as the 5.5-year cycle. As the first phase of either, it is likely to be bullish. That means the low of this first 5.5-year cycle will not likely take out the 1.0339 level that started it in January 2017. And it is likely to be a "right translation" 5.5-year cycle, which means the high will likely happen in the second half of the 5.5-year cycle. The second half (or the new 33-month cycle) began in March 2020. It is next due to bottom in December 2022 +/- 6 months.

Last year's book pointed out the presence of a contracting triangle formation in the monthly chart. The Euro briefly exceeded the downward trendline on that triangle and is still hovering around it (say around 1.1600–1.1700). Last year's book stated, *"That triangle is still in effect, with support along a trendline connecting the 16.5-year cycle lows of 2000 and 2017 (1-3 on the monthly chart). Resistance is along the downward trendline A-B. A close above A-B projects an upside target of 1.5769 +/- .0641."* We will keep that in mind if prices start to accelerate above 1.3000. In the meantime, there may be strong support around the 17- and 26-month moving averages, which start the new year at 1.1250-1.1300.

Shorter-term, the 33-month cycle can subdivide into two 16.5-month phases. Measured from the low of March 2020, the Euro could exhibit a 16.5-month cycle low. If so, it would be due July–August 2021 +/- 3 months. If the Euro closes below 1.1600, then it could fall further to 1.1323 +/- .0164 for this trough. A move above 1.2011 will raise that corrective price zone for a pullback.

GEOCOSMICS FOR DOLLAR/YEN, SWISS FRANC, AND EURO CURRENCIES

The 33-month cycle low in the Euro on March 23, 2020, and the possible 5.5-year cycle crest in the U.S. Dollar on March 20 were only two months following the 32-37-year conjunction of Saturn and Pluto. That was the secondary bottom to the 16.5-year cycle low in January 2017 in the Euro and Swiss Franc and the 16.5-year cycle high in the U.S. Dollar. Sometimes longer-term planetary cycles correlate with the secondary lows or highs rather than the actual lows or highs of a long-term market cycle. It is not unusual.

One other geocosmic factor with some historical correspondence to long-term cycle culminations in currency prices is the Moon's North Node crossing 0° Cancer. This 18.62-year cycle has a possible correspondence to long-term cycle reversals in the U.S. Dollar, as it does when it crosses over 0° Capricorn on the opposite side of the solstice degrees. As discussed in last year's book, *"The Moon's Node will cross over 0° Cancer in June 2020. If this correspondence continues, the U.S. Dollar could make a high, or secondary high to its crest of January 2017, sometime in 2020–September 2022. Based on the U.S. Dollar's 16.5-year cycle, it seems more likely to make a secondary crest in 2020, below the 103.82 high of January 2017."* It did that on March 20, 2020, when it rallied back to 102.99. This was within three months of the Moon's North Node crossing from Cancer into Gemini. In previous Forecast books, we had suggested that currency trends would reverse within nine months of the Nodal crossing of a cardinal point, and usually five months or less. That happened in 2020.

Our attention now shifts to the Jupiter/Saturn conjunction of December 21, 2020, and the three waning square passages of Saturn/Uranus, February–December 2021. In the four cases of the quarter cycle aspects between Saturn and Uranus (conjunction, squares, and opposition) since 1973, all have correlated with 4-year or greater cycles in each market either during the central time band or within five months of its first or last passage. In the last case (November 2008–July 2010), the Dollar/Yen did not complete its cycle until October 2011, but it fell hard through most of that period. The Swiss Franc made an 8-year cycle low then, and the Euro a 5.5-year cycle low. Thus, this signature strongly correlates to a 5.5-year cycle crest or trough happening this time in each market.

The Jupiter/Saturn conjunction unfolds on December 21, 2020. This 20-year planetary cycle has occurred two previous times since our charts began in 1973. In the December 1980–July 1981 instance, the Euro and Swiss Franc both made 4-year cycle lows, while the Dollar/Yen made a 22.5-month cycle trough. The second instance was on May 28, 2000. Both the Euro and Swiss Franc made their 16.5-month cycle troughs less than five months later. The Dollar/Yen made a 5.5-year cycle low five months before.

The last time Saturn and Uranus formed a waning square to one another was October 1975 through April 1977. During that same period, Jupiter was in a T-square with both Saturn and Uranus. That coincided with a 5.5-year cycle trough in the Swiss Franc and crest in the Dollar/Yen (our data on the Euro does not go back that far). These three planets were also in a similar aspect formation to one another in 2000 as they will be in 2021. The Jupiter/Saturn conjunction will be in a square aspect to Uranus with the same signs (Taurus and Aquarius) involved. In 2000, both the Euro and Swiss Franc made their 16.5-year cycle troughs.

There are no 16.5-year cycles due in 2021. However, the presence of both the Jupiter/Saturn and Saturn/Uranus aspects in close proximity to one another suggests that a 5.5-year cycle crest in the Euro and Swiss Franc could happen in 2021, and a 5.5-year cycle low in the Dollar/Yen.

CONCLUSIONS:

Last year's Forecast 2020 Book advised investors to *"... look for opportunities to sell rallies in the U.S. Dollar so long as prices remain below 103.82, and to buy declines in the Euro that remain above 1.0339 and especially above 1.0670. It may even be better to buy the Swiss Franc during this decline to a secondary low due between October 2019 and June 2020."* All of that happened in March 2020 as the Euro and Swiss Franc bottomed and the Dollar topped out.

In 2021, we will look for a high and a pullback in the Euro and Swiss Franc. The next 26-month cycle trough in the Swiss Franc is due June–July 2021 +/- 5 months. The Euro is due for a 16.5-month cycle low, July–August 2021 +/- 3 months. However, these are only expected to be corrective declines, for the 5.5-year greater cycle in each is still pointed higher, indicating that in 2021, each currency will at some point likely exceed the highs of 2020. With the Euro, that means above 1.2011 and probably even 1.2550. In the Swiss Franc, that means above 1.1200, and possibly to the 1.1800 +/-.0200 level.

In the Dollar/Yen, we would not be surprised to see a modest rally back to 109.91 +/- 2.06, probably coinciding with the intermediate-term lows in the Euro and Swiss Franc just mentioned. But longer-term, the third and final 22.5-month cycle phase to the greater 5.5-year cycle trough is not due until September 2021–June 2022, with a good chance of testing or breaking below par (100.00).

The timing of these intermediate-term highs and lows in 2021 will depend on the phasing of the primary cycle in each currency. We will monitor that in our weekly and monthly reports throughout the year. In the meantime, we still like the idea of diversifying one's currency exposure against dollar-denominated assets. Our preferred currency to add to our portfolio continues to be the Swiss Franc.

THREE-STAR CRITICAL REVERSAL DATES FOR 2021 – CURRENCIES

The following is a list of three-star geocosmic critical reversal dates (CRDs) used in MMA's market timing calculations for the Dollar, Yen, Swiss Franc, and Euro. It may pertain to the British Pound too, although we have done no formal studies on that correlation as of yet. They are mostly valid when a market is also in the time band for a primary or half-primary cycle crest or trough. In addition to these dates, one is advised also to use the dates provided in the stock market section that do not match these dates for Currency reversals, for those CRDs apply to several other financial markets too. Allow a range of 3 trading days (sometimes as much as 6) to these dates for a reversal.

In addition to the three-star CRDs, there are also 2- and 1-star geocosmic CRD dates that do not show up here but are reported in the MMA daily, weekly, and monthly reports. These will more often correspond with major or trading cycle lows and highs, which more aggressive traders can use to time short-term trades.

Jan 15 –18, 2021
Feb 8
April 23 –26
June 23
July 9
Aug 6 –9
Sep 23
Dec 22

THE BRITISH POUND for 2021 by MMA Analyst Ulric Aspegrén

REVIEW

The exchange rate of British Pound against the U.S. Dollar is known as the Cable or the Sterling, with the ticker GBP. Last year's report underlined: *"As the UK Parliament has decided to hold a general election on December 12, 2019, the bearish scenario cannot yet be taken off the table. The "No Brexit" deal is therefore still at play, which could even threaten the October 7, 2016 assumed 16-year cycle low at 1.1450 (6)."* This was not our preferred scenario, but during the COVID 19 crisis, the prices collapsed dramatically to 1.1404 on March 20, 2020 (7), and thus, taking out the October 2016 low, by a meager 46 pips.

This March 2020 double bottom was established 18.8 years from the June 2001 previous 16-year cycle trough (3). Last year stated: *"In only one instance out of four has the 16-year cycle been active longer than 17 years and it was then operational for 19 years."* Consequently, it is conceivable that the greater cycle trough is now behind us, as we otherwise would currently be 19.4 years into the greater cycle that started on June 2001 and thus breaking that previous time cycle record. We will therefore assume that the greater 16-year cycle trough has occurred. If this is correct, we should be seeing a long-term bullish trend out of the gates of the March 20 low until the greater cycle crest is established, usually in the middle of the 16-year cycle.

CYCLES

The greater 16-year cycle splits into two 8-year cycles. The 8-year cycle divides into three 34-month (3-year) or/and two 4-year cycles. Since there is a complete cycle reset whenever a new greater cycle is in place, we cannot know at this time if the sub-cycles of the 8-year cycle will be composed of three 3-year cycles or with two 4-year cycles, or with both scenarios, in a combination pattern.

A bullish 3-year cycle crest would be expected in the time frame July 2021-August 2022, which should be followed by the 3-year cycle low, projected to occur sometime June 2022-August 2023. If the 4-year cycle is active, then the next bullish 4-year cycle crest is anticipated in the time range May 2023-March 2024, while the 4-year cycle bottom is expected to happen sometime June 2023-December 2024.

The 4-year cycle breaks into two 24-month intermediate-term cycles and/or three 16-month intermediate-term cycles. The 3-year cycle is most often composed of two 16-month cycles. The 16-month cycle is thus the only sub-cycle that can be operational for both the 3-year and the 4-year cycles. We will therefore assume at first hand that the 16-month cycle is the intermediate-term cycle that is in play at this time.

The bullish 16-month cycle crest should manifest in the time range January-July 2021, which would be tailed by the 16-month cycle bottom sometime March-November 2021. If the 24-month cycle is instead the active intermediate-term cycle, then a bullish 24-month cycle crest is due to unfold in the time frame November 2021-May 2022 and should be shadowed by the 24-month cycle low sometime November 2021-August 2022.

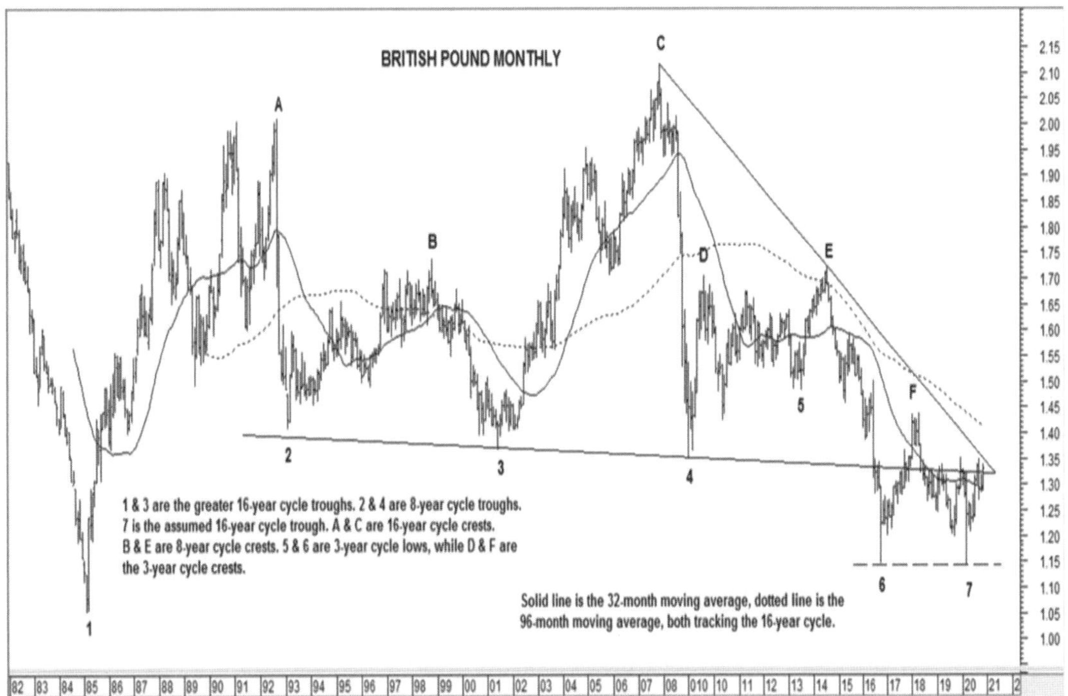

If we look long-term, then the 16-year cycle crest is projected to take place within the overall time span May 2023-March 2028. We can contract this time range, as in 60% of the cases studied, the Cable has reached its 16-year cycle summit between 6.4 and 8.0 years, generating a time frame of August 2026-March 2028. As the Sterling tends to peak out in the middle of its greater cycle, we can further reduce the time frame by overlapping the 16-year cycle crest with the next 8-year cycle crest. The bullish 8-year cycle crest is anticipated to take place sometime August 2026-September 2027. The narrowed down time target for the 16-year cycle crest generated by the overlapping the different projections is thus August 2026-September 2027.

As the 16-year cycle that ended on March 2020 was very much distorted, there is a caveat to the above 16-year cycle crest estimation. The long-term British Pound summit could instead manifest within a time frame estimated from the October 2016 trough. If we do a similar exercise as in the above paragraph from the October 2016 low, we obtain that the 16-year cycle crest could alternatively take place sometime March 2023-April 2024.

GEOCOSMICS

Last year's Forecast Book stated: *"The Brexit saga remains in a very unhinged state. Although, an EU deal looks feasible at this time, Saturn is approaching Pluto and will make an epic conjunction in Capricorn on January 12, 2020. This is a "no prisoners" type of energy, which could speak for a "Hard Brexit" and even a "No Brexit" deal. In any case, the divorce with EU will most likely be much tougher than expected, for everybody."* The UK did leave the EU on January 31, 2020. However, both parties still have to hammer out the terms of this new relationship during a transition phase, which ends on December 31, 2020. The process has been struggling and the deadline for extending the transition period has been passed.

Now, we know that the major concessions in a negotiation process usually take place at the very end, so it is still possible that an agreement can be ironed out. However, the "No Brexit" deal under the WTO terms is a possible scenario, which could push the Cable off the cliff to a triple bottom with the 1.1404 low of March 20, or even lower.

Next year, geocosmically, there is a Saturn square Uranus transit that starts on February 17, 2021 and ends on December 24, 2021. As this planetary pair has a 9-month orb, it is actually active June 2020-September 2022. With a 95.50% correlation, the Saturn-Uranus pair has the highest correspondence to the British Pound long-term cycle events, which is at minimum a 3-year cycle event. As shown in the Cycles segment, the long-term cycle event that could be fully operational during this Saturn-Uranus active period is the 3-year cycle crest. Our preferred outlook is thus that the 8-year cycle will divide, at least, into three 3-year cycles. Overlapping the timing for the 3-year cycle crest with the Saturn-Uranus active period does not narrow down the crest time target span. Consequently, our expectation is that we will get a 34-month cycle crest in the already stated time frame of July 2021-August 2022.

As our preferred view is that the 3-year cycle is active, it reinforces our expectation that the intermediate-term cycle in operation should be the 16-month cycle since the 34-month cycle usually splits in two. However, the Saturn-Uranus correlation to long-term cycle events is not 100%. So although the probability is low, we could instead get a 24-month intermediate-term cycle event that takes place during the Saturn-Uranus period. In this case, the timing for the 24-month cycle crest remains the same as estimated in the Cycles segment.

PRICE

Our assumption is that a 16-year cycle low was made at 1.1404. The prices are thus forecasted via the bullish historical data to rise 15.28%-34.47% to the first 16-month cycle crest, generating a price target span of 1.3146-1.5335. As of this writing in the end of November 2020, the prices have so far reached 1.3482 on September 1, representing an 18.22% increase. Although the prices are now within the 16-month cycle price target span, the expectation is that they will continue higher.

In fact, we are just at the very end of a long-term triangle pattern that started in 2007, shown in the British Pound monthly chart. This area is where the real battle between the bulls and the bears will take place and we are right in it. Our expectation is that the prices should climb sustainably above the upper descending line of the triangle formation that joins the points C and E, right now at 1.3485 and falling. If this turns out to be true, then a British Pound long-term rally should follow, as the 16-year cycle trough is most likely behind us. The actual confirmation that the 16-month and the 34-month cycles are in a bullish trend comes only when the April 2018 peak at 1.4376 is exceeded.

If the prices, on the other hand, are repressed back below the line that joins the points 3 and 4, right now at 1.3217 and falling, then the probability noticeably increases that the 16-year cycle low could still be in front of us.

Once the 16-month cycle crest is in place, the prices should decline to the first 16-month cycle low, expected historically at a descent of 4.42%-12.58%. When the low is established, the prices are anticipated to rise another 15.28%-34.47% to the 3-year cycle crest. If instead the 24-month cycle is active, then the prices should ascend 32.56%-60.11% to the 24-month cycle crest, generating a price target span of 1.5117-1.8259. Once the 24-month cycle crest has unfolded, the prices should decline 7.24%-20.02% to a 24-month cycle low.

Finally, to give a more long-term perspective, the Sterling is anticipated to rise 56.10%-90.31% to reach its 16-year cycle crest, producing a price target span for now of 1.7801-2.1703.

CONCLUSION

Last year's Forecast Book bias: *"The dance between the UK and the EU to make a deal seems to be never ending. Such an unstable situation could normally argue that the great 16-year cycle trough is still ahead. However, my bias is that the greater cycle low is in, as there is a 75% probability that the Cable's 16-year cycle low bottomed out time-wise on October 7, 2016 at 1.1450."* We got a very distorted new 16-year cycle trough candidate on March 20, 2020 at 1.1404, where the low was made after 18.8 years. Due to this extended time band, my bias is that the great 16-year cycle bottom is in with the March 20, 2020 low.

If this is correct, then we should be in a long-term bullish trend, where our first intermediate-term event is expected to be a 16-month cycle crest, forecasted to occur in the time frame January-July 2021, with a price target span of 1.3146-1.5335. There is a good probability that the April 2018 top at 1.4376 will be surpassed. The intermediate-term cycle crest should be followed by a 16-month cycle low, estimated to manifest sometime March-November 2021, at a decline of 4.42%-12.58%.

Meanwhile, a "No Brexit" deal under the WTO terms could precipitate the prices lower. Hence, we cannot exclude the threat of a double bottom to the March 20 low. Even a plunge below the 1.1404 low cannot yet be taken off the table, as the 16-year cycle could set new length records. This event would be the ultimate decline for the bulls, as it would provide a great opportunity to buy at basement prices.

T-NOTES AND INTEREST RATES IN THE U.S.A. IN 2021

By Gianni Di Poce

REVIEW

T-Notes ripped to new all-time highs in early-2020, as a deflationary wave swept over the world economy, largely stemming from the coronavirus lockdowns. This pulled interest rates down to historical lows, which sent bond prices higher, as investors sought the safety of Treasuries due to the economic uncertainty. Forecast 2020's conclusion section stated, "*The low-interest rate environment may continue into much of 2020, even into 2021. However, it appears the long-term cycle high in T-Notes and T-Bonds ended in 2012 and 2016. Sometime within 18 months of January 2020, there may be a secondary high and the possibility of going even higher. However, by mid-2021, long-term planetary cycles indicate a new long-term bearish trend in Treasuries could get underway.*" Indeed, this unfolded in March, as T-Note prices soared to record highs of 140/24.

The major question now is whether this March 2020 high was the final high in the multi-decade, secular bull market in T-Notes, or whether there will be one final blow-off top before the bull market ends. The geocosmics suggest March 2020 may have been the high, but we aren't quite out of the orb yet for another high to occur. Since March 2020, T-Notes have largely traded between 137-140. A resolution from this trading range would likely indicate the next direction for T-Notes. Another big question, of course, is how much firepower the Federal Reserve has left after responding to the coronavirus recession by cutting short-term rates to zero and launching QE-Infinity, which is the purchase of long-term bonds. Throughout the rest of this forecast, we will reference our comments from the previous year, which were written by Raymond Merriman.

THE 18-YEAR CYCLE

Our bias is that an 18-year cycle low occurred on October 8, 2018, at 117/13. Forecast 2020 stated, "*This is only the 2nd year of a new long-term cycle. Even if this cycle is bearish, it is not due to peak until at least years 2 –5, which means T-Notes are likely to test or surpass last year's high of 132/01. The question will then become whether or not T-Notes can make an all-time high. Currently, the all-time high is 135/29, recorded on June 1, 2012. Given that the Saturn/Pluto conjunction cycle will take place on January 12, 2020, and that cycle tends to coincide with long-term cycle lows or highs within 18 months, this new 18-year could peak sometime before the middle of 2021.*" 2021 starts year 3 for this 18-year cycle, which means if this long-term cycle is going to unfold in a bearish manner, there's a good chance that we've already seen the high. An alternative is that it's set to occur by mid-2021, at least according to the geocosmics.

However, we have to be cognizant that longer-term cycles come with stronger trends. T-Notes have been in a bull market since interest rates peaked in 1981, so they've been rallying for decades now. With respect to the possibility that this 18-year cycle could continue to rally for a few more years, Forecast 2020 stated, "*In the event that the new 18-year cycle is going to bullish, T-Notes would not likely top out before the 8th year (2026). In that case, the upside price target could be as high as 159/21 +/- 7/25. My bias is that it will top out somewhere between 133-138…*" T-Notes rallied as high as 140/24 in 2020, slightly above our price target. Prices would need to close back above 140/24 in 2021 to seriously entertain the possibility that prices could rally into 2026. For now, our bias is that the March 2020 high was the 18-year cycle crest. This is largely due to the Capricorn Stellium of 2020, whereby Jupiter, Saturn, and Pluto all conjoined in the sign of Capricorn. The orb for a reversal with these aspects spills into the first six months of 2021. If T-Note prices make a new high after June 2021, then we will have a more serious look at the possibility that the 18-year cycle may unfold in a bullish manner.

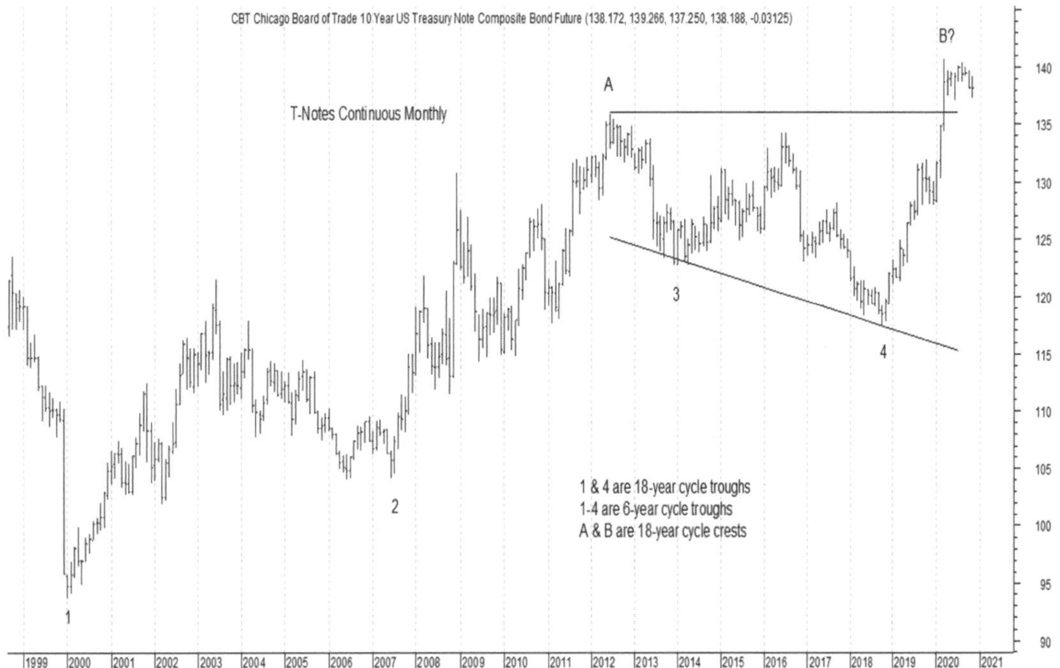

THE 6-YEAR CYCLE

The 18-year cycle breaks down into three 6-year cycles. The range for the 6-year cycle is 5-7 years. In many cases, the last 6-year cycle within the 18-year cycle distorts. This happened with the most recent 6-year cycle that bottomed in October 2018, as the 6-year cycle lasted slightly under five years from the prior low in April 2014. This means that T-Notes start the 3rd year of the first 6-year cycle in 2021. Forecast 2020 stated, "*The crest will likely occur in years 2-5, followed by a decline to the low, due in 2024 +/- 1 year. In most cases, even in bear markets, that decline will not take out the 117/13 low that started the cycle. If it does, it either means the new 18-year cycle has turned bearish, and interest rates will rise for several years, or October 2018 was not the end of the 18- and 6-year cycles. Those cycles might still be unfolding, but due by 2021.*" There is a fair chance that the 6-year cycle high occurred in March 2020 with the rally up to 140/24. If so, we could expect T-Note prices to decline into 2024 +/- 1 year. However, there is ample time remaining for new highs to be made in this 6-year cycle, and so as long as a new high isn't made beyond June 2021, this remains a viable scenario. Another scenario that isn't our preferred bias is that this 6-year cycle is an older one from the April 2014 low. In such a case, a 6-year bottom could occur in what would be its 7th year, no later than April 2021.

THE 3-YEAR CYCLE

The 6-year cycle breaks down into three 2-year cycles or two 3-year cycles. Forecast 2020 stated, "*It is too early yet to tell which of these patterns will unfold, but if the 6-year cycle is to be a classic 3-phase pattern, then a 2-year cycle low is due October 2020 +/- 4 months.*" A meaningful low occurred in June 2020, which in theory, could have been a 2-year cycle low, as it was in orb. However, the rally that followed has been fairly weak, so this is not our preferred bias. The orb for a 2-year cycle low continues until February 2021; otherwise, we could witness a 3-year cycle unfold, in which prices could decline into late-2021 or even early-2022 if it distorts to the long-end. As it stands, it appears that March 2020 was either a 2-year cycle crest or a 3-year cycle crest. Under a 3-year cycle scenario, there is enough time still for a new cycle high to be made, although this is not our preferred bias. If the March 2020 high was the 3-year cycle crest, though, then we could expect a corrective decline to 129-132, and perhaps even down to 126 +/- 0/16.

GEOCOSMICS

The Saturn-Uranus waning square is the major geocosmic on our radar for 2021. There are three passages of this aspect: February 17, 2021, June 14, 2021, and December 24, 2021. Within three weeks of each date, we could anticipate a low to form in either the 2-year or 3-year cycle lows. If T-Notes decline beyond February, then we would look for a 3-year cycle low to form in T-Notes within three weeks of June 14 or December 24. This square aspect will occur with Saturn in the sign of Aquarius and Uranus in the sign of Taurus. Both of these placements carry significance astrologically for bond markets. Saturn rules foundations and structure, and bonds are the foundation of the global monetary system. Taurus rules currencies, and with the Uranus/Aquarius energies present, too, we have to be cognizant of innovative or unexpected disruptions to the monetary system, which would likely impact bond markets significantly.

Forecast 2020 stated, "*The most important long-term geocosmic cycle on the horizon is the Saturn/Pluto conjunction of January 12, 2020. This 31-37 year planetary cycle has an orb of up to 18 months in its correlation with long-term market cycles. Its historical correspondence with U.S. interest rates was covered in detail in the earlier section of this book. The findings in that study demonstrated '... that a historic low, then high, happened at the last two conjunctions of Saturn and Pluto (August 1947 and November 1982, +/- 18 months). That is, within 18 months of the Saturn/ Pluto conjunction in August 1947, interest rates were at a historic low. Rates then began rising and continued rising until they reached a historic peak within 18 months of the next Saturn/Pluto conjunction in November 1982.' This pattern suggests that another historic low in interest rates will be made by*

2021, or a re-test of the lows that occurred in 2012-2016. Following that, rates would be on schedule to increase into the next Saturn/Pluto conjunction, due in 2053-2054… The renewed monetary easing on the part of the Fed throughout much of 2019 could result in a secondary low in rates within 18 months of 2020 when the new Saturn/Pluto cycle gets underway. But according to the Saturn/Pluto cycle, interest rates could reverse and begin a long period of increases into the first quarter phase of the new Saturn/Pluto cycle, which unfolds with their waxing square in 2028-2029."

Indeed, T-Note prices made an all-time high in March 2020, which may have been the crest to coincide with the Saturn/Pluto conjunction. There remains the potential for one final high to be made in 2021, as the 18-month orb of this aspect could last until June 2021. This would likely become a viable scenario if T-Note prices can close back above 140. Until they do, chances are, the 18-year and 6-year highs are likely complete. Forecast 2020 stated, "*…the Saturn/Pluto cycle suggests that this new 18-year cycle will be bearish. That is, T-Notes will top out 2020-2023, or 2-5 years into the new cycle that began October 8, 2018. Then rates will rise (T-Notes will fall) into 2024 +/- 1 year for its 6-year cycle bottom, or perhaps even into 2028-2029 for a 9-year half-cycle trough.*" These comments carry over into 2021.

Last year's forecast also pointed out the correlation between the 13-year Jupiter-Pluto cycle and its correspondence to reversals in interest rates. Forecast 2020 stated, "*This aspect will take place in a three-passage series between April 2020 and November 2020. Each of the last three instances of this aspect occurred in only a single passage, but in each case, it coincided with a long-term cycle low in T-Notes nearby. That is, Jupiter and Pluto conjoined one another on November 2, 1981, which was less than two months after the all-time low in T-Bonds in September 1981. The next instance of this conjunction occurred December 2, 1994, very close to the 6-year cycle low in T-Notes that happened in November 1994. The last time these two planets came together was on December 11, 2007, which is when the Great Recession officially began. That was also just 6 months after another 6-year cycle low in T-Notes. This planetary cycle has correlated more with lows than highs in T-Notes. However, we know that geocosmic signatures are more of a reversal indicator than a specific crest or trough indicator. And since it has correlated with longer-term cycles, and no longer-term cycle lows are due in 2020. Still, a longer-term 6- or 18-year cycle high could be due if the Saturn/Pluto cycle of higher interest rates is going to kick in. There is reason to think that T-Notes could complete an important crest this year.*" The March 2020 high fills the bill here, as it occurred one month before the first passage of Jupiter to Pluto.

Jupiter rules banks, and in 2021, the Great Benefic will transit Aquarius and square Uranus on January 17, 2021. Banks operate as the underwriters for bond markets, so we can see how this ties into the Treasury market too. Aquarius rules innovation, so the blockchain revolution taking place in finance and banking is closely monitored in 2021. Jupiter's square to Uranus can represent an overwhelming disruption to the banking system. Moreover, Jupiter and Saturn's conjunction that occurs in late-2020 will be within orb of squaring Uranus in Taurus, which itself is acting to disrupt currency and banking, presumably through the blockchain revolution.

The last time Saturn transited through Aquarius was February 1991-January 1994. During this time, T-Notes were already rallying off the 1987 lows, and the rally continued higher before forming a peak in September 1993. Prices then declined into a low in November 1994, and by that time, Saturn had already ingressed into Pisces. The last time Jupiter transited through Aquarius was January 2009 to January 2010, and the previous time was January 1997 to February 1998. T-Note prices generally rallied from January 1997 to February 1998, while they generally declined from January 2009 to January 2010. We also note that the United States will experience increasing influence from a Pluto return in 2021, as the nation's natal Pluto rests at 27 degrees Capricorn. The exact conjunction won't happen until early-2022, but the orb of influence for this aspect is basically in effect from February 2019-January 2025. A Pluto return could signify a problem with the country paying its debts, as was the case when the United States was first founded. Hyperinflation occurred not long after the American Revolution as the new nation debased its currency to pay off its war debts. Specifically, inflation rates peaked in 1778, and Pluto was in the first degree of Aquarius by that time.

Keep in mind, however, that Pluto is exalted in Capricorn. The U.S. Treasury is symbolically operating on borrowed (Pluto) time (Capricorn). While the United States did suffer from hyperinflation post-revolution, the Treasury was able to reign in its finances, and the economy stabilized after its war debts were restructured. Therefore, there may be some further economic pain that results from this Pluto return. Still, if the previous occurrence is any indicator, we could see the economy resurrect like the phoenix from the ashes post-2025. Worth noting is that the current national debt and federal deficits are at all-time highs, similar to what the Continental Congress's finances would have looked like back then before the hyperinflationary episode post-war.

CONCLUSION

An 18-year, 6-year, and 3-year or 2-year cycle crest may have occurred in T-Notes in March 2020 at 140/24. The length of the secular bull market in T-Notes that started in 1981, along with the geocosmics of 2020 and 2021, suggests this to be the case. The monthly chart above, however, does display a broadening wedge pattern, from which prices have already broken out to the upside. A measured move from this price pattern suggests that prices could rally as high as 152–155 and suggest that we have yet to see the 18-year, 6-year, or 3-year cycle highs yet. This isn't our preferred bias, but one we need to remain open to nonetheless for 2021. After all, we are talking about a +40-year bull market in bonds, and when it comes to trading, *the trend is your friend.* However, trends last until they don't, and this is where geocosmics provide us an advantage. Between the Saturn – Pluto conjunction, the Jupiter –Pluto conjunction, the U.S. Pluto return in 2021 –2023, and the Jupiter –Uranus and Saturn –Uranus squares in 2021, the stars suggest that this multi-decade bull market is closer to its end than to its beginning.

The biggest question that follows, naturally, is at what *price* the peak will form. Multiple indicators, including technicals, cycles, and geocosmics, suggest that March 2020 is a good candidate for this label.

In the likely event that the March 2020 high at 140/24 was the long-term cycle crest, we could anticipate T-Note prices to decline into the 125-132 range at the least in 2021. If this is the end of the multi-decade long bull market in bonds, then prices will likely decline further, but perhaps not until after 2021. Keep in mind that the Federal Reserve is all in right now through their QE-Infinity program, which is designed to keep long-term interest rates low. Worth noting, however, is that long-term interest rates actually rose after the very first round of QE in November 2008. In fact, they rose until April 2010, which is about 1.5 years. We could see a similar scenario unfold this time around, whereby we decline into a 2-year or 3-year cycle low in 2021, only to see further highs made with respect to the 6-year or 18-year cycles. In summary, the market direction for T-Notes is in a battle between the free market forces of cycle and the monetary policy of the Federal Reserve. The year 2021 may be the year we find out which side has more firepower.

THREE-STAR CRITICAL REVERSAL DATES FOR 2021 – T-NOTES

The following is a list of three-star geocosmic critical reversal dates (CRDs) used in MMA's market timing calculations. They are mostly valid when a market is also in the time band for a primary or half-primary cycle crest or trough. In addition to these dates, one is advised to also use the dates provided in the stock market section that do not match these dates for T-Note reversals, for those CRDs apply to several other financial markets too. Allow a range of 3 trading days (sometime as much as 6) to these dates for a reversal.

In addition to the three-star CRDs, there are also 2- and 1-star geocosmic CRD dates that do not show up here, but are reported in the MMA daily, weekly, and monthly reports. These will more often correspond with major or trading cycle lows and highs which more aggressive traders can use to time short-term trades.

Dec 28, 2020
Jan 15-18, 2021
Jan 27
Feb 8
Feb 15
Mar 19-22
April 23-26
April 30-May 3
June 22-23
July 6-7
Aug 4-5
Aug 17
Sep 20
Nov 5-8
Dec 22

CRUDE OIL, by Gianni Di Poce, MMA Analyst

REVIEW

Crude Oil made history in 2020. After forming its yearly high on January 8 at 65.65, it commenced a historic decline, as it suffered from a hyper deflationary episode in April, which saw prices in this commodity drop as low as $37 per barrel. In this case, the hyperdeflation was derived from a perfect storm. There has been a global supply glut in Crude Oil for years. This bearish dynamic on the supply-side of the price equation was absolutely devastated by the negative demand-shock that stemmed from the coronavirus lockdowns in March–April. The end result was basically that oil producers had to pay someone to take their oil. To our knowledge, the was an unprecedented downside move, and the first time any commodity market fell below the zero bound.

If 2020 taught us anything, it's that rules and perceptions can change quickly. However, we know that bulls tend to capitulate near the lows of a cycle, which lends credence to the notion that the April 21 low in Crude Oil was likely a 36-year, 18-year, 9-year, and 3-year cycle trough. Granted, there was a bit of distortion with some of these cycles that occurred to accompany this historic low, but this happens, especially when multiple long-term cycles come due. As of this writing in mid-November, Crude Oil is trading around the $41.80 mark, and when factoring in the decline into negative price territory, means that an ~$80 rally has occurred, which is very impressive and bullish—the type of behavior witnessed in the early stages of new cycles.

Throughout the rest of this forecast, we will reference our comments from the previous year, written by Nitin Bhandari.

CYCLES

The longest cycle observed in Crude Oil is likely a 36-year cycle. The only problem is that there haven't been enough occurrences to quantify this number to a high degree of statistical confidence. Nonetheless, it seems to fit well within our analysis. A 36-year cycle low formed in April 1986. Our work suggests that the April 2020 low that saw Crude Oil prices decline into negative territory was likely a 36-year cycle low, and it happened to occur 34 years later to the same month. Worth noting is that the 36-year cycle carries a 6-year orb, so unless prices go negative again, we will continue with this label as such.

Next is the 18-year cycle, which also likely exhibited a bottom on April 21. This cycle carries an orb of 3-years, and the previous low occurred in November 2001. This means the cycle lasted 17 years and five months, which is very timely considering its length. The

18-year cycle usually breaks down into two 9-year cycles. April 21 also marked the 9-year cycle low in Crude Oil. However, there was a serious case of cyclical distortion in this cycle from the previous February 2009 low. The 9-year would've lasted 11 years and two months under this label, which is just beyond the 2-year orb that this cycle normally exhibits. The other possibility is that February 2016 was a 9-year cycle low from the February 2009 low, and even though this would only be seven years in length, it still falls within the 2-year cycle orb. If the 9-year bottom happened in April 2020, Crude Oil would be much more bullish than if it occurred in February 2016. The reason behind this is because once cycles close below their starting point, we start to assume a bearish bias until the cycle is complete. In bullish cycles, we expect that the cycle's lowest price is the beginning of the cycle. Therefore, the 9-year cycle could only be construed as bullish if the bottom occurred in April 2020.

A similar situation to the 9-year cycle exists with the intermediate 3-year cycle, or to be more specific, a 32-month cycle with a 5-month orb. A 3-year cycle low occurred in February 2016 at 26.05. A significant low in Crude Oil then formed in December 2018 at 42.36, or 34 months later, which would be within the normal orb of this cycle. Nevertheless, if this label is applied, then it means that the 3-year cycle has turned bearish since the cycle's starting point was exceeded to the downside afterwards, and January 2021 would start the 25th month. This is not our bias, though. It has been observed on numerous occasions that shorter cycles can and do distort when longer-term cycles mature. If we consider that long-term 36-year, 18-year, and 9-year cycles all bottomed in April 2020, it would be plausible to suggest that an intermediate cycle exhibited a case of distortion and bottomed beyond its normal orb. Therefore, our work indicates that April 2020 was a 3-year cycle bottom too, which would be 50 months from the previous low of February 2016.

Last year's forecast stated, "*The 3-year cycle exhibits two 17-month cycle phases. The first 17-month cycle trough is due by May 2020 +/- 3 months. The current 17-month cycle is exhibiting a left-translation pattern, where the high was made in the 4th month in April 2018, and it has been sideways since then. However, the geocosmic studies are suggesting that we may see a sharp rally to a new 17-month cycle high before falling for the 17-month cycle trough. Crude Oil needs to cross above 66.90 to make this 3-year and the 17-month cycle bullish.*" Crude Oil rallied to a high of 65.65 in January 2020, which became the 17-month cycle crest. It then experienced its hyper-deflationary decline, which took prices into negative territory and formed a low in April 2020, within the expected orb for a low to occur.

In summary, Crude Oil likely formed multiple long-term and intermediate-term cycle lows in April 2020. This means that January 2020 would start the 8th month in the 36-year, 18-year, 9-year, 3-year, and 17-month cycles, all of which would still be considered in their early, bullish phases. We could therefore expect the next 36-year cycle low to occur in 2056 +/- 6 years, the next 18-year cycle low to occur in 2038 +/- 3 years, the next 9-year cycle low to occur in 2029 +/- 2 years, the next 3-year cycle low to occur in February 2023 +/- 5 months, and the 17-month cycle in September 2021 +/- 3 months.

GEOCOSMICS

The year 2020 was host to Neptune in Pisces and Jupiter in Capricorn for most of the year. Jupiter and Neptune co-rule Crude Oil, which means we look for aspects and placements with these planets to forecast this market's behavior. Forecast 2020 stated, "*...both rulers of Crude Oil, Jupiter, and Neptune, will be in a sextile aspect in a three-passage series, starting from February 2020 and lasting through October 20202. In 2020, Crude Oil is due for the 17-month cycle crest and trough. The historical study shows that within 3 weeks of this aspect, an important high or low is formed. Another important aspect pertaining to Crude Oil is Jupiter conjunct Pluto. This aspect also will be in effect in a three-passage series, starting from April 2020 and lasting through November 2020. Both these aspects overlap with the time zone for the 17-month cycle trough due by May 2020 +/- 3 months.*" Indeed, an important high occurred during the Jupiter–Neptune sextile, and it was the 17-month crest. The Jupiter/Pluto conjunction also appears to have coincided with the April 2020 low.

From a planetary placement standpoint, we can see how Jupiter in Capricorn during most of 2020 would be construed as bearish for Crude Oil. Capricorn's restrictive, limited nature served to curb demand for the commodity. In contrast, Neptune's placement in Pisces may have served to further the delusion that, "Everything is going to be fine, just keep pumping oil." Looking forward to 2021, we note that Jupiter will spend basically the entire year in the sign of Aquarius (ingress occurs December 19, 2020). Neptune, on the other hand, remains in Pisces until January 2026. Jupiter in Aquarius is an interesting placement, however. The last time Jupiter was in Aquarius was from January 2009 to January 2010, during which prices rallied over 160% from their low at 33.55 in February 2009 to a high of 83.95 in January 2010. The previous occurrence was from January 1997 to February 1998. This period saw prices collapse from 26.74 in January 1997 to a low of 15.20 by February 1998. Note that prices continued their decline in this case into December

1998, when Crude Oil formed at low at 10.65. This suggests that Jupiter's transit through Aquarius can be volatile in nature, or in other words, susceptible to wide price swings. This plays into the theme of Aquarius, ruled by Uranus, and the unpredictable, innovative nature associated with these archetypes. With respect to retrograde motions, we note that Jupiter will be retrograde from June 20, 2021 to October 18, 2021. This change in direction for Jupiter occurs in early Pisces. Neptune begins its retrograde motion on June 25, 2021, which will last until December 1, 2021. Interesting how Crude Oil's co-ruling planets go retrograde within a week of each other in 2021, and perhaps most importantly, they'll both be in Pisces at the time, a ruling sign of Crude Oil.

The significant aspect for Jupiter occurs right before 2020 begins. This is the synodic cycle known as the "Great Chronocrator," which occurs when Jupiter and Saturn meet in conjunction. This particular instance is the first time it will occur in an air sign (Aquarius) in hundreds of years. Previously, these conjunctions were taking place in earth signs. In terms of aspects to each other, Jupiter and Neptune will form their semi-sextile aspect at the beginning of Aries season, or March 21. However, our main focus for 2021 concerns the transit of Jupiter through the sign of Aquarius, while Saturn presides in the same sign too. The Jupiter/Saturn conjunction could cause supply restrictions or disruptions, which would serve to limit supply. Less supply usually means higher prices. We could also see major innovations in energy, perhaps pertaining to infrastructure (Saturn), due to some sort of unexpected supply shock (Aquarius).

CONCLUSIONS

Crude Oil is likely in the early stages of long-term cycles, including the 36-year, 18-year, 9-year cycles. It appears to be in the earlier stage of intermediate-term cycles, too, including the 3-year and 17-month cycles. Given the likely bottom of all aforementioned cycles in April 2020, January 2021 would mark the 9th month in all.

Of these cycles, the only one in which we anticipate a trough to occur in 2021 is the 17-month cycle, which would be due September 2021 +/- 3 months. If this 17-month cycle were bullish, we would anticipate prices to rally above 43.80 at some point starting in January 2021 or beyond (***note**** *- as we go to print in late November, Crude Oil has now traded above here*). This would create a case of "bullish right translation," which is when a market spends more time going up than down. Ideally, we see Crude Oil rallying into the summer solstice, around June 21, to form its 17-month cycle crest. With Jupiter and Neptune both going retrograde in Pisces within a week of each other, we like the idea of a 17-month crest occurring in June 2021 +/- 1 month.

The target for this 17-month cycle crest largely depends on whether Crude Oil can effectively clear current resistance at 42.50–43.00. If it manages to do so, we could see prices rip as high as 70.00 +/- 5.00. This would represent a rally as great as 60–85% higher from the current price level, which is around 40.00 as of this writing in early November 2020. Another significant level of resistance in the 50.00–53.00 area that will need to be cleared before a rally up to 70.00 +/- 5.00 becomes plausible. But if instead, we see prices start to close below 30.00–32.00, we could see prices continue to trade at depressed levels throughout 2021, perhaps even as low as 16.00–17.00 again. Any closure below 16.00–17.00 would likely indicate that the global economy is in serious trouble and at risk of falling into a deflationary depression. Fortunately, however, this is not our bias, which remains bullish in light of the high probability that multiple long-term cycles bottomed in April 2020.

THREE-STAR CRITICAL REVERSAL DATES FOR 2021 – CRUDE OIL

The following a list of three-star geocosmic critical reversal dates (CRDs) used in MMA's market timing calculations. They are mostly valid when a market is also in the time band for a primary or half-primary cycle crest or trough. One should also refer to all the dates given as CRDs in the stock market section, for those dates can affect many markets in addition to stocks, including Crude Oil Allow a range of 3 trading days (sometimes as much as 6) to these dates for a reversal.

In addition to the three-star CRDs, there are also 2- and 1-star geocosmic CRD dates that do not show up here but are reported in the MMA daily, weekly, and monthly reports. These will more often correspond with major or trading cycle lows and highs, which more aggressive traders can use to time short-term trades.

Dec 28, 2020
Jan 15–18, 2021
Jan 26
Mar 12-15
Apr 13
May 27-28
June 18
July 22
Aug 20-23
Sep 8
Oct 15-18
Dec 3-6

GEOCOSMICS AND WEATHER

By Mark Shtayerman & Izabella Suleymanova, San Diego, CA, MMA Analysts

From prehistoric times our ancestors have studied and observed the influence of the celestial bodies on the weather. The fundamental laws of weather prediction were outlined in the *Tetrabiblos* written by Claudius Ptolemy, approximately 19 centuries ago. This text described celestial effects on seasonal temperatures, droughts, cold snaps, heat waves, winds and hurricanes, harvest quantity, and even epidemics. Today we also have other astrologers who have added to the topic of weather predicting. Still, we will utilize a combination of methodologies developed in C.C. Zain's *Weather Predicting* and George J. McCormack's *Text-Book of Long-Range Weather Forecasting.*

The weather is governed by the atmospheric states of temperature, precipitation, and air mass movement, meaning how hot, wet, and windy the atmosphere is. In astrology, the Sun is the chief ruler of temperature and the most important weather assessment based on each season. That is, each season can be evaluated through the temperature chart or a chart that is cast as the Sun enters into the Cardinal sign or the exact time of the solstices and equinoxes. In turn, the moisture chart indicates the general trend of rainfall during the following month and is ruled by the Moon. Finally, the air movement chart indicates the general trend of air movement during the period Mercury is in the sign entered.

When examining any temperature chart, it is important to notice the fourth house. In the Winter Solstice chart (December 21, 2020, Washington D.C., 5:03 am EST), the cusp of the fourth house is in Pisces, and the fourth house has two planets: Neptune and the Moon. Pisces is a cool sign, and in the seasonal or temperature charts, Pisces produces temperatures a bit lower than the norm but not an extreme cold. Neptune can generate "freak" weather occurrences, with sudden changes, some southerly winds, and low barometer events such as storms, fog, haze, and general humidity, so we expect winter to be damp and foggy. The Moon pertains to cooler than normal weather, and like Neptune, it is a wet planet. Therefore, don't expect excessive cold that will injure plant life. However, those southerly winds and sudden temperature changes could cause the trees to go into bloom prematurely, only to be inundated with torrential rains that can damage those blooms and reduce harvest.

The next important element for weather prediction is the sign of the Ascendant. In the above-mentioned chart, the cusp of the first house (Ascendant) is located in Sagittarius. Its influence over temperature is decidedly warm, and we can expect bright, clear, warm days. In the first house, we also have Venus quincunx Uranus in the chart, bringing clear weather conditions. The influence of Uranus is consistently cold temperatures and a tendency toward temperature drops. The effects of Uranus will get reduced as Uranus is in Taurus because Taurus has stabilizing effects as the sign is fixed.

During the winter solstice, Mercury, a planet of wind, is in exact conjunction with the Sun in Capricorn. Capricorn is the sign of storms and extreme cold. Mercury in Capricorn increases wind speed and often brings blizzards. Also, Mercury will go retrograde on January 30, 2021, which could result in strong winds, blizzards, or sleet conditions. The Sun and Mercury will trine Uranus and may bring strong cold snaps with strong north-west winds, gusts, and heavy frost.

Saturn will ingress into Aquarius on December 17, 2020, and Jupiter will ingress into Aquarius on December 20, 2020. That is, on the day of the Winter Solstice, they will be exactly in conjunction at 0 degrees of Aquarius. This conjunction occurs once every twenty years, and this time around, we will only have a single passage. They will be in their orb of conjunction until March 2021. Aquarius is the second coldest sign, and thus we can expect dry, crisp, cold weather. As Jupiter and Saturn are slow-moving planets, their effects will be noticed at a later date and will affect the weather and the economics of the nation. Additionally, this conjunction will cause higher than expected cases of influenza, common cold (coronavirus is one of the causes of the common cold), and pneumonia. This will be due to prolonged periods of dampness that wear down the body's resistance. Expect the seasonal flu and cold to start from the east and migrate west and move from lowlands to highlands. Lastly, this poor weather will affect the growth of fruits and vegetables; thus, we can expect a reduced harvest.

On January 17, Jupiter will square Uranus causing erratic extremes in atmospheric conditions and increasing geomagnetic storms. We will see the Aurora Borealis in parts of the country where it very rarely appears. Increased geomagnetic storms are due to active Uranus, especially January 14 –26, 2021, with various aspects: square with Jupiter on January 17, 2021; Mars conjunct Uranus on January 20, 2021; and Mars square Jupiter January 23, 2021. Uranus will continue affecting winds throughout 2021, with a triple passage square with Saturn on February 17, 2021; June 14, 2021; and December 23, 2021. These strong winds will not be favorable to aviation or harvests, especially wheat.

The vernal equinox will occur on March 20, 2021, at 4:38 am in Washington D.C. The cusp of the fourth house is the sign of Gemini, ruled by Mercury. In the fourth house, we have Mars conjunct with the Moon. Gemini is a cold sign and is considered to favor rapid temperature changes. Mars is considered a hot planet that brings high temperatures, but Mars is making a square to Mercury and trine to Saturn, which will cause it to bring heavy clouds and strong winds, but with slightly higher than average temperatures. Considering that the trine is a harmonious aspect, Mars and Saturn have incompatible qualities: Mars is hot, and Saturn is cold. That combination will bring rapidly changing temperatures. The Moon brings in moisture and some precipitation. Hence we do have conflicting energies that could result in variable weather and possibly destructive storms.

On the cusp of the first house is Aquarius, which is ruled by Uranus, located in Taurus. Uranus symbolizes cold and is the antithesis of the Sun, the dynamic principle of heat. Uranus induces the highest barometric pressure and rapidly declining temperatures and produces strong winds through air currents descending from the higher altitude. Taurus is a fixed sign and provides a stabilizing influence through moderating temperatures and calm winds. However, Uranus is known for unpredictability, so sudden and extreme drops in temperature are possible. In spring, Uranus can bring chilly drizzles and frost at night.

Additionally, Uranus has a parallel aspect with Ascendant, which brings overcast, cold, and blustery weather. As we have mentioned earlier, Aquarius is the coldest sign after Capricorn, meaning we can expect temperatures to drop, with typical February weather, which is dry, crisp, and cold, lasting well into spring. Also, in the first house, we have Mercury, Neptune, Venus, and the Sun. Venus–Sun conjunctions can increase the temperature. Neptune is known for being capricious; thus, don't expect the weather to stay the same. By itself, weather can bring fog and dreary conditions. Yet, when it has a discordant aspect like a sesquiquadrate with Mars, both planets can bring disasters such as storms, torrential rains, and mudslides, particularly around these dates: April 14, 2021; June 24, 2021; November 7, 2021.

Lastly, we will have a total Lunar eclipse or Blood Moon on May 26, 2021, and then an Annular Solar eclipse on June 10, 2021. The earlier event will be seen over most nations in the Far East, such as China, India, Japan, and Australia. It will also be seen over North and South America in the United States, Canada, Mexico, Chile, and Argentina. The later event will have its totality seen by Canada and Russia, but a partial eclipse will be seen in the United States and throughout Europe. From ancient times, eclipses have been associated with events that would harm all harvests and possibly lead to famine in some parts of the world, especially in the region where the event was seen.

The summer solstice will occur on June 20, 2021, at 10:32 pm(EDT) for Washington, D.C. This year both the spring equinox and summer solstice have the same signs at the cusps of the important points: in both cases, Gemini resides in the cusp of the fourth house and Aquarius in the cusp of the first house. Thus, a strong wind situation will continue into summer as well, as Gemini rules over winds. Mercury is in conjunction with the cusp of the fourth house and is in its own sign, which adds to its power. Also, every time Mercury changes signs or changes station (from direct to retrograde and back), the wind direction also changes. Mercury will go retrograde in Gemini from May 29, 2021, to June 22, 2021. Then on July 12, 2021, Mercury will ingress into Cancer, and the winds will die down a bit. After August 12, 2021, Mercury will ingress into Virgo, and the winds will pick up; it will be breezy with variable winds, and the temperature will be lower than usual.

An ascending sign is Aquarius, and, as we discussed earlier, it is characterized by cold, dry weather. During summer, this would indicate a cold spell. Also, we have Jupiter in the first house, whose characteristics make the weather warm to hot, but it is in Pisces from May 14, 2021, and we thus expect the weather to be a bit warmer and not too harsh. From ancient times Jupiter in Pisces, as well as in Aquarius and Cancer, can bring plentiful rains. The two co-rulers of Pisces (Neptune and Jupiter) are in the first house and will bring gentle, mild, and calm weather. Toward the end of July, Jupiter will go retrograde and will ingress back into Aquarius, and the weather will cool again.

The fall equinox will occur on September 22, 2021, at 2:22 pm (EDT) in Washington, D.C. The cusp of the fourth house is in Taurus and is in conjunction with a violent Uranus. Venus, which rules over Taurus, is in opposition to Uranus, meaning that all attempts to soften the violent tendencies of Uranus will not be successful. This opposition is also making a square to a stormy Saturn, a planet of loss and disappointment. Saturn is in the cold sign of Aquarius and in the first house. War-loving Mars is in conjunction with the Sun, both making a trine to Saturn. This conjunction pair will try to warm up the atmosphere as both are hot planets, but they will not be as successful as they are located in the cool sign of Libra and making an aspect to the very cold Saturn. Thus, expect below normal temperatures, cloudy days, and frosty nights. Ascendant is Capricorn, a sign of storms and destructive floods. Pluto is in the first house in a square aspect with Mercury. Pluto is known for being a violent planet and is known to bring extreme conditions. We expect windstorms, tornadoes, hurricanes, blizzards, earthquakes, tsunamis, and other uncommonly destructive weather conditions, as the chart is very discordant and has heavy afflictions. We are expecting destruction of property and of harvests.

We will get another round of events with a Lunar eclipse on November 19, 2021, and then a total Solar eclipse on December 4, 2021. During the Lunar eclipse, Mars, Saturn, and Uranus will form a T-square, combining three destructive signs of Scorpio, Aquarius, and Taurus. During this period, expect destruction of grain and fruit harvests. Also, there may deaths of farm animals from a disease like bovine flu or some other illness. The Lunar eclipse is observed in Australia, Mexico, Canada, Russia, and the United States, so the damage to harvests in those locations will be more pronounced. However, the Solar eclipse is not seen in the United States, so farm animal deaths may be minimal. The partial eclipse will be seen over Antarctica, South Africa, and parts of Australia.

GRAIN MARKETS FOR 2021

In this section of the Forecast 2021 Book, we analyze the outlook for Wheat, Corn, and Soybeans.

WHEAT By Mark Shtayerman & Izabella Suleymanova, San Diego, CA, MMA Analysts

REVIEW

Wheat continued its 2019 rally until a primary top on January 22, 2020, at 592.25. In Forecast 2020, we pointed out that January 12, +/- one week, to expect poor weather and thus rally in prices with Saturn in conjunction with Pluto and a Lunar Eclipse. After that, Wheat declined to a primary bottom at 491.75 on March 16, 2020. This was a 17% decline in under two months. Wheat then rallied to a 587.0 high on March 27, 2020, for the primary cycle top; this was a nearly 20 percent rally in just over a week. This volatility was indicative of an active Uranus. Additionally, Jupiter was in conjunction with Pluto on April 4, 2020, which strongly correlates to reversals. Wheat then had a long decline until June 26, 2020, with a 54-week low of 468.25. This was a 20% decline over three months and coincided with the second passage of Jupiter conjunct Pluto on June 29, 2020. Wheat then went on a tear to 638.25 on October 20, 2020. This was a 36 percent rally in just four months. As of this document's writing, the primary cycle has not been completed and is expected to conclude by the end of the year or by the end of January 2021 at the latest.

CYCLES

Wheat has a long-term 18-year cycle that ranges between 13 and 20 years. Based on cycles analysis, the current 18-year cycle started at the low of 359.5 on August 31, 2016. The last cycle, from a December 1999 low of 222.0 and a crest of 1349.5 in February 2008, was completed in 2016 and lasted almost 17 years, within the expected range. This places the year 2021 in the fifth year of the 18-year cycle, and we have had higher highs and higher lows. With the October 20, 2020 high of 638.25, Wheat has rallied to highs that have not been seen since December 2014. We expect an 18-year high to unfold over the next decade, quite possibly to form a new all-time high as the world production of Wheat peaks due to climatic and economic reasons.

The longer-term 18-year cycle divides into two 9-year half cycles. The year 2021 will start the fifth year of the first 9-year cycle from the August 31, 2016 low of 359.5. A 9-year cycle crest is due over the next few years and then a decline to a 9-year cycle bottom between 2023 at the earliest and 2030 at the latest, with a nominal time frame of 2025. To support the idea of a 9-year cycle crest due over the next few years, we also have the solar minimum, which coincides with low Sun activity, and colder than average temperatures, resulting in lower than expected harvests. In addition, Wheat production competes with industry for water use and will thus lose out. Therefore, we expect a Wheat rally above the July 2012 high of 947.25 and even above the all-time high of 1334 of February 2008.

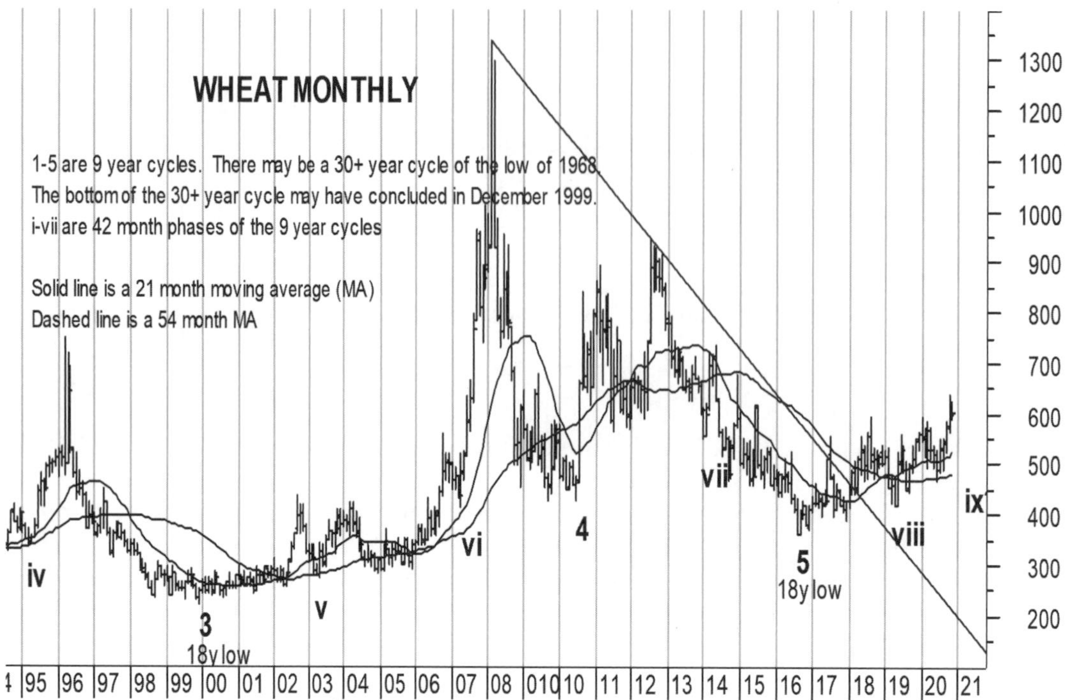

The 9-year cycle subdivides into two or three 42-month cycles, with an orb of 10 months. The best fit is that the first 42-month cycle started from the August 31, 2016, low of 359.50. The first 42-month cycle may have concluded with the 416.25 low on April 30, 2019. The second 42-month cycle within the 9-year cycle is ongoing, and December 2020 will start the 20th month. This implies that the 42-month cycle low will not come until the very end of 2021 at the earliest and quite possibly in the middle of 2022. If this is the case, then the possibility of the rally above the July 2012 high of 947.25 and even above the all-time high of 1334 of February 2008 is there.

An alternative outlook is that the April 30, 2019, low was not the 42-month low, but that would imply that the 42-month cycle low is to extend, with December 2020 being the 52nd month. This would imply that the strongest decline is yet to come, and that Wheat can decline to 499+/-32.75 over the next month. This would make a 22 percent decline in a very short period of time. After that, we will have three years to rally in Wheat.

The 42-month cycle is further subdivided into three or four 54-week cycles with an orb of 17 weeks. The week of December 7, 2020 will start the 23rd week of the second 54-week intermediate cycle from the 468.25 low of June 26, 2019. The orb is 17 weeks, which places a possibility of the 54-week cycle low to occur as early as March 2021 and as late as the end of October 2021. Ideally, the low will occur during the summer months of the harvest. The price expectation is quite wild as Uranus plays quite a prominent role in this cycle, meaning the crests and troughs can be exaggerated. To gauge the market, remember that Corn tends to be a leading indicator for all-grain markets, including Wheat. Therefore, crests and troughs in Corn are repeated in other markets but with a delay by several days or weeks, and even months for longer-term cycles. This provides us an intermarket divergence signal from which the reversal can occur. For more detailed analysis, we cover Wheat market in our International Cycles Report.

CONCLUSIONS

We stated in Forecast 2020: *"Now we are awaiting the 54-week intermediate and 42-month cycle low, ideally January to March 2020, at a price point of double bottom to either the September 3, 2019 low of 443.5+/-6.75 or April 30, 2019 low at 416.25+/-6.25. Price point for the Fibonacci retracement is 476.25+/-27.50…".* The 54-week low of June 26, 2020, was at 468.25. After that, we anticipated the rally: *"After that expect a rally above 559.0 and quite possibly to 636.50 to 1007.75 based on the historical appreciation for the intermediate cycle crests."* We got to 638.25 on October 20, 2020, so far. The price objective for the top of the 42-month cycle is 649+/-27.50 at the very minimum, and we are already there. The next price point is 702.50+/-33.75 based on irregular wave progression. After that, it is 793.46+/-44.50 as a Fibonacci progression, and as high as the 947+/-14.25 as a double top to the July 2012 high.

CORN, by Gianni Di Poce, MMA Analyst

REVIEW

The second half of 2020 was much more beneficial to corn prices than the first. Prices dropped to their lowest level since September 2009 back in April 2020. They reached 309 during a deflationary wave that gripped the global economy together with the coronavirus pandemic. However, this appears to have been the low for multiple long-term cycles, as the snapback rally that came in the following months saw prices rise by over 100, to about 420 as of this writing in mid-November.

There appeared to be a resolution to the trade wars between the United States and China early in 2020. This was supposed to have created a great demand for U.S. agricultural goods overseas, but then the coronavirus pandemic struck. What followed was a collapse in supply chains due to the lockdowns, which resulted in farmers having difficulty bringing products to market. Moreover, a devastating derecho storm struck the corn belt in the U.S. in August. It resulted in over 14 million acres worth of corn and soybean crops being wiped out virtually overnight. This, too, caused a supply shock, which explains the rally off the April lows. Corn prices have been mostly range-bound since mid-2014, trading between 315 and 425. A break above or below this range would signify the next direction of this market. The odds are skewing towards a break above 425, especially as Uranus continues its transit through the agricultural sign of Taurus. Throughout the rest of this forecast, we will reference our comments from the previous year, written by Raymond Merriman.

THE 18-YEAR CYCLE

The April 2020 low at 309 was likely an 18-year cycle trough. The previous 18-year cycle low occurred in August 2000 at 175, which was the lowest price in the last 20 years. The 18-year cycle has a range of 15–21 years, so the April 2020 low fits the bill perfectly. The 18-year cycle low before August 2020 occurred in 1987, which turned out to be a distorted long-term cycle to the short-side (contracted cycle). This was addressed in Forecast 2020, which stated, *"A long-term cycle in corn likely unfolded in August 2000 at*

175, which was its lowest price since 1987, and a low that has not been seen since then. It was tested again in November 2005 when prices dropped back to 186, which could be considered a double bottom and a possible start to an 18-year cycle as measured from the low of 1987. However, until proven otherwise, we will consider the 2005 low as a 6-year cycle phase within a classic three-phase pattern of the 18-year cycle in corn that began in August 2000." The 18-year cycle low from August 2000 was due to bottom in 2018, +/- 3 years, making the April 2020 low at 309 an excellent fit.

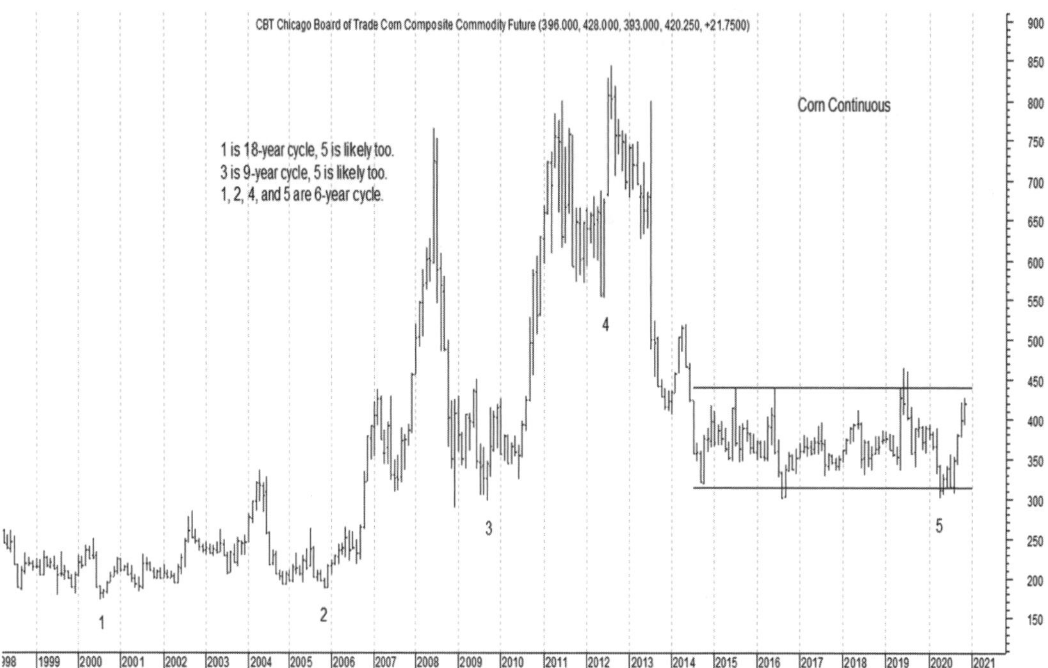

The monthly chart displays a rectangle pattern in which corn prices have traded within a range roughly between 315 and 425 for approximately six years. A monthly close above the upper horizontal trendline, or 425, would be very bullish and all but confirm the April 2020 low at 309 as an 18-year cycle low. Forecast 2020 stated, "*To confirm the bullish labeling for the 18-year cycle, corn needs to start climbing back above 390 before falling under 335. If it does decline below 335, then corn prices could test 300 for an older 18-year cycle that is still due by 2021.*" Prices weren't able to climb back above 390 in early-2020, so we saw that decline into a long-term cycle low. Corn prices fell as low as 309 and took out the low of August 2016 at 314-3/4, which was a previous candidate for an 18-year cycle low. The subsequent rally that followed off the April 2020 low appears promising as long as prices can close back above 425 on a monthly level. If so, we could see prices rip higher throughout 2021, as corn would be in a new, confirmed 18-year cycle.

THE 9-YEAR CYCLE

The April 2020 low at 309 was also very likely a 9-year cycle low in corn. Forecast 2020 stated, "*If the starting point of the current 18-year cycle was August 2000, then a 9-*

year half-cycle trough occurred in September 2009, and the next one would be due September 2018, +/- 18 months. This cycle still allows for a decline below 335 by March 2020." Prices fell below 335 just one month beyond the allowable orb for a 9-year cycle low, which is still fairly accurate.

This means that corn is likely also in a new 9-year cycle as well. This would be confirmed with a close above the upper horizontal trendline of the rectangle pattern, or 425, on the monthly chart above. Markets tend to rally the most when they are in the early-stages of new cycles. Corn is no exception to this rule. Therefore, combined with the 18-year cycle, the 9-year cycle suggests that 2021 could be a very positive year for corn prices.

THE 6-YEAR CYCLE

The 6-year cycle carries a range of 5–7 years. A total of three 6-year cycles also tends to unfold within the longer-term 18-year cycle. The previous two 6-year cycles lasted five years (August 2000–November 2005) and seven years (November 2005–June 2012). This meant that 2020 started the 8th year from the June 2012 low. Forecast 2020 stated, "*The third and final phase was ideally due 2017–2019. However, as it was the third phase of the longer-term 18-year cycle, it could distort slightly, which means it could contract to 4 years (2016) or expand to 8 years (2020). Thus, the 6-year cycle low to complete the 18-year cycle could have occurred in 2016, or it could yet happen in 2020 if prices fall below 335...In the event that Corn falls below 335, it means the 6-,9-, and 18-year cycle lows from 2000, 2009, and 2012 are still underway and due in 2020.*"

Corn prices fell below 335 in 2020, reaching as low as 309 in April. Forecast 2019 actually stated, "*The price target for a new 18-, 9-, and 6-year cycle low, if it is to occur in 2019 (or 2020), would be 278 +/- 21. There may also be support at 300 +/- 10.*" As of this writing, it appears that the support at 300 +/- 10 held excellently and was likely the 18-year, 9-year, and 6-year cycle low. This would also mean that 2021 starts the 1st year of a new 6-year cycle in corn, proving to be a bullish boon for this agricultural commodity.

THE 30-MONTH CYCLE

The 30-month cycle tends to unfold two or three times within the 6-year or 9-year cycles. The orb for this 30-month cycle is seven months. The previous 30-month cycle low occurred in August 2016. Previously, it appeared that a 30-month cycle low occurred in May 2019 at 335-1/2. However, with the 18-year, 9-year, and 6-year cycle lows likely unfolding in April 2020, there's a very fair chance that the 30-month cycle distorted too. This tends to happen more often when longer-term cycles come to fruition. In this case, it would mean that the 30-month cycle low that started in August 2016 distorted to the long-end and bottomed in the 44th month (April 2020). This appears to be the more likely scenario because, under the May 2019 label, prices already fell below the cycle's starting point. Normally, when a cycle unfolds in such a manner, it means it will end up as a bearish cycle, which means it ends lower than it started. This also means that the next 30-month cycle low is due October 2022 +/- 7 months. January 2021 would only start the 9th month in the 30-month cycle as measured from the April 2020 low we are proposing. This would suggest that corn prices have plenty of time to make new higher-highs in 2021.

GEOCOSMICS

The Capricorn Stellium that unfolded in 2020 appears to have affected corn prices significantly. Forecast 2020 stated, "*In 2020, we will have another powerful geocosmic situation that could affect Corn and all grain prices. This is known as the Capricorn Stellium, when Jupiter, Saturn, and Pluto will all conjoin one another in the sign of Capricorn. Saturn and Capricorn both pertain to colder (although sometimes much hotter) than normal temperatures. In the planting and growing season, this can retard the growth of crops, resulting in lower yields per acre than normal. In the fall, it could coincide with an early frost or freeze. This, too, can diminish the harvest of crops. Both of these conditions usually mean less supply than normal, driving prices higher. The last time Saturn was in Capricorn was 1988–1991. Corn soared from an 18-year cycle low of 142 in February 1987 to a 9-year cycle crest of 370 in July 1988. But 2020 could be more threatening to grains because Pluto is conjunct Saturn in Capricorn, and Pluto pertains to damage and even loss of crops, through inclement weather.*" The big story here was the derecho in August 2020 that destroyed millions of acres worth of grain crops. This resulted in a significant reduction in supply, and we saw prices rally not long afterwards.

Then we have transiting Uranus, the boom-bust planet, through the agricultural sign of Taurus. Forecast 2020 stated, "*Uranus is in Taurus 2018–2026, another sign related to agricultural products. With Uranus, prices can explode 4–8 fold from the prior low in sectors ruled by the sign Uranus transits through, sometime in the first 2–5 years of its transit. In this case, we cannot rule out a surge to new all-time highs by 2022, and probably even 2021 when Saturn will square Uranus in Taurus.*" We are still within that 2-5 year orb for a boom to occur in agricultural commodities. If prices simply appreciated 4-fold from the April 2020 low, it would suggest corn prices could reach as high as 1200–1300, which would be an all-time high. 2021 seems to be a bit soon for such a rally to occur, but if 2020 taught anything, it's to expect the unexpected. Nonetheless, new all-time highs for corn prices while Uranus transits Taurus remains our bias, with 2023 being at the back-end of the time band for this to occur.

The agricultural planets in astrology are Venus and Saturn. The agricultural signs are the ones represented by the earth elements: Taurus, Virgo, and Capricorn. So, we look to these areas for 2021 concerning geocosmics. The big aspect in 2021, as alluded to in the previous paragraph, is Uranus (in Taurus) square Saturn, which will be in Aquarius. Uranus rules upheavals, innovation, and revolution. This suggests that an agricultural revolution is occurring at some level, and some of the signs of this are already present. There has been a massive shift in the public's perception of large-scale, industrially-oriented farming, which is falling out of favor with many.

Moreover, we saw in 2020 the fragility of economic supply chains and the devastation it caused to so many farmers, who were unable to take their products to market during the lockdowns. Saturn rules systems, which are essentially an extension of supply chains. Uranus square Saturn suggests an upheaval of existing systems and perhaps a re-localization of agricultural supply chains. New technology could play a role in this, especially blockchain, which is exemplified by Uranus in Taurus. Uranus square Saturn could also mean some sort of natural disaster—earthquake, tornadoes, etc. that causes a serious supply shock, which could be an additional boon for prices.

The last time Saturn transited Aquarius was November 1991–January 1994. During that time, corn prices largely consolidated between 205–305. However, corn prices appreciated significantly not long thereafter, as prices rose from 214 in August 1994 to 554-2/4 in July 1996. However, with the square aspect between Saturn in Aquarius and Uranus in Taurus in 2021, we have a double-influence of boom-bust energy (Uranus and Aquarius) and agriculture (Saturn and Taurus). This could mean 2021 is a very bullish year for grain prices and agricultural commodities overall.

CONCLUSIONS

Corn prices likely formed an 18-year, 9-year, 6-year, and distorted 30-month cycle low in April 2020 at 309. Coupled with Uranus in Taurus and a pending Saturn-Uranus square, our analysis suggests that 2021 should be a very bullish year for grains. A monthly close above the upper horizontal trendline of the rectangle pattern on the monthly chart, or 425, is all that's needed to confirm these long-term cycle lows. An upside resolution from the rectangle pattern would suggest prices could rally as high as 525 +/- 30 in 2021, and perhaps even higher. If the 525 level is cleared, then 650 +/- 30 is the next stop, and maybe even a retest of all-time highs 820 +/- 10. However, when prices reverse and close below the lower horizontal trendline of the rectangle pattern, we could see prices fall as low as 205. This is not our bias and would likely only occur in a scenario whereby the 18-year cycle did not bottom in April 2020 but instead is continuing from August 2000. Nonetheless, multiple indicators, cyclical and geocosmic analysis, and technical analysis suggest a high probability of April 2020 being the final low in these long-term cycles.

Forecast 2020 stated, "*Our strategy, therefore, is to buy Corn anywhere between 335-390, and even down to 275 if offered. It is not possible to predict the high in such a highly charged geocosmic time band as exists in 2020-2021, but our best guess is that the high would be realized in one of these next two years, somewhere well above 500.*" This same strategy and insight carry over into 2021, with an additional component to this strategy—which is to aggressively add to current long positions on a monthly close above 425.

SOYBEANS FOR 2021 – By Gianni Di Poce, MMTA Analyst

REVIEW

Soybean prices broke to multi-year highs in 2020, as this grain commodity continues to resolve higher from multiple long-term cycle lows that occurred in May 2019. Forecast 2020 stated, "*Until soybean prices can sustain trade above resistance from 950–980, prices may remain range bound in a sideways holding pattern or gradual decline.*" Prices closed above 950 on the monthly level in August 2020, the same month a devastating derecho storm wiped out over 14 million acres of farmland in the Great Plains.

There appeared to be a resolution to the trade wars between the United States and China early in 2020, but this was largely overshadowed by the coronavirus pandemic and economic lockdowns that followed. As of this writing in mid-November 2020, soybean prices are trading at their highest level since June 2016 and are poised to close out at their highest monthly level since July 2014. The perfect storm appears to have brewed on the bullish side for this grain, as China agreed to purchase very large amounts of this crop back in January 2020, stimulating demand. Then we had a significant reduction in supply due to the crop damage sustained in August. Higher demand and lower supply are a recipe for higher prices in soybeans. Throughout the rest of this forecast, we will reference our comments from the previous year, written by Kat Powell.

CYCLES

The longest cycle we observe in soybeans is the 16.5-year cycle. This 16.5-year cycle carries an orb of 3 years, and the most recent occurrence was in May 2019, with the low at 780.20. The previous 16.5-year cycle low occurred in July 1999, which means we witnessed a slight distortion to the long-end, as prices bottomed just four months after the normally allowable orb. This is not unusual to witness when long-term cycles come due. Therefore, January 2021 would start only the 20th month in the 16.5-year cycle, which means there is plenty of time for higher prices to be made in this grain market.

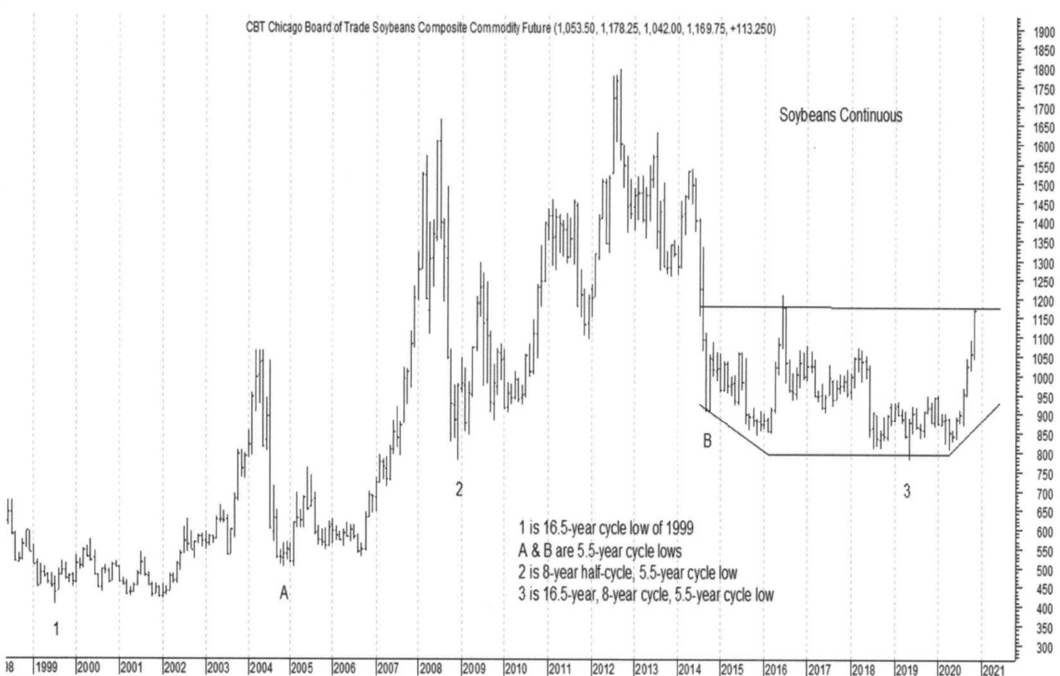

Forecast 2020 stated, "*Since we have a previous example of an extended 20-year cycle from July 1939 to September 1959, we must still consider the potential of an older market cycle that could culminate within 9 months of Saturn/Pluto conjunction in January 2020. The last conjunction was in November 1982, and soybeans made a longer-term cycle low within one month. The orb for these powerful conjunctions can extend months on either side of the exact aspect.*" The May 2019 low falls within this 9-month orb from the Saturn-Pluto conjunction of January 2020, and it's looking very promising as we wrap up 2020.

The 16.5-year cycle then breaks down into two 8-year cycles or three 5.5-year cycles. The 8-year cycle carries a range of 6–11 years, and the 5.5-year cycle carries a range of 4-7 years. The May 2019 low appears to have coincided with 8-year and 5.5-year cycle lows simultaneously with the 16.5-year cycle low. The previous 8-year cycle low bottomed in December 2008 at 776.25 and lasted 10 years and 5 months, within the allowable orb of 6-11 years. The previous 5.5-year cycle low bottomed in October 2014 at 904 and lasted 4 years and 7 months, also within the allowable orb of 4-7 years. Therefore, all of these long-term cycles point to an important low having formed in May 2019 at 780.50. The subsequent rally that has since occurred from this low lends great credence to this thesis. All that's needed at this point is a close above the upper horizontal trendline of the rounding bottom price pattern present on the monthly chart above, or above 1,175 on the monthly level—this would be a strong confirmation signal. It's not far from that mark now as of this writing in mid-November.

GEOCOSMICS

Perhaps the biggest boon for grains in the next few years from a geocosmic perspective is transiting Uranus through Taurus. MMA's studies show there is typically a boom–bust cycle in markets related to the sign Uranus transits through, whereby prices can appreciate 4–8x. Since 2018, Uranus has been in Taurus, which is a ruler of agriculture. <u>Forecast 2020</u> stated, "*Uranus is now transiting through Taurus, which is ruled by Venus, until 2025. Uranus was last in the sign of Taurus in 1934, and then 1935 to 1941–1942 (including retrograde cycles). Looking at charts from that time, we have to respect that soybean prices during that interval formed a triple bottom in 1938–1940.*" A similar pattern appears to have unfolded this time, as soybean prices bounced off support around 850 3–4 times between 2015–2019 before catching a serious bid starting in June 2020.

<u>Forecast 2020</u> also stated, "*Jupiter will be conjunct Pluto in Capricorn on April 4, June 30, and November 12. This planetary pair in hard aspect has a known correlation to problems surrounding over-leveraged debt and bankruptcy. Given that 2019 has seen a tremendous increase in bankruptcies for the farming industry, 2020 may prove even more difficult financially.*" Indeed, the problems for farmers compounded in 2020, with the coronavirus lockdowns decimating supply chains, leaving many farmers without markets to sell their product. This surely added to their financial difficulties, not to mention the derecho storm that wiped out millions of acres worth of crops back in August 2020.

Interestingly, soybean prices started to catch their bid in 2020 in June, which would've been right near the summer solstice and second passage of Jupiter conjunct Pluto. Moreover, Venus, the ruling planet of soybeans, was retrograde in June too. Venus retrograde remains one of the most powerful geocosmics that mark potential reversals in markets.

Looking forward to 2021, we note Saturn will be in Aquarius, squaring Uranus in Taurus. This is especially interesting because we have double-energy of Uranus. It rules Aquarius along with Saturn and Saturn is in Aquarius. Uranus, the planet of boom/bust behavior, is in Taurus which rules agriculture. Major changes are taking place in the agricultural sector, as supply chains are forced to restructure given the unprecedented shortages resulting from the 2020 lockdowns. Uranus rules shocks, and Saturn rules systems. Supply chains act as a form of systems whereby a particular good or service moves from one destination to another. The end result could be a more localized, or even idealist (Uranus) form of agriculture, a stark contrast from many of the farming practices used by "Big-Agri" companies.

Additionally, we have to beware of potential natural disasters related to agriculture—perhaps earthquakes or tornadoes that damage crops. This is especially pertinent given the Saturn-Uranus square, but also when Pluto is in retrograde motion. Pluto has been shown to correlate with crop damage, and we have Pluto resuming its retrograde motion on April 27, 2021, until October 6. Therefore, the main growing season for grains appears to be vulnerable due to Pluto's energies.

When it comes to the ruling planet of soybeans, which is Venus, we note a retrograde motion begins at the end of 2021 in December and lasts into early 2022. But Venus's transit through Aquarius is particularly interesting in 2021 because she will be within orb of conjunction between Jupiter and Saturn while squaring Uranus in Taurus. The noted time band for this geocosmic activity is February 2 through February 14.

CONCLUSION

Soybeans are likely not even through their first year in multiple long-term cycles, including the 16.5-year, 8-year, and 5.5-year cycles. As such, this grain is in the early stages of multiple long-term cycles, when markets are at their most bullish. In short, this means 2021 should prove to be a very bullish year for soybeans. The odds of this would increase greatly, especially if prices can close above 1175 on a monthly level. As of this writing in mid-November 2020, we are not far from that mark now. This would be required in order for a breakout from the rounding bottom pattern drawn on the monthly chart to be confirmed. A resolution from this technical pattern projects prices up to the 1540 zone +/- 30. However, with Uranus in Taurus, and especially with the incoming square from Saturn in 2021, prices could go even higher to test prices in the 1750 +/- 20 area. If we apply the Uranus boom-bust factor to soybean prices, whereby rallies of 4-8x higher can occur, we come up with a price of 3120 from the 780.50 low of May 2019. This just assumes a 4-fold rally, and already, we see this number is well into the all-time high territory. The year 2020 has taught us to expect the unexpected, and while this price target seems a bit farfetched now, it could happen by late-2021 through 2022.

In the event prices struggle to close above the line of resistance on the rounding bottom pattern, we could see soybeans spend some time in sideways price action for some months in 2021 before resolving higher. It would really take a monthly close below 1020–1040 to suggest it needs more time to digest its gains from 2020 and the bull market isn't full steam ahead. This is not our preferred bias, though, as multiple indicators, including technicals, cycles, and geocosmics, all point to a bullish year for soybeans and grain prices overall.

THREE-STAR CRITICAL REVERSAL DATES FOR 2021 – GRAINS

The following a list of three-star geocosmic critical reversal dates (CRDs) for grain markets, especially corn and soybeans. They are mostly valid when a market is also in the time band for a primary or half-primary cycle crest or trough. Traders are advised to also use CRDs provided in the U.S. stock market section that are not included here, for those dates can apply several other financial markets as well. Allow a range of 3 trading days (sometime as much as 6) to these dates for a reversal.

Dec 28, 2020
Jan 15-18, 2021 (especially Wheat)
Jan 28
Feb 8-9
Apr 23-26
May 3
June 22-23
July 7 (July 1-13, maybe different grains during this time)
Aug 4-5
Aug 20-23
Sep 20
Oct 8-11
Nov 5-8
Dec 22

FAVORABLE TIMES, CHALLENGING TIMES FOR 2021

The following is a list of "Favorable Days" and "Challenging Times" for planning in 2021. The "favorable times" indicate favorable periods to schedule important meetings, gatherings (like parties and weddings), or anything you wish to proceed smoothly and harmoniously. The "challenging times" are just the opposite. Tensions and stress tend to be higher than normal, and you may find it best to avoid scheduling social events and important meetings during these times. All dates are based upon Eastern Standard Time. This means that the beginning and ending dates may be one day later in the Far East.

FAVORABLE TIMES	CHALLENGING TIMES
December 24, 2020–January 10, 2021	January 11–27
January 28–February 1 *	February 1–8*
February 9–13*	February 13–23*
February 25–March 21	April 9–May 2
May 6–21	May 21–30
May 30–June 3*	June 4–14*
June 14–23*	June 23–July 10
July 11–15	July 17–August 10
Aug 11–29	August 30–September 6
September 6–11	September 13–23
September 23–29*	October 3–12*
October 13–19 *	October 20–November 17
November 18–30	December 8–24

***Indicates that this period overlaps with Mercury retrograde. If on the "Favorable" side, it is fine for a party, but probably not for a commitment, agreement, or sale.**

Of course, not every day in the “Favorable Times” period will necessarily be good, nor will every day in the “Challenging Times” period necessarily be bad. For help on choosing specific dates for an important event, please consult a professional astrologer.

In 2021, two solar eclipses will be in effect: June 10 at 19° Gemini 47’ (North Node eclipse), and December 4, 2021, at 12° Sagittarius 22’ (South Node eclipse). There will also be two lunar eclipses: May 26 (05° Sagittarius 26’) and November 19 (27° Taurus 14’). In my experience, North Node eclipses tend to be more favorable than South Node ones. Furthermore, it is not wise to plan a major event like a wedding or to open a new business during the two-week period between a lunar and solar eclipse, or vice-versa, which may also coincide with an otherwise “favorable time” as shown above.

MERCURY RETROGRADE PERIODS IN 2021

There will be three retrograde Mercury periods in 2021. They are January 30–February 20 (26°29' Aquarius to 11°01' Aquarius), May 29–June 22 (24°43' Gemini to 16° 09' Gemini), and September 28–October 18 (25° 28' Libra to 10°07' Libra).

As one can see, all retrograde Mercury periods in 2021 will be in air signs, after having been in water signs the prior two years. This means that the thrust of communications has shifted from one that was heavily affected by an emotional and reactive nature, to more of an intellectual bent. Intelligence and objective analysis will be increasingly valued, as will "outside the box" solutions to problems. The difficulty may be that people are willing to try things that are original and inventive but have never been tried before. This was the situation when the unorthodox policies of "quantitative easing" and "zero interest rate policies" were enacted during the Great Recession of 2007–2009 and afterwards. It worked fairly well, but that is not always the case. Sometimes new ideas with Mercury in air signs fail spectacularly due to gross overconfidence in the intellect at the expense of experience. We will know the results of the application of these "out of the box" ideas by the time Mercury starts its retrograde cycle into earth signs the following year.

The plea as Mercury starts its air sign cycle is that we need to do something different because the emotional intensity is too high and must be lessened. We will likely be told that we must change our course of action and behavior, our policies, and our laws, in order to make more intelligent and less emotional decisions. For instance, we need to listen to science, which ultimately may or may not be a good idea if it conflicts with experience or logic. Common sense may be in short supply and relegated to a lesser status than original thinking. This belief will be intensified by the ingress of Jupiter and Saturn into Aquarius, starting a 140-year air sign sequence of this 20-year synodic cycle, as of December 21, 2020.

In air signs, Mercury retrograde brings a greater willingness to try new ideas, even if they seem too radical. At its best, it indicates a greater openness to communications with parties on opposite sides of an issue, rather than an effort to just stifle their thoughts. It presents a favorable time for younger people to make advancements in politics, business, and education. In fact, there may be a baby boom. Major reforms are possible in the field of education, as well as in commerce and trade. New trade deals may be enacted, and old ones discarded (again). It is a favorable period for literary works garnering great recognition and respect. It is a brilliant time to be a writer and invent new ideas, new plans, and new solutions to lingering issues socially and otherwise.

During Mercury retrograde periods, traders are advised to keep in mind that financial and commodity markets can experience indecisiveness, especially at the beginning of the retrograde period. The trend is often unclear. That is because economic data and political pronouncements are often contradictory during Mercury retrograde periods. One set of economic data or political decisions is oftentimes bullish, while another is bearish.

Whipsaws are common during Mercury retrograde as price swings are both sharp and short-lasting. Near the middle section of each period, volatility tends to recede (unless Mars, Jupiter, and/or Uranus aspects are involved), but the direction and trend may still be uncertain. Our rule is that "no trend makes it out alive" without a counter-trend move, usually starting (or ending) around the middle of the retrograde period. After that, one may benefit by selling close-to-expiration, out-of-money options (calls and puts, or "strangles"), given the tendency for market volatility to subside. However, before doing this, one must also make sure that there are no other contradictory signatures present in the second half of the Mercury retrograde interval. For instance, if there are multiple aspects involving Mars or Uranus, or if either is stationary retrograde or stationary direct, this can increase volatility and thus nullify the lower volatility that is normally observed in the latter half of a Mercury retrograde time band. One must either have knowledge of astrology or consult a financial astrologer to determine this.

In addition, technical areas of support and resistance, as well as chart pattern recognition studies, tend to fail more often during Mercury retrograde times. Market prices may not quite reach either support or resistance levels, or they may frequently break through, but only temporarily. These breaks can be sharp, but again they may not last very long. Thus, we have another rule for traders during retrograde Mercury periods: "Take profits too soon." Do not wait until your price objectives are met or until the usual pattern unfolds. As soon as a move in your favor begins to stall, get out. Directional price movements tend to end and reverse about every 1–4 days.

Mercury retrograde periods also affect other areas of life. Typically, one is advised to avoid finalizing agreements or signing contracts. People change their minds frequently. In business, it is not unusual to see a flurry of appointment cancellations or disruptions in telecommunication (i.e., phones and computers go "on the blink"). Be alert in all your communications. Watch what you say and say what you mean. For example, be sure you tell your broker to "sell" and to "buy" when you mean "sell" or "buy." Sometimes the broker will do the opposite of what you mean, and it may be due to your mistake in communicating your wishes or due to the broker's mistake in not executing what you ordered. Have all your orders repeated back to you to make sure what you said is the same as what the other person heard.

On a positive note, the 4-day period before and after Mercury starts its retrograde motion is often a time of great inspiration and/or intuition. I personally feel more inspired and more intuitive. My market calls seem to be very precise and accurate during these periods (well, to me they do ☺). Others seem to be equally inspired and intuitive.

VENUS RETROGRADE PERIOD IN 2021

There will be one retrograde Venus period in effect at the end of 2021, from **December 19, 2021–January 29, 2022.** Venus will start in its retrograde motion at 26° 29' of Capricorn. It continues moving back to 11°01' of Capricorn before returning to its direct motion forward through the signs again. It should be a most interesting period for money and love for Capricorns.

In the study of astrology, Venus corresponds to love, beauty, and financial security. It rules Libra, the sign of beauty and romance, and also Taurus, the sign of savings and security. In mundane terms, Venus is either love or money, or both. It is difficult to have one without the other. Whenever a planet is retrograde, the time is generally *not* favorable for initiating activities in the areas over which that planet rules. Therefore, this period is generally not conducive to major changes in one's appearance, relationships, or the purchase of goods or services whose purpose is to improve one's image. In other words, major changes in one's hairstyle, plastic surgery on the face (or other areas of the body that are supposed to make one look more attractive), breast or lip implants, and liposuction are NOT advised during this time. Furthermore, one is advised against making major purchases for home or office furnishings or for making any major renovations in one's home, office, or building.

In the early part of this period (December 19, +/- 10 days), as well as the end of this period (January 29, +/- 10 days), one may feel romantically inclined. It is favorable for meeting people to whom you are attracted, but in many cases, issues will soon be revealed that may interfere with the longevity of the relationship. Lovers from the past may re-emerge, as a sense of nostalgia about previous relationships comes into one's consciousness. However, these may not work out in the long run, so perhaps it is best to just enjoy them for what they are, and only reminisce about the good times in the past, without weaving complex webs regarding a future together.

In the field of financial markets, Venus retrograde periods often coincide with a very difficult and unpredictable monetary or fiscal environment. It is not unusual to see central banks or government leadership make major policy changes, from accommodative to tightening, or vice-versa. Thus, trends that were up or down prior to the retrograde will frequently reverse during this time. Since the retrograde occurs in Capricorn, we may see reversals of trends in government, banking, business, agriculture, and mining.

This retrograde Venus cycle occurs in Capricorn, conjunct to Pluto in Capricorn. Therefore, it highlights social activities and romance. This combination can be described as seductive and prone to temptations in order to corral the object of one's desire. These activities can also lead to either a deepening of a new relationship if it is satisfying on a sexual level or destructive if either party has an obsessive nature that tends to sabotage all relationships once they enter the arena of intimacy. If not careful, this can become a "fatal attraction" that has a hurtful ending. It can also lead one to engage in sexual activities that are considered taboo by society or the individual him/herself. It is as if one cannot stop from doing something that intuitively they know might be dangerous, harmful, or deliciously exciting and mysterious.

Relationships undertaken at this time may start out as mostly a physical attraction. However, they can evolve into something deeper and more meaningful if there are not unhealthy psychological issues involved. The love either goes beyond the physical to the mental and social factors the parties enjoy together, or it stays totally discreet, hidden, secretive, and sexual. Nevertheless, one must be careful of being too attracted to someone that has a history of bad endings in other relationships, perhaps because of violent emotional or even physical side that was not apparent upon first meeting. You may find out the other person (or maybe it's you) is involved in another relationship that has been kept hidden.

Relationships where money is concerned can also be intense. Pluto rules debt and Venus rules credit, so this is a period where someone may enter into a loan agreement with another. If the borrower doesn't pay back on time, it may fracture the relationship. In fact, relationships can terminate over financial disputes if not careful.

Venus retrograde is generally not a favorable time for stock prices, particularly if the market climate was nervous going into the Venus retrograde (is it ever *not* nervous?). Thus, traders may look for major reversals in almost all financial markets and some commodity markets—like currencies, stocks, soybeans, sugar, coffee, and treasuries—during the period December 19, 2021–January 29, 2022 (the stationary dates), or slightly before or after, as well as right around the middle of this time band (January 8–9, 2022). In the case of stocks, the period around the retrograde has a higher correlation to crests, while the period around the direct date has a higher correlation to troughs. It is not always the case that cycle highs form with the retrograde and troughs with the direct dates. The more important thing to note is that a primary or half-primary cycle crest or trough tends to form within ten trading days of both the stationary retrograde and direct dates.

In terms of stock markets, Venus retrograde, and direct stations are two of the most consistent correlations to primary and greater cycles in the Dow Jones Industrial Average, using an orb of 12 trading days. Within 12 trading days, the Venus retrograde station period has an 80% correlation with primary or greater cycles. The Venus direct station has a 75% correlation with primary or greater cycles within ten trading days.[1]

Another thing to note about Venus retrograde is that every eight years, it takes place in nearly the same sign and degree in the zodiac. The last time Venus went retrograde in this sector of the zodiac was December 21, 2013–January 31, 2014. That was a period when Silver made a healthy rally (over 18%), T-Notes also had a healthy rally (primary cycle low to primary cycle crest), and the DJIA had a sharp decline (7.5%). Soybeans made a primary cycle trough on the day Venus turned direct and began a rally to over $15/bu. over the next four months.

During each 8-year interval, Venus will go retrograde five times, all in different sections of the zodiac, but it will repeat (return to) within two degrees of the same spot every eight years. If you draw a figure through these five points in the heavens, you will see they are approximately 72 degrees apart from one another. If you draw the line of Venus' orbit through these points, you will create an almost perfect pentagram, which was an early symbol of matriarchal (pagan and/or goddess) religions. Interestingly enough, since the advent of Christianity, this early pagan religious symbol (the pentagram) has been reinterpreted in modern times to represent the sign of the devil. However, it is indeed the symbol of the Venus cycle through the cosmos, and astrologically, Venus is most definitely a symbol of the divine, feminine principle.[2]

References:

1. *Merriman, Raymond A., The Ultimate Book on Stock Market Timing Volume 3: Geocosmic Correlations to Trading Cycles, Seek-It Publications, W. Bloomfield, MI, 2001.*
2. *Brown, Dan, The DaVinci Code, Doubleday Publishing, New York, 2003*

SPECIFIC TIMES OF THE YEAR BY SEASONS IN 2021

In this section of the book, we analyze the 2021 seasonal ingress charts for Washington, D.C. We then examine the major planetary aspects—or series of aspects—that occur throughout each season. This provides a collective psychological overview of what is happening in the U.S. and the world. From there, we deduce certain themes and issues that may be highlighted in the political, economic, financial, and mundane realms. We then speculate upon possible events or decisions that may relate to these highlighted themes.

Let's begin where we left off with the last paragraph that ended the "Seasons" section in Forecast 2020 Book. Keep in mind that this was written on October 2, 2019, well before the world turned with the COVID-19 Pandemic that erupted in February 2020.

"In retrospect, people may look back upon 2020 as a year warranting sober assessment of what has really happened, and a commitment to never let things get so "out of order" again. It was likely a very serious year, one filled with many apprehensions, yet many hopes that more practical-minded people would rise to positions of leadership in the world. Politicians and activists will have played on people's fears and campaigned with images of a frightening future unless something radically different was tried. Now it will be, and there will probably be resistance for the next couple of years, maybe even more rebellion in some parts of the world where leaders do not want to relinquish their control over those they rule unjustly. But, if those who are now in leadership roles stand by their promises, a new foundation leading to a more lasting peace and a more civil discourse in societies throughout the world can begin to take shape over the next decade. After all, it is Jupiter and Saturn in Aquarius, and Aquarius rules humanity, equality, and the freedom to pursue Life, Liberty, and Happiness. There is still hope—and change."

WINTER: DECEMBER 21, 2020 – MARCH 19, 2021

Major Geocosmic Signatures:

- December 21, 2020: Jupiter conjunct Saturn 0° Aquarius on the Winter Solstice; Sun/Mercury conjunct 0° Capricorn on the Winter Solstice; Mars square Pluto, exact December 23
- January 6–8: Mars enters Taurus; Mercury enters Aquarius; Venus enters Capricorn
- January 13–20: New Moon; Mars square Saturn; Uranus direct; Sun conjunct Pluto; Jupiter square Uranus; Mars conjunct Uranus
- January 23–February 1: Mars square Jupiter; Sun conjunct Saturn/Jupiter; Sun square Mars/Uranus; Venus conjunct Pluto; Mercury retrograde (January 30–February 20)

- February 6–11: Venus conjunct Jupiter/Saturn, square Uranus
- February 17: Saturn square Uranus
- February 20: Mercury direct
- March 11–14: Sun and Venus conjunct Neptune

THE CAPRICORN INGRESS, WINTER SOLSTICE

The winter ingress for Washington D.C. occurs on December 21, 2020, at 5:03 AM.

WINTER SOLSTICE 2020
Natal Chart
Dec 21 2020, Mon
5:03 am EST +5:00
WASHINGTON, DC
38°N53'42" 077°W02'12"
Geocentric
Tropical
Placidus
Mean Node

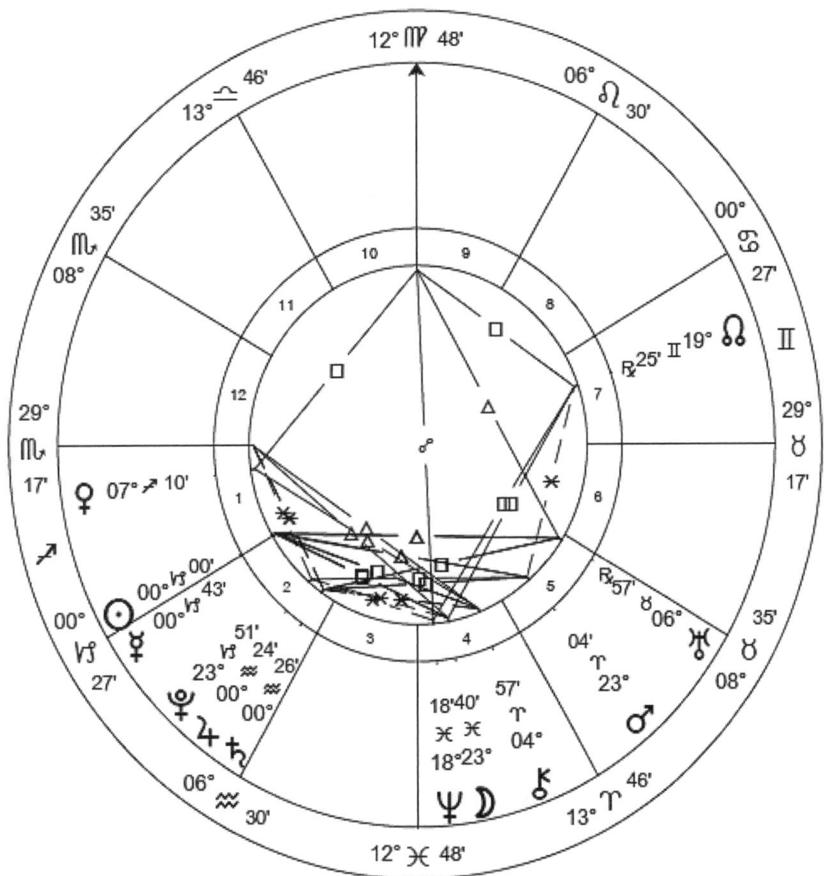

The Sun is on the 2nd house cusp of finances and the economy, conjunct Mercury and forming a wide trine to Uranus in Taurus. This indicates optimism and bright spots in the future of the economy, especially where technology and innovation are concerned.

However, it squares Chiron, so there are also concerns still revolving around illnesses. The health of the population or leader may be in jeopardy. There is a tendency for words to be harsh and critical, whether in the press or statements issued by the president. Chiron pertains to wounds, Mercury to communication and words, and the Sun to the leader. They are in conflict, but innovation and technology lend a positive tone to the economy that seems to cast a more favorable light on the nation's leadership in this area.

However, even though the short-term news of this period may be favorable for the economy and commerce, the longer-term implications of Jupiter conjunct Saturn—also in the second house and square to Uranus in Taurus—paints a more worrisome economic and world trade picture. New ideas are being discussed about building a more progressive and modernistic economy and governmental structure. The future of the government's progressive ideas and its projected economic impact may be more seriously contemplated now. This also pertains to judicial matters, such as the selection of a new Supreme Court jurist. The season may be abuzz about a new direction for the nation in all of these areas: laws, policies, court decisions, even re-organization of political parties and their new platforms for a future America. There is an air of excitement about the future, but also fear of undergoing radical changes just because they sound intelligent. The truth is no one really knows what will happen with these reforms and new directions that are being seriously discussed, and especially how they may affect the economy. With Uranus on the sixth house cusp, there may be a massive undertaking that will affect the nation's employment situation. Many new jobs will be created, probably in the technology sector. But many current jobs may be lost, perhaps in those fields that are traditional office or manufacturing sectors. Uranus is the planet of disruption and revolution. On the cusp of the 6th house, it pertains to the labor force, and it squares Jupiter and Saturn. Job creations and job losses are not evenly balanced, and it may cause demands and disagreements for even more radical changes.

The Ascendant is 29° Scorpio, where the stinger of the Scorpion is located. This is also conjunct Joe Biden's natal Sun and Venus, so he may be favorably highlighted this season, especially if he wins the 2020 election. In the last degree of Scorpio, it is the end of an era. But the old force doesn't go out easily. It has to make a statement of revenge or retaliation. But once the transition takes place, then Venus is rising is Sagittarius. This lends an air of cooperation and agreements, especially in trade deals with other nations.

The Moon is in Pisces in the 4th house of the White House and ruling family matters. It conjoins Neptune, which is the ruler of Pisces. This is a caring and sympathetic combination for the security of the American family. It could indicate the move to develop a universal health care program for the nation, to create a safety net against unexpected catastrophes that could upend a family's financial security. It may place attention on hospitals, women's health clinics, nursing facilities, urgent care units, and counseling services for those suffering from substance abuse and addiction, but not necessarily always in a favorable way as it makes a T-square with the lunar nodes (see below).

In terms of the White House, it can imply several things, ranging from making it a place where music and new cultural activities are presented to the American population. The White House may have a new glamorous look and feel about it.

On the other end of possibilities, the Moon/Neptune in Pisces is in a T-square to the lunar nodes. This could coincide with rumors and scandals that harm the reputation of innocent people. It could also indicate a period of convalescence needed by the occupant of the White House. This T-square can bring attention to mismanagement issues and fraud, perhaps involving well-known personalities or those involved with hospitals, nursing homes, assisted living care facilities, health clinics, jails, and prisons. The lack of disclosure combined with diversionary tactics and unethical practices may come to light. Likewise, this combination could indicate major developments—or secret clandestine activities and agreements—in the field of medicine and pharmaceuticals. The Moon and Neptune in Pisces are tempted to do something undetected by the public. If exposed, it could be highly embarrassing, even scandalous.

Neptune and Pisces also pertain to the nation's waterways: lakes, rivers, and coastlines. It shines a light on the importance of U.S. naval activities in the seas and oceans of the world.

Finally, with Venus rising in Sagittarius, it also appears that several travel restrictions may be lifted during this season.

SPECIFIC PERIODS HIGHLIGHTED IN THE WINTER

The solar year (winter solstice) begins with the Sun and Mercury in conjunction, with both at 0° Capricorn on **December 21**, the same day that the 20-year Jupiter/Saturn conjunction takes place at 0° Aquarius. It is the start of a new era, cosmically speaking. This is more symbolic of a long period starting than an actual event, although this combination emphasizes laws and government acts. It is a combination of optimism (Jupiter and Aquarius) and anxiety (Saturn in Aquarius, square its ruler Uranus in Taurus.) With Mars square Pluto two days later on **December 23**, there could be acts of violence and property destruction (Mars/Pluto) during the holiday season, perhaps aimed at religious or educational institutions (Jupiter). In fact, as important as the state of governance is at this time, so is the future of education, which may be experiencing some financial challenges. Will schools be closed? What about sports (also Jupiter)? Once the aspect passes, restrictions in education, sports, and travel may begin to lift, although it may take several weeks to get well underway.

The year begins with a series of consecutive geocosmic signatures unfolding in short fashion. Mars, Mercury, and Venus all change signs **January 6–8.** Planets changing signs means the focus of the collective's attention changes too. In finances, there may be a shift in sectors that investors suddenly start giving more attention to. A variety of investment strategies are being introduced as portfolio managers restructure their holdings.

January 13–20 then stands out as a potentially very disruptive period in a variety of areas, from social unrest, educational change of plans to the world of finance and investing. Jupiter square Uranus is highlighted (January 17), which is one of the strongest geocosmic correlations to market reversals within an orb of 9 trading days. Uranus also changes directions on January 14, one day after Mars will square Saturn. These are not stable and easy dynamics to navigate. With Uranus highlighted, there may be several areas of social uprising. Protests could get out of hand as radicals demand attention and change. It so happens that on January 20, the day of the USA Presidential Inauguration, Mars will conjunct the stationary Uranus, as well as square Jupiter three days later (January 23). Chaos could get out of control during or around Inauguration Day. Likewise, stock markets may experience huge price movements. If stocks have been rising within ten days of inauguration, they may suddenly and forcefully plummet in reaction to the social unrest signified by these aspects. Does this have to happen? No. But it will require great collective self-control and willingness to see the positives about the future that are being forged now too, and not to be focused on the change from ways that some groups may have become comfortable with. All of these aspects signify the momentum of a new change, and the resistance to it by different groups, some of which may have anarchy, social disruption, and chaos on their agenda. It seems that whatever party won the election, the other side is not willing to accept the result and chooses to act out its disapproval.

The atmosphere of unrest doesn't end there. From **January 24 through January 29,** the Sun will conjoin Jupiter and Saturn, which promises hope and stability, except all three will form a square to Uranus, which means more interruptions, disruptions, and demands for change. Financial markets are still over-excited and prone to large and chaotic price moves.

Mercury turning retrograde **January 30–February 21** may offer distractions from all the chaos, but no one really knows what solution to enact. The retrograde is in air signs, so very smart people are speculating on what to do, but their ideas are not tested ideas. They are more abstract than practical and not based on real experience as much as "thinking out of the box." Yet, promises and agreements may be made only to find out they have to be modified because no one foresaw the consequences.

Right after Mercury turns retrograde, the Sun squares Mars, and Venus conjoins Saturn squaring Uranus, **January 30–February 7.** The volume of dissent is still high, but glimmers of hope are also starting to emerge. In financial markets, we have a rule that any market that is declining into a Venus/Saturn hard aspect is a candidate to reverse and go higher. By **February 11,** Venus will conjoin Jupiter, which is considered an agreeable combination, favorable for financial matters. Even with Mercury retrograde, this may indicate a time when agreements are made, or at least discussed with a sense of optimism.

Yet Saturn is also approaching its first square passage on **February 17,** and this dominates all the smaller aspects. This is a fight between the forces of conservativism and the forces of progressivism, between law and order, versus radical change to "the system." It is symbolic of revolution and overthrow, and indeed this may be witnessed in many areas of the world this year, even this month.

After Mercury turns direct on February 21, the cosmic storm subsides. The major aspect in effect the rest of this season is the Sun and Venus conjunct Neptune in Pisces. This is a peaceful dynamic as if to say we all need a break, to just chill out and relax a bit now. It is a favorable time for a vacation or to engage in any special social events. It is a time highlighting romance and gentleness. It highlights festivals, concerts, and benefits to help others. It can be a very giving and charitable dynamic, just the opposite of what the first two months of the year wrought. It may be inclined to an abundance of rains and possibly floods too. But let's hope the world settles down in March so we can all see life through a more harmonious lens. This aspect wants peace. It does not want war, and it abhors violence. The forces for peace become stronger now.

SPRING: MARCH 20–JUNE 20, 2021

Major Geocosmic Signatures:

- March 20–21: Sun and Venus ingress into Aries
- April 19: Sun and Mercury ingress into Taurus
- April 23–May 3: Venus conjunct Uranus, square Saturn; Pluto retrograde at 26°48' Capricorn; Sun conjunct Uranus, square Saturn
- May 23–26: Saturn retrograde at 13°31' Aquarius; Lunar Eclipse 5° 26'Sagittarius
- May 29–June 5: Mercury retrograde at 24°43' Gemini; Venus ingresses into Cancer; Mars opposition to Pluto
- June 10–20: Solar Eclipse at 14° 47' Gemini; Mars ingresses in Leo; Saturn square Uranus; Jupiter turns retrograde at 2° 11' Pisces

THE ARIES INGRESS, SPRING EQUINOX

The spring equinox for Washington D.C. occurs on March 20, 2021, at 5:39 AM.

This is a very hopeful chart because Jupiter is rising, conjunct the Ascendant, at 21° Aquarius, in a trine aspect to the Moon, which is posited strongly in the 4th house with the lunar North Node. Additionally, Jupiter rules the Midheaven. This combination relates to optimism (Jupiter) about the future (Aquarius). It portends exciting news about trade and travel (Jupiter), innovation, and technology (Aquarius), and it may be favorable for the housing market. Jupiter rising is well-liked, popular, and friendly. It suggests parties, weddings, and large social gatherings. The mood (Moon) is mostly happy (Jupiter). It favors family reunions and celebrations. It may also indicate a large number of new people becoming citizens of the U.S., as immigration policies are relaxed. Families are reunited. Furthermore, it inclines toward good news regarding education and sports.

The Sun falls close to the second house of money and finances in a wide trine to Midheaven. This suggests favorable news regarding the employment situation. More people appear to be working, and wages are rising, perhaps due to new trade deals.

The Moon in the 4th house is strong for domestic and family issues. In Gemini, it relates to advances in communications. There may be uplifting news regarding commerce, auto sales, and home sales. One concern, however, is that the Moon squares Neptune in Pisces, which pertains to more abundance of rains, floods, oil spills, and/or concerns still lingering about contagions. Intellectually, this looks positive, but emotionally, people are still very sensitive. The Moon/Neptune square can also indicate a rumor that is untrue and maligns the reputation of a well-known female, or possibly a scandal involving a female that captures the nation's imagination and interest.

All the planets are tightly compacted between the 12th and 4th houses. This is a very creative and intuitive part of the sky, but also one that wants to start new and exciting projects. America appears to be a leader during this season, and other nations are supportive of its leadership, especially in the fields of education, trade, and technology, and perhaps even outer space exploration.

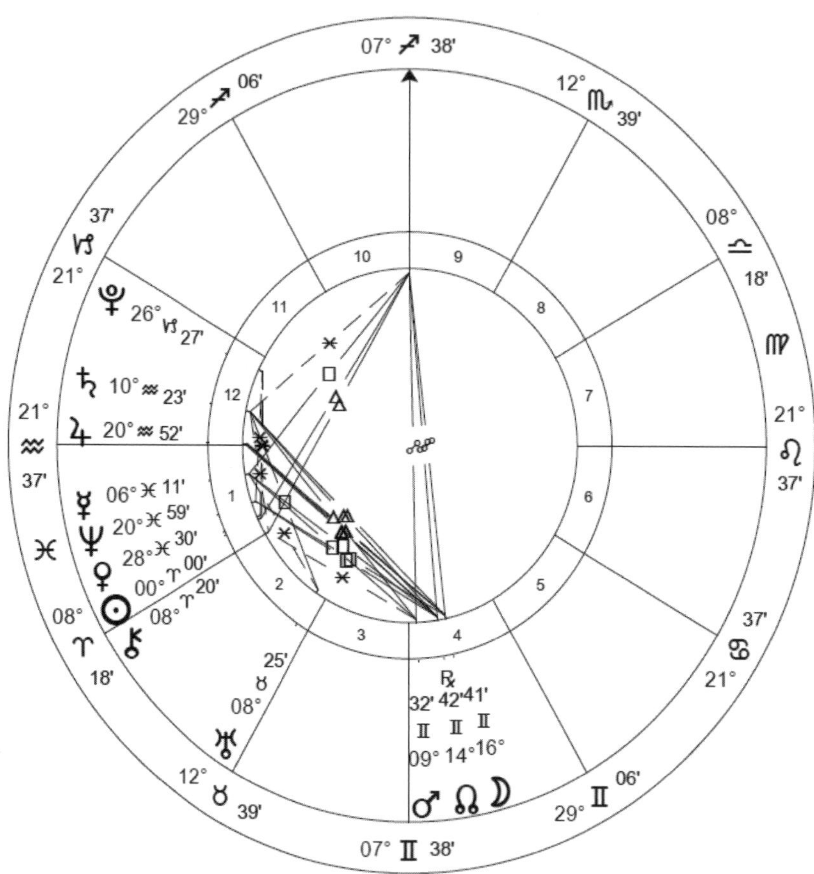

There are two challenging squares this season. The first is the continuation of the Saturn/Uranus fixed square, which falls in the 12th and 2nd houses of the vernal equinox in Washington, D.C. There are still fears of a disturbing financial eruption, but they may remain more fears than realities this season with Jupiter rising in this chart and the Sun close to the 2nd house cusp. However, this could also indicate a cyberattack or electrical grid failure that affects vast numbers of Americans. Inclement weather conditions, such as high winds, tornadoes, even earthquakes, are also a possibility during this season throughout the world. Additionally, with Uranus ruling the chart and in the second house of money, problems with some banks may spring up, or they are there but kept quiet due to the influence of the 12th house (secrets).

The other square involves Mercury in Pisces, in the first house, square Mars in Gemini (ruing sign of Mercury) on the Nadir. This indicates sharp criticism, an outburst of anger, that may be unjustified. It may be coming from the press or the media, and rather than helping a situation, it creates more disturbance and angst. It can be an accident-prone aspect, so one needs to be more careful in auto or airplane travels.

SPECIFIC PERIODS HIGHLIGHTED IN THE SPRING

The relatively peaceful conditions (compared to earlier) that started in March continue in the spring. There are no major aspect clusters until April 23.

The Sun and Venus both ingress into Aries, **March 20–21**, to start the season, which is pleasant, and favors matters of love and romance, and perhaps agreements or harmonious discussions between world leaders. **On April 19,** the Sun and Mercury both ingress into Taurus, another pleasant and harmonious combination suggesting comfortable sharing of ideas about finances and commerce. There may be good news for small businesses. Everything during the first month of spring seems designed to tackle small but easy projects to establish trust and good-will with one another.

The first gathering of multiple planetary dynamics in aspect to one another arises **April 23–May 3**, when Venus in its ruling sign of Taurus hits the Saturn/Uranus square, followed by the Sun doing the same, sandwiched around Pluto turning retrograde in Capricorn. The emphasis on Taurus pertains to money, banking, and agriculture matters. Leaders are getting a little more serious now that the "small ball" period of cooperating on easy issues is over. Taurus indicates that the period of building trust and good-will prior to this time was a good idea, as leaders want to continue that courtesy and respect to one another. But they know there are problems in the financial sector that have to be dealt with, and so now it may start. The ideas proposed may begin to get bold. If so, the boundaries between those who want change and those who want stability start to show. Not all leaders are on the same page, so the spirit of cooperation is there, but the ideas and solutions are not yet ready for a formal compromise. There may be one element that wants a dramatic overhaul and reform of the banking or monetary system. One of the key issues of contention is the worldwide debt. How do we solve it? Out of the box, ideas are presented but may be flatly or courteously rejected. Mother Nature may be highlighted now too, for these are aspects of earth disturbances, such as earthquakes, high winds, tornadoes, and possible threats to the electrical grid or internet/telecom network systems.

Discussions go back and forth for a few weeks, it seems, between **May 4–20**. After that, the differences and boundaries become more well-defined but no closer to solutions through the remainder of this season. Saturn and Mercury turn retrograde **May 23 and 30,** respectively, and in between, there is a lunar eclipse on May 26. There is an air of coolness, both in personal contact and actual weather patterns, suggesting unseasonably cool temperatures. Progress on plans experience delays, which in turn may elicit frustration and disappointment. There may be a sense that things are starting to fall apart again, and opposing sides begin to bring up issues from the past that haunted cooperation efforts before. Differences may become front and center in **late May through June.** Those that want change may feel betrayed or let down by those who start to introduce barriers to change. Decisions may be made that do not consider the wishes of all parties involved. Leaders start to vacillate and make premature pronouncements, which have to be revised later. All those smart ideas are just not working as hoped. It is time to pause and retreat before old wounds begin to resurface and detour the previous efforts and good-will that had started.

Between **June 10 and June 25**, there is a solar eclipse (June 10), Saturn will make its second passage in square to Uranus (June 14, near Donald Trump's birthday), while Jupiter and Neptune turn retrograde and Mercury turns direct. On the one hand, the latter conditions suggest irrational exuberance. Stock markets may be buoyant. But the former indicates vulnerability to a shock, either politically or in financial markets, especially stocks and currencies, but also possibly commodity grain markets. Buoyancy may give way to panic quickly in financial if political or economic expectations turn out to be completely off. Sudden changes of direction may not be well-received, as a shock might be delivered to the global community. It could be in the arena of banking and finances, or it could be related to catastrophic natural events, such as tornadoes and earthquakes. It could coincide with man-made threats, too, such as an outbreak of terrorist activity or a cyberactivity attack, or perhaps even an accident involving space exploration efforts. However, these types of occurrences could erupt anytime during the Saturn/Uranus square, which extends from **February through December.** This middle passage on June 14 may be important however, just because it is the center of the transit. With three planets (Jupiter, Mercury, and Neptune) all changing directions within a five-day period (**June 20–25**), financial market reversals are more likely than usual.

SUMMER: JUNE 20–SEPTEMBER 22, 2021

Major Geocosmic Signatures:

- June 20–27: Jupiter turns retrograde at 2° 11' Pisces; Mercury turns direct at 16° 07' Gemini; Neptune turns retrograde at 23° 11' Pisces; Venus enters Leo
- July 1–13: Mars T-square Saturn and Uranus; Venus T-square Saturn and Uranus; Venus conjunct Mars at 19° 50' Leo
- July 22: Sun enters Leo; Venus enters Virgo, opposition to Jupiter
- July 28–29: Mercury enters Leo; Jupiter retrogrades back into Aquarius; Mars in opposition to Jupiter; Mars enters Virgo
- August 16: Venus enters Libra
- August 19–22: Uranus turns retrograde at 14° 47' Taurus; Sun in opposition to Jupiter; Sun enters Virgo
- August 30–September 10: Heliocentric Mercury in Sagittarius
- September 10: Venus enters Scorpio
- September 14: Mars enters Libra

THE CANCER INGRESS, SUMMER SOLSTICE

The 2021 summer solstice takes place in Washington, D.C. on June 20, 2020, at 11:33 PM, EDT. Once again, it finds 21° Aquarius rising, with Jupiter, the rising planet, which was also the case on the spring equinox. Still, this time Jupiter has advanced to Pisces, one of the two signs it has rulership over, and where it is therefore strong by sign and house placement. This reasserts the theme of developing good relationships with allies, establishing agreeable trade deals, and increasing travel possibilities with other nations. It is also an indication of a large "social heart," which means the wish to be charitable and kind to many nations and many people everywhere. This may favor progress on a universal health insurance program and less restrictive immigration policies. It is as if to say: "We are America, and we are open for business and refuge." It also favors advancements and more opportunities in education and sports.

Summer Solstice
Natal Chart
Jun 20 2021, Sun
11:33 pm EDT +4:00
WASHINGTON, DC
38°N53'42" 077°W02'12"
Geocentric
Tropical
Placidus
Mean Node

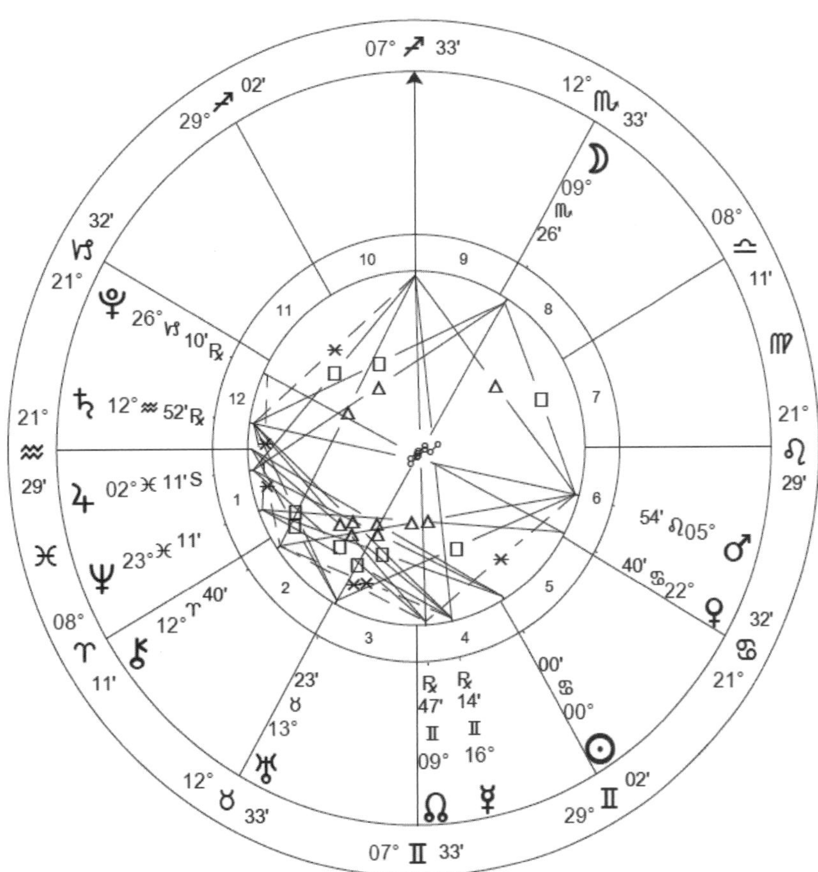

This is an especially fortunate chart pattern because it exhibits a Grand Water Trine between the Sun in Cancer, the Moon in Scorpio, and Jupiter rising in Pisces. This Grand Trine is sympathetic and caring by nature. The Sun is in Cancer near the fifth house cusp of pleasure, entertainment, amusement, romance, and children. All are favored this season, along with weddings, children, education, travel, sports, vacations, and enjoyable social activity. It seems America is a fun place to be in the summer of 2021.

But wait a minute. Behind the exterior of all the fun and good times is another parallel reality. The ruler of the chart is still Uranus, and Uranus is still squared by Saturn in Aquarius. And although it is relatively contained in the 12th house, these two outer planets form a Grand Fixed Square with Mars in Leo and Moon in Scorpio. It is like a cauldron of boiling oil with a tight lid, but ready to explode. And explode it might in some parts of the world where enough of the population is shouting: "Enough is enough. We need to force a change NOW." Nations finding this combination rising, setting, or culminating include India, Pakistan, Afghanistan, Russia, and Mexico. The armies of anarchy and revolution are alive and active, but they are not nearly as highlighted in the U.S. as they were earlier in the year, but they are very active in other regions of the world.

Who is upset in the U.S.? Unions, along with people who work and provide essential services. It appears to be a tale of two cultures in America: those who are happy and joyful, and those who are angry and want more change or money in the jobs' markets. In the U.S., the grievances seem centered on equal rights and equal pay for both minorities and women in the workplace. Yet those who demand change anywhere and everywhere are stubborn and relentless, frustrated, and bitter this summer. But they don't *control* the situation in the U.S. as appears to be the case in other nations. And, with Jupiter rising and ruling the 10th and 1st houses of the chart, financial and career opportunities may be increasing for many demographics, including women and minority groups.

The Moon in Scorpio, in the 8th house (debt), and Venus (money) in opposition to Pluto (debt), may bring matters of the national debt to the surface again. As Pluto rules the 9th house, the complaint about other nations not paying their "fair share" and relying on an unequal financial dependency upon America may also be heard. However, the trine of Venus to Neptune suggests these grievances can be worked out if all parties are sensitive and empathic and stay away from accusations arousing heated passions of dissension.

The Moon in Scorpio stands out by itself, removed from the other nine bodies, no matter where one is in the world. Thus, emotions are strong with cries for reform, especially involving feminist issues. The "Me Too" movement may experience another revival, for Scorpio is the sign of sex, and it is part of a fixed T-square with Mars. There is romance in the air, as shown by Neptune and Venus trine aspect, but there may also be tension between the sexes over violations of fairness and coercion against one's will.

SPECIFIC PERIODS HIGHLIGHTED IN THE SUMMER

Summer starts with three planets changing directions, **June 20–25.** Jupiter begins the parade while it is also in a trine aspect to the Sun, suggesting a spirit of hope and optimism. Mercury then turns direct in its ruling sign of Gemini, indicating a plethora of new ideas are forthcoming designed to stimulate commerce and business. It may also highlight the news media, and perhaps there are journalistic awards announced. The changing of the planets' directions then moves to Neptune turning retrograde in Pisces in a trine aspect with Venus. This is a very romantic, eloquent, and charming dynamic. Symbolically, it represents romantic love, the stuff of which fairy tales are made. The entire period seems very benign and agreeable, and to some, it may seem magical. It could be a good time for world leaders to hold a summit and reach an agreeable consensus on a wide variety of issues. It is also a time in which many financial markets may be readying for a major reversal of trends, such as in Crude Oil, which is co-ruled by Jupiter and Neptune. In terms of stock markets, this can be one of the periods of "irrational exuberance" within the week if new highs are unfolding.

The exuberance, however, may come to an abrupt halt **July 1–August 7.** First, Mars will form a T-square to the Saturn/Uranus square, **July 1–4, +/- 1 week.** This could be a dangerous time for many reasons. With Mars in Leo, a fire sign, there may be another outbreak of wildfires or earthquakes, damaging the environment and threatening human life. This could also be a war-like or terrorist period in which human lives may be endangered. Accident-prone tendencies may be more prominent for the duration. In short, this is a period requiring caution and the need to avoid being careless or overly impulsive in one's actions. Disputes and anger could suddenly erupt, changing the atmosphere from peaceful tranquility to one of great stress.

Venus then enters into a similar T-square with Saturn and Uranus, **July 7–8, followed by its conjunction with Mars in Leo on July 13.** Venus rules money and love, whereas Mars and Uranus can be both passion and disruption. In terms of love matters, this is apt to be a very passionate time, as well; one of the great attractions between people just meeting. That is fine, except in a T-square, it may cause separations in the current state of relationships, whether allies and alliances between nations or partners in business or love. There may be tensions due to jealousy over one's object of attention. Are you giving more attention to those you just met or to those you want to establish a new relationship with at the expense of others who have been your primary allies and supporters? If the latter, then you may experience conflicts of interest, and disloyalty may be alleged regarding your behavior. Diplomacy and loyalty are big issues when Venus is in such an aspect configuration. It is important to show value to those who have supported you, or you may lose their support from this point onward. This is a fixed T-square, so once a decision is made to leave one for the other, it will be hard to get the other back on your side again.

As far as finances, this time band also represents major reversals in many financial markets. Venus rules Currencies, Soybeans, and Sugar, so these are important markets to watch carefully for a change in trend.

Another shift begins to unfold **July 17–29** when five planets change signs, with Venus and Mars forming an opposition to Jupiter. The Sun enters Leo, and Venus enters Virgo on July 22, followed by Mercury entering Leo and Jupiter ingressing into Aquarius on July 28. One day later, Mars will enter Virgo, opposing Jupiter. Whenever a planet changes signs, it signifies a change in attitude about matters pertaining to that planet and the signs it is changing from and to. Thus, we conclude there are a lot of changes in policy and the focus of attention in terms of the future (Sun), a nation's leadership (Sun), its monetary policy and international alliances (Venus), commerce, business, media practices (Mercury), education, foreign affairs (Jupiter), and military situations (Mars). The opposition of Venus and Mars to Jupiter suggests projects will either be completed or reach a turning point in their completion schedule. If there have been issues delaying the completion of the project(s), they may come to the surface now and lead to major changes in any one or a combination of the areas just mentioned.

The changes started in July continue into August. Because this is a summer of many changes, it is not likely to be a time of stability. Many matters are in flux. **August 1–10** finds the Sun in Leo forming a T-square now to the Saturn/Uranus square, forming yet another fixed T-square. This implies more disturbances, unexpected events and disruptions, and possible difficulties caused by inclement weather (hurricanes, tornadoes, high winds, earthquakes, electrical failures, disruptions in the internet, and terrorist activities). One positive cosmic factor is Venus makes a Grand Earth Trine to Uranus and Pluto, and thus there may be compromises to the conflicts discussed in July that help resolve the impasses, at least regarding finances and the workforce.

Yet another round of unexpected events and disruptions follow when Uranus turns retrograde on **August 19,** followed by the Sun/Jupiter opposition the next day, **August 20**. Within a week of this period, financial markets and Mother Nature may hemorrhage, as these are very powerful reversal signatures for global stock markets. This is a time when boundaries are not respected, and "breakouts" occur in financial markets if they are nearing long-term cycle highs or lows. They are apt to break through for a few days, even weeks, and then reverse sharply. However, this can also be an exceptional period for brilliant, new, and innovative ideas that serve to inspire the world or one's community. It is an excellent time to "think outside of the box," but keep in mind your ideas may be far ahead of their time. It will take some discussion before they are ready to implement, so patience will be necessary, and so will the need to make sure others understand you correctly.

Once the Sun enters Virgo on **August 22** and Venus trines Saturn on **August 23**, things begin to take shape, and chaos starts to give way to organization of ideas. There is a sense a major hurdle has been conquered within the week. Heliocentric Mercury will pass through Sagittarius **August 30–September 10**, which may give a lift to currencies and precious metals' prices.

Another interesting period of success in relations and the consummation of agreements is possible **September 4–10.** This is implied by the favorable trine aspects of Venus/Jupiter, Mars/Pluto, and Sun/Uranus. People seem genuinely receptive to working together in an atmosphere of harmony and excitement. It is a fine time to hold meetings or conferences in which new and exciting visions of the future are discussed.

This takes us right up until the start of autumn. The last aspect of the season is Venus square Saturn on **September 17**, and the first aspect of the new season is Venus in opposition to Uranus on **September 23**. Thus, we have another T-square. Just keep in mind any market declining into a Venus/Saturn hard aspect is a candidate for a strong reversal and healthy rally. This may be even more the case with the Venus/Uranus opposition following it. Get ready for a nice trade.

AUTUMN: SEPTEMBER 22–DECEMBER 21, 2021

Major Geocosmic Signatures:

- September 27: Mercury turns retrograde at 25°28' Libra
- October 6–11: Pluto turns direct at 24° 18' Capricorn; Venus enters Sagittarius; Sun conjuncts Mars at 15° 05' Libra; Saturn turns direct at 6° 52' Aquarius
- October 15–19: Sun and Mars trine Jupiter; Mercury turns direct at 10° 07' Libra; Jupiter turns direct at 22° 19' Aquarius
- October 30–November 17: Mars enters Scorpio; Sun square Saturn and opposition to Uranus; Mars square Saturn and opposition to Uranus; Mercury enters Scorpio; Venus enters Capricorn
- November 22–24: Sun and Mercury enter Sagittarius
- November 26–December 7: Heliocentric Mercury transits through Sagittarius
- December 1: Neptune turns direct at 20° 24' Pisces
- December 11–25: Venus conjunct Pluto; Mercury enters Capricorn; Mars enters Sagittarius (December 13); Venus turns retrograde at 26° 29' Capricorn; Saturn square Uranus
- December 29: Jupiter enters Pisces

THE LIBRA INGRESS: AUTUMNAL EQUINOX

The 2021 autumnal equinox in Washington D.C. occurs on September 22, 2021, at 3:22 PM, EDT.

This is a very different chart than the previous three seasons. Here we have the Sun in the 8th house with Mars and ruling the 8th house. Additionally, Pluto is rising in Capricorn, and Pluto has an affinity with 8th house themes of regeneration, rebirth, reform, termination, death, and end of matters. It pertains to structural processes of a major transformation, especially involving the government (Capricorn)

Pluto rising is also in a T-square aspect to Mercury in Libra and Moon in Aries. Mercury, the planet of communication, commerce, and business, is in the 9th house of trade. In Libra, it wants to make a deal. But in a square aspect, it may end up losing or rejecting a major trade deal. With Pluto rising in Capricorn in a T-square involving Moon in Aries, plus the Sun and Mars conjunct in the 8th house, the U.S. leadership may be guilty of being too coercive, trying to force a deal on others who decide it is not a deal in their best interests, and so they (or the U.S.) leave the discussions. The U.S. may be accused of acting like a bully (Mars and Aries highlighted) while insisting it is not, but rather it is just trying to be fair (Libra). However, the words of diplomacy don't match the actions of forcefulness, and the meetings may break down.

Economically, this season brings attention to the 4D's associated with Pluto, Scorpio, and the 8th house: debt, deficits, downgrades, and defaults. Scorpio stands out because Venus is there, in its detriment, on the Midheaven and in opposition to Uranus in Taurus. Venus and Taurus both rule money and finances. Uranus rules the second house of money and finances, plus it is still square to Saturn, as well as Jupiter. This is a very complicated financial situation, challenged even more so by the sudden events and disruptions associated with Uranus. A financial crisis cannot be ruled out during this season.

Autumnal Equinox
Natal Chart
Sep 22 2021, Wed
3:22 pm EDT +4:00
WASHINGTON, DC
38°N53'42" 077°W02'12"
Geocentric
Tropical
Placidus
Mean Node

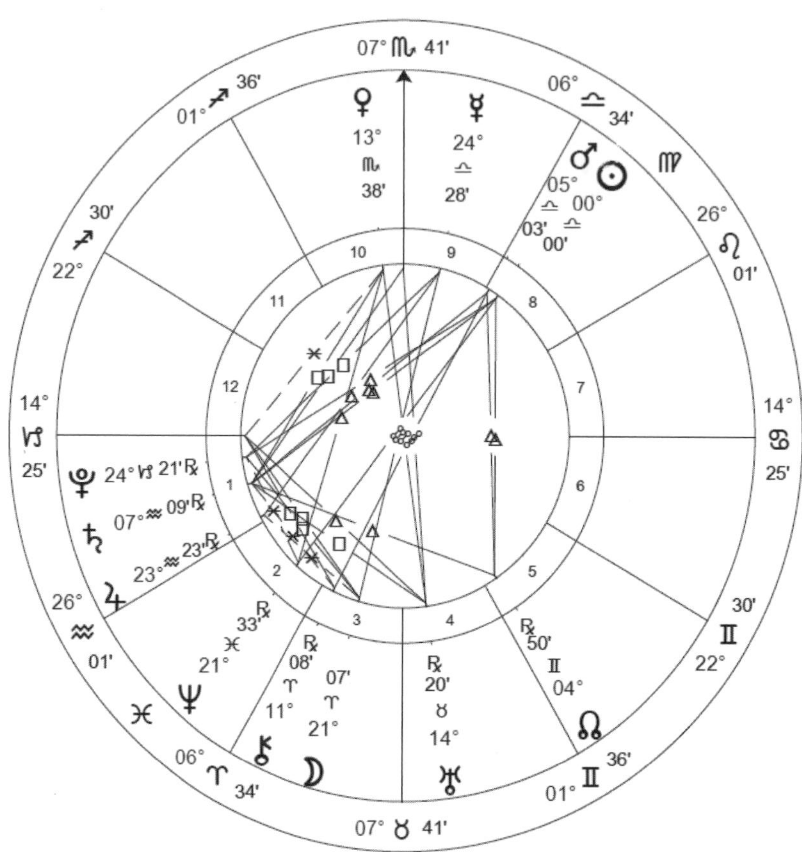

Thus, these two squares indicate a difficult end to the year. The cardinal T-square between Pluto rising and the Moon-Mercury opposition illustrates the possibility of a threat to commerce and trade deals due to being overly aggressive and forceful. The fixed T-square between Jupiter/Saturn to the opposition between Venus and Uranus indicates the possibility of a financial crisis happening during the same period. Financial markets can become riled, especially if financial agreements and trade deals begin to unravel, and debt issues accelerate. Currency markets may undergo large price swings or reversals of trend.

It is possible these breakdowns can be resurrected, especially involving trade deals, because Mercury in the 9th house makes a trine to Jupiter. Compromise over forcefulness will be the key. Mercury, in Libra, wants balance and fairness. The 9th house and Jupiter wish to trade. It requires striking a fair balance. Can Pluto rising in Capricorn, square the Moon in Aries and Mercury in Libra step back and allow that to happen without acting offended? If so, it will make the difference in how international relations unfold this season.

In the end, the final judgment may relate to matters outside anyone's control, such as the health of a world leader or a threat to nature or human lives caused by natural (or even unnatural) conditions. With the Sun and Mars in the 8th house, and Pluto rising also signifying a possible health crisis of a world leader, it is important to treat any signs of physical distress quickly. Pluto also rules dangerous weather conditions or natural forces, such as volcano eruptions or shifts of large landmasses. Perhaps there is a climate crisis.

On the positive side, Pluto in Capricorn also rules the reform and restructuring of government systems. It can represent the repair of the nation's infrastructure (Pluto), which has been promised (Capricorn) for several years. Maybe now it finally gets underway.

SPECIFIC PERIODS HIGHLIGHTED IN THE FALL

Autumn begins with a series of favorable trine aspects, **September 17–29.** The Sun and Mars in Libra trine Saturn, which is a sign of completing an agreement or project. There is a sense of accomplishment for those who have worked hard. Yet, during this same time, Mercury turns retrograde in Libra, **September 27–October 18.** The ideas were agreed upon, but now additional concerns arise that may require revision or modification. And this is where problems might begin. "The devil is in the details" is an old saying that may be appropriate now.

September 30–October 11 finds first Pluto (October 6) and then Saturn (October 11) changing directions, going from retrograde to direct, and during the period, Mercury is retrograde. Sandwiched between the stations of Pluto and Saturn is the Sun conjunct Mars. This latter aspect wants to move forward immediately. It is in a hurry. But Pluto in Capricorn and Saturn in Aquarius want to stop. Here you have a force meeting resistance, and if not careful, the result is a breakdown. Are we going to do this or not? Disputes begin to arise very quickly. If not checked, they can explode into threats, even of war, for Venus is also square Jupiter (exaggeration) on September 30. This, too, can lead to a major decline in world stock prices. These types of market reactions (large price reversals) tend to happen when the Sun and Mars are within 8 degrees of one another, which will be in effect **September 13–October 31.** Price swings of at least 8% are very possible then. Yet if mature temperaments prevail, this can actually be a period when something of importance and value does lift off. After all, Sun and Mars together have great vigor and vitality. For that reason, spectacular accomplishments in sports and other forms of competition may also be evident. Records may be broken.

A window of opportunity emerges **October 13–20** related to favorable Jupiter transits from the Sun and Mars, plus Mercury and Jupiter are both turning direct. There is sudden optimism again. Goodwill between nations can lead to new openings in travel, trade deals, and education. It is a great time to host a summit or conference, where large visions are discussed that generate tremendous excitement and hope for humanity.

After that, the road to progress gets rocky again. There are a series of successive hard aspects between the Sun and Mars to Saturn and Uranus, **October 22–November 17**. The forces of revolution and anarchy are appearing again, as demands for independence and change maybe causing chaos in several different regions of the world. With Uranus and

Saturn, it may not be only a call for new leadership but also a time of natural upheavals like earthquakes, strong winds, wildfires, and threats to the worldwide internet. Rioting and looting are also possible if civil obedience is not restored. This can be a time when angry mobs are on the move. However, these disturbances do not appear to be long-lasting. The chaos they create may be loud and upsetting, but they can be brought under control.

The Sun and Mercury both enter Sagittarius, the sign of optimism, November 22–24, but the entire period of **November 19–December 2** seems festive. People appear to be in a generous, charitable mood, and stock markets tend to be more bullish than bearish now.

Venus will assume prominence **December 10–25**. First, it will conjoin Pluto in Capricorn on December 11. Then it will turn retrograde on December 19, followed by another conjunction to Pluto on December 25. On December 24, Saturn will make its final square to Uranus. Venus and Pluto are money signs. Venus is credit, and Pluto is debt. Plus, Uranus is in Taurus, Venus' ruling sign, also pertaining to money. Therefore, financial matters are highlighted, particularly as it pertains to debt and taxes.

Venus and Pluto also pertain to currency values. There may be renewed talks about changing the role of the U.S. Dollar as the international standard currency, for the Venus/Pluto conjunction falls on the U.S natal Moon/Pluto (see that section of this year's book). Something is in the air about a major reform, restructuring, or change here.

There is something else that may stand out too. Pluto rules the end of matters, and maybe even the end of life. This combination symbolizes death and rebirth, the end of a matter (perhaps financial, perhaps of the life of a very prominent and loved person), and the need to start life on a different course. For individuals, this can also represent a period of transformation in a personal relationship that has served a vital role. This is passion and intensity, and it can also represent a time of too much passion and intensity, to the extent it frightens one or both parties in a relationship. To make your relationships work, to make then survive, you have to give something of yourself up. Something that one has valued has to die to be reborn and healed.

This is something we all realize at the end of the year. To have a life of value, there is something of value we may have to give up. It creates a deep, profound sense of reorganizing our values. Everyone wants to be valued, and yet many feel undervalued. The years 2020 and 2021 will be looked back upon as a time of great personal and societal transformation. We may want to go back to the way it was. But there is no turning back. We are rebuilding a new life, perhaps a better life, with the lessons we have learned over the past two years. Those who rebuild will be reborn and succeed. Those who don't will just have to start over again, and again, and again. Some of this may be fate. Most of it is a choice. That's the nature of Venus and Pluto, especially in the karmic sign of Capricorn as we end the year.

And then Jupiter ingresses into Pisces on December 29 for the greater part of next year, where it will meet up with Neptune, also in Pisces. In fact, Jupiter and Neptune co-rule Pisces, the sign of forgiveness and compassion. There is hope for those who can forgive and feel compassion for others. After all, we are all in the same boat, traversing the same seas in life (all symbols of Jupiter and Neptune in Pisces).

2021 GEOCOSMIC EPHEMERIS AND ASTRO CALENDAR GUIDE

On the following pages you will find the Geocosmic ephemeris (on the left-hand pages) and the Astrological Calendar Guide (on the right-hand pages), for each month between January 2021 and April 2022.

The Ephemeris is provided by Astro Computing Services (ACS) of Epping, New Hampshire. The page is divided into 4 sections. The top section lists the planetary positions as of midnight, GMT (Greenwich Mean Time). The middle section gives the positions of the declinations and latitudes of each planet for each day, as of midnight GMT. The right of this section, and a little lower, are the Moon phenomena. Of most importance are the two right columns, titled "Void of Course Moon" (symbol for the Moon). The farthest right-hand column gives the Moon Ingress, which lists the times when the Moon enters each sign of the zodiac, basis GMT. This is especially important for traders who trade the Solar-Lunar cycles, as I do, and as outlined in The Ultimate Book on Stock Market Timing Volume 4: Solar-Lunar Correlations to Short-Term Reversals and The Sun, The Moon, and The Silver Market: Secrets of a Silver Trader. The bottom part of the page shows the "Daily Aspectarian," which lists the exact time that aspects form between any two planets (including the Sun and Moon). These are important in identifying "Geocosmic Critical Reversal Dates" in the *MMA Monthly Cycles Report,* as well as this Forecasts for 2021 book.

The right-hand page is a day-by-day calendar, showing the times that each aspect and planetary ingress takes place. The times in the calendar have been adjusted for the EST (Eastern Standard Time) zone. It is not adjusted for daylight savings time. Here too one can instantly see if any particular day has more than, or less than, the usual amount of geocosmic activity going on. One can also see when planetary aspects are occurring close in time to one another, which is the basis for identifying a "Critical Reversal Date," as described in The Ultimate Book on Stock Market Timing, Volume 3: Geocosmic Correlations to Trading Cycles.

LONGITUDE

Day	Sid.Time	☉	☽	☽ 12 hour	Mean ☊	True ☊	☿	♀	♂	⚳	♃	♄	⚷	♅	♆	♇
	h m s	° ' "	° ' "	° ' "	° '	° '	° '	° '	° '	° '	° '	° '	° '	° '	° '	° '
1 F	6 43 27	10♑46 44	2♌43 29	9♌17 16	18♊51.4	19♊52.7	17♑42.8	20♐24.6	27♈21.4	11♓59.6	2♒47.0	1♒37.5	5♈03.6	6♉48.0	18♓28.4	24♑11.3
2 Sa	6 47 24	11 47 53	15 54 26	22 34 51	18 48.2	19R 49.3	19 20.6	21 39.8	27 47.5	12 18.2	3 00.7	1 44.3	5 04.5	6R 47.3	18 29.5	24 13.2
3 Su	6 51 21	12 49 01	29 18 24	6♍04 58	18 45.1	19 45.8	20 58.6	22 54.9	28 13.8	12 36.9	3 14.4	1 51.2	5 05.4	6 46.7	18 30.7	24 15.2
4 M	6 55 17	13 50 10	12♍54 25	19 46 36	18 41.9	19 42.6	22 36.8	24 10.1	28 40.4	12 55.8	3 28.2	1 58.1	5 06.4	6 46.1	18 31.9	24 17.2
5 Tu	6 59 14	14 51 19	26 41 25	3♎38 42	18 38.7	19 40.3	24 15.2	25 25.2	29 07.3	13 14.8	3 42.0	2 05.0	5 07.5	6 45.6	18 33.1	24 19.1
6 W	7 03 10	15 52 28	10♎38 20	17 40 10	18 35.5	19D 39.2	25 53.7	26 40.4	29 34.4	13 33.9	3 55.9	2 11.9	5 08.6	6 45.1	18 34.3	24 21.1
7 Th	7 07 07	16 53 37	24 44 03	1♏49 46	18 32.3	19 39.3	27 32.2	27 55.6	0♉01.8	13 53.1	4 09.8	2 18.9	5 09.8	6 44.7	18 35.6	24 23.1
8 F	7 11 03	17 54 47	8♏57 08	16 05 52	18 29.2	19 40.4	29 10.7	29 10.8	0 29.4	14 12.5	4 23.7	2 25.9	5 11.0	6 44.4	18 36.9	24 25.1
9 Sa	7 15 00	18 55 57	23 15 39	0♐26 09	18 26.0	19 41.9	0♒49.1	0♑26.0	0 57.2	14 32.0	4 37.6	2 32.9	5 12.3	6 44.1	18 38.3	24 27.1
10 Su	7 18 56	19 57 07	7♐36 55	14 47 30	18 22.8	19R 43.3	2 27.4	1 41.2	1 25.3	14 51.6	4 51.6	2 39.9	5 13.6	6 43.8	18 39.6	24 29.1
11 M	7 22 53	20 58 16	21 57 22	29 05 57	18 19.6	19 43.7	4 05.3	2 56.4	1 53.7	15 11.3	5 05.6	2 47.0	5 15.0	6 43.6	18 41.0	24 31.1
12 Tu	7 26 50	21 59 26	6♑12 41	13♑16 56	18 16.5	19 42.7	5 42.7	4 11.6	2 22.2	15 31.1	5 19.7	2 54.0	5 16.4	6 43.5	18 42.4	24 33.1
13 W	7 30 46	23 00 36	20 18 09	27 15 46	18 13.3	19 39.9	7 19.5	5 26.9	2 51.0	15 51.1	5 33.7	3 01.1	5 17.9	6 43.4	18 43.9	24 35.1
14 Th	7 34 43	24 01 45	4♒09 17	10♒58 18	18 10.1	19 35.4	8 55.4	6 42.1	3 20.0	16 11.1	5 47.8	3 08.2	5 19.4	6D 43.3	18 45.4	24 37.1
15 F	7 38 39	25 02 54	17 42 27	24 21 30	18 06.9	19 29.5	10 30.2	7 57.3	3 49.2	16 31.3	6 01.9	3 15.3	5 21.0	6 43.3	18 46.9	24 39.1
16 Sa	7 42 36	26 04 02	0♓55 21	7♓23 57	18 03.8	19 23.1	12 03.6	9 12.5	4 18.7	16 51.5	6 16.0	3 22.4	5 22.6	6 43.4	18 48.4	24 41.1
17 Su	7 46 32	27 05 09	13 47 23	20 05 52	18 00.6	19 16.7	13 35.2	10 27.8	4 48.3	17 11.9	6 30.2	3 29.5	5 24.3	6 43.5	18 49.9	24 43.1
18 M	7 50 29	28 06 16	26 19 39	2♈29 08	17 57.4	19 11.2	15 04.7	11 43.0	5 18.1	17 32.4	6 44.3	3 36.6	5 26.0	6 43.7	18 51.5	24 45.1
19 Tu	7 54 25	29 07 21	8♈34 45	14 37 01	17 54.2	19 07.1	16 31.6	12 58.2	5 48.1	17 52.9	6 58.5	3 43.7	5 27.8	6 43.9	18 53.1	24 47.1
20 W	7 58 22	0♒08 26	20 36 29	26 33 45	17 51.0	19D 04.8	17 55.3	14 13.4	6 18.3	18 13.6	7 12.7	3 50.9	5 29.6	6 44.1	18 54.8	24 49.1
21 Th	8 02 19	1 09 31	2♉29 26	8♉24 13	17 47.9	19 04.2	19 15.3	15 28.6	6 48.7	18 34.3	7 26.9	3 58.0	5 31.5	6 44.5	18 56.4	24 51.0
22 F	8 06 15	2 10 34	14 18 44	20 13 40	17 44.7	19 05.0	20 31.0	16 43.8	7 19.2	18 55.2	7 41.1	4 05.2	5 33.4	6 44.8	18 58.1	24 53.0
23 Sa	8 10 12	3 11 36	26 09 37	2♊07 16	17 41.5	19 06.5	21 41.7	17 59.0	7 49.9	19 16.1	7 55.3	4 12.3	5 35.4	6 45.3	18 59.8	24 55.0
24 Su	8 14 08	4 12 37	8♊07 12	14 09 57	17 38.3	19R 08.0	22 46.5	19 14.3	8 20.8	19 37.1	8 09.5	4 19.5	5 37.4	6 45.7	19 01.5	24 57.0
25 M	8 18 05	5 13 38	20 16 05	26 26 01	17 35.2	19 08.5	23 44.6	20 29.5	8 51.8	19 58.2	8 23.8	4 26.6	5 39.4	6 46.3	19 03.3	24 59.0
26 Tu	8 22 01	6 14 37	2♋40 10	8♋58 49	17 32.0	19 07.5	24 35.3	21 44.7	9 22.9	20 19.4	8 38.0	4 33.7	5 41.5	6 46.9	19 05.0	25 00.9
27 W	8 25 58	7 15 36	15 22 12	21 50 27	17 28.8	19 04.3	25 17.7	22 59.9	9 54.3	20 40.7	8 52.3	4 40.9	5 43.6	6 47.5	19 06.8	25 02.9
28 Th	8 29 54	8 16 33	28 23 34	5♌01 31	17 25.6	18 58.8	25 50.9	24 15.1	10 25.7	21 02.0	9 06.5	4 48.0	5 45.8	6 48.2	19 08.7	25 04.9
29 F	8 33 51	9 17 30	11♌44 05	18 31 01	17 22.5	18 51.3	26 14.2	25 30.2	10 57.3	21 23.4	9 20.8	4 55.2	5 48.0	6 48.9	19 10.5	25 06.8
30 Sa	8 37 48	10 18 25	25 21 56	2♍16 25	17 19.3	18 42.5	26R 27.0	26 45.4	11 29.1	21 44.9	9 35.0	5 02.3	5 50.3	6 49.7	19 12.3	25 08.8
31 Su	8 41 44	11♒19 20	9♍13 58	16 14 04	17♊16.1	18♊33.3	26♒28.8	28♑00.6	12♉00.9	22♓06.5	9♒49.3	5♒09.4	5♈52.6	6♉50.6	19♓14.2	25♑10.7

1st of Month

Julian Day # 2459215.5
Obliquity 23°26'13"
SVP 4♓58'15"
GC 27♐08.0
Eris 23♈27.7R

Day	⚴
1	7♒51.1
6	9 30.7
11	11 11.1
16	12 52.1
21	14 33.5
26	16 15.2
31	17 57.0

Day	⚵
1	4♐15.0
6	5 48.1
11	7 19.4
16	8 48.5
21	10 15.3
26	11 39.5
31	13 00.8

Day	⚶
1	20♍08.5
6	20 43.1
11	21 07.5
16	21 21.0
21	21 23.0R
26	21 13.3R
31	20 51.7R

DECLINATION and LATITUDE

Day	☉ Decl	☽ Decl	☽ Lat	☽ 12h Decl	☿ Decl	☿ Lat	♀ Decl	♀ Lat	♂ Decl	♂ Lat	⚳ Decl	⚳ Lat	♃ Decl	♃ Lat	♄ Decl	♄ Lat
1 F	22S60	23N01	3N34	21N46	24S21	2S06	22S26	0N39	11N21	0N52	15S43	9S23	20S01	0S29	20S10	0S23
2 Sa	22 55	20 13	4 21	18 23	24 09	2 07	22 34	0 37	11 31	0 53	15 34	9 21	19 58	0 29	20 09	0 23
3 Su	22 49	16 18	4 55	14 00	23 55	2 08	22 40	0 35	11 42	0 55	15 24	9 18	19 55	0 30	20 08	0 23
4 M	22 43	11 31	5 12	8 52	23 39	2 09	22 47	0 32	11 52	0 56	15 15	9 16	19 51	0 30	20 06	0 23
5 Tu	22 37	6 05	5 12	3 13	23 22	2 09	22 52	0 29	12 03	0 57	15 05	9 14	19 48	0 30	20 05	0 24
6 W	22 30	0 17	4 53	2S39	23 04	2 08	22 57	0 27	12 13	0 58	14 56	9 12	19 45	0 30	20 03	0 24
7 Th	22 22	5S35	4 17	8 28	22 44	2 07	23 01	0 24	12 24	0 59	14 46	9 09	19 42	0 30	20 02	0 24
8 F	22 14	11 14	3 25	13 52	22 22	2 06	23 04	0 22	12 35	0 60	14 37	9 07	19 39	0 30	20 00	0 24
9 Sa	22 06	16 20	2 20	18 33	21 59	2 04	23 07	0 19	12 45	1 01	14 27	9 05	19 35	0 30	19 58	0 24
10 Su	21 57	20 30	1 06	22 07	21 34	2 01	23 09	0 17	12 56	1 02	14 17	9 03	19 32	0 30	19 57	0 24
11 M	21 48	23 24	0S12	24 17	21 08	1 58	23 10	0 14	13 07	1 03	14 08	9 00	19 29	0 30	19 55	0 24
12 Tu	21 39	24 46	1 29	24 51	20 41	1 54	23 11	0 12	13 17	1 04	13 58	8 58	19 25	0 30	19 54	0 24
13 W	21 29	24 32	2 39	23 49	20 12	1 49	23 11	0 09	13 28	1 04	13 48	8 56	19 22	0 30	19 52	0 24
14 Th	21 18	22 45	3 39	21 23	19 42	1 44	23 10	0 06	13 39	1 05	13 38	8 54	19 19	0 30	19 51	0 24
15 F	21 07	19 43	4 25	17 49	19 11	1 38	23 08	0 04	13 50	1 06	13 28	8 52	19 15	0 30	19 49	0 24
16 Sa	20 56	15 44	4 55	13 29	18 38	1 31	23 06	0 01	14 00	1 07	13 19	8 50	19 12	0 30	19 48	0 24
17 Su	20 44	11 08	5 09	8 41	18 05	1 24	23 03	0S01	14 11	1 08	13 09	8 48	19 08	0 30	19 46	0 24
18 M	20 32	6 10	5 08	3 38	17 31	1 15	22 59	0 04	14 22	1 08	12 59	8 46	19 05	0 31	19 44	0 24
19 Tu	20 20	1 05	4 53	1N27	16 56	1 06	22 55	0 06	14 33	1 09	12 49	8 44	19 01	0 31	19 43	0 24
20 W	20 07	3N57	4 25	6 24	16 21	0 56	22 49	0 09	14 43	1 10	12 39	8 42	18 58	0 31	19 41	0 24
21 Th	19 54	8 48	3 46	11 06	15 45	0 45	22 44	0 11	14 54	1 11	12 29	8 40	18 54	0 31	19 40	0 25
22 F	19 40	13 18	2 58	15 23	15 10	0 33	22 37	0 14	15 05	1 11	12 19	8 38	18 51	0 31	19 38	0 25
23 Sa	19 26	17 19	2 01	19 06	14 35	0 20	22 30	0 16	15 15	1 12	12 09	8 36	18 47	0 31	19 36	0 25
24 Su	19 12	20 41	0 59	22 03	14 01	0 06	22 22	0 19	15 26	1 13	11 59	8 34	18 43	0 31	19 35	0 25
25 M	18 58	23 11	0N06	24 03	13 28	0N09	22 13	0 21	15 36	1 13	11 49	8 32	18 40	0 31	19 33	0 25
26 Tu	18 43	24 37	1 12	24 53	12 57	0 24	22 04	0 24	15 47	1 14	11 39	8 31	18 36	0 31	19 31	0 25
27 W	18 27	24 49	2 17	24 25	12 28	0 40	21 54	0 26	15 58	1 14	11 29	8 29	18 33	0 31	19 30	0 25
28 Th	18 12	23 40	3 15	22 35	12 01	0 57	21 44	0 28	16 08	1 15	11 19	8 27	18 29	0 31	19 28	0 25
29 F	17 56	21 11	4 05	19 28	11 37	1 14	21 32	0 31	16 19	1 16	11 08	8 25	18 25	0 31	19 26	0 25
30 Sa	17 39	17 28	4 41	15 14	11 16	1 32	21 20	0 33	16 29	1 16	10 58	8 23	18 21	0 32	19 25	0 25
31 Su	17S23	12N46	5N02	10N07	10S59	1N49	21S08	0S35	16N39	1N17	10S48	8S22	18S18	0S32	19S23	0S25

Day	⚷ Decl	⚷ Lat	♅ Decl	♅ Lat	♆ Decl	♆ Lat	♇ Decl	♇ Lat
1	4N21	2N33	13N21	0S27	5S33	1S05	22S27	1S12
6	4 22	2 32	13 21	0 27	5 31	1 05	22 26	1 12
11	4 23	2 31	13 20	0 27	5 28	1 05	22 24	1 13
16	4 26	2 30	13 20	0 27	5 25	1 05	22 23	1 13
21	4 28	2 29	13 21	0 26	5 22	1 04	22 22	1 13
26	4 31	2 28	13 22	0 26	5 18	1 04	22 20	1 14
31	4N35	2N27	13N23	0S26	5S15	1S04	22S19	1S14

Day	⚴ Decl	⚴ Lat	⚵ Decl	⚵ Lat	⚶ Decl	⚶ Lat	Eris Decl	Eris Lat
1	0S31	18N21	11S33	9N36	9N43	6N19	1S39	11S34
6	0 31	17 58	11 39	9 46	9 49	6 41	1 39	11 34
11	0 28	17 35	11 43	9 56	10 00	7 04	1 38	11 33
16	0 23	17 14	11 45	10 08	10 16	7 27	1 37	11 32
21	0 16	16 54	11 45	10 20	10 37	7 51	1 36	11 31
26	0 06	16 34	11 44	10 33	11 03	8 15	1 35	11 30
31	0N04	16N16	11S40	10N46	11N34	8N39	1S34	11S30

Moon Phenomena

Max/0 Decl

dy	hr mn	
6	1:11	0 S
12	8:18	24S52
19	5:08	0 N
26	15:40	24N54

Max/0 Lat

dy	hr mn	
4	11:51	5N14
10	20:16	0 S
17	10:22	5S11
24	21:48	0 N
31	15:48	5N06

Perigee/Apogee

dy	hr m		kilometers
9	15:38	p	367389
21	13:12	a	404357

PH	dy	hr mn	
☾	6	9:38	16♎17
●	13	5:01	23♑13
☽	20	21:03	1♉02
○	28	19:17	9♌06

Void of Course Moon

Last Aspect			☽ Ingress		
2 22:01	♂	△	♍	3	1:14
4 21:35	♀	□	♎	5	5:43
7 5:56	♀	⚹	♏	7	8:55
9 2:00	♇	⚹	♐	9	11:16
10 18:30	♆	□	♑	11	13:31
13 7:23	♇	☌	♒	13	16:45
14 9:29	☿	☌	♓	15	22:18
18 3:46	☉	⚹	♈	18	7:08
20 8:30	♇	□	♉	20	18:57
22 21:29	♇	△	♊	23	7:44
25 7:18	☿	△	♋	25	18:53
27 17:56	♇	☍	♌	28	2:55
30 1:54	☿	☍	♍	30	8:04

DAILY ASPECTARIAN

1 F	☽ ☍ ♃	0:07
	☉ ⋕ ☽	0:17
	☽ ⚼ ♆	1:23
	♀ ∥ ♇	2:56
	☽ △ ⚷	4:17
	☽ ⚼ ♀	5:27
	☽ ⋕ ♀	5:43
	☽ ⋕ ♇	5:52
	☽ □ ♅	7:27
	☿ ⚹ ♆	11:19
	☉ ⚻ ☽	15:56
	☽ ⚻ ⚳	17:19
2 Sa	☽ ⋕ ♄	0:29
	☽ ⋕ ♃	1:49
	♀ ⚼ ♅	2:23
	☽ ⚻ ♆	4:40
	☽ ⚻ ☿	7:03
	☽ ⚼ ⚷	7:31
	☽ △ ♀	11:25
	☽ ⚻ ♇	14:58
	☉ ⚹ ⚳	17:08
	☉ ⚼ ☽	21:08
	☽ △ ♂	22:01
3 Su	☽ ⚻ ♄	4:34
	☽ ⋕ ⚳	5:00
	☽ ⚻ ♃	7:06
	☽ ⚻ ⚷	10:16
	☽ △ ♅	13:13
	☽ ⚼ ☿	13:26
	☽ ∥ ♅	15:14
	☉ ∥ ♀	17:10
	☽ ⚼ ♇	17:38
	☽ ∥ ♂	22:23
4 M	☽ ☍ ⚳	0:02
	☽ ⚼ ♂	1:23
	☉ △ ☽	1:46
	♀ ⚺ ♇	2:20
	♃ ∠ ♆	6:59
	☽ ⚼ ♄	7:10
	☽ ☍ ♆	9:51
	☽ ⚼ ♃	9:53
	☽ ⚼ ♅	15:27
	☽ △ ☿	19:13
	☽ △ ♇	19:53
	☽ □ ♀	21:35
5 Tu	☿ ☌ ♇	0:59
	☽ ⋕ ♆	2:23
	☽ ⚻ ♂	4:21
	☽ ∥ ⚷	7:15
	☽ △ ♄	9:23
	☽ △ ♃	12:18
	☽ ☍ ⚷	14:34
	☽ ⚻ ♅	17:21
6 W	☽ ⚻ ⚳	5:07
	☿ ∥ ♀	7:01
	☉ □ ☽	9:38
	☊ D	9:45
	☉ ∥ ♇	13:17
	☽ ⚻ ♆	13:33
	☽ ⋕ ⚷	19:00
	♂ ♉	22:28
	☽ □ ♇	23:24
	☽ ∥ ♆	23:40
7 Th	☽ □ ☿	5:22
	☽ ⚹ ♀	5:56
	☽ ⚼ ⚳	7:11
	☽ ☍ ♂	9:16
	☽ □ ♄	12:55
	☽ ⚼ ♆	15:00
	☽ □ ♃	16:12
	☽ ⚻ ⚷	17:39
	☽ ☍ ♅	20:17
	☿ ∥ ♇	20:40
8 F	☿ ⚺ ♀	0:05
	☿ ∠ ⚳	0:32
	☽ ⋕ ♂	6:13
	☽ △ ⚳	9:02
	☽ ⋕ ♅	9:31
	☽ ∠ ♀	9:38
	☿ ♒	12:01
	☉ ∥ ☿	12:48
	☽ ∥ ⚳	15:01
	♀ ♑	15:42
	☉ ⚹ ☽	16:12
	☽ △ ♆	16:15
	☉ ⚹ ♆	16:54
	☽ ⚼ ⚷	18:53
9 Sa	☽ ⚹ ♇	2:00
	☿ □ ♂	2:46
	☽ ⚺ ♀	13:09
	☽ ⚻ ♂	13:18
	☽ ⚹ ☿	14:16
	☽ ⚹ ♄	15:39
	♀ △ ♂	15:54
	☽ ∥ ♃	17:56
	☉ ∠ ☽	19:12
	☽ ⚹ ♃	19:19
	☽ △ ⚷	20:00
	☽ ∥ ♄	20:29
	☽ ⚻ ♅	22:31
10 Su	☽ ∠ ♇	3:08
	☿ ☌ ♄	3:18
	☽ ∥ ☿	6:46
	☉ ∥ ☽	10:09
	☽ □ ⚳	12:24
	☽ ∥ ♇	14:26
	☽ ⚼ ♂	15:14
	☽ ∠ ♄	16:57
	☿ ∠ ♆	17:57
	☽ □ ♆	18:30
	☽ ∠ ☿	18:35
	☊ R	20:19
	♀ ⚺ ♄	20:40
	☽ ∠ ♃	20:50
	☽ ∥ ♀	21:35
	☉ ⚺ ☽	22:13
	☽ ⚼ ♅	23:37
11 M	☽ ⚺ ♇	4:19
	☽ △ ♂	17:17
	☿ ☌ ♃	17:21
	☿ ⚹ ⚷	17:24
	♃ ⚹ ⚷	17:49
	☽ ⚺ ♄	18:22
	☽ ☌ ♀	20:16
	☽ □ ⚷	22:25
	☽ ⚺ ♃	22:29
	☽ ⚺ ☿	23:03
12 Tu	☽ △ ♅	0:52
	♂ ∥ ♅	6:32
	☿ □ ♅	15:01
	☽ ⚹ ⚳	16:12
	♀ □ ⚷	21:05
	☽ ⚹ ♆	21:18
13 W	♀ ⚺ ♃	2:41
	☉ ☌ ☽	5:01
	☽ ☌ ♇	7:23
	♂ □ ♄	11:03
	☿ ∥ ♄	16:37
	☽ ∠ ⚳	18:41
	☽ ∥ ♀	19:49
	☽ ☌ ♄	22:12
	☽ □ ♂	22:31
	☽ ∠ ♆	23:18
	♂ ⋕ ⚳	23:19
14 Th	♀ △ ♅	0:23
	☽ ⚹ ⚷	2:03
	☽ ☌ ♃	2:56
	☽ ∥ ♇	3:27
	☽ □ ♅	4:30
	☽ ⚺ ♀	4:55
	♅ D	8:37
	☽ ☌ ☿	9:29
	☉ ∥ ☽	13:21
	☉ ☌ ♇	14:20
	☿ ∥ ♃	20:04
	☽ ⚺ ⚳	21:49
	♂ ∠ ♆	21:56
	☽ ∥ ♄	23:19
15 F	☽ ⚺ ♆	1:56
	☽ ∥ ♃	3:08
	☽ ∥ ☿	4:11
	☽ ∠ ⚷	4:46
	☽ ∠ ♀	10:27
	☽ ⚺ ♇	12:34
	☉ ⚺ ☽	14:22
	⚳ ⋕ ♅	19:36
16 Sa	☽ ⚺ ♄	4:34
	☽ ⚹ ♂	6:30
	☽ ⚺ ⚷	8:15
	☽ ⋕ ♂	8:58
	☽ ⚺ ♃	10:05
	☽ ⚹ ♅	10:45
	☽ ⋕ ♅	12:47
	☽ ∥ ⚳	13:25
	☽ ∠ ♇	16:19
	☽ ⚹ ♀	17:03
	☉ ∠ ☽	20:30
	☽ ⚺ ☿	23:34
17 Su	☽ ☌ ⚳	6:39
	☽ ∠ ♄	9:01
	☽ ☌ ♆	9:36
	☽ ∠ ♂	11:55
	☽ ∠ ♃	14:59
	☽ ∠ ♅	15:07
	☽ ⚹ ♇	20:57
	♃ □ ♅	22:51
18 M	☽ ∥ ♆	3:41
	☉ ⚹ ☽	3:46
	♂ ⚺ ⚷	6:45
	☽ ⋕ ⚷	8:10
	☽ ∠ ☿	8:17
	☽ ⚹ ♄	14:21
	☽ ☌ ⚷	17:50
	☽ ⚺ ♂	18:17
	☽ ⚺ ♅	20:21
	☽ ⚹ ♃	20:46
19 Tu	⚶ R	8:55
	☽ □ ♀	9:44
	☽ ⚹ ☿	17:55
	☽ ⚺ ⚳	19:05
	☽ ⚺ ♆	20:35
	☉ ♒	20:41
20 W	☽ ∥ ⚷	2:29
	☽ ⋕ ♆	6:55
	☿ ⚺ ⚳	7:13
	☽ □ ♇	8:30
	♄ ∠ ♆	16:59
	☿ ⚺ ♆	18:05
	♂ ☌ ♅	20:39
	☊ D	20:50
	☉ □ ☽	21:03
21 Th	☽ ∠ ⚳	2:16
	☽ ∠ ♆	2:57
	☽ □ ♄	3:01
	☽ ⚺ ⚷	6:10
	☽ ☌ ♅	8:38
	☽ ☌ ♂	9:10
	☽ □ ♃	10:16
	☽ ⋕ ⚳	18:44
22 F	☽ ∥ ♅	0:16
	☿ ∠ ⚷	0:48
	☿ ⋕ ♂	2:52
	⚳ ☌ ♆	3:39
	☉ ∥ ♄	4:55
	☽ △ ♀	5:29
	☽ ⋕ ☿	9:22
	☽ ⚹ ♆	9:28
	☽ ⚹ ⚳	9:38
	☽ ∥ ♂	10:38
	☽ ∠ ⚷	12:42
	☽ □ ☿	14:00
	⚳ ∠ ♄	17:25
	☽ △ ♇	21:29
23 Sa	♂ □ ♃	7:50
	☽ ⋕ ♃	9:37
	☉ ⋕ ☽	13:30
	☽ ⚼ ♀	15:20
	☉ △ ☽	15:28
	☽ ⋕ ♄	15:33
	☽ △ ♄	16:20
	☽ ⚹ ⚷	19:00
	☉ ∠ ♆	19:30
	♀ ⚹ ♆	19:50
	☽ ⚺ ♅	21:17
24 Su	☽ △ ♃	0:05
	☽ ⚺ ♂	0:28
	☉ ☌ ♄	3:03
	♀ ∥ ♇	3:29
	☽ ⚼ ♇	3:39
	♀ ⚹ ⚳	10:08
	☽ ⋕ ♀	14:15
	☉ ∠ ⚳	14:43
	☽ ⋕ ♇	14:52
	☽ □ ♆	21:37
	☊ R	21:50
	☽ ⚼ ♄	22:22
	☽ □ ⚳	23:24
	☉ ⚼ ☽	23:55
25 M	☽ ⚻ ♀	0:29
	☽ ∠ ♅	2:56
	☿ ⋕ ♅	4:57
	☽ ⚼ ♃	6:13
	☽ △ ☿	7:18
	☽ ∠ ♂	7:19
	☽ ⚻ ♇	9:13
	☉ ⚹ ⚷	10:30
26 Tu	☽ ⚻ ♄	3:39
	☽ □ ⚷	5:47
	☉ ⚻ ☽	7:25
	☽ ⚹ ♅	7:50
	☽ ⚻ ♃	11:34
	☉ □ ♅	12:49
	☽ ⚹ ♂	13:18
	☉ ∥ ♃	13:22
	☽ ⚼ ☿	13:57
	☿ ⚺ ♇	14:36
27 W	☽ △ ♆	6:59
	☽ △ ⚳	10:08
	☽ ☍ ♀	15:38
	☽ ☍ ♇	17:56
	☽ ⚻ ☿	19:11
28 Th	☽ ⚼ ♆	10:26
	☽ ☍ ♄	11:42
	☽ △ ⚷	13:22
	☽ ⚼ ⚳	14:11
	☽ ⋕ ♇	14:25
	☽ □ ♅	15:12
	♀ ☌ ♇	16:19
	☉ ☍ ☽	19:17
	☽ ☍ ♃	19:40
	☽ ⋕ ♀	20:59
	☽ □ ♂	22:33
29 F	☉ ☌ ♃	1:41
	☽ ⋕ ♄	12:15
	☽ ⚻ ♆	13:11
	☽ ⚼ ⚷	16:03
	☿ ⚺ ♀	17:20
	☽ ⚻ ⚳	17:30
	☽ ⋕ ♃	18:47
	☉ ⋕ ☽	22:53
	☽ ⚻ ♇	23:37
30 Sa	☽ ☍ ☿	1:54
	☽ ⚻ ♀	2:40
	☽ ∥ ♂	5:14
	⚳ ∠ ♅	5:32
	☿ R	15:53
	☽ ⚻ ♄	16:55
	☽ ⚻ ⚷	18:12
	☽ △ ♅	19:53
	☽ ∥ ♅	21:03
31 Su	☽ ⚻ ♃	1:02
	☽ ⚼ ♇	1:38
	☉ ⚻ ☽	3:52
	☽ △ ♂	4:58
	☽ ⚼ ♀	7:07
	☽ ⋕ ☿	8:34
	☽ ⋕ ⚳	9:16
	☽ ☍ ♆	17:10
	☽ ⚼ ♄	18:51
	☽ ⚼ ♅	21:36
	☽ ☍ ⚳	22:36

January 2021:Modify New York Stock Exchange Zone:-5

Sunday	Monday	Tuesday	Wednesday	Thursday	Friday	Saturday
					1 6:17AM ☿ ⚹ ♆	2 8:11PM ☽-> 0♍00
3	4 7:57PM ☿ ☌ ♇	5 12:40AM ☽-> 0♎00	6 5:25PM ♂-> 0♉00	7 3:52AM ☽-> 0♏00	8 6:59AM ☿-> 0♒00 10:40AM ♀-> 0♑00 11:52AM ☉ ⚹ ♆ 9:44PM ☿ □ ♂	9 6:14AM ☽-> 0♐00 10:52AM ♀ △ ♂ 10:16PM ☿ ☌ ♄
10	11 8:28AM ☽-> 0♑00 12:19PM ☿ ☌ ♃	12 9:59AM ☿ □ ♅ 11:59PM New Moon♑	13 5:59AM ♂ □ ♄ 11:42AM ☽-> 0♒00 7:21PM ♀ △ ♅	14 3:34AM ♅Direct 9:18AM ☉ ☌ ♇	15 5:16PM ☽-> 0♓00	16
17 5:49PM ♃ □ ♅	18 2:06AM ☽-> 0♈00	19 3:39PM ☉-> 0♒00	20 1:55PM ☽-> 0♉00 3:36PM ♂ ☌ ♅	21	22	23 2:42AM ☽-> 0♊00 2:46AM ♂ □ ♃ 2:48PM ♀ ⚹ ♆ 10:00PM ☉ ☌ ♄
24	25 1:50PM ☽-> 0♋00	26 7:47AM ☉ □ ♅	27 9:53PM ☽-> 0♌00	28 11:17AM ♀ ☌ ♇ 2:15PM Full Moon♌ 8:39PM ☉ ☌ ♃	29	30 3:01AM ☽-> 0♍00 10:51AM ☿ ℞26♒
31						

December 2020

S	M	T	W	T	F	S
		1	2	3	4	5
6	7	8	9	10	11	12
13	14	15	16	17	18	19
20	21	22	23	24	25	26
27	28	29	30	31		

February

S	M	T	W	T	F	S
	1	2	3	4	5	6
7	8	9	10	11	12	13
14	15	16	17	18	19	20
21	22	23	24	25	26	27
28						

February 2021

LONGITUDE

Day	Sid.Time	☉	☽	☽ 12 hour	Mean☊	True☊	☿	♀	♂	⚳	♃	♄	⚷	♅	♆	♇
	h m s	° ' "	° ' "	° ' "	° '	° '	° '	° '	° '	° '	° '	° '	° '	° '	° '	° '
1 M	8 45 41	12♒20 13	23♍16 11	0♎19 47	17♊12.9	18♊24.7	26♒19.4	29♑15.8	12♉32.9	22♓28.2	10♒03.5	5♒16.5	5♈54.9	6♉51.5	19♓16.1	25♑12.6
2 Tu	8 49 37	13 21 06	7♎24 23	14 29 32	17 09.7	18R 17.8	25R 58.7	0♒31.0	13 05.0	22 49.9	10 17.8	5 23.6	5 57.3	6 52.4	19 18.0	25 14.5
3 W	8 53 34	14 21 58	21 34 50	28 39 57	17 06.6	18 13.2	25 27.1	1 46.2	13 37.3	23 11.7	10 32.0	5 30.7	5 59.7	6 53.4	19 20.0	25 16.5
4 Th	8 57 30	15 22 49	5♏44 36	12♏48 37	17 03.4	18D 10.8	24 45.4	3 01.3	14 09.6	23 33.6	10 46.2	5 37.8	6 02.2	6 54.4	19 21.9	25 18.4
5 F	9 01 27	16 23 40	19 51 48	26 54 03	17 00.2	18 10.5	23 54.5	4 16.5	14 42.1	23 55.5	11 00.5	5 44.9	6 04.7	6 55.5	19 23.9	25 20.3
6 Sa	9 05 23	17 24 29	3♐55 16	10♐55 22	16 57.0	18 11.1	22 55.8	5 31.7	15 14.7	24 17.2	11 14.7	5 52.0	6 07.2	6 56.7	19 25.9	25 22.1
7 Su	9 09 20	18 25 18	17 54 16	24 51 50	16 53.9	18R 11.6	21 51.0	6 46.9	15 47.4	24 39.6	11 28.9	5 59.0	6 09.8	6 57.9	19 27.9	25 24.0
8 M	9 13 17	19 26 06	1♑47 58	8♑42 27	16 50.7	18 10.8	20 42.0	8 02.1	16 20.2	25 01.7	11 43.1	6 06.0	6 12.4	6 59.1	19 29.9	25 25.9
9 Tu	9 17 13	20 26 53	15 35 08	22 25 43	16 47.5	18 07.7	19 30.7	9 17.2	16 53.2	25 23.9	11 57.3	6 13.1	6 15.0	7 00.4	19 31.9	25 27.7
10 W	9 21 10	21 27 39	29 13 58	5♒59 33	16 44.3	18 01.8	18 19.2	10 32.4	17 26.2	25 46.2	12 11.5	6 20.1	6 17.7	7 01.8	19 34.0	25 29.6
11 Th	9 25 06	22 28 23	12♒42 12	19 21 37	16 41.2	17 53.1	17 09.4	11 47.5	17 59.4	26 08.5	12 25.7	6 27.0	6 20.4	7 03.2	19 36.1	25 31.4
12 F	9 29 03	23 29 06	25 57 30	2♓29 39	16 38.0	17 42.2	16 02.9	13 02.7	18 32.6	26 30.9	12 39.8	6 34.0	6 23.2	7 04.6	19 38.1	25 33.2
13 Sa	9 32 59	24 29 48	8♓57 51	15 22 00	16 34.8	17 29.9	15 01.2	14 17.8	19 06.0	26 53.4	12 54.0	6 40.9	6 26.0	7 06.1	19 40.2	25 35.0
14 Su	9 36 56	25 30 28	21 42 03	27 58 02	16 31.6	17 17.6	14 05.4	15 33.0	19 39.4	27 15.9	13 08.1	6 47.8	6 28.8	7 07.6	19 42.3	25 36.8
15 M	9 40 52	26 31 07	4♈10 06	10♈18 25	16 28.4	17 06.2	13 16.4	16 48.1	20 13.0	27 38.4	13 22.2	6 54.7	6 31.6	7 09.2	19 44.5	25 38.6
16 Tu	9 44 49	27 31 44	16 23 17	22 25 05	16 25.3	16 56.9	12 34.8	18 03.2	20 46.6	28 01.0	13 36.3	7 01.6	6 34.5	7 10.8	19 46.6	25 40.4
17 W	9 48 46	28 32 19	28 24 13	4♉21 12	16 22.1	16 50.1	12 00.8	19 18.3	21 20.3	28 23.7	13 50.3	7 08.4	6 37.4	7 12.5	19 48.7	25 42.1
18 Th	9 52 42	29 32 53	10♉16 35	16 10 59	16 18.9	16 46.0	11 34.6	20 33.4	21 54.1	28 46.4	14 04.3	7 15.2	6 40.3	7 14.2	19 50.9	25 43.8
19 F	9 56 39	0♓33 25	22 05 02	27 59 23	16 15.7	16D 44.2	11 16.1	21 48.5	22 28.0	29 09.2	14 18.3	7 22.0	6 43.3	7 16.0	19 53.1	25 45.5
20 Sa	10 00 35	1 33 55	3♊54 45	9♊51 48	16 12.6	16 43.9	11 05.1	23 03.5	23 02.0	29 32.0	14 32.3	7 28.8	6 46.3	7 17.8	19 55.2	25 47.2
21 Su	10 04 32	2 34 23	15 51 16	21 53 49	16 09.4	16R 44.1	11D 01.4	24 18.6	23 36.0	29 54.8	14 46.3	7 35.5	6 49.3	7 19.7	19 57.4	25 48.9
22 M	10 08 28	3 34 49	28 00 06	4♋10 45	16 06.2	16 43.6	11 04.5	25 33.6	24 10.1	0♈17.7	15 00.2	7 42.2	6 52.4	7 21.6	19 59.6	25 50.6
23 Tu	10 12 25	4 35 14	10♋26 18	16 47 16	16 03.0	16 41.5	11 14.1	26 48.7	24 44.3	0 40.7	15 14.1	7 48.8	6 55.5	7 23.5	20 01.8	25 52.2
24 W	10 16 21	5 35 37	23 14 01	29 46 51	15 59.8	16 36.9	11 29.8	28 03.7	25 18.6	1 03.7	15 27.9	7 55.5	6 58.6	7 25.5	20 04.1	25 53.9
25 Th	10 20 18	6 35 58	6♌25 54	13♌11 11	15 56.7	16 29.5	11 51.2	29 18.7	25 52.9	1 26.7	15 41.7	8 02.1	7 01.7	7 27.5	20 06.3	25 55.5
26 F	10 24 15	7 36 16	20 02 33	26 59 41	15 53.5	16 19.6	12 17.9	0♓33.7	26 27.3	1 49.8	15 55.5	8 08.6	7 04.8	7 29.6	20 08.5	25 57.1
27 Sa	10 28 11	8 36 34	4♍02 08	11♍09 18	15 50.3	16 07.9	12 49.6	1 48.7	27 01.8	2 12.9	16 09.2	8 15.1	7 08.0	7 31.7	20 10.8	25 58.6
28 Su	10 32 08	9♓36 49	18 20 25	25 34 39	15♊47.1	15♊55.6	13♒25.8	3♓03.7	27♉36.3	2♈36.0	16♒23.0	8♒21.6	7♈11.2	7♉33.8	20♓13.0	26♑00.2

1st of Month

Julian Day # 2459246.5
Obliquity 23°26'14"
SVP 4♓58'10"
GC 27♐08.0
Eris 23♈29.7

Day	⚴
1	18♒17.4
6	19 59.2
11	21 41.0
16	23 22.4
21	25 03.4
26	26 43.8

Day	⚵
1	13♐16.8
6	14 34.4
11	15 48.6
16	16 59.0
21	18 05.3
26	19 07.2

Day	⚶
1	20♍45.9R
6	20 10.1R
11	19 23.1R
16	18 25.8R
21	17 19.9R
26	16 07.3R

DECLINATION and LATITUDE

Day	☉ Decl	☽ Decl	☽ Lat	☽12h Decl	☿ Decl	☿ Lat	♀ Decl	♀ Lat	♂ Decl	♂ Lat	⚳ Decl	⚳ Lat	♃ Decl	♃ Lat	♄ Decl	♄ Lat
1 M	17S06	7N20	5N05	4N27	10S46	2N06	20S55	0S37	16N50	1N17	10S38	8S20	18S14	0S32	19S21	0S25
2 Tu	16 49	1 29	4 49	1S29	10 37	2 23	20 41	0 39	16 60	1 18	10 28	8 18	18 10	0 32	19 20	0 25
3 W	16 31	4S27	4 16	7 22	10 32	2 39	20 26	0 42	17 10	1 18	10 18	8 17	18 06	0 32	19 18	0 26
4 Th	16 13	10 11	3 27	12 52	10 32	2 54	20 11	0 44	17 20	1 19	10 07	8 15	18 03	0 32	19 17	0 26
5 F	15 55	15 22	2 26	17 39	10 37	3 07	19 56	0 46	17 30	1 19	9 57	8 13	17 59	0 32	19 15	0 26
6 Sa	15 37	19 42	1 16	21 26	10 45	3 18	19 40	0 48	17 40	1 20	9 47	8 12	17 55	0 32	19 13	0 26
7 Su	15 18	22 52	0 02	23 56	10 57	3 28	19 23	0 50	17 50	1 20	9 37	8 10	17 51	0 32	19 12	0 26
8 M	14 59	24 38	1S12	24 56	11 12	3 35	19 05	0 52	18 00	1 20	9 26	8 08	17 47	0 32	19 10	0 26
9 Tu	14 40	24 51	2 21	24 24	11 30	3 39	18 48	0 54	18 10	1 21	9 16	8 07	17 43	0 32	19 08	0 26
10 W	14 21	23 34	3 20	22 25	11 49	3 41	18 29	0 56	18 20	1 21	9 06	8 05	17 40	0 33	19 07	0 26
11 Th	14 01	20 57	4 08	19 14	12 10	3 41	18 10	0 57	18 30	1 21	8 56	8 04	17 36	0 33	19 05	0 26
12 F	13 41	17 16	4 41	15 07	12 32	3 39	17 51	0 59	18 39	1 22	8 45	8 02	17 32	0 33	19 03	0 26
13 Sa	13 21	12 49	4 59	10 24	12 55	3 34	17 31	1 01	18 49	1 22	8 35	8 01	17 28	0 33	19 02	0 26
14 Su	13 01	7 54	5 01	5 21	13 17	3 28	17 10	1 03	18 58	1 23	8 25	7 59	17 24	0 33	18 60	0 26
15 M	12 41	2 46	4 49	0 11	13 38	3 20	16 49	1 04	19 08	1 23	8 14	7 58	17 20	0 33	18 58	0 26
16 Tu	12 20	2N23	4 24	4N54	13 59	3 11	16 28	1 06	19 17	1 23	8 04	7 56	17 16	0 33	18 57	0 27
17 W	11 59	7 22	3 47	9 45	14 18	3 00	16 06	1 07	19 26	1 24	7 54	7 55	17 12	0 33	18 55	0 27
18 Th	11 38	12 02	3 01	14 12	14 36	2 49	15 43	1 09	19 35	1 24	7 43	7 53	17 08	0 33	18 53	0 27
19 F	11 16	16 14	2 07	18 07	14 53	2 37	15 21	1 10	19 44	1 24	7 33	7 52	17 04	0 33	18 52	0 27
20 Sa	10 55	19 49	1 08	21 20	15 08	2 24	14 57	1 12	19 53	1 24	7 23	7 51	17 00	0 34	18 50	0 27
21 Su	10 33	22 36	0 05	23 39	15 21	2 12	14 34	1 13	20 02	1 25	7 12	7 49	16 56	0 34	18 48	0 27
22 M	10 12	24 25	0N59	24 53	15 33	1 59	14 10	1 14	20 11	1 25	7 02	7 48	16 52	0 34	18 47	0 27
23 Tu	9 50	25 03	2 02	24 54	15 43	1 46	13 45	1 15	20 20	1 25	6 52	7 47	16 48	0 34	18 45	0 27
24 W	9 28	24 24	3 00	23 34	15 51	1 33	13 20	1 16	20 28	1 25	6 41	7 45	16 44	0 34	18 43	0 27
25 Th	9 05	22 23	3 51	20 53	15 57	1 20	12 55	1 17	20 37	1 26	6 31	7 44	16 40	0 34	18 42	0 27
26 F	8 43	19 04	4 30	16 57	16 02	1 07	12 30	1 18	20 45	1 26	6 21	7 43	16 36	0 34	18 40	0 27
27 Sa	8 20	14 35	4 54	11 59	16 05	0 55	12 04	1 19	20 53	1 26	6 10	7 41	16 32	0 34	18 39	0 28
28 Su	7S58	9N13	5N00	6N17	16S07	0N42	11S38	1S20	21N01	1N26	6S00	7S40	16S28	0S35	18S37	0S28

Day	⚷ Decl	⚷ Lat	♅ Decl	♅ Lat	♆ Decl	♆ Lat	♇ Decl	♇ Lat
1	4N36	2N27	13N23	0S26	5S14	1S04	22S19	1S14
6	4 40	2 26	13 25	0 26	5 10	1 04	22 17	1 15
11	4 44	2 25	13 28	0 26	5 06	1 04	22 16	1 15
16	4 49	2 25	13 30	0 26	5 02	1 04	22 15	1 16
21	4 55	2 24	13 33	0 26	4 58	1 04	22 14	1 17
26	5N00	2N23	13N37	0S25	4S53	1S04	22S13	1S17

Day	⚴ Decl	⚴ Lat	⚵ Decl	⚵ Lat	⚶ Decl	⚶ Lat	Eris Decl	Eris Lat
1	0N07	16N13	11S39	10N49	11N41	8N44	1S34	11S29
6	0 20	15 55	11 33	11 04	12 17	9 08	1 33	11 29
11	0 34	15 39	11 25	11 19	12 56	9 30	1 32	11 28
16	0 51	15 23	11 16	11 35	13 38	9 51	1 31	11 27
21	1 08	15 09	11 05	11 52	14 21	10 10	1 29	11 27
26	1N27	14N54	10S51	12N10	15N05	10N26	1S28	11S26

Moon Phenomena

Max/0 Decl

dy	hr mn	
2	6:00	0 S
8	15:32	24S57
15	12:51	0 N
23	0:13	25N03

Perigee/Apogee

dy	hr m		kilometers
3	19:04	p	370116
18	10:23	a	404465

Max/0 Lat

dy	hr mn	
7	0:30	0 S
13	15:46	5S02
21	1:46	0 N
27	20:03	5N00

PH	dy	hr mn	
☾	4	17:38	16♏08
●	11	19:07	23♒17
☽	19	18:48	1♊21
○	27	8:18	8♍57

Void of Course Moon

Last Aspect			☽ Ingress	
1 11:11	♀	△	♎	1 11:26
3 6:16	☿	△	♏	3 14:16
5 9:21	♇	⚹	♐	5 17:18
7 6:17	☿	⚹	♑	7 20:53
9 17:23	♇	☌	♒	10 1:21
11 19:07	☉	☌	♓	12 7:24
14 7:30	♇	⚹	♈	14 15:55
17 0:18	☉	⚹	♉	17 3:13
19 7:29	♇	△	♊	19 16:05
21 18:40	♀	△	♋	22 3:54
24 4:55	♇	☍	♌	24 12:24
26 11:33	♂	□	♍	26 17:08
28 15:59	♂	△	♎	28 19:18

DAILY ASPECTARIAN

1 M ☽⚼♃ 3:06, ☽△♇ 3:19, ☽⚻☿ 5:06, ☉⚼☽ 7:27, ☽⚼♂ 7:34, ☽⋕♆ 8:47, ☉□♂ 10:35, ☽△♀ 11:11, ☽∥⚷ 11:21, ♀ ♒ 14:07, ☉⋕♂ 14:13, ☽△♄ 20:34, ☽☍⚷ 21:32, ☽⚻♅ 23:06

2 Tu ☽△♃ 4:59, ☽⚼☿ 5:52, ☽⚻♂ 10:00, ☉△☽ 10:51, ☽⚻♆ 20:11

3 W ☽⋕⚷ 0:42, ☽⚻⚳ 2:48, ☽∥♆ 3:04, ☽□♇ 6:16, ☽△☿ 6:16, ☿⚺♇ 6:23, ☽□♀ 18:56, ☽⚼♆ 21:39, ☽∥⚳ 23:46, ☽□♄ 23:48

4 Th ☽⚻⚷ 0:30, ☽∥☿ 1:35, ☽☍♅ 1:59, ☽⚼⚳ 4:54, ☽□♃ 8:41, ☽⋕♅ 14:35, ☽☍♂ 14:52, ☉□☽ 17:38, ☊ D 17:42, ☽△♆ 23:12, ☿⚺⚳ 23:40

5 F ☽⚼⚷ 2:05, ♀∠♆ 2:25, ☉∥☽ 2:38, ☽□☿ 6:28, ☽△⚳ 7:06, ☽⚹♇ 9:21, ☽⋕♂ 11:38, ☽∥♃ 13:37, ☽∥♄ 21:05, ☽∥♀ 23:48

6 Sa ☽⚹♀ 3:01, ☽⚹♄ 3:21, ☽△⚷ 3:47, ☽⚻♅ 5:11, ♀☌♄ 7:08, ☽∠♇ 11:04, ♀⚹⚷ 11:44, ☽⚹♃ 12:46, ☽∥♇ 18:49, ☽⚻♂ 20:13

7 Su ☊ R 0:32, ☉⚹☽ 0:58, ♂⋕♃ 1:20, ☽□♆ 2:42, ♀□♅ 3:34, ☽∠♄ 5:21, ☽⚹☿ 6:17, ☽⚼♅ 7:00, ☽∠♀ 7:20, ☽□⚳ 11:58, ☽⚺♇ 12:57, ☿∠⚷ 13:56, ☽∠♃ 15:03, ♀∥♄ 17:23, ☽⚼♂ 23:10

8 M ☉⚺♆ 1:33, ☉∠☽ 4:56, ☽∠☿ 6:14, ☽⚺♄ 7:32, ☽□⚷ 7:40, ☽△♅ 9:01, ☽⚺♀ 11:55, ☉☌☿ 13:49, ☽⚺♃ 17:33, ☿⚺♆ 23:36

9 Tu ☽△♂ 2:22, ⚳⚹♇ 4:28, ☽⚺☿ 6:20, ☽⚹♆ 6:56, ☉⚺☽ 9:12, ♄⚹⚷ 11:00, ☽☌♇ 17:23, ☽⚹⚳ 17:43, ☉∠⚷ 19:54

10 W ♀∠⚳ 6:17, ♀⋕♂ 7:45, ☽∠♆ 9:29, ☿□♂ 12:17, ☽⚹⚷ 12:35, ☽☌♄ 12:43, ☽∥♇ 13:17, ☽□♅ 13:52, ☽∠⚳ 21:07, ☽☌♀ 22:12, ☽☌♃ 23:30

11 Th ☽☌☿ 7:23, ☽□♂ 9:56, ☽⚺♆ 12:28, ☽∥♄ 13:02, ♀☌♃ 15:01, ☽∠⚷ 15:39, ☽⋕♂ 15:58, ☉☌☽ 19:07, ☽∥♀ 20:18, ☽∥♃ 22:26, ☽⚺♇ 23:16

12 F ☽⚺⚳ 1:03, ☉⋕♅ 15:33, ☽⚺⚷ 19:16, ☽⚺♄ 19:43, ☽⚹♅ 20:32, ☽⋕♅ 20:39, ☉∥☽ 21:04, ☽∥☿ 23:34

13 Sa ☽∠♇ 3:02, ♀∥♃ 4:03, ☽⚺♃ 7:30, ☿☌♀ 7:49, ☽⚺☿ 10:33, ☽⚺♀ 11:05, ☉∥☿ 15:03, ☽⚹♂ 19:56, ☽☌♆ 20:12, ☽∥⚳ 21:30

14 Su ☽∠♄ 0:11, ☽∠♅ 0:49, ♂⚹♆ 2:14, ☉⚺♇ 2:35, ♂⋕♄ 3:26, ☽⚹♇ 7:30, ☉⚺☽ 7:55, ☽☌⚳ 10:59, ☽∠♃ 12:34, ☽∠☿ 13:16, ☽∥♆ 13:23, ☿⋕♅ 14:02, ☽⋕⚷ 14:34, ☽∠♀ 18:53, ☿☌♃ 21:41

15 M ☽∠♂ 2:08, ☽☌⚷ 4:37, ☽⚹♄ 5:24, ☽⚺♅ 5:50, ☿∠⚳ 13:51, ☉∠☽ 15:41, ☽⚹☿ 16:51, ☽⚹♃ 18:23

16 Tu ☽⚹♀ 3:41, ☽⚺♆ 6:45, ☽⚺♂ 9:09, ☽∥⚷ 11:39, ☽⋕♆ 12:34, ☉⚺⚳ 18:33, ☽□♇ 18:34, ☽⚺⚳ 23:59

17 W ☉⚹☽ 0:18, ☽⋕⚳ 2:32, ♀⚺♆ 10:01, ☽∠♆ 12:58, ♂∠⚷ 13:18, ☽⚺⚷ 16:40, ☽□♄ 17:49, ☽☌♅ 17:49, ♄□♅ 19:10, ☉⋕☽ 21:59

18 Th ☽□☿ 2:34, ☽∠⚳ 7:20, ☽□♃ 7:52, ☽∥♅ 8:10, ☉ ♓ 10:45, ☽⋕☿ 15:19, ☽⋕♀ 19:04, ☽⚹♆ 19:31, ♀∠⚷ 22:17, ☽∠⚷ 23:16, ☽□♀ 23:22

19 F ☽☌♂ 0:49, ☽⋕♃ 5:05, ☽△♇ 7:29, ☽⚹⚳ 14:50, ☽⋕♄ 16:55, ☿∥♀ 17:19, ☊ D 18:36, ☉□☽ 18:48, ♀□♂ 23:05

20 Sa ☽∥♂ 0:31, ⚳∠♃ 0:52, ☽⚹⚷ 5:48, ☽⚺♅ 6:51, ☽△♄ 7:16, ☽⚼♇ 13:53, ☽△☿ 14:21, ☽⋕♇ 20:16, ☽△♃ 21:48

21 Su ☿ D 0:53, ☊ R 1:47, ⚳ ♈ 5:24, ☽□♆ 8:11, ☽∠♅ 12:53, ☽⚼♄ 13:30, ☽⚺♂ 16:07, ☽△♀ 18:40, ☽⚻♇ 19:46, ☽⚼☿ 20:12

22 M ☽⚼♃ 3:59, ☽□⚳ 4:37, ♀⚺♇ 5:32, ☉△☽ 11:48, ♆⋕⚷ 12:24, ☽□⚷ 17:15, ☽⚹♅ 18:10, ☽⚻♄ 18:57, ☽∠♂ 22:36

23 Tu ☽⚻☿ 1:33, ☽⚼♀ 2:54, ☽⚻♃ 9:15, ♀⋕♅ 10:07, ☽△♆ 18:07, ☉⚼☽ 18:42

24 W ☽⚹♂ 4:00, ☽☍♇ 4:55, ☽⚻♀ 9:48, ☽△⚳ 14:45, ☽⚼♆ 21:37

25 Th ☉⚻☽ 0:19, ☽△⚷ 1:04, ☽⋕♇ 1:27, ☽□♅ 1:50, ♂△♇ 1:53, ☽☍♄ 2:53, ☽☍☿ 9:57, ☉⚺⚷ 10:48, ♀ ♓ 13:13, ☽∥♂ 13:21, ☽☍♃ 16:41, ☽⚼⚳ 18:14, ☉⚹♅ 21:14

26 F ☽⚻♆ 0:10, ☽⋕♄ 2:22, ☽⚼⚷ 3:33, ☽⚻♇ 10:14, ☽□♂ 11:33, ☽⋕♃ 14:02, ☉⚺♄ 14:26, ☽⋕☿ 16:35, ☽☍♀ 19:51, ☽⚻⚳ 20:49

27 Sa ☽∥♅ 4:33, ☽⚻⚷ 5:15, ☽△♅ 5:55, ☽⚻♄ 7:11, ☉☍☽ 8:18, ♀⚺⚳ 11:11, ☽⚼♇ 11:43, ☽⋕♀ 12:41, ☽⚻☿ 15:26, ☽⚻♃ 20:41

28 Su ☽☍♆ 3:08, ☉⋕☽ 5:32, ☽⚼♅ 7:02, ☽⚼♄ 8:24, ☽△♇ 12:44, ☽⋕⚳ 13:31, ☽△♂ 15:59, ☽∥⚷ 16:55, ☽⚼☿ 17:31, ☽⋕♆ 17:44, ☽⚼♃ 21:55

February 2021:Modify New York Stock Exchange Zone:-5

Sunday	Monday	Tuesday	Wednesday	Thursday	Friday	Saturday
	1 5:34AM ☉ □ ♂ 6:24AM ☽-> 0♎00 9:04AM ♀-> 0♒00	2	3 9:13AM ☽-> 0♏00	4	5 12:15PM ☽-> 0♐00	6 2:06AM ♀ ☌ ♄ 10:32PM ♀ □ ♅
7 3:50PM ☽-> 0♑00	8 8:46AM ☉ ☌ ☿	9 8:19PM ☽-> 0♒00	10 7:14AM ♂ □ ☿	11 9:59AM ♀ ☌ ♃ 2:04PM New Moon♒	12 2:22AM ☽-> 0♓00	13 2:47AM ♀ ☌ ☿ 9:11PM ♂ ⚹ ♆
14 10:53AM ☽-> 0♈00 4:38PM ♃ ☌ ☿	15	16 10:10PM ☽-> 0♉00	17 2:07PM ♄ □ ♅	18 5:43AM ☉-> 0♓00	19 11:02AM ☽-> 0♊00 6:03PM ♀ □ ♂	20 7:50PM ☿ Direct
21 10:51PM ☽-> 0♋00	22	23	24 7:21AM ☽-> 0♌00 8:50PM ♂ △ ♇	25 8:10AM ♀-> 0♓00 4:12PM ☉ ⚹ ♅	26 12:06PM ☽-> 0♍00	27 3:16AM Full Moon♍
28 2:15PM ☽-> 0♎00						

January

S	M	T	W	T	F	S
					1	2
3	4	5	6	7	8	9
10	11	12	13	14	15	16
17	18	19	20	21	22	23
24	25	26	27	28	29	30
31						

March

S	M	T	W	T	F	S
	1	2	3	4	5	6
7	8	9	10	11	12	13
14	15	16	17	18	19	20
21	22	23	24	25	26	27
28	29	30	31			

LONGITUDE

March 2021

Day	Sid.Time	☉	☽	☽ 12 hour	Mean ☊	True ☊	☿	♀	♂	⚳	♃	♄	⚷	♅	♆	♇
	h m s	° ' "	° ' "	° ' "	° '	° '	° '	° '	° '	° '	° '	° '	° '	° '	° '	° '
1 M	10 36 04	10♓37 02	2♎51 08	10♎08 55	15♊44.0	15♊43.9	14♒06.2	4♓18.6	28♉10.8	2♈59.2	16♒36.6	8♒28.0	7♈14.4	7♉36.0	20♓15.2	26♑01.7
2 Tu	10 40 01	11 37 14	17 27 07	24 44 54	15 40.8	15R 34.3	14 50.6	5 33.6	28 45.5	3 22.4	16 50.2	8 34.4	7 17.6	7 38.2	20 17.5	26 03.3
3 W	10 43 57	12 37 24	2♏01 29	9♏16 15	15 37.6	15 27.3	15 38.7	6 48.5	29 20.2	3 45.7	17 03.8	8 40.8	7 20.9	7 40.5	20 19.8	26 04.7
4 Th	10 47 54	13 37 33	16 28 39	23 38 18	15 34.4	15 23.2	16 30.1	8 03.5	29 54.9	4 08.9	17 17.4	8 47.1	7 24.2	7 42.8	20 22.0	26 06.2
5 F	10 51 50	14 37 41	0♐44 55	7♐48 21	15 31.2	15 21.5	17 24.7	9 18.4	0♊29.7	4 32.3	17 30.9	8 53.4	7 27.4	7 45.2	20 24.3	26 07.7
6 Sa	10 55 47	15 37 46	14 48 30	21 45 24	15 28.1	15 21.2	18 22.2	10 33.3	1 04.6	4 55.6	17 44.3	8 59.6	7 30.8	7 47.5	20 26.6	26 09.1
7 Su	10 59 44	16 37 51	28 39 04	5♑29 38	15 24.9	15 21.0	19 22.5	11 48.2	1 39.5	5 19.0	17 57.8	9 05.8	7 34.1	7 50.0	20 28.8	26 10.5
8 M	11 03 40	17 37 54	12♑17 11	19 01 48	15 21.7	15 19.6	20 25.4	13 03.1	2 14.5	5 42.4	18 11.1	9 11.9	7 37.4	7 52.4	20 31.1	26 11.9
9 Tu	11 07 37	18 37 55	25 43 36	2♒22 38	15 18.5	15 15.8	21 30.7	14 18.0	2 49.5	6 05.9	18 24.4	9 18.0	7 40.8	7 54.9	20 33.4	26 13.3
10 W	11 11 33	19 37 54	8♒58 57	15 32 31	15 15.4	15 09.0	22 38.2	15 32.9	3 24.6	6 29.3	18 37.7	9 24.0	7 44.2	7 57.4	20 35.7	26 14.6
11 Th	11 15 30	20 37 52	22 03 22	28 31 24	15 12.2	14 59.2	23 47.9	16 47.7	3 59.7	6 52.9	18 50.9	9 30.0	7 47.6	8 00.0	20 37.9	26 16.0
12 F	11 19 26	21 37 48	4♓56 36	11♓18 52	15 09.0	14 47.1	24 59.7	18 02.6	4 34.8	7 16.4	19 04.1	9 36.0	7 51.0	8 02.6	20 40.2	26 17.3
13 Sa	11 23 23	22 37 42	17 38 10	23 54 27	15 05.8	14 33.4	26 13.3	19 17.4	5 10.1	7 39.9	19 17.2	9 41.9	7 54.4	8 05.2	20 42.5	26 18.6
14 Su	11 27 19	23 37 34	0♈07 42	6♈17 57	15 02.6	14 19.5	27 28.9	20 32.2	5 45.3	8 03.5	19 30.2	9 47.7	7 57.8	8 07.9	20 44.8	26 19.8
15 M	11 31 16	24 37 24	12 25 15	18 29 46	14 59.5	14 06.5	28 46.1	21 47.1	6 20.7	8 27.1	19 43.2	9 53.5	8 01.3	8 10.6	20 47.1	26 21.0
16 Tu	11 35 13	25 37 12	24 31 38	0♉31 08	14 56.3	13 55.6	0♓05.1	23 01.8	6 56.0	8 50.7	19 56.2	9 59.2	8 04.7	8 13.3	20 49.3	26 22.2
17 W	11 39 09	26 36 58	6♉28 34	12 24 17	14 53.1	13 47.3	1 25.7	24 16.6	7 31.4	9 14.4	20 09.0	10 04.8	8 08.2	8 16.1	20 51.6	26 23.4
18 Th	11 43 06	27 36 41	18 18 44	24 12 23	14 49.9	13 42.0	2 47.9	25 31.4	8 06.9	9 38.1	20 21.8	10 10.5	8 11.7	8 18.9	20 53.9	26 24.6
19 F	11 47 02	28 36 23	0♊05 46	5♊59 30	14 46.8	13 39.2	4 11.7	26 46.1	8 42.3	10 01.7	20 34.6	10 16.0	8 15.1	8 21.7	20 56.1	26 25.7
20 Sa	11 50 59	29 36 02	11 54 10	17 50 27	14 43.6	13D 38.4	5 36.9	28 00.8	9 17.9	10 25.5	20 47.2	10 21.5	8 18.6	8 24.5	20 58.4	26 26.8
21 Su	11 54 55	0♈35 40	23 49 00	29 50 32	14 40.4	13R 38.6	7 03.6	29 15.5	9 53.4	10 49.2	20 59.8	10 26.9	8 22.1	8 27.4	21 00.6	26 27.9
22 M	11 58 52	1 35 14	5♋55 44	12♋05 17	14 37.2	13 38.7	8 31.7	0♈30.2	10 29.0	11 12.9	21 12.4	10 32.3	8 25.6	8 30.3	21 02.9	26 29.0
23 Tu	12 02 48	2 34 47	18 19 49	24 39 58	14 34.0	13 37.5	10 01.3	1 44.9	11 04.6	11 36.7	21 24.9	10 37.6	8 29.1	8 33.2	21 05.1	26 30.0
24 W	12 06 45	3 34 17	1♌06 16	7♌39 09	14 30.9	13 34.3	11 32.2	2 59.5	11 40.3	12 00.4	21 37.3	10 42.8	8 32.6	8 36.2	21 07.4	26 31.0
25 Th	12 10 42	4 33 45	14 18 57	21 05 51	14 27.7	13 28.7	13 04.6	4 14.2	12 16.0	12 24.2	21 49.6	10 48.0	8 36.2	8 39.2	21 09.6	26 32.0
26 F	12 14 38	5 33 11	27 59 53	5♍00 53	14 24.5	13 20.8	14 38.3	5 28.8	12 51.7	12 48.0	22 01.8	10 53.1	8 39.7	8 42.2	21 11.8	26 32.9
27 Sa	12 18 35	6 32 34	12♍08 32	19 22 14	14 21.3	13 11.2	16 13.3	6 43.4	13 27.5	13 11.8	22 14.0	10 58.2	8 43.2	8 45.2	21 14.1	26 33.8
28 Su	12 22 31	7 31 56	26 41 17	4♎04 45	14 18.2	13 00.8	17 49.8	7 57.9	14 03.2	13 35.6	22 26.1	11 03.2	8 46.7	8 48.3	21 16.3	26 34.7
29 M	12 26 28	8 31 15	11♎31 36	19 00 41	14 15.0	12 50.9	19 27.6	9 12.5	14 39.0	13 59.4	22 38.1	11 08.1	8 50.2	8 51.3	21 18.5	26 35.6
30 Tu	12 30 24	9 30 32	26 30 51	4♏00 53	14 11.8	12 42.6	21 06.8	10 27.0	15 14.9	14 23.2	22 50.1	11 12.9	8 53.7	8 54.4	21 20.7	26 36.4
31 W	12 34 21	10♈29 47	11♏29 42	18 56 17	14♊08.6	12♊36.7	22♓47.3	11♈41.5	15♊50.7	14♈47.0	23♒01.9	11♒17.7	8♈57.3	8♉57.6	21♓22.8	26♑37.3

1st of Month

Julian Day #
2459274.5
Obliquity
23°26'14"
SVP 4♓58'07"
GC 27♐08.1
Eris 23♈40.0

Day	⚴
1	27♒43.7
6	29 22.9
11	1♓01.3
16	2 38.5
21	4 14.6
26	5 49.3
31	7 22.5

Day	⚵
1	19♐42.1
6	20 36.2
11	21 24.9
16	22 07.7
21	22 44.4
26	23 14.4
31	23 37.5

Day	⚶
1	15♍21.6R
6	14 03.3R
11	12 44.8R
16	11 29.0R
21	10 18.5R
26	9 15.5R
31	8 21.9R

DECLINATION and LATITUDE

Day	☉ Decl	☽ Decl	☽ Lat	☽ 12h Decl	☿ Decl	☿ Lat	♀ Decl	♀ Lat	♂ Decl	♂ Lat	⚳ Decl	⚳ Lat	♃ Decl	♃ Lat	♄ Decl	♄ Lat
1 M	7S35	3N16	4N47	0N11	16S06	0N31	11S11	1S21	21N09	1N26	5S50	7S39	16S24	0S35	18S35	0S28
2 Tu	7 12	2S55	4 16	5S58	16 05	0 19	10 44	1 22	21 17	1 27	5 40	7 38	16 20	0 35	18 34	0 28
3 W	6 49	8 56	3 27	11 46	16 01	0 08	10 17	1 23	21 25	1 27	5 29	7 37	16 16	0 35	18 32	0 28
4 Th	6 26	14 26	2 26	16 52	15 56	0S03	9 50	1 23	21 33	1 27	5 19	7 35	16 12	0 35	18 31	0 28
5 F	6 03	19 04	1 16	20 57	15 50	0 14	9 22	1 24	21 40	1 27	5 09	7 34	16 08	0 35	18 29	0 28
6 Sa	5 40	22 31	0 03	23 45	15 42	0 24	8 55	1 24	21 48	1 27	4 58	7 33	16 04	0 35	18 28	0 28
7 Su	5 17	24 35	1S10	25 04	15 32	0 33	8 27	1 25	21 55	1 27	4 48	7 32	16 00	0 35	18 26	0 28
8 M	4 53	25 09	2 17	24 51	15 21	0 43	7 58	1 25	22 02	1 28	4 38	7 31	15 56	0 36	18 25	0 28
9 Tu	4 30	24 12	3 16	23 13	15 09	0 52	7 30	1 26	22 09	1 28	4 28	7 30	15 52	0 36	18 23	0 29
10 W	4 06	21 55	4 03	20 20	14 55	1 00	7 01	1 26	22 16	1 28	4 17	7 28	15 49	0 36	18 22	0 29
11 Th	3 43	18 31	4 37	16 29	14 40	1 08	6 32	1 26	22 23	1 28	4 07	7 27	15 45	0 36	18 20	0 29
12 F	3 19	14 17	4 56	11 56	14 23	1 16	6 03	1 26	22 30	1 28	3 57	7 26	15 41	0 36	18 19	0 29
13 Sa	2 56	9 29	4 60	6 57	14 05	1 23	5 34	1 26	22 36	1 28	3 47	7 25	15 37	0 36	18 17	0 29
14 Su	2 32	4 22	4 49	1 46	13 45	1 30	5 04	1 26	22 43	1 28	3 36	7 24	15 33	0 36	18 16	0 29
15 M	2 08	0N50	4 25	3N25	13 25	1 37	4 35	1 26	22 49	1 28	3 26	7 23	15 29	0 36	18 14	0 29
16 Tu	1 44	5 57	3 49	8 25	13 03	1 43	4 05	1 26	22 55	1 28	3 16	7 22	15 25	0 37	18 13	0 29
17 W	1 21	10 47	3 03	13 03	12 39	1 48	3 35	1 26	23 01	1 28	3 06	7 21	15 21	0 37	18 11	0 29
18 Th	0 57	15 12	2 10	17 11	12 14	1 53	3 05	1 26	23 07	1 29	2 56	7 20	15 17	0 37	18 10	0 29
19 F	0 33	19 00	1 11	20 38	11 48	1 58	2 35	1 25	23 13	1 29	2 46	7 19	15 13	0 37	18 09	0 30
20 Sa	0 10	22 04	0 09	23 15	11 21	2 03	2 05	1 25	23 18	1 29	2 35	7 18	15 09	0 37	18 07	0 30
21 Su	0N14	24 11	0N54	24 51	10 53	2 06	1 35	1 24	23 24	1 29	2 25	7 17	15 05	0 37	18 06	0 30
22 M	0 38	25 14	1 56	25 18	10 23	2 10	1 05	1 24	23 29	1 29	2 15	7 16	15 01	0 37	18 04	0 30
23 Tu	1 02	25 03	2 53	24 28	9 52	2 13	0 35	1 23	23 34	1 29	2 05	7 15	14 57	0 38	18 03	0 30
24 W	1 25	23 33	3 44	22 19	9 20	2 16	0 05	1 23	23 39	1 29	1 55	7 14	14 54	0 38	18 02	0 30
25 Th	1 49	20 45	4 25	18 53	8 46	2 18	0N26	1 22	23 44	1 29	1 45	7 13	14 50	0 38	18 00	0 30
26 F	2 12	16 44	4 52	14 19	8 11	2 19	0 56	1 21	23 48	1 29	1 35	7 12	14 46	0 38	17 59	0 30
27 Sa	2 36	11 40	5 03	8 49	7 36	2 21	1 26	1 21	23 53	1 29	1 25	7 11	14 42	0 38	17 58	0 30
28 Su	2 59	5 49	4 55	2 42	6 59	2 21	1 56	1 20	23 57	1 29	1 15	7 11	14 38	0 38	17 57	0 31
29 M	3 23	0S28	4 26	3S40	6 21	2 22	2 27	1 19	24 02	1 29	1 05	7 10	14 35	0 39	17 55	0 31
30 Tu	3 46	6 49	3 40	9 52	5 41	2 21	2 57	1 18	24 06	1 29	0 55	7 09	14 31	0 39	17 54	0 31
31 W	4N09	12S47	2N38	15S29	5S01	2S21	3N27	1S17	24N10	1N29	0S45	7S08	14S27	0S39	17S53	0S31

Day	⚷ Decl	⚷ Lat	♅ Decl	♅ Lat	♆ Decl	♆ Lat	♇ Decl	♇ Lat
1	5N04	2N23	13N39	0S25	4S51	1S04	22S13	1S17
6	5 10	2 22	13 43	0 25	4 46	1 04	22 12	1 18
11	5 16	2 22	13 47	0 25	4 42	1 04	22 11	1 19
16	5 22	2 21	13 51	0 25	4 37	1 04	22 10	1 19
21	5 29	2 21	13 56	0 25	4 33	1 04	22 10	1 20
26	5 35	2 20	14 01	0 25	4 28	1 04	22 10	1 20
31	5N42	2N20	14N06	0S25	4S24	1S04	22S09	1S21

Day	⚴ Decl	⚴ Lat	⚵ Decl	⚵ Lat	⚶ Decl	⚶ Lat	Eris Decl	Eris Lat
1	1N38	14N46	10S43	12N22	15N30	10N35	1S27	11S26
6	1 59	14 33	10 27	12 41	16 11	10 46	1 26	11 25
11	2 20	14 21	10 10	13 01	16 49	10 53	1 24	11 25
16	2 42	14 09	9 51	13 22	17 22	10 57	1 23	11 24
21	3 04	13 57	9 31	13 44	17 49	10 58	1 21	11 24
26	3 27	13 47	9 10	14 07	18 11	10 55	1 20	11 23
31	3N51	13N36	8S48	14N30	18N26	10N49	1S18	11S23

Moon Phenomena

Max/0 Decl
dy hr mn
1 12:41 0 S
7 20:41 25S09
14 20:07 0 N
22 8:36 25N19
28 22:14 0 S

Max/0 Lat
dy hr mn
6 0:57 0 S
12 18:15 5S00
20 3:32 0 N
27 1:44 5N03

Perigee/Apogee
dy hr m kilometers
2 5:19 p 365425
18 5:04 a 405252
30 6:17 p 360312

PH dy hr mn
☾ 6 1:31 15♐42
● 13 10:22 23♓04
☽ 21 14:42 1♋12
○ 28 18:49 8♎18

Void of Course Moon

Last Aspect	☽ Ingress
2 14:11 ♇ □	♏ 2 20:39
4 16:11 ♇ ⚹	♐ 4 22:44
6 9:45 ♆ □	♑ 7 2:21
9 0:54 ♇ ☌	♒ 9 7:42
11 3:33 ☿ ☌	♓ 11 14:45
13 16:39 ♇ ⚹	♈ 13 23:45
16 3:41 ♇ □	♉ 16 10:57
18 20:41 ☉ ⚹	♊ 18 23:48
21 12:05 ♀ □	♋ 21 12:19
23 15:27 ♇ ☍	♌ 23 21:57
25 13:29 ♃ ☍	♍ 26 3:27
27 23:49 ♇ △	♎ 28 5:23
30 0:09 ♇ □	♏ 30 5:34

DAILY ASPECTARIAN

1 M ☽☍⚳ 0:14
☽⚻♀ 2:38
☽☍⚷ 7:15
☽⚻♅ 7:50
☽△♄ 9:18
☉∠♇ 10:06
☉⚻☽ 13:43
☽⚼♂ 17:41
☽△☿ 19:29
☽△♃ 22:58

2 Tu ☽⚻♆ 4:41
☽⚼♀ 5:35
☽∥♆ 7:30
☽⋕⚷ 8:32
☽∥⚳ 10:30
☽□♇ 14:11
☉∥☽ 15:57
☉⚼☽ 16:12
☽⚻♂ 19:23

3 W ☽⚻⚳ 2:57
☽∥♀ 5:16
☽⚼♆ 5:29
☽△♀ 8:40
☽⚻⚷ 8:51
☽☍♅ 9:23
♀⚺⚷ 10:50
☽□♄ 11:06
♀⚹♅ 17:10
☉△☽ 18:53
☽⋕♅ 20:33

4 Th ☽□☿ 0:03
☽□♃ 1:23
♂ ♊ 3:31
☽⚼⚳ 4:36
☽△♆ 6:32
☽∥☿ 7:09
☽∥♃ 8:31
☽⚼⚷ 9:58
♀⚺♄ 15:15
☽⚹♇ 16:11
☽∥♄ 20:44
☽☍♂ 23:33

5 F ⚳⋕⚷ 0:42
☿☌♃ 3:28
☽△⚳ 6:37
☽△⚷ 11:27
☽⚻♅ 11:57
☽⚹♄ 13:57
☽□♀ 15:59
☽∠♇ 17:43
☽⋕♂ 17:53
☽∥♇ 21:16

6 Sa ☉□☽ 1:31
☽⚹♃ 5:08
☽⚹☿ 6:37
☽□♆ 9:45
♀∠♇ 11:42
☽⚼♅ 13:50
☽∠♄ 16:00
☽⚺♇ 19:40

7 Su ☽⚻♂ 5:30
☉⋕⚷ 5:43
⚳∥♆ 7:21
☽∠♃ 7:41
☽∠☿ 10:51
☽□⚳ 12:02
☽□⚷ 15:43
☽△♅ 16:10
☽⚺♄ 18:30
♀ ♓ 21:07

8 M ☽⚹♀ 1:30
☿⚺♆ 2:13
☽⚼♂ 9:12
☉∥♆ 9:29
☿∠⚳ 9:56
☉⚹☽ 10:16
☽⚺♃ 10:40
☽⚹♆ 14:42
☽⚺☿ 15:46
☉⚺♃ 17:05

9 Tu ☽☌♇ 0:54
☉∥⚳ 4:04
♂⋕♇ 6:35
☽∠♀ 7:06
☽△♂ 13:24
☉∠☽ 15:26
☽∠♆ 17:49
☽⚹⚳ 19:19
☽⋕♂ 21:05
☽∥♇ 21:42
☽⚹⚷ 21:43
☽□♅ 22:08

10 W ☽☌♄ 0:46
☿∠⚷ 2:11
☽⚺♀ 13:17
☽☌♃ 17:59
☉⚺☽ 21:09
☽⚺♆ 21:22
☽∠⚳ 23:40

11 Th ☉☌♆ 0:02
☽∥♄ 1:07
☽∠⚷ 1:22
☽☌☿ 3:33
☽⚺♇ 7:49
☽∥♃ 16:23
☽□♂ 23:17
☽∥☿ 23:25

12 F ☽⋕♅ 2:32
☽⚺⚳ 4:31
☽⚺⚷ 5:29
☽⚹♅ 5:51
☽⚺♄ 8:50
☽∠♇ 11:58
♀⚺♃ 23:54

13 Sa ☿⚺♇ 1:42
☽⚺♃ 3:12
☽☌♀ 3:30
☽☌♆ 5:53
☉☌☽ 10:22
☽∠♅ 10:28
☉∠♅ 11:33
♀⋕⚷ 12:04
☽∠♄ 13:38
☽⚹♇ 16:39
⚳☌⚷ 17:13
☽⚺☿ 18:18
☿⋕♅ 19:32
☽⋕⚷ 19:35
☽∥♀ 20:24
☽∥♆ 22:41

14 Su ☽∥⚳ 3:37
♀☌♆ 4:09
⚳⚺♅ 5:01
☽∠♃ 8:39
☉∥☽ 9:09
☽⚹♂ 11:29
☽☌⚷ 15:20
☽⚺♅ 15:38
☽☌⚳ 15:57
☽⚹♄ 18:59
♀∥♆ 21:08

15 M ☽∠☿ 2:58
☉⋕☽ 5:35
☉∠♄ 7:08
☽⋕⚳ 11:42
☽⚹♃ 14:42
☽⋕♀ 15:55
☽⚺♆ 16:36
☽⋕♆ 17:41
☽∠♂ 18:34
☽⚺♀ 20:40
☽∥⚷ 21:12
☿ ♓ 22:28

16 Tu ☉⚺☽ 2:23
☽□♇ 3:41
♀∠♅ 3:49
☽⚹☿ 12:32
☉⚹♇ 18:27
☽∠♆ 22:45

17 W ☽⚺♂ 2:14
☽⚺⚷ 3:22
☽☌♅ 3:38
☽⚺⚳ 5:47
☽∠♀ 6:20
☽□♄ 7:21
☽⋕☿ 9:00
☉∠☽ 11:21
☽∥♅ 16:31
♀∠♄ 16:45

18 Th ☽⋕♃ 0:30
♂⚹⚷ 3:36
☽□♃ 4:15
☽⚹♆ 5:17
♂⚺♅ 8:49
☽∠⚷ 9:59
♀∥⚳ 11:39
☽∠⚳ 13:19
☽⚹♀ 16:25
☽△♇ 16:31
♀⚹♇ 17:21
☽⋕♄ 18:12
☉⚹☽ 20:41

19 F ☽□☿ 9:29
☽⚹⚷ 16:41
☽⚺♅ 16:53
☽☌♂ 18:26
⚳⚹♄ 18:48
☽△♄ 20:51
☽⚹⚳ 20:54
☽⚼♇ 23:04

20 Sa ☽⋕♇ 0:59
☊ D 3:31
☉ ♈ 9:39
☽∥♂ 13:10
☽△♃ 18:15
☽□♆ 18:22
☽∠♅ 23:17

21 Su ♃⚺♆ 1:52
☽⚼♄ 3:17
☽⚻♇ 5:18
☽□♀ 12:05
♀ ♈ 14:17
☊ R 14:33
☉□☽ 14:42
☿⚺⚷ 22:17
☿⚹♅ 23:36

22 M ☽⚼♃ 0:33
♂△♄ 2:36
☽□⚷ 4:55
☽⚹♅ 5:03
☽△☿ 5:47
☽⚻♄ 9:04
☽⚺♂ 9:20
☽□⚳ 10:39
☉⋕♀ 12:06

23 Tu ☽△♆ 5:15
☽⚻♃ 5:58
☿⚺♄ 10:13
☽⚼☿ 14:22
☽∠♂ 15:21
☽☍♇ 15:27
♂⚼♇ 17:33
☽∥♂ 22:59
☿∠♇ 23:40

24 W ☿□♂ 3:27
☽△♀ 3:51
☉△☽ 4:55
☽⚼♆ 9:14
☿⚺⚳ 9:56
☽⋕♇ 13:19
☽△⚷ 13:41
☽□♅ 13:47
☽☍♄ 17:39
☽⚹♂ 20:10
☽△⚳ 20:28
☉⋕⚳ 21:24
☽⚻☿ 21:30

25 Th ☽⚼♀ 9:36
☉⚼☽ 10:02
☽⚻♆ 12:08
☽☍♃ 13:29
☽⚼⚷ 16:27
♂⚹⚳ 16:29
☽⋕♄ 17:11
☽⚻♇ 21:30
☽⚼⚳ 23:39

26 F ☉☌♀ 6:59
☽⋕♃ 9:59
☽∥♅ 13:24
☉⚻☽ 13:53
☽⚻♀ 14:01
☽⚻⚷ 18:14
☽△♅ 18:18
☽⚻♄ 22:02
☽⚼♇ 23:02
♀⋕⚳ 23:26

27 Sa ☽⚻⚳ 1:49
☽□♂ 2:17
☽☍☿ 7:38
♀∠♃ 11:47
☽☍♆ 15:06
☽⚻♃ 16:57
☽⋕☿ 18:54
☽⚼♅ 19:16
☉∠♃ 21:03
☽⚼♄ 22:57
☽△♇ 23:49

28 Su ☽∥⚷ 0:45
☽⋕♆ 5:21
☉∥☽ 10:17
☽∥♀ 13:49
♀☌⚷ 16:29
♀⚺♅ 16:54
☽⚼♃ 17:39
☽⋕⚳ 17:58
☉☍☽ 18:49
☽☍⚷ 19:39
☽⚻♅ 19:41
☽☍♀ 19:56
☽△♄ 23:22

29 M ☽∥⚳ 2:16
☽☍⚳ 4:04
☽△♂ 5:13
☽⋕♀ 8:02
☉☌⚷ 8:10
☉⚺♅ 8:35
☉⋕☽ 11:39
☽⚻☿ 14:17
☽∥♆ 14:53
☽⚻♆ 15:43
☽△♃ 18:02
☽⋕⚷ 19:37
☽∥☿ 20:06

30 Tu ☽□♇ 0:09
☿⋕⚷ 0:33
☿☌♆ 3:25
☽⚼♂ 6:13
☽⚼♆ 15:46
♀⚹♄ 15:48
☽⚼☿ 17:18
☽⚻⚷ 19:54
☽☍♅ 19:55
☉⚻☽ 22:17
☽□♄ 23:41

31 W ☽⚻♀ 0:21
☿⚺♃ 3:55
☽⚻⚳ 5:26
☽⋕♅ 5:44
☽∥♃ 7:13
☽⚻♂ 7:18
☉⋕♆ 14:52
☽△♆ 16:00
☿∠♅ 17:06
♅⚺⚷ 18:12
☽□♃ 18:53
☉⋕☿ 19:14
☽⚼⚷ 20:13
☽△☿ 20:37
☉⚹♄ 21:06
☿∥♆ 21:48
☽∥♄ 23:35

March 2021:Modify New York Stock Exchange Zone:-5

Sunday	Monday	Tuesday	Wednesday	Thursday	Friday	Saturday
	1	2 3:37PM ☽-> 0♏00	3 12:08PM ♀ ⚹ ♅ 10:28PM ♂-> 0♊00	4 5:41PM ☽-> 0♐00 10:26PM ☿ ☌ ♃	5	6 9:19PM ☽-> 0♑00
7	8	9 2:39AM ☽-> 0♒00	10 7:00PM ☉ ☌ ♆	11 9:42AM ☽-> 0♓00	12	13 5:20AM New Moon♓ 6:42PM ☽-> 0♈00 11:07PM ♀ ☌ ♆
14	15 5:25PM ☿-> 0♓00	16 5:55AM ☽-> 0♉00 1:25PM ☉ ⚹ ♇	17	18 12:19PM ♀ ⚹ ♇ 6:46PM ☽-> 0♊00	19	20 4:36AM ☉-> 0♈00
21 7:16AM ☽-> 0♋00 9:15AM ♀-> 0♈00 6:34PM ☿ ⚹ ♅ 9:33PM ♂ △ ♄	22	23 4:55PM ☽-> 0♌00 10:25PM ☿ □ ♂	24	25 10:24PM ☽-> 0♍00	26 1:57AM ♀ ☌ ☉	27
28 12:21AM ☽-> 0♎00 1:47PM Full Moon♎	29 10:23PM ☿ ☌ ♆	30 12:32AM ☽-> 0♏00 10:46AM ♀ ⚹ ♄	31 4:03PM ☉ ⚹ ♄			

February

S	M	T	W	T	F	S
	1	2	3	4	5	6
7	8	9	10	11	12	13
14	15	16	17	18	19	20
21	22	23	24	25	26	27
28						

April

S	M	T	W	T	F	S
				1	2	3
4	5	6	7	8	9	10
11	12	13	14	15	16	17
18	19	20	21	22	23	24
25	26	27	28	29	30	

April 2021

LONGITUDE

Day	Sid.Time	☉	☽	☽ 12 hour	Mean☊	True☊	☿	♀	♂	⚳	♃	♄	⚷	♅	♆	♇
	h m s	° ' "	° ' "	° ' "	° '	° '	° '	° '	° '	° '	° '	° '	° '	° '	° '	° '
1 Th	12 38 17	11♈29 00	26♏19 46	3♐39 26	14♊05.4	12♊33.4	24♓29.2	12♈56.0	16♊26.6	15♈10.9	23♒13.7	11♒22.4	9♈00.8	9♉00.7	21♓25.0	26♑38.0
2 F	12 42 14	12 28 12	10♐54 44	18 05 18	14 02.3	12D 32.4	26 12.6	14 10.5	17 02.5	15 34.7	23 25.4	11 27.0	9 04.3	9 03.9	21 27.2	26 38.8
3 Sa	12 46 10	13 27 21	25 10 52	2♑11 22	13 59.1	12 32.8	27 57.3	15 25.0	17 38.4	15 58.6	23 37.0	11 31.6	9 07.8	9 07.0	21 29.3	26 39.5
4 Su	12 50 07	14 26 30	9♑06 49	15 57 18	13 55.9	12R 33.5	29 43.5	16 39.4	18 14.4	16 22.5	23 48.6	11 36.1	9 11.3	9 10.2	21 31.5	26 40.2
5 M	12 54 04	15 25 36	22 43 01	29 24 10	13 52.7	12 33.3	1♈31.1	17 53.9	18 50.4	16 46.3	24 00.0	11 40.5	9 14.8	9 13.5	21 33.6	26 40.9
6 Tu	12 58 00	16 24 41	6♒01 00	12♒33 47	13 49.6	12 31.5	3 20.1	19 08.3	19 26.4	17 10.2	24 11.4	11 44.8	9 18.4	9 16.7	21 35.7	26 41.6
7 W	13 01 57	17 23 43	19 02 46	25 28 12	13 46.4	12 27.3	5 10.5	20 22.7	20 02.4	17 34.1	24 22.6	11 49.1	9 21.9	9 20.0	21 37.8	26 42.2
8 Th	13 05 53	18 22 44	1♓50 18	8♓09 18	13 43.2	12 20.8	7 02.5	21 37.1	20 38.5	17 58.0	24 33.8	11 53.3	9 25.3	9 23.2	21 39.9	26 42.8
9 F	13 09 50	19 21 43	14 25 21	20 38 39	13 40.0	12 12.4	8 55.8	22 51.5	21 14.6	18 21.9	24 44.9	11 57.4	9 28.8	9 26.5	21 42.0	26 43.3
10 Sa	13 13 46	20 20 41	26 49 19	2♈57 31	13 36.8	12 02.9	10 50.6	24 05.9	21 50.7	18 45.7	24 55.8	12 01.4	9 32.3	9 29.8	21 44.1	26 43.9
11 Su	13 17 43	21 19 36	9♈03 23	15 07 02	13 33.7	11 53.0	12 46.9	25 20.2	22 26.8	19 09.6	25 06.7	12 05.4	9 35.8	9 33.1	21 46.1	26 44.4
12 M	13 21 39	22 18 29	21 08 37	27 08 18	13 30.5	11 43.9	14 44.6	26 34.5	23 03.0	19 33.5	25 17.5	12 09.3	9 39.2	9 36.5	21 48.1	26 44.9
13 Tu	13 25 36	23 17 20	3♉06 15	9♉02 43	13 27.3	11 36.2	16 43.7	27 48.8	23 39.2	19 57.4	25 28.2	12 13.0	9 42.7	9 39.8	21 50.2	26 45.3
14 W	13 29 33	24 16 10	14 57 54	20 52 06	13 24.1	11 30.6	18 44.2	29 03.1	24 15.4	20 21.3	25 38.7	12 16.8	9 46.1	9 43.2	21 52.2	26 45.7
15 Th	13 33 29	25 14 57	26 45 39	2♊38 54	13 21.0	11 27.2	20 45.9	0♉17.4	24 51.6	20 45.1	25 49.2	12 20.4	9 49.5	9 46.5	21 54.1	26 46.1
16 F	13 37 26	26 13 42	8♊32 17	14 26 13	13 17.8	11D 25.9	22 49.0	1 31.6	25 27.9	21 09.0	25 59.6	12 23.9	9 53.0	9 49.9	21 56.1	26 46.5
17 Sa	13 41 22	27 12 25	20 21 13	26 17 49	13 14.6	11 26.2	24 53.1	2 45.8	26 04.1	21 32.9	26 09.8	12 27.4	9 56.4	9 53.3	21 58.1	26 46.8
18 Su	13 45 19	28 11 06	2♋16 34	8♋18 04	13 11.4	11 27.5	26 58.4	4 00.1	26 40.4	21 56.7	26 20.0	12 30.7	9 59.8	9 56.7	22 00.0	26 47.1
19 M	13 49 15	29 09 45	14 22 56	20 31 46	13 08.2	11 29.0	29 04.5	5 14.2	27 16.7	22 20.6	26 30.0	12 34.0	10 03.1	10 00.1	22 01.9	26 47.4
20 Tu	13 53 12	0♉08 22	26 45 12	3♌03 50	13 05.1	11R 29.9	1♉11.4	6 28.4	27 53.0	22 44.4	26 39.9	12 37.2	10 06.5	10 03.5	22 03.8	26 47.6
21 W	13 57 08	1 06 56	9♌28 14	15 58 54	13 01.9	11 29.6	3 18.9	7 42.5	28 29.3	23 08.2	26 49.7	12 40.3	10 09.8	10 07.0	22 05.7	26 47.8
22 Th	14 01 05	2 05 28	22 36 15	29 20 39	12 58.7	11 27.7	5 26.8	8 56.7	29 05.7	23 32.1	26 59.4	12 43.4	10 13.2	10 10.4	22 07.5	26 48.0
23 F	14 05 02	3 03 58	6♍12 16	13♍11 10	12 55.5	11 24.2	7 34.7	10 10.8	29 42.1	23 55.9	27 09.0	12 46.3	10 16.5	10 13.8	22 09.4	26 48.2
24 Sa	14 08 58	4 02 26	20 17 11	27 30 02	12 52.4	11 19.5	9 42.5	11 24.8	0♋18.4	24 19.7	27 18.5	12 49.2	10 19.8	10 17.3	22 11.2	26 48.3
25 Su	14 12 55	5 00 51	4♎49 09	12♎13 51	12 49.2	11 14.1	11 49.9	12 38.9	0 54.8	24 43.4	27 27.8	12 51.9	10 23.1	10 20.7	22 13.0	26 48.4
26 M	14 16 51	5 59 15	19 43 11	27 16 07	12 46.0	11 08.9	13 56.5	13 52.9	1 31.2	25 07.2	27 37.0	12 54.6	10 26.3	10 24.2	22 14.8	26 48.4
27 Tu	14 20 48	6 57 36	4♏51 26	12♏27 54	12 42.8	11 04.5	16 02.1	15 06.9	2 07.6	25 31.0	27 46.1	12 57.2	10 29.5	10 27.6	22 16.5	26R 48.5
28 W	14 24 44	7 55 56	20 04 15	27 39 13	12 39.6	11 01.6	18 06.4	16 20.9	2 44.1	25 54.7	27 55.1	12 59.6	10 32.8	10 31.1	22 18.3	26 48.5
29 Th	14 28 41	8 54 14	5♐11 40	12♐40 33	12 36.5	11D 00.2	20 09.0	17 34.9	3 20.5	26 18.4	28 03.9	13 02.0	10 36.0	10 34.5	22 20.0	26 48.5
30 F	14 32 37	9♉52 31	20 05 02	27 24 22	12♊33.3	11♊00.4	22♉09.6	18♉48.9	3♋57.0	26♈42.1	28♒12.7	13♒04.4	10♈39.1	10♉38.0	22♓21.7	26♑48.4

1st of Month

Julian Day # 2459305.5
Obliquity 23°26'15"
SVP 4♓58'04"
GC 27♐08.2
Eris 23♈57.9

Day	⚴
1	7♓41.0
6	9 12.2
11	10 41.6
16	12 09.0
21	13 34.1
26	14 56.7

Day	⚵
1	23♐41.2
6	23 55.4
11	24 01.8
16	24 00.0R
21	23 49.9R
26	23 31.6R

Day	⚶
1	8♍12.5R
6	7 31.8R
11	7 02.8R
16	6 46.1R
21	6 41.7
26	6 49.3

DECLINATION and LATITUDE

Day	☉ Decl	☽ Decl	☽ Lat	☽12h Decl	☿ Decl	☿ Lat	♀ Decl	♀ Lat	♂ Decl	♂ Lat	⚳ Decl	⚳ Lat	♃ Decl	♃ Lat	♄ Decl	♄ Lat
1 Th	4N33	17S57	1N26	20S06	4S20	2S20	3N57	1S16	24N13	1N29	0S36	7S07	14S23	0S39	17S52	0S31
2 F	4 56	21 56	0 09	23 24	3 37	2 18	4 27	1 14	24 17	1 29	0 26	7 06	14 20	0 39	17 51	0 31
3 Sa	5 19	24 28	1S07	25 08	2 54	2 16	4 57	1 13	24 20	1 29	0 16	7 05	14 16	0 39	17 49	0 31
4 Su	5 42	25 24	2 17	25 17	2 09	2 13	5 26	1 12	24 24	1 29	0 06	7 05	14 12	0 40	17 48	0 31
5 M	6 04	24 47	3 18	23 55	1 23	2 10	5 56	1 11	24 27	1 29	0N04	7 04	14 09	0 40	17 47	0 31
6 Tu	6 27	22 45	4 06	21 17	0 37	2 07	6 25	1 09	24 30	1 29	0 13	7 03	14 05	0 40	17 46	0 32
7 W	6 50	19 33	4 41	17 37	0N11	2 02	6 55	1 08	24 32	1 29	0 23	7 02	14 02	0 40	17 45	0 32
8 Th	7 12	15 30	5 01	13 13	0 59	1 58	7 24	1 06	24 35	1 29	0 33	7 02	13 58	0 40	17 44	0 32
9 F	7 35	10 50	5 06	8 20	1 49	1 53	7 53	1 05	24 37	1 29	0 42	7 01	13 54	0 40	17 43	0 32
10 Sa	7 57	5 47	4 56	3 12	2 39	1 47	8 22	1 03	24 40	1 29	0 52	7 00	13 51	0 41	17 42	0 32
11 Su	8 19	0 35	4 33	2N01	3 30	1 41	8 51	1 02	24 42	1 29	1 02	6 59	13 47	0 41	17 41	0 32
12 M	8 41	4N35	3 57	7 06	4 22	1 34	9 19	1 00	24 44	1 29	1 11	6 59	13 44	0 41	17 40	0 32
13 Tu	9 03	9 32	3 12	11 53	5 14	1 27	9 47	0 58	24 45	1 28	1 21	6 58	13 41	0 41	17 39	0 32
14 W	9 25	14 07	2 18	16 13	6 07	1 20	10 15	0 57	24 47	1 28	1 30	6 57	13 37	0 41	17 38	0 33
15 Th	9 46	18 09	1 19	19 55	7 00	1 12	10 43	0 55	24 49	1 28	1 40	6 56	13 34	0 42	17 37	0 33
16 F	10 07	21 28	0 16	22 48	7 54	1 03	11 11	0 53	24 50	1 28	1 49	6 56	13 31	0 42	17 36	0 33
17 Sa	10 29	23 53	0N48	24 43	8 48	0 54	11 38	0 51	24 51	1 28	1 59	6 55	13 27	0 42	17 36	0 33
18 Su	10 50	25 16	1 51	25 31	9 42	0 45	12 05	0 49	24 52	1 28	2 08	6 54	13 24	0 42	17 35	0 33
19 M	11 11	25 28	2 49	25 06	10 36	0 35	12 32	0 47	24 53	1 28	2 17	6 54	13 21	0 42	17 34	0 33
20 Tu	11 31	24 25	3 41	23 26	11 30	0 25	12 58	0 45	24 53	1 28	2 27	6 53	13 18	0 43	17 33	0 33
21 W	11 52	22 07	4 24	20 31	12 23	0 15	13 24	0 43	24 54	1 28	2 36	6 52	13 14	0 43	17 32	0 33
22 Th	12 12	18 37	4 55	16 27	13 16	0 04	13 50	0 41	24 54	1 28	2 45	6 52	13 11	0 43	17 32	0 34
23 F	12 32	14 02	5 10	11 23	14 08	0N06	14 15	0 39	24 54	1 28	2 54	6 51	13 08	0 43	17 31	0 34
24 Sa	12 52	8 33	5 07	5 34	14 60	0 17	14 40	0 37	24 54	1 28	3 04	6 51	13 05	0 43	17 30	0 34
25 Su	13 12	2 27	4 45	0S44	15 50	0 28	15 05	0 34	24 54	1 27	3 13	6 50	13 02	0 44	17 30	0 34
26 M	13 31	3S57	4 04	7 08	16 38	0 39	15 29	0 32	24 53	1 27	3 22	6 49	12 59	0 44	17 29	0 34
27 Tu	13 50	10 14	3 05	13 12	17 25	0 49	15 53	0 30	24 52	1 27	3 31	6 49	12 56	0 44	17 28	0 34
28 W	14 09	15 58	1 52	18 27	18 11	0 60	16 17	0 28	24 52	1 27	3 40	6 48	12 53	0 44	17 28	0 34
29 Th	14 28	20 39	0 32	22 28	18 54	1 10	16 40	0 25	24 51	1 27	3 49	6 48	12 50	0 44	17 27	0 35
30 F	14N46	23S53	0S50	24S53	19N35	1N20	17N03	0S23	24N50	1N27	3N58	6S47	12S48	0S45	17S27	0S35

Day	⚷ Decl	⚷ Lat	♅ Decl	♅ Lat	♆ Decl	♆ Lat	♇ Decl	♇ Lat
1	5N43	2N20	14N07	0S25	4S23	1S04	22S09	1S21
6	5 50	2 20	14 12	0 25	4 19	1 05	22 09	1 22
11	5 56	2 20	14 17	0 24	4 15	1 05	22 09	1 23
16	6 03	2 19	14 22	0 24	4 11	1 05	22 10	1 23
21	6 10	2 19	14 28	0 24	4 08	1 05	22 10	1 24
26	6 16	2 19	14 33	0 24	4 04	1 05	22 11	1 25

Day	⚴ Decl	⚴ Lat	⚵ Decl	⚵ Lat	⚶ Decl	⚶ Lat	Eris Decl	Eris Lat
1	3N55	13N34	8S44	14N35	18N29	10N48	1S18	11S23
6	4 19	13 24	8 20	14 58	18 36	10 39	1 17	11 23
11	4 43	13 15	7 57	15 22	18 38	10 29	1 15	11 22
16	5 06	13 05	7 32	15 47	18 33	10 17	1 14	11 22
21	5 30	12 56	7 08	16 10	18 22	10 04	1 13	11 22
26	5 53	12 48	6 44	16 34	18 07	9 50	1 11	11 22

Moon Phenomena

Max/0 Decl
dy hr mn
4 2:05 25S25
11 2:43 0 N
18 16:03 25N32
25 9:15 0 S

Perigee/Apogee
dy hr m kilometers
14 17:47 a 406119
27 15:24 p 357383

PH dy hr mn
☾ 4 10:04 14♑51
● 12 2:32 22♈25
☽ 20 7:00 0♌25
○ 27 3:33 7♏06

Max/0 Lat
dy hr mn
2 2:43 0 S
8 19:48 5S06
16 5:54 0 N
23 8:55 5N11
29 9:19 0 S

Void of Course Moon

Last Aspect	☽ Ingress
1 0:30 ♇ ⚹	♐ 1 6:00
3 5:25 ☿ □	♑ 3 8:14
5 7:06 ♇ ☌	♒ 5 13:05
7 10:06 ♃ ☌	♓ 7 20:32
9 23:49 ♇ ⚹	♈ 10 6:12
12 12:08 ♀ ☌	♉ 12 17:45
15 0:01 ♇ △	♊ 15 6:36
17 15:04 ☉ ⚹	♋ 17 19:26
20 0:05 ♇ ☍	♌ 20 6:12
22 12:06 ♂ ⚹	♍ 22 13:09
24 10:51 ♇ △	♎ 24 16:07
26 12:41 ♃ △	♏ 26 16:19
28 12:33 ♃ □	♐ 28 15:44
30 13:28 ♃ ⚹	♑ 30 16:17

DAILY ASPECTARIAN

1 Th
☉⚼☽ 0:16
☽⚹♇ 0:30
☽⚼♀ 2:52
☽⚼⚳ 6:28
☿#♀ 7:36
♀#♆ 20:46
☽⊼♅ 20:55
☽△⚷ 20:56

2 F
☽⚹♄ 0:54
☽∠♇ 1:13
☽∥♇ 1:38
☊ D 2:42
☉△☽ 2:47
☿∠♄ 3:29
☽△♀ 5:57
☿⚹♇ 6:05
☽△⚳ 8:01
☽☍♂ 10:41
☽□♆ 17:43
☽⚹♃ 21:18
☽⚼♅ 22:11
☽#♂ 22:14

3 Sa
☽∠♄ 2:18
☽⊻♇ 2:31
☽□☿ 5:25
♀☌⚳ 15:57
☽∠♃ 23:28

4 Su
☽△♅ 0:06
☽□⚷ 0:08
☿ ♈ 3:42
☽⊻♄ 4:22
☉∥⚷ 6:11
☉□☽ 10:04
☊ R 10:15
☽□⚳ 13:08
♃#♅ 13:45
☽□♀ 14:34
☽⊼♂ 16:47
♀∥⚷ 17:40
☽⚹♆ 21:56

5 M
☽⊻♃ 2:20
☽#♂ 5:05
☽☌♇ 7:06
☽⚹☿ 18:20
☽⚼♂ 20:59

6 Tu
☽∠♆ 1:04
☽∥♇ 5:05
☽□♅ 5:59
☽⚹⚷ 6:02
☉∥♀ 6:08
☿#⚳ 9:47
☽☌♄ 10:33
♀⚹♂ 11:19
☉⚹☽ 20:41
☽⚹⚳ 21:10
♃∠⚷ 21:36

7 W
☽△♂ 1:56
☽∠☿ 2:27
☽⚹♀ 2:45
☽⊻♆ 4:50
☉☌⚳ 7:05
☿∥⚳ 7:37
☽∠⚷ 9:58
☽☌♃ 10:06
☽∥♄ 11:16
☽⊻♇ 14:20

8 Th
♀⊻♆ 0:56
☽∠⚳ 2:12
☉∠☽ 3:10
☽#♅ 6:44
☽∥♃ 8:15
☽∠♀ 10:04
☽⊻☿ 11:37
☽⚹♅ 14:25
☽⊻⚷ 14:29
☽∠♇ 18:49
☽⊻♄ 19:15

9 F
☿⊻♅ 6:38
☿☌⚷ 7:09
☽⊻⚳ 7:51
☉⊻☽ 10:20
☿∠♃ 11:23
☽#♀ 12:56
☽□♂ 13:50
☽☌♆ 14:05
☉#☽ 14:33
☽⊻♀ 18:06
♂□♆ 19:19
☽∠♅ 19:27
☽⊻♃ 20:16
☽#⚷ 23:24
☽⚹♇ 23:49

10 Sa
☽∠♄ 0:24
☽∥♆ 7:04
☽#☿ 12:30
☿⚹♄ 15:10
♀⚹♃ 18:54
☽#⚳ 22:02

11 Su
☽⊻♅ 0:59
☽☌⚷ 1:04
☽∠♃ 2:07
☽⚹♄ 6:02
☽∥⚳ 7:42
☽☌☿ 8:47
☉⊻♆ 11:11
☽☌⚳ 20:44
☿#♆ 20:47
☽#♆ 22:25
☽∥☿ 22:45

12 M
☽⊻♆ 1:19
☉☌☽ 2:32
♀□♇ 3:22
☽⚹♂ 4:01
☽∥⚷ 6:35
☽⚹♃ 8:25
⚵ R 10:14
☽□♇ 11:13
☽☌♀ 12:08
☉∥☽ 21:21

13 Tu
☽∥♀ 1:23
☽∠♆ 7:33
☽∠♂ 11:48
☽☌♅ 13:19
☽⊻⚷ 13:25
☽□♄ 18:31
☿∥⚷ 21:04
☽#♃ 21:16
☉⚹♂ 23:10

14 W
☽∥♅ 1:12
☽⊻☿ 9:15
☽⊻⚳ 11:20
☽⚹♆ 14:05
♀ ♉ 18:23
☽⊻♂ 19:55
☽∠⚷ 20:02
♂∠♅ 20:18
☽#♄ 20:35
☉⊻☽ 20:38
☽□♃ 22:03
☿☌⚳ 23:48

15 Th
☽△♇ 0:01
☽⊻♀ 8:02
☿⊻♆ 13:33
☉⚹♃ 17:00
☽∠⚳ 18:58
☽∠☿ 22:13

16 F
☽⊻♅ 2:39
☽⚹⚷ 2:45
☊ D 5:53
☉∠☽ 5:58
☽#♇ 5:59
☽⚼♇ 6:35
☽△♄ 7:54
☉□♇ 13:28
☽∠♀ 18:08

17 Sa
☽⚹⚳ 2:30
☽□♆ 3:16
♂△♃ 5:15
☽∠♅ 9:12
☽⚹☿ 11:06
☽△♃ 11:54
☽☌♂ 12:09
☽⊼♇ 12:59
☽⚼♄ 14:24
☽∥♂ 14:37
☉⚹☽ 15:04
☿⚹♃ 16:01
☿⚹♂ 19:10
☿□♇ 21:50

18 Su
⚳⊻♆ 3:35
☽⚹♀ 3:50
♂⊼♇ 4:27
☽⚹♅ 15:20
☽□⚷ 15:26
☽⚼♃ 18:15
☽⊼♄ 20:25

19 M
☉☌☿ 1:51
☿ ♉ 10:30
♂⚼♄ 12:34
☽△♆ 14:57
☽□⚳ 16:02
☽∥♂ 16:31
☉ ♉ 20:35
☽⊼♃ 23:50

20 Tu
☽☍♇ 0:05
☉∥☿ 1:02
☽⊻♂ 2:16
☊ R 6:55
☉□☽ 7:00
⚶ D 7:07
☽□☿ 10:09
♀∠♆ 11:45
♀#♃ 15:56
♃⊻♇ 19:10
☽⚼♆ 19:34
☽□♀ 20:22
☽#♇ 23:37

21 W
☽□♅ 1:12
☽△⚷ 1:18
☽☍♄ 5:57
☽∠♂ 7:47
☿#♃ 21:51
☽⊼♆ 23:08

22 Th
☽△⚳ 1:43
☽⚼⚷ 4:42
☽#♄ 6:12
☽⊼♇ 7:30
☽☍♃ 7:56
☽⚹♂ 12:06
☉△☽ 18:07
☿∠♆ 19:11
☽∥♅ 21:45
☽∥♀ 23:00
☽∥☿ 23:33

23 F
♀☌♅ 1:02
♀⊻⚷ 1:56
☽△☿ 2:48
☽#♃ 4:12
☽⚼⚳ 4:51
☿∥♀ 6:19
☉∥☽ 6:30
☽△♅ 6:58
☽⊼⚷ 7:03
☽△♀ 7:31
☽⚼♇ 9:38
☿∥♅ 10:17
☽⊼♄ 11:20
♂ ♋ 11:50
♀∥♅ 14:38
☉⚼☽ 21:45

24 Sa
☽☍♆ 3:11
☿☌♅ 6:43
☽⊼⚳ 6:56
☿⊻⚷ 7:12
☽⚼♅ 8:22
☽⚼☿ 8:39
☽∥⚷ 9:21
☽△♇ 10:51
☽⚼♀ 11:09
☽⊼♃ 11:48
☽⚼♄ 12:34
☉#♃ 13:56
☽□♂ 17:20
☽#♆ 17:44
☽∥⚳ 21:10

25 Su
☉⊼☽ 0:20
♀□♄ 4:23
☽⊼♅ 9:00
☽☍⚷ 9:03
☿□♄ 11:59
☽⚼♃ 12:30
☽△♄ 13:04
☽⊼☿ 13:14
☽⊼♀ 13:49
☽#⚳ 21:46
☿☌♀ 22:20

26 M
☽∥♆ 0:28
☽⊼♆ 4:02
☽#⚷ 8:44
☽☍⚳ 8:49
☽□♇ 11:16
☽△♃ 12:41
☽△♂ 19:31

27 Tu
☿#♄ 1:29
☉☍☽ 3:33
☽⚼♆ 3:49
☉∠♆ 8:01
☽☍♅ 8:52
☽⊼⚷ 8:55
☽∥♃ 10:49
☽□♄ 12:48
☉#☽ 15:34
☽☍♀ 17:36
☿∠♂ 17:52
☽#♅ 17:54
♇ R 20:04
☽⚼♂ 20:09
☽☍☿ 20:25

28 W
☽#♀ 1:36
☽△♆ 3:32
☽∥♄ 7:03
☽⚼⚷ 8:41
☽⊼⚳ 9:29
☽⚹♇ 10:40
☽□♃ 12:33
☽#☿ 12:33
☽⊼♂ 20:55

29 Th
☉⊼☽ 6:21
☽⊼♅ 8:39
☽△⚷ 8:41
☊ D 9:17
☽∥♇ 9:59
☽⚼⚳ 10:04
☽∠♇ 10:36
☉∥♅ 11:50
☽⚹♄ 12:37
☽⊼♀ 21:45

30 F
☿⚹♆ 2:28
☽□♆ 3:43
☽⊼☿ 3:55
♀∠♂ 5:11
⚳□♇ 6:20
☉⚼☽ 8:24
☽⚼♅ 9:07
⚳#♆ 10:05
☽#♂ 10:59
☽⊻♇ 11:01
☽△⚳ 11:09
☽∠♄ 13:08
☽⚹♃ 13:28
☉☌♅ 19:55
☉⊻⚷ 20:18
☽☍♂ 23:52

April 2021:Modify New York Stock Exchange Zone:-5

Sunday	Monday	Tuesday	Wednesday	Thursday	Friday	Saturday
March S M T W T F S 1 2 3 4 5 6 7 8 9 10 11 12 13 14 15 16 17 18 19 20 21 22 23 24 25 26 27 28 29 30 31	May S M T W T F S 1 2 3 4 5 6 7 8 9 10 11 12 13 14 15 16 17 18 19 20 21 22 23 24 25 26 27 28 29 30 31			1 12:57AM ☽-> 0♐00	2 1:03AM ☿ ⚹ ♇	3 3:11AM ☽-> 0♑00 10:40PM ☿ -> 0♈00
4	5 8:02AM ☽-> 0♒00	6 6:17AM ♀ ⚹ ♂	7 3:29PM ☽-> 0♓00	8	9 2:16PM ♂ □ ♆	10 1:10AM ☽-> 0♈00 10:08AM ☿ ⚹ ♄ 1:52PM ♀ ⚹ ♃
11 9:29PM New Moon♈ 10:19PM ♀ □ ♇	12 12:42PM ☽-> 0♉00	13 6:09PM ☉ ⚹ ♂	14 1:21PM ♀ -> 0♉00	15 1:33AM ☽-> 0♊00 11:57AM ☉ ⚹ ♃	16 8:25AM ☉ □ ♇	17 12:12AM ♂ △ ♃ 10:59AM ☿ ⚹ ♃ 2:08PM ☿ ⚹ ♂ 2:24PM ☽-> 0♋00 4:48PM ☿ □ ♇
18 8:48PM ☿ ☌ ☉	19 5:28AM ☿ -> 0♉00 3:32PM ☉-> 0♉00	20 1:09AM ☽-> 0♌00	21	22 8:07AM ☽-> 0♍00 8:00PM ♀ ☌ ♅	23 6:47AM ♂-> 0♋00	24 1:41AM ☿ ☌ ♅ 11:04AM ☽-> 0♎00 11:21PM ♀ □ ♄
25 6:57AM ☿ □ ♄ 5:18PM ☿ ☌ ♀	26 11:17AM ☽-> 0♏00 10:30PM Full Moon♏	27 3:04PM ♇ ℞ 26♑	28 10:41AM ☽-> 0♐00	29 9:25PM ☿ ⚹ ♆	30 11:15AM ☽-> 0♑00 2:53PM ☉ ☌ ♅	

LONGITUDE

Day	Sid.Time	☉	☽	☽ 12 hour	Mean☊	True☊	☿	♀	♂	⚳	♃	♄	⚷	♅	♆	♇
	h m s	° ' "	° ' "	° ' "	° '	° '	° '	° '	° '	° '	° '	° '	° '	° '	° '	° '
1 Sa	14 36 34	10♉50 46	4♑38 03	11♑45 44	12♊30.1	11♊01.5	24♉08.0	20♉02.8	4♋33.4	27♈05.8	28♒21.2	13♒06.6	10♈42.3	10♉41.4	22♓23.3	26♑48.3
2 Su	14 40 31	11 48 59	18 47 13	25 42 27	12 26.9	11 03.0	26 03.9	21 16.7	5 09.9	27 29.5	28 29.7	13 08.7	10 45.4	10 44.9	22 25.0	26R 48.2
3 M	14 44 27	12 47 11	2♒31 31	9♒14 37	12 23.8	11R 04.1	27 57.0	22 30.6	5 46.4	27 53.2	28 38.0	13 10.7	10 48.5	10 48.4	22 26.6	26 48.1
4 Tu	14 48 24	13 45 22	15 51 58	22 23 55	12 20.6	11 04.5	29 47.2	23 44.5	6 22.9	28 16.8	28 46.2	13 12.7	10 51.6	10 51.8	22 28.2	26 48.0
5 W	14 52 20	14 43 31	28 50 49	5♓13 04	12 17.4	11 03.7	1♊34.2	24 58.4	6 59.4	28 40.5	28 54.3	13 14.5	10 54.7	10 55.3	22 29.8	26 47.8
6 Th	14 56 17	15 41 39	11♓31 02	17 45 08	12 14.2	11 01.7	3 18.0	26 12.3	7 36.0	29 04.1	29 02.2	13 16.2	10 57.7	10 58.7	22 31.3	26 47.5
7 F	15 00 13	16 39 45	23 55 45	0♈03 15	12 11.1	10 58.7	4 58.3	27 26.1	8 12.5	29 27.7	29 10.0	13 17.9	11 00.7	11 02.2	22 32.9	26 47.3
8 Sa	15 04 10	17 37 49	6♈08 01	12 10 23	12 07.9	10 55.1	6 35.1	28 39.9	8 49.1	29 51.3	29 17.6	13 19.4	11 03.7	11 05.6	22 34.3	26 47.0
9 Su	15 08 06	18 35 52	18 10 39	24 09 09	12 04.7	10 51.4	8 08.2	29 53.7	9 25.6	0♉14.8	29 25.1	13 20.9	11 06.6	11 09.1	22 35.8	26 46.7
10 M	15 12 03	19 33 54	0♉06 10	6♉01 58	12 01.5	10 47.9	9 37.6	1♊07.5	10 02.2	0 38.3	29 32.5	13 22.2	11 09.6	11 12.5	22 37.3	26 46.4
11 Tu	15 16 00	20 31 54	11 56 49	17 50 59	11 58.3	10 45.1	11 03.2	2 21.3	10 38.8	1 01.8	29 39.7	13 23.5	11 12.5	11 15.9	22 38.7	26 46.0
12 W	15 19 56	21 29 53	23 44 45	29 38 21	11 55.2	10 43.2	12 25.0	3 35.0	11 15.5	1 25.3	29 46.7	13 24.7	11 15.3	11 19.4	22 40.1	26 45.6
13 Th	15 23 53	22 27 50	5♊32 05	11♊26 14	11 52.0	10D 42.3	13 42.7	4 48.8	11 52.1	1 48.8	29 53.6	13 25.7	11 18.2	11 22.8	22 41.5	26 45.2
14 F	15 27 49	23 25 46	17 21 07	23 17 04	11 48.8	10 42.3	14 56.5	6 02.5	12 28.7	2 12.2	0♓00.4	13 26.7	11 21.0	11 26.2	22 42.8	26 44.8
15 Sa	15 31 46	24 23 40	29 14 27	5♋13 37	11 45.6	10 43.1	16 06.2	7 16.2	13 05.4	2 35.6	0 07.0	13 27.6	11 23.8	11 29.6	22 44.1	26 44.3
16 Su	15 35 42	25 21 33	11♋14 59	17 18 59	11 42.5	10 44.3	17 11.8	8 29.9	13 42.1	2 58.9	0 13.4	13 28.4	11 26.5	11 33.0	22 45.4	26 43.8
17 M	15 39 39	26 19 23	23 26 04	29 36 40	11 39.3	10 45.6	18 13.2	9 43.5	14 18.8	3 22.3	0 19.7	13 29.0	11 29.2	11 36.4	22 46.7	26 43.3
18 Tu	15 43 35	27 17 13	5♌51 18	12♌10 24	11 36.1	10 46.8	19 10.4	10 57.2	14 55.5	3 45.6	0 25.9	13 29.6	11 31.9	11 39.7	22 47.9	26 42.8
19 W	15 47 32	28 15 00	18 34 28	25 03 53	11 32.9	10R 47.5	20 03.2	12 10.8	15 32.2	4 08.9	0 31.8	13 30.1	11 34.6	11 43.1	22 49.1	26 42.2
20 Th	15 51 29	29 12 46	1♍39 06	8♍20 25	11 29.8	10 47.6	20 51.6	13 24.4	16 08.9	4 32.1	0 37.6	13 30.5	11 37.2	11 46.4	22 50.3	26 41.6
21 F	15 55 25	0♊10 30	15 08 06	22 02 19	11 26.6	10 47.3	21 35.6	14 38.0	16 45.6	4 55.3	0 43.3	13 30.8	11 39.8	11 49.8	22 51.4	26 41.0
22 Sa	15 59 22	1 08 12	29 03 05	6♎10 19	11 23.4	10 46.5	22 15.1	15 51.5	17 22.3	5 18.5	0 48.8	13 30.9	11 42.3	11 53.1	22 52.5	26 40.3
23 Su	16 03 18	2 05 53	13♎23 43	20 42 53	11 20.2	10 45.6	22 50.0	17 05.0	17 59.1	5 41.6	0 54.1	13R 31.0	11 44.8	11 56.4	22 53.6	26 39.6
24 M	16 07 15	3 03 32	28 07 12	5♏35 54	11 17.0	10 44.7	23 20.3	18 18.6	18 35.8	6 04.7	0 59.2	13 31.0	11 47.3	11 59.7	22 54.7	26 38.9
25 Tu	16 11 11	4 01 10	13♏08 02	20 42 34	11 13.9	10 44.0	23 45.9	19 32.0	19 12.6	6 27.8	1 04.2	13 30.9	11 49.7	12 02.9	22 55.7	26 38.2
26 W	16 15 08	4 58 46	28 18 22	5♐54 13	11 10.7	10D 43.6	24 06.8	20 45.5	19 49.3	6 50.8	1 09.0	13 30.7	11 52.1	12 06.2	22 56.7	26 37.5
27 Th	16 19 04	5 56 21	13♐28 55	21 01 19	11 07.5	10 43.5	24 22.9	21 59.0	20 26.1	7 13.8	1 13.7	13 30.4	11 54.5	12 09.4	22 57.7	26 36.7
28 F	16 23 01	6 53 56	28 30 21	5♑55 02	11 04.3	10 43.6	24 34.3	23 12.4	21 02.9	7 36.7	1 18.2	13 30.0	11 56.8	12 12.7	22 58.6	26 35.9
29 Sa	16 26 58	7 51 29	13♑14 34	20 28 18	11 01.2	10 43.9	24R 41.0	24 25.8	21 39.7	7 59.7	1 22.5	13 29.5	11 59.1	12 15.9	22 59.5	26 35.1
30 Su	16 30 54	8 49 01	27 35 45	4♒36 37	10 58.0	10 44.1	24 43.0	25 39.2	22 16.5	8 22.5	1 26.6	13 28.9	12 01.3	12 19.1	23 00.4	26 34.3
31 M	16 34 51	9♊46 32	11♒30 45	18 18 09	10♊54.8	10♊44.2	24♊40.5	26♊52.6	22♋53.3	8♉45.4	1♓30.6	13♒28.3	12♈03.6	12♉22.2	23♓01.2	26♑33.4

1st of Month

Julian Day # 2459335.5
Obliquity 23°26'14"
SVP 4♓58'00"
GC 27♐08.2
Eris 24♈17.4

Day	⚴
1	16♓16.8
6	17 34.0
11	18 48.2
16	19 58.9
21	21 06.0
26	22 09.1
31	23 08.1

Day	⚵
1	23♐04.9R
6	22 30.2R
11	21 47.8R
16	20 58.2R
21	20 02.5R
26	19 01.7R
31	17 57.0R

Day	⚶
1	7♍08.5
6	7 38.8
11	8 19.4
16	9 09.8
21	10 09.3
26	11 17.2
31	12 32.8

DECLINATION and LATITUDE

Day	☉ Decl	☽ Decl	☽ Lat	☽12h Decl	☿ Decl	☿ Lat	♀ Decl	♀ Lat	♂ Decl	♂ Lat	⚳ Decl	⚳ Lat	♃ Decl	♃ Lat	♄ Decl	♄ Lat
1 Sa	15N05	25S27	2S06	25S35	20N15	1N29	17N25	0S21	24N48	1N27	4N07	6S46	12S45	0S45	17S26	0S35
2 Su	15 23	25 18	3 13	24 37	20 51	1 38	17 47	0 18	24 47	1 27	4 15	6 46	12 42	0 45	17 26	0 35
3 M	15 40	23 35	4 06	22 14	21 26	1 46	18 08	0 16	24 45	1 27	4 24	6 45	12 39	0 45	17 25	0 35
4 Tu	15 58	20 36	4 44	18 44	21 57	1 54	18 29	0 14	24 43	1 26	4 33	6 45	12 37	0 46	17 25	0 35
5 W	16 15	16 40	5 07	14 26	22 27	2 01	18 50	0 11	24 41	1 26	4 42	6 44	12 34	0 46	17 24	0 35
6 Th	16 32	12 05	5 14	9 37	22 54	2 07	19 09	0 09	24 39	1 26	4 50	6 44	12 32	0 46	17 24	0 35
7 F	16 49	7 06	5 06	4 31	23 18	2 13	19 29	0 06	24 37	1 26	4 59	6 43	12 29	0 46	17 24	0 36
8 Sa	17 05	1 55	4 44	0N41	23 40	2 17	19 48	0 04	24 34	1 26	5 08	6 43	12 27	0 46	17 23	0 36
9 Su	17 21	3N16	4 10	5 49	23 59	2 21	20 06	0 02	24 32	1 26	5 16	6 42	12 24	0 47	17 23	0 36
10 M	17 37	8 18	3 26	10 42	24 16	2 24	20 24	0N01	24 29	1 26	5 25	6 42	12 22	0 47	17 23	0 36
11 Tu	17 53	13 00	2 32	15 11	24 31	2 26	20 41	0 03	24 26	1 25	5 33	6 41	12 20	0 47	17 23	0 36
12 W	18 08	17 13	1 32	19 05	24 43	2 28	20 58	0 06	24 23	1 25	5 42	6 41	12 17	0 47	17 22	0 36
13 Th	18 23	20 45	0 29	22 13	24 54	2 28	21 14	0 08	24 19	1 25	5 50	6 40	12 15	0 48	17 22	0 36
14 F	18 38	23 27	0N37	24 25	25 02	2 27	21 29	0 11	24 16	1 25	5 58	6 40	12 13	0 48	17 22	0 37
15 Sa	18 52	25 07	1 41	25 32	25 08	2 26	21 44	0 13	24 12	1 25	6 07	6 39	12 11	0 48	17 22	0 37
16 Su	19 06	25 38	2 41	25 27	25 12	2 24	21 59	0 16	24 08	1 25	6 15	6 39	12 09	0 48	17 22	0 37
17 M	19 20	24 56	3 35	24 07	25 15	2 20	22 12	0 18	24 04	1 24	6 23	6 39	12 07	0 49	17 22	0 37
18 Tu	19 33	23 00	4 20	21 36	25 15	2 16	22 25	0 21	23 60	1 24	6 31	6 38	12 05	0 49	17 22	0 37
19 W	19 46	19 54	4 54	17 57	25 14	2 10	22 38	0 23	23 56	1 24	6 39	6 38	12 03	0 49	17 22	0 37
20 Th	19 59	15 45	5 13	13 20	25 11	2 04	22 50	0 25	23 51	1 24	6 47	6 37	12 01	0 49	17 22	0 37
21 F	20 11	10 43	5 16	7 55	25 07	1 57	23 01	0 28	23 46	1 24	6 55	6 37	11 59	0 50	17 22	0 38
22 Sa	20 23	4 59	5 01	1 56	25 01	1 49	23 11	0 30	23 41	1 24	7 03	6 37	11 58	0 50	17 22	0 38
23 Su	20 35	1S11	4 27	4S19	24 54	1 40	23 21	0 33	23 36	1 23	7 11	6 36	11 56	0 50	17 22	0 38
24 M	20 46	7 27	3 35	10 30	24 46	1 29	23 30	0 35	23 31	1 23	7 19	6 36	11 54	0 50	17 22	0 38
25 Tu	20 57	13 26	2 27	16 11	24 36	1 18	23 39	0 37	23 26	1 23	7 26	6 35	11 53	0 51	17 22	0 38
26 W	21 08	18 40	1 09	20 51	24 25	1 07	23 47	0 40	23 20	1 23	7 34	6 35	11 51	0 51	17 23	0 38
27 Th	21 18	22 40	0S15	24 05	24 13	0 54	23 54	0 42	23 15	1 23	7 42	6 35	11 50	0 51	17 23	0 38
28 F	21 28	25 03	1 37	25 34	23 60	0 40	24 00	0 44	23 09	1 22	7 49	6 34	11 49	0 51	17 23	0 39
29 Sa	21 37	25 37	2 51	25 14	23 45	0 26	24 06	0 47	23 03	1 22	7 57	6 34	11 47	0 52	17 23	0 39
30 Su	21 46	24 26	3 52	23 16	23 30	0 11	24 11	0 49	22 57	1 22	8 05	6 34	11 46	0 52	17 24	0 39
31 M	21N55	21S46	4S37	19S60	23N15	0S05	24N15	0N51	22N50	1N22	8N12	6S33	11S45	0S52	17S24	0S39

Day	⚷ Decl	⚷ Lat	♅ Decl	♅ Lat	♆ Decl	♆ Lat	♇ Decl	♇ Lat
1	6N22	2N19	14N39	0S24	4S01	1S05	22S11	1S25
6	6 28	2 19	14 44	0 24	3 58	1 05	22 12	1 26
11	6 34	2 19	14 49	0 24	3 55	1 06	22 13	1 27
16	6 40	2 19	14 55	0 24	3 53	1 06	22 14	1 27
21	6 45	2 19	14 60	0 24	3 51	1 06	22 15	1 28
26	6 50	2 20	15 05	0 24	3 49	1 06	22 17	1 28
31	6N55	2N20	15N10	0S24	3S47	1S06	22S18	1S29

Day	⚴ Decl	⚴ Lat	⚵ Decl	⚵ Lat	⚶ Decl	⚶ Lat	Eris Decl	Eris Lat
1	6N15	12N39	6S20	16N56	17N46	9N35	1S10	11S22
6	6 37	12 31	5 57	17 18	17 21	9 21	1 09	11 22
11	6 58	12 22	5 36	17 37	16 52	9 06	1 08	11 22
16	7 17	12 14	5 16	17 54	16 20	8 52	1 07	11 22
21	7 36	12 06	4 57	18 09	15 44	8 37	1 06	11 22
26	7 52	11 58	4 41	18 21	15 05	8 23	1 05	11 22
31	8N08	11N49	4S28	18N30	14N23	8N10	1S05	11S23

Moon Phenomena

Max/0 Decl

dy hr mn	
1 9:40	25S35
8 8:51	0 N
15 22:24	25N38
22 19:29	0 S
28 19:26	25S39

Max/0 Lat

dy hr mn	
5 23:05	5S14
13 10:31	0 N
20 16:21	5N17
26 19:38	0 S

Perigee/Apogee

dy hr m		kilometers
11 21:54	a	406512
26 1:51	p	357312

PH	dy hr mn	
☾	3 19:51	13♒35
●	11 19:01	21♉18
☽	19 19:14	29♌01
○	26 11:15	5♐26
●	26 11:20	T 1.009

Void of Course Moon

Last Aspect			☽ Ingress		
2 14:39	☿	△	♒	2	19:32
5 0:07	♃	☌	♓	5	2:10
7 7:37	♀	✶	♈	7	11:54
9 22:51	♃	✶	♉	9	23:48
12 12:24	♃	□	♊	12	12:44
14 10:52	♆	□	♋	15	1:32
17 6:24	♇	☍	♌	17	12:45
19 19:14	☉	□	♍	19	21:00
21 19:57	♇	△	♎	22	1:57
23 21:38	♇	□	♏	24	3:02
25 21:21	♇	✶	♐	26	2:40
27 17:37	☿	☍	♑	28	2:25
29 22:16	♇	☌	♒	30	4:05

DAILY ASPECTARIAN

1 Sa: ☽⚼♀ 0:45; ♀#♄ 1:13; ☽⚼☿ 8:45; ☽△♅ 10:14; ☽□⚷ 10:15; ☉△☽ 11:13; ☽⊻♄ 14:20; ☽∠♃ 14:51; ☿∠⚷ 20:02

2 Su: ☽△♀ 4:43; ☽✶♆ 6:17; ☿△♇ 9:20; ☽#♂ 9:48; ☽☌♇ 13:55; ☽△☿ 14:39; ☽□⚳ 15:34; ☽⊻♃ 17:04; ♀✶♆ 22:40; ☿⊻⚳ 22:58

3 M: ☽⊼♂ 6:03; ☽∠♆ 8:47; ☿□♃ 9:35; ☉□♄ 10:03; ♅⊻⚷ 10:47; ☽∥♇ 12:17; ☽✶⚷ 14:53; ☽□♅ 14:53; ☽#☿ 15:33; ☽☌♄ 19:09; ☉□☽ 19:51; ☊ R 20:05

4 Tu: ☿ ♊ 2:50; ☽⚼♂ 10:37; ☿#♇ 11:30; ☽⊻♆ 12:09; ☽#♀ 12:25; ☽□♀ 16:01; ☽∠⚷ 18:30; ☽∥♄ 19:48; ☽⊻♇ 20:10; ☽✶⚳ 23:40

5 W: ☽☌♃ 0:07; ☉#☽ 2:08; ☽□☿ 5:56; ☽#♅ 10:30; ☽△♂ 16:09; ♀∠⚷ 19:04; ⚳✶♃ 21:08; ☽∥♃ 21:45; ☽⊻⚷ 22:56; ☽✶♅ 22:58

6 Th: ☽∠♇ 0:32; ☽⊻♄ 3:22; ☽∠⚳ 5:03; ☉✶☽ 8:42; ♀△♇ 11:26; ☽☌♆ 21:18

7 F: ☽#⚷ 2:49; ☽∠♅ 4:08; ☽✶♇ 5:35; ☽✶♀ 7:37; ☽∠♄ 8:34; ☽#⚳ 9:35; ☽⊻♃ 10:22; ☽⊻⚳ 11:12; ☽∥♆ 14:37; ☉∠☽ 16:29

8 Sa: ☽✶☿ 1:02; ☽□♂ 5:36; ⚳ ♉ 8:55; ☽☌⚷ 9:50; ☽⊻♅ 9:54; ♀□♃ 13:39; ☽✶♄ 14:19; ☽∠♃ 16:24; ☽∠♀ 16:41

9 Su: ☉⊻☽ 0:55; ♀ ♊ 2:02; ☉#♄ 2:28; ☽#♆ 3:09; ☽⊻♆ 8:53; ☽∥⚳ 9:42; ♀⊻⚳ 10:04; ☽∠☿ 11:24; ☽∥⚷ 15:30; ☽□♇ 17:17; ☽✶♃ 22:51

10 M: ☽☌⚳ 1:07; ☽⊻♀ 2:18; ☿⊻♂ 11:49; ☽∠♆ 15:15; ☿∥♂ 16:49; ☽#♃ 20:26; ☽✶♂ 21:13; ☽⊻☿ 21:57; ☽⊻⚷ 22:30; ☽☌♅ 22:37

11 Tu: ☿✶⚷ 2:45; ☽□♄ 2:56; ☿⊻♅ 3:49; ☽∥♅ 10:01; ☿⚼♇ 12:22; ☉☌☽ 19:01; ☽✶♆ 21:48; ♂□⚷ 23:55

12 W: ☽#♄ 0:59; ♂✶♅ 2:49; ☽∠⚷ 5:08; ☽∠♂ 5:24; ☽△♇ 6:08; ☉∥☽ 6:11; ☽□♃ 12:24; ☽⊻⚳ 16:10; ☿△♄ 18:35; ☽☌♀ 22:22

13 Th: ☽∥♀ 4:04; ☉✶♆ 5:46; ☊ D 10:29; ☽✶⚷ 11:46; ☽⊻♅ 11:56; ☽#♇ 12:04; ☽⚼♇ 12:38; ☽⊻♂ 13:35; ☽△♄ 16:04; ☽☌☿ 18:34; ♃ ♓ 22:37; ☽∠⚳ 23:41

14 F: ☽∥♂ 9:32; ☽□♆ 10:52; ☉⊻☽ 13:23; ☽∠♅ 18:27; ☽⊼♇ 18:58; ☽⚼♄ 22:26

15 Sa: ☽∥☿ 0:23; ☽△♃ 1:47; ☽✶⚳ 6:57; ♂⊼♄ 14:50; ☽⊻♀ 17:54; ☉∠☽ 22:05

16 Su: ☽□⚷ 0:23; ☽✶♅ 0:36; ☽⊼♄ 4:25; ☽☌♂ 5:07; ☽⚼♃ 7:56; ☽⊻☿ 12:52; ☽∥☿ 17:50; ☽△♆ 22:43

17 M: ☽∠♀ 2:48; ♀#♇ 3:27; ☉∠⚷ 4:17; ☉✶☽ 6:06; ☿∠⚳ 6:09; ☽☍♇ 6:24; ☉△♇ 9:50; ☽∥♂ 13:08; ☽⊼♃ 13:30; ☽□⚳ 19:52; ☽∠☿ 20:31

18 Tu: ☽⚼♆ 3:43; ☽∥♀ 4:53; ☽#♇ 6:48; ☽✶♀ 10:44; ☽△⚷ 10:50; ☽□♅ 11:05; ♀✶⚷ 11:45; ☽☍♄ 14:30; ♀⊻♅ 14:32; ♀⚼♇ 14:45; ☽⊻♂ 18:02; ♂⚼♃ 23:44

19 W: ☉∥☽ 0:52; ☽✶☿ 2:56; ☽⊼♆ 7:53; ⚳∥⚷ 13:03; ☽⚼⚷ 14:49; ☽⊼♇ 14:59; ☽#♄ 15:21; ☊ R 19:11; ☉□☽ 19:14; ☽☍♃ 22:08; ☽∠♂ 23:03

20 Th: ♀△♄ 2:00; ☽∥♅ 3:56; ☽△⚳ 5:21; ☽⊼⚷ 17:52; ☽⚼♇ 17:56; ☽△♅ 18:10; ☽#♃ 18:14; ☉ ♊ 19:38; ☽⊼♄ 21:09; ☽□♀ 23:02

21 F: ☽✶♂ 2:58; ☽⚼⚳ 8:35; ☽□☿ 11:48; ☽☍♆ 13:26; ☉□♃ 15:05; ☽∥⚳ 15:47; ☽∥⚷ 16:47; ☽△♇ 19:57; ☽⚼♅ 20:18; ☽⚼♄ 23:05

22 Sa: ☽⊼♃ 3:00; ☉△☽ 3:47; ☽#♆ 4:33; ☽⊼⚳ 10:51; ☽☍⚷ 21:16; ☽⊼♅ 21:35

23 Su: ☽△♄ 0:12; ☿□♆ 2:44; ☽⚼♃ 4:09; ☉⚼☽ 6:31; ☽△♀ 6:37; ☽□♂ 7:52; ♄ R 9:20; ☽∥♆ 10:06; ☽⊼♆ 15:34; ☽△☿ 16:00; ☽#⚷ 21:29; ☽□♇ 21:38; ☽#⚳ 23:27

24 M: ♀∥♂ 1:28; ☽△♃ 4:38; ☉⊼☽ 8:29; ☽⚼♀ 9:05; ♀⊻♂ 11:17; ☽☍⚳ 13:06; ☽⚼♆ 15:42; ☽⚼☿ 16:52; ☽∥♃ 17:34; ☽⊼⚷ 21:55; ☽☍♅ 22:16

25 Tu: ☽□♄ 0:36; ☽#♅ 7:03; ☽△♂ 10:02; ☽⊼♀ 11:02; ☉∠♂ 13:08; ☽△♆ 15:31; ☽⊼☿ 17:14; ☽∥♄ 17:37; ☽✶♇ 21:21; ☽⚼⚷ 21:43

26 W: ☽□♃ 4:31; ☽⚼♂ 10:43; ☉☍☽ 11:15; ☽⊼⚳ 13:50; ☉#☽ 14:19; ☊ D 19:23; ☽∠♇ 21:02; ☽∥♇ 21:12; ☽△⚷ 21:30; ☽⊼♅ 21:53

27 Th: ☽✶♄ 0:02; ☽#♂ 4:21; ♀∠⚳ 7:03; ☽#♀ 10:44; ☽⊼♂ 11:32; ☽#☿ 12:17; ☽⚼⚳ 14:18; ☽☍♀ 14:44; ☽□♆ 15:07; ☽☍☿ 17:37; ♀□♆ 19:26; ☽⊻♇ 20:56; ☽⚼♅ 21:55; ☿∥♀ 23:19; ☽∠♄ 23:59

28 F: ☽✶♃ 4:32; ☉⊼☽ 14:33; ☽△⚳ 15:10; ☽□⚷ 21:55; ☽△♅ 22:23; ⚳∠♆ 23:49

29 Sa: ☽⊻♄ 0:25; ☽∠♃ 5:12; ☿☌♀ 5:14; ☉⊻⚳ 5:40; ☽☍♂ 14:37; ☽✶♆ 16:15; ☉⚼☽ 17:09; ☽⊼☿ 19:08; ☽⊼♀ 20:24; ☽☌♇ 22:16; ☿ R 22:35

30 Su: ☽#♀ 2:48; ☽⊻♃ 6:36; ☽#☿ 10:50; ☽#♂ 15:19; ♀⊼♇ 17:48; ☽∠♆ 17:54; ☽□⚳ 19:03; ☽∥♇ 20:01; ☉△☽ 20:44; ☽⚼☿ 20:48; ☉#☽ 22:58

31 M: ☽⚼♀ 0:42; ☽✶⚷ 0:58; ☽□♅ 1:31; ☽☌♄ 3:26; ♂△♆ 5:17; ♀∠♅ 10:08; ☽⊻♆ 20:29; ☽⊼♂ 21:12; ☽△☿ 23:15

May 2021:Modify New York Stock Exchange Zone:-5

Sunday	Monday	Tuesday	Wednesday	Thursday	Friday	Saturday
						1
2 4:18AM ☿ △ ♇ 2:29PM ☽-> 0♒00 5:37PM ♀ ⚹ ♆	3 4:32AM ☿ □ ♃ 5:00AM ☉ □ ♄ 9:48PM ☿-> 0♊00	4 9:07PM ☽-> 0♓00	5	6 6:23AM ♀ △ ♇	7 6:51AM ☽-> 0♈00	8 8:37AM ♀ □ ♃ 9:00PM ♀-> 0♊00
9 6:45PM ☽-> 0♉00	10	11 1:58PM New Moon♉[9:46PM ♂ ⚹ ♅	12 7:41AM ☽-> 0♊00 1:32PM ☿ △ ♄	13 12:44AM ☉ ⚹ ♆ 5:34PM ♃-> 0♓00	14 8:29PM ☽-> 0♋00	15
16	17 4:47AM ☉ △ ♇ 7:42AM ☽-> 0♌00	18	19 3:58PM ☽-> 0♍00 8:57PM ♀ △ ♄	20 2:36PM ☉-> 0♊00	21 10:02AM ☉ □ ♃ 8:34PM ☽-> 0♎00	22 9:42PM ☿ □ ♆
23 4:19AM ♄ ℞13♒ 9:59PM ☽-> 0♏00	24	25 9:38PM ☽-> 0♐00	26 6:12AM Full Moon♐	27 2:24PM ♀ □ ♆ 9:22PM ☽-> 0♑00	28	29 12:12AM ♀ ☌ ☿ 5:33PM ☿ ℞24♊ 11:03PM ☽-> 0♒00
30	31 12:14AM ♂ △ ♆				April	June

April

S	M	T	W	T	F	S
				1	2	3
4	5	6	7	8	9	10
11	12	13	14	15	16	17
18	19	20	21	22	23	24
25	26	27	28	29	30	

June

S	M	T	W	T	F	S
		1	2	3	4	5
6	7	8	9	10	11	12
13	14	15	16	17	18	19
20	21	22	23	24	25	26
27	28	29	30			

June 2021

LONGITUDE

Day	Sid.Time	☉	☽	☽ 12 hour	Mean☊	True ☊	☿	♀	♂	⚳	♃	♄	⚷	♅	♆	♇
	h m s	° ' "	° ' "	° ' "	° '	° '	° '	° '	° '	° '	° '	° '	° '	° '	° '	° '
1 Tu	16 38 47	10♊44 03	24♒58 56	1♓33 23	10♊51.6	10♊44.3	24♊33.5	28♊05.9	23♋30.1	9♉08.2	1♓34.4	13♒27.5	12♈05.7	12♉25.4	23♓02.0	26♑32.5
2 W	16 42 44	11 41 32	8♓01 48	14 24 36	10 48.5	10D 44.3	24R 22.3	29 19.3	24 07.0	9 30.9	1 38.0	13R 26.6	12 07.9	12 28.5	23 02.8	26R 31.6
3 Th	16 46 40	12 39 01	20 42 15	26 55 13	10 45.3	10 44.3	24 07.0	0♋32.6	24 43.8	9 53.6	1 41.4	13 25.6	12 09.9	12 31.6	23 03.6	26 30.7
4 F	16 50 37	13 36 29	3♈04 02	9♈09 13	10 42.1	10 44.4	23 48.0	1 45.9	25 20.7	10 16.3	1 44.6	13 24.6	12 12.0	12 34.7	23 04.3	26 29.7
5 Sa	16 54 33	14 33 56	15 11 18	21 10 47	10 38.9	10 44.7	23 25.6	2 59.2	25 57.6	10 38.9	1 47.7	13 23.4	12 14.0	12 37.8	23 05.0	26 28.8
6 Su	16 58 30	15 31 23	27 08 09	3♉03 54	10 35.7	10 45.2	23 00.1	4 12.5	26 34.4	11 01.5	1 50.6	13 22.1	12 16.0	12 40.8	23 05.6	26 27.8
7 M	17 02 27	16 28 49	8♉58 28	14 52 17	10 32.6	10 45.8	22 31.9	5 25.7	27 11.3	11 24.0	1 53.3	13 20.8	12 17.9	12 43.8	23 06.3	26 26.8
8 Tu	17 06 23	17 26 14	20 45 45	26 39 14	10 29.4	10 46.3	22 01.7	6 39.0	27 48.3	11 46.5	1 55.8	13 19.3	12 19.8	12 46.8	23 06.9	26 25.7
9 W	17 10 20	18 23 39	2♊33 06	8♊27 38	10 26.2	10R 46.7	21 29.7	7 52.2	28 25.2	12 08.9	1 58.1	13 17.8	12 21.6	12 49.8	23 07.4	26 24.7
10 Th	17 14 16	19 21 03	14 23 10	20 19 58	10 23.0	10 46.8	20 56.7	9 05.4	29 02.1	12 31.3	2 00.2	13 16.2	12 23.4	12 52.8	23 08.0	26 23.6
11 F	17 18 13	20 18 26	26 18 19	2♋18 27	10 19.9	10 46.4	20 23.1	10 18.6	29 39.1	12 53.6	2 02.2	13 14.5	12 25.1	12 55.7	23 08.4	26 22.5
12 Sa	17 22 09	21 15 48	8♋20 37	14 25 04	10 16.7	10 45.6	19 49.6	11 31.7	0♌16.0	13 15.9	2 03.9	13 12.7	12 26.8	12 58.6	23 08.9	26 21.4
13 Su	17 26 06	22 13 10	20 32 03	26 41 48	10 13.5	10 44.2	19 16.7	12 44.9	0 53.0	13 38.1	2 05.5	13 10.8	12 28.5	13 01.5	23 09.3	26 20.3
14 M	17 30 02	23 10 31	2♌54 34	9♌10 35	10 10.3	10 42.6	18 44.9	13 58.0	1 30.0	14 00.3	2 06.8	13 08.8	12 30.1	13 04.3	23 09.7	26 19.2
15 Tu	17 33 59	24 07 51	15 30 07	21 53 27	10 07.2	10 40.8	18 14.9	15 11.1	2 07.0	14 22.4	2 08.0	13 06.7	12 31.7	13 07.1	23 10.1	26 18.0
16 W	17 37 56	25 05 09	28 20 48	4♍52 26	10 04.0	10 39.2	17 47.0	16 24.2	2 44.0	14 44.4	2 09.0	13 04.5	12 33.2	13 09.9	23 10.4	26 16.9
17 Th	17 41 52	26 02 28	11♍28 35	18 09 29	10 00.8	10 38.1	17 21.9	17 37.3	3 21.0	15 06.4	2 09.8	13 02.3	12 34.6	13 12.6	23 10.7	26 15.7
18 F	17 45 49	26 59 45	24 55 19	1♎46 12	9 57.6	10D 37.6	16 59.9	18 50.3	3 58.1	15 28.3	2 10.4	13 00.0	12 36.1	13 15.4	23 11.0	26 14.5
19 Sa	17 49 45	27 57 01	8♎42 13	15 43 21	9 54.5	10 37.8	16 41.3	20 03.3	4 35.1	15 50.1	2 10.8	12 57.6	12 37.4	13 18.1	23 11.2	26 13.2
20 Su	17 53 42	28 54 17	22 49 33	0♏00 34	9 51.3	10 38.7	16 26.6	21 16.3	5 12.2	16 11.9	2R 11.0	12 55.1	12 38.8	13 20.7	23 11.4	26 12.0
21 M	17 57 38	29 51 31	7♏16 07	14 35 45	9 48.1	10 39.9	16 15.9	22 29.2	5 49.2	16 33.6	2 11.1	12 52.5	12 40.0	13 23.4	23 11.6	26 10.8
22 Tu	18 01 35	0♋48 45	21 58 53	29 24 50	9 44.9	10 41.1	16D 09.5	23 42.2	6 26.3	16 55.3	2 10.9	12 49.9	12 41.3	13 26.0	23 11.8	26 09.5
23 W	18 05 32	1 45 59	6♐52 46	14♐21 46	9 41.7	10R 41.7	16 07.6	24 55.1	7 03.4	17 16.9	2 10.5	12 47.1	12 42.4	13 28.5	23 11.9	26 08.2
24 Th	18 09 28	2 43 12	21 50 52	29 19 01	9 38.6	10 41.5	16 10.3	26 08.0	7 40.5	17 38.4	2 10.0	12 44.3	12 43.6	13 31.1	23 11.9	26 06.9
25 F	18 13 25	3 40 25	6♑45 12	14♑08 25	9 35.4	10 40.1	16 17.7	27 20.8	8 17.6	17 59.9	2 09.2	12 41.5	12 44.7	13 33.6	23R 12.0	26 05.7
26 Sa	18 17 21	4 37 37	21 27 44	28 42 20	9 32.2	10 37.7	16 29.9	28 33.6	8 54.7	18 21.3	2 08.3	12 38.5	12 45.7	13 36.0	23 12.0	26 04.3
27 Su	18 21 18	5 34 49	5♒51 31	12♒54 44	9 29.0	10 34.5	16 46.8	29 46.5	9 31.8	18 42.6	2 07.2	12 35.5	12 46.7	13 38.5	23 12.0	26 03.0
28 M	18 25 14	6 32 01	19 51 36	26 41 54	9 25.9	10 30.9	17 08.5	0♌59.2	10 09.0	19 03.9	2 05.9	12 32.4	12 47.6	13 40.9	23 11.9	26 01.7
29 Tu	18 29 11	7 29 13	3♓25 34	10♓02 38	9 22.7	10 27.5	17 35.0	2 12.0	10 46.1	19 25.0	2 04.4	12 29.2	12 48.5	13 43.3	23 11.8	26 00.4
30 W	18 33 07	8♋26 25	16 33 21	22 58 00	9♊19.5	10♊24.7	18♊06.2	3♌24.7	11♌23.3	19♉46.1	2♓02.7	12♒26.0	12♈49.4	13♉45.6	23♓11.7	25♑59.0

1st of Month

Julian Day # 2459366.5
Obliquity 23°26'14"
SVP 4♓57'55"
GC 27♐08.3
Eris 24♈34.9

Day	⚴	Day	⚵	Day	⚶
1	23♓19.3	1	17♐43.7R	1	12♍48.8
6	24 12.7	6	16 36.2R	6	14 12.7
11	25 01.0	11	15 28.1R	11	15 43.2
16	25 43.8	16	14 21.0R	16	17 19.6
21	26 20.8	21	13 16.4R	21	19 01.4
26	26 51.6	26	12 15.8R	26	20 48.2

DECLINATION and LATITUDE

Day	☉ Decl	☽ Decl	☽ Lat	☽12h Decl	☿ Decl	☿ Lat	♀ Decl	♀ Lat	♂ Decl	♂ Lat	⚳ Decl	⚳ Lat	♃ Decl	♃ Lat	♄ Decl	♄ Lat
1 Tu	22N03	17S59	5S06	15S48	22N58	0S21	24N19	0N53	22N44	1N22	8N19	6S33	11S44	0S52	17S24	0S39
2 W	22 11	13 28	5 17	11 01	22 41	0 38	24 22	0 56	22 37	1 21	8 27	6 33	11 43	0 53	17 25	0 39
3 Th	22 19	8 29	5 13	5 53	22 23	0 55	24 24	0 58	22 31	1 21	8 34	6 32	11 42	0 53	17 25	0 39
4 F	22 26	3 17	4 54	0 40	22 05	1 13	24 25	0 60	22 24	1 21	8 41	6 32	11 41	0 53	17 26	0 40
5 Sa	22 33	1N57	4 22	4N31	21 47	1 30	24 26	1 02	22 17	1 21	8 48	6 32	11 40	0 53	17 26	0 40
6 Su	22 39	7 02	3 40	9 29	21 28	1 47	24 26	1 04	22 09	1 21	8 55	6 31	11 39	0 54	17 27	0 40
7 M	22 45	11 50	2 48	14 05	21 09	2 04	24 25	1 06	22 02	1 20	9 03	6 31	11 39	0 54	17 27	0 40
8 Tu	22 51	16 11	1 49	18 09	20 51	2 21	24 24	1 08	21 54	1 20	9 10	6 31	11 38	0 54	17 28	0 40
9 W	22 56	19 55	0 46	21 30	20 33	2 37	24 22	1 10	21 47	1 20	9 16	6 31	11 37	0 55	17 28	0 40
10 Th	23 01	22 51	0N20	23 58	20 15	2 53	24 19	1 11	21 39	1 20	9 23	6 30	11 37	0 55	17 29	0 40
11 F	23 05	24 48	1 25	25 22	19 58	3 07	24 15	1 13	21 31	1 19	9 30	6 30	11 36	0 55	17 29	0 41
12 Sa	23 09	25 37	2 27	25 34	19 42	3 21	24 11	1 15	21 23	1 19	9 37	6 30	11 36	0 55	17 30	0 41
13 Su	23 13	25 13	3 23	24 32	19 27	3 34	24 06	1 17	21 15	1 19	9 44	6 30	11 36	0 56	17 31	0 41
14 M	23 16	23 34	4 10	22 18	19 13	3 45	24 00	1 18	21 06	1 19	9 50	6 29	11 35	0 56	17 31	0 41
15 Tu	23 18	20 45	4 46	18 56	19 00	3 56	23 54	1 20	20 58	1 19	9 57	6 29	11 35	0 56	17 32	0 41
16 W	23 21	16 52	5 09	14 36	18 49	4 04	23 47	1 22	20 49	1 18	10 03	6 29	11 35	0 56	17 33	0 41
17 Th	23 23	12 08	5 16	9 29	18 39	4 12	23 39	1 23	20 40	1 18	10 10	6 29	11 35	0 57	17 34	0 41
18 F	23 24	6 42	5 07	3 49	18 31	4 18	23 30	1 25	20 31	1 18	10 16	6 28	11 35	0 57	17 35	0 42
19 Sa	23 25	0 50	4 39	2S12	18 25	4 23	23 21	1 26	20 22	1 18	10 23	6 28	11 35	0 57	17 35	0 42
20 Su	23 26	5S14	3 55	8 15	18 20	4 26	23 11	1 27	20 13	1 17	10 29	6 28	11 36	0 58	17 36	0 42
21 M	23 26	11 11	2 54	13 60	18 17	4 28	23 01	1 29	20 04	1 17	10 35	6 28	11 36	0 58	17 37	0 42
22 Tu	23 26	16 37	1 42	19 01	18 16	4 29	22 50	1 30	19 54	1 17	10 41	6 28	11 36	0 58	17 38	0 42
23 W	23 26	21 07	0 21	22 51	18 16	4 28	22 38	1 31	19 45	1 17	10 47	6 27	11 36	0 58	17 39	0 42
24 Th	23 25	24 12	1S01	25 07	18 18	4 26	22 26	1 32	19 35	1 16	10 53	6 27	11 37	0 59	17 40	0 42
25 F	23 23	25 34	2 19	25 34	18 22	4 23	22 12	1 33	19 25	1 16	10 59	6 27	11 37	0 59	17 41	0 42
26 Sa	23 21	25 07	3 26	24 14	18 27	4 19	21 59	1 34	19 15	1 16	11 05	6 27	11 38	0 59	17 42	0 43
27 Su	23 19	22 59	4 19	21 23	18 34	4 14	21 44	1 35	19 05	1 16	11 11	6 27	11 39	0 60	17 43	0 43
28 M	23 17	19 30	4 54	17 23	18 42	4 08	21 30	1 36	18 55	1 15	11 17	6 26	11 39	0 60	17 44	0 43
29 Tu	23 14	15 05	5 12	12 39	18 52	4 01	21 14	1 36	18 44	1 15	11 23	6 26	11 40	1 00	17 45	0 43
30 W	23N10	10S06	5S12	7S29	19N03	3S53	20N58	1N37	18N34	1N15	11N28	6S26	11S41	1S00	17S46	0S43

Day	⚷ Decl	⚷ Lat	♅ Decl	♅ Lat	♆ Decl	♆ Lat	♇ Decl	♇ Lat
1	6N56	2N20	15N11	0S24	3S47	1S07	22S18	1S29
6	6 60	2 20	15 15	0 24	3 46	1 07	22 20	1 30
11	7 04	2 20	15 20	0 24	3 45	1 07	22 21	1 30
16	7 07	2 21	15 24	0 24	3 44	1 07	22 23	1 31
21	7 10	2 21	15 28	0 24	3 44	1 07	22 25	1 32
26	7 12	2 21	15 32	0 24	3 44	1 08	22 26	1 32

Day	⚴ Decl	⚴ Lat	⚵ Decl	⚵ Lat	⚶ Decl	⚶ Lat	Eris Decl	Eris Lat
1	8N10	11N47	4S25	18N31	14N14	8N07	1S05	11S23
6	8 23	11 39	4 15	18 35	13 29	7 54	1 04	11 23
11	8 34	11 29	4 09	18 36	12 42	7 41	1 04	11 23
16	8 42	11 20	4 05	18 33	11 53	7 29	1 03	11 24
21	8 47	11 10	4 05	18 27	11 02	7 17	1 03	11 24
26	8 49	10 59	4 08	18 17	10 10	7 06	1 03	11 24

Moon Phenomena

Max/0 Decl
dy hr mn
4 15:02 0 N
12 4:09 25N38
19 3:18 0 S
25 5:52 25S38

Max/0 Lat
dy hr mn
2 5:05 5S18
9 16:43 0 N
16 22:29 5N16
23 6:08 0 S
29 12:43 5S14

Perigee/Apogee
dy hr m kilometers
8 2:28 a 406228
23 9:56 p 359960

PH dy hr mn
☾ 2 7:26 11♓59
● 10 10:54 19♊47
◐ 10 643:05A 03'51"
☽ 18 3:55 27♍09
○ 24 18:41 3♑28

Void of Course Moon

Last Aspect			☽ Ingress		
1 6:15	♀	△	♓	1	9:09
3 11:12	♇	⚹	♈	3	18:00
5 22:48	♂	□	♉	6	5:47
8 15:08	♂	⚹	♊	8	18:49
10 17:39	♆	□	♋	11	7:24
13 11:17	♇	☍	♌	13	18:24
15 17:28	☉	⚹	♍	16	3:03
18 3:55	☉	□	♎	18	8:55
20 10:53	☉	△	♏	20	11:59
22 6:44	♇	⚹	♐	22	12:57
24 2:10	♆	□	♑	24	13:06
26 12:51	♀	☍	♒	26	14:10
27 19:09	☿	△	♓	28	17:52

DAILY ASPECTARIAN

1 Tu
☊R 1:29
☽⚺♇ 2:50
☽∥♄ 3:17
☽∠⚷ 3:51
☽△♀ 6:15
♀⚼♄ 6:58
☽☌♃ 12:05
☽⋕♅ 15:12
☿∠⚳ 18:10
☉⚼♇ 19:55

2 W
☽⚼♂ 2:08
☽⚹⚳ 2:52
☽∠♇ 6:33
☿⚺♂ 7:15
☉□☽ 7:26
☊D 7:26
☽⚺⚷ 7:43
☿∥♂ 7:45
☽⚹♅ 8:23
☽∥♃ 8:38
☽⚺♄ 10:10
☉⚹⚷ 11:24
♀ ♋ 13:20
☉⚺♅ 20:44
☽⋕⚳ 23:35

3 Th
☉⋕♇ 0:19
☉∥☿ 4:12
☽☌♆ 4:32
☿⋕♇ 5:41
☽□☿ 6:25
☽⋕⚷ 7:04
☽△♂ 8:10
☽∠⚳ 8:20
☽⚹♇ 11:12
☽∠♅ 13:14
☽∠♄ 14:55
☉△♄ 19:07
☉∥♂ 20:12
☽□♀ 21:10
☽⚺♃ 21:24
☽∥♆ 21:45
♀△♃ 23:34

4 F
☽⚺⚳ 14:40
♂⋕♇ 14:55
☽☌⚷ 18:06
☽⚺♅ 18:53
☽⚹♄ 20:25
☉⚹☽ 22:39

5 Sa
☽∠♃ 3:13
☽⋕♆ 8:28
☽⚺♆ 15:51
☽⚹☿ 15:58
☿□♆ 19:06
♂☍♇ 19:46
☽□♇ 22:39
☽□♂ 22:48
☽∥⚷ 23:48

6 Su
☉∠☽ 7:27
☽∥⚳ 9:27
☽⚹♃ 9:34
☽⚹♀ 15:58
☽∠☿ 21:11
☽∠♆ 22:14
☽⋕♃ 22:59

7 M
☽☌⚳ 5:06
☽⚺⚷ 6:47
☽☌♅ 7:40
☽□♄ 8:53
☉⚺☽ 16:38
☽∥♅ 18:45

8 Tu
☽∠♀ 2:01
☽⚺☿ 2:28
☽⚹♆ 4:48
☽⋕♄ 7:42
☽△♇ 11:31
☽∠⚷ 13:25
☽⚹♂ 15:08
☽□♃ 22:49

9 W
☽∥☿ 4:10
☽⚺♀ 12:03
☽∥♂ 13:42
⚳⚺⚷ 14:46
☊R 16:48
☽⚼♇ 17:57
☽⋕♇ 19:16
☽⚹⚷ 19:57
☽⚺⚳ 20:06
☽⚺♅ 20:56
☽△♄ 21:45
☽∠♂ 23:15

10 Th
☉∥☽ 1:35
☉☌☽ 10:54
☽☌☿ 12:38
☽∥♀ 16:03
☽□♆ 17:39

11 F
☽⚻♇ 0:08
☉☌☿ 1:14
⚳☌♅ 2:33
☽∠♅ 3:16
☽∠⚳ 3:17
☽⚼♄ 3:52
☽⚺♂ 7:04
☽△♃ 11:29
♂ ♌ 13:35
⚳□♄ 20:47

12 Sa
☽☌♀ 7:00
☽□⚷ 8:08
☽⚹♅ 9:12
☽⚻♄ 9:36
☽⚹⚳ 10:02
☽⚼♃ 17:15
♀□⚷ 18:29
☽⚺☿ 21:39

13 Su
☉⚺☽ 3:34
☽△♆ 5:07
♀⚹♅ 5:39
♀⚻♄ 8:16
☽☍♇ 11:17
☽∥♀ 18:46
☽☌♂ 21:09
☽⚻♃ 22:28
☉□♆ 23:41

14 M
♀⚹⚳ 1:03
☽∠☿ 1:33
☉∥☽ 3:03
☽⚼♆ 10:04
☉∠☽ 10:55
☽⋕♇ 11:18
☽△⚷ 18:22
☽□♅ 19:29
☽☍♄ 19:29
☽□⚳ 21:48
♄□♅ 22:02
☽∥♂ 22:21
☽⚺♀ 23:20

15 Tu
♂⚻♃ 0:40
☽⚹☿ 4:59
☽∥☿ 12:07
☽⚻♆ 14:24
☉⚹☽ 17:28
☽⚻♇ 20:11
☽⋕♄ 20:13
☽⚼⚷ 22:32

16 W
☿∠♂ 1:08
☽∠♀ 6:13
☽☍♃ 7:01
☽∥♅ 7:51
☽⚺♂ 8:29
♀⚼♃ 14:53
☿⚺♀ 20:12
☽⚼♇ 23:37

17 Th
☽⚻⚷ 1:59
☽⋕♃ 2:32
☽⚻♄ 2:49
☽△♅ 3:08
☉⚻♇ 5:25
☽△⚳ 6:43
☽∥⚳ 8:49
☽□☿ 10:17
☽⚹♀ 12:08
☽∠♂ 12:56
☽☍♆ 20:56
☽∥⚷ 22:11

18 F
☽△♇ 2:19
☊D 3:49
☉□☽ 3:55
☽⚼♄ 5:24
☽⚼♅ 5:53
☽⚼⚳ 10:00
☽⋕♆ 12:18
☽⚻♃ 12:43
☉∥♀ 14:47
☽⚹♂ 16:33

19 Sa
☉⚼♄ 0:13
☽☍⚷ 6:44
☽△♄ 7:16
☽⚻♅ 7:54
☉∠♅ 9:15
☽⚻⚳ 12:31
☽△☿ 13:24
☽⚼♃ 14:29
☽∥♆ 18:03
☽□♀ 21:08

20 Su
☽⚻♆ 0:37
☽□♇ 5:39
☽⋕⚷ 7:36
☿⚺⚳ 10:28
☉△☽ 10:53
☽⚼☿ 14:11
♃R 15:06
☽△♃ 15:36
☽⋕⚳ 21:27
☽□♂ 21:31

21 M
☽⚼♆ 1:31
☽∥♃ 1:42
☉ ♋ 3:33
☽⚻⚷ 8:52
☽□♄ 9:10
☽☍♅ 10:04
☉⚼☽ 13:17
♀△♆ 13:58
☽⚻☿ 14:36
☽☍⚳ 15:35
☽⋕♅ 18:39

22 Tu
☽△♆ 1:58
☽△♀ 3:02
☽∥♄ 4:55
☽⚹♇ 6:44
☽⋕☿ 8:05
☽⚼⚷ 9:14
☉⚻☽ 15:13
☽⋕♂ 16:15
☽□♃ 16:27
☿D 22:01

23 W
☽△♂ 0:18
☽⚼♀ 5:18
☊R 6:12
☽∠♇ 6:49
☽∥♇ 8:49
☽△⚷ 9:21
☽⚹♄ 9:27
☽⋕♀ 9:44
☉△♃ 10:12
☽⚻♅ 10:36
☽☍☿ 14:51
☉⋕☽ 16:34
☽⚻⚳ 17:05
☉∠⚳ 20:48
♀☍♇ 23:40
♀⋕♇ 23:41

24 Th
☽⚼♂ 1:23
☽□♆ 2:10
♄⚹⚷ 4:31
☽⚺♇ 6:51
☽⚻♀ 7:29
☽∠♄ 9:26
☽⚼♅ 10:45
☽⚹♃ 16:35
☽⚼⚳ 17:47
☉☍☽ 18:41
♂⚼♆ 20:23

25 F
☽⚻♂ 2:36
☽⚺♄ 9:36
☽□⚷ 9:44
☽△♅ 11:05
☽⚻☿ 15:43
☽∠♃ 16:55
☽△⚳ 18:46
♆R 19:22

26 Sa
☽⚹♆ 2:52
☽☌♇ 7:37
☽☍♀ 12:51
☽⚼☿ 16:59
☽⚺♃ 17:43
☉⋕☽ 21:01
☉⚻☽ 23:30

27 Su
☽∠♆ 3:58
☽∥♇ 4:16
♀ ♌ 4:28
☽☍♂ 6:31
☽⋕♀ 10:14
☽☌♄ 11:25
☽⚹⚷ 11:47
☽□♅ 13:17
☽△☿ 19:09
☽□⚳ 22:35

28 M
☉⚼☽ 3:08
☽⋕♂ 3:39
☽⋕☿ 4:30
☽⚺♆ 5:50
☽∥♄ 10:07
☽⚺♇ 10:48
☽∠⚷ 13:57
☿∥♂ 14:45
♀⚻♃ 21:32
☽⋕♅ 21:34
☽☌♃ 21:35
☽⚻♀ 21:35

29 Tu
☉△☽ 7:55
☿∠♀ 12:57
☽∠♇ 13:44
☽⚻♂ 13:59
☽⚺♄ 16:25
☽∥♃ 16:36
☽⚺⚷ 17:05
☽⋕⚳ 17:41
☽⚹♅ 18:49

30 W
☽□☿ 3:01
☽⚼♀ 3:49
☽⚹⚳ 6:10
☽☌♆ 12:26
☽⋕⚷ 13:07
☽⚹♇ 17:41
☽⚼♂ 19:26
☽∠♄ 20:23
☽∠♅ 23:04

June 2021:Modify New York Stock Exchange Zone:-5

Sunday	Monday	Tuesday	Wednesday	Thursday	Friday	Saturday
		1 4:06AM ☽-> 0♓00	2 8:18AM ♀-> 0♋00	3 12:57PM ☽-> 0♈00 2:04PM ☉ △ ♄ 6:32PM ♀ △ ♃	4	5 2:04PM ♆ □ ☿ 2:44PM ♂ ☍ ♇
6 12:45AM ☽-> 0♉00	7	8 1:46PM ☽-> 0♊00	9	10 5:51AM New Moon ♊[8:12PM ☉ ☌ ☿	11 2:21AM ☽-> 0♋00 8:32AM ♂-> 0♌00	12
13 12:37AM ♀ ⚹ ♅ 1:21PM ☽-> 0♌00 6:38PM ☉ □ ♆	14 5:00PM ♅ □ ♄	15 10:00PM ☽-> 0♍00	16	17	18 3:52AM ☽-> 0♎00	19
20 6:56AM ☽-> 0♏00 10:05AM ♃ ℞ 2♓ 10:31PM ☉-> 0♋00	21 8:56AM ♀ △ ♆	22 7:54AM ☽-> 0♐00 4:59PM ☿ Direct	23 5:10AM ☉ △ ♃ 6:38PM ♀ ☍ ♆	24 8:03AM ☽-> 0♑00 1:38PM Full Moon♑	25 2:21PM ♆ ℞ 23♓	26 9:07AM ☽-> 0♒00 11:26PM ♀-> 0♌00
27	28 12:49PM ☽-> 0♓00	29	30 8:20PM ☽-> 0♈00		May S M T W T F S 1 2 3 4 5 6 7 8 9 10 11 12 13 14 15 16 17 18 19 20 21 22 23 24 25 26 27 28 29 30 31	July S M T W T F S 1 2 3 4 5 6 7 8 9 10 11 12 13 14 15 16 17 18 19 20 21 22 23 24 25 26 27 28 29 30 31

LONGITUDE

July 2021

Day	Sid.Time	☉	☽	☽ 12 hour	Mean☊	True☊	☿	♀	♂	⚳	♃	♄	⚷	♅	♆	♇
	h m s	° ' "	° ' "	° ' "	° '	° '	° '	° '	° '	° '	° '	° '	° '	° '	° '	° '
1 Th	18 37 04	9♋23 37	29♓16 59	5♈30 49	9♊16.3	10♊23.1	18♊42.1	4♌37.4	12♌00.4	20♉07.2	2♓00.8	12♒22.7	12♈50.1	13♉47.9	23♓11.5	25♑57.6
2 F	18 41 01	10 20 49	11♈40 00	17 45 08	9 13.2	10D 22.6	19 22.7	5 50.1	12 37.6	20 28.1	1R 58.7	12R 19.3	12 50.9	13 50.1	23R 11.4	25R 56.3
3 Sa	18 44 57	11 18 02	23 46 49	29 45 39	9 10.0	10 23.2	20 07.9	7 02.8	13 14.8	20 49.0	1 56.4	12 15.9	12 51.6	13 52.3	23 11.1	25 54.9
4 Su	18 48 54	12 15 14	5♉42 16	11♉37 16	9 06.8	10 24.7	20 57.6	8 15.4	13 52.1	21 09.8	1 54.0	12 12.4	12 52.2	13 54.5	23 10.9	25 53.5
5 M	18 52 50	13 12 27	17 31 13	23 24 44	9 03.6	10 26.4	21 51.8	9 28.0	14 29.3	21 30.5	1 51.3	12 08.8	12 52.8	13 56.7	23 10.6	25 52.1
6 Tu	18 56 47	14 09 40	29 18 19	5♊12 29	9 00.5	10R 27.8	22 50.5	10 40.6	15 06.6	21 51.1	1 48.5	12 05.2	12 53.3	13 58.8	23 10.3	25 50.7
7 W	19 00 43	15 06 53	11♊07 42	17 04 24	8 57.3	10 28.4	23 53.5	11 53.2	15 43.8	22 11.6	1 45.5	12 01.5	12 53.8	14 00.8	23 09.9	25 49.3
8 Th	19 04 40	16 04 07	23 02 56	29 03 40	8 54.1	10 27.6	25 00.8	13 05.7	16 21.1	22 32.1	1 42.3	11 57.8	12 54.2	14 02.9	23 09.6	25 47.9
9 F	19 08 36	17 01 21	5♋06 53	11♋12 48	8 50.9	10 25.1	26 12.4	14 18.3	16 58.4	22 52.4	1 38.9	11 54.0	12 54.6	14 04.9	23 09.2	25 46.5
10 Sa	19 12 33	17 58 35	17 21 39	23 33 33	8 47.8	10 20.9	27 28.2	15 30.8	17 35.8	23 12.7	1 35.3	11 50.2	12 54.9	14 06.8	23 08.7	25 45.0
11 Su	19 16 30	18 55 49	29 48 39	6♌07 00	8 44.6	10 15.2	28 48.1	16 43.2	18 13.1	23 32.9	1 31.6	11 46.3	12 55.2	14 08.7	23 08.3	25 43.6
12 M	19 20 26	19 53 03	12♌28 39	18 53 39	8 41.4	10 08.7	0♋12.1	17 55.6	18 50.5	23 52.9	1 27.7	11 42.3	12 55.4	14 10.6	23 07.7	25 42.2
13 Tu	19 24 23	20 50 17	25 22 00	1♍53 41	8 38.2	10 01.8	1 40.1	19 08.0	19 27.8	24 12.9	1 23.6	11 38.4	12 55.6	14 12.4	23 07.2	25 40.7
14 W	19 28 19	21 47 32	8♍28 42	15 07 03	8 35.0	9 55.5	3 12.0	20 20.4	20 05.2	24 32.8	1 19.3	11 34.3	12 55.7	14 14.2	23 06.7	25 39.3
15 Th	19 32 16	22 44 46	21 48 43	28 33 41	8 31.9	9 50.5	4 47.7	21 32.7	20 42.6	24 52.6	1 14.9	11 30.3	12R 55.8	14 15.9	23 06.1	25 37.9
16 F	19 36 12	23 42 00	5♎21 58	12♎13 33	8 28.7	9 47.2	6 27.1	22 45.1	21 20.0	25 12.3	1 10.3	11 26.1	12 55.8	14 17.6	23 05.4	25 36.4
17 Sa	19 40 09	24 39 15	19 08 27	26 06 36	8 25.5	9D 45.7	8 10.0	23 57.3	21 57.4	25 31.8	1 05.5	11 22.0	12 55.7	14 19.2	23 04.8	25 35.0
18 Su	19 44 05	25 36 29	3♏07 59	10♏12 30	8 22.3	9 45.8	9 56.4	25 09.5	22 34.9	25 51.3	1 00.6	11 17.8	12 55.7	14 20.9	23 04.1	25 33.5
19 M	19 48 02	26 33 44	17 20 00	24 30 17	8 19.2	9 46.7	11 45.9	26 21.7	23 12.3	26 10.6	0 55.5	11 13.6	12 55.5	14 22.4	23 03.4	25 32.1
20 Tu	19 51 59	27 30 59	1♐43 03	8♐57 57	8 16.0	9R 47.7	13 38.5	27 33.9	23 49.8	26 29.9	0 50.3	11 09.3	12 55.3	14 23.9	23 02.7	25 30.7
21 W	19 55 55	28 28 14	16 14 30	23 32 08	8 12.8	9 47.8	15 33.8	28 46.0	24 27.3	26 49.0	0 45.0	11 05.1	12 55.1	14 25.4	23 01.9	25 29.2
22 Th	19 59 52	29 25 30	0♑50 13	8♑08 01	8 09.6	9 46.1	17 31.6	29 58.1	25 04.8	27 08.0	0 39.4	11 00.8	12 54.8	14 26.8	23 01.1	25 27.8
23 F	20 03 48	0♌22 46	15 24 46	22 39 39	8 06.5	9 42.3	19 31.6	1♍10.1	25 42.3	27 27.0	0 33.8	10 56.4	12 54.4	14 28.2	23 00.3	25 26.3
24 Sa	20 07 45	1 20 02	29 51 53	7♒00 39	8 03.3	9 36.2	21 33.6	2 22.2	26 19.8	27 45.8	0 28.0	10 52.1	12 54.0	14 29.6	22 59.4	25 24.9
25 Su	20 11 41	2 17 19	14♒05 16	21 05 06	8 00.1	9 28.5	23 37.0	3 34.1	26 57.4	28 04.4	0 22.0	10 47.7	12 53.6	14 30.9	22 58.6	25 23.5
26 M	20 15 38	3 14 37	27 59 38	4♓48 30	7 56.9	9 19.9	25 41.8	4 46.0	27 35.0	28 23.0	0 15.9	10 43.3	12 53.1	14 32.1	22 57.7	25 22.1
27 Tu	20 19 34	4 11 55	11♓31 27	18 08 23	7 53.7	9 11.4	27 47.4	5 57.9	28 12.5	28 41.4	0 09.7	10 38.9	12 52.5	14 33.3	22 56.7	25 20.6
28 W	20 23 31	5 09 14	24 39 20	1♈04 27	7 50.6	9 04.0	29 53.6	7 09.8	28 50.1	28 59.7	0 03.[illegible]	10 34.5	12 51.9	14 34.5	22 55.8	25 19.2
29 Th	20 27 28	6 06 35	7♈24 02	13 38 27	7 47.4	8 58.2	2♌00.1	8 21.6	29 27.8	29 17.9	29♒57.[illegible]	10 30.1	12 51.3	14 35.6	22 54.8	25 17.8
30 F	20 31 24	7 03 56	19 48 10	25 53 43	7 44.2	8 54.6	4 06.7	9 33.3	0♍05.4	29 36.0	29 50.4	10 25.6	12 50.6	14 36.6	22 53.8	25 16.4
31 Sa	20 35 21	8♌01 18	1♉55 42	7♉54 44	7♊41.0	8♊52.9	6♌12.9	10♍45.1	0♍43.1	29♉53.9	29♒43.7	10♒21.2	12♈49.8	14♉37.6	22♓52.7	25♑15.0

1st of Month

Julian Day # 2459396.5
Obliquity 23°26'14"
SVP 4♓57'50"
GC 27♐08.4
Eris 24♈45.3

Day	⚴	Day	⚵	Day	⚶
1	27♓15.7	1	11♓20.3R	1	22♍39.5
6	27 32.6	6	10 31.1R	6	24 35.0
11	27 41.9	11	9 49.1R	11	26 34.5
16	27 43.3R	16	9 14.8R	16	28 37.6
21	27 36.3R	21	8 48.7R	21	0♎44.0
26	27 20.8R	26	8 31.1R	26	2 53.5
31	26 56.6R	31	8 21.9R	31	5 05.8

DECLINATION and LATITUDE

Day	☉ Decl	☽ Decl	☽ Lat	☽12h Decl	☿ Decl	☿ Lat	♀ Decl	♀ Lat	♂ Decl	♂ Lat	⚳ Decl	⚳ Lat	♃ Decl	♃ Lat	♄ Decl	♄ Lat
1 Th	23N06	4S50	4S57	2S10	19N14	3S44	20N41	1N38	18N23	1N15	11N34	6S26	11S42	1S01	17S47	0S43
2 F	23 02	0N29	4 29	3N07	19 27	3 35	20 24	1 38	18 12	1 14	11 40	6 26	11 43	1 01	17 48	0 43
3 Sa	22 57	5 41	3 49	8 11	19 40	3 25	20 06	1 39	18 01	1 14	11 45	6 26	11 44	1 01	17 49	0 44
4 Su	22 52	10 36	2 59	12 55	19 54	3 14	19 48	1 39	17 50	1 14	11 50	6 26	11 45	1 01	17 50	0 44
5 M	22 47	15 06	2 02	17 08	20 09	3 03	19 29	1 39	17 39	1 13	11 56	6 25	11 46	1 02	17 51	0 44
6 Tu	22 41	19 01	1 01	20 42	20 24	2 51	19 09	1 40	17 28	1 13	12 01	6 25	11 48	1 02	17 52	0 44
7 W	22 35	22 10	0N04	23 24	20 39	2 39	18 49	1 40	17 17	1 13	12 06	6 25	11 49	1 02	17 53	0 44
8 Th	22 28	24 23	1 08	25 06	20 54	2 27	18 29	1 40	17 05	1 13	12 11	6 25	11 50	1 02	17 55	0 44
9 F	22 21	25 31	2 10	25 37	21 09	2 14	18 08	1 40	16 54	1 13	12 17	6 25	11 52	1 03	17 56	0 44
10 Sa	22 14	25 24	3 07	24 53	21 24	2 01	17 47	1 40	16 42	1 12	12 22	6 25	11 53	1 03	17 57	0 44
11 Su	22 06	24 02	3 56	22 53	21 38	1 48	17 25	1 40	16 30	1 12	12 27	6 25	11 55	1 03	17 58	0 44
12 M	21 58	21 27	4 34	19 44	21 51	1 35	17 02	1 40	16 19	1 12	12 31	6 25	11 57	1 04	17 59	0 45
13 Tu	21 49	17 46	4 59	15 34	22 04	1 22	16 39	1 39	16 07	1 11	12 36	6 25	11 58	1 04	18 01	0 45
14 W	21 40	13 10	5 09	10 36	22 16	1 08	16 16	1 39	15 54	1 11	12 41	6 24	12 00	1 04	18 02	0 45
15 Th	21 31	7 53	5 03	5 03	22 26	0 55	15 53	1 39	15 42	1 11	12 46	6 24	12 02	1 04	18 03	0 45
16 F	21 22	2 09	4 39	0S49	22 35	0 42	15 29	1 38	15 30	1 10	12 50	6 24	12 04	1 05	18 04	0 45
17 Sa	21 12	3S48	3 60	6 45	22 42	0 29	15 04	1 38	15 18	1 10	12 55	6 24	12 06	1 05	18 05	0 45
18 Su	21 01	9 39	3 05	12 27	22 47	0 17	14 39	1 37	15 05	1 10	12 60	6 24	12 08	1 05	18 07	0 45
19 M	20 50	15 07	1 58	17 34	22 51	0 04	14 14	1 36	14 53	1 09	13 04	6 24	12 10	1 05	18 08	0 45
20 Tu	20 39	19 48	0 44	21 43	22 52	0N08	13 48	1 35	14 40	1 09	13 08	6 24	12 12	1 06	18 09	0 45
21 W	20 28	23 18	0S35	24 30	22 51	0 19	13 23	1 34	14 27	1 09	13 13	6 24	12 14	1 06	18 11	0 46
22 Th	20 16	25 17	1 51	25 38	22 47	0 30	12 56	1 33	14 14	1 09	13 17	6 24	12 16	1 06	18 12	0 46
23 F	20 04	25 31	2 60	24 59	22 41	0 40	12 30	1 32	14 01	1 08	13 21	6 24	12 18	1 06	18 13	0 46
24 Sa	19 52	24 01	3 56	22 41	22 32	0 50	12 03	1 31	13 48	1 08	13 25	6 24	12 21	1 06	18 14	0 46
25 Su	19 39	21 01	4 37	19 03	22 20	0 59	11 36	1 30	13 35	1 08	13 30	6 24	12 23	1 07	18 16	0 46
26 M	19 26	16 52	5 00	14 29	22 06	1 07	11 08	1 29	13 22	1 07	13 34	6 24	12 25	1 07	18 17	0 46
27 Tu	19 12	11 57	5 06	9 19	21 49	1 14	10 40	1 27	13 09	1 07	13 38	6 24	12 28	1 07	18 18	0 46
28 W	18 59	6 38	4 55	3 55	21 30	1 21	10 12	1 26	12 55	1 07	13 41	6 23	12 30	1 07	18 20	0 46
29 Th	18 45	1 12	4 30	1N30	21 08	1 27	9 44	1 24	12 42	1 06	13 45	6 23	12 33	1 08	18 21	0 46
30 F	18 30	4N10	3 52	6 45	20 43	1 32	9 16	1 23	12 28	1 06	13 49	6 23	12 35	1 08	18 22	0 46
31 Sa	18N16	9N15	3S05	11N39	20N16	1N36	8N47	1N21	12N15	1N06	13N53	6S23	12S38	1S08	18S23	0S47

Day	⚷ Decl	⚷ Lat	♅ Decl	♅ Lat	♆ Decl	♆ Lat	♇ Decl	♇ Lat
1	7N14	2N21	15N35	0S24	3S44	1S08	22S28	1S33
6	7 16	2 22	15 39	0 24	3 45	1 08	22 30	1 33
11	7 17	2 22	15 42	0 24	3 46	1 08	22 32	1 34
16	7 17	2 22	15 44	0 25	3 48	1 09	22 34	1 34
21	7 17	2 23	15 46	0 25	3 49	1 09	22 35	1 35
26	7 17	2 23	15 48	0 25	3 51	1 09	22 37	1 35
31	7N16	2N23	15N50	0S25	3S53	1S09	22S39	1S36

Day	⚴ Decl	⚴ Lat	⚵ Decl	⚵ Lat	⚶ Decl	⚶ Lat	Eris Decl	Eris Lat
1	8N48	10N47	4S14	18N04	9N15	6N55	1S03	11S25
6	8 43	10 35	4 23	17 48	8 20	6 44	1 03	11 25
11	8 34	10 21	4 36	17 30	7 23	6 34	1 03	11 26
16	8 21	10 06	4 51	17 10	6 24	6 23	1 03	11 26
21	8 03	9 49	5 08	16 49	5 25	6 14	1 04	11 27
26	7 40	9 30	5 27	16 27	4 25	6 04	1 04	11 27
31	7N11	9N10	5S49	16N04	3N25	5N55	1S05	11S27

Moon Phenomena

Max/0 Decl

dy	hr mn	
1	21:46	0 N
9	10:05	25N37
16	8:42	0 S
22	15:11	25S38
29	5:17	0 N

Max/0 Lat

dy	hr mn	
6	22:41	0 N
14	2:37	5N09
20	13:23	0 S
26	19:52	5S06

Perigee/Apogee

dy	hr m		kilometers
5	14:48	a	405340
21	10:26	p	364523

PH	dy	hr mn	
☾	1	21:12	10♈14
●	10	1:18	18♋02
☽	17	10:12	25♎04
○	24	2:38	1♒26
☾	31	13:17	8♉33

Void of Course Moon

Last Aspect			☽ Ingress		
30 17:41	♇	⚹	♈	1	1:22
3 4:16	♇	□	♉	3	12:29
5 16:58	♇	△	♊	6	1:25
8 4:21	☿	☌	♋	8	13:52
10 16:11	♇	☍	♌	11	0:22
12 12:30	♂	☌	♍	13	8:32
15 6:47	♇	△	♎	15	14:33
17 11:05	♇	□	♏	17	18:39
19 16:31	☉	△	♐	19	21:09
21 22:27	♀	☍	♑	21	22:37
23 16:35	♇	☌	♒	24	0:14
25 23:15	♂	☍	♓	26	3:31
28 1:14	♇	⚹	♈	28	9:59
30 19:39	♃	⚹	♉	30	20:09

DAILY ASPECTARIAN

1 Th ☽∥♆ 4:54; ☽⚺♃ 5:13; ☽△♀ 11:23; ☽∠⚳ 11:34; ♂☍♄ 13:09; ☉□☽ 21:12; ☊ D 21:21

2 F ☽⚹♄ 1:17; ☽△♂ 1:59; ☽☌⚷ 2:19; ☽⚺♅ 4:17; ♂△⚷ 8:43; ☽∠♃ 10:26; ☽#♆ 14:55; ☽⚹☿ 16:13; ☽⚺⚳ 17:55; ⚳#♃ 19:08; ☽⚺♆ 22:49

3 Sa ☽□♇ 4:16; ☽∥⚷ 7:28; ☽⚹♃ 16:20; ☿∥♀ 19:10; ♀⚼♆ 22:30; ☉⚻♄ 22:52

4 Su ☽∠☿ 0:34; ♂#♄ 0:51; ♂□♅ 1:41; ☽∠♆ 5:01; ☽□♀ 5:46; ☽#♃ 5:55; ☽∥⚳ 6:28; ☿⚺⚳ 9:04; ☽□♄ 13:07; ☉⚹☽ 14:27; ☽⚺⚷ 14:33; ☉□⚷ 15:40; ☽☌♅ 16:42; ☽□♂ 17:29

5 M ☽∥♅ 3:04; ☽☌⚳ 8:22; ☽⚺☿ 9:38; ☽⚹♆ 11:31; ☽∥♂ 14:30; ☽#♄ 16:31; ☽△♇ 16:58; ☉⚹♅ 19:15; ☽∠⚷ 21:07; ☉∠☽ 23:41

6 Tu ☽∥♀ 0:54; ☽□♃ 5:04; ☿□♆ 7:41; ☽∥☿ 10:35; ☊ R 22:43; ☽⚼♇ 23:23

7 W ☽⚹♀ 1:42; ☽△♄ 1:48; ♀☍♄ 2:37; ☽#♇ 3:05; ☽⚹⚷ 3:35; ☉∥☽ 3:36; ☽⚺♅ 5:51; ☉⚺☽ 8:45; ☽⚹♂ 9:48; ☉#♇ 15:19; ♀△⚷ 20:10; ☽⚺⚳ 22:56

8 Th ☽□♆ 0:13; ☽☌☿ 4:21; ☽⚻♇ 5:29; ☽⚼♄ 7:47; ☽∠♀ 11:12; ☽∠♅ 12:00; ☉⚼♃ 15:07; ☿⚻♇ 15:37; ☽△♃ 17:10; ☽∠♂ 17:27; ♀□♅ 19:26; ☉⚺♂ 20:30

9 F ☽∠⚳ 5:36; ☿⚼♄ 12:41; ♀#♄ 13:03; ☽⚻♄ 13:17; ☽□⚷ 15:20; ☽⚹♅ 17:39; ⚳⚹♆ 19:23; ☽⚺♀ 20:01; ☽⚼♃ 22:30

10 Sa ☽⚺♂ 0:29; ☉☌☽ 1:18; ☽△♆ 11:12; ☽⚹⚳ 11:39; ☽☍♇ 16:11; ☽⚺☿ 21:50

11 Su ☽⚻♃ 3:16; ☿∠♅ 6:08; ☽#♇ 15:08; ☽⚼♆ 15:49; ☉∥☽ 19:44; ☿ ♋ 20:36; ☽∥☿ 21:02; ☽☍♄ 22:33

12 M ☽△⚷ 0:50; ☽□♅ 3:12; ☽∠☿ 5:45; ☉∥☿ 7:25; ☽☌♀ 11:15; ☽☌♂ 12:30; ☉⚺☽ 14:57; ☿△♃ 19:46; ☽⚻♆ 19:51; ☽□⚳ 21:49; ☽#♄ 22:34

13 Tu ☽⚻♇ 0:35; ☽⚼⚷ 4:43; ☽∥♀ 6:45; ☽∥♂ 9:33; ☽☍♃ 11:01; ☽∥♅ 11:12; ☽⚹☿ 13:06; ♀☌♂ 13:34; ☉∠☽ 20:42

14 W ☽∥⚳ 2:16; ☽⚼♇ 3:56; ☽#♃ 5:30; ☽⚻♄ 5:35; ⚴ R 7:41; ☽⚻⚷ 8:03; ☽△♅ 10:26; ♂∥♅ 21:21; ☽⚺♂ 21:56; ☽⚺♀ 23:29

15 Th ☉⚹☽ 1:48; ☽☍♆ 2:18; ☽∥⚷ 2:33; ☽△⚳ 5:36; ☽△♇ 6:47; ☽⚼♄ 8:19; ♀∥♅ 8:47; ☉△♆ 8:50; ☽⚼♅ 13:16; ☽⚻♃ 16:39; ⚷ R 16:42; ☽#♆ 17:15; ☿#♇ 20:56; ♀∥♂ 21:06; ☿∠♂ 21:20

16 F ☽∠♂ 1:47; ☽□☿ 2:10; ☽∠♀ 4:35; ♀⚻♆ 6:43; ☽⚼⚳ 8:41; ☽△♄ 10:34; ☽☍⚷ 13:14; ☽⚻♅ 15:38; ☽⚼♃ 18:45

17 Sa ☽∥♆ 0:00; ⚳△♇ 3:37; ☽⚹♂ 5:05; ☽⚻♆ 6:47; ☽⚹♀ 9:05; ☊ D 10:02; ☉□☽ 10:12; ☽□♇ 11:05; ☽⚻⚳ 11:16; ☽#⚷ 14:11; ☽△♃ 20:24; ☉☍♇ 22:48

18 Su ♀⚻♇ 7:49; ☽⚼♆ 8:22; ☿∠♀ 8:42; ☉⚹⚳ 9:23; ☽∥♃ 10:38; ☽△☿ 13:14; ☽□♄ 13:46; ☽#⚳ 14:34; ☿∠⚳ 14:43; ☽⚻⚷ 16:35; ☿⚻♄ 17:15; ♂⚻♆ 18:23; ♀□⚳ 18:57; ☽☍♅ 19:01; ☽#♀ 20:15; ☽#♂ 22:57

19 M ☽#♅ 3:04; ⚶ ♎ 6:32; ☽△♆ 9:34; ☽□♂ 10:17; ☽⚹♇ 13:42; ☿□⚷ 14:53; ☽∥♄ 14:58; ☽☍⚳ 15:07; ☽□♀ 16:28; ☉△☽ 16:31; ☽⚼⚷ 17:42; ☽⚼☿ 18:07; ☉⚺♀ 19:18; ☽□♃ 22:33

20 Tu ☉#☽ 4:55; ♀⚼⚷ 7:06; ☿⚹♅ 9:39; ☊ R 13:25; ☽∠♇ 14:32; ☽⚹♄ 15:32; ☽∥♇ 18:17; ☽△⚷ 18:31; ☉⚼☽ 19:07; ☽#☿ 20:17; ☽⚻♅ 21:00; ☽⚻☿ 22:43

21 W ☿⚼♃ 2:11; ♀∥⚳ 7:41; ☽□♆ 11:10; ☽△♂ 14:07; ☽⚺♇ 15:11; ☽∠♄ 16:07; ☽⚻⚳ 17:47; ☉⚻☽ 21:31; ☽⚼♅ 21:43; ☽△♀ 22:27; ☽⚹♃ 23:42

22 Th ♀ ♍ 0:38; ♀☍♃ 12:46; ♂⚻♇ 14:10; ☉ ♌ 14:28; ☽⚼♂ 15:53; ☽⚺♄ 16:40; ☽⚼⚳ 19:00; ☽□⚷ 19:52; ☽△♅ 22:26

23 F ☽∠♃ 0:15; ☽⚼♀ 1:22; ☉⚻♃ 4:11; ☽☍☿ 7:55; ♀#♃ 9:24; ☿#♇ 12:27; ☽⚹♆ 12:34; ☽☌♇ 16:35; ☽⚻♂ 17:50; ☽△⚳ 20:25

24 Sa ☽⚺♃ 1:00; ☉☍☽ 2:38; ☽⚻♀ 4:35; ⚳∠⚷ 10:22; ☽∥♇ 12:34; ☽∠♆ 13:38; ☽#☿ 14:02; ☿△♆ 16:36; ☽☌♄ 18:26; ☽⚹⚷ 21:58

25 Su ☽□♅ 0:44; ♂∥⚳ 7:47; ☉#☽ 9:01; ☽⚺♆ 15:15; ☽∥♄ 16:23; ☽⚻☿ 19:17; ☽⚺♇ 19:26; ☿☍♇ 20:16; ☽☍♂ 23:15; ☽∠⚷ 23:49

26 M ☽□⚳ 0:42; ☽☌♃ 3:57; ☽#♅ 5:24; ☉⚻☽ 9:56; ♂⚼⚷ 11:24; ☽☍♀ 13:05; ☽#⚳ 16:13; ☽#♂ 18:09; ☽∥♃ 21:38; ☽∠♇ 21:53; ☽⚺♄ 22:26

27 Tu ☽⚺⚷ 2:26; ☽⚼☿ 2:43; ☽⚹♅ 5:29; ☽#♀ 6:27; ☿⚺♂ 6:49; ☿⚹⚳ 12:02; ☉⚼☽ 15:02; ☽☌♆ 20:48; ☽#⚷ 21:10

28 W ☿ ♌ 1:13; ☽⚹♇ 1:14; ☽∠♄ 1:42; ☿⚻♃ 1:46; ☽⚻♂ 8:12; ☽⚹⚳ 8:18; ☽∠♅ 9:12; ☽⚺♃ 10:00; ☽△☿ 11:43; ♂□⚳ 11:52; ☽∥♆ 12:13; ♃R♒ 12:44; ☉△☽ 21:20

29 Th ☽⚻♀ 2:02; ☽⚹♄ 5:54; ☽☌⚷ 10:28; ☽∠⚳ 13:36; ♂#♃ 13:44; ☽⚺♅ 13:52; ☽⚼♂ 14:19; ☽∠♃ 14:25; ♂☍♃ 15:51; ♂ ♍ 20:34; ☽#♆ 22:42

30 F ☽⚺♆ 6:04; ☽⚼♀ 10:22; ☽□♇ 10:45; ☉#♄ 12:13; ⚳□♃ 14:04; ♀⚼♇ 14:08; ☽∥⚷ 14:27; ♀⚻♄ 16:28; ☽⚹♃ 19:39; ☽⚺⚳ 19:51; ☉⚼♆ 20:29; ☽△♂ 21:27; ☽∥♀ 21:55

31 Sa ⚳ ♊ 8:14; ☽□☿ 10:25; ☽∠♆ 11:55; ☉□☽ 13:17; ☊ D 13:25; ☽∥♂ 14:21; ☽□♄ 16:49; ☽#♃ 17:13; ☿⚼♆ 18:53; ☽△♀ 19:42; ☽⚺⚷ 21:54

July 2021:Modify New York Stock Exchange Zone:-5

Sunday	Monday	Tuesday	Wednesday	Thursday	Friday	Saturday
June S M T W T F S 1 2 3 4 5 6 7 8 9 10 11 12 13 14 15 16 17 18 19 20 21 22 23 24 25 26 27 28 29 30	August S M T W T F S 1 2 3 4 5 6 7 8 9 10 11 12 13 14 15 16 17 18 19 20 21 22 23 24 25 26 27 28 29 30 31			1 8:07AM ♂ ☍ ♄	2	3 7:26AM ☽-> 0♉00 8:38PM ♂ □ ♅
4	5 2:13PM ☉ ⚹ ♅ 8:22PM ☽-> 0♊00	6 2:38AM ☿ □ ♆ 9:35PM ♀ ☍ ♄	7	8 8:49AM ☽-> 0♋00 2:24PM ♀ □ ♅	9 8:15PM New Moon♋[	10 7:19PM ☽-> 0♌00
11 3:34PM ☿ -> 0♋00	12 2:44PM ☿ △ ♃	13 3:29AM ☽-> 0♍00 8:32AM ♀ ☌ ♂	14	15 3:48AM ☉ △ ♆ 9:30AM ☽-> 0♎00	16	17 1:37PM ☽-> 0♏00 5:45PM ☉ ☍ ♇
18	19 4:06PM ☽-> 0♐00	20 4:36AM ☿ ⚹ ♅	21 5:35PM ☽-> 0♑00 7:36PM ♀-> 0♍00	22 7:44AM ♀ ☍ ♃ 9:25AM ☉-> 0♌00	23 7:11PM ☽-> 0♒00 9:35PM Full Moon♒	24 11:34AM ☿ △ ♆
25 3:13PM ☿ ☍ ♇ 10:28PM ☽-> 0♓00	26	27 8:10PM ☿ -> 0♌00	28 4:56AM ☽-> 0♈00 7:42AM ♃-> 0♓00	29 10:49AM ♂ ☍ ♃ 3:31PM ♂-> 0♍00	30 3:07PM ☽-> 0♉00	31

August 2021

LONGITUDE

Day	Sid.Time	☉	☽	☽ 12 hour	Mean ☊	True ☊	☿	♀	♂	⚳	♃	♄	⚷	♅	♆	♇
	h m s	° ' "	° ' "	° ' "	° '	° '	° '	° '	° '	° '	° '	° '	° '	° '	° '	° '
1 Su	20 39 17	8♌58 41	13♉51 29	19♉46 36	7♊37.9	8♊52.8	8♌18.7	11♍56.7	1♍20.7	0♊11.7	29♒36.9	10♒16.7	12♈49.0	14♉38.6	22♓51.7	25♑13.6
2 M	20 43 14	9 56 06	25 40 47	1♊34 40	7 34.7	8 53.5	10 23.8	13 08.4	1 58.4	0 29.3	29R 30.0	10R 12.2	12R 48.1	14 39.5	22R 50.6	25R 12.2
3 Tu	20 47 10	10 53 31	7♊28 55	13 24 10	7 31.5	8R 54.0	12 28.0	14 20.0	2 36.2	0 46.8	29 23.0	10 07.8	12 47.2	14 40.4	22 49.5	25 10.8
4 W	20 51 07	11 50 58	19 20 59	25 19 56	7 28.3	8 53.5	14 31.2	15 31.6	3 13.9	1 04.2	29 15.9	10 03.3	12 46.3	14 41.2	22 48.4	25 09.4
5 Th	20 55 03	12 48 26	1♋21 30	7♋26 07	7 25.2	8 51.1	16 33.2	16 43.1	3 51.7	1 21.4	29 08.7	9 58.8	12 45.3	14 42.0	22 47.2	25 08.1
6 F	20 59 00	13 45 55	13 34 11	19 45 59	7 22.0	8 46.2	18 34.1	17 54.6	4 29.5	1 38.5	29 01.4	9 54.4	12 44.2	14 42.7	22 46.0	25 06.7
7 Sa	21 02 57	14 43 25	26 01 44	2♌21 35	7 18.8	8 38.9	20 33.5	19 06.0	5 07.3	1 55.4	28 54.1	9 49.9	12 43.1	14 43.4	22 44.8	25 05.4
8 Su	21 06 53	15 40 57	8♌45 37	15 13 47	7 15.6	8 29.4	22 31.6	20 17.4	5 45.1	2 12.2	28 46.7	9 45.5	12 42.0	14 44.0	22 43.6	25 04.1
9 M	21 10 50	16 38 29	21 46 02	28 22 10	7 12.4	8 18.4	24 28.3	21 28.8	6 22.9	2 28.8	28 39.2	9 41.1	12 40.8	14 44.6	22 42.4	25 02.7
10 Tu	21 14 46	17 36 02	5♍01 59	11♍45 13	7 09.3	8 07.0	26 23.5	22 40.1	7 00.8	2 45.2	28 31.6	9 36.7	12 39.5	14 45.1	22 41.1	25 01.4
11 W	21 18 43	18 33 37	18 31 34	25 20 44	7 06.1	7 56.3	28 17.2	23 51.3	7 38.7	3 01.5	28 24.0	9 32.3	12 38.3	14 45.6	22 39.8	25 00.1
12 Th	21 22 39	19 31 12	2♎12 24	9♎06 16	7 02.9	7 47.4	0♍09.5	25 02.5	8 16.6	3 17.6	28 16.3	9 27.9	12 36.9	14 46.0	22 38.5	24 58.8
13 F	21 26 36	20 28 48	16 02 05	22 59 35	6 59.7	7 40.9	2 00.2	26 13.7	8 54.6	3 33.6	28 08.6	9 23.6	12 35.5	14 46.3	22 37.2	24 57.6
14 Sa	21 30 32	21 26 25	29 58 34	6♏58 53	6 56.6	7 37.1	3 49.4	27 24.8	9 32.5	3 49.4	28 00.9	9 19.2	12 34.1	14 46.7	22 35.9	24 56.3
15 Su	21 34 29	22 24 03	14♏00 22	21 02 55	6 53.4	7D 35.5	5 37.2	28 35.8	10 10.5	4 05.0	27 53.1	9 14.9	12 32.6	14 46.9	22 34.5	24 55.1
16 M	21 38 26	23 21 42	28 06 26	5♐10 48	6 50.2	7R 35.4	7 23.4	29 46.8	10 48.5	4 20.4	27 45.3	9 10.7	12 31.1	14 47.2	22 33.1	24 53.8
17 Tu	21 42 22	24 19 23	12♐15 53	19 21 31	6 47.0	7 35.4	9 08.2	0♎57.7	11 26.5	4 35.6	27 37.4	9 06.4	12 29.6	14 47.4	22 31.7	24 52.6
18 W	21 46 19	25 17 04	26 27 31	3♑33 36	6 43.8	7 34.4	10 51.6	2 08.6	12 04.5	4 50.7	27 29.6	9 02.2	12 28.0	14 47.5	22 30.3	24 51.4
19 Th	21 50 15	26 14 46	10♑39 26	17 44 39	6 40.7	7 31.2	12 33.5	3 19.4	12 42.6	5 05.6	27 21.7	8 58.1	12 26.3	14 47.6	22 28.9	24 50.2
20 F	21 54 12	27 12 29	24 48 48	1♒51 22	6 37.5	7 25.4	14 13.9	4 30.2	13 20.7	5 20.3	27 13.8	8 54.0	12 24.7	14R 47.6	22 27.4	24 49.1
21 Sa	21 58 08	28 10 14	8♒51 50	15 49 39	6 34.3	7 16.8	15 53.0	5 40.9	13 58.8	5 34.7	27 06.0	8 49.9	12 22.9	14 47.6	22 26.0	24 47.9
22 Su	22 02 05	29 07 59	22 44 17	29 35 14	6 31.1	7 05.9	17 30.6	6 51.5	14 36.9	5 49.0	26 58.1	8 45.8	12 21.2	14 47.5	22 24.5	24 46.8
23 M	22 06 01	0♍05 47	6♓22 03	13♓04 21	6 28.0	6 53.8	19 06.8	8 02.0	15 15.0	6 03.1	26 50.3	8 41.8	12 19.4	14 47.4	22 23.0	24 45.6
24 Tu	22 09 58	1 03 35	19 41 52	26 14 25	6 24.8	6 41.7	20 41.6	9 12.5	15 53.2	6 17.0	26 42.4	8 37.9	12 17.5	14 47.2	22 21.5	24 44.5
25 W	22 13 55	2 01 25	2♈41 55	9♈04 25	6 21.6	6 30.7	22 15.1	10 22.9	16 31.4	6 30.7	26 34.6	8 33.9	12 15.6	14 47.0	22 20.0	24 43.5
26 Th	22 17 51	2 59 17	15 22 03	21 35 05	6 18.4	6 21.7	23 47.2	11 33.3	17 09.6	6 44.2	26 26.8	8 30.1	12 13.7	14 46.7	22 18.5	24 42.4
27 F	22 21 48	3 57 10	27 43 51	3♉48 46	6 15.2	6 15.3	25 17.8	12 43.6	17 47.9	6 57.5	26 19.1	8 26.3	12 11.8	14 46.4	22 16.9	24 41.3
28 Sa	22 25 44	4 55 05	9♉50 20	15 49 07	6 12.1	6 11.5	26 47.1	13 53.8	18 26.1	7 10.6	26 11.3	8 22.5	12 09.8	14 46.0	22 15.4	24 40.3
29 Su	22 29 41	5 53 02	21 45 42	27 40 46	6 08.9	6 09.8	28 15.0	15 04.0	19 04.4	7 23.4	26 03.7	8 18.8	12 07.7	14 45.6	22 13.8	24 39.3
30 M	22 33 37	6 51 01	3♊34 57	9♊28 58	6 05.7	6 09.4	29 41.5	16 14.1	19 42.7	7 36.0	25 56.1	8 15.2	12 05.7	14 45.1	22 12.2	24 38.3
31 Tu	22 37 34	7♍49 01	15 23 29	21 19 12	6♊02.5	6♊09.3	1♎06.6	17♎24.1	20♍21.1	7♊48.4	25♒48.5	8♒11.6	12♈03.6	14♉44.6	22♓10.6	24♑37.4

1st of Month

Julian Day # 2459427.5
Obliquity 23°26'15"
SVP 4♓57'45"
GC 27♐08.4
Eris 24♈46.8R

Day	⚴	Day	⚵	Day	⚶
1	26♓50.7R	1	8♐21.1R	1	5♎32.5
6	26 15.9R	6	8 21.9	6	7 48.0
11	25 32.4R	11	8 31.0	11	10 05.9
16	24 40.7R	16	8 48.0	16	12 26.1
21	23 41.5R	21	9 12.5	21	14 48.3
26	22 35.6R	26	9 44.3	26	17 12.5
31	21 24.2R	31	10 22.8	31	19 38.5

DECLINATION and LATITUDE

Day	☉ Decl	☽ Decl	☽ Lat	☽ 12h Decl	☿ Decl	☿ Lat	♀ Decl	♀ Lat	♂ Decl	♂ Lat	⚳ Decl	⚳ Lat	♃ Decl	♃ Lat	♄ Decl	♄ Lat
1 Su	18N01	13N56	2S10	16N04	19N48	1N40	8N18	1N19	12N01	1N05	13N56	6S23	12S40	1S08	18S25	0S47
2 M	17 45	18 02	1 10	19 50	19 17	1 43	7 49	1 17	11 47	1 05	13 60	6 23	12 43	1 08	18 26	0 47
3 Tu	17 30	21 26	0 08	22 48	18 44	1 44	7 19	1 15	11 33	1 05	14 04	6 23	12 45	1 09	18 27	0 47
4 W	17 14	23 56	0N56	24 48	18 10	1 46	6 50	1 13	11 19	1 04	14 07	6 23	12 48	1 09	18 29	0 47
5 Th	16 58	25 23	1 57	25 40	17 34	1 46	6 20	1 11	11 05	1 04	14 10	6 23	12 51	1 09	18 30	0 47
6 F	16 42	25 38	2 54	25 16	16 56	1 46	5 50	1 09	10 51	1 04	14 14	6 23	12 53	1 09	18 31	0 47
7 Sa	16 25	24 36	3 43	23 36	16 18	1 45	5 20	1 07	10 37	1 03	14 17	6 23	12 56	1 09	18 32	0 47
8 Su	16 08	22 18	4 23	20 42	15 38	1 44	4 50	1 04	10 23	1 03	14 20	6 23	12 59	1 09	18 34	0 47
9 M	15 51	18 49	4 50	16 41	14 58	1 42	4 20	1 02	10 08	1 03	14 23	6 23	13 02	1 10	18 35	0 47
10 Tu	15 33	14 20	5 02	11 48	14 16	1 39	3 49	0 60	9 54	1 02	14 27	6 23	13 05	1 10	18 36	0 47
11 W	15 16	9 06	4 57	6 16	13 34	1 36	3 19	0 57	9 40	1 02	14 30	6 23	13 07	1 10	18 38	0 47
12 Th	14 58	3 20	4 36	0 21	12 51	1 32	2 48	0 54	9 25	1 02	14 33	6 23	13 10	1 10	18 39	0 48
13 F	14 40	2S39	3 58	5S38	12 08	1 28	2 18	0 52	9 11	1 01	14 36	6 23	13 13	1 10	18 40	0 48
14 Sa	14 21	8 34	3 05	11 24	11 25	1 24	1 47	0 49	8 56	1 01	14 38	6 23	13 16	1 10	18 41	0 48
15 Su	14 03	14 06	2 02	16 38	10 41	1 19	1 16	0 46	8 41	1 01	14 41	6 23	13 19	1 10	18 42	0 48
16 M	13 44	18 55	0 50	20 57	9 56	1 14	0 45	0 43	8 27	1 00	14 44	6 23	13 21	1 11	18 44	0 48
17 Tu	13 25	22 40	0S25	24 02	9 12	1 08	0 14	0 40	8 12	1 00	14 47	6 23	13 24	1 11	18 45	0 48
18 W	13 06	25 02	1 38	25 36	8 27	1 02	0S17	0 37	7 57	0 60	14 49	6 23	13 27	1 11	18 46	0 48
19 Th	12 46	25 46	2 45	25 29	7 43	0 56	0 48	0 34	7 42	0 59	14 52	6 23	13 30	1 11	18 47	0 48
20 F	12 26	24 48	3 42	23 44	6 58	0 49	1 19	0 31	7 27	0 59	14 55	6 23	13 33	1 11	18 48	0 48
21 Sa	12 07	22 18	4 25	20 33	6 13	0 43	1 50	0 28	7 12	0 59	14 57	6 23	13 35	1 11	18 49	0 48
22 Su	11 46	18 31	4 51	16 16	5 29	0 36	2 20	0 25	6 57	0 58	14 59	6 23	13 38	1 11	18 50	0 48
23 M	11 26	13 49	5 01	11 15	4 44	0 28	2 51	0 22	6 42	0 58	15 02	6 23	13 41	1 11	18 52	0 48
24 Tu	11 06	8 34	4 53	5 50	4 00	0 21	3 22	0 18	6 27	0 58	15 04	6 23	13 44	1 11	18 53	0 48
25 W	10 45	3 04	4 30	0 18	3 16	0 13	3 53	0 15	6 12	0 57	15 06	6 23	13 47	1 11	18 54	0 48
26 Th	10 24	2N27	3 55	5N07	2 33	0 05	4 24	0 11	5 57	0 57	15 09	6 23	13 49	1 12	18 55	0 48
27 F	10 04	7 44	3 08	10 14	1 50	0S03	4 54	0 08	5 41	0 56	15 11	6 23	13 52	1 12	18 56	0 48
28 Sa	9 42	12 38	2 15	14 53	1 07	0 11	5 25	0 04	5 26	0 56	15 13	6 22	13 55	1 12	18 57	0 48
29 Su	9 21	16 59	1 16	18 55	0 24	0 19	5 55	0 01	5 11	0 56	15 15	6 22	13 57	1 12	18 58	0 48
30 M	8 60	20 39	0 14	22 10	0S18	0 28	6 26	0S03	4 55	0 55	15 17	6 22	13 60	1 12	18 59	0 48
31 Tu	8N38	23N27	0N49	24N29	0S60	0S36	6S56	0S07	4N40	0N55	15N19	6S22	14S03	1S12	18S60	0S49

Day	⚷ Decl	⚷ Lat	♅ Decl	♅ Lat	♆ Decl	♆ Lat	♇ Decl	♇ Lat
1	7N16	2N23	15N50	0S25	3S54	1S09	22S39	1S36
6	7 14	2 23	15 51	0 25	3 56	1 09	22 41	1 36
11	7 12	2 24	15 52	0 25	3 59	1 10	22 43	1 36
16	7 09	2 24	15 52	0 25	4 01	1 10	22 44	1 37
21	7 06	2 24	15 53	0 25	4 04	1 10	22 45	1 37
26	7 03	2 24	15 52	0 25	4 07	1 10	22 47	1 37
31	6N59	2N24	15N52	0S25	4S11	1S10	22S48	1S38

Day	⚴ Decl	⚴ Lat	⚵ Decl	⚵ Lat	⚶ Decl	⚶ Lat	Eris Decl	Eris Lat
1	7N05	9N05	5S53	15N60	3N12	5N53	1S05	11S28
6	6 30	8 42	6 16	15 37	2 11	5 45	1 06	11 28
11	5 50	8 17	6 40	15 14	1 09	5 36	1 06	11 28
16	5 04	7 49	7 05	14 51	0 07	5 28	1 07	11 29
21	4 13	7 19	7 31	14 28	0S55	5 19	1 08	11 29
26	3 17	6 46	7 58	14 06	1 58	5 11	1 09	11 29
31	2N17	6N11	8S24	13N44	2S60	5N04	1S10	11S30

Moon Phenomena

Max/0 Decl

dy	hr mn	
5	16:48	25N41
12	13:25	0 S
18	22:22	25S46
25	13:17	0 N

Max/0 Lat

dy	hr mn	
3	2:53	0 N
10	5:27	5N02
16	16:05	0 S
23	0:56	5S01
30	5:15	0 N

Perigee/Apogee

dy	hr m		kilometers
2	7:36	a	404408
17	9:17	p	369124
30	2:23	a	404099

PH	dy	hr mn	
●	8	13:51	16♌14
☽	15	15:21	23♏01
○	22	12:03	29♒37
☾	30	7:14	7♊09

Void of Course Moon

Last Aspect			☽ Ingress		
2 7:42	♃	□	♊	2	8:47
4 19:39	♃	△	♋	4	21:18
6 22:13	♇	☍	♌	7	7:33
9 12:24	♃	☍	♍	9	14:57
11 11:23	♇	△	♎	11	20:09
13 20:40	♃	△	♏	14	0:02
16 3:06	♀	✶	♐	16	3:13
18 1:44	♃	✶	♑	18	5:59
20 0:00	♇	☌	♒	20	8:50
22 12:03	☉	☍	♓	22	12:44
24 9:14	♇	✶	♈	24	18:58
26 21:16	♃	✶	♉	27	4:28
29 15:00	☿	△	♊	29	16:43

DAILY ASPECTARIAN

1 Su	☽ ∥ ⚳	0:04
	☽ ☌ ♅	1:35
	☽ ∥ ♅	10:41
	☉ ☌ ☿	14:09
	♀ ⚻ ⚷	17:18
	☽ ✶ ♆	18:14
	☿ ☍ ♄	21:51
	☉ ∥ ☽	22:20
	☽ △ ♇	23:02
2 M	☽ # ♄	2:33
	☽ ∠ ⚷	4:19
	☉ ☍ ♄	6:16
	☽ ∥ ☿	7:04
	☽ □ ♃	7:42
	☽ ☌ ⚳	10:02
	☽ □ ♂	13:32
	⚵ D	23:44
3 Tu	☊ R	2:54
	♀ ∥ ⚷	3:39
	☿ △ ⚷	3:42
	☽ △ ♄	5:20
	☽ ⚼ ♇	5:28
	♀ △ ♅	6:55
	☉ ✶ ☽	7:31
	☽ # ♇	10:43
	☽ ✶ ⚷	10:44
	☿ # ♄	11:18
	☽ ✶ ☿	12:14
	☽ ⚺ ♅	14:35
	☽ □ ♀	15:26
4 W	☿ □ ♅	1:58
	☽ □ ♆	6:56
	☽ ⚼ ♄	11:22
	☽ ⚻ ♇	11:38
	☉ ∠ ☽	16:20
	☽ △ ♃	19:39
	☽ ∠ ♅	20:42
	☉ △ ⚷	22:42
	☽ ⚺ ⚳	24:00
5 Th	☽ ∠ ☿	0:28
	☿ ⚺ ♀	4:45
	☽ ✶ ♂	5:14
	☽ ⚻ ♄	16:53
	☽ □ ⚷	22:23
6 F	☉ ⚺ ☽	0:25
	☽ ⚼ ♃	0:53
	☽ ✶ ♅	2:13
	☽ ∠ ⚳	6:06
	☽ ✶ ♀	9:19
	☽ ⚺ ☿	11:32
	☽ ∠ ♂	12:05
	☉ ∥ ☿	16:21
	☽ △ ♆	17:44
	☽ ☍ ♇	22:13
	☉ □ ♅	23:58
7 Sa	☽ ⚻ ♃	5:24
	☽ ✶ ⚳	11:26
	☿ ∥ ♅	16:00
	☽ ∠ ♀	16:51
	☽ ⚺ ♂	18:05
	☽ # ♇	20:38
	☽ ⚼ ♆	22:04
8 Su	☽ ☍ ♄	1:51
	☿ ⚻ ♆	2:26
	☽ △ ⚷	7:19
	☽ □ ♅	11:05
	☉ ☌ ☽	13:51
	☉ ∥ ♅	22:42
	☽ ⚺ ♀	23:25
9 M	☽ # ♄	1:23
	☽ ⚻ ♆	1:43
	☽ ☌ ☿	5:46
	☽ ⚻ ♇	5:58
	☿ ⚻ ♇	7:04
	☽ ⚼ ⚷	10:44
	☽ ☍ ♃	12:24
	☽ ∥ ♅	16:20
	♀ # ♆	17:17
	☉ ∥ ☽	17:30
	☿ ∥ ⚳	18:31
	☽ □ ⚳	19:49
	☽ ∥ ⚳	23:30
10 Tu	♀ ☍ ♆	0:21
	☽ ∥ ☿	0:23
	☽ ☌ ♂	3:43
	☽ # ♃	6:01
	☽ ⚻ ♄	8:08
	☽ ⚼ ♇	8:54
	☽ ⚻ ⚷	13:35
	☿ ⚼ ⚷	15:50
	☽ △ ♅	17:20
	☽ ∥ ♂	21:25
11 W	☉ ⚺ ☽	0:04
	☿ ☍ ♃	1:21
	☽ ☍ ♆	7:17
	☽ ∥ ⚷	8:06
	☽ ☌ ♀	10:17
	☽ ⚼ ♄	10:32
	☽ △ ♇	11:23
	♀ ⚼ ♄	13:00
	☿ # ♃	14:12
	☽ ⚻ ♃	17:11
	☽ ⚼ ♅	19:44
	☽ ⚺ ☿	19:52
	☽ # ♆	21:22
	☿ ♍	21:58
	♀ △ ♇	22:47
12 Th	☽ △ ⚳	1:56
	☽ ∥ ♀	2:22
	☉ ∠ ☽	4:20
	☽ ⚺ ♂	11:04
	☽ △ ♄	12:34
	☽ ☍ ⚷	18:03
	☽ ⚼ ♃	19:03
	☽ ⚻ ♅	21:49
	☽ # ♀	22:41
13 F	☽ ∠ ☿	1:56
	☽ ⚼ ⚳	4:27
	☉ ∥ ⚳	4:42
	☽ ∥ ♆	5:24
	☉ ✶ ☽	8:14
	☽ ⚻ ♆	11:20
	☽ ∠ ♂	14:13
	☽ □ ♇	15:22
	♂ ⚻ ♄	16:28
	☽ # ⚷	18:15
	☽ ⚺ ♀	19:12
	☽ △ ♃	20:40
	☿ □ ⚳	23:59
14 Sa	☽ # ♂	1:28
	☽ ⚻ ⚳	6:43
	☽ ✶ ☿	7:34
	☽ # ☿	10:37
	♀ ⚻ ♃	10:59
	☽ ⚼ ♆	13:02
	♂ ⚼ ♇	14:33
	☽ □ ♄	15:55
	☽ ✶ ♂	17:09
	☽ ∥ ♃	20:22
	☽ ⚻ ⚷	21:31
	☽ ∠ ♀	23:14
	☉ # ☽	23:44
15 Su	☽ ☍ ♅	1:19
	☽ # ⚳	2:43
	☉ ⚻ ♆	4:15
	☽ # ♅	8:19
	☽ △ ♆	14:34
	☊ D	15:09
	☉ □ ☽	15:21
	☽ ✶ ♇	18:33
	☽ ∥ ♄	22:55
	☽ ⚼ ⚷	23:00
	☽ □ ♃	23:24
16 M	♀ ⚼ ♅	0:07
	☽ ✶ ♀	3:06
	♀ ♎	4:28
	☽ ☍ ⚳	10:46
	☊ R	16:08
	☽ □ ☿	17:58
	☽ ✶ ♄	18:41
	☽ ∠ ♇	19:58
	☽ □ ♂	22:33
	☿ ⚻ ♄	23:36
17 Tu	☽ △ ⚷	0:23
	☽ ∥ ♇	0:32
	☉ # ♃	0:38
	☽ ⚻ ♅	4:16
	☿ ⚼ ♇	10:09
	☉ ⚻ ♇	13:33
	☽ □ ♆	17:20
	☽ ∠ ♄	19:56
	☽ ⚺ ♇	21:18
	☉ △ ☽	21:52
18 W	☽ ✶ ♃	1:44
	☽ ⚼ ♅	5:38
	♃ ∠ ⚷	6:08
	☽ □ ♀	10:29
	♂ ⚻ ⚷	14:10
	☽ ⚻ ⚳	14:25
	☽ ⚺ ♄	21:09
	☿ ⚻ ⚷	22:20
19 Th	☿ ∥ ♂	0:18
	☉ ⚼ ☽	1:04
	☽ ∠ ♃	2:51
	☽ □ ⚷	3:01
	☿ ☌ ♂	3:29
	☽ △ ♂	3:38
	☽ △ ☿	3:39
	☽ △ ♅	7:00
	☽ ⚼ ⚳	16:16
	☿ ∥ ⚷	19:10
	☽ ✶ ♆	20:00
20 F	☽ ☌ ♇	0:00
	☉ ☍ ♃	0:30
	♅ R	1:41
	☽ ⚺ ♃	4:05
	☉ ⚻ ☽	4:22
	☉ ⚼ ⚷	4:55
	☽ ⚼ ♂	6:18
	☿ △ ♅	8:07
	☽ ⚼ ☿	8:32
	☽ △ ♀	18:02
	☽ △ ⚳	18:16
	☽ ∥ ♇	20:27
	♀ △ ⚳	21:24
	☽ ∠ ♆	21:33
	☽ ☌ ♄	23:57
21 Sa	☽ ✶ ⚷	6:02
	☽ ⚻ ♂	9:14
	☽ □ ♅	10:13
	♂ ∥ ⚷	10:14
	☽ ⚻ ☿	13:43
	☽ ∥ ♄	22:12
	☽ ⚼ ♀	22:19
	☽ ⚺ ♆	23:26
22 Su	☽ ⚺ ♇	3:34
	♂ △ ♅	6:39
	☽ ☌ ♃	7:20
	☽ ∠ ⚷	8:03
	☉ ☍ ☽	12:03
	☽ # ♅	13:58
	☽ # ⚳	18:13
	☉ ♍	21:36
	☽ □ ⚳	23:26
23 M	☽ ∥ ♃	0:40
	☽ ⚻ ♀	3:15
	☽ ⚺ ♄	4:08
	☽ ∠ ♇	6:03
	☽ ⚺ ⚷	10:38
	☉ # ☽	11:54
	♀ △ ♄	12:49
	☽ ✶ ♅	15:06
	☽ ☍ ♂	16:44
	☿ # ♆	20:53
24 Tu	☽ ☍ ☿	2:04
	☽ ☌ ♆	4:51
	☽ # ⚷	6:37
	☽ ∠ ♄	7:10
	☽ ✶ ♇	9:14
	☽ # ♂	9:45
	☿ # ♀	12:14
	☽ ⚺ ♃	12:44
	☽ ∠ ♅	18:34
	☽ ∥ ♆	19:27
	☽ ∥ ♀	20:44
	☉ ⚻ ☽	22:38
	☽ # ☿	22:56
25 W	☿ ☍ ♆	1:15
	☽ ✶ ⚳	7:17
	♀ ∥ ♆	10:57
	☽ ✶ ♄	10:59
	☽ ☍ ♀	15:58
	☽ ∠ ♃	16:35
	☽ ☌ ⚷	18:01
	☿ ⚼ ♄	19:42
	♀ ⚼ ♃	22:00
	☽ ⚺ ♅	22:52
26 Th	☽ ∥ ☿	0:25
	☽ ⚻ ♂	3:38
	☉ ⚼ ☽	5:28
	☽ # ♆	7:30
	☽ # ♀	9:38
	☽ ∠ ⚳	12:31
	☽ ⚺ ♆	13:23
	♀ ☍ ⚷	13:25
	☿ △ ♇	14:24
	☽ ∥ ♂	15:00
	☽ □ ♇	18:03
	☽ ⚻ ☿	18:34
	☽ ∥ ⚷	20:45
	☽ ✶ ♃	21:16
27 F	☉ ∥ ☽	10:23
	☽ ⚼ ♂	10:33
	☉ △ ☽	13:21
	☿ ⚻ ♃	15:06
	☽ ⚺ ⚳	18:35
	☽ ∠ ♆	18:51
	☽ □ ♄	21:05
28 Sa	♀ # ♂	0:33
	☽ ⚼ ☿	4:27
	☽ ⚺ ⚷	4:38
	☽ # ♃	6:46
	☽ ⚻ ♀	9:01
	☽ ☌ ♅	9:53
	☽ ∥ ⚳	13:56
	☽ ∥ ♅	17:28
	♀ ⚻ ♅	17:45
	☽ △ ♂	18:15
29 Su	☽ ✶ ♆	0:57
	☽ △ ♇	5:51
	☽ □ ♃	8:37
	☽ ∠ ⚷	10:51
	☽ # ♄	12:24
	☽ △ ☿	15:00
	☽ ⚼ ♀	18:42
30 M	☿ ⚼ ♅	1:01
	☿ ♎	5:11
	☉ □ ☽	7:14
	☽ ☌ ⚳	8:19
	☽ △ ♄	9:27
	☽ ⚼ ♇	12:18
	☽ ✶ ⚷	17:15
	☽ # ♇	17:40
	☽ ⚺ ♅	22:41
	☉ □ ⚳	23:40
31 Tu	♀ # ⚷	2:01
	☽ △ ♀	4:31
	☉ ⚻ ♄	8:47
	☽ □ ♂	10:37
	☽ □ ♆	13:42
	☽ ⚼ ♄	15:42
	☽ ⚻ ♇	18:38
	☽ △ ♃	20:50

August 2021:Modify New York Stock Exchange Zone:-5

Sunday	Monday	Tuesday	Wednesday	Thursday	Friday	Saturday
1 9:06AM ☿ ☌ ☉ 4:49PM ☿ ☍ ♄	2 1:13AM ☉ ☍ ♄ 3:45AM ☽-> 0♊00	3 1:52AM ♀ △ ♅ 8:56PM ☿ □ ♅	4 4:16PM ☽-> 0♋00	5	6 6:56PM ☉ □ ♅	7 2:30AM ☽-> 0♌00
8 8:49AM New Moon♌[	9 9:54AM ☽-> 0♍00 7:19PM ♀ ☍ ♆	10 8:19PM ☿ ☍ ♃	11 3:06PM ☽-> 0♎00 4:56PM ☿-> 0♍00 5:44PM ♀ △ ♇	12	13 7:00PM ☽-> 0♏00	14
15 10:10PM ☽-> 0♐00 11:26PM ♀-> 0♎00	16	17	18 12:56AM ☽-> 0♑00 10:26PM ☿ ☌ ♂	19 7:27PM ☉ ☍ ♃ 8:40PM ♅ ℞⎕14♉	20 3:05AM ☿ △ ♅ 3:47AM ☽-> 0♒00	21
22 1:37AM ♂ △ ♅ 7:00AM Full Moon♒ 7:41AM ☽-> 0♓00 4:34PM ☉-> 0♍00	23 7:47AM ♀ △ ♄	24 1:55PM ☽-> 0♈00 8:12PM ☿ ☍ ♆	25	26 9:22AM ☿ △ ♇ 11:25PM ☽-> 0♉00	27	28
29 11:40AM ☽-> 0♊00	30 12:09AM ☿-> 0♎00	31			July	September

July

S	M	T	W	T	F	S
				1	2	3
4	5	6	7	8	9	10
11	12	13	14	15	16	17
18	19	20	21	22	23	24
25	26	27	28	29	30	31

September

S	M	T	W	T	F	S
			1	2	3	4
5	6	7	8	9	10	11
12	13	14	15	16	17	18
19	20	21	22	23	24	25
26	27	28	29	30		

LONGITUDE — September 2021

Day	Sid.Time	☉	☽	☽ 12 hour	Mean☊	True ☊	☿	♀	♂	⚳	♃	♄	⚷	♅	♆	♇
	h m s	° ' "	° ' "	° ' "	° '	° '	° '	° '	° '	° '	° '	° '	° '	° '	° '	° '
1 W	22 41 30	8♍47 04	27♊16 48	3♋16 55	5♊59.4	6♊08.4	2♎30.2	18♎34.1	20♍59.5	8♊00.5	25♒41.0	8♒08.0	12♈01.4	14♉44.1	22♓09.1	24♑36.4
2 Th	22 45 27	9 45 08	9♋20 11	15 27 07	5 56.2	6R 05.8	3 52.3	19 44.0	21 37.9	8 12.4	25R 33.6	8R 04.6	11R 59.3	14R 43.4	22R 07.5	24R 35.5
3 F	22 49 24	10 43 15	21 38 16	27 54 01	5 53.0	6 00.7	5 12.9	20 53.8	22 16.3	8 24.1	25 26.2	8 01.2	11 57.1	14 42.8	22 05.8	24 34.6
4 Sa	22 53 20	11 41 23	4♌14 43	10♌40 35	5 49.8	5 53.0	6 32.0	22 03.5	22 54.8	8 35.5	25 18.9	7 57.8	11 54.9	14 42.1	22 04.2	24 33.7
5 Su	22 57 17	12 39 33	17 11 45	23 48 13	5 46.7	5 42.9	7 49.5	23 13.2	23 33.2	8 46.7	25 11.7	7 54.6	11 52.6	14 41.3	22 02.6	24 32.8
6 M	23 01 13	13 37 45	0♍29 53	7♍16 30	5 43.5	5 31.2	9 05.3	24 22.8	24 11.8	8 57.6	25 04.6	7 51.4	11 50.3	14 40.5	22 01.0	24 32.0
7 Tu	23 05 10	14 35 58	14 07 43	21 03 05	5 40.3	5 18.9	10 19.4	25 32.3	24 50.3	9 08.3	24 57.6	7 48.2	11 48.0	14 39.7	21 59.3	24 31.2
8 W	23 09 06	15 34 14	28 02 06	5♎04 10	5 37.1	5 07.3	11 31.8	26 41.8	25 28.9	9 18.7	24 50.7	7 45.2	11 45.6	14 38.8	21 57.7	24 30.4
9 Th	23 13 03	16 32 30	12♎08 39	19 14 58	5 33.9	4 57.5	12 42.2	27 51.1	26 07.5	9 28.8	24 43.9	7 42.2	11 43.3	14 37.8	21 56.0	24 29.6
10 F	23 16 59	17 30 49	26 22 29	3♏30 39	5 30.8	4 50.4	13 50.8	29 00.4	26 46.1	9 38.7	24 37.2	7 39.3	11 40.9	14 36.8	21 54.4	24 28.9
11 Sa	23 20 56	18 29 09	10♏38 59	17 47 02	5 27.6	4 46.1	14 57.2	0♏09.6	27 24.7	9 48.2	24 30.6	7 36.5	11 38.4	14 35.8	21 52.7	24 28.2
12 Su	23 24 53	19 27 31	24 54 28	2♐00 59	5 24.4	4D 44.3	16 01.5	1 18.7	28 03.4	9 57.5	24 24.2	7 33.7	11 36.0	14 34.7	21 51.1	24 27.5
13 M	23 28 49	20 25 55	9♐06 23	16 10 29	5 21.2	4R 44.1	17 03.4	2 27.7	28 42.1	10 06.6	24 17.8	7 31.0	11 33.5	14 33.6	21 49.4	24 26.8
14 Tu	23 32 46	21 24 20	23 13 13	0♑14 26	5 18.0	4 44.2	18 02.9	3 36.6	29 20.8	10 15.3	24 11.6	7 28.5	11 31.0	14 32.4	21 47.8	24 26.2
15 W	23 36 42	22 22 46	7♑14 06	14 12 08	5 14.9	4 43.5	18 59.8	4 45.4	29 59.6	10 23.7	24 05.6	7 26.0	11 28.5	14 31.2	21 46.1	24 25.6
16 Th	23 40 39	23 21 15	21 08 25	28 02 49	5 11.7	4 40.7	19 53.8	5 54.1	0♎38.4	10 31.9	23 59.6	7 23.5	11 26.0	14 30.0	21 44.5	24 25.0
17 F	23 44 35	24 19 44	4♒55 13	11♒45 25	5 08.5	4 35.4	20 44.9	7 02.7	1 17.2	10 39.7	23 53.8	7 21.2	11 23.5	14 28.7	21 42.8	24 24.4
18 Sa	23 48 32	25 18 16	18 33 13	25 18 22	5 05.3	4 27.5	21 32.6	8 11.2	1 56.0	10 47.3	23 48.2	7 18.9	11 20.9	14 27.3	21 41.2	24 23.9
19 Su	23 52 28	26 16 49	2♓00 37	8♓39 44	5 02.2	4 17.4	22 16.9	9 19.6	2 34.9	10 54.5	23 42.7	7 16.8	11 18.3	14 25.9	21 39.5	24 23.4
20 M	23 56 25	27 15 24	15 15 29	21 47 39	4 59.0	4 06.1	22 57.5	10 27.9	3 13.8	11 01.4	23 37.3	7 14.7	11 15.7	14 24.5	21 37.9	24 22.9
21 Tu	0 00 22	28 14 00	28 16 03	4♈40 36	4 55.8	3 54.7	23 34.0	11 36.0	3 52.7	11 08.0	23 32.1	7 12.7	11 13.1	14 23.1	21 36.2	24 22.4
22 W	0 04 18	29 12 39	11♈01 13	17 17 56	4 52.6	3 44.3	24 06.1	12 44.0	4 31.6	11 14.3	23 27.1	7 10.8	11 10.5	14 21.6	21 34.6	24 22.0
23 Th	0 08 15	0♎11 19	23 30 48	29 40 01	4 49.4	3 35.8	24 33.5	13 52.0	5 10.6	11 20.3	23 22.2	7 09.0	11 07.8	14 20.0	21 33.0	24 21.6
24 F	0 12 11	1 10 02	5♉45 46	11♉48 24	4 46.3	3 29.7	24 55.8	14 59.7	5 49.6	11 25.9	23 17.5	7 07.3	11 05.2	14 18.4	21 31.3	24 21.2
25 Sa	0 16 08	2 08 47	17 48 15	23 45 47	4 43.1	3 26.1	25 12.6	16 07.4	6 28.7	11 31.3	23 13.0	7 05.6	11 02.5	14 16.8	21 29.7	24 20.8
26 Su	0 20 04	3 07 34	29 41 29	5♊35 53	4 39.9	3D 24.7	25 23.6	17 15.0	7 07.7	11 36.2	23 08.6	7 04.1	10 59.8	14 15.2	21 28.1	24 20.5
27 M	0 24 01	4 06 23	11♊29 34	17 23 11	4 36.7	3 24.9	25R 28.3	18 22.4	7 46.9	11 40.9	23 04.4	7 02.7	10 57.2	14 13.5	21 26.5	24 20.2
28 Tu	0 27 57	5 05 15	23 17 21	29 12 44	4 33.6	3 25.8	25 26.3	19 29.7	8 26.0	11 45.1	23 00.4	7 01.3	10 54.5	14 11.7	21 24.9	24 20.0
29 W	0 31 54	6 04 09	5♋10 03	11♋09 56	4 30.4	3R 26.3	25 17.4	20 36.8	9 05.2	11 49.1	22 56.5	7 00.1	10 51.8	14 10.0	21 23.3	24 19.7
30 Th	0 35 51	7♎03 05	17 13 04	23 20 05	4♊27.2	3♊25.7	25♎01.1	21♏43.8	9♎44.4	11♊52.7	22♒52.9	6♒58.9	10♈49.1	14♉08.2	21♓21.7	24♑19.5

1st of Month

Julian Day #
2459458.5
Obliquity
23°26'15"
SVP 4♓57'41"
GC 27♐08.5
Eris 24♈38.7R

Day	⚴
1	21♓09.4R
6	19 53.2R
11	18 34.8R
16	17 15.9R
21	15 58.5R
26	14 44.1R

Day	⚵
1	10♐31.3
6	11 17.5
11	12 09.7
16	13 07.6
21	14 10.6
26	15 18.5

Day	⚶
1	20♎07.9
6	22 35.9
11	25 05.5
16	27 36.6
21	0♏09.0
26	2 42.5

DECLINATION and LATITUDE

Day	☉ Decl	☽ Decl	☽ Lat	☽12h Decl	☿ Decl	☿ Lat	♀ Decl	♀ Lat	♂ Decl	♂ Lat	⚳ Decl	⚳ Lat	♃ Decl	♃ Lat	♄ Decl	♄ Lat
1 W	8N17	25N14	1N49	25N42	1S41	0S45	7S26	0S10	4N24	0N55	15N21	6S22	14S05	1S12	19S01	0S49
2 Th	7 55	25 52	2 46	25 43	2 21	0 53	7 56	0 14	4 09	0 54	15 23	6 22	14 08	1 12	19 02	0 49
3 F	7 33	25 15	3 36	24 28	3 01	1 02	8 26	0 18	3 53	0 54	15 25	6 22	14 10	1 12	19 03	0 49
4 Sa	7 11	23 21	4 17	21 56	3 41	1 11	8 56	0 22	3 38	0 53	15 27	6 22	14 13	1 12	19 04	0 49
5 Su	6 49	20 13	4 45	18 13	4 19	1 19	9 25	0 26	3 22	0 53	15 28	6 22	14 15	1 12	19 04	0 49
6 M	6 26	15 58	4 60	13 29	4 57	1 28	9 55	0 30	3 07	0 53	15 30	6 22	14 18	1 12	19 05	0 49
7 Tu	6 04	10 49	4 57	7 59	5 34	1 37	10 24	0 34	2 51	0 52	15 32	6 22	14 20	1 12	19 06	0 49
8 W	5 41	5 01	4 37	1 59	6 11	1 46	10 53	0 38	2 35	0 52	15 33	6 22	14 22	1 12	19 07	0 49
9 Th	5 19	1S06	4 00	4S12	6 46	1 54	11 21	0 42	2 20	0 51	15 35	6 21	14 24	1 12	19 08	0 49
10 F	4 56	7 15	3 08	10 13	7 21	2 03	11 50	0 46	2 04	0 51	15 37	6 21	14 27	1 12	19 09	0 49
11 Sa	4 33	13 03	2 04	15 43	7 54	2 11	12 18	0 50	1 48	0 51	15 38	6 21	14 29	1 12	19 09	0 49
12 Su	4 10	18 09	0 52	20 20	8 27	2 19	12 46	0 54	1 32	0 50	15 40	6 21	14 31	1 12	19 10	0 49
13 M	3 47	22 12	0S23	23 43	8 58	2 28	13 14	0 58	1 17	0 50	15 41	6 21	14 33	1 12	19 11	0 49
14 Tu	3 24	24 52	1 36	25 37	9 29	2 36	13 41	1 02	1 01	0 49	15 42	6 21	14 35	1 12	19 11	0 49
15 W	3 01	25 58	2 43	25 53	9 58	2 44	14 09	1 06	0 45	0 49	15 44	6 20	14 37	1 12	19 12	0 49
16 Th	2 38	25 24	3 40	24 32	10 25	2 51	14 35	1 10	0 29	0 49	15 45	6 20	14 39	1 12	19 13	0 49
17 F	2 15	23 17	4 23	21 44	10 51	2 58	15 02	1 14	0 14	0 48	15 46	6 20	14 41	1 12	19 13	0 49
18 Sa	1 52	19 52	4 51	17 46	11 16	3 05	15 28	1 18	0S02	0 48	15 48	6 20	14 43	1 12	19 14	0 49
19 Su	1 29	15 27	5 02	12 59	11 39	3 12	15 54	1 23	0 18	0 47	15 49	6 19	14 45	1 12	19 14	0 49
20 M	1 05	10 22	4 57	7 40	11 60	3 18	16 20	1 27	0 34	0 47	15 50	6 19	14 46	1 12	19 15	0 49
21 Tu	0 42	4 55	4 36	2 08	12 19	3 24	16 45	1 31	0 50	0 47	15 51	6 19	14 48	1 12	19 16	0 49
22 W	0 19	0N39	4 02	3N24	12 36	3 30	17 10	1 35	1 06	0 46	15 52	6 19	14 50	1 12	19 16	0 49
23 Th	0S05	6 05	3 16	8 42	12 50	3 34	17 35	1 39	1 21	0 46	15 54	6 18	14 51	1 11	19 16	0 49
24 F	0 28	11 12	2 22	13 35	13 02	3 38	17 59	1 43	1 37	0 45	15 55	6 18	14 53	1 11	19 17	0 49
25 Sa	0 51	15 49	1 23	17 53	13 11	3 42	18 22	1 47	1 53	0 45	15 56	6 17	14 54	1 11	19 17	0 49
26 Su	1 15	19 46	0 20	21 26	13 18	3 44	18 46	1 51	2 09	0 44	15 57	6 17	14 55	1 11	19 18	0 49
27 M	1 38	22 52	0N43	24 04	13 21	3 45	19 09	1 56	2 25	0 44	15 58	6 17	14 57	1 11	19 18	0 49
28 Tu	2 01	25 01	1 45	25 40	13 20	3 46	19 31	1 60	2 41	0 44	15 59	6 16	14 58	1 11	19 18	0 49
29 W	2 25	26 02	2 42	26 06	13 16	3 45	19 53	2 04	2 56	0 43	15 60	6 16	14 59	1 11	19 19	0 49
30 Th	2S48	25N51	3N33	25N17	13S08	3S43	20S15	2S08	3S12	0N43	16N01	6S15	15S00	1S11	19S19	0S49

Day	⚷ Decl	⚷ Lat	♅ Decl	♅ Lat	♆ Decl	♆ Lat	♇ Decl	♇ Lat
1	6N58	2N24	15N51	0S25	4S11	1S10	22S48	1S38
6	6 53	2 24	15 50	0 25	4 14	1 10	22 49	1 38
11	6 49	2 24	15 49	0 25	4 18	1 10	22 50	1 38
16	6 44	2 24	15 47	0 25	4 21	1 10	22 51	1 38
21	6 39	2 24	15 45	0 25	4 24	1 10	22 52	1 39
26	6 33	2 24	15 43	0 25	4 28	1 10	22 52	1 39

Day	⚴ Decl	⚴ Lat	⚵ Decl	⚵ Lat	⚶ Decl	⚶ Lat	Eris Decl	Eris Lat
1	2N04	6N04	8S29	13N40	3S12	5N02	1S10	11S30
6	0 60	5 26	8 56	13 19	4 14	4 54	1 11	11 30
11	0S07	4 46	9 22	12 59	5 15	4 47	1 12	11 30
16	1 16	4 06	9 48	12 40	6 16	4 40	1 13	11 30
21	2 24	3 24	10 13	12 22	7 16	4 32	1 14	11 31
26	3 32	2 42	10 38	12 04	8 15	4 25	1 15	11 31

Moon Phenomena

Max/0 Decl
dy hr mn
2 0:25 25N52
8 19:42 0 S
15 3:46 25S59
21 21:10 0 N
29 8:28 26N07

Max/0 Lat
dy hr mn
6 8:47 5N01
12 16:36 0 S
19 4:03 5S02
26 7:34 0 N

Perigee/Apogee
dy hr m kilometers
11 10:05 p 368462
26 21:45 a 404640

PH dy hr mn
● 7 0:53 14♍38
☽ 13 20:41 21♐16
○ 20 23:56 28♓14
☾ 29 1:58 6♋09

Void of Course Moon

Last Aspect			☽ Ingress	
31 20:50	♃	△	♋	1 5:27
3 5:39	♇	☍	♌	3 15:59
5 14:23	♃	☍	♍	5 23:07
7 19:25	♂	☌	♎	8 3:22
10 4:49	♀	☌	♏	10 6:06
12 5:34	♂	⚹	♐	12 8:36
14 10:59	♂	□	♑	14 11:35
16 5:41	♇	☌	♒	16 15:24
18 9:16	♃	☌	♓	18 20:24
20 23:56	☉	☍	♈	21 3:14
23 2:06	☿	☍	♉	23 12:39
25 13:10	♇	△	♊	26 0:38
28 4:19	☿	△	♋	28 13:35

DAILY ASPECTARIAN

1 W
☽∠♅ 4:55
⚳△♄ 11:40
☽□☿ 11:48
♂#♆ 19:38
☉⚼♇ 20:04
☽⚻♄ 21:31
☽⚺⚳ 21:44
☉#♀ 23:20
☉∥⚷ 17:25
☽□♅ 19:25
☿∥♆ 20:33

2 Th
☉⚹☽ 0:53
☽⚼♃ 2:23
☽□⚷ 5:12
☽⚹♅ 10:34
♂☍♆ 17:44
☽□♀ 22:25

3 F
☽△♆ 0:53
☽⚹♂ 1:17
☽∠⚳ 3:27
☽☍♇ 5:39
☽⚻♃ 7:14
☉∠☽ 8:30
☿#♂ 22:48

4 Sa
♀⚻♆ 0:14
♂⚼♄ 1:46
☽⚹☿ 4:46
☽#♇ 4:49
☽⚼♆ 5:17
☉⚻⚷ 5:21
☽☍♄ 6:56
☽∠♂ 7:13
☽⚹⚳ 8:15
☽△⚷ 14:15
☉⚺☽ 15:00

5 Su
☿△♄ 1:32
☽#♄ 6:59
☽⚻♆ 8:48
☽∠☿ 11:19
☽⚹♀ 12:00
☽⚺♂ 12:08
☽⚻♇ 13:20
♀⚼⚳ 13:43
☽☍♃ 14:23
♀⚺♂ 15:27
☽⚼⚷ 17:29
☿△⚳ 21:08

6 M
☽∥♅ 0:37
☽∥⚳ 2:17
♀□♇ 3:08
☽#♃ 8:08
♂△♇ 12:21
☽⚻♄ 12:58
♀△♃ 13:06
☽□⚳ 15:10
☽⚼♇ 15:57
☽⚺☿ 16:42
☽∠♀ 17:09
☿⚼♃ 17:29
☽⚻⚷ 19:57

7 Tu
☉☌☽ 0:53
☽△♅ 0:56
☉△♅ 1:30
☽#♀ 1:40
♂⚻♃ 3:51
☉#☿ 11:59
☽☍♆ 13:35
☽⚼♄ 14:58
☽∥⚷ 16:34
☽△♇ 17:57
☽⚻♃ 18:34
☽☌♂ 19:25
☽#☿ 19:47
☉∥☽ 21:09
☽⚺♀ 21:30

8 W
☽⚼♅ 2:45
☽#♆ 3:01
☿☍⚷ 4:31
☽∥♂ 10:03
☽△♄ 16:30
☽△⚳ 19:26
☽⚼♃ 19:57
☽☍⚷ 23:17

9 Th
☽☌☿ 1:02
⚳⚼♇ 1:50
☿#⚷ 3:01
☽⚻♅ 4:12
☽#♂ 4:32
☉⚺☽ 7:59
☽∥♆ 12:19
☉#☽ 15:24
☽⚻♆ 16:30
☽□♇ 20:49
☽⚼⚳ 21:03
☽△♃ 21:04
☽#⚷ 22:20

10 F
☽∥☿ 0:25
☽⚺♂ 0:42
☽☌♀ 4:49
☉∠☽ 11:05
☿⚻♅ 16:18
☽⚼♆ 17:40
☽□♄ 18:54
☽∥♀ 20:28
♀ ♏ 20:40
☽⚻⚳ 22:34

11 Sa
☽⚻⚷ 1:40
☽∠♂ 3:06
☽∥♃ 6:23
☽☍♅ 6:38
☽⚺☿ 7:50
♃⚺♇ 10:07
☽#⚳ 11:41
☽#♅ 12:28
☉⚹☽ 14:09
☉#♆ 15:47
☽△♆ 18:52
☽□♃ 23:09
☽⚹♇ 23:15

12 Su
☽⚼⚷ 2:51
☽∥♄ 5:25
☽⚹♂ 5:34
☽∠☿ 11:09
☽⚺♀ 11:46
☊ D 16:35
☽⚹♄ 21:19

13 M
☽∠♇ 0:35
☽☍⚳ 1:43
☽△⚷ 4:09
☽∥♇ 4:46
☽⚻♅ 9:15
☽⚹☿ 14:32
☽∠♀ 15:27
☊ R 20:35
☉□☽ 20:41
☽□♆ 21:35
☽∠♄ 22:44

14 Tu
☽⚹♃ 1:39
☽⚺♇ 2:04
♂⚼♅ 6:58
☉☍♆ 9:22
☽⚼♅ 10:47
☽□♂ 10:59
☽⚹♀ 19:22

15 W
♂ ♎ 0:15
☽⚺♄ 0:20
☉⚼♄ 1:15
☽∠♃ 3:10
☽⚻⚳ 5:29
☽□⚷ 7:17
☽△♅ 12:32
☽□☿ 21:42

16 Th
☽⚹♆ 1:02
♀∥♃ 3:33
☉△☽ 4:08
☽⚺♃ 4:55
☽☌♇ 5:41
☽⚼⚳ 7:42
☉⚻♃ 14:19
♀⚼♆ 17:12
☽△♂ 17:20

17 F
☉△♇ 1:54
☽∠♆ 3:08
☽∥♇ 3:37
⚳∥♅ 4:01
☽□♀ 4:04
☽☌♄ 4:15
♀□♄ 6:16
☉⚼☽ 8:19
☽△⚳ 10:10
☽⚹⚷ 11:19
☽□♅ 16:46
☽⚼♂ 20:59

18 Sa
☽∥♄ 3:48
☿⚻♆ 4:19
☽⚺♆ 5:33
☽△☿ 5:37
☽☌♃ 9:16
☽⚺♇ 10:22
☉⚻☽ 12:56
☽∠⚷ 13:49
♀#♅ 16:19
♀#⚳ 18:46
☽∥♀ 21:56
☽#⚳ 22:13
☽#♅ 22:27

19 Su
☽⚻♂ 1:05
☽∥♃ 3:30
☽⚺♄ 9:28
☽⚼☿ 10:02
☽∠♇ 13:19
☽△♀ 14:27
☽□⚳ 16:13
☽⚺⚷ 16:44
☽∥☿ 17:02
☽⚹♅ 22:27

20 M
☽☌♆ 11:41
☽∠♄ 12:48
♀⚻⚳ 13:06
☽⚻☿ 14:52
☽⚺♃ 15:17
♀⚻⚷ 16:14
☽#⚷ 16:28
☽⚹♇ 16:46
⚶ ♏ 16:58
☉#♂ 19:20
☽⚼♀ 20:36
☿△♃ 22:54
☉☍☽ 23:56

21 Tu
☽∠♅ 2:05
☽∥♆ 2:10
☽☍♂ 11:04
⚳⚹⚷ 13:29
☽⚹♄ 16:44
☽∥♂ 16:48
☽∠♃ 19:09
☉#☽ 19:30
☉∥☽ 22:38

22 W
☽☌⚷ 0:18
☽⚹⚳ 0:25
☽#♂ 2:00
☉⚼♅ 3:33
☽⚻♀ 3:35
☽⚺♅ 6:21
☿□♇ 13:13
☽#♆ 16:32
☉ ♎ 19:22
☽⚺♆ 20:12
☽⚹♃ 23:43

23 Th
☽□♇ 1:39
☽☍☿ 2:06
☽∥⚷ 2:20
☽∠⚳ 5:32
♀☍♅ 9:42
☉⚻☽ 14:09

24 F
☽⚻♂ 0:08
☽∠♆ 1:30
☽□♄ 2:41
☽#☿ 9:31
☽⚺⚷ 10:32
☽⚺⚳ 11:20
☽☌♅ 16:57
☽#♃ 18:57
☽☍♀ 20:17
☉⚼☽ 22:34
☽∥♅ 23:28

25 Sa
☽∥⚳ 0:38
☽⚹♆ 7:24
☽⚼♂ 7:49
☽□♃ 10:50
☽△♇ 13:10
☽⚻☿ 15:11
☽∠⚷ 16:33
☽#♀ 16:45
☽#♄ 20:55
♂△♄ 21:51

26 Su
☊ D 7:34
☉△☽ 7:36
☽△♄ 14:58
☽△♂ 16:00
☽⚼♇ 19:37
☽⚼☿ 21:55
☽⚹⚷ 22:54
☽#♇ 24:00

27 M
☽☌⚳ 0:23
☿ R 5:11
☽⚺♅ 5:33
♂⚼♃ 9:45
♀∥♄ 10:07
☽⚻♀ 15:29
☽□♆ 20:12
☽⚼♄ 21:26
☽△♃ 23:26

28 Tu
☽⚻♇ 2:07
☽△☿ 4:19
☽∠♅ 11:56

29 W
☽⚼♀ 0:59
☉□☽ 1:58
☊ R 2:10
☽⚻♄ 3:40
☽⚼♃ 5:32
☽□♂ 8:18
☽□⚷ 11:21
☽⚺⚳ 13:22
♀△♆ 16:15
☽⚹♅ 17:55
☉△♄ 22:21

30 Th
☽△♆ 8:08
☽△♀ 9:45
☽⚻♃ 11:04
☽☍♇ 13:56
☽□☿ 14:50
☽∠⚳ 18:58
☉⚼♃ 19:08
♀□♃ 23:32

September 2021:Modify New York Stock Exchange Zone:-5

Sunday	Monday	Tuesday	Wednesday	Thursday	Friday	Saturday
			1 12:24AM ☽-> 0♋00	2 12:42PM ♂ ☍ ♆	3 10:57AM ☽-> 0♌00	4 8:29PM ☿ △ ♄
5 6:04PM ☽-> 0♍00 10:06PM ♀ □ ♇	6 7:19AM ♂ △ ♇ 8:04AM ♀ △ ♃ 7:50PM New Moon♍ 8:28PM ☉ △ ♅	7 10:19PM ☽-> 0♎00	8	9	10 1:03AM ☽-> 0♏00 3:38PM ♀-> 0♏00	11
12 3:33AM ☽-> 0♐00	13	14 4:20AM ☉ ☍ ♆ 6:33AM ☽-> 0♑00 7:13PM ♂-> 0♎00	15	16 10:22AM ☽-> 0♒00 8:52PM ☉ △ ♇	17 1:14AM ♀ □ ♄	18 3:21PM ☽-> 0♓00
19	20 5:52PM ☿ △ ♃ 6:53PM Full Moon♓ 10:11PM ☽-> 0♈00	21	22 8:11AM ☿ □ ♇ 2:20PM ☉-> 0♎00	23 4:40AM ♀ ☍ ♅ 7:37AM ☽-> 0♉00	24	25 4:49PM ♂ △ ♄ 7:35PM ☽-> 0♊00
26	27 12:09AM ☿ ℞25♎	28 8:33AM ☽-> 0♋00	29 11:13AM ♀ △ ♆ 5:18PM ☉ △ ♄	30 6:30PM ♀ □ ♃ 7:52PM ☽-> 0♌00	August S M T W T F S 1 2 3 4 5 6 7 8 9 10 11 12 13 14 15 16 17 18 19 20 21 22 23 24 25 26 27 28 29 30 31	October S M T W T F S 1 2 3 4 5 6 7 8 9 10 11 12 13 14 15 16 17 18 19 20 21 22 23 24 25 26 27 28 29 30 31

October 2021

LONGITUDE

Day	Sid.Time	☉	☽	☽ 12 hour	Mean☊	True☊	☿	♀	♂	⚳	♃	♄	⚷	♅	♆	♇
	h m s	° ' "	° ' "	° ' "	° '	° '	° '	° '	° '	° '	° '	° '	° '	° '	° '	° '
1 F	0 39 47	8♎02 03	29♋31 36	5♌48 08	4♊24.0	3♊23.3	24♎37.3	22♏50.7	10♎23.6	11♊55.9	22♒49.4	6♒57.9	10♈46.4	14♉06.3	21♓20.1	24♑19.3
2 Sa	0 43 44	9 01 04	12♌10 10	18 38 05	4 20.9	3R 18.7	24R 05.8	23 57.5	11 02.9	11 58.7	22R 46.1	6R 56.9	10R 43.7	14R 04.5	21R 18.6	24R 19.2
3 Su	0 47 40	10 00 06	25 12 10	1♍52 32	4 17.7	3 12.1	23 26.7	25 04.0	11 42.2	12 01.2	22 43.0	6 56.0	10 40.9	14 02.5	21 17.0	24 19.1
4 M	0 51 37	10 59 11	8♍39 13	15 32 05	4 14.5	3 04.1	22 40.2	26 10.5	12 21.5	12 03.3	22 40.0	6 55.3	10 38.2	14 00.6	21 15.5	24 19.0
5 Tu	0 55 33	11 58 19	22 30 49	29 34 59	4 11.3	2 55.4	21 46.9	27 16.8	13 00.9	12 05.1	22 37.3	6 54.6	10 35.5	13 58.6	21 13.9	24 18.9
6 W	0 59 30	12 57 28	6♎44 00	13♎57 08	4 08.1	2 47.2	20 47.3	28 22.9	13 40.3	12 06.4	22 34.8	6 54.0	10 32.8	13 56.6	21 12.4	24D 18.9
7 Th	1 03 26	13 56 39	21 13 36	28 32 30	4 05.0	2 40.3	19 42.7	29 28.8	14 19.7	12 07.4	22 32.4	6 53.6	10 30.1	13 54.6	21 10.9	24 18.9
8 F	1 07 23	14 55 53	5♏52 57	13♏14 03	4 01.8	2 35.4	18 34.3	0♐34.6	14 59.2	12 08.0	22 30.3	6 53.2	10 27.4	13 52.6	21 09.4	24 18.9
9 Sa	1 11 19	15 55 08	20 34 57	27 54 51	3 58.6	2D 32.9	17 23.8	1 40.2	15 38.7	12R 08.2	22 28.3	6 52.9	10 24.7	13 50.5	21 08.0	24 18.9
10 Su	1 15 16	16 54 25	5♐13 04	12♐29 00	3 55.4	2 32.3	16 12.9	2 45.6	16 18.2	12 08.1	22 26.6	6 52.8	10 22.0	13 48.4	21 06.5	24 19.0
11 M	1 19 13	17 53 45	19 42 12	26 52 16	3 52.2	2 33.1	15 03.6	3 50.8	16 57.8	12 07.5	22 25.0	6D 52.7	10 19.3	13 46.2	21 05.1	24 19.1
12 Tu	1 23 09	18 53 06	3♑58 56	11♑02 02	3 49.1	2 34.4	13 57.9	4 55.9	17 37.4	12 06.6	22 23.7	6 52.8	10 16.6	13 44.1	21 03.6	24 19.3
13 W	1 27 06	19 52 28	18 01 29	24 57 13	3 45.9	2R 35.1	12 57.8	6 00.7	18 17.0	12 05.2	22 22.5	6 52.9	10 14.0	13 41.9	21 02.2	24 19.4
14 Th	1 31 02	20 51 53	1♒49 16	8♒37 39	3 42.7	2 34.5	12 04.9	7 05.3	18 56.7	12 03.5	22 21.6	6 53.1	10 11.3	13 39.7	21 00.9	24 19.6
15 F	1 34 59	21 51 19	15 22 26	22 03 41	3 39.5	2 32.2	11 20.6	8 09.7	19 36.4	12 01.4	22 20.8	6 53.5	10 08.7	13 37.4	20 59.5	24 19.9
16 Sa	1 38 55	22 50 46	28 41 29	5♓15 53	3 36.4	2 28.1	10 46.3	9 13.8	20 16.1	11 58.9	22 20.3	6 53.9	10 06.1	13 35.2	20 58.1	24 20.1
17 Su	1 42 52	23 50 16	11♓46 57	18 14 43	3 33.2	2 22.4	10 22.5	10 17.7	20 55.9	11 56.0	22 19.9	6 54.5	10 03.4	13 32.9	20 56.8	24 20.4
18 M	1 46 48	24 49 47	24 39 16	1♈00 37	3 30.0	2 15.9	10D 09.8	11 21.4	21 35.7	11 52.7	22D 19.8	6 55.1	10 00.8	13 30.6	20 55.5	24 20.7
19 Tu	1 50 45	25 49 20	7♈18 49	13 33 57	3 26.8	2 09.3	10 08.3	12 24.8	22 15.5	11 49.0	22 19.8	6 55.9	9 58.2	13 28.3	20 54.2	24 21.1
20 W	1 54 42	26 48 55	19 46 05	25 55 19	3 23.6	2 03.3	10 17.7	13 27.9	22 55.3	11 44.9	22 20.1	6 56.7	9 55.7	13 25.9	20 52.9	24 21.5
21 Th	1 58 38	27 48 32	2♉01 47	8♉05 37	3 20.5	1 58.5	10 37.7	14 30.8	23 35.2	11 40.4	22 20.5	6 57.7	9 53.1	13 23.6	20 51.7	24 21.9
22 F	2 02 35	28 48 12	14 07 01	20 06 14	3 17.3	1 55.2	11 07.7	15 33.4	24 15.2	11 35.6	22 21.2	6 58.7	9 50.6	13 21.2	20 50.4	24 22.3
23 Sa	2 06 31	29 47 53	26 03 32	1♊59 14	3 14.1	1D 53.7	11 46.9	16 35.7	24 55.1	11 30.3	22 22.1	6 59.8	9 48.1	13 18.9	20 49.2	24 22.8
24 Su	2 10 28	0♏47 36	7♊53 42	13 47 21	3 10.9	1 53.7	12 34.5	17 37.7	25 35.1	11 24.7	22 23.1	7 01.1	9 45.6	13 16.5	20 48.1	24 23.3
25 M	2 14 24	1 47 22	19 40 36	25 33 58	3 07.8	1 54.9	13 29.7	18 39.4	26 15.2	11 18.6	22 24.4	7 02.4	9 43.1	13 14.1	20 46.9	24 23.8
26 Tu	2 18 21	2 47 09	1♋27 57	7♋23 07	3 04.6	1 56.6	14 31.7	19 40.7	26 55.2	11 12.2	22 25.8	7 03.9	9 40.7	13 11.6	20 45.8	24 24.3
27 W	2 22 17	3 46 59	13 20 04	19 19 22	3 01.4	1 58.4	15 39.6	20 41.8	27 35.3	11 05.4	22 27.5	7 05.4	9 38.2	13 09.2	20 44.7	24 24.9
28 Th	2 26 14	4 46 51	25 21 40	1♌27 33	2 58.2	1R 59.7	16 52.7	21 42.5	28 15.5	10 58.3	22 29.3	7 07.1	9 35.8	13 06.8	20 43.6	24 25.5
29 F	2 30 11	5 46 46	7♌37 39	13 52 32	2 55.1	2 00.1	18 10.2	22 42.8	28 55.7	10 50.7	22 31.4	7 08.8	9 33.5	13 04.3	20 42.5	24 26.2
30 Sa	2 34 07	6 46 42	20 12 47	26 38 52	2 51.9	1 59.3	19 31.5	23 42.8	29 35.9	10 42.8	22 33.7	7 10.7	9 31.1	13 01.9	20 41.5	24 26.8
31 Su	2 38 04	7♏46 40	3♍11 13	9♍50 10	2♊48.7	1♊57.4	20♎56.1	24♐42.4	0♏16.2	10♊34.5	22♒36.1	7♒12.6	9♈28.8	12♉59.4	20♓40.5	24♑27.5

1st of Month

Julian Day # 2459488.5
Obliquity 23°26'16"
SVP 4♓57'37"
GC 27♐08.6
Eris 24♈23.7R

Day	⚴
1	13♓34.4R
6	12 30.7R
11	11 34.3R
16	10 46.3R
21	10 07.1R
26	9 37.1R
31	9 16.6R

Day	⚵
1	16♐31.0
6	17 47.7
11	19 08.4
16	20 32.9
21	22 00.6
26	23 31.6
31	25 05.5

Day	⚶
1	5♏17.3
6	7 53.2
11	10 30.1
16	13 07.8
21	15 46.4
26	18 25.6
31	21 05.6

DECLINATION and LATITUDE

Day	☉ Decl	☽ Decl	☽ Lat	☽12h Decl	☿ Decl	☿ Lat	♀ Decl	♀ Lat	♂ Decl	♂ Lat	⚳ Decl	⚳ Lat	♃ Decl	♃ Lat	♄ Decl	♄ Lat
1 F	3S11	24N24	4N15	23N13	12S56	3S39	20S36	2S12	3S28	0N42	16N02	6S15	15S01	1S11	19S19	0S49
2 Sa	3 34	21 43	4 46	19 56	12 39	3 34	20 57	2 16	3 44	0 42	16 02	6 14	15 02	1 11	19 20	0 49
3 Su	3 58	17 53	5 04	15 34	12 18	3 27	21 17	2 19	3 60	0 41	16 03	6 14	15 03	1 11	19 20	0 49
4 M	4 21	13 02	5 05	10 18	11 53	3 18	21 37	2 23	4 15	0 41	16 04	6 13	15 04	1 11	19 20	0 49
5 Tu	4 44	7 24	4 49	4 22	11 23	3 07	21 56	2 27	4 31	0 41	16 05	6 12	15 05	1 10	19 20	0 49
6 W	5 07	1 14	4 15	1S57	10 49	2 55	22 15	2 31	4 47	0 40	16 06	6 12	15 06	1 10	19 20	0 49
7 Th	5 30	5S07	3 24	8 16	10 11	2 40	22 33	2 35	5 02	0 40	16 07	6 11	15 06	1 10	19 20	0 49
8 F	5 53	11 18	2 19	14 11	9 30	2 24	22 51	2 38	5 18	0 39	16 08	6 10	15 07	1 10	19 21	0 49
9 Sa	6 16	16 52	1 04	19 17	8 47	2 07	23 08	2 42	5 34	0 39	16 08	6 10	15 07	1 10	19 21	0 49
10 Su	6 39	21 24	0S14	23 11	8 02	1 48	23 25	2 46	5 49	0 38	16 09	6 09	15 08	1 10	19 21	0 49
11 M	7 01	24 34	1 32	25 32	7 17	1 28	23 41	2 49	6 05	0 38	16 10	6 08	15 08	1 10	19 21	0 49
12 Tu	7 24	26 05	2 42	26 11	6 33	1 07	23 57	2 53	6 20	0 37	16 11	6 07	15 09	1 10	19 21	0 49
13 W	7 46	25 53	3 42	25 10	5 50	0 47	24 12	2 56	6 36	0 37	16 11	6 06	15 09	1 09	19 21	0 49
14 Th	8 09	24 05	4 27	22 40	5 11	0 26	24 26	2 59	6 51	0 36	16 12	6 05	15 09	1 09	19 21	0 49
15 F	8 31	20 57	4 57	18 58	4 35	0 06	24 40	3 03	7 07	0 36	16 13	6 04	15 09	1 09	19 20	0 49
16 Sa	8 53	16 46	5 10	14 23	4 04	0N13	24 53	3 06	7 22	0 35	16 13	6 03	15 09	1 09	19 20	0 49
17 Su	9 15	11 51	5 06	9 13	3 39	0 30	25 06	3 09	7 38	0 35	16 14	6 02	15 09	1 09	19 20	0 49
18 M	9 37	6 31	4 47	3 46	3 18	0 47	25 18	3 12	7 53	0 35	16 15	6 01	15 09	1 09	19 20	0 49
19 Tu	9 59	0 60	4 14	1N46	3 04	1 02	25 30	3 15	8 08	0 34	16 15	5 60	15 09	1 09	19 20	0 49
20 W	10 20	4N30	3 30	7 09	2 55	1 15	25 41	3 18	8 24	0 34	16 16	5 58	15 09	1 09	19 20	0 49
21 Th	10 42	9 44	2 36	12 12	2 52	1 27	25 51	3 20	8 39	0 33	16 17	5 57	15 09	1 08	19 19	0 49
22 F	11 03	14 33	1 36	16 44	2 55	1 37	26 01	3 23	8 54	0 33	16 18	5 56	15 08	1 08	19 19	0 49
23 Sa	11 24	18 45	0 32	20 34	3 02	1 46	26 10	3 26	9 09	0 32	16 18	5 54	15 08	1 08	19 19	0 49
24 Su	11 45	22 10	0N33	23 32	3 14	1 53	26 19	3 28	9 24	0 32	16 19	5 53	15 07	1 08	19 18	0 49
25 M	12 06	24 38	1 36	25 28	3 31	1 58	26 27	3 30	9 39	0 31	16 20	5 52	15 07	1 08	19 18	0 49
26 Tu	12 26	26 01	2 35	26 16	3 51	2 02	26 34	3 32	9 54	0 31	16 20	5 50	15 06	1 08	19 18	0 49
27 W	12 47	26 14	3 28	25 52	4 14	2 05	26 41	3 35	10 09	0 30	16 21	5 48	15 05	1 08	19 17	0 49
28 Th	13 07	25 13	4 13	24 15	4 41	2 07	26 47	3 37	10 24	0 30	16 22	5 47	15 05	1 07	19 17	0 49
29 F	13 27	22 59	4 47	21 26	5 09	2 08	26 52	3 38	10 38	0 29	16 23	5 45	15 04	1 07	19 16	0 49
30 Sa	13 47	19 37	5 08	17 32	5 40	2 07	26 57	3 40	10 53	0 29	16 23	5 43	15 03	1 07	19 16	0 49
31 Su	14S06	15N13	5N15	12N42	6S13	2N06	27S01	3S42	11S08	0N28	16N24	5S41	15S02	1S07	19S16	0S49

Day	⚷ Decl	⚷ Lat	♅ Decl	♅ Lat	♆ Decl	♆ Lat	♇ Decl	♇ Lat
1	6N28	2N23	15N40	0S25	4S31	1S10	22S53	1S39
6	6 22	2 23	15 37	0 25	4 34	1 10	22 53	1 39
11	6 16	2 23	15 34	0 25	4 37	1 10	22 53	1 40
16	6 11	2 22	15 31	0 25	4 39	1 10	22 53	1 40
21	6 05	2 22	15 27	0 25	4 42	1 10	22 53	1 40
26	5 60	2 21	15 24	0 25	4 44	1 10	22 53	1 40
31	5N54	2N20	15N20	0S25	4S46	1S10	22S52	1S40

Day	⚴ Decl	⚴ Lat	⚵ Decl	⚵ Lat	⚶ Decl	⚶ Lat	Eris Decl	Eris Lat
1	4S37	1N59	11S01	11N47	9S13	4N18	1S16	11S31
6	5 40	1 18	11 24	11 31	10 10	4 11	1 17	11 31
11	6 39	0 37	11 46	11 16	11 06	4 04	1 18	11 31
16	7 34	0S03	12 06	11 01	12 00	3 58	1 19	11 30
21	8 25	0 41	12 25	10 48	12 52	3 51	1 20	11 30
26	9 10	1 18	12 43	10 34	13 43	3 44	1 21	11 30
31	9S50	1S53	12S59	10N22	14S32	3N38	1S21	11S30

Moon Phenomena

Max/0 Decl (dy hr mn)
6 4:40 0 S
12 9:10 26S12
19 4:18 0 N
26 16:07 26N17

Max/0 Lat (dy hr mn)
3 14:14 5N07
9 19:36 0 S
16 6:51 5S10
23 11:49 0 N
30 21:46 5N15

Perigee/Apogee (dy hr m kilometers)
8 17:29 p 363388
24 15:29 a 405614

PH dy hr mn
● 6 11:07 13♎25
☽ 13 3:26 20♑01
○ 20 14:58 27♈26
☾ 28 20:06 5♌37

Void of Course Moon

Last Aspect	☽ Ingress
30 14:50 ☿ □	♌ 1 0:55
2 23:44 ♀ □	♍ 3 8:39
5 8:47 ♀ ⚹	♎ 5 12:42
7 5:04 ♇ □	♏ 7 14:23
9 6:06 ♇ ⚹	♐ 9 15:25
11 4:32 ♃ ⚹	♑ 11 17:16
13 10:54 ♇ ☌	♒ 13 20:48
15 12:34 ☉ △	♓ 16 2:23
17 23:25 ♇ ⚹	♈ 18 10:05
20 14:58 ☉ ☍	♉ 20 20:00
22 20:36 ♇ △	♊ 23 7:58
25 14:12 ♂ △	♋ 25 21:01
28 6:03 ♂ □	♌ 28 9:08
30 7:06 ♀ △	♍ 30 18:11

DAILY ASPECTARIAN

1 F: ☽⚼♆ 12:59; ♂☍⚷ 13:01; ☽☍♄ 14:11; ☿□♇ 14:27; ☽#♇ 14:55; ☉⚹☽ 17:35; ☽△⚷ 21:18; ☽⚹♂ 21:47; ☽⚹⚳ 23:39

2 Sa: ☿⚺♀ 1:58; ☽□♅ 3:33; ☽#♀ 4:58; ♀⚹♇ 7:49; ☉∠♀ 11:24; ☽#♄ 15:43; ☽⚻♆ 16:53; ☽☍♃ 19:30; ☽⚹☿ 20:58; ☽⚻♇ 22:24; ☉∠☽ 23:36; ☽□♀ 23:44

3 Su: ☽⚼⚷ 0:52; ☽∠♂ 2:51; ☉∥♂ 6:04; ☽∥⚳ 9:34; ☽∥♅ 11:39; ♂△⚳ 12:18; ♀⚼⚷ 12:48; ☽#♃ 14:30; ☉☍⚷ 15:52; ☽⚻♄ 20:57; ☽∠☿ 22:22

4 M: ☿△♃ 0:06; ☽⚼♇ 1:10; ☽⚻⚷ 3:28; ☉⚺☽ 4:24; ☽#☿ 5:40; ☽□⚳ 5:58; ☽⚺♂ 6:48; ☽△♅ 9:20; ☉∥♆ 12:27; ☽☍♆ 21:49; ☽⚺☿ 22:50; ☽⚼♄ 22:58

5 Tu: ☽⚻♃ 0:11; ☉△⚳ 2:49; ☽△♇ 3:04; ♂∥♆ 3:19; ☽∥⚷ 4:04; ☽⚹♀ 8:47; ☉#☽ 9:56; ☽#♂ 10:56; ☽⚼♅ 10:57; ☽#♆ 11:14; ☿⚻♆ 13:54

6 W: ☽△♄ 0:17; ☽⚼♃ 1:24; ☽☍⚷ 6:20; ☽△⚳ 8:57; ♂⚻♅ 9:28; ☉☌☽ 11:07; ☽⚻♅ 11:57; ☽∠♀ 11:58; ☽☌♂ 12:05; ♀∠♂ 15:45; ♇ D 18:30; ☽☌☿ 21:41; ☽∥♆ 21:54; ☉⚻♅ 23:12; ☽∥♂ 23:40; ☽⚻♆ 23:56

7 Th: ☉∥☽ 1:31; ☽△♃ 2:09; ☽#⚷ 4:38; ☽□♇ 5:04; ☽⚼⚳ 9:41; ♀ ♐ 11:22; ☽⚺♀ 14:38; ☽∥☿ 17:35

8 F: ☽⚼♆ 0:27; ☽□♄ 1:38; ♀∥♇ 2:43; ☉☌♂ 4:02; ☽⚻⚷ 7:27; ☽⚻⚳ 10:13; ☽☍♅ 13:01; ☽⚺♂ 15:33; ☉⚺☽ 15:50; ☽∥♃ 16:06; ☽#♅ 18:11; ☽⚺☿ 19:11; ☽#⚳ 20:39

9 Sa: ☽△♆ 0:54; ⚳ R 1:32; ☉#⚷ 2:45; ☽□♃ 3:05; ☽⚹♇ 6:06; ☿∠♀ 7:39; ☽⚼⚷ 7:53; ☽∥♄ 12:19; ☉☌☿ 16:19; ☽∠♂ 17:16; ☽∠☿ 17:54; ☉∠☽ 18:10; ☊ D 19:35; ☽☌♀ 19:38; ☿☌♂ 22:50

10 Su: ☽⚹♄ 2:44; ☽∠♇ 6:46; ☽△⚷ 8:28; ☽∥♇ 9:51; ☽☍⚳ 11:25; ☽⚻♅ 14:10; ☽∥♀ 15:15; ☽⚹☿ 16:50; ☽⚹♂ 19:13; ☉⚹☽ 20:46

11 M: ☽□♆ 2:18; ♄ D 2:18; ☽∠♄ 3:38; ☽⚹♃ 4:32; ☉∥☿ 5:34; ☽⚺♇ 7:43; ☽⚼♅ 15:09; ♂#⚷ 16:17

12 Tu: ☽⚺♀ 1:45; ☽⚺♄ 4:55; ☿∥♂ 4:56; ☿⚻♅ 5:31; ☽∠♃ 5:47; ☿#⚷ 9:58; ☽□⚷ 10:40; ☽⚻⚳ 13:49; ☽□☿ 15:52; ☽△♅ 16:35

13 W: ☽□♂ 0:28; ☊ R 3:23; ☉□☽ 3:26; ☽⚹♆ 5:12; ☽∠♀ 5:36; ☽⚺♃ 7:31; ☽☌♇ 10:54; ☽⚼⚳ 15:41; ♀⚹♄ 19:28; ☽∥♀ 20:50

14 Th: ☿△⚳ 0:41; ☉⚻♆ 3:33; ☽∠♆ 7:22; ☽☌♄ 8:55; ☽⚹♀ 10:04; ☽∥♇ 10:18; ☽⚹⚷ 14:43; ☽△☿ 17:10; ☽△⚳ 18:03; ☽□♅ 20:53; ☿∥♆ 21:29

15 F: ☽△♂ 7:59; ☽∥♄ 9:49; ☽⚺♆ 10:03; ☉△♃ 11:47; ☽☌♃ 12:30; ☉△☽ 12:34; ☽⚺♇ 16:06; ☽∠⚷ 17:31; ☽⚼☿ 18:54

16 Sa: ♀∠♇ 2:23; ☽#⚳ 2:46; ☽#♅ 6:25; ☽∥♃ 8:11; ☽⚼♂ 12:39; ☽⚺♄ 15:01; ☉⚼☽ 18:07; ♀△⚷ 18:50; ☽∠♇ 19:29; ☽⚺⚷ 20:49; ☽□♀ 21:01; ☽⚻☿ 21:28

17 Su: ☽□⚳ 0:17; ♂⚻♆ 0:33; ☿⚹♀ 1:25; ☽⚹♅ 3:16; ☉∥☽ 11:08; ☉□♇ 12:14; ☽☌♆ 17:01; ☽⚻♂ 17:57; ☽∥♂ 18:15; ☽∠♄ 18:52; ☽⚺♃ 19:38; ☽⚹♇ 23:25

18 M: ☉⚻☽ 0:21; ☽#⚷ 1:40; ♃ D 5:31; ☽∠♅ 7:15; ☽∥♆ 8:03; ♀☍⚳ 11:12; ☽∥☿ 14:40; ☿ D 15:18; ☽⚹♄ 23:16

19 Tu: ☽∠♃ 0:02; ♂△♃ 2:38; ☽☌⚷ 5:04; ☽☍☿ 5:27; ☽⚹⚳ 8:35; ☽△♀ 10:41; ☽⚺♅ 11:47; ☽#☿ 17:12; ☉⚼⚳ 22:29; ♀⚻♅ 23:17

20 W: ☽#♆ 0:52; ☽⚺♆ 2:10; ☽⚹♃ 5:00; ☽☍♂ 6:29; ☽∥⚷ 7:11; ☽□♇ 8:57; ☽∠⚳ 13:32; ☉☍☽ 14:58; ☽⚼♀ 18:35; ☽#♂ 18:37

21 Th: ☉#☽ 4:56; ☽∠♆ 7:34; ☽□♄ 9:46; ☽⚺⚷ 15:30; ☽⚻☿ 17:45; ☽⚺⚳ 19:00; ☽☌♅ 22:29

22 F: ☽#♃ 3:08; ☽⚻♀ 3:09; ♂□♇ 4:21; ☽∥♅ 4:47; ☽∥⚳ 9:32; ☽⚹♆ 13:28; ☿△⚳ 15:37; ☽□♃ 16:33; ☽△♇ 20:36; ☽∠⚷ 21:28; ☽⚻♂ 21:34

23 Sa: ☽⚼☿ 1:33; ☽#♄ 3:35; ☉ ♏ 4:52; ☉⚻☽ 8:15; ☊ D 11:49; ☽△♄ 22:13

24 Su: ☽⚼♇ 3:02; ☽⚹⚷ 3:47; ☽⚼♂ 5:48; ☽#♇ 6:03; ☽☌⚳ 7:06; ☽△☿ 10:18; ☽⚺♅ 10:55; ☉⚼☽ 17:34; ☿⚻♅ 17:46; ☽☍♀ 21:43

25 M: ♂⚼⚳ 1:48; ☽□♆ 2:15; ☽⚼♄ 4:50; ☽△♃ 5:34; ☽⚻♇ 9:38; ☽△♂ 14:12; ☽∠♅ 17:22

26 Tu: ☉△☽ 2:56; ☽⚻♄ 11:23; ☽⚼♃ 12:07; ☽□⚷ 16:35; ☽⚺⚳ 19:32; ☽⚹♅ 23:38

27 W: ♀□♆ 1:07; ☽□☿ 5:11; ☽△♆ 14:49; ☽⚻♀ 16:05; ☽⚻♃ 18:17; ☽☍♇ 22:09

28 Th: ☽∠⚳ 1:12; ☿∥♆ 3:40; ☽□♂ 6:03; ♀∠♄ 10:03; ♀⚹♃ 19:17; ☉□☽ 20:06; ☽⚼♆ 20:17; ☊ R 20:21; ☉⚼♆ 22:20; ☽☍♄ 23:04

29 F: ☽⚼♀ 0:11; ☽#♇ 0:54; ☽△⚷ 3:43; ☽⚹⚳ 6:08; ☽□♅ 10:26; ☽⚹☿ 22:33

30 Sa: ☽⚻♆ 0:54; ☽#♄ 2:08; ☽☍♃ 4:25; ☽△♀ 7:06; ☽⚻♇ 7:55; ☽⚼⚷ 8:02; ☉□♄ 9:55; ☿#⚷ 10:47; ♂ ♏ 14:22; ♀⚺♇ 17:55; ☽∥⚳ 18:05; ☽⚹♂ 18:23; ☿⚻♆ 19:41; ☽∥♅ 23:28

31 Su: ☽#♃ 0:56; ☉#☽ 5:06; ☽∠☿ 5:35; ☽⚻♄ 7:18; ☉⚹☽ 8:59; ☽⚻⚷ 11:20; ☽⚼♇ 11:20; ☽□⚳ 13:11; ☽△♅ 17:34; ☽#♂ 18:11; ☽∠♂ 22:47

October 2021:Modify New York Stock Exchange Zone:-5

Sunday	Monday	Tuesday	Wednesday	Thursday	Friday	Saturday
					1 9:25AM ♇ □ ☿	2 2:47AM ♀ ⚹ ♇
3 3:36AM ☽-> 0♍00 7:03PM ♃ △ ☿	4	5 7:39AM ☽-> 0♎00	6 6:04AM New Moon♎ 1:26PM ♇Direct	7 6:20AM ♀-> 0♐00 9:21AM ☽-> 0♏00 11:00PM ☉ ☌ ♂	8	9 10:23AM ☽-> 0♐00 11:17AM ☉ ☌ ☿ 5:47PM ♂ ☌ ☿
10 9:16PM ♄Direct	11 12:13PM ☽-> 0♑00	12	13 2:26PM ♀ ⚹ ♄ 3:46PM ☽-> 0♒00	14	15 6:45AM ☉ △ ♃ 9:20PM ☽-> 0♓00	16 8:22PM ♀ ⚹ ☿
17 7:11AM ☉ □ ♇	18 12:29AM ♃Direct 5:02AM ☽-> 0♈00 10:15AM ☿Direct 9:35PM ♂ △ ♃	19	20 9:55AM Full Moon♈ 2:57PM ☽-> 0♉00	21 11:18PM ♂ □ ♇	22 11:50PM ☉-> 0♏00	23 2:56AM ☽-> 0♊00
24	25 3:59PM ☽-> 0♋00	26 8:05PM ♀ □ ♆	27	28 4:06AM ☽-> 0♌00 2:15PM ♀ ⚹ ♃	29	30 4:52AM ☉ □ ♄ 9:20AM ♂-> 0♏00 1:08PM ☽-> 0♍00
31 11:17PM ☿ △ ♃						

September

S	M	T	W	T	F	S
			1	2	3	4
5	6	7	8	9	10	11
12	13	14	15	16	17	18
19	20	21	22	23	24	25
26	27	28	29	30		

November

S	M	T	W	T	F	S
	1	2	3	4	5	6
7	8	9	10	11	12	13
14	15	16	17	18	19	20
21	22	23	24	25	26	27
28	29	30				

LONGITUDE

Day	Sid.Time	☉	☽	☽ 12 hour	Mean☊	True☊	☿	♀	♂	⚳	♃	♄	⚷	♅	♆	♇
	h m s	° ' "	° ' "	° ' "	° '	° '	° '	° '	° '	° '	° '	° '	° '	° '	° '	° '
1 M	2 42 00	8♏46 41	16♍35 56	23♍28 36	2♊45.5	1♊54.7	22♎23.3	25♐41.7	0♏56.5	10♊25.9	22♒38.7	7♒14.6	9♈26.5	12♉56.9	20♓39.5	24♑28.3
2 Tu	2 45 57	9 46 44	0♎28 05	7♎34 09	2 42.3	1R 51.5	23 52.7	26 40.5	1 36.8	10R 16.9	22 41.6	7 16.8	9R 24.3	12R 54.5	20R 38.5	24 29.0
3 W	2 49 53	10 46 49	14 46 23	22 04 12	2 39.2	1 48.4	25 24.0	27 38.9	2 17.2	10 07.6	22 44.6	7 19.0	9 22.0	12 52.0	20 37.6	24 29.8
4 Th	2 53 50	11 46 56	29 26 51	6♏53 26	2 36.0	1 45.8	26 56.8	28 36.9	2 57.6	9 57.9	22 47.8	7 21.3	9 19.8	12 49.5	20 36.7	24 30.6
5 F	2 57 46	12 47 04	14♏22 57	21 54 18	2 32.8	1 44.1	28 30.7	29 34.4	3 38.0	9 47.9	22 51.3	7 23.8	9 17.7	12 47.0	20 35.8	24 31.4
6 Sa	3 01 43	13 47 15	29 26 23	6♐58 03	2 29.6	1D 43.5	0♏05.6	0♑31.4	4 18.5	9 37.6	22 54.9	7 26.3	9 15.6	12 44.5	20 35.0	24 32.3
7 Su	3 05 40	14 47 27	14♐28 14	21 55 58	2 26.5	1 43.8	1 41.1	1 28.0	4 59.0	9 27.0	22 58.7	7 28.9	9 13.5	12 42.1	20 34.2	24 33.2
8 M	3 09 36	15 47 42	29 20 22	6♑40 42	2 23.3	1 44.7	3 17.2	2 24.1	5 39.6	9 16.0	23 02.7	7 31.6	9 11.4	12 39.6	20 33.4	24 34.1
9 Tu	3 13 33	16 47 57	13♑56 22	21 06 56	2 20.1	1 45.9	4 53.7	3 19.6	6 20.2	9 04.8	23 06.9	7 34.4	9 09.4	12 37.1	20 32.7	24 35.1
10 W	3 17 29	17 48 14	28 12 05	5♒11 41	2 16.9	1 46.9	6 30.5	4 14.5	7 00.8	8 53.3	23 11.2	7 37.3	9 07.4	12 34.7	20 31.9	24 36.0
11 Th	3 21 26	18 48 33	12♒05 40	18 54 06	2 13.8	1R 47.5	8 07.3	5 08.9	7 41.5	8 41.6	23 15.8	7 40.3	9 05.5	12 32.2	20 31.2	24 37.0
12 F	3 25 22	19 48 53	25 37 08	2♓14 57	2 10.6	1 47.6	9 44.3	6 02.7	8 22.2	8 29.6	23 20.5	7 43.4	9 03.6	12 29.7	20 30.6	24 38.1
13 Sa	3 29 19	20 49 14	8♓47 50	15 16 04	2 07.4	1 47.0	11 21.2	6 55.8	9 02.9	8 17.3	23 25.4	7 46.5	9 01.7	12 27.3	20 29.9	24 39.1
14 Su	3 33 15	21 49 36	21 39 58	27 59 50	2 04.2	1 46.0	12 58.1	7 48.3	9 43.7	8 04.9	23 30.5	7 49.8	8 59.9	12 24.8	20 29.3	24 40.2
15 M	3 37 12	22 50 00	4♈16 00	10♈28 48	2 01.0	1 44.8	14 34.9	8 40.1	10 24.5	7 52.2	23 35.8	7 53.1	8 58.1	12 22.4	20 28.8	24 41.3
16 Tu	3 41 09	23 50 26	16 38 31	22 45 28	1 57.9	1 43.6	16 11.5	9 31.2	11 05.3	7 39.3	23 41.3	7 56.6	8 56.4	12 20.0	20 28.2	24 42.4
17 W	3 45 05	24 50 52	28 49 56	4♉52 10	1 54.7	1 42.6	17 48.0	10 21.5	11 46.2	7 26.2	23 46.9	8 00.1	8 54.7	12 17.6	20 27.7	24 43.6
18 Th	3 49 02	25 51 21	10♉52 26	16 51 01	1 51.5	1 41.9	19 24.3	11 11.1	12 27.1	7 13.0	23 52.7	8 03.7	8 53.0	12 15.2	20 27.3	24 44.7
19 F	3 52 58	26 51 50	22 48 08	28 44 02	1 48.3	1D 41.5	21 00.4	11 59.8	13 08.1	6 59.6	23 58.6	8 07.4	8 51.4	12 12.8	20 26.8	24 45.9
20 Sa	3 56 55	27 52 22	4♊38 59	10♊33 15	1 45.2	1 41.5	22 36.3	12 47.8	13 49.0	6 46.1	24 04.8	8 11.2	8 49.8	12 10.5	20 26.4	24 47.2
21 Su	4 00 51	28 52 55	16 27 05	22 20 48	1 42.0	1 41.6	24 12.1	13 34.8	14 30.1	6 32.4	24 11.1	8 15.0	8 48.3	12 08.1	20 26.0	24 48.4
22 M	4 04 48	29 53 29	28 14 42	4♋09 07	1 38.8	1 41.8	25 47.6	14 21.0	15 11.1	6 18.6	24 17.6	8 19.0	8 46.9	12 05.8	20 25.7	24 49.7
23 Tu	4 08 44	0♐54 05	10♋04 24	16 00 57	1 35.6	1R 41.9	27 23.0	15 06.2	15 52.3	6 04.8	24 24.2	8 23.0	8 45.4	12 03.5	20 25.4	24 51.0
24 W	4 12 41	1 54 43	21 59 11	27 59 31	1 32.5	1 42.0	28 58.1	15 50.4	16 33.4	5 50.8	24 31.0	8 27.1	8 44.0	12 01.2	20 25.1	24 52.3
25 Th	4 16 38	2 55 22	4♌02 26	10♌08 24	1 29.3	1 41.9	0♐33.1	16 33.6	17 14.6	5 36.8	24 37.9	8 31.3	8 42.7	11 58.9	20 24.9	24 53.7
26 F	4 20 34	3 56 03	16 17 55	22 31 31	1 26.1	1 41.7	2 08.0	17 15.7	17 55.8	5 22.7	24 45.1	8 35.6	8 41.4	11 56.6	20 24.7	24 55.0
27 Sa	4 24 31	4 56 45	28 49 40	5♍12 53	1 22.9	1D 41.6	3 42.7	17 56.7	18 37.1	5 08.6	24 52.3	8 39.9	8 40.2	11 54.4	20 24.5	24 56.4
28 Su	4 28 27	5 57 29	11♍41 36	18 16 17	1 19.7	1 41.6	5 17.2	18 36.6	19 18.4	4 54.5	24 59.8	8 44.4	8 39.0	11 52.2	20 24.4	24 57.8
29 M	4 32 24	6 58 15	24 57 15	1♎44 48	1 16.6	1 41.8	6 51.7	19 15.3	19 59.7	4 40.4	25 07.4	8 48.9	8 37.9	11 50.0	20 24.3	24 59.3
30 Tu	4 36 20	7♐59 02	8♎39 05	15 40 09	1♊13.4	1♊42.3	8♐26.0	19♑52.8	20♏41.1	4♊26.3	25♒15.1	8♒53.5	8♈36.8	11♉47.9	20♓24.2	25♑00.7

1st of Month

Julian Day # 2459519.5
Obliquity 23°26'16"
SVP 4♓57'34"
GC 27♐08.7
Eris 24♈05.4R

Day	⚴	Day	⚵	Day	⚶
1	9♓13.6R	1	25♐24.6	1	21♏37.6
6	9 04.4R	6	27 01.9	6	24 18.3
11	9 04.6	11	28 41.6	11	26 59.5
16	9 13.8	16	0♑23.7	16	29 41.0
21	9 31.6	21	2 07.8	21	2♐22.8
26	9 57.6	26	3 53.9	26	5 04.8

DECLINATION and LATITUDE

Day	☉ Decl	☽ Decl	☽ Lat	☽12h Decl	☿ Decl	☿ Lat	♀ Decl	♀ Lat	♂ Decl	♂ Lat	⚳ Decl	⚳ Lat	♃ Decl	♃ Lat	♄ Decl	♄ Lat
1 M	14S26	9N58	5N05	7N04	6S47	2N04	27S05	3S43	11S22	0N28	16N25	5S39	15S01	1S07	19S15	0S49
2 Tu	14 45	4 03	4 37	0 55	7 23	2 02	27 08	3 44	11 37	0 27	16 25	5 37	15 00	1 07	19 14	0 49
3 W	15 03	2S16	3 51	5S28	7 59	1 59	27 11	3 46	11 51	0 27	16 26	5 35	14 59	1 07	19 14	0 49
4 Th	15 22	8 38	2 49	11 43	8 36	1 55	27 12	3 47	12 05	0 26	16 27	5 33	14 58	1 06	19 13	0 49
5 F	15 40	14 39	1 35	17 22	9 13	1 51	27 14	3 47	12 20	0 26	16 27	5 31	14 57	1 06	19 13	0 49
6 Sa	15 59	19 49	0 13	21 57	9 51	1 46	27 14	3 48	12 34	0 25	16 28	5 29	14 55	1 06	19 12	0 49
7 Su	16 16	23 42	1S10	25 01	10 29	1 41	27 14	3 49	12 48	0 25	16 29	5 27	14 54	1 06	19 11	0 49
8 M	16 34	25 53	2 27	26 18	11 07	1 36	27 14	3 49	13 02	0 24	16 30	5 24	14 52	1 06	19 11	0 49
9 Tu	16 51	26 14	3 33	25 45	11 44	1 30	27 13	3 49	13 16	0 23	16 30	5 22	14 51	1 06	19 10	0 49
10 W	17 08	24 50	4 24	23 33	12 22	1 24	27 11	3 49	13 30	0 23	16 31	5 19	14 49	1 06	19 09	0 49
11 Th	17 25	21 56	4 59	20 03	12 59	1 18	27 09	3 49	13 43	0 22	16 32	5 17	14 48	1 06	19 08	0 49
12 F	17 41	17 55	5 15	15 36	13 36	1 12	27 06	3 49	13 57	0 22	16 33	5 14	14 46	1 05	19 08	0 49
13 Sa	17 58	13 08	5 15	10 33	14 12	1 05	27 03	3 48	14 10	0 21	16 33	5 12	14 44	1 05	19 07	0 49
14 Su	18 13	7 52	4 58	5 09	14 48	0 59	26 59	3 47	14 24	0 21	16 34	5 09	14 42	1 05	19 06	0 49
15 M	18 29	2 24	4 28	0N21	15 23	0 52	26 55	3 46	14 37	0 20	16 35	5 06	14 41	1 05	19 05	0 49
16 Tu	18 44	3N05	3 45	5 45	15 58	0 45	26 50	3 45	14 50	0 20	16 36	5 03	14 39	1 05	19 04	0 49
17 W	18 59	8 22	2 53	10 53	16 31	0 38	26 45	3 44	15 04	0 19	16 37	5 00	14 37	1 05	19 03	0 49
18 Th	19 13	13 18	1 53	15 34	17 04	0 32	26 39	3 42	15 17	0 19	16 38	4 57	14 35	1 05	19 02	0 49
19 F	19 27	17 41	0 49	19 36	17 37	0 25	26 33	3 40	15 30	0 18	16 38	4 54	14 32	1 04	19 01	0 49
20 Sa	19 41	21 20	0N16	22 50	18 08	0 18	26 26	3 38	15 42	0 18	16 39	4 51	14 30	1 04	19 00	0 49
21 Su	19 54	24 06	1 21	25 05	18 39	0 11	26 19	3 36	15 55	0 17	16 40	4 48	14 28	1 04	18 59	0 49
22 M	20 08	25 48	2 22	26 13	19 08	0 04	26 12	3 33	16 08	0 16	16 41	4 45	14 26	1 04	18 58	0 49
23 Tu	20 20	26 20	3 18	26 09	19 37	0S03	26 04	3 30	16 20	0 15	16 42	4 41	14 23	1 04	18 57	0 49
24 W	20 33	25 40	4 05	24 53	20 05	0 09	25 56	3 27	16 32	0 15	16 43	4 38	14 21	1 04	18 56	0 49
25 Th	20 44	23 48	4 42	22 27	20 32	0 16	25 47	3 24	16 45	0 15	16 44	4 34	14 19	1 04	18 55	0 49
26 F	20 56	20 49	5 07	18 57	20 57	0 23	25 38	3 20	16 57	0 14	16 45	4 31	14 16	1 03	18 54	0 49
27 Sa	21 07	16 50	5 18	14 31	21 22	0 29	25 28	3 16	17 09	0 14	16 46	4 27	14 14	1 03	18 53	0 49
28 Su	21 18	11 60	5 13	9 19	21 46	0 36	25 19	3 12	17 21	0 13	16 47	4 24	14 11	1 03	18 52	0 49
29 M	21 28	6 28	4 52	3 31	22 09	0 42	25 08	3 07	17 32	0 13	16 48	4 20	14 08	1 03	18 50	0 49
30 Tu	21S38	0N28	4N14	2S38	22S30	0S48	24S58	3S02	17S44	0N12	16N49	4S16	14S06	1S03	18S49	0S49

Day	⚷ Decl	⚷ Lat	♅ Decl	♅ Lat	♆ Decl	♆ Lat	♇ Decl	♇ Lat
1	5N53	2N20	15N19	0S25	4S46	1S10	22S52	1S40
6	5 48	2 19	15 16	0 25	4 48	1 10	22 52	1 41
11	5 44	2 19	15 12	0 25	4 49	1 10	22 51	1 41
16	5 39	2 18	15 08	0 25	4 50	1 09	22 50	1 41
21	5 35	2 17	15 05	0 25	4 51	1 09	22 49	1 41
26	5 32	2 16	15 01	0 25	4 52	1 09	22 49	1 42

Day	⚴ Decl	⚴ Lat	⚵ Decl	⚵ Lat	⚶ Decl	⚶ Lat	Eris Decl	Eris Lat
1	9S57	1S60	13S02	10N20	14S41	3N36	1S22	11S30
6	10 31	2 33	13 16	10 08	15 27	3 30	1 22	11 29
11	11 00	3 04	13 29	9 57	16 11	3 23	1 23	11 29
16	11 24	3 33	13 40	9 46	16 53	3 17	1 23	11 28
21	11 43	4 01	13 49	9 36	17 32	3 10	1 24	11 28
26	11 58	4 28	13 56	9 27	18 08	3 03	1 24	11 27

Moon Phenomena

Max/0 Decl (dy hr mn)
2 15:28 0 S
8 16:34 26S19
15 10:28 0 N
22 22:46 26N21
30 1:49 0 S

Max/0 Lat (dy hr mn)
6 3:39 0 S
12 11:10 5S17
19 18:00 0 N
27 5:25 5N18

Perigee/Apogee (dy hr m kilometers)
5 22:19 p 358845
21 2:14 a 406279

PH (dy hr mn)
● 4 21:16 12♏40
☽ 11 12:47 19♒21
○ 19 8:59 27♉14
● 19 9:04 P 0.974
☾ 27 12:29 5♍28

Void of Course Moon

Last Aspect	☽ Ingress
1 17:01 ♀ □	♎ 1 23:12
3 22:33 ♀ ⚹	♏ 4 0:54
5 16:11 ♇ ⚹	♐ 6 0:54
7 13:45 ♃ ⚹	♑ 8 1:05
9 17:53 ♇ ☌	♒ 10 3:04
11 19:53 ♃ ☌	♓ 12 7:55
14 5:41 ♇ ⚹	♈ 14 15:49
16 15:52 ♇ □	♉ 17 2:19
19 8:59 ☉ ☍	♊ 19 14:34
21 15:53 ♃ △	♋ 22 3:34
24 5:47 ♇ ☍	♌ 24 16:00
26 16:25 ♃ ☍	♍ 27 2:13
29 0:04 ♇ △	♎ 29 8:56

DAILY ASPECTARIAN

1 M	☿△♃	4:19
	☽☍♆	7:06
	☽⚼♄	9:53
	☽⚻♃	10:36
	☽⚺☿	11:19
	☽#☿	11:58
	☉∠☽	13:29
	☽△♇	13:44
	☉⚻⚷	15:21
	☽∥⚷	16:48
	☽□♀	17:01
	☽⚼♅	19:38
	☽#♆	21:09
2 Tu	☽⚺♂	2:03
	☿□♇	9:40
	☉⚻⚳	10:27
	☽△♄	11:33
	☽⚼♃	12:15
	☽☍⚷	15:02
	☽△⚳	16:22
	☉⚺☽	16:52
	☉∥♃	18:34
	☿⚼⚳	20:07
	☽⚻♅	20:51
3 W	♀⚼♅	5:11
	☽∥♆	9:26
	☽⚻♆	9:38
	☽△♃	13:09
	☽#⚷	13:24
	☽□♇	15:58
	☽⚼⚳	16:48
	☉#♅	17:40
	☽☌☿	19:28
	☽⚹♀	22:33
	☽∥☿	23:50
4 Th	☽☌♂	5:57
	☽⚼♆	9:56
	☽□♄	12:47
	☽∥♂	14:02
	☽⚻⚷	15:53
	☽⚻⚳	16:45
	☉☌☽	21:16
	☽☍♅	21:27
	☉☍♅	23:59
5 F	☽∠♀	0:20
	☽∥♃	1:15
	☽#♅	2:39
	☉∥☽	4:40
	☽#⚳	7:52
	☽△♆	9:54
	♀ ♑	10:45
	☽□♃	13:34
	☽⚼⚷	15:46
	☽⚹♇	16:11
	☽∥♄	20:49
	☿ ♏	22:36
6 Sa	☽⚺☿	1:10
	☽⚺♀	1:51
	☊ D	3:36
	☽⚺♂	8:07
	⚳⚼♇	11:06
	☽⚹♄	12:47
	☽△⚷	15:37
	☿⚹♀	16:00
	☽☍⚳	16:04
	☽∠♇	16:07
	☽∥♇	17:57
	☽⚻♅	21:10
7 Su	☉⚺☽	0:33
	☽∠☿	3:59
	☽∠♂	9:17
	☽□♆	9:48
	☽∠♄	12:56
	☽⚹♃	13:45
	☽⚺♇	16:15
	☉#⚳	17:41
	♂⚼♆	20:25
	☽⚼♅	21:17
8 M	☉∠☽	2:33
	☽☌♀	5:20
	☽⚹☿	7:14
	⚴ D	9:24
	☽⚹♂	10:50
	⚳⚹⚷	12:10
	☽⚺♄	13:26
	☽∠♃	14:19
	☽⚻⚳	16:04
	☽□⚷	16:06
	☽△♅	21:49
9 Tu	☉⚹☽	5:07
	☿⚼♆	9:36
	☽⚹♆	11:02
	☽⚺♃	15:27
	☽⚼⚳	16:47
	☽☌♇	17:53
10 W	☽⚺♀	11:05
	☽∠♆	12:34
	☿☌♂	12:58
	☽□♂	15:56
	☽□☿	16:09
	☽☌♄	16:16
	☿□♄	17:05
	☽∥♇	17:29
	☽△⚳	18:09
	☽⚹⚷	18:46
	♂□♄	23:15
11 Th	☽□♅	0:46
	☿⚻⚳	7:33
	☊ R	12:47
	☉□☽	12:47
	☿⚻⚷	14:07
	☽⚺♆	14:52
	☽∠♀	15:14
	☽∥♄	17:20
	☽☌♃	19:53
	☽∠⚷	21:12
	☽⚺♇	22:14
12 F	☉∥☽	1:10
	♂⚻⚳	3:22
	☽#⚳	7:13
	☽#♅	14:07
	☽∥♃	16:14
	☉△♆	16:25
	☽∥♂	19:14
	☽∥☿	19:25
	☽⚹♀	20:19
	☽⚺♄	22:07
	☿∥♂	22:09
	☽□⚳	23:05
	♂⚻⚷	23:20
13 Sa	☽⚺⚷	0:26
	☽△♂	0:29
	☽∠♇	1:35
	☽△☿	5:24
	☽⚹♅	6:45
	☿☍♅	15:58
	☿∥♃	20:27
	☽☌♆	21:47
14 Su	☉△☽	0:20
	♀⚺♄	0:44
	☽∠♄	2:12
	☽⚺♃	3:30
	☽⚹♇	5:41
	☽⚼♂	6:07
	♀⚻⚳	6:09
	☽#⚷	9:41
	☽∠♅	10:51
	☽∥♆	13:22
	☽⚼☿	13:42
	☿#♅	14:28
	⚵ ♑	20:24
	♀∠♃	21:46
	⚳△♄	22:35
15 M	♂∥♃	5:13
	☽⚹⚳	6:50
	☽⚹♄	7:01
	☉⚼☽	7:29
	♀□⚷	8:08
	☽∠♃	8:25
	☽☌⚷	9:03
	☽□♀	9:07
	☽⚻♂	12:33
	☽⚺♅	15:38
	☉□♃	19:59
	☽⚻☿	22:59
16 Tu	☉⚼⚷	2:18
	☽⚺♆	7:30
	☽#♆	7:53
	☽∥⚷	11:31
	☽∠⚳	11:35
	☽⚹♃	13:56
	⚶ ♐	14:08
	☉⚻☽	15:24
	☽□♇	15:52
	☉⚹♇	21:03
17 W	☿#⚳	4:00
	♂#♅	6:43
	☉∥♄	6:58
	☽∠♆	13:10
	☽⚺⚳	16:49
	♂☍♅	17:24
	☽□♄	18:21
	☽⚺⚷	20:01
18 Th	☽△♀	0:40
	♃∠⚷	1:06
	☽☌♅	2:45
	☽☍♂	3:21
	☽#♃	6:38
	☽∥♅	9:31
	☽#♂	10:58
	☿△♆	15:39
	☽∥⚳	17:58
	☽⚹♆	19:15
	☽☍☿	19:49
	☽#☿	23:32
19 F	☽∠⚷	2:08
	☽□♃	2:24
	☽△♇	3:59
	♀△♅	6:09
	☽#♄	8:12
	☉☍☽	8:59
	☽⚼♀	9:06
	☉#☽	11:44
	☉∠♀	15:27
	☊ D	17:54
20 Sa	☽☌⚳	4:13
	☽△♄	7:13
	☽⚹⚷	8:29
	☽⚼♇	10:27
	☽#♇	11:55
	☽⚺♅	15:15
	☽⚻♀	17:45
	☿⚼⚷	18:08
	☽⚻♂	19:47
	☿□♃	23:44
21 Su	☽□♆	8:06
	☿⚹♇	9:15
	☽⚼♄	13:55
	☽△♃	15:53
	☿∥♄	16:11
	☽⚻♇	17:02
	☽⚻☿	18:14
	☽∠♅	21:40
22 M	☉ ♐	2:35
	☉⚻☽	3:40
	☽⚼♂	4:11
	☽#♀	9:12
	☽⚺⚳	16:04
	☽⚻♄	20:34
	☽□⚷	21:20
	☽⚼♃	22:38
23 Tu	☽⚹♅	4:00
	☽⚼☿	5:23
	☽☍♀	10:50
	☽△♂	12:25
	☉⚼☽	12:52
	☽#♀	17:41
	☊ R	19:49
	☽△♆	20:51
	☽∠⚳	21:46
24 W	☽⚻♃	5:07
	☽☍♇	5:47
	☿ ♐	15:38
	☽△☿	16:03
	☉△☽	21:35
	♂#⚳	22:49
25 Th	☽⚼♆	2:43
	☽⚹⚳	3:03
	☽☍♄	8:53
	☽#♇	8:59
	☽△⚷	9:11
	☽□♅	15:33
	☉∥☿	21:45
	☽#☿	23:10
	☉#☽	23:15
26 F	☽⚻♀	1:59
	☽□♂	3:21
	☿∠♀	3:29
	☽⚻♆	7:56
	☽#♄	12:19
	☽⚼⚷	14:12
	☽☍♃	16:25
	☽⚻♇	16:36
	☽#♂	22:23
27 Sa	☽∥⚳	0:21
	♄⚹⚷	1:05
	☉☍⚳	3:49
	☽⚼♀	8:11
	☽∥♅	9:33
	☽□☿	10:29
	☽□⚳	11:39
	☉□☽	12:29
	☊ D	12:32
	☽#♃	13:32
	♃⚺♇	16:17
	☽⚻⚷	18:24
	☽⚻♄	18:31
	☿☍⚳	18:59
	☽⚼♇	20:48
28 Su	☽△♅	0:19
	☽△♀	13:16
	☽⚹♂	14:38
	☽☍♆	15:51
	☽⚼♄	21:57
29 M	☽△♇	0:04
	☽⚻♃	0:18
	☽⚼♅	3:20
	☽∥⚷	4:00
	☉☌☿	4:41
	☽#♆	6:36
	♀⚼⚳	11:37
	♂△♆	14:11
	☽△⚳	16:49
	☽∠♂	18:36
	☉⚹☽	22:45
	☽⚹☿	23:35
	☽☍⚷	23:56
30 Tu	☽△♄	0:25
	☿△⚷	2:42
	☽⚼♃	2:47
	☽⚻♅	5:23
	☿⚹♄	7:20
	☉△⚷	14:39
	☽⚼⚳	18:04
	☽□♀	19:57
	☽⚻♆	19:59
	☿∥♇	20:25
	☽∥♆	20:31
	♀⚹♆	20:47
	☽⚺♂	21:30
	☽#⚷	22:54
	☉⚹♄	23:16

November 2021:Modify New York Stock Exchange Zone:-5

Sunday	Monday	Tuesday	Wednesday	Thursday	Friday	Saturday
	1 6:09PM ☽-> 0♎00	2 4:38AM ☿ □ ♇	3 7:51PM ☽-> 0♏00	4 4:13PM New Moon♏[6:57PM ☉ ☍ ♅	5 5:43AM ♀-> 0♑00 5:34PM ☿-> 0♏00 7:51PM ☽-> 0♐00	6 10:57AM ☿ ⚹ ♀
7 8:02PM ☽-> 0♑00	8	9 10:02PM ☽-> 0♒00	10 7:55AM ☿ ☌ ♂ 12:03PM ☿ □ ♄ 6:13PM ♂ □ ♄	11	12 2:52AM ☽-> 0♓00 11:23AM ☉ △ ♆	13 10:55AM ☿ ☍ ♅
14 10:47AM ☽-> 0♈00	15 2:57PM ☉ □ ♃	16 4:01PM ☉ ⚹ ♇ 9:16PM ☽-> 0♉00	17 12:22PM ♂ ☍ ♅	18 10:36AM ☿ △ ♆	19 1:07AM ♀ △ ♅ 3:56AM Full Moon ♉ 9:31AM ☽-> 0♊00	20 6:42PM ☿ □ ♃
21 4:13AM ☿ ⚹ ♇ 9:33PM ☉-> 0♐00 10:31PM ☽-> 0♋00	22	23	24 10:35AM ☿-> 0♐00 10:57AM ☽-> 0♌00	25	26 9:10PM ☽-> 0♍00	27
28 11:38PM ☿ ☌ ☉	29 3:53AM ☽-> 0♎00 9:09AM ♂ △ ♆	30 2:18AM ☿ ⚹ ♄ 3:45PM ♀ ⚹ ♆ 6:14PM ☉ ⚹ ♄			October	December

October

S	M	T	W	T	F	S
					1	2
3	4	5	6	7	8	9
10	11	12	13	14	15	16
17	18	19	20	21	22	23
24	25	26	27	28	29	30
31						

December

S	M	T	W	T	F	S
			1	2	3	4
5	6	7	8	9	10	11
12	13	14	15	16	17	18
19	20	21	22	23	24	25
26	27	28	29	30	31	

December 2021

LONGITUDE

Day	Sid.Time	☉	☽	☽ 12 hour	Mean ☊	True ☊	☿	♀	♂	⚳	♃	♄	⚷	♅	♆	♇
	h m s	° ' "	° ' "	° ' "	° '	° '	° '	° '	° '	° '	° '	° '	° '	° '	° '	° '
1 W	4 40 17	8♐59 50	22♎47 55	0♏02 05	1♊10.2	1♊43.0	10♐00.3	20♑28.9	21♏22.6	4♊12.3	25♒23.0	8♒58.1	8♈35.7	11♉45.7	20♓24.2	25♑02.2
2 Th	4 44 13	10 00 40	7♏22 13	14 47 42	1 07.0	1 43.6	11 34.5	21 03.7	22 04.0	3R 58.3	25 31.0	9 02.8	8R 34.8	11R 43.6	20D 24.1	25 03.7
3 F	4 48 10	11 01 32	22 17 42	29 51 16	1 03.9	1R 44.1	13 08.6	21 37.1	22 45.5	3 44.3	25 39.2	9 07.6	8 33.8	11 41.5	20 24.2	25 05.2
4 Sa	4 52 07	12 02 24	7♐27 18	15♐04 34	1 00.7	1 44.2	14 42.7	22 09.1	23 27.1	3 30.5	25 47.6	9 12.5	8 32.9	11 39.5	20 24.3	25 06.7
5 Su	4 56 03	13 03 18	22 41 50	0♑17 50	0 57.5	1 43.7	16 16.8	22 39.5	24 08.7	3 16.8	25 56.1	9 17.5	8 32.1	11 37.5	20 24.4	25 08.3
6 M	5 00 00	14 04 13	7♑51 20	15 21 13	0 54.3	1 42.5	17 50.8	23 08.4	24 50.3	3 03.2	26 04.7	9 22.5	8 31.3	11 35.5	20 24.5	25 09.9
7 Tu	5 03 56	15 05 09	22 46 29	0♒06 18	0 51.2	1 40.9	19 24.9	23 35.6	25 32.0	2 49.7	26 13.5	9 27.6	8 30.6	11 33.5	20 24.7	25 11.4
8 W	5 07 53	16 06 06	7♒20 01	14 27 10	0 48.0	1 39.1	20 59.0	24 01.1	26 13.7	2 36.4	26 22.4	9 32.8	8 30.0	11 31.6	20 24.9	25 13.1
9 Th	5 11 49	17 07 03	21 27 30	28 20 54	0 44.8	1 37.4	22 33.0	24 24.8	26 55.4	2 23.3	26 31.4	9 38.0	8 29.4	11 29.7	20 25.1	25 14.7
10 F	5 15 46	18 08 01	5♓07 25	11♓47 15	0 41.6	1 36.2	24 07.2	24 46.6	27 37.2	2 10.4	26 40.6	9 43.3	8 28.8	11 27.9	20 25.4	25 16.3
11 Sa	5 19 43	19 09 00	18 20 42	24 48 09	0 38.5	1D 35.8	25 41.3	25 06.6	28 19.0	1 57.6	26 49.9	9 48.6	8 28.3	11 26.0	20 25.7	25 18.0
12 Su	5 23 39	20 09 59	1♈10 04	7♈26 55	0 35.3	1 36.1	27 15.5	25 24.5	29 00.8	1 45.1	26 59.3	9 54.0	8 27.8	11 24.3	20 26.1	25 19.7
13 M	5 27 36	21 10 58	13 39 15	19 47 35	0 32.1	1 37.2	28 49.7	25 40.4	29 42.7	1 32.8	27 08.9	9 59.5	8 27.4	11 22.5	20 26.4	25 21.4
14 Tu	5 31 32	22 11 58	25 52 27	1♉54 23	0 28.9	1 38.8	0♑24.0	25 54.2	0♐24.6	1 20.8	27 18.6	10 05.1	8 27.1	11 20.8	20 26.9	25 23.1
15 W	5 35 29	23 12 59	7♉53 52	13 51 24	0 25.7	1 40.5	1 58.4	26 05.8	1 06.6	1 09.0	27 28.4	10 10.7	8 26.8	11 19.1	20 27.3	25 24.8
16 Th	5 39 25	24 14 00	19 47 24	25 42 17	0 22.6	1 41.9	3 32.7	26 15.1	1 48.6	0 57.5	27 38.4	10 16.3	8 26.6	11 17.5	20 27.8	25 26.5
17 F	5 43 22	25 15 02	1♊36 27	7♊30 15	0 19.4	1R 42.4	5 07.1	26 22.2	2 30.6	0 46.2	27 48.4	10 22.1	8 26.4	11 15.9	20 28.3	25 28.3
18 Sa	5 47 18	26 16 05	13 23 59	19 17 58	0 16.2	1 41.8	6 41.5	26 26.9	3 12.7	0 35.3	27 58.6	10 27.8	8 26.3	11 14.3	20 28.9	25 30.1
19 Su	5 51 15	27 17 08	25 12 27	1♋07 42	0 13.0	1 39.8	8 15.9	26R 29.2	3 54.8	0 24.7	28 08.9	10 33.7	8D 26.2	11 12.8	20 29.5	25 31.8
20 M	5 55 12	28 18 11	7♋03 56	13 01 22	0 09.9	1 36.5	9 50.3	26 29.0	4 37.0	0 14.3	28 19.3	10 39.6	8 26.2	11 11.4	20 30.1	25 33.6
21 Tu	5 59 08	29 19 16	19 00 15	25 00 46	0 06.7	1 32.0	11 24.6	26 26.4	5 19.1	0 04.3	28 29.9	10 45.5	8 26.2	11 09.9	20 30.7	25 35.5
22 W	6 03 05	0♑20 21	1♌03 11	7♌07 42	0 03.5	1 26.8	12 58.7	26 21.3	6 01.4	29♉54.7	28 40.5	10 51.5	8 26.3	11 08.6	20 31.4	25 37.3
23 Th	6 07 01	1 21 26	13 14 35	19 24 07	0 00.3	1 21.4	14 32.7	26 13.7	6 43.7	29 45.3	28 51.3	10 57.6	8 26.5	11 07.2	20 32.2	25 39.1
24 F	6 10 58	2 22 32	25 36 35	1♍52 17	29♉57.2	1 16.5	16 06.4	26 03.6	7 26.0	29 36.4	29 02.1	11 03.7	8 26.7	11 05.9	20 32.9	25 41.0
25 Sa	6 14 54	3 23 39	8♍11 35	14 34 47	29 54.0	1 12.6	17 39.7	25 51.0	8 08.3	29 27.7	29 13.1	11 09.8	8 27.0	11 04.7	20 33.7	25 42.8
26 Su	6 18 51	4 24 46	21 02 17	27 34 24	29 50.8	1 10.1	19 12.6	25 35.9	8 50.7	29 19.5	29 24.2	11 16.0	8 27.3	11 03.4	20 34.5	25 44.7
27 M	6 22 47	5 25 54	4♎11 30	10♎53 53	29 47.6	1D 09.2	20 44.9	25 18.5	9 33.1	29 11.6	29 35.3	11 22.3	8 27.7	11 02.3	20 35.4	25 46.6
28 Tu	6 26 44	6 27 02	17 41 51	24 35 36	29 44.5	1 09.6	22 16.4	24 58.6	10 15.6	29 04.0	29 46.6	11 28.5	8 28.1	11 01.2	20 36.3	25 48.4
29 W	6 30 41	7 28 11	1♏35 15	8♏40 50	29 41.3	1 11.0	23 47.0	24 36.6	10 58.1	28 56.9	29 58.0	11 34.9	8 28.6	11 00.1	20 37.2	25 50.3
30 Th	6 34 37	8 29 21	15 52 13	23 09 10	29 38.1	1 12.5	25 16.5	24 12.3	11 40.7	28 50.2	0♓09.5	11 41.3	8 29.1	10 59.1	20 38.1	25 52.2
31 F	6 38 34	9♑30 31	0♐31 13	7♐57 47	29♉34.9	1♊13.2	26♑44.5	23♑46.0	12♐23.3	28♉43.8	0♓21.1	11♒47.7	8♈29.7	10♉58.1	20♓39.1	25♑54.2

1st of Month

Julian Day #
2459549.5
Obliquity
23°26'15"
SVP 4♓57'29"
GC 27♐08.7
Eris 23♈50.1R

Day	⚴
1	10♓31.4
6	11 12.5
11	12 00.6
16	12 55.1
21	13 55.5
26	15 01.5
31	16 12.7

Day	⚵
1	5♑41.9
6	7 31.5
11	9 22.7
16	11 15.2
21	13 09.0
26	15 03.8
31	16 59.7

Day	⚶
1	7♐47.1
6	10 29.5
11	13 11.8
16	15 54.0
21	18 36.0
26	21 17.8
31	23 59.3

DECLINATION and LATITUDE

Day	☉ Decl	☽ Decl	☽ Lat	☽12h Decl	☿ Decl	☿ Lat	♀ Decl	♀ Lat	♂ Decl	♂ Lat	⚳ Decl	⚳ Lat	♃ Decl	♃ Lat	♄ Decl	♄ Lat
1 W	21S48	5S46	3N20	8S52	22S50	0S54	24S47	2S57	17S55	0N11	16N51	4S13	14S03	1S03	18S48	0S49
2 Th	21 57	11 54	2 11	14 48	23 10	1 00	24 36	2 51	18 07	0 11	16 52	4 09	13 60	1 03	18 47	0 49
3 F	22 06	17 30	0 52	19 57	23 28	1 06	24 25	2 45	18 18	0 10	16 53	4 05	13 57	1 03	18 46	0 49
4 Sa	22 14	22 04	0S32	23 49	23 45	1 12	24 14	2 39	18 29	0 10	16 54	4 01	13 54	1 03	18 44	0 49
5 Su	22 22	25 08	1 54	25 58	24 00	1 17	24 02	2 32	18 40	0 09	16 55	3 57	13 51	1 02	18 43	0 49
6 M	22 29	26 19	3 07	26 11	24 15	1 22	23 50	2 25	18 50	0 08	16 57	3 54	13 48	1 02	18 42	0 49
7 Tu	22 36	25 34	4 07	24 31	24 28	1 27	23 38	2 18	19 01	0 08	16 58	3 50	13 45	1 02	18 40	0 49
8 W	22 43	23 05	4 49	21 19	24 40	1 32	23 26	2 10	19 11	0 07	16 60	3 46	13 42	1 02	18 39	0 49
9 Th	22 49	19 16	5 12	16 59	24 51	1 37	23 14	2 02	19 22	0 07	17 01	3 42	13 39	1 02	18 37	0 49
10 F	22 54	14 32	5 16	11 56	24 60	1 42	23 02	1 53	19 32	0 06	17 02	3 37	13 35	1 02	18 36	0 49
11 Sa	22 60	9 16	5 03	6 31	25 08	1 46	22 49	1 44	19 42	0 05	17 04	3 33	13 32	1 02	18 35	0 49
12 Su	23 04	3 45	4 36	0 59	25 14	1 50	22 37	1 35	19 52	0 05	17 05	3 29	13 29	1 02	18 33	0 49
13 M	23 09	1N46	3 55	4N28	25 20	1 54	22 24	1 25	20 01	0 04	17 07	3 25	13 25	1 02	18 32	0 49
14 Tu	23 12	7 07	3 05	9 40	25 23	1 57	22 11	1 15	20 11	0 04	17 09	3 21	13 22	1 01	18 30	0 49
15 W	23 16	12 08	2 08	14 27	25 26	2 00	21 59	1 04	20 20	0 03	17 10	3 17	13 18	1 01	18 29	0 49
16 Th	23 19	16 38	1 05	18 39	25 26	2 03	21 46	0 53	20 29	0 02	17 12	3 13	13 15	1 01	18 27	0 49
17 F	23 21	20 28	0 01	22 05	25 26	2 06	21 33	0 42	20 38	0 02	17 14	3 09	13 11	1 01	18 26	0 49
18 Sa	23 23	23 28	1N04	24 35	25 24	2 08	21 21	0 30	20 47	0 01	17 16	3 04	13 08	1 01	18 24	0 49
19 Su	23 25	25 27	2 06	26 01	25 20	2 10	21 08	0 17	20 55	0 00	17 18	3 00	13 04	1 01	18 23	0 49
20 M	23 26	26 17	3 02	26 15	25 15	2 11	20 56	0 04	21 04	0S00	17 20	2 56	13 00	1 01	18 21	0 49
21 Tu	23 26	25 54	3 51	25 15	25 09	2 12	20 43	0N09	21 12	0 01	17 22	2 52	12 57	1 01	18 19	0 49
22 W	23 26	24 19	4 30	23 05	25 01	2 13	20 31	0 22	21 20	0 01	17 24	2 48	12 53	1 01	18 18	0 49
23 Th	23 26	21 35	4 57	19 50	24 51	2 13	20 18	0 36	21 28	0 02	17 26	2 44	12 49	1 01	18 16	0 49
24 F	23 25	17 51	5 11	15 40	24 40	2 13	20 06	0 51	21 36	0 03	17 28	2 39	12 45	1 00	18 14	0 49
25 Sa	23 24	13 17	5 10	10 45	24 27	2 12	19 54	1 05	21 43	0 03	17 30	2 35	12 41	1 00	18 13	0 49
26 Su	23 22	8 03	4 54	5 15	24 13	2 11	19 42	1 20	21 50	0 04	17 33	2 31	12 37	1 00	18 11	0 49
27 M	23 20	2 21	4 22	0S37	23 57	2 09	19 31	1 35	21 57	0 05	17 35	2 27	12 33	1 00	18 09	0 49
28 Tu	23 17	3S38	3 35	6 38	23 40	2 06	19 19	1 51	22 04	0 05	17 37	2 23	12 29	1 00	18 08	0 49
29 W	23 14	9 36	2 35	12 30	23 22	2 03	19 08	2 06	22 11	0 06	17 40	2 19	12 25	1 00	18 06	0 49
30 Th	23 10	15 16	1 23	17 51	23 02	1 59	18 57	2 22	22 18	0 07	17 42	2 15	12 21	0 60	18 04	0 49
31 F	23S06	20S12	0N04	22S14	22S41	1S55	18S46	2N37	22S24	0S07	17N45	2S11	12S17	0S60	18S02	0S49

Day	⚷ Decl	⚷ Lat	♅ Decl	♅ Lat	♆ Decl	♆ Lat	♇ Decl	♇ Lat
1	5N29	2N15	14N58	0S25	4S52	1S09	22S47	1S42
6	5 26	2 14	14 55	0 25	4 51	1 09	22 46	1 42
11	5 24	2 14	14 52	0 25	4 51	1 09	22 45	1 42
16	5 23	2 13	14 50	0 25	4 50	1 09	22 44	1 43
21	5 22	2 12	14 47	0 25	4 48	1 08	22 42	1 43
26	5 21	2 11	14 45	0 24	4 47	1 08	22 41	1 43
31	5N21	2N10	14N44	0S24	4S45	1S08	22S40	1S44

Day	⚴ Decl	⚴ Lat	⚵ Decl	⚵ Lat	⚶ Decl	⚶ Lat	Eris Decl	Eris Lat
1	12S08	4S53	14S01	9N18	18S42	2N57	1S24	11S27
6	12 15	5 17	14 04	9 10	19 13	2 50	1 25	11 26
11	12 17	5 40	14 06	9 02	19 40	2 44	1 25	11 26
16	12 17	6 02	14 05	8 54	20 05	2 37	1 24	11 25
21	12 13	6 23	14 02	8 47	20 27	2 30	1 24	11 24
26	12 06	6 44	13 58	8 41	20 46	2 24	1 24	11 23
31	11S56	7S04	13S51	8N34	21S01	2N17	1S24	11S23

Moon Phenomena

Max/0 Decl
dy hr mn
6 2:32 26S20
12 16:16 0 N
20 4:36 26N18
27 9:30 0 S

Max/0 Lat
dy hr mn
3 14:59 0 S
9 17:45 5S17
17 0:13 0 N
24 10:48 5N13
31 1:08 0 S

Perigee/Apogee
dy hr m kilometers
4 10:05 p 356800
18 2:16 a 406320

PH dy hr mn
● 4 7:44 12♐22
● 4 454:36T 01'55"
☽ 11 1:37 19♓13
○ 19 4:37 27♊29
☾ 27 2:25 5♎32

Void of Course Moon

Last Aspect				☽ Ingress		
1	4:21	♃	△	♏	1	11:57
3	5:23	♃	□	♐	3	12:14
5	5:09	♃	⚹	♑	5	11:32
7	4:43	♂	⚹	♒	7	11:50
9	10:01	♂	□	♓	9	14:54
11	19:41	♂	△	♈	11	21:47
14	2:53	♃	⚹	♉	14	8:12
16	16:10	♃	□	♊	16	20:44
19	6:03	♃	△	♋	19	9:43
21	14:45	♀	☍	♌	21	21:55
24	6:41	♃	☍	♍	24	8:25
26	8:41	♇	△	♎	26	16:25
28	21:12	♃	△	♏	28	21:17
30	17:11	☿	⚹	♐	30	23:09

DAILY ASPECTARIAN

1 W
☿∠♇ 0:29
☉∠☽ 2:09
☽□♇ 3:44
☽∠☿ 4:08
☽△♃ 4:21
♆D 13:23
☽⚻⚳ 18:33
☽⚼♆ 20:48

2 Th
☉∠♇ 1:13
☽⚻⚷ 1:58
☿⚻♅ 2:16
☽□♄ 2:44
☉⚺☽ 4:36
☽☍♅ 7:02
☽⚺☿ 7:37
☽∥♃ 8:33
☽⋕♅ 12:39
☽△♆ 20:59
☽⋕⚳ 21:09
☽⚹♀ 22:53

3 F
☽☌♂ 0:46
☽⚼⚷ 2:01
☽∥♂ 3:54
☽⚹♇ 4:27
☽□♃ 5:23
☽∥♄ 5:58
☊R 15:05
☉⚻♅ 15:15
☽☍⚳ 17:52
☽∠♀ 23:30

4 Sa
☉∥☽ 1:02
☽△⚷ 1:43
☽⚹♄ 2:47
♂⚼⚷ 3:19
☽∠♇ 4:12
☽∥♇ 4:33
☽⚻♅ 6:36
☉☌☽ 7:44
☽∥☿ 12:35
☽☌☿ 12:44
☽∥♀ 14:26
☽□♆ 20:23
☽⚺♀ 23:56

5 Su
☿∥♀ 1:36
☽⚺♂ 2:23
☽∠♄ 2:32
☽⚺♇ 3:51
☽⚹♃ 5:09
☽⚼♅ 6:11
♂∥♄ 6:23
☽⚻⚳ 16:29

6 M
☽□⚷ 1:04
☽⚺♄ 2:26
☽∠♂ 3:19
☽∠♃ 5:12
☽△♅ 5:57
☉⚺☽ 10:40
♂⚹♇ 11:42
☽⚼⚳ 16:06
☽⚺☿ 17:54
☽⚹♆ 20:10

7 Tu
☽☌♀ 1:22
☽☌♇ 3:57
☽⚹♂ 4:43
☽⚺♃ 5:41
☽∥☿ 11:33
☉∠☽ 12:52
☿□♆ 15:17
☽△⚳ 16:15
☽∠♆ 20:48
☽∥♀ 21:07
☽∠☿ 21:28

8 W
☽⚹⚷ 1:57
☽∥♇ 2:21
☉∥☽ 2:38
☽☌♄ 3:44
♂□♃ 6:23
☽□♅ 7:02
☉∥♇ 11:31
☉⚹☽ 15:58
☽⚺♆ 22:12
☽∥♂ 23:28

9 Th
☽⚹☿ 2:08
☽∥♄ 3:30
☽∠⚷ 3:31
☽⚺♀ 5:16
☽⚺♇ 6:35
☽☌♃ 8:54
☽□♂ 10:01
☽⋕⚳ 11:47
☽□⚳ 18:50
☽⋕♅ 22:20

10 F
☽∥♃ 4:28
☽⚺⚷ 6:01
☽⚺♄ 8:19
☽∠♀ 8:35
☽∠♇ 9:16
☿∠♄ 9:46
☉∥♀ 9:46
☽⚹♅ 11:23
☿⚺♀ 12:51
☿⚺♇ 17:57

11 Sa
☊D 1:29
☉□☽ 1:37
☽☌♆ 3:51
♀∥♇ 8:04
☿⚼♅ 11:11
☽∠♄ 12:06
☽⚹♀ 12:53
☽⚹♇ 12:58
☽∠♅ 15:02
☽□☿ 15:34
☽⚺♃ 16:00
♀☌♇ 16:30
☽⋕⚷ 16:52
☽∥♆ 19:16
☿⚹♃ 19:25
☽△♂ 19:41

12 Su
☽⚹⚳ 1:05
☉□♆ 6:22
☽☌⚷ 13:57
☽⚹♄ 16:51
☽⚺♅ 19:35
☽∠♃ 21:02

13 M
☽⚼♂ 2:11
☽∠⚳ 5:33
♂ ♐ 9:54
☽⚺♆ 13:17
☽⋕♆ 13:38
☉△☽ 16:04
☽∥⚷ 16:07
☿ ♑ 17:53
☽□♇ 23:02

14 Tu
☽□♀ 0:04
☿⚺♂ 0:17
☽⚹♃ 2:53
☽⚻♂ 9:34
☽△☿ 10:21
☽⚺⚳ 10:42
☿⚻⚳ 12:50
☽∠♆ 19:06

15 W
☉⚼☽ 0:42
♂☍⚳ 1:04
☽⚺⚷ 1:06
☽□♄ 4:37
☽⋕♃ 5:56
☽☌♅ 6:52
☽∥♅ 14:00
☽⚼☿ 21:06

16 Th
☽⚹♆ 1:22
☽∥⚳ 3:19
☽∠⚷ 7:24
☉⚻☽ 9:52
☽⋕♄ 10:43
☽△♇ 11:30
☽△♀ 13:15
☽□♃ 16:10
☽☌⚳ 22:19

17 F
☊R 0:14
☽⋕♂ 1:11
☽☍♂ 1:57
☉∠♄ 3:03
☉⚺♇ 5:22
☽⋕♀ 7:23
☽⚻☿ 8:15
☽⚹⚷ 13:54
☽⋕♇ 17:17
☽△♄ 17:59
☽⚼♇ 18:05
☽⚺♅ 19:37
☽⚼♀ 20:00
☉⋕☽ 23:14
☉⚼♅ 23:20

18 Sa
☉⚺♀ 4:29
☽□♆ 14:25
☽⋕☿ 22:20

19 Su
☽⚻♇ 0:39
☽⚼♄ 0:43
☽∠♅ 2:02
☽⚻♀ 2:36
☿□⚷ 2:36
☉☍☽ 4:37
☽△♃ 6:03
☽⚺⚳ 10:24
♀R 10:37
♀∥♂ 14:35
⚷D 16:34
☽⚻♂ 18:45

20 M
☉⚹♃ 0:33
☽□⚷ 2:46
☽☍☿ 6:26
☽⚻♄ 7:18
☽⚹♅ 8:18
☽⚼♃ 12:47
☿⚺♄ 13:23
☽∠⚳ 16:13
☿△♅ 20:19

21 Tu
☽⚼♂ 2:48
☽△♆ 3:01
⚳R♉ 10:40
☽☍♇ 13:11
☽⋕☿ 14:44
☽☍♀ 14:45
☉⚻⚳ 15:17
☉ ♑ 16:00
☽⚻♃ 19:13
☽⚹⚳ 21:46
☉⚻☽ 22:27

22 W
☉⋕☽ 8:48
☽⚼♆ 8:51
☽△♂ 10:26
☿∠♃ 12:02
☽△⚷ 14:35
☽⋕♇ 15:16
☽☍♄ 19:29
☽□♅ 19:51

23 Th
☽⋕♂ 0:51
☽⚻☿ 2:55
☿⚼⚳ 2:57
☉⚼☽ 6:38
☽⋕♀ 9:27
☽⚻♆ 14:13
☽⚼⚷ 19:50
☽⋕♄ 21:45

24 F
☽⚻♇ 0:08
☽⚻♀ 0:51
☽∥⚳ 2:12
☽☍♃ 6:41
♄□♅ 7:18
☽□⚳ 7:35
☽⚼☿ 12:02
☉△☽ 14:06
☽∥♅ 16:39
☽□♂ 23:53

25 Sa
☽⚻⚷ 0:29
☽⋕♃ 2:56
☽⚼♇ 4:46
☽⚼♀ 4:55
☽△♅ 5:26
☽⚻♄ 5:39
♂△⚷ 10:38
♀☌♇ 12:03
⚳□♃ 18:07
☽△☿ 20:10
☽☍♆ 23:09

26 Su
☽△♀ 8:13
☽△♇ 8:41
☽⚼♅ 9:13
☽⚼♄ 9:41
☽∥⚷ 11:33
☽⋕♆ 13:58
☽△⚳ 15:02
☽⚻♃ 15:33
☿⚹♆ 21:30

27 M
☉□☽ 2:25
☊D 2:35
☽☍⚷ 7:40
☽⚹♂ 10:08
☽⚻♅ 12:14
☽△♄ 12:56
♀∠♂ 17:33
☽⚼⚳ 17:40
☽⚼♃ 18:48

28 Tu
☽∥♆ 4:32
☽⚻♆ 5:05
☽⋕⚷ 6:53
☽□☿ 8:58
☽□♀ 12:21
☽∠♂ 13:51
☽□♇ 14:08
♂∠♇ 19:24
☽⚻⚳ 19:32
☽△♃ 21:12

29 W
♂⚻♅ 1:05
♃ ♓ 4:11
☽⚼♆ 6:51
☿☌♀ 10:29
☉⚹☽ 10:44
☽∥♃ 11:31
☽⚻⚷ 11:40
☉∥☿ 12:21
☽☍♅ 15:52
☽⚺♂ 16:40
☽□♄ 16:59
☽⋕♅ 21:38
☉□⚷ 23:54

30 Th
♂⚹♄ 0:23
☽△♆ 7:53
☿☌♇ 9:55
☽⋕⚳ 11:23
☽⚼⚷ 12:33
☽∥♄ 12:59
☽⚹♀ 13:20
☉∠☽ 13:29
☽⚹♇ 16:29
☽∥♀ 16:46
☽⚹☿ 17:11
☽☍⚳ 21:07
☽□♃ 23:43

31 F
☊R 1:10
☿∥♇ 1:19
☽△⚷ 12:52
☽∠♀ 12:53
☽∥♂ 13:26
☽∥☿ 13:32
☿∥♂ 14:22
☽∥♇ 14:46
☉⚺☽ 15:32
☽∠♇ 16:45
☽⚻♅ 16:48
☉∥☽ 17:25
☽⚹♄ 18:16
☽∠☿ 19:58
☽☌♂ 20:02
☿∠♂ 21:13

December 2021:Modify New York Stock Exchange Zone:-5

Sunday	Monday	Tuesday	Wednesday	Thursday	Friday	Saturday
November S M T W T F S 1 2 3 4 5 6 7 8 9 10 11 12 13 14 15 16 17 18 19 20 21 22 23 24 25 26 27 28 29 30	January 2022 S M T W T F S 1 2 3 4 5 6 7 8 9 10 11 12 13 14 15 16 17 18 19 20 21 22 23 24 25 26 27 28 29 30 31		1 6:54AM ☽-> 0♏00 8:19AM ♆Direct	2	3 7:11AM ☽-> 0♐00	4 2:42AM New Moon♐
5 6:29AM ☽-> 0♑00	6 6:40AM ♂ ⚹ ♇	7 6:47AM ☽-> 0♒00 10:15AM ☿ □ ♆	8 1:21AM ♂ □ ♃	9 9:52AM ☽-> 0♓00	10	11 11:28AM ♀ ☌ ♇ 2:23PM ☿ ⚹ ♃ 4:45PM ☽-> 0♈00
12 1:20AM ☉ □ ♆	13 4:52AM ♂-> 0♐00 12:51PM ☿ -> 0♑00	14 3:09AM ☽-> 0♉00	15	16 3:41PM ☽-> 0♊00	17	18 11:34PM Full Moon♊
19 4:40AM ☽-> 0♋00 5:35AM ♀ ℞26♑ 7:31PM ☉ ⚹ ♃	20 3:18PM ☿ △ ♅	21 10:58AM ☉-> 0♑00 4:52PM ☽-> 0♌00	22	23	24 2:16AM ♄ □ ♅ 3:23AM ☽-> 0♍00	25 7:01AM ♇ ☌ ♀
26 11:22AM ☽-> 0♎00 4:28PM ☿ ⚹ ♆	27	28 4:15PM ☽-> 0♏00 11:08PM ♃-> 0♓00	29 5:27AM ☿ ☌ ♀ 7:21PM ♂ ⚹ ♄	30 4:53AM ☿ ☌ ♇ 6:07PM ☽-> 0♐00	31	

LONGITUDE

January 2022

Day	Sid.Time	☉	☽	☽ 12 hour	Mean ☊	True ☊	☿	♀	♂	⚳	♃	♄	⚷	♅	♆	♇
	h m s	° ' "	° ' "	° ' "	° '	° '	° '	° '	° '	° '	° '	° '	° '	° '	° '	° '
1 Sa	6 42 30	10♑31 41	15♐28 04	23♐01 07	29♉31.7	1♊12.4	28♑10.9	23♑17.7	13♐05.9	28♉37.9	0♓32.7	11♒54.2	8♈30.4	10♉57.2	20♓40.1	25♑56.1
2 Su	6 46 27	11 32 52	0♑35 49	8♑11 00	29 28.6	1R 09.7	29 35.2	22R 47.7	13 48.6	28R 32.3	0 44.5	12 00.7	8 31.1	10R 56.3	20 41.2	25 58.0
3 M	6 50 23	12 34 03	15 45 21	23 17 39	29 25.4	1 04.9	0♒57.1	22 16.1	14 31.3	28 27.2	0 56.4	12 07.2	8 31.8	10 55.5	20 42.3	25 59.9
4 Tu	6 54 20	13 35 14	0♒46 38	8♒11 13	29 22.2	0 58.5	2 16.1	21 43.1	15 14.1	28 22.4	1 08.3	12 13.8	8 32.6	10 54.7	20 43.4	26 01.9
5 W	6 58 17	14 36 25	15 30 24	22 43 24	29 19.1	0 51.3	3 31.7	21 08.8	15 56.8	28 18.1	1 20.4	12 20.4	8 33.5	10 54.0	20 44.5	26 03.8
6 Th	7 02 13	15 37 35	29 49 37	6♓48 40	29 15.9	0 44.3	4 43.2	20 33.6	16 39.7	28 14.2	1 32.5	12 27.1	8 34.4	10 53.3	20 45.7	26 05.8
7 F	7 06 10	16 38 45	13♓40 22	20 24 43	29 12.7	0 38.4	5 50.1	19 57.6	17 22.5	28 10.7	1 44.7	12 33.8	8 35.4	10 52.6	20 46.9	26 07.8
8 Sa	7 10 06	17 39 55	27 01 54	3♈32 13	29 09.5	0 34.1	6 51.5	19 21.1	18 05.4	28 07.7	1 57.0	12 40.5	8 36.4	10 52.1	20 48.2	26 09.7
9 Su	7 14 03	18 41 04	9♈56 06	16 14 04	29 06.3	0D 31.9	7 46.7	18 44.4	18 48.3	28 05.0	2 09.4	12 47.3	8 37.5	10 51.5	20 49.4	26 11.7
10 M	7 17 59	19 42 13	22 26 44	28 34 41	29 03.2	0 31.5	8 34.8	18 07.6	19 31.3	28 02.8	2 21.8	12 54.1	8 38.6	10 51.1	20 50.7	26 13.7
11 Tu	7 21 56	20 43 21	4♉38 36	10♉39 09	29 00.0	0 32.4	9 15.0	17 31.2	20 14.3	28 01.0	2 34.4	13 00.9	8 39.8	10 50.6	20 52.0	26 15.6
12 W	7 25 52	21 44 29	16 36 59	22 32 44	28 56.8	0 33.7	9 46.3	16 55.2	20 57.3	27 59.6	2 47.0	13 07.8	8 41.1	10 50.3	20 53.4	26 17.6
13 Th	7 29 49	22 45 37	28 27 02	4♊20 27	28 53.6	0R 34.5	10 07.9	16 20.0	21 40.4	27 58.6	2 59.7	13 14.6	8 42.4	10 49.9	20 54.8	26 19.6
14 F	7 33 45	23 46 43	10♊13 33	16 06 48	28 50.5	0 33.9	10R 18.9	15 45.8	22 23.5	27D 58.0	3 12.4	13 21.5	8 43.7	10 49.7	20 56.2	26 21.6
15 Sa	7 37 42	24 47 50	22 00 41	27 55 34	28 47.3	0 31.3	10 18.7	15 12.8	23 06.6	27 57.8	3 25.3	13 28.5	8 45.1	10 49.5	20 57.6	26 23.5
16 Su	7 41 39	25 48 55	3♋51 50	9♋49 47	28 44.1	0 26.1	10 07.0	14 41.3	23 49.8	27 58.1	3 38.1	13 35.4	8 46.5	10 49.3	20 59.1	26 25.5
17 M	7 45 35	26 50 00	15 49 39	21 51 38	28 40.9	0 18.4	9 43.4	14 11.4	24 33.0	27 58.7	3 51.1	13 42.4	8 48.0	10 49.2	21 00.6	26 27.5
18 Tu	7 49 32	27 51 05	27 55 55	4♌02 37	28 37.8	0 08.6	9 08.3	13 43.3	25 16.3	27 59.8	4 04.1	13 49.4	8 49.6	10D 49.1	21 02.1	26 29.5
19 W	7 53 28	28 52 09	10♌11 50	16 23 37	28 34.6	29♉57.3	8 22.3	13 17.2	25 59.6	28 01.3	4 17.2	13 56.4	8 51.2	10 49.1	21 03.6	26 31.5
20 Th	7 57 25	29 53 12	22 38 02	28 55 09	28 31.4	29 45.5	7 26.4	12 53.2	26 42.9	28 03.1	4 30.4	14 03.5	8 52.8	10 49.2	21 05.2	26 33.5
21 F	8 01 21	0♒54 15	5♍15 00	11♍37 40	28 28.2	29 34.5	6 22.1	12 31.5	27 26.3	28 05.4	4 43.6	14 10.5	8 54.5	10 49.3	21 06.8	26 35.4
22 Sa	8 05 18	1 55 18	18 03 14	24 31 47	28 25.0	29 25.1	5 11.4	12 12.0	28 09.7	28 08.0	4 56.9	14 17.6	8 56.2	10 49.4	21 08.4	26 37.4
23 Su	8 09 15	2 56 20	1♎03 28	7♎38 25	28 21.9	29 18.1	3 56.5	11 55.0	28 53.1	28 11.1	5 10.2	14 24.7	8 58.0	10 49.6	21 10.0	26 39.4
24 M	8 13 11	3 57 21	14 16 50	20 58 54	28 18.7	29 13.9	2 39.6	11 40.4	29 36.6	28 14.5	5 23.6	14 31.8	8 59.8	10 49.9	21 11.7	26 41.4
25 Tu	8 17 08	4 58 22	27 44 48	4♏34 44	28 15.5	29D 12.0	1 23.1	11 28.2	0♑20.1	28 18.3	5 37.1	14 38.9	9 01.7	10 50.2	21 13.4	26 43.3
26 W	8 21 04	5 59 22	11♏28 53	18 27 20	28 12.3	29 11.9	0 09.2	11 18.6	1 03.7	28 22.5	5 50.6	14 46.0	9 03.6	10 50.5	21 15.1	26 45.3
27 Th	8 25 01	7 00 23	25 30 10	2♐37 20	28 09.2	29R 12.3	28♑59.9	11 11.5	1 47.3	28 27.1	6 04.1	14 53.2	9 05.6	10 50.9	21 16.8	26 47.2
28 F	8 28 57	8 01 22	9♐48 41	17 03 58	28 06.0	29 12.0	27 56.6	11 06.9	2 30.9	28 32.0	6 17.7	15 00.3	9 07.6	10 51.4	21 18.6	26 49.2
29 Sa	8 32 54	9 02 21	24 22 45	1♑44 27	28 02.8	29 09.7	27 00.7	11D 04.8	3 14.6	28 37.3	6 31.4	15 07.5	9 09.6	10 51.9	21 20.4	26 51.2
30 Su	8 36 50	10 03 20	9♑08 22	16 33 36	27 59.6	29 04.7	26 12.8	11 05.1	3 58.3	28 43.0	6 45.1	15 14.7	9 11.7	10 52.5	21 22.2	26 53.1
31 M	8 40 47	11♒04 17	23 59 12	1♒24 06	27♉56.5	28♉56.8	25♑33.6	11♑07.8	4♑42.1	28♉49.0	6♓58.9	15♒21.9	9♈13.9	10♉53.1	21♓24.0	26♑55.0

1st of Month

Julian Day # 2459580.5
Obliquity 23°26'15"
SVP 4♓57'23"
GC 27♐08.8
Eris 23♈41.7R

Day	⚴
1	16♓27.5
6	17 44.6
11	19 06.0
16	20 31.5
21	22 00.8
26	23 33.6
31	25 09.8

Day	⚵
1	17♑23.0
6	19 19.9
11	21 17.6
16	23 15.8
21	25 14.5
26	27 13.6
31	29 13.1

Day	⚶
1	24♐31.6
6	27 12.5
11	29 52.9
16	2♑32.6
21	5 11.5
26	7 49.6
31	10 26.8

DECLINATION and LATITUDE

Day	☉ Decl	☽ Decl	☽ Lat	☽12h Decl	☿ Decl	☿ Lat	♀ Decl	♀ Lat	♂ Decl	♂ Lat	⚳ Decl	⚳ Lat	♃ Decl	♃ Lat	♄ Decl	♄ Lat
1 Sa	23S01	23S55	1S17	25S11	22S18	1S49	18S35	2N53	22S30	0S08	17N48	2S07	12S13	0S60	18S01	0S49
2 Su	22 56	25 59	2 33	26 18	21 55	1 43	18 25	3 09	22 36	0 09	17 50	2 03	12 08	0 60	17 59	0 49
3 M	22 51	26 07	3 38	25 27	21 30	1 36	18 14	3 24	22 42	0 09	17 53	1 59	12 04	0 60	17 57	0 49
4 Tu	22 45	24 20	4 28	22 48	21 05	1 28	18 04	3 39	22 47	0 10	17 56	1 55	11 60	0 60	17 55	0 50
5 W	22 38	20 56	4 58	18 45	20 39	1 19	17 55	3 54	22 52	0 11	17 59	1 51	11 55	0 60	17 53	0 50
6 Th	22 31	16 21	5 09	13 46	20 12	1 09	17 45	4 09	22 57	0 11	18 02	1 47	11 51	0 59	17 52	0 50
7 F	22 24	11 03	5 01	8 15	19 46	0 59	17 37	4 23	23 02	0 12	18 05	1 43	11 47	0 59	17 50	0 50
8 Sa	22 16	5 25	4 37	2 34	19 19	0 47	17 28	4 37	23 07	0 13	18 08	1 39	11 42	0 59	17 48	0 50
9 Su	22 08	0N16	3 59	3N03	18 52	0 34	17 20	4 51	23 11	0 13	18 11	1 35	11 38	0 59	17 46	0 50
10 M	21 59	5 47	3 11	8 25	18 26	0 20	17 12	5 03	23 15	0 14	18 14	1 31	11 33	0 59	17 44	0 50
11 Tu	21 50	10 57	2 15	13 21	18 01	0 05	17 04	5 16	23 19	0 15	18 18	1 27	11 29	0 59	17 42	0 50
12 W	21 41	15 37	1 15	17 43	17 37	0N11	16 57	5 27	23 23	0 15	18 21	1 24	11 24	0 59	17 40	0 50
13 Th	21 31	19 38	0 11	21 21	17 15	0 28	16 51	5 38	23 27	0 16	18 25	1 20	11 19	0 59	17 38	0 50
14 F	21 21	22 50	0N52	24 05	16 55	0 46	16 45	5 48	23 30	0 17	18 28	1 16	11 15	0 59	17 36	0 50
15 Sa	21 10	25 04	1 53	25 47	16 38	1 04	16 39	5 57	23 33	0 17	18 32	1 13	11 10	0 59	17 34	0 50
16 Su	20 59	26 12	2 49	26 18	16 23	1 23	16 34	6 06	23 36	0 18	18 35	1 09	11 05	0 59	17 32	0 50
17 M	20 47	26 06	3 38	25 36	16 11	1 41	16 29	6 13	23 38	0 19	18 39	1 05	11 01	0 59	17 30	0 50
18 Tu	20 35	24 47	4 18	23 40	16 03	1 60	16 25	6 20	23 41	0 19	18 43	1 02	10 56	0 59	17 29	0 50
19 W	20 23	22 16	4 46	20 37	15 58	2 17	16 22	6 27	23 43	0 20	18 46	0 58	10 51	0 59	17 27	0 50
20 Th	20 10	18 43	5 01	16 35	15 56	2 34	16 19	6 32	23 45	0 21	18 50	0 55	10 46	0 59	17 25	0 50
21 F	19 57	14 16	5 02	11 46	15 57	2 49	16 16	6 36	23 46	0 22	18 54	0 51	10 41	0 59	17 23	0 50
22 Sa	19 44	9 08	4 48	6 23	16 01	3 03	16 14	6 40	23 48	0 22	18 58	0 48	10 36	0 59	17 21	0 50
23 Su	19 30	3 32	4 19	0 38	16 08	3 14	16 12	6 44	23 49	0 23	19 02	0 44	10 31	0 59	17 19	0 50
24 M	19 16	2S19	3 35	5S16	16 16	3 23	16 11	6 46	23 50	0 24	19 06	0 41	10 26	0 59	17 16	0 50
25 Tu	19 01	8 12	2 39	11 03	16 27	3 29	16 10	6 48	23 51	0 24	19 10	0 38	10 21	0 59	17 14	0 50
26 W	18 46	13 48	1 33	16 24	16 39	3 33	16 10	6 49	23 51	0 25	19 14	0 34	10 16	0 59	17 12	0 50
27 Th	18 31	18 49	0 20	20 59	16 52	3 34	16 10	6 49	23 51	0 26	19 18	0 31	10 11	0 58	17 10	0 51
28 F	18 16	22 51	0S56	24 22	17 05	3 33	16 10	6 49	23 51	0 27	19 23	0 28	10 06	0 58	17 08	0 51
29 Sa	17 60	25 28	2 10	26 09	17 19	3 30	16 11	6 49	23 51	0 27	19 27	0 25	10 01	0 58	17 06	0 51
30 Su	17 44	26 22	3 15	26 06	17 33	3 25	16 12	6 48	23 51	0 28	19 31	0 22	9 56	0 58	17 04	0 51
31 M	17S27	25S22	4S08	24S12	17S46	3N19	16S13	6N46	23S50	0S29	19N36	0S18	9S51	0S58	17S02	0S51

Day	⚷ Decl	⚷ Lat	♅ Decl	♅ Lat	♆ Decl	♆ Lat	♇ Decl	♇ Lat
1	5N21	2N10	14N44	0S24	4S44	1S08	22S39	1S44
6	5 22	2 09	14 43	0 24	4 42	1 08	22 38	1 44
11	5 24	2 08	14 42	0 24	4 40	1 08	22 36	1 44
16	5 25	2 07	14 42	0 24	4 37	1 08	22 35	1 45
21	5 28	2 06	14 42	0 24	4 33	1 08	22 33	1 45
26	5 31	2 05	14 42	0 24	4 30	1 07	22 32	1 46
31	5N34	2N04	14N43	0S23	4S27	1S07	22S31	1S46

Day	⚴ Decl	⚴ Lat	⚵ Decl	⚵ Lat	⚶ Decl	⚶ Lat	Eris Decl	Eris Lat
1	11S54	7S08	13S49	8N33	21S04	2N16	1S23	11S23
6	11 42	7 27	13 40	8 27	21 16	2 09	1 23	11 22
11	11 27	7 46	13 29	8 22	21 25	2 02	1 22	11 21
16	11 10	8 04	13 16	8 17	21 30	1 55	1 21	11 20
21	10 51	8 23	13 01	8 12	21 33	1 47	1 21	11 19
26	10 31	8 41	12 44	8 07	21 32	1 40	1 20	11 19
31	10S10	8S59	12S26	8N03	21S29	1N33	1S19	11S18

Moon Phenomena

Max/0 Decl

dy	hr mn	
2	13:36	26S18
8	22:52	0 N
16	10:19	26N18
23	14:33	0 S
29	23:24	26S22

Max/0 Lat

dy	hr mn	
6	1:33	5S09
13	4:20	0 N
20	13:24	5N04
27	6:16	0 S

Perigee/Apogee

dy	hr m		kilometers
1	22:57	p	358033
14	9:27	a	405804
30	7:12	p	362255

PH	dy	hr mn	
●	2	18:35	12♑20
☽	9	18:12	19♈27
○	17	23:50	27♋51
☾	25	13:42	5♏33

Void of Course Moon

Last Aspect			☽ Ingress	
1 8:17	♆	□	♑	1 23:03
3 16:22	♇	☌	♒	3 22:45
5 0:46	♂	⚹	♓	6 0:18
7 22:24	♇	⚹	♈	8 5:27
10 7:24	♇	□	♉	10 14:48
12 19:40	♇	△	♊	13 3:09
15 2:23	♂	☍	♋	15 16:12
17 23:50	☉	☍	♌	18 4:04
20 8:17	♂	△	♍	20 14:03
22 19:47	♂	□	♎	22 22:04
24 22:11	♇	□	♏	25 3:58
27 5:29	☿	⚹	♐	27 7:36
28 19:01	♆	□	♑	29 9:10
31 4:45	♇	☌	♒	31 9:44

DAILY ASPECTARIAN

1 Sa
☿△⚳ 7:08
☽□♆ 8:17
☉△♅ 9:51
☽⚺♀ 12:03
☽⚼♅ 16:38
☽⚺♇ 16:39
☽∠♄ 18:17
☽⚻⚳ 20:46
☽⚺☿ 22:14

2 Su
☽⚹♃ 0:14
☿ ♒ 7:11
☉⚺♄ 12:13
☽□⚷ 12:32
♂∥♇ 12:41
☽△♅ 16:21
☽⚺♄ 18:12
☉☌☽ 18:35
☽⚼⚳ 20:22
☽⚺♂ 21:57
☿⚺♃ 23:45

3 M
☽∠♃ 0:18
☽⚹♆ 7:53
☽☌♀ 10:00
☽☌♇ 16:22
☉∥♂ 19:04
☉⚼⚳ 19:20
⚳⋕♄ 20:00
☽△⚳ 20:09
☽∠♂ 23:05

4 Tu
☽⚺♃ 0:35
☽☌☿ 2:38
☽∠♆ 8:00
☽∥♂ 11:50
☽⚹⚷ 12:36
☉∥☽ 12:49
☽∥♇ 13:09
♀⋕⚳ 16:04
☽□♅ 16:26
☽☌♄ 18:45
☉⚺☽ 22:24

5 W
☉∥♇ 0:13
☽⚹♂ 0:46
☽∥☿ 1:49
♀∥♄ 4:28
☽⚺♆ 8:42
☽⚺♀ 9:00
☽∠⚷ 13:25
☽⋕⚳ 15:48
♀⚹♆ 16:04
☽∥♄ 16:33
☽∥♀ 16:52
☽⚺♇ 17:40
☽□⚳ 21:19

6 Th
☉∠☽ 1:28
☽☌♃ 2:58
☽⋕♅ 7:42
☽⚺☿ 9:08
☽∠♀ 9:26
☽⚺⚷ 15:05
☽⚹♅ 19:05
☽∠♇ 19:31
☽∥♃ 20:47
☽⚺♄ 22:02
☿∠♆ 22:49

7 F
☉∠♃ 2:56
☉⚹☽ 5:42
☽□♂ 6:56
☽⚹♀ 10:42
☽☌♆ 12:41
☽∠☿ 13:51
☽∠♅ 21:53
☽⚹♇ 22:24

8 Sa
☽⋕⚷ 0:09
☽∠♄ 1:11
☽⚹⚳ 2:00
☽∥♆ 3:05
☽⚺♃ 9:12
☽⚹☿ 19:38
☽☌⚷ 21:31
♀⚺♂ 22:49

9 Su
☉☌♀ 0:49
☽⚺♅ 1:45
☽⚹♄ 5:28
☽∠⚳ 5:57
☉⚺♂ 9:33
☽∠♃ 14:00
☽□♀ 16:02
☽△♂ 17:59
☊ D 18:02
☉□☽ 18:12
☽⋕♆ 19:05
☽⚺♆ 20:53
☽∥⚷ 22:16

10 M
☿⚹⚷ 2:08
☽□♇ 7:24
☿⋕⚳ 9:41
☽⚺⚳ 10:56
☽⚹♃ 19:49
♀∠♃ 22:25

11 Tu
☽⚼♂ 1:15
☽∠♆ 2:26
☽⋕♃ 2:34
☉⚹♆ 3:29
⚶ ♑ 5:20
☽⚺⚷ 8:02
☽□☿ 9:39
☽☌♅ 12:23
☽□♄ 16:54
☽∥♅ 19:03
☿∥♄ 20:34
♂□♆ 21:44

12 W
☽△♀ 0:35
☽⋕♀ 7:23
☽⚹♆ 8:40
☽⚻♂ 9:20
☽⋕☿ 10:30
☉△☽ 11:21
☽⋕♄ 11:40
☽∠⚷ 14:20
☽∥⚳ 16:07
☽△♇ 19:40
☽☌⚳ 23:02

13 Th
☊ R 4:21
☽⚼♀ 5:36
☽□♃ 9:25
☉⋕☽ 12:39
☉⚼☽ 20:46
☽⚹⚷ 20:56
☽⋕♇ 21:55

14 F
☽△☿ 0:11
☽⚺♅ 1:14
☽⚼♇ 2:19
☽⋕♂ 6:12
☽△♄ 6:27
☽⚻♀ 10:47
☿ R 11:43
☿∥♀ 20:41
⚳ D 21:21
☽□♆ 21:52

15 Sa
☽☍♂ 2:23
☉⚻☽ 6:11
☽⚼☿ 6:38
☽∠♅ 7:44
☽⚻♇ 8:55
☽⚺⚳ 12:05
☽⚼♄ 13:14
☽△♃ 23:32

16 Su
☽□⚷ 9:54
☽⚻☿ 12:13
☽⚹♅ 13:59
☉☌♇ 14:52
☽∠⚳ 18:18
☽⚻♄ 19:43
☽☍♀ 20:51

17 M
☿∠♂ 3:23
☽⚼♃ 6:08
☽△♆ 10:20
☽⚻♂ 18:25
♀⚺♄ 19:45
☽☍♇ 21:09
☉☍☽ 23:50

18 Tu
☽⚹⚳ 0:08
☉△⚳ 3:30
☿⚹⚷ 10:05
☽⋕♂ 11:44
☽⚻♃ 12:16
♅ D 15:28
☽⚼♆ 15:55
♂⚼♅ 18:12
☊R♉ 18:22
☽☍☿ 20:40
☽△⚷ 21:23
☽⋕♇ 21:39

19 W
☽□♅ 1:12
☽⚼♂ 1:39
☽⚻♀ 5:48
☽☍♄ 7:20
☉⋕☽ 14:21
♀⚼⚳ 14:38
♂⚺♇ 18:31
☽⚻♆ 21:02
☽∥⚳ 23:16

20 Th
☽⚼⚷ 2:23
☉ ♒ 2:40
☽⚻♇ 7:31
☽⋕♄ 7:33
☽△♂ 8:17
☽⚼♀ 9:45
☽□⚳ 10:23
☽⋕♀ 13:37
☉⚻☽ 15:03
☽⋕☿ 15:28
☽∥♅ 21:51
☽☍♃ 23:00

21 F
☽⚻☿ 1:56
☿∠♆ 5:15
☽⚻⚷ 6:55
☽△♅ 10:29
☽⚼♇ 11:58
☽△♀ 13:20
☽⚻♄ 16:55
☽⋕♃ 17:17
☉⚼☽ 21:43
♂⚻⚳ 23:01

22 Sa
☽⚼☿ 3:38
☿⚺♃ 4:01
☽☍♆ 5:45
☽⚼♅ 14:23
☽∥⚷ 15:51
☽△♇ 15:54
☽△⚳ 18:43
☽□♂ 19:47
☽⋕♆ 19:49
☽⚼♄ 20:57

23 Su
☉△☽ 3:44
☽△☿ 4:48
☽⚻♃ 7:38
☉☌☿ 10:29
☿∥♀ 11:27
☽☍⚷ 14:26
☽⚻♅ 17:47
☽□♀ 19:23
♂∠♄ 20:49
☽⚼⚳ 22:07

24 M
☽△♄ 0:27
☽∥♆ 8:56
☽⚼♃ 11:08
☽⚻♆ 12:24
☉⋕⚳ 12:48
♂ ♑ 12:54
☽⋕⚷ 12:55
☽□♇ 22:11

25 Tu
☽⚻⚳ 0:59
☽⚹♂ 4:49
☽□☿ 5:52
☽∥♃ 8:56
☿⚺♂ 12:47
☉□☽ 13:42
☊ D 13:48
☽△♃ 14:03
☽⚼♆ 14:54
☉⚺♃ 19:33
☽⚻⚷ 19:48
☽☍♅ 22:54
☽⚹♀ 23:42

26 W
☿R♑ 3:06
☽⋕♅ 4:04
☽□♄ 5:43
☉∠♆ 6:22
☽∠♂ 8:20
☽∥♀ 10:50
☽∥☿ 13:45
☽∥♄ 15:45
☽△♆ 16:49
☽⚼⚷ 21:36
☉∥☽ 22:32

27 Th
☽∠♀ 1:10
☽⚹♇ 2:11
☽⋕⚳ 2:38
☽☍⚳ 5:01
☽⚹☿ 5:29
☊ R 6:18
☽⚺♂ 11:10
☿△⚳ 11:17
☽□♃ 18:03
☉⚹☽ 20:48
☽∥♇ 21:47
☽△⚷ 22:52

28 F
☽⚻♅ 1:44
☽⚺♀ 2:09
☽∠♇ 3:20
☿∥♄ 4:31
☽∠☿ 4:52
☽∥♂ 7:41
☽⚹♄ 8:40
☽□♆ 19:01
☉∠☽ 23:24

29 Sa
☽⚼♅ 2:26
☉⚹⚷ 2:58
☽⚺♇ 4:03
☽⚺☿ 4:04
☿☌♇ 4:17
☽⚻⚳ 6:58
♀ D 8:47
☽∠♄ 9:27
☽☌♂ 15:11
☽⚹♃ 20:04

30 Su
☽□⚷ 0:05
☉⚺☽ 1:36
☽△♅ 2:49
☽☌♀ 3:09
☽⚼⚳ 7:27
☉∥☿ 8:28
☽⚺♄ 9:57
☉□♅ 19:33
☽⚹♆ 19:49
☽∠♃ 20:42

31 M
☉⚺♀ 1:30
☽☌☿ 2:27
☽☌♇ 4:45
☽△⚳ 7:52
☽∥♂ 15:06
☽⚺♂ 18:15
☽∠♆ 20:09
☽⚺♃ 21:24

January 2022:Modify New York Stock Exchange Zone:-5

Sunday	Monday	Tuesday	Wednesday	Thursday	Friday	Saturday
						1 4:49AM ☉ △ ♅ 6:01PM ☽-> 0♑00
2 2:09AM ☿ -> 0♒00 1:32PM New Moon♑	3 5:42PM ☽-> 0♒00	4	5 11:02AM ♆ ⚹ ♀ 7:15PM ☽-> 0♓00	6	7	8 12:24AM ☽-> 0♈00 7:47PM ☉ ☌ ♀
9	10 9:45AM ☽-> 0♉00 10:27PM ☉ ⚹ ♆	11 4:42PM ♂ □ ♆	12 10:07PM ☽-> 0♊00	13	14 6:40AM ☿ ℞10♒	15 11:09AM ☽-> 0♋00
16 9:50AM ☉ ☌ ♇	17 6:47PM Full Moon♋ 11:01PM ☽-> 0♌00	18 10:26AM ♅Direct	19 9:38PM ☉-> 0♒00	20 9:01AM ☽-> 0♍00	21	22 5:01PM ☽-> 0♎00
23 5:27AM ☉ ☌ ☿	24 7:52AM ♂-> 0♑00 10:56PM ☽-> 0♏00	25 10:03PM ☿ -> 0♒00	26	27 2:33AM ☽-> 0♐00	28 11:14PM ♇ ☌ ☿	29 3:45AM ♀Direct 4:07AM ☽-> 0♑00
30 2:31PM ☉ □ ♅	31 4:41AM ☽-> 0♒00					

December 2021

S	M	T	W	T	F	S
			1	2	3	4
5	6	7	8	9	10	11
12	13	14	15	16	17	18
19	20	21	22	23	24	25
26	27	28	29	30	31	

February

S	M	T	W	T	F	S
		1	2	3	4	5
6	7	8	9	10	11	12
13	14	15	16	17	18	19
20	21	22	23	24	25	26
27	28					

February 2022

LONGITUDE

Day	Sid.Time	☉	☽	☽ 12 hour	Mean☊	True☊	☿	♀	♂	⚳	♃	♄	⚷	♅	♆	♇
	h m s	° ' "	° ' "	° ' "	° '	° '	° '	° '	° '	° '	° '	° '	° '	° '	° '	° '
1 Tu	8 44 44	12♒05 14	8♒47 13	16♒07 28	27♉53.3	28♉46.5	25♑03.1	11♑12.9	5♑25.8	28♉55.5	7♓12.7	15♒29.1	9♈16.1	10♉53.8	21♓25.9	26♑57.0
2 W	8 48 40	13 06 09	23 23 49	0♓35 22	27 50.1	28R 34.8	24R 41.3	11 20.3	6 09.6	29 02.2	7 26.5	15 36.3	9 18.3	10 54.5	21 27.7	26 58.9
3 Th	8 52 37	14 07 04	7♓41 21	14 41 10	27 46.9	28 23.0	24 27.9	11 30.0	6 53.5	29 09.3	7 40.4	15 43.5	9 20.6	10 55.3	21 29.6	27 00.8
4 F	8 56 33	15 07 57	21 34 24	28 20 49	27 43.7	28 12.4	24D 22.7	11 41.8	7 37.4	29 16.8	7 54.4	15 50.7	9 22.9	10 56.1	21 31.5	27 02.7
5 Sa	9 00 30	16 08 49	5♈00 22	11♈33 10	27 40.6	28 04.0	24 25.1	11 55.8	8 21.3	29 24.6	8 08.3	15 57.9	9 25.2	10 57.0	21 33.5	27 04.6
6 Su	9 04 26	17 09 39	17 59 30	24 19 44	27 37.4	27 58.2	24 34.7	12 11.8	9 05.2	29 32.7	8 22.4	16 05.0	9 27.6	10 57.9	21 35.4	27 06.5
7 M	9 08 23	18 10 28	0♉34 23	6♉44 00	27 34.2	27 55.1	24 50.9	12 29.9	9 49.2	29 41.2	8 36.4	16 12.2	9 30.1	10 58.9	21 37.4	27 08.4
8 Tu	9 12 19	19 11 16	12 49 14	18 50 46	27 31.0	27D 53.9	25 13.2	12 49.8	10 33.2	29 50.0	8 50.5	16 19.4	9 32.5	11 00.0	21 39.3	27 10.3
9 W	9 16 16	20 12 02	24 49 17	0♊45 29	27 27.9	27R 53.8	25 41.3	13 11.7	11 17.2	29 59.1	9 04.6	16 26.6	9 35.0	11 01.0	21 41.3	27 12.1
10 Th	9 20 13	21 12 47	6♊40 06	12 33 48	27 24.7	27 53.7	26 14.5	13 35.4	12 01.2	0♊08.6	9 18.7	16 33.8	9 37.6	11 02.2	21 43.4	27 14.0
11 F	9 24 09	22 13 30	18 27 15	24 21 05	27 21.5	27 52.2	26 52.5	14 00.8	12 45.3	0 18.3	9 32.9	16 41.0	9 40.2	11 03.4	21 45.4	27 15.8
12 Sa	9 28 06	23 14 11	0♋15 53	6♋12 12	27 18.3	27 48.6	27 34.9	14 28.0	13 29.5	0 28.4	9 47.1	16 48.2	9 42.8	11 04.6	21 47.4	27 17.6
13 Su	9 32 02	24 14 51	12 10 31	18 11 15	27 15.2	27 42.2	28 21.3	14 56.7	14 13.6	0 38.8	10 01.4	16 55.3	9 45.5	11 05.9	21 49.5	27 19.4
14 M	9 35 59	25 15 30	24 14 44	0♌21 17	27 12.0	27 33.0	29 11.3	15 27.1	14 57.8	0 49.5	10 15.6	17 02.5	9 48.1	11 07.2	21 51.6	27 21.2
15 Tu	9 39 55	26 16 07	6♌31 07	12 44 21	27 08.8	27 21.2	0♒04.8	15 58.9	15 42.0	1 00.4	10 29.9	17 09.6	9 50.9	11 08.6	21 53.7	27 23.0
16 W	9 43 52	27 16 42	19 01 04	25 21 18	27 05.6	27 07.7	1 01.3	16 32.2	16 26.3	1 11.7	10 44.2	17 16.8	9 53.6	11 10.0	21 55.8	27 24.8
17 Th	9 47 48	28 17 16	1♍44 58	8♍11 59	27 02.4	26 53.6	2 00.7	17 06.9	17 10.6	1 23.2	10 58.5	17 23.9	9 56.4	11 11.5	21 57.9	27 26.6
18 F	9 51 45	29 17 48	14 42 13	21 15 31	26 59.3	26 40.2	3 02.8	17 43.0	17 54.9	1 35.0	11 12.9	17 31.0	9 59.2	11 13.0	22 00.0	27 28.3
19 Sa	9 55 42	0♓18 19	27 51 42	4♎30 36	26 56.1	26 28.6	4 07.3	18 20.4	18 39.2	1 47.1	11 27.3	17 38.1	10 02.1	11 14.6	22 02.1	27 30.0
20 Su	9 59 38	1 18 48	11♎12 05	17 56 00	26 52.9	26 19.8	5 14.1	18 59.0	19 23.6	1 59.5	11 41.7	17 45.1	10 05.0	11 16.2	22 04.3	27 31.8
21 M	10 03 35	2 19 16	24 42 16	1♏30 49	26 49.7	26 14.1	6 23.0	19 38.8	20 08.0	2 12.1	11 56.1	17 52.2	10 07.9	11 17.9	22 06.5	27 33.5
22 Tu	10 07 31	3 19 43	8♏21 37	15 14 39	26 46.5	26 11.2	7 33.9	20 19.8	20 52.5	2 25.0	12 10.5	17 59.2	10 10.8	11 19.6	22 08.6	27 35.1
23 W	10 11 28	4 20 08	22 09 58	29 07 33	26 43.4	26 10.4	8 46.7	21 01.9	21 36.9	2 38.2	12 24.9	18 06.3	10 13.8	11 21.3	22 10.8	27 36.8
24 Th	10 15 24	5 20 32	6♐07 25	13♐09 35	26 40.2	26 10.4	10 01.3	21 45.0	22 21.4	2 51.6	12 39.4	18 13.3	10 16.8	11 23.1	22 13.0	27 38.5
25 F	10 19 21	6 20 55	20 13 58	27 20 27	26 37.0	26 09.8	11 17.5	22 29.2	23 06.0	3 05.3	12 53.8	18 20.2	10 19.8	11 25.0	22 15.2	27 40.1
26 Sa	10 23 17	7 21 17	4♑28 49	11♑38 48	26 33.8	26 07.6	12 35.3	23 14.3	23 50.6	3 19.2	13 08.3	18 27.2	10 22.9	11 26.9	22 17.4	27 41.7
27 Su	10 27 14	8 21 37	18 50 00	26 01 54	26 30.7	26 02.7	13 54.6	24 00.4	24 35.2	3 33.4	13 22.8	18 34.1	10 25.9	11 28.8	22 19.6	27 43.3
28 M	10 31 11	9♓21 55	3♒13 56	10♒25 26	26♉27.5	25♉54.9	15♒15.4	24♑47.3	25♑19.8	3♊47.8	13♓37.3	18♒41.0	10♈29.0	11♉30.8	22♓21.9	27♑44.9

1st of Month

Julian Day # 2459611.5
Obliquity 23°26'16"
SVP 4♓57'17"
GC 27♐08.9
Eris 23♈43.5

Day	⚴	Day	⚵	Day	⚶
1	25♓29.4	1	29♑37.0	1	10♑58.2
6	27 09.3	6	1♒36.6	6	13 34.0
11	28 51.9	11	3 36.2	11	16 08.7
16	0♈37.2	16	5 35.8	16	18 42.0
21	2 24.9	21	7 35.1	21	21 13.9
26	4 14.9	26	9 34.2	26	23 44.3

DECLINATION and LATITUDE

Day	☉ Decl	☽ Decl	☽ Lat	☽ 12h Decl	☿ Decl	☿ Lat	♀ Decl	♀ Lat	♂ Decl	♂ Lat	⚳ Decl	⚳ Lat	♃ Decl	♃ Lat	♄ Decl	♄ Lat
1 Tu	17S10	22S37	4S43	20S41	17S60	3N11	16S15	6N44	23S49	0S29	19N40	0S15	9S46	0S58	17S00	0S51
2 W	16 53	18 26	5 00	15 57	18 12	3 02	16 17	6 42	23 48	0 30	19 44	0 12	9 41	0 58	16 58	0 51
3 Th	16 36	13 17	4 57	10 28	18 24	2 52	16 19	6 39	23 46	0 31	19 49	0 09	9 36	0 58	16 56	0 51
4 F	16 18	7 35	4 37	4 39	18 35	2 41	16 21	6 36	23 45	0 32	19 54	0 06	9 30	0 58	16 54	0 51
5 Sa	15 60	1 43	4 02	1N12	18 46	2 31	16 23	6 32	23 43	0 32	19 58	0 03	9 25	0 58	16 52	0 51
6 Su	15 41	4N03	3 15	6 50	18 55	2 19	16 26	6 29	23 41	0 33	20 03	0 00	9 20	0 58	16 50	0 51
7 M	15 23	9 30	2 19	12 02	19 04	2 08	16 28	6 24	23 38	0 34	20 07	0N02	9 15	0 58	16 48	0 51
8 Tu	15 04	14 26	1 19	16 40	19 11	1 56	16 31	6 20	23 36	0 35	20 12	0 05	9 09	0 58	16 45	0 51
9 W	14 45	18 42	0 16	20 33	19 18	1 44	16 33	6 15	23 33	0 35	20 17	0 08	9 04	0 58	16 43	0 51
10 Th	14 26	22 11	0N46	23 34	19 23	1 33	16 36	6 11	23 29	0 36	20 22	0 11	8 59	0 58	16 41	0 51
11 F	14 06	24 42	1 47	25 34	19 27	1 21	16 38	6 06	23 26	0 37	20 26	0 14	8 53	0 58	16 39	0 51
12 Sa	13 46	26 09	2 42	26 25	19 30	1 10	16 41	6 00	23 23	0 37	20 31	0 17	8 48	0 58	16 37	0 52
13 Su	13 26	26 23	3 31	26 03	19 32	0 58	16 43	5 55	23 19	0 38	20 36	0 19	8 43	0 58	16 35	0 52
14 M	13 06	25 23	4 11	24 25	19 33	0 47	16 46	5 49	23 15	0 39	20 41	0 22	8 37	0 58	16 33	0 52
15 Tu	12 46	23 10	4 40	21 37	19 32	0 37	16 48	5 43	23 10	0 40	20 46	0 25	8 32	0 58	16 31	0 52
16 W	12 25	19 49	4 57	17 46	19 30	0 26	16 50	5 37	23 06	0 40	20 50	0 27	8 26	0 58	16 29	0 52
17 Th	12 04	15 30	4 59	13 02	19 27	0 16	16 52	5 31	23 01	0 41	20 55	0 30	8 21	0 58	16 27	0 52
18 F	11 43	10 24	4 45	7 39	19 23	0 06	16 53	5 25	22 56	0 42	21 00	0 32	8 15	0 58	16 25	0 52
19 Sa	11 22	4 46	4 17	1 50	19 17	0S04	16 55	5 19	22 51	0 43	21 05	0 35	8 10	0 58	16 22	0 52
20 Su	11 00	1S09	3 34	4S09	19 11	0 13	16 56	5 13	22 45	0 43	21 10	0 37	8 05	0 58	16 20	0 52
21 M	10 39	7 07	2 38	10 01	19 02	0 23	16 57	5 06	22 39	0 44	21 15	0 40	7 59	0 58	16 18	0 52
22 Tu	10 17	12 50	1 33	15 29	18 53	0 31	16 57	4 60	22 33	0 45	21 20	0 42	7 54	0 58	16 16	0 52
23 W	9 55	17 58	0 21	20 13	18 42	0 40	16 58	4 53	22 27	0 46	21 25	0 45	7 48	0 58	16 14	0 52
24 Th	9 33	22 11	0S52	23 51	18 30	0 48	16 58	4 47	22 21	0 46	21 30	0 47	7 43	0 58	16 12	0 53
25 F	9 11	25 08	2 04	26 01	18 17	0 56	16 58	4 40	22 14	0 47	21 35	0 50	7 37	0 58	16 10	0 53
26 Sa	8 49	26 29	3 08	26 31	18 02	1 03	16 57	4 33	22 07	0 48	21 40	0 52	7 31	0 58	16 08	0 53
27 Su	8 26	26 05	4 01	25 13	17 46	1 10	16 56	4 26	22 00	0 49	21 45	0 54	7 26	0 58	16 06	0 53
28 M	8S03	23S56	4S38	22S17	17S29	1S17	16S55	4N20	21S53	0S49	21N50	0N57	7S20	0S59	16S04	0S53

Day	⚷ Decl	⚷ Lat	♅ Decl	♅ Lat	♆ Decl	♆ Lat	♇ Decl	♇ Lat
1	5N35	2N04	14N43	0S23	4S26	1S07	22S30	1S46
6	5 38	2 04	14 45	0 23	4 22	1 07	22 29	1 47
11	5 43	2 03	14 47	0 23	4 18	1 07	22 28	1 47
16	5 47	2 02	14 49	0 23	4 14	1 07	22 26	1 48
21	5 52	2 01	14 51	0 23	4 10	1 07	22 25	1 49
26	5N58	2N01	14N54	0S23	4S05	1S07	22S24	1S49

Day	⚴ Decl	⚴ Lat	⚵ Decl	⚵ Lat	⚶ Decl	⚶ Lat	Eris Decl	Eris Lat
1	10S05	9S03	12S22	8N02	21S28	1N31	1S18	11S18
6	9 42	9 21	12 01	7 59	21 22	1 24	1 17	11 17
11	9 18	9 39	11 39	7 55	21 12	1 16	1 16	11 16
16	8 53	9 57	11 15	7 51	21 01	1 08	1 15	11 16
21	8 27	10 15	10 49	7 48	20 47	0 60	1 13	11 15
26	8S00	10S34	10S22	7N45	20S31	0N51	1S12	11S14

Moon Phenomena

Max/0 Decl
dy hr mn
5 7:02 0 N
12 16:47 26N26
19 19:22 0 S
26 6:34 26S33

Max/0 Lat
dy hr mn
2 8:31 5S01
9 6:13 0 N
16 15:04 5N00
23 6:55 0 S

Perigee/Apogee
dy hr m kilometers
11 2:38 a 404896
26 22:26 p 367789

PH dy hr mn
● 1 5:47 12♒20
☽ 8 13:51 19♉46
○ 16 16:58 28♌00
☾ 23 22:34 5♐17

Void of Course Moon

Last Aspect			☽ Ingress	
1 11:02	♄	☌	♓	2 11:01
4 9:42	♇	⚹	♈	4 14:58
6 17:22	♇	□	♉	6 22:54
9 4:49	♇	△	♊	9 10:28
11 8:24	☉	△	♋	11 23:28
14 10:28	☿	☍	♌	14 11:18
16 16:58	☉	☍	♍	16 20:44
18 23:21	♇	△	♎	19 3:52
21 5:03	♇	□	♏	21 9:20
23 9:25	♇	⚹	♐	23 13:30
25 3:26	♆	□	♑	25 16:29
27 14:51	♇	☌	♒	27 18:37

DAILY ASPECTARIAN

1 Tu
☽ ∥ ♇ 0:45
☽ ⚹ ⚷ 0:47
☽ □ ♅ 3:27
☽ ⚺ ♀ 3:59
☉ ☌ ☽ 5:47
☽ ☌ ♄ 11:02
☉ ∥ ♄ 16:02
☽ ⋕ ⚳ 17:18
☽ ∠ ♂ 20:06
☽ ⚺ ♆ 20:47
⚵ ♒ 23:06

2 W
☽ ∥ ☿ 1:08
☽ ∠ ⚷ 1:31
☽ ⚺ ☿ 2:06
☽ ∠ ♀ 4:57
☽ ⚺ ♇ 5:59
☽ ∥ ♄ 7:17
☉ ∥ ☽ 8:06
☽ □ ⚳ 9:29
☽ ∥ ♀ 10:25
☽ ⋕ ♅ 17:35
☽ ⚹ ♂ 22:34
☽ ☌ ♃ 23:58

3 Th
☽ ⚺ ⚷ 2:50
☽ ∠ ☿ 3:00
☽ ⚹ ♅ 5:32
☽ ⚹ ♀ 6:36
☽ ∠ ♇ 7:25
☉ ⚺ ☽ 11:53
☽ ⚺ ♄ 13:55
☽ ∥ ♃ 15:56
☉ ∥ ♀ 20:13
☽ ☌ ♆ 23:55

4 F
☿ D 4:14
☽ ⚹ ☿ 4:57
☽ ∠ ♅ 7:43
☽ ⋕ ⚷ 8:03
☽ ⚹ ♇ 9:42
☽ ∥ ♆ 13:05
♂ ⚹ ♃ 13:39
☽ ⚹ ⚳ 13:48
☉ ∠ ☽ 16:27
☽ ∠ ♄ 16:38
☉ ☌ ♄ 19:06

5 Sa
☽ ⚺ ♃ 5:49
☽ □ ♂ 6:28
☽ ☌ ⚷ 8:06
☽ ⚺ ♅ 10:54
☽ □ ♀ 12:57
☽ ∠ ⚳ 17:29
☽ ⚹ ♄ 20:23
☉ ⚹ ☽ 22:18

6 Su
☽ ⋕ ♆ 1:19
☽ ⚺ ♆ 6:49
☽ ∥ ⚷ 6:50
☽ ∠ ♃ 10:22
☽ □ ☿ 12:43
♂ □ ⚷ 12:58
☽ □ ♇ 17:22
☽ ⚺ ⚳ 22:16
☽ ⋕ ♃ 22:52

7 M
☽ ∠ ♆ 11:49
☽ ⚹ ♃ 15:59
☽ ⚺ ⚷ 17:30
☽ △ ♂ 19:14
☽ ☌ ♅ 20:23

8 Tu
☽ △ ♀ 0:01
☽ ∥ ♅ 1:43
☉ ⋕ ☽ 3:08
☽ □ ♄ 7:02
☽ ⋕ ♀ 11:17
☽ ⋕ ♄ 12:27
☊ D 13:39
☉ □ ☽ 13:51
♂ △ ♅ 14:58
☽ ⚹ ♆ 17:41
☉ ⋕ ♅ 22:58
☽ ∠ ⚷ 23:31

9 W
☽ △ ☿ 1:50
⚳ ♊ 2:14
☽ ⚼ ♂ 3:09
☽ ⋕ ☿ 3:46
☽ △ ♇ 4:49
☊ R 6:14
☽ ⚼ ♀ 7:02
☽ ∥ ⚳ 10:21
☽ ☌ ⚳ 10:34

10 Th
☽ ⋕ ♇ 2:17
☽ □ ♃ 5:29
☽ ⚹ ⚷ 6:02
☽ ⚺ ♅ 8:54
☽ ⚼ ☿ 9:49
☽ ⋕ ♂ 11:01
☽ ⚼ ♇ 11:21
☽ ⚻ ♂ 11:37
☉ ⚺ ♆ 12:30
☽ ⚻ ♀ 14:37
☽ △ ♄ 20:21

11 F
♀ ∥ ♄ 4:00
☽ □ ♆ 6:44
☉ △ ☽ 8:24
☿ ☌ ♇ 14:05
♃ ⚺ ⚷ 15:02
☽ ∠ ♅ 15:29
☽ ⚻ ♇ 17:58
☽ ⚻ ☿ 18:12

12 Sa
☽ ⚺ ⚳ 0:26
☽ ⚼ ♄ 3:09
☉ ⚼ ☽ 17:35
☽ □ ⚷ 19:08
☽ △ ♃ 19:36
☽ ⚹ ♅ 21:50

13 Su
☽ ☍ ♂ 4:22
☽ ☍ ♀ 5:47
☽ ∠ ⚳ 7:02
☽ ⚻ ♄ 9:35
☉ ∠ ⚷ 12:40
☽ △ ♆ 19:16

14 M
☽ ⚼ ♃ 2:02
☉ ⚻ ☽ 2:11
♀ ♈ 5:54
☽ ☍ ♇ 6:08
☽ ☍ ☿ 10:28
☽ ⚹ ⚳ 13:07
☿ ♒ 21:55
☽ ⋕ ♂ 23:57

15 Tu
☽ ⚼ ♆ 0:44
♀ ⚼ ⚳ 1:42
☽ ⋕ ♇ 5:52
☽ △ ⚷ 6:28
☽ ⚻ ♃ 7:50
☽ □ ♅ 8:57
♂ ⚼ ⚳ 13:21
☽ ∥ ⚳ 17:32
☽ ⚻ ♂ 18:47
☽ ⚻ ♀ 19:03
☽ ☍ ♄ 20:39

16 W
☽ ⋕ ☿ 1:55
☉ ⚺ ♇ 3:19
☿ △ ⚳ 5:18
☽ ⚻ ♆ 5:33
☽ ⚼ ⚷ 11:10
♀ ☌ ♂ 14:30
☽ ⚻ ♇ 15:55
☽ ⋕ ♀ 16:57
☉ ☍ ☽ 16:58
☽ ⋕ ♄ 19:04
☽ □ ⚳ 23:19

17 Th
☽ ⚻ ☿ 0:32
☽ ⚼ ♀ 0:43
☽ ⚼ ♂ 0:51
☽ ∥ ♅ 3:22
♂ ⚺ ♄ 8:36
♀ ⚺ ♄ 14:10
☽ ⚻ ⚷ 15:17
☽ ☍ ♃ 17:27
☽ △ ♅ 17:34
☉ ⋕ ☽ 17:40
☽ ⚼ ♇ 19:53

18 F
♃ ⚹ ♅ 0:14
☽ ⚻ ♄ 5:12
☽ △ ♀ 5:48
☽ △ ♂ 6:14
☽ ⚼ ☿ 6:40
☽ ⋕ ♃ 9:32
☽ ☍ ♆ 13:23
☉ ♓ 16:44
☽ ∥ ⚷ 19:36
☽ ⚼ ♅ 21:04
☽ △ ♇ 23:21

19 Sa
☽ ⋕ ♆ 2:25
☉ ⚻ ☽ 4:47
☽ △ ⚳ 7:12
☽ ⚼ ♄ 8:42
☽ △ ☿ 12:19
☽ ☍ ⚷ 21:59

20 Su
☽ ⚻ ♅ 0:07
☽ ⚻ ♃ 0:54
☉ ⚼ ☽ 9:51
☽ ⚼ ⚳ 10:29
☽ △ ♄ 11:47
☽ ∥ ♆ 12:04
☽ □ ♀ 14:35
☽ □ ♂ 15:26
☽ ⋕ ⚷ 18:56
☽ ⚻ ♆ 19:24
☉ □ ⚳ 20:25

21 M
☽ ∥ ♃ 3:29
☽ ⚼ ♃ 4:00
☽ □ ♇ 5:03
☽ ⚻ ⚳ 13:25
☉ ∥ ☽ 13:45
☉ △ ☽ 14:29
☿ ∠ ♆ 15:14
☽ ⚼ ♆ 21:52
☽ □ ☿ 22:29

22 Tu
☽ ⚻ ⚷ 3:11
☽ ☍ ♅ 5:11
☽ △ ♃ 6:47
☽ ⋕ ♅ 9:08
☽ ∥ ♄ 15:34
☽ □ ♄ 16:54
☽ ∥ ♀ 19:01
☽ ⚹ ♀ 21:56
☽ ⚹ ♂ 23:00

23 W
☽ △ ♆ 0:01
☽ ∥ ☿ 3:38
☽ ⚼ ⚷ 5:19
♂ ∥ ♇ 9:16
☽ ⚹ ♇ 9:25
☽ ☍ ⚳ 18:19
♂ ⚹ ♆ 19:13
☽ ⋕ ⚳ 19:31
♃ ∠ ♇ 22:18
☉ □ ☽ 22:34

24 Th
☽ ∥ ♂ 1:01
☽ ∠ ♀ 1:08
☽ ∥ ♇ 1:29
☽ ∠ ♂ 2:14
☿ ⚹ ⚷ 5:07
☽ △ ⚷ 7:07
☽ ⚹ ☿ 7:19
☽ ⚻ ♅ 9:00
☽ ∠ ♇ 11:08
☽ □ ♃ 11:20
♀ ⚹ ♆ 16:05
☽ ⚹ ♄ 20:46

25 F
☿ □ ♅ 2:23
☽ □ ♆ 3:26
☽ ⚺ ♀ 4:01
☽ ⚺ ♂ 5:07
☽ ⚼ ♅ 10:28
☽ ∠ ☿ 11:15
☽ ⚺ ♇ 12:34
☽ ⚻ ⚳ 22:01
☽ ∠ ♄ 22:16

26 Sa
☉ ⚹ ☽ 5:11
☽ □ ⚷ 9:55
☽ △ ♅ 11:42
☿ ⚺ ♃ 12:17
☽ ⚹ ♃ 14:44
☽ ⚺ ☿ 14:57
☽ ⚼ ⚳ 23:32
☽ ⚺ ♄ 23:33

27 Su
☽ ⚹ ♆ 5:50
☉ ∠ ☽ 8:07
☽ ☌ ♀ 9:07
☽ ☌ ♂ 10:07
☽ ☌ ♇ 14:51
☽ ∠ ♃ 16:11

28 M
☽ △ ⚳ 0:57
♂ ⋕ ⚳ 4:59
☽ ∠ ♆ 6:55
☉ ⚺ ☽ 11:00
☽ ∥ ♇ 11:14
☽ ⚹ ⚷ 12:09
☽ □ ♅ 13:51
☽ ⋕ ⚳ 14:31
☽ ∥ ♂ 15:03
☽ ⚺ ♃ 17:39
☽ ☌ ☿ 22:12

February 2022:Modify New York Stock Exchange Zone:-5

Sunday	Monday	Tuesday	Wednesday	Thursday	Friday	Saturday
		1 12:45AM New Moon♒	2 5:58AM ☽-> 0♓00	3 11:11PM ☿ Direct	4 8:37AM ♂ ✶ ♃ 9:55AM ☽-> 0♈00 2:04PM ☉ ☌ ♄	5
6 5:51PM ☽-> 0♉00	7	8 9:56AM ♂ △ ♅	9 5:25AM ☽-> 0♊00	10	11 9:03AM ☿ ☌ ♇ 6:25PM ☽-> 0♋00	12
13	14 6:16AM ☽-> 0♌00 4:53PM ☿ -> 0♒00	15	16 9:27AM ♂ ☌ ♀ 11:55AM Full Moon♌ 3:41PM ☽-> 0♍00	17 7:12PM ♃ ✶ ♅	18 11:42AM ☉-> 0♓00 10:49PM ☽-> 0♎00	19
20	21 4:18AM ☽-> 0♏00	22	23 8:27AM ☽-> 0♐00 2:11PM ♂ ✶ ♆	24 11:03AM ♀ ✶ ♆ 9:20PM ☿ □ ♅	25 11:26AM ☽-> 0♑00	26
27 1:34PM ☽-> 0♒00	28					

January

S	M	T	W	T	F	S
						1
2	3	4	5	6	7	8
9	10	11	12	13	14	15
16	17	18	19	20	21	22
23	24	25	26	27	28	29
30	31					

March

S	M	T	W	T	F	S
		1	2	3	4	5
6	7	8	9	10	11	12
13	14	15	16	17	18	19
20	21	22	23	24	25	26
27	28	29	30	31		

March 2022

LONGITUDE

Day	Sid.Time	☉	☽	☽ 12 hour	Mean☊	True☊	☿	♀	♂	⚳	♃	♄	⚷	♅	♆	♇
	h m s	° ' "	° ' "	° ' "	° '	° '	° '	° '	° '	° '	° '	° '	° '	° '	° '	° '
1 Tu	10 35 07	10♓22 12	17♒35 39	24♒43 50	26♉24.3	25♉44.7	16♒37.6	25♑35.1	26♑04.4	4♊02.4	13♓51.8	18♒47.9	10♈32.2	11♉32.8	22♓24.1	27♑46.5
2 W	10 39 04	11 22 28	1♓49 15	8♓51 09	26 21.1	25R 33.0	18 01.1	26 23.8	26 49.1	4 17.3	14 06.3	18 54.8	10 35.3	11 34.8	22 26.3	27 48.0
3 Th	10 43 00	12 22 41	15 48 55	22 41 57	26 18.0	25 21.1	19 25.9	27 13.2	27 33.8	4 32.4	14 20.9	19 01.6	10 38.5	11 36.9	22 28.6	27 49.5
4 F	10 46 57	13 22 53	29 29 50	6♈12 15	26 14.8	25 10.1	20 52.0	28 03.4	28 18.5	4 47.8	14 35.4	19 08.4	10 41.7	11 39.1	22 30.8	27 51.1
5 Sa	10 50 53	14 23 03	12♈49 00	19 20 04	26 11.6	25 01.2	22 19.3	28 54.3	29 03.3	5 03.3	14 49.9	19 15.2	10 44.9	11 41.3	22 33.1	27 52.5
6 Su	10 54 50	15 23 11	25 45 31	2♉05 34	26 08.4	24 54.9	23 47.9	29 45.9	29 48.1	5 19.1	15 04.4	19 21.9	10 48.1	11 43.5	22 35.4	27 54.0
7 M	10 58 46	16 23 16	8♉20 33	14 30 51	26 05.2	24 51.3	25 17.6	0♒38.1	0♒32.9	5 35.1	15 18.9	19 28.6	10 51.4	11 45.7	22 37.6	27 55.4
8 Tu	11 02 43	17 23 20	20 37 01	26 39 33	26 02.1	24D 50.0	26 48.5	1 31.0	1 17.7	5 51.3	15 33.5	19 35.3	10 54.7	11 48.0	22 39.9	27 56.9
9 W	11 06 39	18 23 22	2♊39 07	8♊36 20	25 58.9	24 50.1	28 20.6	2 24.6	2 02.5	6 07.7	15 48.0	19 41.9	10 58.0	11 50.4	22 42.2	27 58.3
10 Th	11 10 36	19 23 21	14 31 52	20 26 25	25 55.7	24R 50.7	29 53.9	3 18.7	2 47.4	6 24.3	16 02.5	19 48.5	11 01.3	11 52.8	22 44.4	27 59.7
11 F	11 14 33	20 23 19	26 20 41	2♋15 19	25 52.5	24 50.6	1♓28.3	4 13.4	3 32.3	6 41.2	16 17.0	19 55.1	11 04.6	11 55.2	22 46.7	28 01.0
12 Sa	11 18 29	21 23 14	8♋11 00	14 08 22	25 49.4	24 48.9	3 03.9	5 08.6	4 17.2	6 58.2	16 31.5	20 01.6	11 08.0	11 57.6	22 49.0	28 02.3
13 Su	11 22 26	22 23 07	20 07 59	26 10 25	25 46.2	24 45.1	4 40.7	6 04.4	5 02.1	7 15.4	16 46.0	20 08.1	11 11.4	12 00.1	22 51.3	28 03.7
14 M	11 26 22	23 22 58	2♌16 10	8♌25 37	25 43.0	24 38.9	6 18.6	7 00.7	5 47.0	7 32.8	17 00.4	20 14.5	11 14.7	12 02.6	22 53.6	28 05.0
15 Tu	11 30 19	24 22 47	14 39 10	20 57 02	25 39.8	24 30.5	7 57.7	7 57.5	6 32.0	7 50.3	17 14.9	20 20.9	11 18.1	12 05.2	22 55.8	28 06.2
16 W	11 34 15	25 22 33	27 19 25	3♍46 23	25 36.6	24 20.5	9 38.0	8 54.8	7 17.0	8 08.1	17 29.3	20 27.2	11 21.5	12 07.8	22 58.1	28 07.5
17 Th	11 38 12	26 22 18	10♍17 56	16 53 58	25 33.5	24 10.0	11 19.5	9 52.5	8 02.0	8 26.0	17 43.8	20 33.6	11 25.0	12 10.4	23 00.4	28 08.7
18 F	11 42 08	27 22 00	23 34 16	0♎18 35	25 30.3	23 59.8	13 02.2	10 50.7	8 47.0	8 44.1	17 58.2	20 39.8	11 28.4	12 13.1	23 02.7	28 09.9
19 Sa	11 46 05	28 21 40	7♎06 36	13 57 56	25 27.1	23 51.2	14 46.1	11 49.3	9 32.1	9 02.4	18 12.6	20 46.0	11 31.8	12 15.7	23 04.9	28 11.0
20 Su	11 50 02	29 21 19	20 52 11	27 48 55	25 23.9	23 44.7	16 31.3	12 48.3	10 17.2	9 20.9	18 27.0	20 52.2	11 35.3	12 18.5	23 07.2	28 12.2
21 M	11 53 58	0♈20 55	4♏47 44	11♏48 15	25 20.8	23 40.7	18 17.7	13 47.8	11 02.3	9 39.5	18 41.4	20 58.3	11 38.7	12 21.2	23 09.5	28 13.3
22 Tu	11 57 55	1 20 30	18 50 05	25 52 56	25 17.6	23D 39.2	20 05.3	14 47.6	11 47.4	9 58.3	18 55.7	21 04.4	11 42.2	12 24.0	23 11.7	28 14.4
23 W	12 01 51	2 20 03	2♐56 30	10♐00 33	25 14.4	23 39.4	21 54.3	15 47.8	12 32.5	10 17.2	19 10.0	21 10.4	11 45.7	12 26.8	23 14.0	28 15.5
24 Th	12 05 48	3 19 34	17 04 53	24 09 18	25 11.2	23 40.4	23 44.5	16 48.4	13 17.7	10 36.3	19 24.4	21 16.4	11 49.2	12 29.6	23 16.2	28 16.5
25 F	12 09 44	4 19 04	1♑13 39	8♑17 46	25 08.0	23R 41.1	25 36.0	17 49.3	14 02.9	10 55.6	19 38.6	21 22.4	11 52.7	12 32.5	23 18.5	28 17.6
26 Sa	12 13 41	5 18 32	15 21 29	22 24 36	25 04.9	23 40.7	27 28.8	18 50.5	14 48.1	11 15.0	19 52.9	21 28.2	11 56.2	12 35.4	23 20.7	28 18.6
27 Su	12 17 37	6 17 58	29 26 56	6♒28 13	25 01.7	23 38.5	29 22.8	19 52.1	15 33.3	11 34.5	20 07.1	21 34.1	11 59.7	12 38.3	23 23.0	28 19.5
28 M	12 21 34	7 17 22	13♒28 11	20 26 31	24 58.5	23 34.1	1♈18.2	20 54.0	16 18.5	11 54.2	20 21.4	21 39.8	12 03.2	12 41.3	23 25.2	28 20.5
29 Tu	12 25 31	8 16 45	27 22 52	4♓16 53	24 55.3	23 28.0	3 14.8	21 56.2	17 03.7	12 14.1	20 35.5	21 45.5	12 06.7	12 44.3	23 27.4	28 21.4
30 W	12 29 27	9 16 05	11♓08 12	17 56 26	24 52.2	23 20.8	5 12.6	22 58.7	17 49.0	12 34.1	20 49.7	21 51.2	12 10.2	12 47.3	23 29.6	28 22.3
31 Th	12 33 24	10♈15 24	24 41 16	1♈22 24	24♉49.0	23♉13.3	7♈11.7	24♒01.5	18♒34.3	12♊54.2	21♓03.8	21♒56.8	12♈13.7	12♉50.3	23♓31.8	28♑23.1

1st of Month

Julian Day # 2459639.5
Obliquity 23°26'17"
SVP 4♓57'14"
GC 27♐08.9
Eris 23♈53.7

Day	⚴
1	5♈22.0
6	7 15.4
11	9 10.8
16	11 08.0
21	13 06.8
26	15 07.3
31	17 09.4

Day	⚵
1	10♒45.5
6	12 43.9
11	14 41.6
16	16 38.6
21	18 34.8
26	20 30.0
31	22 24.1

Day	⚶
1	25♑13.7
6	27 41.2
11	0♒06.8
16	2 30.2
21	4 51.3
26	7 10.1
31	9 26.2

DECLINATION and LATITUDE

Day	☉ Decl	☽ Decl	☽ Lat	☽12h Decl	☿ Decl	☿ Lat	♀ Decl	♀ Lat	♂ Decl	♂ Lat	⚳ Decl	⚳ Lat	♃ Decl	♃ Lat	♄ Decl	♄ Lat
1 Tu	7S41	20S17	4S58	18S00	17S11	1S24	16S53	4N13	21S45	0S50	21N55	0N59	7S15	0S59	16S02	0S53
2 W	7 18	15 29	4 59	12 46	16 51	1 30	16 50	4 06	21 37	0 51	22 00	1 01	7 09	0 59	15 60	0 53
3 Th	6 55	9 56	4 42	6 60	16 30	1 35	16 48	3 59	21 29	0 52	22 05	1 03	7 04	0 59	15 58	0 53
4 F	6 32	4 01	4 09	1 02	16 08	1 41	16 45	3 52	21 21	0 52	22 10	1 06	6 58	0 59	15 56	0 53
5 Sa	6 09	1N56	3 24	4N50	15 44	1 46	16 42	3 45	21 13	0 53	22 15	1 08	6 53	0 59	15 54	0 53
6 Su	5 46	7 39	2 28	10 21	15 19	1 50	16 38	3 39	21 04	0 54	22 20	1 10	6 47	0 59	15 52	0 54
7 M	5 22	12 55	1 27	15 19	14 53	1 54	16 34	3 32	20 55	0 55	22 25	1 12	6 41	0 59	15 50	0 54
8 Tu	4 59	17 33	0 22	19 34	14 26	1 58	16 29	3 25	20 46	0 55	22 30	1 14	6 36	0 59	15 48	0 54
9 W	4 35	21 22	0N42	22 56	13 57	2 02	16 24	3 18	20 37	0 56	22 35	1 17	6 30	0 59	15 46	0 54
10 Th	4 12	24 15	1 43	25 17	13 27	2 05	16 19	3 11	20 27	0 57	22 40	1 19	6 25	0 59	15 44	0 54
11 F	3 48	26 03	2 40	26 31	12 56	2 07	16 13	3 05	20 18	0 58	22 45	1 21	6 19	0 59	15 42	0 54
12 Sa	3 25	26 40	3 30	26 32	12 24	2 10	16 06	2 58	20 08	0 58	22 50	1 23	6 13	0 59	15 40	0 54
13 Su	3 01	26 04	4 11	25 18	11 50	2 12	15 59	2 51	19 58	0 59	22 55	1 25	6 08	0 59	15 38	0 54
14 M	2 38	24 13	4 42	22 51	11 15	2 13	15 52	2 44	19 47	0 60	22 60	1 27	6 02	0 59	15 36	0 54
15 Tu	2 14	21 13	4 60	19 18	10 39	2 14	15 44	2 38	19 37	1 01	23 05	1 29	5 57	0 59	15 34	0 55
16 W	1 50	17 09	5 04	14 47	10 02	2 15	15 36	2 31	19 26	1 01	23 09	1 31	5 51	0 59	15 32	0 55
17 Th	1 27	12 13	4 52	9 29	9 23	2 15	15 27	2 24	19 15	1 02	23 14	1 33	5 46	0 59	15 30	0 55
18 F	1 03	6 37	4 25	3 38	8 44	2 14	15 18	2 18	19 04	1 03	23 19	1 35	5 40	0 59	15 28	0 55
19 Sa	0 39	0 35	3 43	2S30	8 03	2 13	15 08	2 11	18 53	1 03	23 24	1 37	5 34	0 59	15 26	0 55
20 Su	0 15	5S34	2 46	8 37	7 21	2 12	14 58	2 05	18 42	1 04	23 29	1 39	5 29	0 60	15 24	0 55
21 M	0N08	11 33	1 40	14 22	6 38	2 10	14 47	1 59	18 30	1 05	23 33	1 41	5 23	0 60	15 23	0 55
22 Tu	0 32	17 01	0 26	19 25	5 53	2 08	14 36	1 52	18 18	1 05	23 38	1 43	5 18	0 60	15 21	0 55
23 W	0 56	21 34	0S50	23 23	5 08	2 05	14 25	1 46	18 06	1 06	23 43	1 44	5 12	0 60	15 19	0 55
24 Th	1 19	24 51	2 03	25 55	4 21	2 02	14 13	1 40	17 54	1 07	23 47	1 46	5 07	0 60	15 17	0 56
25 F	1 43	26 34	3 08	26 47	3 34	1 59	14 00	1 34	17 42	1 08	23 52	1 48	5 01	0 60	15 15	0 56
26 Sa	2 07	26 34	4 02	25 55	2 45	1 54	13 47	1 27	17 29	1 09	23 56	1 50	4 56	0 60	15 14	0 56
27 Su	2 30	24 51	4 41	23 24	1 55	1 50	13 34	1 21	17 16	1 09	24 01	1 52	4 50	1 00	15 12	0 56
28 M	2 54	21 37	5 03	19 32	1 05	1 44	13 20	1 15	17 04	1 10	24 05	1 54	4 45	1 00	15 10	0 56
29 Tu	3 17	17 11	5 07	14 38	0 13	1 38	13 06	1 09	16 51	1 11	24 10	1 55	4 39	1 00	15 08	0 56
30 W	3 40	11 55	4 54	9 04	0N40	1 32	12 51	1 04	16 37	1 11	24 14	1 57	4 34	1 00	15 07	0 56
31 Th	4N04	6S08	4S23	3S10	1N33	1S25	12S36	0N58	16S24	1S12	24N19	1N59	4S28	1S00	15S05	0S57

Day	⚷ Decl	⚷ Lat	♅ Decl	♅ Lat	♆ Decl	♆ Lat	♇ Decl	♇ Lat
1	6N01	2N00	14N56	0S23	4S03	1S07	22S24	1S49
6	6 07	1 60	14 60	0 23	3 58	1 07	22 23	1 50
11	6 13	1 59	15 03	0 22	3 54	1 07	22 22	1 51
16	6 19	1 59	15 07	0 22	3 49	1 07	22 21	1 51
21	6 25	1 58	15 11	0 22	3 45	1 07	22 21	1 52
26	6 32	1 58	15 16	0 22	3 40	1 07	22 20	1 53
31	6N38	1N58	15N20	0S22	3S36	1S07	22S20	1S53

Day	⚴ Decl	⚴ Lat	⚵ Decl	⚵ Lat	⚶ Decl	⚶ Lat	Eris Decl	Eris Lat
1	7S44	10S45	10S06	7N43	20S20	0N46	1S11	11S14
6	7 17	11 04	9 37	7 41	20 01	0 37	1 10	11 13
11	6 50	11 24	9 07	7 38	19 40	0 28	1 08	11 13
16	6 23	11 43	8 36	7 36	19 18	0 19	1 07	11 12
21	5 56	12 04	8 04	7 33	18 54	0 09	1 05	11 12
26	5 30	12 24	7 31	7 31	18 30	0S01	1 04	11 12
31	5S03	12S45	6S57	7N29	18S05	0S11	1S02	11S11

Moon Phenomena

Max/0 Decl (dy hr mn)
4 16:08 0 N
12 0:15 26N40
19 2:18 0 S
25 11:54 26S47

Max/0 Lat (dy hr mn)
1 13:32 5S01
8 8:22 0 N
15 18:29 5N04
22 8:13 0 S
28 17:17 5S08

Perigee/Apogee (dy hr m kilometers)
10 23:05 a 404268
23 23:39 p 369760

PH dy hr mn
● 2 17:36 12♓07
☽ 10 10:47 19♊50
○ 18 7:19 27♍40
☾ 25 5:38 4♑33

Void of Course Moon

Last Aspect	☽ Ingress
1 2:02 ♄ ☌	♓ 1 20:55
3 21:46 ♂ ⚹	♈ 4 0:54
6 4:03 ♇ □	♉ 6 8:01
8 14:36 ♇ △	♊ 8 18:41
10 16:44 ♆ □	♋ 11 7:25
13 15:45 ♇ ☍	♌ 13 19:33
15 10:57 ♄ ☍	♍ 16 5:00
18 8:12 ♇ △	♎ 18 11:27
20 12:41 ♇ □	♏ 20 15:46
22 16:02 ♇ ⚹	♐ 22 19:00
24 13:00 ♆ □	♑ 24 21:55
26 23:52 ☿ ⚹	♒ 27 0:56
28 14:12 ♄ ☌	♓ 29 4:33
31 6:38 ♇ ⚹	♈ 31 9:32

DAILY ASPECTARIAN

1 Tu ☽☌♄ 2:02; ☉⊻⚷ 4:11; ☽⊻♆ 8:06; ☽∠⚷ 13:25; ☽⊻♀ 14:15; ☽⊻♂ 15:03; ☽∥☿ 17:09; ☽⊻♇ 17:10; ☽∥♀ 17:35; ☽∥♄ 21:37

2 W ☿∥♀ 0:26; ☽#♅ 2:25; ☉∠♀ 2:50; ☽□⚳ 4:17; ☉⚹♅ 5:06; ☉∥♃ 11:55; ☽⊻⚷ 15:02; ☿☌♄ 16:34; ☽⚹♅ 16:44; ☽∠♀ 17:24; ☉☌☽ 17:36; ☽∠♂ 18:04; ☽∠♇ 18:49; ☽☌♃ 21:25

3 Th ☽⊻♄ 5:38; ☽⊻☿ 7:01; ♂☌♇ 8:44; ☉∠♇ 10:59; ☽☌♆ 11:39; ☽∥♃ 11:55; ☉∥☽ 13:11; ☽#⚷ 15:45; ☉∠♂ 17:15; ♀☌♇ 17:57; ☽∠♅ 18:57; ☽⚹♇ 21:04; ☽⚹♀ 21:16; ☽⚹♂ 21:46

4 F ☽∥♆ 0:04; ☽∠♄ 8:22; ☽⚹⚳ 9:39; ☽∠☿ 12:47; ☿∥♄ 13:34; ☽☌⚷ 20:13; ☽⊻♅ 21:56

5 Sa ☉⊻☽ 3:07; ☉#⚷ 3:10; ☽⊻♃ 3:46; ☿⊻♆ 3:51; ☽#♆ 8:25; ☽⚹♄ 11:57; ☽∠⚳ 13:37; ☉☌♃ 14:08; ☉#☽ 16:24; ☽∥⚷ 17:21; ☽⊻♆ 18:03; ☽⚹☿ 19:50; ☽#♃ 20:18

6 Su ☽□♇ 4:03; ♂ ♒ 6:24; ♀ ♒ 6:31; ♀☌♂ 7:14; ☽□♂ 8:07; ☽□♀ 8:08; ☽∠♃ 8:19; ☉∠☽ 9:30; ⚳#♇ 11:34; ♀∠♃ 11:50; ♂∠♃ 12:58; ☿#♅ 17:42; ☽⊻⚳ 18:34; ☽∠♆ 22:37

7 M ☽⊻⚷ 4:54; ☽☌♅ 6:39; ☽#☿ 8:55; ☿∠⚷ 9:17; ☽∥♅ 10:24; ☽⚹♃ 13:51; ☽#♄ 14:32; ☉⚹☽ 17:04; ☽#♀ 18:17; ☽□♄ 21:57

8 Tu ☽⚹♆ 4:04; ☊ D 8:23; ☽∠⚷ 10:33; ☽□☿ 14:06; ☽△♇ 14:36; ☿⊻♇ 18:07; ☽#♂ 19:01; ☽△♂ 22:42; ☽△♀ 23:28

9 W ☽☌⚳ 7:10; ☽#♇ 7:27; ☽∥⚳ 9:25; ☽⚹⚷ 16:51; ☽⊻♅ 18:36; ☽⚼♇ 20:53

10 Th ☿ ♓ 1:33; ☽□♃ 3:08; ☽⚼♂ 7:04; ☽⚼♀ 8:19; ☊ R 10:37; ☉□☽ 10:47; ☽△♄ 10:49; ☉⊻♄ 11:18; ☽□♆ 16:44; ⚶ ♒ 18:23; ☉∥♆ 18:31

11 F ☽∠♅ 1:10; ☽⊼♇ 3:24; ☽△☿ 12:02; ☽⊼♂ 15:35; ☽⊼♀ 17:20; ☽⚼♄ 17:33; ☽⊻⚳ 21:29; ♃#⚷ 22:19

12 Sa ☽□⚷ 5:59; ☽⚹♅ 7:39; ☽△♃ 17:08; ☽⚼☿ 22:57

13 Su ☽⊼♄ 0:00; ☽∠⚳ 4:20; ☉△☽ 4:53; ☽△♆ 5:26; ☿⊻♂ 9:45; ☉☌♆ 11:44; ☽☍♇ 15:45; ☽⚼♃ 23:29

14 M ☽☍♂ 7:19; ☽⊼☿ 9:06; ☽☍♀ 10:01; ☽⚹⚳ 10:32; ☽∥⚳ 10:35; ☽⚼♆ 11:00; ☉⚼☽ 12:57; ☽#♇ 15:51; ☽△⚷ 17:32; ☽□♅ 19:03; ♀△⚳ 19:38; ☿□⚳ 21:50; ♀∠♆ 23:16; ☿⊻♀ 23:52

15 Tu ☽⊼♃ 5:04; ☽#♂ 10:36; ☽☍♄ 10:57; ☽⊼♆ 15:47; ☉⊼☽ 20:02; ☽⚼⚷ 22:11

16 W ☽⊼♇ 1:30; ☽#♀ 8:13; ☽#♄ 8:21; ☽∥♅ 10:18; ♀∥♄ 13:47; ☽⊼♂ 19:36; ☽□⚳ 20:30; ♂∠♆ 23:05; ☽⊼♀ 23:10

17 Th ☿⊻⚷ 1:19; ☽⊼⚷ 2:03; ☽☍☿ 2:09; ☽△♅ 3:26; ☽⚼♇ 5:12; ☿⚹♅ 12:15; ☽☍♃ 13:45; ☽#☿ 14:01; ☽⊼♄ 18:45; ☉∠♅ 20:14; ♂△⚳ 21:24; ☽☍♆ 23:03

18 F ☽⚼♂ 0:24; ☽∥⚷ 1:02; ☿∠♇ 1:48; ☽#♃ 3:54; ☽⚼♀ 4:23; ☽⚼♅ 6:32; ☉☍☽ 7:19; ☽△♇ 8:12; ☽#♆ 11:25; ♀⚹⚷ 16:25; ☉⚹♇ 19:38; ♀#♅ 20:38; ☽⚼♄ 21:37; ☉#☽ 23:44

19 Sa ☽△⚳ 3:28; ☽△♂ 4:30; ☉∥☽ 4:32; ☽☍⚷ 7:47; ☽△♀ 8:54; ☽⊼♅ 9:03; ♀□♅ 11:18; ☽⊼☿ 15:21; ☽∥♆ 16:56; ☽⊼♃ 19:44; ☽∥♃ 23:39

20 Su ☽△♄ 0:00; ☽#⚷ 3:15; ☽⊼♆ 3:54; ☽⚼⚳ 6:09; ☽∥☿ 6:15; ☽□♇ 12:41; ☉ ♈ 15:35; ☉⊼☽ 15:47; ☽⚼☿ 21:03; ☽⚼♃ 22:04

21 M ☽⚼♆ 5:47; ☿☌♃ 6:07; ☿#⚷ 6:37; ☽⊼⚳ 8:31; ☽□♂ 11:18; ☽⊼⚷ 11:47; ☽☍♅ 12:59; ☽∥♀ 13:24; ☽#♅ 15:40; ☽∥♄ 16:23; ☽□♀ 16:35; ☉⚼☽ 19:26; ♂⚹⚷ 21:01

22 Tu ☽△♃ 0:10; ☽△☿ 2:27; ☽□♄ 3:51; ☽∥♂ 6:02; ☽△♆ 7:27; ☊ D 8:13; ☽⚼⚷ 13:27; ☿⊻♄ 13:49; ☽⚹♇ 16:02; ♂□♅ 20:45; ☿∥♃ 21:28; ☉△☽ 22:53

23 W ☽∥♇ 4:54; ☽☍⚳ 12:45; ☽#⚳ 14:50; ☽△⚷ 15:02; ☽⊼♅ 16:11; ☽⚹♂ 17:13; ☽∠♇ 17:32; ☿☌♆ 17:45; ☽⚹♀ 23:30

24 Th ☽□♃ 4:01; ☽⚹♄ 7:10; ☽□♆ 10:32; ☽□☿ 13:00; ☽⚼♅ 17:43; ☽⊻♇ 19:01; ☽∠♂ 20:06; ☿∥♆ 20:11

25 F ☽∠♀ 2:55; ♄#♅ 4:04; ☉□☽ 5:38; ☊ R 5:50; ☽∠♄ 8:48; ☽⊼⚳ 16:51; ☽□⚷ 18:10; ☽△♅ 19:17; ☽⊻♂ 23:00

26 Sa ☿∠♅ 1:27; ☽⊻♀ 6:23; ☽⚹♃ 7:50; ☽⊻♄ 10:28; ☿⚹♇ 10:36; ☉#☿ 12:38; ☽⚹♆ 13:38; ☽⚼⚳ 18:59; ☽☌♇ 22:05; ☽⚹☿ 23:52

27 Su ☽#⚳ 7:04; ☉∠♄ 7:12; ♀⊻♃ 7:35; ☿ ♈ 7:46; ☽∠♃ 9:51; ☉⚹☽ 12:36; ☽∠♆ 15:19; ☽∥♇ 19:25; ☽△⚳ 21:15; ☽⚹⚷ 21:33; ☽□♅ 22:39

28 M ☿∠♂ 0:06; ☽☌♂ 5:09; ☽∠☿ 5:39; ☽⊻♃ 12:03; ⚳⚹⚷ 13:10; ☽☌♀ 13:49; ☽☌♄ 14:12; ☉∠☽ 16:21; ☽⊻♆ 17:11; ♀☌♄ 19:28; ☽∠⚷ 23:32

29 Tu ☽⊻♇ 1:42; ☽∥♂ 1:45; ☽#♅ 8:52; ☽∥♄ 9:44; ☽⊻☿ 11:53; ☽∥♀ 19:43; ☉⊻☽ 20:28; ☉#♆ 20:32

30 W ☽⊻⚷ 1:50; ☽□⚳ 2:35; ☽⚹♅ 2:55; ☽∠♇ 3:56; ♀⊻♆ 12:17; ☽⊻♂ 12:29; ☽☌♃ 17:26; ⚳⊻♅ 18:29; ☽⊻♄ 19:05; ☿∠♄ 20:52; ☽☌♆ 21:56; ☽#⚷ 21:59; ☽⊻♀ 22:43

31 Th ☽∠♅ 5:40; ☽⚹♇ 6:38; ☽∥♃ 6:52; ☉#☽ 7:53; ☽∥♆ 10:17; ☽#☿ 16:05; ☽∠♂ 16:56; ☉#♃ 20:24; ☽∠♄ 22:15

March 2022:Modify New York Stock Exchange Zone:-5

Sunday	Monday	Tuesday	Wednesday	Thursday	Friday	Saturday
		1 3:52PM ☽-> 0♓00	2 12:04AM ☉ ✶ ♅ 11:32AM ☿ ☌ ♄ 12:33PM New Moon♓	3 3:42AM ♂ ☌ ♇ 12:55PM ♀ ☌ ♇ 7:51PM ☽-> 0♈00	4	5 9:05AM ☉ ☌ ♃
6 1:22AM ♂-> 0♒00 1:29AM ♀-> 0♒00 2:12AM ♀ ☌ ♂ 2:58AM ☽-> 0♉00	7	8 1:38PM ☽-> 0♊00	9 8:31PM ☿-> 0♓00	10	11 2:23AM ☽-> 0♋00	12
13 6:42AM ☉ ☌ ♆ 2:30PM ☽-> 0♌00	14	15 11:57PM ☽-> 0♍00	16	17 7:12AM ☿ ✶ ♅	18 2:16AM Full Moon♍ 6:24AM ☽-> 0♎00 2:36PM ☉ ✶ ♇	19 6:15AM ♀ □ ♅
20 10:32AM ☉-> 0♈00 10:43AM ☽-> 0♏00	21 1:05AM ☿ ☌ ♃	22 1:57PM ☽-> 0♐00 3:43PM ♂ □ ♅	23 12:43PM ☿ ☌ ♆	24 4:52PM ☽-> 0♑00	25	26 5:34AM ☿ ✶ ♇ 7:54PM ☽-> 0♒00
27 2:43AM ☿-> 0♈00	28 2:26PM ♀ ☌ ♄ 11:30PM ☽-> 0♓00	29	30	31 4:29AM ☽-> 0♈00		

February

S	M	T	W	T	F	S
		1	2	3	4	5
6	7	8	9	10	11	12
13	14	15	16	17	18	19
20	21	22	23	24	25	26
27	28					

April

S	M	T	W	T	F	S
					1	2
3	4	5	6	7	8	9
10	11	12	13	14	15	16
17	18	19	20	21	22	23
24	25	26	27	28	29	30

April 2022

LONGITUDE

Day	Sid.Time	☉	☽	☽ 12 hour	Mean☊	True☊	☿	♀	♂	⚳	♃	♄	⚷	♅	♆	♇
	h m s	° ' "	° ' "	° ' "	° '	° '	° '	° '	° '	° '	° '	° '	° '	° '	° '	° '
1 F	12 37 20	11♈14 40	7♈59 33	14♈32 33	24♉45.8	23♉06.4	9♈11.8	25♒04.5	19♒19.5	13♊14.5	21♓17.9	22♒02.3	12♈17.3	12♉53.3	23♓34.0	28♑24.0
2 Sa	12 41 17	12 13 55	21 01 16	27 25 40	24 42.6	23R 00.8	11 13.0	26 07.8	20 04.8	13 34.9	21 32.0	22 07.8	12 20.8	12 56.4	23 36.2	28 24.8
3 Su	12 45 13	13 13 08	3♉45 45	10♉01 40	24 39.4	22 57.1	13 15.2	27 11.3	20 50.1	13 55.5	21 46.0	22 13.2	12 24.3	12 59.5	23 38.4	28 25.6
4 M	12 49 10	14 12 18	16 13 36	22 21 48	24 36.3	22D 55.3	15 18.3	28 15.0	21 35.4	14 16.2	22 00.0	22 18.6	12 27.8	13 02.6	23 40.6	28 26.3
5 Tu	12 53 06	15 11 26	28 26 37	4♊28 28	24 33.1	22 55.2	17 22.1	29 19.0	22 20.7	14 37.0	22 13.9	22 23.9	12 31.3	13 05.8	23 42.7	28 27.1
6 W	12 57 03	16 10 33	10♊27 47	16 25 05	24 29.9	22 56.4	19 26.4	0♓23.3	23 06.0	14 58.0	22 27.8	22 29.1	12 34.9	13 09.0	23 44.9	28 27.8
7 Th	13 01 00	17 09 36	22 20 55	28 15 52	24 26.7	22 58.1	21 31.2	1 27.7	23 51.4	15 19.0	22 41.7	22 34.2	12 38.4	13 12.1	23 47.0	28 28.4
8 F	13 04 56	18 08 38	4♋10 33	10♋05 34	24 23.6	22 59.7	23 36.0	2 32.4	24 36.7	15 40.2	22 55.5	22 39.3	12 41.9	13 15.3	23 49.1	28 29.1
9 Sa	13 08 53	19 07 38	16 01 34	21 59 11	24 20.4	23R 00.6	25 40.8	3 37.2	25 22.0	16 01.5	23 09.3	22 44.4	12 45.4	13 18.6	23 51.2	28 29.7
10 Su	13 12 49	20 06 35	27 59 02	4♌01 43	24 17.2	23 00.3	27 45.1	4 42.3	26 07.4	16 22.9	23 23.1	22 49.3	12 48.9	13 21.8	23 53.3	28 30.3
11 M	13 16 46	21 05 29	10♌07 50	16 17 53	24 14.0	22 58.6	29 48.8	5 47.5	26 52.7	16 44.5	23 36.8	22 54.2	12 52.4	13 25.1	23 55.4	28 30.8
12 Tu	13 20 42	22 04 22	22 32 23	28 51 44	24 10.8	22 55.6	1♉51.5	6 52.9	27 38.1	17 06.1	23 50.4	22 59.0	12 55.9	13 28.3	23 57.5	28 31.4
13 W	13 24 39	23 03 12	5♍16 15	11♍46 12	24 07.7	22 51.5	3 52.8	7 58.5	28 23.4	17 27.9	24 04.0	23 03.8	12 59.4	13 31.6	23 59.6	28 31.9
14 Th	13 28 35	24 02 00	18 21 44	25 02 53	24 04.5	22 47.0	5 52.4	9 04.3	29 08.8	17 49.8	24 17.6	23 08.5	13 02.9	13 34.9	24 01.6	28 32.3
15 F	13 32 32	25 00 46	1♎49 33	8♎41 33	24 01.3	22 42.6	7 50.0	10 10.3	29 54.1	18 11.7	24 31.1	23 13.1	13 06.3	13 38.2	24 03.6	28 32.8
16 Sa	13 36 29	25 59 29	15 38 35	22 40 11	23 58.1	22 38.8	9 45.2	11 16.4	0♓39.5	18 33.8	24 44.5	23 17.6	13 09.8	13 41.6	24 05.6	28 33.2
17 Su	13 40 25	26 58 11	29 45 53	6♏55 02	23 55.0	22 36.1	11 37.7	12 22.7	1 24.8	18 56.0	24 57.9	23 22.1	13 13.2	13 44.9	24 07.6	28 33.6
18 M	13 44 22	27 56 51	14♏07 01	21 21 08	23 51.8	22D 34.8	13 27.1	13 29.1	2 10.2	19 18.3	25 11.2	23 26.4	13 16.7	13 48.3	24 09.6	28 33.9
19 Tu	13 48 18	28 55 29	28 36 40	5♐52 55	23 48.6	22 34.6	15 13.2	14 35.7	2 55.6	19 40.6	25 24.5	23 30.8	13 20.1	13 51.6	24 11.5	28 34.2
20 W	13 52 15	29 54 05	13♐09 13	20 24 56	23 45.4	22 35.5	16 55.8	15 42.5	3 40.9	20 03.1	25 37.8	23 35.0	13 23.5	13 55.0	24 13.5	28 34.5
21 Th	13 56 11	0♉52 40	27 39 31	4♑52 28	23 42.2	22 36.8	18 34.5	16 49.4	4 26.3	20 25.7	25 51.0	23 39.2	13 26.9	13 58.4	24 15.4	28 34.8
22 F	14 00 08	1 51 13	12♑03 21	19 11 48	23 39.1	22 38.1	20 09.2	17 56.5	5 11.7	20 48.4	26 04.1	23 43.2	13 30.3	14 01.8	24 17.3	28 35.1
23 Sa	14 04 04	2 49 44	26 17 33	3♒20 20	23 35.9	22R 38.9	21 39.7	19 03.7	5 57.1	21 11.1	26 17.1	23 47.2	13 33.7	14 05.2	24 19.2	28 35.3
24 Su	14 08 01	3 48 14	10♒20 00	17 16 25	23 32.7	22 38.9	23 05.8	20 11.0	6 42.4	21 34.0	26 30.1	23 51.2	13 37.0	14 08.7	24 21.1	28 35.5
25 M	14 11 58	4 46 42	24 09 28	0♓59 07	23 29.5	22 38.0	24 27.3	21 18.5	7 27.8	21 56.9	26 43.1	23 55.0	13 40.4	14 12.1	24 22.9	28 35.6
26 Tu	14 15 54	5 45 08	7♓45 18	14 27 59	23 26.4	22 36.4	25 44.3	22 26.0	8 13.2	22 20.0	26 55.9	23 58.8	13 43.7	14 15.5	24 24.8	28 35.7
27 W	14 19 51	6 43 33	21 07 11	27 42 52	23 23.2	22 34.4	26 56.5	23 33.7	8 58.5	22 43.1	27 08.7	24 02.4	13 47.0	14 19.0	24 26.6	28 35.8
28 Th	14 23 47	7 41 56	4♈15 04	10♈43 47	23 20.0	22 32.2	28 03.8	24 41.6	9 43.9	23 06.3	27 21.5	24 06.0	13 50.3	14 22.4	24 28.4	28 35.9
29 F	14 27 44	8 40 17	17 09 04	23 30 57	23 16.8	22 30.2	29 06.3	25 49.5	10 29.2	23 29.6	27 34.2	24 09.5	13 53.6	14 25.9	24 30.1	28R 35.9
30 Sa	14 31 40	9♉38 37	29 49 31	6♉04 50	23♉13.6	22♉28.8	0♊03.7	26♓57.5	11♓14.5	23♊53.0	27♓46.8	24♒13.0	13♈56.8	14♉29.3	24♓31.9	28♑35.9

1st of Month

Julian Day #
2459670.5
Obliquity
23°26'17"
SVP 4♓57'11"
GC 27♐09.0
Eris 24♈11.5

Day	⚴
1	17♈34.0
6	19 37.9
11	21 43.1
16	23 49.6
21	25 57.3
26	28 06.3

Day	⚵
1	22♒46.8
6	24 39.3
11	26 30.3
16	28 19.7
21	0♓07.2
26	1 52.8

Day	⚶
1	9♒53.0
6	12 05.6
11	14 15.0
16	16 20.9
21	18 23.2
26	20 21.6

DECLINATION and LATITUDE

Day	☉ Decl	☽ Decl	☽ Lat	☽12h Decl	☿ Decl	☿ Lat	♀ Decl	♀ Lat	♂ Decl	♂ Lat	⚳ Decl	⚳ Lat	♃ Decl	♃ Lat	♄ Decl	♄ Lat
1 F	4N27	0S11	3S39	2N46	2N27	1S18	12S21	0N52	16S11	1S13	24N23	2N01	4S23	1S01	15S03	0S57
2 Sa	4 50	5N40	2 44	8 28	3 22	1 10	12 05	0 46	15 57	1 13	24 27	2 02	4 17	1 01	15 02	0 57
3 Su	5 13	11 10	1 42	13 43	4 17	1 02	11 48	0 41	15 43	1 14	24 32	2 04	4 12	1 01	15 00	0 57
4 M	5 36	16 07	0 36	18 19	5 13	0 53	11 32	0 35	15 29	1 15	24 36	2 06	4 06	1 01	14 58	0 57
5 Tu	5 59	20 18	0N30	22 04	6 09	0 44	11 14	0 30	15 15	1 16	24 40	2 08	4 01	1 01	14 57	0 57
6 W	6 22	23 34	1 34	24 49	7 05	0 34	10 57	0 25	15 01	1 16	24 44	2 09	3 55	1 01	14 55	0 57
7 Th	6 44	25 46	2 34	26 26	8 01	0 24	10 39	0 20	14 47	1 17	24 48	2 11	3 50	1 01	14 54	0 58
8 F	7 07	26 48	3 26	26 52	8 57	0 14	10 21	0 14	14 32	1 18	24 52	2 13	3 45	1 01	14 52	0 58
9 Sa	7 29	26 37	4 10	26 03	9 53	0 03	10 02	0 09	14 18	1 18	24 56	2 14	3 39	1 01	14 51	0 58
10 Su	7 52	25 12	4 44	24 02	10 48	0N08	9 43	0 04	14 03	1 19	24 60	2 16	3 34	1 01	14 49	0 58
11 M	8 14	22 36	5 05	20 53	11 42	0 19	9 24	0S01	13 48	1 20	25 04	2 18	3 29	1 02	14 48	0 58
12 Tu	8 36	18 55	5 13	16 43	12 36	0 30	9 04	0 05	13 33	1 20	25 07	2 19	3 23	1 02	14 46	0 58
13 W	8 58	14 19	5 05	11 42	13 28	0 41	8 44	0 10	13 18	1 21	25 11	2 21	3 18	1 02	14 45	0 58
14 Th	9 19	8 56	4 42	6 01	14 18	0 53	8 24	0 15	13 03	1 22	25 15	2 23	3 13	1 02	14 44	0 59
15 F	9 41	2 60	4 03	0S06	15 07	1 04	8 03	0 19	12 47	1 22	25 18	2 24	3 08	1 02	14 42	0 59
16 Sa	10 02	3S15	3 09	6 23	15 55	1 14	7 42	0 24	12 32	1 23	25 22	2 26	3 02	1 02	14 41	0 59
17 Su	10 24	9 29	2 02	12 29	16 40	1 25	7 21	0 28	12 16	1 23	25 26	2 27	2 57	1 02	14 39	0 59
18 M	10 45	15 20	0 46	17 59	17 23	1 35	6 59	0 32	12 01	1 24	25 29	2 29	2 52	1 02	14 38	0 59
19 Tu	11 05	20 23	0S33	22 29	18 04	1 45	6 37	0 36	11 45	1 25	25 32	2 31	2 47	1 02	14 37	0 59
20 W	11 26	24 13	1 51	25 32	18 43	1 54	6 15	0 40	11 29	1 25	25 36	2 32	2 42	1 03	14 36	0 59
21 Th	11 47	26 13	3 01	26 53	19 19	2 02	5 53	0 44	11 13	1 26	25 39	2 34	2 37	1 03	14 34	0 60
22 F	12 07	26 52	3 60	26 25	19 52	2 10	5 30	0 48	10 57	1 27	25 42	2 35	2 32	1 03	14 33	0 60
23 Sa	12 27	25 31	4 43	24 14	20 23	2 17	5 07	0 52	10 41	1 27	25 45	2 37	2 26	1 03	14 32	0 60
24 Su	12 47	22 35	5 08	20 38	20 52	2 24	4 44	0 56	10 25	1 28	25 48	2 38	2 21	1 03	14 31	1 00
25 M	13 07	18 25	5 15	15 59	21 18	2 29	4 21	0 59	10 08	1 28	25 51	2 40	2 16	1 03	14 30	1 00
26 Tu	13 26	13 22	5 05	10 37	21 41	2 34	3 58	1 03	9 52	1 29	25 54	2 41	2 11	1 03	14 29	1 00
27 W	13 46	7 46	4 37	4 52	22 02	2 38	3 34	1 06	9 35	1 30	25 57	2 43	2 06	1 04	14 28	1 01
28 Th	14 05	1 55	3 56	1N01	22 20	2 40	3 10	1 09	9 19	1 30	25 60	2 45	2 02	1 04	14 27	1 01
29 F	14 23	3N55	3 03	6 45	22 36	2 42	2 46	1 12	9 02	1 31	26 03	2 46	1 57	1 04	14 26	1 01
30 Sa	14N42	9N30	2S02	12N08	22N49	2N43	2S22	1S15	8S45	1S31	26N05	2N48	1S52	1S04	14S25	1S01

Day	⚷ Decl	⚷ Lat	♅ Decl	♅ Lat	♆ Decl	♆ Lat	♇ Decl	♇ Lat
1	6N40	1N58	15N21	0S22	3S35	1S07	22S20	1S54
6	6 46	1 57	15 26	0 22	3 31	1 08	22 20	1 54
11	6 53	1 57	15 31	0 22	3 27	1 08	22 20	1 55
16	6 59	1 57	15 36	0 22	3 23	1 08	22 20	1 56
21	7 06	1 57	15 41	0 22	3 19	1 08	22 21	1 56
26	7 12	1 56	15 46	0 22	3 16	1 08	22 21	1 57

Day	⚴ Decl	⚴ Lat	⚵ Decl	⚵ Lat	⚶ Decl	⚶ Lat	Eris Decl	Eris Lat
1	4S58	12S50	6S50	7N29	17S59	0S14	1S02	11S11
6	4 33	13 12	6 16	7 27	17 34	0 25	1 01	11 11
11	4 08	13 34	5 42	7 25	17 08	0 36	0 59	11 11
16	3 45	13 57	5 07	7 23	16 42	0 48	0 58	11 10
21	3 22	14 21	4 32	7 21	16 16	1 00	0 57	11 10
26	3 00	14 45	3 57	7 19	15 51	1 13	0 55	11 10

Moon Phenomena

Max/0 Decl
dy hr mn
1 0:46 0 N
8 8:16 26N53
15 11:35 0 S
21 17:39 26S56
28 7:51 0 N

Max/0 Lat
dy hr mn
4 13:06 0 N
12 0:45 5N13
18 14:02 0 S
24 21:21 5S15

Perigee/Apogee
dy hr m kilometers
7 19:12 a 404437
19 15:15 p 365146

PH dy hr mn
● 1 6:26 11♈31
☽ 9 6:49 19♋24
○ 16 18:56 26♎46
☾ 23 11:58 3♒19
● 30 20:29 10♉28
• 30 1242:3P 0.640

Void of Course Moon

Last Aspect	☽ Ingress
2 13:52 ♇ □	♉ 2 16:51
5 1:54 ♀ □	♊ 5 3:05
7 3:16 ♂ △	♋ 7 15:31
10 1:02 ♇ ☍	♌ 10 4:01
12 10:18 ♂ ☍	♍ 12 14:09
14 18:13 ♇ △	♎ 14 20:47
16 21:58 ♇ □	♏ 17 0:24
18 23:56 ♇ ⚹	♐ 19 2:18
20 20:57 ♃ □	♑ 21 3:53
23 3:54 ♇ ☌	♒ 23 6:18
25 0:35 ☿ □	♓ 25 10:16
27 13:37 ♇ ⚹	♈ 27 16:11
29 21:40 ♇ □	♉ 30 0:20

DAILY ASPECTARIAN

1 F
☽☌☿ 2:36
☽∠♀ 4:08
☉☌☽ 6:26
☽☌⚷ 7:53
☽⚺♅ 9:00
☽⚹⚳ 9:52
⚳⚼♇ 11:36
☽∥☿ 12:41
☽#♆ 15:20
☽#♃ 18:21
☉∥☽ 20:17
☿∠♀ 21:49
☽⚹♂ 22:08

2 Sa
☽⚺♃ 0:58
☽⚹♄ 2:05
☉☌⚷ 2:58
☽∥⚷ 4:19
☽⚺♆ 4:50
☿#♆ 5:25
☽⚹♀ 10:25
☿☌⚷ 13:43
☽□♇ 13:52
☽∠⚳ 14:34
☉⚺♅ 18:11
☿⚺♅ 20:51
☿#♃ 21:55
☉☌☿ 23:12

3 Su
☽#♀ 2:47
♀∠⚷ 5:12
☽∠♃ 5:51
☽∠♆ 9:22
☿⚹⚳ 9:27
☽⚺⚷ 16:40
☽☌♅ 17:48
☽#♄ 18:13
☉⚺☽ 19:44
☽⚺⚳ 20:05
☽∥♅ 20:21
☽#♂ 20:56
☽⚺☿ 21:51

4 M
☉⚹⚳ 2:26
♀⚺♇ 4:17
♂#♅ 8:04
☽□♂ 11:10
☽⚹♃ 11:30
☽□♄ 11:59
☊ D 13:06
☽⚹♆ 14:38
☉∥☿ 16:58
♂⚺♃ 18:48
☽∠⚷ 22:10

5 Tu
☽△♇ 0:01
♂☌♄ 1:52
☽□♀ 1:54
☉∠☽ 3:46
☽∠☿ 9:25
☽#♇ 14:02
♀ ♓ 15:19
☿∥⚷ 15:49

6 W
♃⚺♄ 3:25
☽⚹⚷ 4:17
☽⚺♅ 5:26
☽⚼♇ 6:03
☽☌⚳ 9:21
♂∥♄ 10:44
☽∥⚳ 11:30
☉⚹☽ 12:33
♂⚺♆ 21:35
☽⚹☿ 21:58

7 Th
☽△♄ 0:27
☽□♃ 0:43
☽□♆ 2:55
☽△♂ 3:16
☉∥⚷ 3:32
☽∠♅ 11:56
☽⚻♇ 12:26
☿⚹♄ 12:39
☿⚺♃ 15:15
☽△♀ 20:21

8 F
☿⚺♆ 2:34
☽⚼♄ 7:07
☽⚼♂ 11:47
☽□⚷ 17:22
☿⚹♂ 18:20
☽⚹♅ 18:29
☽⚺⚳ 24:00

9 Sa
☿#♀ 3:00
☽⚼♀ 5:45
☊ R 6:43
☉□☽ 6:49
☽⚻♄ 13:36
☽△♃ 14:38
☽△♆ 15:48
☽⚻♂ 20:02
☽□☿ 23:27

10 Su
☽☍♇ 1:02
☽∥⚳ 2:11
☽∠⚳ 6:58
☿□♇ 8:47
☽⚻♀ 14:39
☽⚼♃ 20:58
☽⚼♆ 21:38

11 M
☽#♇ 1:57
☿ ♉ 2:11
☽△⚷ 5:23
☽□♅ 6:26
♃∥♆ 9:29
☽⚹⚳ 13:14
☉△☽ 23:02

12 Tu
☽☍♄ 0:51
☽⚻♃ 2:32
☽⚻♆ 2:43
☿∠⚳ 3:30
♂∠⚷ 10:14
☽⚼⚷ 10:17
☽☍♂ 10:18
☽⚻♇ 11:22
♃☌♆ 14:44
☉#♀ 16:11
☽∥♅ 17:58
☿#♂ 20:29
☽△☿ 20:56
☽#♄ 21:53

13 W
☉⚹♄ 0:15
☽∥☿ 3:26
♂⚺♇ 4:31
☽#♂ 5:00
☽☍♀ 5:29
☉⚼☽ 5:35
☽⚻⚷ 14:18
☽⚼♇ 15:14
☽△♅ 15:17
☉∠♀ 16:08
☉∥☽ 22:27
☽□⚳ 23:01
☉⚺♆ 23:50

14 Th
☽#♀ 2:24
☽⚼☿ 5:19
☽∥⚷ 8:12
☉⚺♃ 8:15
☽⚻♄ 8:39
☽☍♆ 10:12
☽☍♃ 10:50
☉⚻☽ 10:59
☿#♄ 11:51
☽△♇ 18:13
☽⚼♅ 18:21
☽⚻♂ 20:25
☽#♆ 22:25
☽#♃ 23:28

15 F
♂ ♓ 3:07
☽⚼♄ 11:14
☽⚻☿ 12:13
☿∥♅ 14:12
☿∠♆ 15:33
☽⚻♀ 15:49
☽☍⚷ 19:43
☽⚻♅ 20:38
☽∥♃ 23:13
☿∠♃ 23:50

16 Sa
☽⚼♂ 0:02
☽∥♆ 0:31
☽△⚳ 5:08
☽△♄ 13:08
☽#⚷ 14:21
☽⚻♆ 14:27
☽⚻♃ 15:46
☽∥♀ 16:08
☉☍☽ 18:56
☽⚼♀ 19:38
☽□♇ 21:58

17 Su
☽△♂ 2:56
☉#☽ 3:49
☽⚼⚳ 7:11
☽∥♂ 10:40
☽⚼♆ 15:44
☽⚼♃ 17:21
♀⚺⚷ 19:15
☽∥♄ 21:00
♀#⚷ 21:08
☿⚺⚷ 21:36
☽⚻⚷ 22:36
☽☍☿ 22:44
☽△♀ 22:52
☽☍♅ 23:29

18 M
☿⚹♀ 1:10
☽#♅ 1:19
♀∠♇ 1:44
☿☌♅ 4:53
♀⚹♅ 7:16
☽⚻⚳ 8:50
☽#☿ 10:36
☊ D 14:01
☉□♇ 15:15
☽□♄ 15:32
☽△♆ 16:41
☽△♃ 18:38
☽⚼⚷ 23:33
☽⚹♇ 23:56

19 Tu
☉⚻☽ 0:33
☽□♂ 7:31
☽∥♇ 11:10

20 W
☽△⚷ 0:24
☽∠♇ 0:42
☽⚻♅ 1:16
☉#♂ 1:49
☉ ♉ 2:25
☉⚼☽ 3:06
☽□♀ 4:34
☽⚻☿ 7:03
☽☍⚳ 11:42
☽#⚳ 12:57
⚵ ♓ 15:52
☽⚹♄ 17:20
☽□♆ 18:21
☽□♃ 20:57

21 Th
☽⚺♇ 1:32
☽⚼♅ 2:12
☉△☽ 5:44
☽⚼☿ 11:04
☽⚹♂ 11:54
☽∠♄ 18:24

22 F
☽□⚷ 2:26
☽△♅ 3:19
☽⚹♀ 10:44
☿⚺⚳ 13:42
☽∠♂ 14:27
☽⚻⚳ 15:07
☽△☿ 15:15
☽⚺♄ 19:44
☽⚹♆ 20:39
☽#⚳ 21:22
☽⚹♃ 23:59

23 Sa
☽☌♇ 3:54
☉□☽ 11:58
☊ R 12:14
☽∠♀ 14:23
☽⚼⚳ 17:21
☽⚺♂ 17:25
☽∠♆ 22:18

24 Su
☽∥♇ 1:35
☽∠♃ 2:03
☽⚹⚷ 5:41
☽□♅ 6:36
☽#☿ 9:40
☿□♄ 13:51
☽⚺♀ 18:35
☽△⚳ 20:02
☿⚹♆ 22:38
☽☌♄ 23:35

25 M
☽⚺♆ 0:24
☽□☿ 0:35
☽⚺♃ 4:34
☽⚺♇ 7:47
☽∠⚷ 7:57
☽#♅ 13:02
☽∥♄ 18:58
☉⚹☽ 20:10
♀□⚳ 20:44
☉#☽ 23:42

26 Tu
☽☌♂ 0:53
☽∠♇ 10:26
☽⚺⚷ 10:43
☽⚹♅ 11:41
☽∥♂ 15:59

27 W
☉∠☽ 1:11
☽#⚷ 2:15
☽□⚳ 2:59
☽☌♀ 4:51
☿⚹♃ 5:13
☽⚺♄ 5:20
☽☌♆ 6:03
♀⚺♄ 10:44
☽☌♃ 11:08
☽⚹☿ 11:36
☽⚹♇ 13:37
☽∠♅ 15:00
☽∥♀ 18:33
☽∥♆ 18:37
♀☌♆ 19:13
♀∥♆ 19:36
☽∥♃ 23:34

28 Th
☿#♇ 2:09
☉⚺☽ 6:53
☽∠♄ 9:01
☽⚺♂ 10:46
☿△♇ 12:06
☽#♃ 15:57
☉∠⚳ 16:41
☽∠☿ 17:48
☽☌⚷ 17:52
☿∠⚷ 18:41
☽⚺♅ 18:53
☽#♀ 19:32
☽#♆ 21:09

29 F
☉#♄ 2:33
☽⚹⚳ 12:20
☽⚹♄ 13:17
☽⚺♆ 13:54
☽∥⚷ 14:16
☽∠♂ 16:44
☽⚺♀ 18:00
♇ R 18:38
☽⚺♃ 20:02
☽#♂ 20:51
☉∠♆ 21:08
☽□♇ 21:40
☿ ♊ 22:24

30 Sa
☽⚺☿ 0:29
⚴ ♉ 8:51
☽∠⚳ 17:59
☽∠♆ 18:42
☉☌☽ 20:29
♀☌♃ 21:15
☽#♄ 22:50
☽⚹♂ 23:24
⚳△♄ 23:50

April 2022:Modify New York Stock Exchange Zone:-5

Sunday	Monday	Tuesday	Wednesday	Thursday	Friday	Saturday
March S M T W T F S 1 2 3 4 5 6 7 8 9 10 11 12 13 14 15 16 17 18 19 20 21 22 23 24 25 26 27 28 29 30 31	May S M T W T F S 1 2 3 4 5 6 7 8 9 10 11 12 13 14 15 16 17 18 19 20 21 22 23 24 25 26 27 28 29 30 31				1 1:23AM New Moon♈	2 11:49AM ☽-> 0♉00 6:10PM ☿ ☌ ☉
3	4 8:50PM ♂ ☌ ♄ 10:03PM ☽-> 0♊00	5 10:16AM ♀-> 0♓00	6	7 7:36AM ☿ ⚹ ♄ 10:29AM ☽-> 0♋00	8 1:17PM ☿ ⚹ ♂	9 10:58PM ☽-> 0♌00
10 3:44AM ☿ □ ♇ 9:08PM ☿-> 0♉00	11	12 9:06AM ☽-> 0♍00 9:41AM ♃ ☌ ♆ 7:13PM ☉ ⚹ ♄	13	14 3:44PM ☽-> 0♎00 10:04PM ♂-> 0♓00	15	16 1:54PM Full Moon♎ 7:21PM ☽-> 0♏00
17 8:08PM ☿ ⚹ ♀ 11:50PM ☿ ☌ ♅	18 2:14AM ♀ ⚹ ♅ 10:13AM ☉ □ ♇ 9:15PM ☽-> 0♐00	19 9:23PM ☉-> 0♉00	20 10:51PM ☽-> 0♑00	21	22	23 1:16AM ☽-> 0♒00
24 8:49AM ☿ □ ♄ 5:36PM ☿ ⚹ ♆	25 5:13AM ☽-> 0♓00	26	27 12:10AM ☿ ⚹ ♃ 11:08AM ☽-> 0♈00 2:10PM ♀ ☌ ♆	28 7:03AM ☿ △ ♇	29 1:34PM ♇ ℞ 28♑ 5:22PM ☿-> 0♊00 7:17PM ☽-> 0♉00	30 3:27PM New Moon♉ 4:13PM ♀ ☌ ♃

Rave Reviews for
VOLUME 1 of The Ultimate Book On Stock Market Timing: Cycles And Patterns In The Indexs.

"The Ultimate Book on Stock Market Timing Volume I: Cycles and Patterns in the Indexes" by Raymond Merriman is literally the ultimate book on the analysis of the stock market. We are especially impressed with various waves of long-term cycles for more than 200 years, which we have never seen before... a marvelous job."

- T. Kaburagi, *Toshi Nippou Ltd.* (Japan's major commodities' newspaper).

"As the first volume in what is designated to be a five-volume series, Ray Merriman has not only provided a unique and in-depth analysis of various cycles in the stock market indices, but he has done so with a clarity and enthusiasm that makes reading this "technical" book an exciting and illuminating journey into the cyclical ups and downs of the stock market. Guiding the reader through the complexities of cyclical analysis, Merriman explains step by step what defines a market cycle; the orb of time a cycle can take to unfold; reasons why a cycle might contract or expand; and most importantly, how to read the characteristics of a cycle to determine whether it is bullish or bearish."

"That Merriman has so generously shared this knowledge with us in this first volume, gives the reader/investor one of the most valuable market timing tools available. It is a book based not on subjectivity but on data that has revealed a complexity of market cycles to Merriman's unrelenting search to know "the soul of the stock market." For those who are fascinated with (market) cycles, this book is a classic. And for those who invest, this book is a must."

- Geraldine Hannon; Reviewer for *The Mountain Astrologer*

"Do stock markets rise and fall in accordance with some readily identifiable cycle? Most are familiar with the so-called "Presidential Election" or four year cycle, some are familiar with the 54-year Kondratieff Cycle. Author Raymond Merriman searches through centuries of stock market history with charts and data going back as far as 1695 to prove the existence of these as well as both short and longer stock market cycles.

"Analyzed in depth is the entire history of the New York Stock Exchange from 1789-1997 and the Japanese Nikkei Index from 1949-1997. The charts of these markets alone are fascinating!"

"From all this data, we are provided with details on 15 separate long and short term recurring cycles, and a description of the patterns occurring in each one. Not only are we taught when to expect a cycle to unfold, but also how to recognize it when it does."

"Merriman also provides us with...(studies) on technical analysis, and helps us integrate the two together whether our time frame is next year - or 300 years."

I recommend this book for all those interested in markets. I can't wait for Volume 2!"

- Ted Kunzog; Reviewer for *Technically Speaking,* newsletter for the Market Technicians Association (MTA), and editor of *The Asset Allocator* market letter.

"If you are done with Fourier transform cycle printouts, and cycles sent down from Sanai, this is your book. Raymond Merriman teaches you how to isolate and prove historical cycles: in an eighteen year cycle prices will do "this" at a certain point, but they will NOT do "that." In setting long (and short) term positions, what you want to know is what ARE the cycles and how do they perform? Merriman puts you in control and doesn't mandate a computing environment more complex than you and your pencil."

- Dr. Thomas Drake, Tenorio Research; Editor of the *Gold Fax Market Letter.*

Rave Reviews for

VOLUME 2 of The Ultimate Book On Stock Market Timing: Geocosmic Correlations To Investment Cycles.

"Once in a great while a truly revolutionary trading book is published that creates and redefines a method of analysis."

-David Wierzba, Willow Financial, Atlanta, GA

"I just finished Volume 2 of The Ultimate Book on Stock Market Timing: Geocosmic Correlation to Investment Cycles, by Raymond A. Merriman. It is everything I was expecting and looking for, and is a landmark in research."

-Lukman Clark, Signal Hill, CA - The Future Works, and member of ISAR, Inc.

"Raymond Merriman has written an exceptional book on the correlation of stock market cycles with planetary alignments that is of tremendous value to market analysts and investors. It is a well researched and easy to read correlation of stock market tops and bottoms with planetary movements...If you often consider the possibilities of what the stock market is likely to do over the next 10-15 years, read this book. It will help you anticipate longer-term tops and bottoms of the stock market, and point out some time periods when you should be out of the market. With so much gloom and doom published today about the world economy it was very refreshing to read Merriman's longer term outlook for 2000-2015, based on well researched historical precedents. This book is a MUST for the serous investor."

-Walter J. Bressert, Chicago, IL - World-renowned cycles analyst

---

"Words can't even begin to express how extraordinary I think this volume is. (Merriman) has indeed handed over to us investors and market timers a blue-chip portfolio of substantive and ground-breaking research and information. This book is phenomenal!"

-Geraldine Hannon, Reviewer for *The Mountain Astrologer*

---

*"When it comes to applying the principles of financial astrology to active analysis of the markets, few people have more credibility than Raymond Merriman. Merriman's latest contribution is **Geocosmic Correlations To Investment Cycles**, a great financial astrology tool that will save you incredible amounts of research time.*

Merriman's work is meticulously researched, carefully documented, and extremely helpful if you're trying to make meaningful and well-reasoned forecasts for the U.S. stock market. Since overall market direction has a huge impact on the fortunes of most individual equities, this is also important information if you hope to make wise investment decisions. Understanding cycles and developing market forecasts is a fairly complex task, but Ray Merriman does an excellent job of making the work accessible.

*An especially useful section of **Geocosmic Correlations To Investment Cycles** is the closing chapter on "The Art of Integration: Combining Long-Term Cycles in Stocks with Long-Term Geocosmic Cycles." In it, Ray Merriman guides you step-by-step in the process of developing a long-range market forecast, then illustrates his methodology with a couple of extremely detailed examples. This chapter alone is worth the price of the book.*

*If you really want to sink your teeth into financial astrology as a vital, rigorous discipline, **Geocosmic Correlations To Investment Cycles** comes highly recommended, along with Ray Merriman's companion volumes. When you get your hands on these books, get ready for a lot of intensive study-- and a lot of profitable understanding too!"*

- Tim Bost, editor of *Financial*, Sarasota, FL

MMA SUBSCRIPTION SERVICES REPORTS	MMA Daily Cycles	MMA Weekly Cycles	Monthly MMA Cycles	Monthly ICR FINANCIALS	Monthly ICR COMMODITIES
Geocosmic Critical Reversal Dates (CRDs)	★	★	★	★	★
MARKETS COVERED					
DJIA - Cash	★	★	★		
S&P E-MINI - FNC**	★	★	★		
NASDAQ E-MINI - FNC	★	★			
ASX - Australian Stock Index				★	
RUT - Russell 2000 - Cash				★	
HSI - Hang Seng Index				★	
SSE - Chinese Shanghai Stock Composite				★	
Euro Cash		★	★		
Euro / USD - FNC	★	★			
Euro / Yen Spread - Cash		★			
Japanese Yen / USD - FNC	★	★			
USD / Yen - Cash		★			
Swiss Franc / USD - FNC		★			
AUD / USD - Australian Dollar				★	
DXY - U.S. Dollar				★	
GBP / USD - British Pound				★	
Bitcoin - FNC	★				
Bitcoin - CASH		★			
T-Notes - FNC	★	★	★		
Crude Oil - FNC and CF***		★	★		
Soybeans - FNC and CF		★	★		
LC - Live Cattle - FNC and CF					★
MJ - Cannabis ETF					★
KT - Coffee - CF					★
KA - Sugar - CF					★
C - Corn - CF					★
W - Wheat - CF					★
Gold - FNC	★	★	★		
GLD - Gold SPDR ETF	★	★			
Silver - FNC	★	★	★		
SLV - ishares Silver Trust ETF	★	★			
XAU - Gold & Silver Miners					★
SUBSCRIPTION PRICING					
Annual Rate	$3,600*	$1,650	$325	$325	$325
Payment Plans	$995/3mos	$495/3mos	$95/3-mo	$95/3-mo	$95/3-mo
	$360/mo	$185/mo	$35/mo	$35/mo	$35/mo
	* Daily sub includes weekly				

Daily and Weekly Reports of Select Markets Also Available - please see our website for details.

**FNC - Futures Nearby Contract ***CF - Continuous Futures

phone: 800-662-3349 I 248-626-3034 | www.mmacycles.com | customerservice@mmacycles.com